Arizona
FOR
DUMMIES®
1ST EDITION

by Edie Jarolim

IDG Books Worldwide, Inc.
An International Data Group Company

Foster City, CA ✦ Chicago, IL ✦ Indianapolis, IN ✦ New York, NY

Arizona For Dummies,® 1st Edition

Published by
IDG Books Worldwide, Inc.
An International Data Group Company
919 E. Hillsdale Blvd.
Suite 300
Foster City, CA 94404
www.idgbooks.com (IDG Books Worldwide Web Site)
www.dummies.com (Dummies Press Web Site)

Library of Congress Control Number: 00-109140

ISBN: 0-7645-6196-0

ISSN: 1531-1503

Printed in the United States of America

10 9 8 7 6 5 4 3 2 1

1B/RT/RR/QQ/IN

Distributed in the United States by IDG Books Worldwide, Inc.

Distributed by CDG Books Canada Inc. for Canada; by Transworld Publishers Limited in the United Kingdom; by IDG Norge Books for Norway; by IDG Sweden Books for Sweden; by IDG Books Australia Publishing Corporation Pty. Ltd. for Australia and New Zealand; by TransQuest Publishers Pte Ltd. for Singapore, Malaysia, Thailand, Indonesia, and Hong Kong; by Gotop Information Inc. for Taiwan; by ICG Muse, Inc. for Japan; by Intersoft for South Africa; by Eyrolles for France; by International Thomson Publishing for Germany, Austria and Switzerland; by Distribuidora Cuspide for Argentina; by LR International for Brazil; by Galileo Libros for Chile; by Ediciones ZETA S.C.R. Ltda. for Peru; by WS Computer Publishing Corporation, Inc., for the Philippines; by Contemporanea de Ediciones for Venezuela; by Express Computer Distributors for the Caribbean and West Indies; by Micronesia Media Distributor, Inc. for Micronesia; by Chips Computadoras S.A. de C.V. for Mexico; by Editorial Norma de Panama S.A. for Panama; by American Bookshops for Finland.

For general information on IDG Books Worldwide's books in the U.S., please call our Consumer Customer Service department at 800-762-2974. For reseller information, including discounts and premium sales, please call our Reseller Customer Service department at 800-434-3422.

For information on where to purchase IDG Books Worldwide's books outside the U.S., please contact our International Sales department at 317-572-3993 or fax 317-572-4002.

For consumer information on foreign language translations, please contact our Customer Service department at 1-800-434-3422, fax 317-572-4002, or e-mail rights@idgbooks.com.

For information on licensing foreign or domestic rights, please phone +1-650-653-7098.

For sales inquiries and special prices for bulk quantities, please contact our Order Services department at 800-434-4322 or write to the address above.

For information on using IDG Books Worldwide's books in the classroom or for ordering examination copies, please contact our Educational Sales department at 800-434-2086 or fax 317-572-4005.

For press review copies, author interviews, or other publicity information, please contact our Public Relations department at 650-653-7000 or fax 650-653-7500.

For authorization to photocopy items for corporate, personal, or educational use, please contact Copyright Clearance Center, 222 Rosewood Drive, Danvers, MA 01923, or fax 978-750-4470.

is a registered trademark under exclusive license to IDG Books Worldwide, Inc., from International Data Group, Inc.

About the Author

Edie Jarolim has worn many hats — not counting the sombrero she donned on a certain one-margarita-too-many night. . . . She has a Ph.D. in American literature from New York University (which explains the occasional highbrow literary allusion) and was a senior editor at Frommer's travel guides in New York before being lured by the warm sun and endless vistas — not to mention the inexpensive real estate — to Tucson, Arizona, in 1992. She has since written about the Southwest and Mexico for a variety of national publications, ranging from the *America West Airlines Magazine, Art & Antiques,* and *Brides* to the *New York Times Book Review* and the *Wall Street Journal.* In addition to *Arizona For Dummies,* she's the author of *Frommer's San Antonio and Austin* and the *Complete Idiot's Travel Guide to Mexico's Beach Resorts.*

ABOUT IDG BOOKS WORLDWIDE

Welcome to the world of IDG Books Worldwide.

IDG Books Worldwide, Inc., is a subsidiary of International Data Group, the world's largest publisher of computer-related information and the leading global provider of information services on information technology. IDG was founded more than 30 years ago by Patrick J. McGovern and now employs more than 9,000 people worldwide. IDG publishes more than 290 computer publications in over 75 countries. More than 90 million people read one or more IDG publications each month.

Launched in 1990, IDG Books Worldwide is today the #1 publisher of best-selling computer books in the United States. We are proud to have received eight awards from the Computer Press Association in recognition of editorial excellence and three from Computer Currents' First Annual Readers' Choice Awards. Our best-selling *...For Dummies®* series has more than 50 million copies in print with translations in 31 languages. IDG Books Worldwide, through a joint venture with IDG's Hi-Tech Beijing, became the first U.S. publisher to publish a computer book in the People's Republic of China. In record time, IDG Books Worldwide has become the first choice for millions of readers around the world who want to learn how to better manage their businesses.

Our mission is simple: Every one of our books is designed to bring extra value and skill-building instructions to the reader. Our books are written by experts who understand and care about our readers. The knowledge base of our editorial staff comes from years of experience in publishing, education, and journalism — experience we use to produce books to carry us into the new millennium. In short, we care about books, so we attract the best people. We devote special attention to details such as audience, interior design, use of icons, and illustrations. And because we use an efficient process of authoring, editing, and desktop publishing our books electronically, we can spend more time ensuring superior content and less time on the technicalities of making books.

You can count on our commitment to deliver high-quality books at competitive prices on topics you want to read about. At IDG Books Worldwide, we continue in the IDG tradition of delivering quality for more than 30 years. You'll find no better book on a subject than one from IDG Books Worldwide.

John J. Kilcullen

John Kilcullen
Chairman and CEO
IDG Books Worldwide, Inc.

Eighth Annual
Computer Press
Awards ≥1992

Ninth Annual
Computer Press
Awards ≥1993

Tenth Annual
Computer Press
Awards ≥1994

Eleventh Annual
Computer Press
Awards ≥1995

Author Acknowledgments:

It's been a long time since Marjorie Magnusson and Leia James of the Arizona Office of Tourism warmly welcomed a flustered travel writer who, new to the state and to the many mysteries of automobiles, showed up more than an hour late for her first lunch in Scottsdale with them. My driving and ability to judge distances between cities are a bit better these days, but the helpfulness and good spirits of everyone I've worked with at the Arizona Office of Tourism have remained unchanged over the years. In addition to Marjorie — who even put me up at her home one night when all the hotels were full — I'd particularly like to thank Laura McMurchie (now with the city of Scottsdale) and Kristen Jarnagin for making my research so much fun.

If I could individually thank all the hoteliers, innkeepers, restaurateurs, park rangers, shopkeepers, and other tourism personnel who assisted me in getting me to know Arizona, this book would be twice the size, so I'll restrict myself to just those with the most direct relationship to this guide. They are (in alphabetical order by destination): Sandra Perl of the Grand Canyon National Park service and Bruce Bossman of Grand Canyon National Park Lodges; Kathie Curley of Navajo Tourism; Joan Stavely, of the Page-Lake Powell Chamber of Commerce; Jennifer Franklin and Brent DeRaad of the Phoenix Convention and Visitors Bureau; Susan Schepman of Prescott; Tom Kelley of the Sedona-Oak Creek Chamber of Commerce; Erika Breckel of the Sierra Vista Chamber of Commerce; Julie Henig of the Tempe Convention and Visitors Bureau; Terry Grady of the Tombstone Chamber of Commerce; and Julie Brooks of the Wickenburg Chamber of Commerce, who variously toured me around, helped arrange my travel, and/or answered scores of annoying questions. I ask forgiveness — and beg detail overload — from anyone I might have overlooked.

My gratitude, too, to Nikki Buchanan for agreeing to lend her expertise to the Greater Phoenix dining section and for being such a fun fellow foodie.

Finally, special thanks to Jean McKnight of the Metropolitan Tucson Convention and Visitors Bureau for her endless research assistance and her friendship. All my best wishes for happiness in your upcoming marriage, girlfriend — you deserve it!

Publisher's Acknowledgments

We're proud of this book; please register your comments through our IDG Books Worldwide Online Registration Form located at http://my2cents.dummies.com.

Some of the people who helped bring this book to market include the following:

Editorial

Editors: Kathleen A. Dobie, Lisa Torrance

Copy Editors: Ellen Considine, Robert Annis

Cartographer: Roberta Stockwell

Editorial Manager: Christine Meloy Beck

Editorial Assistant: Jennifer Young

Production

Project Coordinator: Dale White

Layout and Graphics: Beth Brooks, LeAndra Johnson, Jill Piscitelli

Proofreaders: Laura Albert, John Bitter, Laura L. Bowman, Carl Pierce

Indexer: Southwest Indexing

General and Administrative

IDG Books Worldwide, Inc.: John Kilcullen, CEO; Bill Barry, President and COO

IDG Books Consumer Reference Group

    Business: Kathleen A. Welton, Vice President and Publisher; Kevin Thornton, Acquisitions Manager

    Cooking/Gardening: Jennifer Feldman, Associate Vice President and Publisher

    Education/Reference: Diane Graves Steele, Vice President and Publisher; Greg Tubach, Publishing Director

    Lifestyles: Kathleen Nebenhaus, Vice President and Publisher; Tracy Boggier, Managing Editor

    Pets: Dominique De Vito, Associate Vice President and Publisher; Tracy Boggier, Managing Editor

    Travel: Michael Spring, Vice President and Publisher; Suzanne Jannetta, Editorial Director; Brice Gosnell, Managing Editor

IDG Books Consumer Editorial Services: Kathleen Nebenhaus, Vice President and Publisher; Kristin A. Cocks, Editorial Director; Cindy Kitchel, Editorial Director

IDG Books Consumer Production: Debbie Stailey, Production Director

IDG Books Packaging: Marc J. Mikulich, Vice President, Brand Strategy and Research

♦

The publisher would like to give special thanks to Patrick J. McGovern, without whom this book would not have been possible.

♦

Contents at a Glance

Cartoons at a Glance

By Rich Tennant

"I think we should arrange to be there for Garlic-Anchovy-Chili Bean Week, and then shoot over to the Breathmint-Antacid Festival."

page 241

"Yeah, this is the Painted Desert. Try to stay on the drop clothe, okay?"

page 7

"Oh, it's okay if you're into neo-romanticist art. Personally, I prefer the soaring perspectives of David Hockney or the controlled frenzy of Gerhard Richter."

page 97

"Careful! There's a diamondback coiled behind that rock. I think it's Greg Swindell, so he might strike."

page 59

"Of all the stuff we came back from Arizona with, I think these adobe bathrobes were the least well-thought-out."

page 429

Fax: 978-546-7747
E-mail: richtennant@the5thwave.com
World Wide Web: www.the5thwave.com

Maps at a Glance

Table of Contents

Introduction

*I*t's always fun to hear friends who have never been to Arizona give their impressions of my adopted home state: "It's all desert, isn't it?" they say, or "It's all canyons," or "It's all Indians living on reservations," or "It's all fat cats playing golf."

Kind of reminds me of the story of the group of blindfolded men who, when asked to describe an elephant after having examined a small section of one, each come up with a completely different, fantastical description of it.

Like an elephant, Arizona is very large and can't be characterized by any one of its parts. But just because you haven't visited the state or have had only a limited experience with it, you don't have to take after those short-sighted pachyderm probers. This book is designed to give you the big picture in enough detail to provide a clear image, while sparing you the irrelevant and confusing aspects.

About This Book

Forget all those other guidebooks where you have to wade through a small forest's worth of paper to find out the one thing you wanted to know. *Arizona For Dummies* is a reference book as well as a guide, which means that you don't have to read it from cover to cover — or even from front to back. Each section and chapter is as self-contained as possible so you can concentrate on what's important to you at the moment. You can always go back to a different section later if you feel like it. Honest.

Just because the chapters are self-contained, though, it doesn't mean that I keep repeating myself; I've been cornered at enough weddings by bores who want to keep telling me the same stories about their trip to Hawaii to know better (of course, trips to Arizona are endlessly fascinating). If I cover a topic that interests you in one section of the book, I refer you to that area rather than waste your time — and mine — by going over the information again.

Maybe you want an honest evaluation of the hotels near the Grand Canyon's South Rim, and then want to find the best way to book the one you chose — and at the best rate. No problem. Simply go to the "Where to Stay" section of the Grand Canyon's South Rim in Chapter 17 to find a hotel, and then skip back to Chapter 8 for tips on getting a great hotel deal. Or say you're traveling with children and want to follow the kid-friendly itinerary outlined in Chapter 3, but don't know which restaurants would welcome you when you turn up with the brood. Just consult the different chapters mentioned in that itinerary, flip to the "Where to Dine" sections, and look for the Kid Friendly icon. (I explain all the icons [those funny symbols in the margins] a little later in this Introduction.)

Please be advised that travel information is subject to change at any time — and this is especially true of prices. I therefore suggest that you write or call ahead for confirmation when making your travel plans. The authors, editors, and publisher cannot be held responsible for the experiences of readers while traveling. Your safety is important to us, however, so we encourage you to stay alert and be aware of your surroundings. Keep a close eye on cameras, purses, and wallets, all favorite targets of thieves and pickpockets.

Conventions Used in This Book

In this book, I include lists of hotels and restaurants. These are usually divided into two categories — my personal favorites and those that don't quite make my preferred list but still get my hearty seal of approval. Don't be shy about considering these "runner-up" spots. If you're unable to get a room or table at one of my favorites, or if your preferences differ from mine, the runner-up locations are all worthy of your consideration.

I also include some general pricing information to help you as you decide where to unpack your bags or dine on the local cuisine. I use a system of dollar signs to show a range of costs for one night in a hotel (the price refers to a double-occupancy room) or a meal for one at a restaurant (without alcohol). Check out the following table to decipher the dollar signs:

Cost	Hotel	Restaurant
$	$75 or less	$10 or less
$$	$76–$125	$11–$20
$$$	$126–$175	$21–$35
$$$$	$176 or more	$36 or more

Throughout the book, I also use abbreviations for credit cards. Sorry, I only had room for the biggies, so though your local discount club or gas card may well be accepted in Arizona, I couldn't include *everything*. The plastic that appears in these pages is:

AE	American Express
CB	Carte Blanche
DC	Diners Club
DISC	Discover Card
MC	MasterCard
V	Visa

To make pertinent information stand out, attractions and main telephone numbers (usually toll-free) are in **bold** typeface. The telephone numbers have little, tiny telephones next to them, too.

Foolish Assumptions

As I wrote this book, I made some assumptions about you and what your needs may be as a traveler. Here's what I assumed about you:

- ✔ You may be an inexperienced traveler looking for guidance when determining whether to take a trip to Arizona and how to plan for it.

- ✔ You may be an experienced traveler who hasn't had much time to explore Arizona and wants expert advice when you finally do get a chance to enjoy that particular locale.

- ✔ You're not looking for a book that provides all the information available about Arizona or that lists every hotel, restaurant, or attraction available to you. Instead, you're looking for a book that focuses on the places that will give you the best or most unique experiences in this beautiful state.

If you fit any of this criteria, then *Arizona For Dummies* gives you the information you're looking for!

How This Book Is Organized

The information in this book is methodically arranged in an easy-to-use, logical fashion (it's a good thing you can't see the stacks of paper piled on the floor of my home office). First of all, it's divvied up into five parts, each one covering a major aspect of your trip. Those parts are then further subdivided into chapters that cover more specific topics, so you can zoom in on the one you're interested in. The sections break down as follows.

Part I: Getting Started

In this part, I introduce you to Arizona and fill you in on what you need to consider when planning a trip to the state — everything from the dates of major festivals to the weather at different times of the year to the portion of your budget you need to allot to transportation. I even offer several possible itineraries for you. Although much of the advice in Part I applies to everyone, it's also designed to take individual differences into account, offering special tips for you whether you're going solo or leading the pack.

Part II: Ironing Out the Details

This nitty-gritty section walks you through those potentially difficult trip-planning stages, covering the top ways to make travel arrangements, whether you decide to go it on your own, book an escorted tour, or do something in-between; the types of transportation you'll find in Arizona; your accommodation options; and the best methods of dealing with money matters and (heaven forbid) illness while you're on the road. It also helps you wrap up those last-minute details — everything from buying travel insurance to packing.

Part III: Exploring the Big Cities

Here you find out all about Greater Phoenix and Tucson, getting the lowdown on hotels, restaurants, sights, tours, activities, shops, and nightlife in Arizona's two major cities. I don't overload you with choices, though: I cut to the chase with the best options plus some alternatives in each category. I also explain why I think they're prime — that way you can decide whether you agree (in other words, I can't make you like Garth Brooks, but I can tell you I think a bar is great because it plays his music all the time). Two additional chapters in this section give you the details on fun side trips you can take from each of the cities.

Part IV: Exploring the Regions

This part does for Arizona's top touring regions what Part III does for the cities, only on a larger scale. I pare down info even more than in the city chapters. For example, because there's no nightlife to speak of near the Grand Canyon, I don't speak of it — that is, I don't include a section on nightlife. For details on the regions I chose and the reasons I chose them, see Chapter 2 (see, I told you I wasn't going to repeat myself).

Part V: The Part of Tens

No, this is not something out of Star Trek, though Seven of Nine may come to mind (if you're a bit of a trekkie as — I confess — I am). Perhaps David Letterman's Top Ten list is somewhat closer to the mark. It's a fun section that highlights things that are characteristic of — some might say peculiar to — Arizona, including the top crafts to buy, the key foods to identify, and the prime ways for you to blend in with the locals.

Quick Concierge

You also find two other elements near the back of this book. I include an appendix — your Quick Concierge — containing lots of handy information about services in Arizona, such as phone numbers and Web sites for airlines, hotel chains, car rental agencies, local newspapers and magazines, and tourist information centers. You also find contact information for area hospitals, pharmacies, and police. Check out this appendix when searching for answers to lots of little questions that may come up as you travel, or even before you leave.

I also include a bunch of *worksheets* to make your travel planning easier — among other things, you can determine your travel budget, create specific itineraries, and keep a log of your favorite restaurants so you can hit them again next time you're in town. You can find these worksheets easily because they're printed on yellow paper.

Icons Used in This Book

Brevity is the soul of wit, the Bard said, and who doesn't want to be witty? Thus, the cute little drawings in the margins throughout this book (well, I think they're cute — and even if you don't, you're probably going to have to admit they're useful). They serve as a kind of shorthand or code. Here's the encryption key:

This book is entirely devoted to giving you useful advice, but this symbol lets you know when you should really pay attention if you want to make the most of your time and energy.

A tip off to rip-offs, tourist traps, and other things you should keep an eye out for, lest they interfere with your general sense of well-being.

A green light for attractions, hotels, restaurants, and activities that are particularly kid-friendly.

This alerts you to money-saving tips (like "Never buy retail" — oops, that's another book) and/or great deals.

A gentle nudge in the ribs to point out stuff you're unlikely to see outside of the Southwest. These tend mostly to be historic, but sometimes new things manage to achieve that ineffable quality of Arizona-ness.

Smooch-potential alert. Along with spectacular sunsets and starry, starry nights, this state has lots of other ways to help create that lovin' feeling, and this icon tells you what and where they are.

Where to Go from Here

Well, to Arizona of course. Oh, you want me to be a little more specific? Just dip into these pages as you would into a Phoenix swimming pool in February — one toe at a time until you realize just how inviting the water is and you take the plunge. Most of all, get yourself prepared to have a blast. We like everything from clothing styles to tequila shots kicked back here in Arizona, and a little hootin' and hollerin' is definitely permitted.

Part I
Getting Started

The 5th Wave   By Rich Tennant

"Yeah, this is the Painted Desert. Try to stay on the drop cloths, okay?"

In this part. . .

So you think you want to go to Arizona — but what's it really like, anyway? When's the best time to go? What are the top travel routes? What resources are available to you if you're (fill in the blank) single, traveling with a family, gay, mobility impaired? So many questions — and so many answers. Let's just call this part Arizona 101, a quick introduction to the state's geography, travel economics, and more.

Chapter 1

Discovering the Best of Arizona

. . . .

In This Chapter

▶ Getting to know the old, new, and eternal West

▶ Shopping indoors or playing outdoors

▶ Reviewing the best sleeps and eats

. . . .

*P*icture a land of silent, manly men and spirited, sun-worn women leaving clouds of dust in the wake of their pickups as they hightail it through rugged canyon lands and parched, sparse deserts. Of noble braves in touch with Earth's ancient wisdom. Of lonely Mexican cantinas and rundown roadside cafes. . . .

Then give it a name: Arizona.

Okay. You've obviously been watching too many westerns and truck commercials.

Me, too. Before I moved to Tucson, nearly a decade ago, I had many of the same preconceptions about the state.

As it happens, the men in Arizona are far more likely to golf, hike, or mountain bike than to rope cattle, and the sassiest females are generally from New York City, like me. Women here know better than to go outdoors without slathering on sunscreen, and if their skin gets parched they head for the nearest spa. More contrasts to your possible preconceived notions: Arizona's Sonoran Desert is lush with vegetation, much of the income of the southern Native American nations comes from casinos, and a long line often forms for the best Mexican restaurants, which tend to be in lively downtown barrios.

But . . . the scenery is as spectacular as anything you'd ever imagine (more than 80 percent of the state is undeveloped), ancient traditions are alive and well on the Indian reservations, and several cattle ranches are still active; some even rent their rooms.

And Arizona has long stretches of open roads and a highway speed limit of 75 mph. Zooming down those long, wide roads in a convertible with music blaring on the radio is not a bad way to spend an afternoon.

Arizona

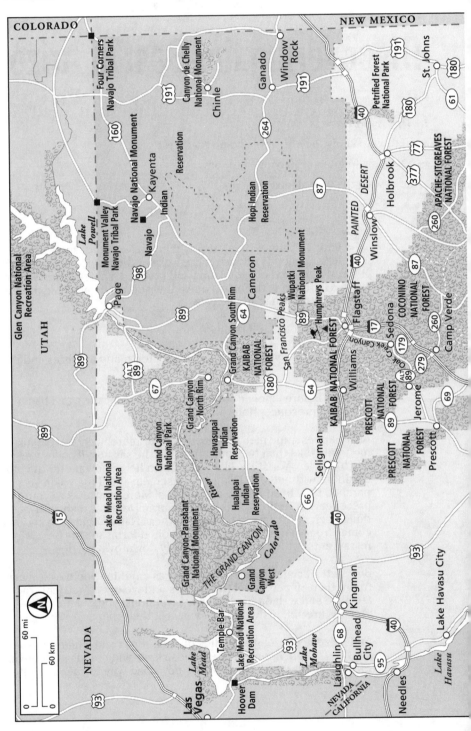

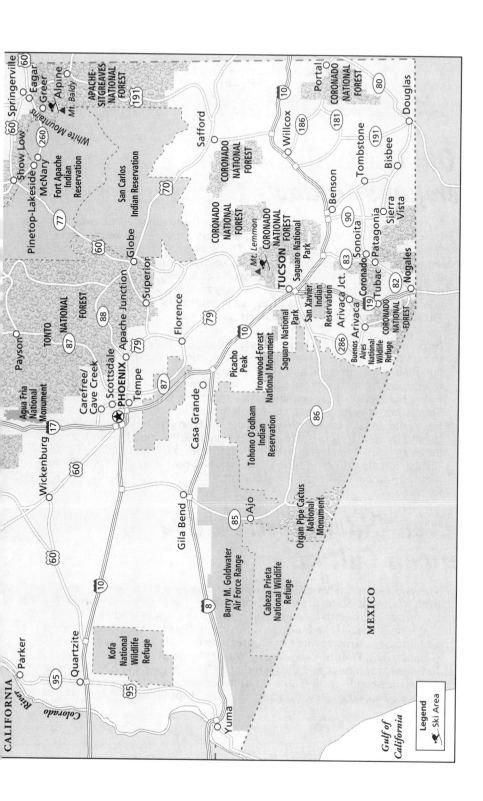

The Art of the State

You are in for a real treat. As a result of my love of Arizona and my years of arduous statewide research — hey, all that sightseeing, trekking, jeep touring, dining, resort-ing, and spa-ing isn't easy — I now know the best and I spare you the rest.

The Old West: Missionaries, Miners, and Outlaws

No real showdowns are in Arizona's streets these days — not counting the occasional shouting match over a parking spot — but remnants of the state's colorful history abound. The Spanish — the first European settlers — left their marks throughout southern Arizona, most notably in the beautiful missions of **Tumacacori** (Chapter 15) and **San Xavier del Bac** in Tucson (Chapter 13). You may also see sections of the adobe *presidios* (fortresses) at **Tubac Presidio State Park** and the **Tucson Museum of Art and Historic Block.**

Next came the seekers of gold, silver, and copper riches and they tended to be a rowdy bunch — which gave mining boomtowns like **Tombstone** and **Bisbee** (Chapter 15) and **Wickenburg** and **Jerome** (Chapter 16) their rough 'n' tumble reputations. All of these towns thrive on tourism today, but plenty of the genuine historical article is still left. And while Tombstone may have been "too tough to die," lots of other get-quick-rich towns did, in fact, expire; check out the skeletons these settlements left behind by visiting some of the ghost towns nearby. For a look into the industry behind the legends, tour the underground copper mine in Bisbee, not shut down until 1975, and the still-operating open pit copper mine at **Asarco,** south of Tucson (Chapter 15).

The Even Older West: Native American Culture

The people the Spanish padres were on a mission to convert — and from whom the Spanish needed protection — were the land's original inhabitants: the Native Americans. You can see traces of civilizations that long predated the Europeans' arrival in these parts in such central and northern Arizona sites as **Montezuma's Castle** and **Tuzigoot** (Chapter 16), **Walnut Canyon** and **Wupatki** (Chapter 17), and **Navajo National Monument** and **Canyon de Chelly** (Chapter 18). The cultures of their descendents still flourish in the state, which is home to most of the huge **Navajo reservation** and all of the **Hopi lands** (Chapter 18).

For background into the past (and present) of the Southwest native peoples, the world-class **Heard Museum** in Phoenix (Chapter 11) is the best — hands down. Other good resources include Flagstaff's **Northern Arizona Museum** (Chapter 17) and the **Amerind Foundation Museum** in the Dragoon Mountains (Chapter 15), both in wonderful historic buildings, and the newer annex of Tucson's **Arizona State Museum.**

The New and (Maybe) Future West

The arrival of the railroad in the 1880s not only made hauling copper and silver ore more efficient, but the railroad also brought new industries to Arizona — including, in the north, lumber. (At Flagstaff's **Riordan Mansion State Park,** see Chapter 17, you may see just how lucrative wood chucking can be.) Rail lines also helped jumpstart the state's ongoing tourism boom, which has lately entered a steam engine–nostalgia phase: Service has been restored on the **Grand Canyon Railway** (Chapter 17) and a one-time mining line near Jerome has been pressed into service for the scenic **Verde Canyon Railroad** excursion (Chapter 16).

Williams (Chapter 17), the Grand Canyon Railway's point of departure, is also the last town on **Old Route 66** to be bypassed by I-40 (in 1985) — which makes it a hot spot for both railroad and Mother Road buffs. You find cool neon signs on the northeast side of the state, where you also see giant jackrabbits, dinosaurs, and wigwams on Route 66 in and around **Winslow** and **Holbrook** (Chapter 18).

Not surprisingly, the idea of driving through Arizona did not take hold until the advent of air-conditioning after World War II. Architect Frank Lloyd Wright, however, appreciated desert living, as tours of his house and studio, **Taliesen West,** outside of Scottsdale (Chapter 12), prove. His student, Paolo Solieri, took the idea of desert habitation one step further at **Arcosanti** (Chapter 12), a yet-to-be completed study of a self-sustaining community.

Of course Arizona's most famous — and perhaps strangest — experiment in self-sufficiency was **Biosphere 2,** north of Tucson (Chapter 14). Columbia University later gave the project scientific validity, but you can still see (and even enter) the giant terrarium where eight people holed up for two years in the early 1990s. The science center's new **astronomical observatory** joins many others in southern Arizona, which has — and helps create — some of the world's most advanced sky-search instruments. You can tour top-rated facilities at **Kitt Peak, Mt. Graham** (Chapter 14), **Mt. Hopkins** (Chapter 15), and their Flagstaff predecessor in the north, **Lowell Observatory** (Chapter 17), where the planet Pluto was discovered.

Amazing Landscapes of the Eternal West

Civilizations and scientific theories come and go over the centuries, but scenery generally lasts a bit longer, and Arizona has some of the most striking, often startling, landscapes on this planet. Only Arizona and Mexico grow the gigantic saguaro cactus, and Tucson's **Saguaro National Park** hosts many of these prickly plants. You may visit its skinnier-armed cousin, the organ pipe cactus, at **Organ Pipe National Monument** in Ajo (Chapter 14). Other prime cacti spots are Tucson's **Arizona-Sonora Desert Museum,** Phoenix's **Desert Botanical Garden,** and the **Boyce Thompson Southwestern Arboretum** near Superior (Chapter 12).

Are you bowled over by boulders? Check out the eerie, weirdly balanced stones at **Chiricahua National Monument** (Chapter 15); the astonishingly **red cliffs of Sedona** (Chapter 16); the strangely shaped spires and mesas at **Monument Valley** (Chapter 18); and the rocks-formerly-known-as-wood at **Petrified National Forest** (Chapter 18), which have the lovely pastel-hued **Painted Desert** as a backdrop.

The down (and down) side? Canyons, for one thing. In addition to the superstar hole that gave Arizona its nickname — the **Grand Canyon State** (Chapter 17) — there's also the less dramatic but equally beautiful **Canyon de Chelly** (Chapter 18). At **Lake Powell** (also Chapter 18), you can see what happens when you take gorgeous gorges like these and add water. And these days you can also go batty over **Kartchner Caverns,** a living cave — still dripping water to form stalactites and stalagmites — near Benson (Chapter 15), which opened to the public in late 1999.

Getting Artsy and Craftsy: The Retail West

Something about the quality of the light — not to mention the quantity of the (lower) rents — draws creative types to Arizona. The tiny towns of **Tubac** (Chapter 15) and **Jerome** (Chapter 16) may have the most **crafters** per capita in the nation. **Fine art galleries** abound in **Tucson** (Chapter 13) but the concentrations are greater in **Scottsdale** (Chapter 11) and **Sedona** (Chapter 16), both renowned for their western paintings and sculptures.

You're bound to find mucho Mexican crafts in a state that straddles the border, but why not go to the source — or at least the more authentic clearinghouse — **Nogales, Mexico** (Chapter 15), right across the border from Nogales, Arizona. Bargaining in this Mexican city is part of the elaborate shopping dance. Don't like to stray from the U. S. of A.? You can get many of the same items — at prices not all that much higher — in nearby **Tubac** (Chapter 15) as well as in the **Lost Barrio** section of Tucson (Chapter 13).

Although you find Native American crafts for sale in practically every nook and cranny of Arizona, you're better off buying directly from the Indian reservations. Several old trading posts on the **Navajo Nation,** especially the **Hubbell Trading Post National Historic Site** (Chapter 18), are great places to rationalize your purchases in the name of historic research. And you may use the "cultural exchange" excuse when buying directly from **artisans' homes** on the **Hopi reservation** (also Chapter 18). You may have a harder time finding the baskets of the **Tohono O'odham** tribe of southwest Arizona; the best place to try is the gift shop of **Kitt Peak National Observatory** (Chapter 14), on land owned by the tribe.

Get your kitsch on Route 66. **Williams** (Chapter 17) is a prime source of highway nostalgia tchotchkes and home of the official Route 66 store (where a magazine devoted to the road is published). You can also find great tacky souvenirs that aren't quite so self-referential in and around Holbrook.

Playing Outdoors: The Active West

Arizona abounds with outdoor playgrounds, from landscaped greens to starry skies.

Both Tucson and the greater Phoenix area are meccas for **desert golf,** which is played on desert courses and often called "target golf" because it emphasizes aim rather than distance. But if you prefer traditional courses to cacti fields, both cities also offer plenty of wide, rolling greens for those a bit, well, greener about playing through prickly stuff. Expect state-of-the-art scenery and stunning equipment on the newest courses.

Nearly every spot I mention in the previous "Amazing Landscapes of the Eternal West" section is great for **hiking;** the exceptions are the desert areas in summer and Lake Powell itself (as opposed to the non-flooded canyons nearby). Saguaro National Park East in Tucson, South Mountain Park in Phoenix, and the red rock areas around Sedona stand out when it comes to **mountain biking. Jeep touring** is another key desert activity; nature outfitters are as common as cactus in the Valley of the Sun (the Phoenix area) and Tucson. Navajo-guided four-wheeling in Monument Valley is great, too, but for scenic off-roading, you can't beat Sedona, where the rocks are red and the jeeps are pink.

You can **horseback ride** off into the sunset to your heart's content if you stay at a guest ranch (see "From Horse Courts to Golf Resorts: The Bunkhouse West" later in this chapter). You can also book day rides into the desert (try Tucson, Phoenix, or Wickenburg); into the craggier regions around Sedona and Prescott (Chapter 16); or into northern plateau lands like Monument Valley and Canyon de Chelly. Most famous of the four-legged tours, however, are the mule rides into the Grand Canyon, where the animals get the epithet "sure-footed."

If winging it is your thing, you are in heaven in southeast Arizona (Chapter 15), one of this country's top five **bird-watching** spots. On their yearly jaunts between their summer and winter homes in Canada and Mexico, nearly 500 avian species like to hang out at watering holes like Madera Canyon, the Patagonia-Sonoita Creek Preserve, the Ramsey Canyon Creek Preserve, the San Pedro Riparian National Conservation Area, and the Willcox Playa.

No need to stop looking up after dark, however: The **stargazing** is stellar in Arizona. The scientists bogart most of the telescopes at the major observatories (see the previous "The New and (Maybe) Future West," section), but you may catch night-sky viewing programs in the south at the Flandrau Planetarium at Tucson's University of Arizona, at Biosphere 2, at Kitt Peak, at the Gov Aker Observatory near Mt. Graham, and at Flagstaff's Lowell Observatory in the north.

I won't try to pass Arizona off as a major **ski** center, but Snowbowl near Flagstaff has the right stuff when it has the white stuff (Snowbowl doesn't make its own snow); Tucson's Mount Lemmon boasts this continent's southernmost ski area — which means you can sometimes schuss in shorts. Having "waterfront property in Arizona" is another supposed joke — but outfitters who run **river-rafting** trips along the Colorado River in the Grand Canyon laugh all the way to the bank, as do the water-toy and speedboat concessionaires at Lake Powell.

From Horse Courts to Golf Resorts: The Bunkhouse West

Most of Arizona's old dude ranches are gone (and the dudes are now called guests — at least to their faces), but several of those that remain are winners. Some of the top places to hole up with a horse include **Tanque Verde Ranch** and **White Stallion Ranch** in Tucson (Chapter 13), **Grapevine Canyon Ranch** near Chiricahua National Monument (Chapter 15), **Circle Z Ranch** in Patagonia (Chapter 15), and **Kay El Bar** and **Merv Griffin's Wickenburg Inn and Dude Ranch** in Wickenburg (Chapter 16).

Southern Arizona's modern **luxury resorts** are equipped with great golf courses, tony spas, and pools that may make you forget you're in the desert. These resorts are travel goals in themselves, not just means to a (sightseeing) end. Some of my favorite miniature pamper cities are **The Boulders,** the **Fairmont Scottsdale Princess,** and the **Four Seasons** in Scottsdale (Chapter 11) and the **Sheraton El Conquistador, Loew's Ventana Canyon,** and the **Westin La Paloma** in Tucson (Chapter 13). Tucson also hosts two of the world's top **destination spas** — **Canyon Ranch** and **Miraval.** Outside the DRZ (Desert Resort Zone), but equally impressive, is **Enchantment** in Sedona (substitute jeep touring for golf, though) (Chapter 16).

You don't have to exchange luxury for historic character in Arizona. Some of the state's top resorts and hotels keep their very venerable pasts polished — and modernized. In Tucson (Chapter 13), these accommodations include **Westward Look,** a full-service resort; the **Arizona Inn,** the city's most gracious hotel; and the **Hacienda del Sol,** which falls somewhere in between the luxury and historic categories. In the Valley of the Sun (Chapter 11), the **Arizona Biltmore** and **Marriott's Camelback Inn** can't have more (or better) posh amenities, while the **Royal Palms** and the **Hermosa Inn** are boutique hotel charmers.

If you care more about Lewis & Clark than Crabtree & Evelyn, you're likely to be happy in digs with more character than cachet — not to mention lower prices. In fact, Bisbee's **Copper Queen** (Chapter 15), the **Hassayampa Inn** in Prescott (Chapter 16), **La Posada** in Holbrook (Chapter 18), the **El Tovar** at the Grand Canyon's South Rim, and the **Grand Canyon Lodge** at the North Rim (see Chapter 17 for both) were all tops of the tourist luxury lines in their heydays (the first half of the twentieth century). Lodgings that never aspire to more than rustic comfort, but which go far beyond basic, include the **Thunderbird Lodge** at the Canyon de Chelly (Chapter 18), **Goulding's Lodge** near Monument Valley (Chapter 18), and the **Bright Angel Lodge** on the Grand Canyon's South Rim (Chapter 17).

Arizona is nothing if not colorful and that's evident in some of its more unusual B&Bs, which cater to special interests. Birders love to watch the hummingbirds flitting outside the windows of the **Ramsey Canyon Bed & Breakfast,** near the nature preserve (Chapter 15). Do your tastes run to things celestial? Try the **Skywatcher's Inn** outside of Benson (Chapter 15), which has its own observatory. Winter sports and canine buffs alike go barking mad for the **Sled Dog Inn** near Flagstaff (Chapter 17), with its resident team of Siberian huskies. The **Red Garter Inn** in Williams (Chapter 17) is a converted bordello, but the hottest happenings these days are in the downstairs bakery.

Speaking of heat, my picks for the most romantic B&Bs are Tucson's **Catalina Park Inn** (Chapter 13); Sedona's **Wishing Well** (Chapter 16); **Rocamadour,** just outside of Prescott (Chapter 16); and Flagstaff's **Inn at Four Ten** (Chapter 17).

Eating the West: The Tastes of the Southwest

The restaurants in Arizona's big cities — Phoenix and Tucson — cover a wide and sophisticated culinary range. But I recommend sampling the specialties of the state — foods you're not likely to find (or find done as well) in other places. (You don't eat Chinese food in France, do you?) Many culinary possibilities are available for your palate to explore: Mexican, Southwestern, new Southwestern, and Native American cuisines.

Arizona borders the northern Mexican state of Sonora, where beef is big, chiles tend to be not quite incendiary, and cheese is a major ingredient. In Nogales, Mexico you can enjoy the genuine items in a romantic atmosphere at **La Roca** (Chapter 15). For far-flung regional dishes not prepared in most other places, Tucson's **Café Poca Cosa** is tops; if you like local flavor, try one of the restaurants on the city's South 4th Avenue — say, **Mi Nidito** (Chapter 13 for both). **Los Dos Molinos** in south Phoenix specializes in spicier New Mexican dishes — definitely not for those who walk on the mild side; central Phoenix's **San Carlos Bay** caters to seafood lovers; while **La Hacienda** in Scottsdale is the most upscale — and most creative — of the Valley of the Sun bunch (Chapter 11 for all three). North of the Valley, you pretty much pass the cutoff line for good, authentic Mexican food (ooh, will I get flak for that statement!), but **Oaxaca,** in Sedona, is a notable, cheerful exception (Chapter 16).

New Southwestern cuisine (so termed by chefs to distinguish it from the plainer Mexican and cowboy fare folks associate with the old Southwest) is known for its use of local ingredients like blue corn and (deprickled) cactus pads, a creative melange of cooking styles, and visually stimulating presentations. Primo practitioners of this (usually) upscale mix-it-up cuisine in Tucson are **Janos,** where the food has a slight French accent; **J-Bar,** the same chef's less expensive, more Mexicano cafe; and **Café Terra Cotta,** where Native America and Asia meet (Chapter 13 for all three). Asia also puts in a strong appearance at Phoenix's **RoxSand** (Chapter 11). In Scottsdale, **Norman's Arizona** describes itself as Nueva Mexicana and the **Roaring Fork** does innovative takes on steak and other Old West staples (Chapter 11 for both). Get a low-key (and low-budget) introduction to this type of cooking at **Sam's Café,** with three branches in the Valley (Chapter 11). In Sedona, **Heartline Café** and the **Yavapai Room** are the best keepers of the New Southwestern flame (Chapter 16 for both).

On the opposite end of the spectrum is the food of **Native America,** which tends to cozy up with Mexico. The fare is not light (one of its staples is fry bread, which is exactly what it says it is), but it's tasty and inexpensive. My vote for the top Navajo taco in the best setting goes to the **Cameron Trading Post** restaurant near the Grand Canyon's South Rim (Chapter 17). The Navajo lamb stew is fine at **Goulding's** restaurant, close to Monument Valley (Chapter 18). For Hopi specialties like piki bread, the restaurant at the **Hopi Cultural Center** on Second Mesa — the only full-menu eatery on that reservation — wins by default, but the food's good, too (Chapter 18).

Chapter 2

Deciding When and Where to Go

. . . .

In This Chapter

▶ What I cover in this book — and why

▶ The pros and cons of the different seasons

▶ Arizona's top festivals and events

▶ A few trip-planning tips

. . . .

1'm not going to try to fool you (you'd figure it out, anyway, when you look at a map): I don't cover every inch of Arizona in this book. That would require a volume twice this size and half as useful. Besides, who has that much time?

I don't even cover every single great spot. Some places are so far out of the way that, getting to these locations, you miss out on places that are even better. And some places are fine for Arizonans — for example, the White Mountains in the eastern part of the state are a great escape from the lower reaches' summer heat — but these mountains may not thrill you if you come to see landscapes that can't be found anywhere except in the Southwest.

I select the top cities (okay, so that selection doesn't require the smarts of a rocket scientist because Arizona only has two major cities) and regions (you *can* give me some credit for choosing these areas). Within these locations, I cover the best attractions to see and events to do so that you don't waste a minute of your hard-earned vacation time going anywhere unworthy.

The Cities

Be prepared: Arizona's major urban areas are not the compact, strol-lable spaces that most travelers associate with the term "city." Both Phoenix and Tucson came of age while America was romancing the auto and their original historic centers did not hold. Take these two sprawling Sonoran Desert metropolises for what they are — the (heat)

waves of the future. Incidentally, though Tucson is farther south than Phoenix, it's generally about 5 degrees cooler — in part because its 2,100-foot elevation is 1,000 feet higher than Phoenix's and because it has less heat-retaining concrete.

The Valley of the Sun (Also known as Greater Phoenix)

Arizona's largest, most populous city (and its state capital) is actually a metropolitan complex. The two best-known components of this complex are Phoenix and Scottsdale. (I cover the Valley in more depth in Chapter 11.) Growing rapidly and adding great restaurants, shopping centers, and resorts, but subtracting desert terrain, the Valley of the Sun is quintessentially New West. Side trips from the Valley (check out Chapter 12) explore a far more pristine landscape (the **Apache Trail**), visit Arizona's Hohokam past (**Casa Grande**), and provide a possible antidote against future shock (**Arcosanti**), among other things.

Tucson

The state's "second city" is first in terms of history and culture. Established almost a century earlier than Phoenix, Tucson still has lots of Old West and Spanish character. (I tell you all about it in Chapter 13.) Tucson also has more protected land, including a national park devoted to cacti. But the urban math formula works here too: Unbridled growth adds leisure amenities, while diminishing natural beauty. Side trips from Tucson (which I explore in detail in Chapter 14) lead to an observatory and more cacti (**Kitt Peak/Organ Pipe**) and to a place where people once lived in a glass house (**Biosphere 2**).

The Regions

The east central and far northwestern portions of the state have their appeal but don't significantly add to a first-time visitor's experience. The remaining areas of the state can be broken down into the following prime touring regions. Starting from the south . . .

Don't Try to See It All

You can't relax when you're trying to cover the entire state. Unless your vacation spans more than a week, concentrate on either northern or southern Arizona. The terrain within each region is really varied; no room for boredom, I promise. And if you fall in love with the state, you can always come back (like I did — permanently).

The Southeast

The region southeast of Tucson has it all: Old West color, including Tombstone and several remote guest ranches; venerable Spanish missions and new wineries; outdoor activities from horseback riding to birding; the state's latest underground attraction, Kartchner Caverns; and great shopping down Mexico way. I give you the details in Chapter 15.

Central

Within the up-and-down area northwest of Phoenix, renowned for its red rocks, granite dells, and spreading desert, Sedona vies with Scottsdale for the state's "ritziest little town" title; Prescott, the one-time territorial capital, is rich with Victoriana; and Wickenburg keeps its mining legends alive through its many dude ranches. Near Sedona, the Verde Valley offers a lively ghost town, a great train ride, and two well-preserved Indian ruins. Find more info on all of this in Chapter 16.

The Grand Canyon and the Northwest

The Grand Canyon speaks — or should I say gapes? — for itself, but the rest of the northwest area may surprise you. For example, Flagstaff, Arizona's third-largest city, has a kick-back college-town charm; the town is also home to ancient dwellings that were left behind in a land ravaged, and then fertilized, by some not-so-ancient volcanoes. Check out Chapter 17 for in-depth information.

The Northeast and Indian Country

One of Arizona's most remote and intriguing regions has landscapes that define the Southwest, including Monument Valley, Canyon de Chelly, and Petrified National Forest; the native cultures of the Navajo and the Hopi that keep its spiritual heart beating; and splashy attractions like Lake Powell. You can get your Route 66 kicks (and more) by turning to Chapter 18.

The Secrets of the Seasons

Because of Arizona's size and its varied topography, vacationing in the northern, Colorado Plateau part of the state is a completely different experience from touring the Sonoran Desert in the south. The areas differ greatly in temperatures and altitudes. In fact, these two regions are practically mirror opposites of each other — meaning Arizona always has great weather *somewhere*.

Central Arizona's climate? Of the three towns covered in Chapter 16, Sedona and Prescott tend to follow the northern area's weather patterns (though these towns are a bit warmer), while Wickenburg's weather goes as the south goes. Tables 2-1 and 2-2 give you a month-by-month breakdown of average temperatures and rainfall for Phoenix and Flagstaff, respectively.

Table 2-1   Phoenix's Average Temperatures (°F) and Rainfall (In Days)

	Jan	Feb	Mar	Apr	May	June	July	Aug	Sept	Oct	Nov	Dec
High	65	69	75	84	93	102	105	102	98	88	75	66
Low	38	41	45	52	60	68	78	76	69	57	45	39
Rain	4	4	3	2	1	1	4	5	3	3	2	4

Table 2-2   Flagstaff's Average Temperatures (°F) and Rainfall (In Days)

	Jan	Feb	Mar	Apr	May	June	July	Aug	Sept	Oct	Nov	Dec
High	41	44	48	57	67	76	81	78	74	63	51	43
Low	14	17	20	27	34	40	50	49	41	31	22	16
Rain	7	6	8	6	3	3	12	11	6	5	5	6

Southern Arizona

If you're like me and don't mind the heat — but, honey, when southern Arizona is hot, it's hot — you can't find a bad time of the year to visit this part of the state. Spring — when the mercury doesn't peak, but room prices do — is prime; unless the winter's unusually dry, the desert blooms with wildflowers.

Winter is wonderful because . . .
- ✔ The weather's glorious — sunny and warm — and perfect for sightseeing and anything else you want to do.
- ✔ Everything's happening — events, festivals, music, and theater programs . . . you name it.

But keep in mind . . .
- ✔ Room prices are at their highest.
- ✔ Crowds are at their largest — which means lots of traffic, too.

Spring is special because . . .
- ✔ The desert is usually a flowering wonderland.
- ✔ Room rates start to dip.

But keep in mind . . .

> ✔ Temperatures are beginning to creep up; it can get uncomfortably warm and you may enjoy better weather in your hometown.

> ✔ Prices are not as low as they're going to be soon.

Summer sizzles because . . .

> ✔ You may try the resort of your dreams for rock-bottom rates — and fancy restaurants run summer specials.

> ✔ The streets are uncrowded, what with both the students and the snowbirds (long-term winter visitors) gone.

But keep in mind . . .

> ✔ The sizzling is literal.

> ✔ Desert tours, hikes, and other activities slow or cease; many restaurants in the southeast close when their owners head for the hills.

Fall is fabulous because . . .

> ✔ The room rates are still fairly low.

> ✔ Activities like concerts and shows are coming back on track.

But keep in mind . . .

> ✔ It takes a while to cure that heat hangover; temperatures may still be uncomfortable.

> ✔ The University of Arizona and Arizona State University freshmen are beginners at driving around the streets of Tucson and Phoenix.

Northern Arizona

Northern Arizona doesn't have any loser seasons — even the cold isn't very cold — but fall is prime because the crowds thin and the weather's crisp and comfortable. Stay away from the Grand Canyon in summer, though, if you want to bond with nature more than with your fellow human beings' elbows.

Summer sizzles because . . .

> ✔ The weather is great — sunny, warm, and clear.

> ✔ Everything's open and everything's happening.

But keep in mind . . .

> ✔ This season is when everyone wants to visit; the Grand Canyon is a zoo.

> ✔ The room rates are as high as the sun in the sky.

Fall is fabulous because . . .

 ✔ The crowds go back to school and work.

 ✔ The weather's still sunny and an actual autumn season begins — colored leaves and all.

But keep in mind . . .

 ✔ Many places begin observing shorter hours; services start to close.

 ✔ The rates aren't at their lowest yet.

Winter is wonderful because . . .

 ✔ No scenery is prettier than the snow against the Grand Canyon (and Flagstaff is a winter sports mecca). If no snow is on the ground, the weather is crisp and clear.

 ✔ The room rates — and the crowds — bottom out; you enjoy your pick of lodgings.

But keep in mind . . .

 ✔ The Grand Canyon's North Rim is closed and you can't swim in Lake Powell without freezing your patooties off.

 ✔ Fewer services are offered than at any other time of year.

Spring is special because . . .

 ✔ Facilities reopen but the crowds aren't present.

 ✔ The weather is warming up.

But keep in mind . . .

 ✔ Mother Nature's erratic; snow may fall, the roads may close, and the temperature's still not warm enough to dip into Lake Powell.

 ✔ The rates are beginning to warm up, too.

Arizona's Calendar of Events

In addition to the typical American holiday festivities and the events listed below, expect celebrations in southern Arizona for *Cinco de Mayo* (May 5), commemorating Mexico's victory over the French in an 1862 battle, and, to a lesser extent, for the Day of the Dead (All Soul's Day), in early November. Christmas in the southern part of the state also has a Mexican accent, with *luminarias* (candles in small paper bags) lighting the paths to many churches and homes.

January

Fiesta Bowl Football Classic, Tempe (Chapter 11). January 1–4, Sun Devil Stadium. College football's biggest competition — and biggest post-game bash. Getting tickets is as tough as the guys on the teams; put yourself on the waiting list in August or September at the latest (☎ **480-350-0911;** Internet: www.tostitosfiestabowl.com).

Phoenix Open: Scottsdale (Chapter 11). Tournament Players Club of Scottsdale. Late January. One of the PGA Tour's top events, with the world's top golfers competing (☎ **602-870-4431;** Internet: www.phoenixopen.com).

Parada Del Sol Rodeo: Scottsdale (Chapter 11). Late January/early February. Rodeos, line dances, live country music, games, a huge parade . . . the whole Western shebang (☎ **480-502-1880** or 480-990-3179; Internet: www.rawhide.com).

February

Winterfest: Flagstaff (Chapter 17). Entire month of February. More than 100 events include sled-dog races, llama games, skiing, sleigh rides, snow sculpture . . . pretty much any way you can think of to play in the snow (or, absent that, cold) (☎ **520-774-4505;** Internet: www.flagstaff.az.us).

Tucson Gem and Mineral Show: Tucson (Chapter 13). First two weeks in February. The convention center and downtown hotel rooms load up with fabulous stones, jewels, and fossils in a huge, multi-faceted event. Keep these dates in mind even if you don't care about crystals or dinosaurs; hotel rooms are hard to nab (☎ **520-322-5773**).

Festival of the Arts: Tubac (Chapter 15). First full week of February. This artsy town is in full glory with juried art shows, crafts demonstrations — and, of course, food booths (☎ **520-398-2371;** Internet: www.tubacaz.com).

O'odham Tash: Casa Grande (Chapter 12). Mid-February. Dozens of tribes gather for arts and crafts exhibits, dance performances, and rodeos at one of the country's largest annual Native American festivals (☎ **602-444-8000**).

La Fiesta De Los Vaqueros Rodeo & Parade: Tucson (Chapter 13). Final full week of February. A Tucson school kids' favorite: All classes are suspended for the kickoff of America's largest annual winter rodeo. Visiting young 'uns also like the marching bands, floats, and one of the world's longest parades with horse-drawn floats (☎ **520-741-2233**).

March

Guild Indian Fair and Market: Phoenix (Chapter 11). First weekend in March. Today's most talented Native American artists gather for a juried competition, preceded by a reception, followed by sales (☎ 602-252-8840; Internet: www.heard.org/visit/cal.html).

Festival of the West: Scottsdale (Chapter 11). Mid-March. This one's major: Cowboy poets, Western films, shooting contests, chuck wagon cook-off . . . yee-HAW (☎ 602-996-4387; Internet: www.festivalofthewest.com).

O'odham Day Celebration: Ajo (Chapter 14). Third Saturday in March. The Tohono O'odham, the country's second-largest Indian tribe, demonstrate everything from basket weaving to the *toka* game — a kind of women's land hockey played with willow pucks. A kid's corner has hands-on activities (☎ 520-387-6849).

Welcome Back Buzzards: Superios (Chapter 12). Late March, Boyce Thompson Arboretum. The resident flock of turkey vultures returns to their roosts in the eucalyptus grove to great hoopla (yes, there's a bird of prey send-off, too, in September) (☎ 520-689-2723).

April

International Mariachi Conference: Tucson (Chapter 13). Last or second-to-last weekend in April. This lively festival, with folk dancers, workshops, and mariachi star-studded concerts, often gets hometown girl Linda Ronstadt up on stage. Viva mariachi! (☎ 520-884-9920 ext. 243; Internet: www.azstarnet.com/~timc).

May

Wyatt Earp Days: Tombstone (Chapter 15). Memorial Day weekend. Chili cook-off, Country & Western bands, and general gunslinger-style rowdiness, including a replay of the you-know-what at the you-know-where (think Wyatt Earp and Doc Holliday versus the Clantons) (☎ 800-457-3423).

Rendezvous Days: Williams (Chapter 17). Memorial Day weekend. A festive re-enactment of the springtime regrouping of the trappers known as mountain men (but the actors are townsfolk who, presumably, take a few showers over the winter) (☎ 520-635-4061).

Phippen Western Art Show and Sale: Prescott (Chapter 16). Memorial Day weekend. A major Western art event, drawing artists from Canada, Mexico, and the U.S. working in the Lonesome Cowboy mode (☎ **520-778-1385**).

Paseo de Casas: Jerome (Chater 16). Third weekend in May. Tours of historic homes and public buildings ranging from ritzy Victorians to renovated miner's shacks, plus art shows and photos from the Jerome Historical Society Archives (☎ **520-634-2900** or 520-634-5477).

June

Heritage Days: Flagstaff (Chapter 17). Last weeks of June. Celebrating the region's history in ranching, railroading, and Route 66 hot-rodding (☎ **520-779-5300** or 520-779-0384). The **Pine Country Pro Rodeo** takes place around the same dates and sometimes falls under the aegis of Heritage Days (☎ **800-842-7293** or 800-KOA-FLAG).

July

Frontier Days & World's Oldest Rodeo: Prescott (Chapter 16). July 4th weekend. It's hard to prove that "world's oldest" claim — who started keeping rodeo records, anyway? — but the parade, fireworks, melodramas, bands, and more are rip roarin' fun (☎ **520-445- 3103** or 800-266-7534).

The Museum of Northern Arizona kicks off its summer-long (Flagstaff, Chapter 17, early July through mid-September) schedule of events with the **Hopi Marketplace,** featuring sales of Native American artwork, crafts demonstrations, and tribal dances. The **Navajo Marketplace** is in early August, the **Zuni Marketplace** in early September, and the **Pai Marketplace** in mid-September (☎ **520-774-5213;** Internet: www.musnaz.org/Calendar).

August

Southwest Wings Birding Festival: Sierra Vista (Chapter 15). Mid-August. Hummingbirds rule, but bats and owls are among the other winged birds touted on field trips, displays, and lectures (☎ **800-946- 4777** or 520-378-0233).

September

Navajo Nation Fair: Window Rock (Chapter 18). Early September. The tribe's prime powwow — literally — with arts and crafts demonstrations, horse racing, rodeo, traditional songs and dances, a fry bread contest, and more (☎ **520-871-6478**).

Grand Canyon Music Festival: Grand Canyon (Chapter 17). From early to late September. A more glorious setting for this annual series of evening concerts, ranging from classical to jazz, is hard to imagine (☎ **800-997-8285** or 520-638-9215; Internet: www. grandcanyonmusicfest.org).

Jazz on the Rocks: Sedona (Chapter 16). Late September. The red rocks — and the resorts and restaurant — are alive with the sounds of America's coolest music. This international event is very popular; if you want to attend, you should purchase your tickets up to two months in advance (☎ **520-282-1985;** Internet: www.sedonajazz.com).

Also see the Museum of Northern Arizona events in the "July" section.

October

Rex Allen Days: Willcox (Chapter 15). Early October. Rex Allen, Sr., was one of the silver screen's last great singing cowboys and Willcox celebrates her favorite son with four days of films, cowboy poetry, stunt riding, rodeos, and more. Dad died in 1999, but Rex Allen, Jr. and other country crooners are still in the saddle for this event (☎ **877-234-4111** or 520-384-4583).

Helldorado Days: Tombstone (Chapter 15). Third weekend in October. A public hanging, ladies' fashion show, gunfight under the stars, Indian dancers . . . just some typical events in the life of an 1880s western town (☎ **888-457-3929** or 520-457-9317).

Anza Days: Nogales/Tubac (Chapter 15). Late October. Riders dressed as Spanish soldiers re-enact the 1776 Juan Bautista expedition to California — at least the stretch of it between Nogales and Tubac (so, no, you don't end up at the Golden Gate Bridge). Food and entertainment celebrate the conquistadors' success (☎ **520-398-2704**).

La Fiesta de los Chiles: Tucson (Chapter 13). Late October. Chile-laden dishes, chile roasting, chile pot holders, chile planters . . . and the bands are hot, too (☎ **520-326-9686;** Internet: www. tucsonbotanical.org).

November

Thunderbird Balloon Classic: Scottsdale (Chapter 11). Early November. Up, up, and away with more than 150 beautiful hot-air balloons (☎ **602-978-7797;** Internet: www.t-birdballoonclassic.com).

Red Rock Fantasy of Lights: Sedona (Chapter 16). Mid-November through early January. Twinkle, twinkle, little lights — more than a million of them go into creating 60 themed displays that you stroll through while enjoying classical holiday music (☎ **520-282-1777**).

December

 Festival of Lights Boat Parade: Page (Chapter 18). First Saturday in December. Dock yourself at Wahweap Marina or anywhere on the five-mile long Lakeshore Drive to watch a dazzling array of boats floating in formation on Lake Powell (☎ 520-645-2741).

 La Fiesta de Tumacacori: Tumacacori (Chapter 15). First weekend in December. The lovely Spanish mission at Tumacacori throws a cultural heritage bash, with food; crafts; folklorico and Native American dancing; and Mexican, Indian, and old-time Arizona music (☎ 520-398-2341 ext. 0).

Chapter 3

Five Great Itineraries

● ●

In This Chapter

▶ Southern Arizona's hot spots in 1 week

▶ Northern Arizona's high (and low) points in 1 week

▶ The great Arizona 2-week combination plate

▶ Arizona for youngsters (and youngsters-at-heart)

▶ The best of Arizona's Old West

● ●

*Y*ou may already know exactly what you want to do in Arizona —
park yourself at a Scottsdale resort and get spa treatments for the
first week of your vacation and go white-water rafting on the Colorado
River during the second week. Ain't decisiveness great? But, if you're
like most people, you may not be quite that sure of what you want out
of your Arizona vacation, especially faced with the terrific array of
escape opportunities. I would like to have known at the outset of my
many trips around the state which places I absolutely had to visit —
and which ones I could have skipped. Still, the fun is in finding out —
and sharing my travel tips.

Thus, I offer the following itineraries. Your contributions to this cause
include an automobile (rented or otherwise) and a willingness to get
up and out of your room early.

Because you can't do the entire state in a single week — you just get
super stressed if you try — I devise two separate weeklong "Greatest
Hits" itineraries. One itinerary is for the northern half of the state and
one is for the southern part. I also suggest combination itineraries for
those of you lucky enough to spend 2 weeks in the state, traveling with
kids, or interested in exploring the Old West, Arizona style.

For all these itineraries, I assume you're flying into Sky Harbor Airport
in Phoenix, which has the greatest number of flights in the state (see
Chapter 6 for info on who flies to Phoenix). In addition, I assume that
you're renting a car (see the section on renting a car in Chapter 7 for
info on how to do that).

Greatest Hits: Arizona in 1 Week

With both northern and southern route options, which should you choose? Look at the info on Arizona's seasons in Chapter 2. If you're interested in beating the crowds and keeping your costs down, try the northern Arizona itinerary in winter or the southern Arizona itinerary in summer. If you're dying for a winter getaway to a warm place and money is not the main issue, go to southern Arizona in winter and . . . well, you get the picture.

Southern Arizona in 1 Week

Because the distances between attractions aren't as great in the southern part of the state, during a 1-week tour of the south you may even be able to fit in a little pool time. But you're still on the move. Part of the allure of southern Arizona for many people is kicking back at a top resort or a dude ranch, but if you follow my proposed schedule, you're not going to get much bang for your buck from these lodgings. If you opt for this itinerary, choose economical or historic digs, not ones with tons of built-in activities.

Assuming you're not completely wiped out on **Day 1** when you arrive in **Phoenix,** spend the afternoon exploring **Old Scottsdale's** historic buildings and boutiques and visiting the **Scottsdale Museum of Contemporary Art;** if you're more interested in architecture than shops or contemporary art, head for **Taliesen West,** Frank Lloyd Wright's home and architecture school, instead. (For information on all these sights, see Chapter 11.) Your first evening is a good night for a low-key dinner, so go to a western steakhouse or a funky Mexican restaurant near your hotel.

Spend **Day 2** following the 1-day Phoenix itinerary in Chapter 11 — but skip the Desert Botanical Gardens. You'll see plenty of cacti in Tucson during the next couple of days.

On **Day 3,** take the slow, scenic back route (Hwy. 87/287 to Hwy. 79 to Hwy. 77) down to Tucson, stopping at the **Casa Grande Ruins National Monument,** with its mysterious **Hohokam** structures, and in the town of **Florence,** which has the greatest number of homes on the National Historic Register — and the most prisons — in Arizona. (See Chapter 12 for information on both places.) Eat lunch in Florence, then drive down to **Biosphere 2,** a big (and once very weird) science project in the desert (see Chapter 14). Spend the rest of the afternoon at the center. Then drive down to your **Tucson** hotel, eat dinner near your hotel, and make it an early evening — you need to prepare for a jam-packed Day 4.

On **Day 4,** follow the 1-day itinerary for **Tucson** outlined in Chapter 13.

On **Day 5,** drive south from Tucson along I-19. Choose between the **Titan Missile Museum,** where you can descend into the former control center of a nuclear warhead, and the town of **Tubac,** with its historic fortress and myriad crafts shops. By choosing either the museum or a tour of Tubac, you may have time to stop at the moody, ruined mission at **Tumacácori National Historical Park** and get down to **Nogales, Mexico** for lunch. Do a bit of bargaining and cross back over the border. Then take Hwy. 82 northeast to the sleepy one-time ranching town of **Patagonia;** if you're not shopped out, browse a few more crafts boutiques. You may spend the night here or in nearby **Sonoita,** which is even smaller — both have interesting lodgings and good restaurants, plus at least one cowboy bar. (See Chapter 15 for information on the attractions in this paragraph.)

Divide **Day 6** between **Bisbee,** a Victorian-style mining town, and **Tombstone** (yes, that one, famous for the shootout at the OK Corral). Plan on spending the night in the last town you visit for the day; these towns are not very far from each other, but why drive back to your hotel at night when you can walk, for a change? (See Chapter 15 for information on both towns.)

Spend the morning of **Day 7** trekking among the strangely balanced boulders at **Chiricahua National Monument.** To get to the monument from Tombstone, take Hwy. 80 to I-10; then go east to Hwy. 186 south. From Bisbee, take Hwy. 90 east to Hwy. 191 north; then go east on Hwy. 181. Try to arrive at the monument in time for the daily 10 a.m. **Faraway Ranch** tour; enjoy a piece of apple pie for lunch in **Willcox** (you earn it after all that exercise); and visit the **Rex Allen Cowboy Museum and Theater.** In the afternoon, descend into Arizona's newest attraction, **Kartchner Caverns State Park,** near Benson — which puts you back on I-10, and in a position to zip back to Tucson where you can spend your last night if you don't have an early plane out the next day, or to Phoenix, if you do. (See Chapter 15 for the attractions mentioned in this paragraph.)

Getting tickets for Kartchner Caverns is not always easy, so you may fiddle with the Day 6 and Day 7 itineraries to allow time for when (and if) you can obtain entry. Adjusting your travel schedule around these towns is not a problem; distances are not too great in this area.

Northern Arizona in 1 Week

Pick up your rental car at the Phoenix airport on **Day 1** and hit the road — I-17, that is — heading north. If you arrive reasonably early in the afternoon, stop for a half hour at the Indian cliff dwellings of **Montezuma Castle National Monument** en route to **Sedona** (see Chapter 16). In Sedona, you may splurge on an upscale dinner and room; from this point on, most of the accommodations are without frills.

Take a jeep tour around the red rocks in the morning of **Day 2,** lunch at the lively ghost town of **Jerome** (see Chapter 16), and enjoy a gorgeous mid-afternoon drive along Hwy. 89A through Oak Creek Canyon to **Flagstaff** (see Chapter 17). "Flag" is your last chance for anything resembling nightlife, so visit one of the brew pubs or savor a nice dinner; then hit the **Museum Club** for some country music.

On **Day 3,** take the southwestern route from Flagstaff (via Williams and Hwy. 64) to the **Grand Canyon's South Rim,** where you spend the day and night. See Chapter 17 for ideas on how to organize your canyon activities. Be sure to book a meal at the **El Tovar,** no matter where you stay.

Leave the Grand Canyon vicinity early in the morning on **Day 4** and take the eastern route via Hwy. 64 out to Hwy. 89A, stopping at the **Cameron Trading Post** (see Chapter 17) to browse the Native American crafts — but don't spend too long. You want to be close to **Monument Valley Navajo Tribal Park** via Hwy. 160 to 163 by lunchtime. Eat a Navajo taco at **Goulding's Lodge** or at the visitor center's restaurant and tour the strange mesas and spires, either on your own or with a guide; prepare to leave by late afternoon so you can arrive at **Canyon de Chelly** (via Hwy. 191 south) at a reasonable hour and enjoy a leisurely dinner at the **Thunderbird Lodge.** (For the last four sights in bold, see Chapter 18.)

On the morning of **Day 5,** take the two **Canyon de Chelly** rim drives or hike down the White House Trail. Lunch near the canyon before heading east via Hwy. 191 to Hwy. 264 for the **Hubbell Trading Post,** where you can ogle Navajo rugs and, if you're lucky, catch the last tour of trader Lorenzo Hubbell's house. From here you have a choice: You can either head west along Hwy. 264 toward the **Hopi Mesas** and spend a quiet night on Second Mesa at the Hopi Cultural Center or head south and hole up in either **Holbrook** or **Winslow** along I-40; these towns are very close to one another. Your evening isn't going to be super exciting in these towns, either, but Holbrook and Winslow offer more restaurant choices. You can enjoy a beer in these towns because you're off the reservations (which don't allow alcohol). Dine at the historic **La Posada hotel** in Winslow or at one of the Route 66 restaurants in Holbrook. (See Chapter 18 for all the sights in this paragraph.)

If you wake up on Second Mesa on **Day 6,** explore the **Hopi villages** in the morning; you already enjoyed your blue corn piki bread at the Hopi Cultural Center the night before, so plan on lunch in either **Winslow** or **Holbrook.** Spend the rest of the afternoon browsing the kitschy **Route 66** souvenir shops in and around Holbrook. Alternatively, if you start your day in Holbrook or Winslow, go to the **Hopi mesas,** have lunch at the Hopi Cultural Center, and return to the Route 66 area in time for dinner in either Winslow or Holbrook; then spend the night in one of the two towns. (See Chapter 18 for all the sights in this paragraph.)

On **Day 7,** you backtrack a little bit on I-40 to the **Petrified National Forest and Painted Desert** (see Chapter 18), where you spend a nice leisurely morning and lunchtime among the dead wood. If your flight departs in the early morning from Phoenix the next day, you want to sleep in the Valley of the Sun; take the scenic Hwy. 87 route back from Winslow to Hwy. 260 to Hwy. 17. If you haven't already done so on the way up, stop at **Montezuma Castle** (see Chapter 16) in the late afternoon. Enjoy a blowout farewell-to-Arizona dinner at a new Southwest or authentic Mexican restaurant in the Valley (if you're not wiped out). Alternatively, if your flight leaves at noon or later the following day, after a morning at the Petrified National Forest, stop at **Meteor Crater** (see Chapter 18) and **Walnut Canyon National Monument** (see Chapter 17) off of I-40, before retiring for dinner in Flagstaff (which seems like a gourmet mecca by now). Get a good night's sleep in Flagstaff so you're refreshed for your morning drive to Phoenix and the flight back home.

A Leisurely Drive-Through: Arizona in 2 Weeks

Sorry, you can't just combine the 1-week northern and southern Arizona itineraries to get a perfect 2-week tour: In this case, one and one don't quite add up to two. Those itineraries are built around getting you back to the Phoenix airport, which you don't need to do in the middle of your 2-week jaunt.

Follow the southern Arizona itinerary (see the "Southern Arizona in 1 Week" section) for the first 6 days. On **Day 7,** skip the detour to Chiricahua National Monument and Willcox and head to **Prescott** (Chapter 16) via I-10 to I-17 to Hwy. 69. (If you can get into Kartchner Caverns in the morning or still haven't toured Tombstone, fine, but don't go too far south or east.) The drive from Benson to Prescott takes 5 hours. Prescott is Arizona's one-time territorial capital, where you can spend the night in a historic hotel or B&B. If you need to stretch your legs en route, the **Casa Grande** or **New River Outlet malls** (off I-10 and I-17, respectively) make useful — if potentially expensive — walkabouts (see Chapter 12 for both).

On **Day 8,** travel to **Jerome;** then spend the rest of the afternoon and evening in **Sedona** (see Chapter 16).

On the morning of **Day 9,** drive through **Oak Creek Canyon** (see Chapter 16) on Hwy. 89A and turn west on I-40, before you get to Flagstaff; then take Hwy. 64 north until you reach the **Grand Canyon** (see Chapter 17). From here, follow the itinerary from Days 3 through 7 from "Northern Arizona in 1 Week."

Touring Arizona with Kids

This itinerary is based on the assumption that you want to get in as many top sights as possible — without pushing your family's travel endurance to the limit — in a single week. If you don't feel compelled to see the Grand Canyon, however, you may choose to spend a relaxing family vacation in southern Arizona. You and your family may unwind at a resort with a good kids' program in the Valley of the Sun (the Phoenix area) for half of your vacation and stay at a guest ranch in Tucson for the other half. From the Valley of the Sun or Tucson, you may take daily excursions to the top children's sights in those areas. When you stay in the Valley, visit all the attractions recommended in the following itinerary except the Desert Botanical Gardens, because

Tucson's **Arizona-Sonora Desert Museum** covers the same territory, but better. Also, be sure your family doesn't miss **Old Tucson Studios.** (I mark other kid-friendly attractions in both places with the Kid-Friendly icon in this book.) For the state's "greatest family hits" tour, use the following agenda.

After you arrive in Phoenix, devote the afternoon of **Day 1** to just one activity — either the **Heard Museum** or the **Desert Botanical Garden;** then eat dinner near your hotel. Alternatively, if you don't care about doing anything typically Southwestern but just want to show your kids that you aren't in the boonies, head over to **GameWorks** at the Arizona Mills mall. Gameworks is an amazing two-story family fun center designed by Stephen Spielberg's Dreamworks/Sega/Universal Studios. Naturally, the mall has a huge food court, too. (See Chapter 11 for the sights in this paragraph.)

On **Day 2** in **Phoenix,** spend the morning at the **Arizona Science Center;** chow down on a fast-food lunch at the center, then spend the afternoon at the **Desert Botanical Gardens** if you haven't already been there. Time permitting, you can also visit the **Phoenix Zoo,** right next door. Dine at a family steakhouse like **Pinnacle Peak.** (See Chapter 11 for attractions on this day.)

Hit the road on **Day 3** by heading north on I-17. Stop off at the **Deer Valley Rock Art Center,** where you can view hundreds of *petroglyphs* (Indian rock art), or the Williamsburg-gone-West **Pioneer Arizona Living History Museum.** Both are close to the **Rock Springs Café and Bakery,** a former stagecoach stop with lots of kid-friendly lunch food (see Chapter 12 for these sights). Get up to **Clarkdale** on Hwy. 260 in time to board the **Verde Canyon Railroad** for a scenic and fun after-noon train ride. If you're visiting from Wednesday to Sunday, go for the pony rides, a chuck-wagon supper, and a western show at the **Blazin' M Ranch** in **Cottonwood** — which is, in any case, a convenient and eco-nomical place to spend the night. (See Chapter 16 for attractions in Clarkdale and Cottonwood.)

Spend **Day 4** in **Sedona.** If the temperature is warm enough, swim at **Slide Rock State Park** in the morning before the crowds descend. If the weather is too cool for a dip, start the day with a jeep tour; then go fishing at the **Rainbow Trout Farm** in Oak Creek in the afternoon. The scenic drive north through **Oak Creek Canyon** on Hwy. 89A gets you to **Flagstaff,** which has loads of family restaurants and inexpensive chain hotels. (See Chapters 16 and 17 for information on Sedona and Flagstaff, respectively.)

On **Day 5,** drive to the **Grand Canyon's South Rim** (via I-40 and Hwy. 64) and spend the day and night there. For suggestions on things to do, see the "The Canyon for Kids" sidebar in Chapter 17. Alternatively, if your kids get a kick out of the Verde Canyon train ride, consider repris-ing the event by using the **Grand Canyon Railway** as transport. You don't have to hassle with parking and you can stay overnight at **Williams** (also in Chapter 17), where the train depot has lots of fun railroad and forest toys (including cute Smokey Bear replicas).

Day 6 and night 6 should be spent back in **Flagstaff,** where kid-friendly attractions include the **Museum of Northern Arizona,** which has a dinosaur exhibit (enough said); the **Lowell Observatory,** with lots of fun hands-on science displays (better still if you come at night when the observatory offers telescope viewing); and **Snowbowl.** If the white stuff is on the ground, consider some family skiing; the slopes on Mt. Agassiz are not intimidating. If you're visiting in summer, take the ski lift to the top of Mt. Agassiz and walk around.

On **Day 7,** drive east on I-40 to **Meteor Crater** — not quite as deep as the Grand Canyon but created a lot more quickly — and **Petrified Forest National Park,** where young dinosaur buffs can ogle more fossils (see Chapter 18 for both attractions). You can eat lunch at the national park or in Holbrook, where the "retro" Route 66 diners are the genuine items. If you're through early enough in the afternoon, take the scenic Hwy. 87 route from Winslow to Hwy. 260 to Hwy. 17. Stop at a not-very-taxing-on-the-weary **Montezuma Castle** (see Chapter 16) or, if you didn't visit it on the way up, the **Pioneer Arizona Living History Museum** (see Chapter 12; the museum is closer to Phoenix). If the time is late or you're all tuckered out, just drive straight east on I-40 to I-17 and zip down to Phoenix to spend your last evening unwinding.

How the West Was Dug: Touring Arizona's Mining History

This Old West itinerary takes you around Arizona's past (and maybe future) mining towns. Does this sound like as big a yawn as one of the open mine pits? Think again. Most of the famous towns of the West rose and fell around mineral wealth. Greed, rowdiness, and, in southern Arizona, clashes with the Native Americans — whose land was being encroached on — are the stuff of America's legends and Hollywood's westerns.

Oh yes, I should mention that those mines happen to be in some mighty purty territory. And although I focus on the mining sights, I include plenty of other stuff to do if your interests lie more above ground.

On **Day 1,** head straight from the Phoenix airport (northwest on Hwy. 60) to **Wickenburg** (see Chapter 16), home to what was once the richest gold mine in the state. If the museum is still open, stop at the **Desert Caballeros Western Museum** for some town background (and art); if not, the **Jail Tree** and **The Old Wishing Well** never close and you may stroll around **Frontier Street,** with its intact early 1900s buildings. It's not worth it for you to stay at one of Wickenburg's famed guest ranches for a single night, because you wouldn't have time to enjoy the activities, but you can have dinner at one of them or at a historic cowboy bar.

You spend a good part of **Day 2** in Wickenburg. Visit the museum if you haven't already done so; then drive to the **Robson's Arizona Mining World,** which re-creates an old mining camp; take a jeep tour or mule ride into the surrounding mining territory; or take a self-guided tour of the **Vulture Mine.** Be sure to leave the Wickenburg area by late afternoon, so you can fully enjoy the scenery along the long and winding mountain roads (Hwy. 89 to Hwy. 89A) up to **Jerome** (see Chapter 16), a not-very-dead ghost town where you can spend the night.

Jerome isn't a very large town, but among such sights as the **Jerome State Historic Park** (a one-time mine owner's mansion), the **Jerome Historical Society and Mine Museum,** and the **Gold King Mine and Ghost Town,** you find plenty of attractions to fill the morning of **Day 3** (and I didn't even mention the steep streets lined with rows of crafts shops). In the afternoon, come down from the mountain to nearby **Clarkdale** (see Chapter 16) and ride the **Verde Canyon Railroad,** which runs along tracks formerly used to haul minerals from Jerome (the haulers probably didn't appreciate the stunning vistas as much as you do). From here, drive back down along I-17 to the **Valley of the Sun** (Chapter 11), where you spend the night. Except for **Old Scottsdale,** you don't find much authentic western history here, but this place is the best jumping-off point for next morning's excursion. If you need a break from standard American fare, go for some good, authentic Mexican food.

You may visit two sights east of Phoenix on **Day 4:** the **Apache Trail** and **Lost Dutchman State Park,** the location of a world-famous gold mine that may never have existed. If you'd rather relax and enjoy the scenery than drive along sometimes harrowing mountain roads, book a full-day tour of the Apache Trail (see Chapter 12 for some options) and spend a second night in the greater Phoenix area. If you don't mind a little adrenaline pumping, take the Apache Trail drive described in Chapter 12, only instead of going back to the Valley, bunk in the town of **Globe,** still a more or less active mining area.

If, on **Day 5,** you wake up in Globe, take the scenic route (Hwy. 77, south towards I-10) and stop for lunch before you get to Tucson; you pass plenty of casual restaurants (try **Cibaria** if you're up for Italian). If you begin the day in the Phoenix area, pick up I-10 there and, before you get to downtown Tucson, detour to the **Arizona-Sonora Desert Museum** (no mining stuff here, but it's a top sight) and lunch among the desert flora and fauna (see Chapter 13). However you begin the day, eventually get back on I-10 and head southwest until you reach the turnoff for **Tombstone** (see Chapter 15), a town that rose from the riches of the Lucky Cuss silver mine. That's where you spend the night (in the town, not the mine — the mine doesn't exist any more).

On the morning of **Day 6,** finish exploring **Tombstone.** The **Tombstone Courthouse State Historic Park** is the best place to get the truth behind the tourist hype. Then head down to **Bisbee,** a mining mecca. Not only can you take a terrific miner-led tour of the defunct **Copper Queen mine,** but you may also gaze into the great gaping **Lavender**

mine pit (which may be resuscitated if copper prices rise). The most obvious lodging choice is the Copper Queen Hotel, but several other hotels and B&Bs in town hearken back to Bisbee's mining heyday. (See Chapter 15 for information on Bisbee.)

On **Day 7,** you may take your pick of destinations. You may drive east from Bisbee to **Douglas** (which once hosted the smelters for Bisbee's mines) and visit the historic **Gadsen Hotel;** then go north along 191 and visit the mining ghost towns of **Gleeson, Pearce,** and **Courtland;** and finally detour a short bit farther east on I-10 to explore the **Rex Allen cowboy museum** in downtown **Willcox** (which also happens to be Arizona's apple pie capital). Or you can head west from Bisbee, stopping for lunch and a stroll in sleepy **Patagonia** (where silver was once transported from the railroad depot); then, if your vehicle has good suspension, explore the ruins of **Dusquesne** or, if you're not up for back-roading, pick up I-19 in Nogales and drive north to the **Asarco Mineral Discovery Center,** between **Green Valley** and **Tucson.** At the center, you can see modern copper strip-mining in action. Either way, you end up pretty close to Tucson, where you may spend your last starry Arizona night — unless you're booked on an early flight, in which case, you better hightail it back to **Phoenix.** (See Chapter 15 for the attractions on this day.)

Chapter 4

Planning Your Budget

. . . .

In This Chapter

▶ Estimating your trip costs

▶ Ferreting out the sneaky charges

▶ Cutting expenses without cutting corners

. . . .

*Y*ou may dislike paying for fun you've already had — who doesn't? — but if you plan ahead, there's no reason for you to go into credit card shock when you return from Arizona.

Adding Up the Elements

Budgeting for an Arizona vacation isn't hard. Use the budget worksheet in the yellow pages at the end of the book to help get an approximation of how much your trip will cost. (Sticking to your budget after you actually arrive is another thing entirely, of course. Speaking sharply to yourself when you're about to make that impulse purchase may help — or it may just get you really weird looks.)

A good way to get a handle on the total amount you'll end up spending, if you do everything you want to do, is to start the metaphorical meter ticking from the moment you leave home. Begin with transportation to the airport, then add your flight costs (see Chapter 6 for tips on how to fly for less), car rental, gas, hotel rates, meals (exclude breakfast if it's included in the hotel rate), admission prices to attractions, and the cost of the activities you're interested in (golf or jeep tours, for example). If you've been coveting an only-in-Arizona item, include the cost of that also. After you do all that, add on another 15 percent to 20 percent for good measure.

Transportation

Transportation is a large part of your trip costs, although it's easy to budget for. After you figure your rental car costs, tally in the taxes (see "Keeping a Lid on Hidden Expenses," later in this chapter), and approximate gas expenses (do that as close to departure time as possible; your guess is as good as mine as to what the price of gas will be when you're traveling), you have your transportation figured out. Of course, you may decide to fly from location to location within the state, in which case transportation costs are an even larger percentage of your trip costs. Check out Chapter 7 for details about flying within Arizona and for ways to keep rental car charges down.

Lodging

How much you spend on sleeping accommodations is really up to you. You can spend as little or as much as you want, depending on what you're looking for — and when you're traveling. A fancy resort in Scottsdale during the high season is gonna take a huge bite out of your budget (more than airfare, even). If, on the other hand, you want to stay at a chain motel or modest B&B off-season, you can get away pretty darn cheap. In general, summer is high season in northern Arizona, while winter is high season in southern Arizona; see Chapter 2 for details on both. See Chapter 8 for specifics about lodging categories and costs.

Dining

The range of dining options particular to Arizona — everything from Navajo tacos to gourmet New Southwestern fare (see Chapter 1) — leads to a wide range of costs. So you can choose to spend as little or as much as you like on meals. Consider the loads of chain restaurants, which may not be anyone's idea of haute cuisine, but are just the ticket if you're traveling with kids.

What Things Cost in Phoenix

This list gives you the approximate cost of a variety of touristy expenses:

- Double room at the Arizona Biltmore resort ($$$$, Very Expensive): February: $380; July: $165

- Double room at the all-suites Phoenix Inn ($$–$$$, Moderate): February: $99; July: $59

- Dinner for two at RoxSand (New Southwestern; $$$–$$$$, Very Expensive), without drinks, tax, or tip: $120

- Dinner for two at San Carlos Bay (Mexican; $–$$, Inexpensive to Moderate), without drinks, tax, or tip: $25

- Long-neck beer at Toolies: $2

- Adult admission to the Heard Museum: $7

- Greens fees at The Boulders golf course on a winter weekend: $225 (without cart)

- Greens fees at the Papago Municipal golf course on a winter weekend: $28 ($50 extra for cart)

- Trail ride at South Mountain Park: $17/hour

What Things Cost in Flagstaff

From rooms to dinner to lift tickets, this list gives you a sampling of prices in "Flag":

✔ Double room at the Little America Flagstaff ($$, Moderate): Summer: $119; Winter: $89

✔ Double room at The Inn at Northern Arizona Univeristy ($$, Moderate): Summer, $99; Winter, $69

✔ Dinner for two at Cottage Place (Continental; $$$, Expensive), without drinks, tax, or tip: $75

✔ Dinner for two at Beaver Street Brewery ($–$$, Inexpensive to Moderate), without brew, tax, or tip: $25

✔ Pint of pale ale at the Mogollon Brewing Co.: $3

✔ Per person admission to both Sunset Crater Volcano and Wupatki National Monuments: $3

✔ Weekend all-day ski lift ticket at Snowbowl (adult): $37

✔ Ski lift to the top of Mt. Agassiz (Snowbowl) when there's no snow (adult): $9

It's almost impossible to find a city or region where you can't get a low-key (and low-cost) dinner, including, in some cases, authentic Mexican food, for $10 or under per person, excluding alcohol. This is the inexpensive ($) range. Move up to the moderate ($$) range, which runs you $20 or under per person, and you have an even wider choice of non-chain, non-pizza options. Outside of Greater Phoenix, Tucson, and Sedona, an evening meal at even the most expensive restaurants shouldn't run you more than $35 apiece ($$$), sans that bottle of Dom Perignon champagne; even in the big cities most good restaurants fall into that category. If you want to try the real dining dazzlers, the domains of the cutting-edge chefs, it'll cost you $36 or more ($$$$), and often more than $50, which still is not nearly as much as you'd pay for an equivalent meal in, say, New York, Chicago, or San Francisco.

When budgeting for meals on the Indian reservations, you don't need to include the cost of alcohol, which isn't served.

Attractions

Visiting Arizona's top sights won't break your bank. Very few attractions in the state cost more than $10. The Grand Canyon entry fee is $20 per vehicle, not per person — and it's good for a week. There's also lots to do in the state that's free (or close to it). Visiting Saguaro National Park East won't cost you a dime, nor will most of the museums on the University of Arizona campus — to offer just two Tucson examples.

Activities and Tours

Recreation and tours, on the other hand, can take you into rough financial terrain. Greens fees are very expensive at the top resort golf courses (as high as $200), spa treatments start at about $60 for 50 minutes, and a 10-minute helicopter buzz around Sedona runs you $35 — to name just a few possibilities. Choose carefully. Some activities, such as helicopter rides and jeep tours, are never discounted, but prices for others, like golf, go way down in the off-season. And you can save on other things, such as spa treatments, if you book them as part of a hotel package (see Chapter 6 for details).

Shopping

Shopping is the real wild card in your vacation budget. You can spend tons of money on Western art or Indian crafts if you're not careful — and even if you are. If you've always wanted a Navajo rug, you won't find a better place to buy one than in Arizona. Just be sure that you can really afford to spend thousands of dollars (or hundreds on even the smallest ones).

Rugs aside, visitors can find plenty of things to buy in Arizona that aren't budget destroyers — pretty tin-work candlesticks from Mexico, for example (see Chapter 19). You can even consider a great pair of cowboy boots, which you may ultimately get a lot of use out of (I sure do out of mine). Bottom line: Think about what you want to purchase in advance so as to avoid impulse buys.

Nightlife

Keeping your costs down when it comes to evening activities is no problem. If you're a culture vulture, Phoenix and Tucson have plenty of shows and concerts to see, and tickets won't cost you an arm and a leg (rarely above $40 for the best theater or ballet seats). But if you come back and say you didn't attend the Scottsdale Symphony, no one will be as shocked as if, say, you didn't make it to the Grand Canyon. A couple of beers at a cowboy bar won't set you back a whole lot, and it's easy to spend the entire evening in the big cities at a nice dinner. And all those wonderful stars up there in the sky are free.

Keeping a Lid on Hidden Expenses

You no doubt already are aware that the price you're quoted isn't necessarily the whole price you pay. In this section, I clue you in to some charges you may not be expecting.

Tipping Tips

Tipping isn't much different in Arizona than it is anywhere else. I give guidelines in the following list.

- ✔ **Restaurants:** If the service is good in an upscale restaurant, you're expected to tip about 20 percent (though no one will come yelling after you if you don't — as once happened to me in Manhattan, when a European friend offered to pick up the tab and, assuming service was included, didn't add a gratuity). In low-key restaurants, 15 percent is fine if the service didn't wow you (but be generous if it did — the wait staff doesn't get paid more here than anywhere else).

- ✔ **Indian reservations:** You're not permitted to take photographs on the Hopi reservation, but you usually are on the Navajo reservation — if you ask. You're expected to tip a dollar or two if permission is granted, which is also what you should pay if someone guides you around a sight on a free, informal tour.

- ✔ **Resorts:** In a fancy-shmancy resort, you're expected to leave something behind for the room cleaning staff, assuming you stay a few nights: $5 per night is fine, more if they turn down your sheets twice a day or provide any extra services — for example, bringing you the additional towels you've requested or cleaning up that bottle of aftershave you broke in the bathroom. Valet parking is free at many greater Phoenix area and most Tucson resorts, but you're expected to tip at least $1; if loading luggage is involved, add on $1 per piece.

Dialing Costs Dollars

In addition, don't forget to check the price of phone calls before you pick up the receiver and dial. Many of the nicer hotels and resorts in the big cities charge from 75¢ to $1 or more per call — even if you're just calling a toll-free number or contacting a long-distance operator to use your telephone credit card. If you have a cell phone with unlimited (or a large amount of included) minutes, that may be the way to go in Tucson and the Valley of the Sun. In the smaller towns, on the other hand, you're likely to incur roaming charges — and, except in Sedona, the hotels in the more remote areas are less likely to slap on those hefty fees, anyway.

Watching Out for Costly Room Perks

Finally, regard the minibar in your hotel room as a cold, little money-grubbing bandit; its contents are likely to cost double what they do at a convenience store across the road. Don't open that pint-sized refrigerator except to stash the less expensive drinks and snacks that you bought elsewhere. And beware especially of the new, even sneakier type of "perks" that I've come across in several hotels recently: A basket full of goodies that sits on top of the refrigerator or even a bureau, pretending to be a gift. Some expensive hotels *do* welcome guests with fruit or other gifts of food — which makes these snack arrays doubly duplicitous. Always check around for a list of charges, or a welcome note from the manager in its stead.

Tips for Cutting Costs

The destination chapters in Parts III and IV all include money-saving tips specific to those places; here I give you some additional general advice — and it's free, too (talk about bargains!):

- ✔ **Go off-season.** Luckily it's always off-season somewhere in Arizona. If you visit southern Arizona in summer or northern Arizona in winter, you can cut room costs by as much as 50 percent; prices on things like greens fees on golf courses go way down, too.

- ✔ **Travel midweek.** If you can travel on a Tuesday, Wednesday, or Thursday, you may find cheaper flights to your destination. When you ask about airfares, see if you can get a cheaper rate by flying on a different day.

- ✔ **Check the package tours.** There aren't many air/hotel/sightseeing bundlings for travelers to Arizona (see Chapter 6), but lots of resorts include things like greens fees at their on-site courses, spa treatments, breakfast, champagne — you name it — in special packages. Always ask when you're booking a room if there are any deals; they may just fit your interests to a (golf) tee.

- ✔ **Reserve a room with a refrigerator and coffeemaker.** You don't have to slave over a hot stove to cut a few costs; lots of motels have mini-fridges and coffeemakers. Buying supplies for breakfast the night before will save you money — and probably calories — while packing a picnic lunch is not only economical in itself, but provides an opportunity for an inexpensive midday activity.

- ✔ **Invest in a cheap cooler.** You'll quickly recover the costs if you buy large bottles of water and six-packs of soft drinks from a grocery store rather than buying individual drinks at more expensive roadside convenience stores. Give the cooler away to someone you like at the end of your trip — or to the clerk at the car rental company; most everyone in this state can use an extra ice chest.

- ✔ **Always ask for discount rates.** Membership in AAA, frequent flyer plans, trade unions, AARP, or other groups may qualify you for savings on car rentals, plane tickets, hotel rooms, even meals. Ask about everything; you may be pleasantly surprised.

- ✔ **Ask if your kids can stay in the room with you.** A room with two double beds usually doesn't cost any more than one with a queen-size bed. And many hotels won't charge you the additional person rate if the additional person is pint-sized and related to you. Even if you have to pay $10 or $15 extra for a rollaway bed, you'll save hundreds by not taking two rooms.

✔ **Try expensive restaurants at lunch instead of dinner.** In the Phoenix area and in Tucson, a lunch tab at a top restaurant is usually far lower than a dinner tab, although the menu often boasts many of the same specialties.

✔ **Don't rent a gas guzzler.** Renting a smaller car is cheaper, and you'll save on gas to boot. Unless you're traveling with kids and need lots of space, there's no reason for you to go beyond economy size (and, hey, the valet parking guy will be less inspired to take your car for a spin if it's not exciting).

✔ **Cut back on the costly activities and tours.** If you're a golfer, eliminate one round — or try a municipal course instead of a resort course. Or buy a book about something you're interested in — Old West history, say, or desert plants — and devise a self-guided driving tour or a hike rather than paying for a guide or something expensive like a helicopter fly-by.

✔ **Reign in the trinkets — and the drinkettes.** As I said in this chapter's shopping section, I wouldn't suggest you cut out consuming altogether; just be sure to plan for it and don't bother with things you can get anywhere, like key chains and T-shirts. And be careful: Arizona's shopping centers often include nice restaurants, and there's nothing like alcohol for loosening those purse strings. Skip the margaritas until after you make your purchases.

Chapter 5

Tips for Travelers with Special Interests

. . . .

. . . .

*I*f you have special needs, interests, or concerns — and almost every-one does — it's your turn to grab some attention. I may not be able to address every question you have on a particular topic, but I can at least help direct you to some additional information sources.

We Are Family: Traveling with Kids

Arizona is a great place for a family vacation, no matter what sort of travel you decide on. Just want to chill out at a resort? Most of the major ones have full menus of children's activities — fun for them, and relaxing for you. Throughout this book, the Kid Friendly icon highlights places and activities particularly geared toward or welcoming to children, but when it comes to accommodations, even the cheapest motels in southern Arizona have swimming pools to keep kids happily splashing. Lots of places also let children as old as 18, depending on the hotel policy, stay in your room for free, so don't forget to ask when you're booking.

Food is no problem, either. Every chain restaurant you can think of is represented in the state, but you don't have to restrict yourselves to them if you don't want to. Nearly every city has Western steakhouses offering pint-sized plates and a fun, rowdy atmosphere; friendly, inexpensive Mexican eateries that always include something on the menu for even the pickiest eater (including hamburgers); casual roadside diners — you name it. Again, I use the handy icon to mark restaurants especially suited for children but, except for the really fancy places, you and your brood will be warmly welcomed nearly everywhere. When you're ready to hit the road, you can stock up on healthful snacks in the cities' huge supermarkets, and everywhere you go, there are convenience stores galore (where you can stock up on not-so-healthful supplies).

You can find the requisite water parks in and around the big cities and video arcades in nearly every mall. Arizona doesn't have a whole lot of theme parks per se (Old Tucson Studios, in the Tucson area, of course, is the only one that comes close). What it does have, however, is far better: Tons of places where kids can engage with nature and history in a fun (but sneakily educational) way. Most are inexpensive to begin with and are even less costly when you subtract children's discounts. Chapter 3 offers an itinerary especially suited for families, but wherever you go you'll find activities to keep kids occupied, mind and body (the especially appropriate ones are tagged with icons in this book).

Some Quick Travel-with-Kids Tips

About to explore Arizona with a car full of kids? Use these tips to increase their enjoyment and comfort while on the road.

In advance:

✔ Take along some of your youngest kids' favorite books and toys, even if they add bulk to your luggage; going to unfamiliar places can be hard on even the most outgoing youngsters and security blankets of all sorts help.

✔ Have your children read up on Arizona in advance. If they're young, a book such as Susan Howell's *Three Little Javelinas* is great; older kids can go for Zane Grey western romances, nature books on the Sonoran Desert, or even corny films about Wyatt Earp and the OK Corral, of which there are 28 celluloid versions. Kids will get a kick out of seeing the real thing later in Tombstone, where you can help separate myth from fact.

✔ Bring along lots of protective gear — hats, sunglasses, and sunscreen (though you won't have a hard time finding these items in Arizona). Kids' skin is super-sensitive to Arizona's powerful rays.

✔ Dig up fun car games from the recesses of your mind — or any other available sources (identifying license plates is always good in a pinch); you're going to be putting in lots of road time.

✔ If your kids are small, be sure to arrange with the car rental companies for child safety seats.

When you're there:

✔ Don't forget to stock up on plain crackers (you never know when carsickness may hit).

✔ Don't ever let young children play in even a shallow pool unsupervised; tragedy can hit quickly.

✔ When in the desert, don't leave kids in a locked car for even two minutes to run in for a few things; temperatures can rise to dangerously high levels before you know it.

✔ Don't overwhelm them with activities. Kids get sore muscles, too. Swimming, going on a tour, and having dinner at a Western restaurant may be too much. Gear activities to your child's age, physical condition, and attention span.

Planning with Publications

The **Family Travel Times** newsletter, *Travel with Your Children,* (40 Fifth Avenue, New York, NY 10011; ☎ **888-822-4388** or 212-477-5524; Internet: www.familytraveltimes.com. Subscription: $39/year), published six times a year, offers good general information, as well as destination specific articles (for example, the June/July 1999 issue contained a piece on spa vacations with kids that included several resorts in Scottsdale).

Marty Campbell's *Arizona Family Field Trips* (World Publishing), available at most major bookstores, is an excellent resource for kid-friendly sights and activities throughout the state. The Phoenix-based monthly, *Raising Arizona Kids,* (4545 E. Shea Blvd., Suite 201, Phoenix, AZ 85028; ☎ **602-953-KIDS;** Internet: www.razkids.com), concentrates on activities in the Valley of the Sun, but also includes a statewide calendar of events geared toward children. Copies are available at both the Valley's major bookstores and local Basha's grocery stores for $1.95 per issue, and by subscription for $14.95 per year.

A similarly city-focused publication, *Tucson Family Magazine,* (177 N. Church Ave., No. 200, Tucson, AZ 85701; ☎ **520-792-1382;** Internet: www.tucsonfamily.com), is available on-line or by subscription. You can also pick up your free copy at local Toys 'R' Us and Wal-Mart stores.

It Pays to Be Gray: Advice for the Mature Traveler

With its several huge Sun City retirement communities and cadres of retired "snow-birds" migrating down from colder climes come winter, Arizona is extremely senior friendly. The state caters to older travelers with everything from great golf courses to great medical facilities. The only thing missing is widespread early-bird specials for dinner — but that's probably because everyone in the state eats early anyway.

Most of the attractions in Arizona offer discounts to seniors (sometimes as young as 60); if available, these rates are indicated in this book with the other price listings. And anyone age 62 or older can get a lifetime Golden Age Pass to all the U.S. National Parks by showing proof of age and paying a one-time $10 fee — which waives all future entry fees to the national parks.

In addition, most major domestic airlines, including American, United, Continental, US Airways, and TWA all offer discount programs for senior travelers; be sure to ask whenever you book a flight. Not yet 60? You can still reap the benefits of the maturity that your birth certificate indicates you've achieved. One of them is membership in the **AARP (American Association of Retired Persons)** (601 E St. NW, Washington, DC 20049; ☎ **800-424-3410** or 202-434-AARP; Internet: www.aarp.org) — yes, first-wave baby boomers, you only have to be 50 to join. For only $10 a year, you can get discounts on package tours, air fares, car rentals, and hotels — to mention only the travel-related items.

The Mature Traveler, a monthly newsletter on senior travel is another valuable resource. It's available by subscription ($30 a year); for a free sample, send a postcard with your name and address to GEM Publishing Group (Box 50400, Reno, NV 89513; E-mail: maturetrav@aol.com). GEM also publishes *The Book of Deals* ($9.95), a collection of more than 1,000 senior discounts on airlines, lodging, tours, and attractions around the country; phone ☎ **800-460-6676** to order a copy.

Some tour operators gear their trips toward a graying crowd. **SAGA Holidays,** (222 Berkeley St., Boston, MA 02116; ☎ **800-343-0273;** Internet: www.sagaholidays.com), specializes in package tours and cruises for those 50 and older, including, for example, a week-long Scottsdale-based holiday; prices, including airfare and accommodations, range from $800 to $1,150, depending on point and date of departure. **Maupin Tour** bus tours suitable for older travelers are detailed more in-depth in Chapter 6, and the Prime Time Travel division of **GORPtravel,** discussed in the same chapter, includes an 8-day Arizona Desert Trails walking tour for the 50 plus crowd ($1,695, not including airfare).

Advice for Travelers with Disabilities

A disability shouldn't stop anybody from traveling. Thanks to anti-discrimination laws and the increased accessibility of most attractions and sights, the disabled can travel with less stress than ever before.

National Resources

Several national organizations provide disabled travelers with the information and tools they need to experience the world.

Access-Able Travel Source (Internet: www.access-able.com) is a comprehensive database of travel agents who specialize in travel for the disabled; it's also a clearinghouse for information about accessible destinations around the world, including Arizona.

Many major car rental companies now offer hand-controlled cars for disabled drivers. Avis can provide such a vehicle at any of its locations in the United States with 48-hour advance notice; Hertz requires between 24 and 72 hours of advance reservation at most of its locations. **Wheelchair Getaways** (☎ 800-536-5518 or 606-873-4973; Internet: www.wheelchair-getaways.com) rents specialized vans with wheelchair lifts and other features for the disabled in more than 35 states, including Arizona, where the main distributor is at 6700 E. Solano Dr., Paradise Valley (near Scottsdale) (☎ 888-824-7413 or 480-348-9219; E-mail: AzAccVans@aol.com).

A World of Options, a 658-page book of resources for disabled travelers, covers everything from biking trips to scuba outfitters. It costs $35 and is available from **Mobility International USA** (P.O. Box 10767, Eugene, OR, 97440; ☎ 541-343-1284, voice and TTY; Internet: www.miusa.org). You may also want to consider joining a tour that caters specifically to folks with disabilities. One such company is **FEDCAP Rehabilitation Services** (211 W. 14th St., New York, NY 10011; ☎ 212-727-4200; Fax: 212-727-4373).

Vision-impaired travelers can get information on traveling with seeing-eye dogs from the **American Foundation for the Blind** (11 Penn Plaza, Suite 300, New York, NY 10001; ☎ 800-232-5463).

Arizona Resources

Because of Arizona's aging population (resident and visitor), the state has good resources for the mobility impaired, as well as, in the two big cities, excellent medical facilities. The **Arizona Office for Americans with Disabilities,** (1700 W. Washington St., Suite 3320, Phoenix, AZ 85007; ☎ 602-542-6276; TTY: 602-542-6686; Fax 602-542-1220), offers free statewide travel information and referrals. **ABAL, the Architectural Barriers Action League, Inc.** (P.O. Box 57008, Tucson, AZ 85732; ☎ 520-721-1633 or 520-296-0922), publishes an access guide for the Tucson area, and the **Arizona Easter Seal Society** (903 North Second St., Phoenix, AZ 85004; ☎ 602-252-6061) distributes the *Access Northern Arizona* guide.

The **Golden Access Passport,** a lifetime free-entry pass into national parks and monuments, is available, free, to any U.S. citizen or permanent resident who is medically certified as disabled or blind; all you need to do is go to one of the parks or monuments with proof of disability status to be issued a pass on the spot.

Of the resorts reviewed in this book (see the individual destination chapters for details), Access-Able Travel Source lists the following as suited to those using wheelchairs:

- ✔ **Phoenix area:** Sunburst, the Phoenician, the Fairmont Scottsdale Princess, and the Ritz-Carlton
- ✔ **Tucson:** Westin La Paloma and the Doubletree Hotel
- ✔ **The Grand Canyon:** the Grand Canyon Lodge, El Tovar, Kachina, Thunderbird, and Yavapai lodges

The Wahweap Lodge and the houseboats at Lake Powell Resorts and Marina near Page also accommodate wheelchairs. The Super 8 motels in Sedona and Flagstaff are also listed as accessible. For other options in the Greater Phoenix and Tucson areas, and for specifics on the facilities in this section, click on the "search world cities" option of www.access-able.com/tips/ and then find your way through North America to the Arizona portion of the map.

Going Solo: Advice for Singles

You may be independent-minded but not independently wealthy. Hotels and packages that offer discounts for singles are rarer than original come-on lines at pick-up bars. If you don't want to shell out for a room for two, consider finding someone to share costs through the **Travel Companion Exchange** (P.O. Box 833, Amityville, NY 11701; ☎ 800-392-1256 or 631-454-0880; Fax 631-454-0170; Internet: www.whytravelalone.com). If you join — prices range from $159 to $298 a year — you get a newsletter that lists other members' profiles and travel interests. Spot someone who seems compatible, and the organization enables you to contact them directly, so you can get to know them before deciding to take up close quarters.

There are no restrictions. If you want to travel with someone of the opposite gender, it ain't nobody's business but your own. On the other hand, even though they have a Web site, this organization is careful to make sure members have genuine mailing addresses (as opposed to, say, an e-mail address in prison), often corresponding with you via the U.S. mail for that purpose.

The newsletter also offers other types of travel information for singles, including safety tips. If you're not looking for a roomie, you can subscribe to the publication alone for $48 a year.

Arizona Outings: Advice for Gays and Lesbians

In most states, the cities with universities tend to have the most resources for gays and lesbians; in Arizona, these include Phoenix and Tucson and, to a lesser degree, Flagstaff and Prescott. Tucson, the most politically liberal city in a generally conservative state, is probably the gay-friendliest of the four. There are no gay or lesbian residential neighborhoods or nightlife areas in any of these cities, just specific clubs.

In Phoenix, the best source of information is the **Gay and Lesbian Community Center** (24 W. Camelback Rd., Suite C) where you can find copies of the two local gay papers, *Echo* and *Heat Stroke*. **Wingspan** (300 E. Sixth St.; ☎ 520-624-1779) is Tucson's official lesbian, gay, and bisexual community center, but **Antigone Bookstore** (411 N. Fourth Ave.; ☎ 520-792-3715) is also a good information source, especially for lesbians. Both carry the local gay tabloid, the *Observer*.

The top travel information resource online is www.outandabout.com, which has a comprehensive list of travel agents catering to gays and lesbians, a calendar of gay travel events, and links to other useful Web sites and health resources. The monthly newsletter ($49 per year for a regular subscription, $99 for unlimited access to all back issues online) has articles about specific destinations and events.

From Astronomy to Zoology: Finding Your Bliss in Arizona

Guest ranching (see Chapter 8) and golfing are just two of the state's specialties; other Arizona vacations cater to less obvious — but equally engaging — interests.

Adventure

Whether you want a low-impact, women-only outdoor experience or a macho extreme sports marathon, the **Arizona Adventure Travel Network** (AATN), (☎ **480-951-6525;** Internet: www.arizonaguide. com/azadventuretravel) can help. This non-profit organization offers a complete listing of the state's adventure tour providers, usefully organized by adventure type and destination as well as by company name.

Astronomy

Several of the astronomical observatories that you can visit on a daily (or nightly) basis are detailed in Chapter 14. Like to extend your inter-galactic adventure? The University of Arizona's Alumni Association and the Steward Observatory run a series of beginner and advanced astronomy camps each May, June, and October for adults and teens. Campers bunk on Mt. Lemmon, just north of Tucson, and have access to advanced telescopes; prices range from $350 to $550, including meals and lodging. For details, call ☎ **800-BEAT-ASU** (outside AZ), 520-621- 4079, or 520-621-5233; or log on to http://ethel.as. arizona.edu/astro_camp.

Birding

Chapter 15 details many of the excellent birdwatching spots in southeast Arizona and lists various local resources and festivals. If you want to take avian awareness even further, contact the southeast Arizona-based **Hilonesome Ecotours** (570 S. Little Bar Trail, Sierra Vista, AZ 85635; ☎ **800-743-2668;** Internet: www.hilonesome.com), which runs guided birding trips in the region; several last around a week, but personalized single or half-day trips are options, too. You have to sign on for longer excursions if you go with the Tucson-based **Borderland Tours** (2550 W. Calle Padilla, AZ 85745; ☎ 800-525-7753 or 520-882-7650; Internet: www.borderland-tours.com) or with **Field Guides** (9433 Bee Cave Rd., Suite 150, Austin, TX 78733; ☎ 800-728-4953 or 512-263-7295; Internet: www.fieldguides.com), both of which run several southeast Arizona trips. None of the longer trips run cheap; expect to pay upwards of $1,295, including food and nests — but not flights.

Educational

The Ventures program of Flagstaff's **Museum of Northern Arizona** (☎ 520-774-5211, ext. 220; Internet: www.musnaz.org — click on "What's Fun" and then on "Ventures") offers a variety of educational vacations in the Four Corners area, with topics ranging from paleontology to prehistoric warfare in central Arizona. The adventure level is wide-ranging too; you can spend three days at the Grand Canyon's South Rim exploring historic mysteries and sleeping at the El Tovar hotel ($475 including lodging) or kayak for six days in the wild country west of Monument Valley ($1,195, with camping). Most programs depart from the museum.

See also the Grand Canyon Field Institutes, in the South Rim of the Grand Canyon section of Chapter 17.

Golf

Many resorts in Scottsdale and, to a lesser degree Phoenix and Tucson, bundle golf deals in with their room rates. (I discuss golf packages in more detail in Chapter 5.) If you want someone to customize a complete duffer's dream trip for you, contact **America West Golf Vacations** (☎ 888-AWA-GOLF; Internet: www.awagolf.com), which offers a wide range of Arizona air/hotel/and green fees packages. **SGH Golf Inc.** (☎ 800-284-8884; Internet: www.sghgolf.com) tends to specialize in European greens, but does offer Scottsdale deals. If you're devoted to improving your game, check out **Resort Golf Schools** (☎ 888-373-7555; Internet: www.resortgolf.com), with programs in Scottsdale, Phoenix, and Tucson. Prices range widely depending on your point of departure, interest in upscale accommodations, and how much time you want to spend on the greens.

Native American Culture

If you're interested in Native American culture, **Largo Navajoland Tours** (☎ 888-726-9084 or 505-863-0050; Internet: www.navajolandtours.com) offers a unique opportunity to visit Arizona's Indian reservations with insider guides. Most of the tours focus on Navajo Nation sights, but the Navajo tour operators also work with the Hopi, Hualapai, and White Mountain Apache tribes. Tours, which require a minimum of 8 people and last 8 days, vary greatly in price and specifics depending on the group's needs and interests, but always include an interesting assortment of activities and cultural events — everything from sweat lodge ceremonies to horseback riding in remote backcountry.

Photography

Arizona Highways magazine is renowned for its excellent photographs of the state's spectacular landscapes — and faces. If you go on one of the **Friends of Arizona Highways** photography trips (☎ **888-790-7042** or 602-712-2004; Internet: www.friendsofazhighways.com), you may not end up with pictures quite as expert as those of the guides, but you'll get some great photo tips and be guaranteed incredible scenery. Offered February through May and September through November in different parts of the state, photo tours range from 5 to 12 days, with prices starting at about $1,300, including round-trip transportation from Phoenix and, in most cases, all meals and accommodations. Less extensive — and less expensive — one-day workshops are available, too.

Part II
Ironing Out the Details

The 5th Wave   By Rich Tennant

Careful! There's a diamondback coiled behind that rock. I think it's Greg Swindell, so he might strike.

In this part...

You're Arizona bound, and you even have an idea of which parts of the state you want to visit and when. This section deals with the ways to get there (with a group, on your own, by plane, by train . . .); your means of transportation once you arrive; the types of rooms available and the rates you can expect to pay for them; methods of dealing with your finances while you're on the road; as well as assorted odds and ends from packing to planning for emergencies. In fact, about the only thing this "Ironing Out the Details" section doesn't deal with is actual ironing — which is one subject I refuse to discuss.

Chapter 6

Getting to Arizona

● ●

In This Chapter

▶ Talking with a travel agent

▶ Exploring the package and escorted tour routes

▶ Going it alone

▶ Riding the wheels and rails

● ●

*F*iguring out how to approach your Arizona vacation is one of the toughest — and earliest — decisions you need to make about your trip. Only you can decide whether you want to go it alone (relatively speaking — you have me to give you advice), let someone else call the shots, or devise a combination strategy.

Travel Agent: Friend, Fiend, or In Between?

A good travel agent is like a good mechanic or good plumber: Hard to find, but invaluable when you locate the right one. The best way to find a good travel agent is the same way you find a good plumber or mechanic or doctor — word of mouth.

To get the most out of a travel agent, do a little homework. Read up on your destination (you've already made a sound decision by buying this book) and pick out some accommodations and attractions that appeal to you. You can get a comprehensive travel guide such as *Frommer's Arizona* (IDG Books Worldwide, Inc.). If you have access to the Internet, check prices on the Web yourself (see "Getting the Best Airfare" later in this chapter for ideas) to get a sense of ballpark figures. Then take your guidebook and Web information to the travel agent and ask him or her to make the arrangements for you. Because they have access to more resources than even the most complete travel Web site, travel agents generally can get you a better price than you can get by yourself. And they can issue your tickets and vouchers right in the agency. If they can't get you into the hotel of your choice, they can recommend an alternative, and you can look for an objective review in your guidebook.

Travel agents work on commission. The good news is that *you* don't pay the commission — the airlines, accommodations, and tour companies do. The bad news is that unscrupulous travel agents will try to persuade you to book the vacations that nab them the most money in commissions. But over the past few years, some airlines and resorts have begun to limit or eliminate these commissions altogether. The immediate result has been that travel agents don't bother booking certain services unless the customer specifically requests them. Some travel agents have started charging customers for their services. When that practice becomes more commonplace, the best agents should prove even harder to find.

Choosing an Escorted or Package Tour

Say the words "escorted tour" or "package tour" and you may automatically feel as though you're being forced to choose: Your money or your lifestyle. Think again, my friends. Times — and tours — have changed.

An escorted tour does, in fact, involve an escort, but that doesn't mean it has to be dull — or even tame. Escorted tours range from cushy bus trips, where you sit back and let the driver worry about the traffic, to adventures that include river rafting or trekking in the Grand Canyon — activities that most of us can use a bit of guidance with. You do, however, travel with a group, which may be just the thing if you're single and want company. In general, your costs are taken care of after you arrive at your destination, but you still have to cover the airfare.

Which brings us to package tours. Unlike escorted tours, these generally package costs rather than people. There *are* companies that bundle every aspect of your trip, including tours to various sights, but most deal just with selected aspects, allowing you to get good deals by putting together an airfare and hotel arrangement, say, or an airfare and greens fee package. Most packages tend to leave you a lot of leeway, while saving you a lot of money.

How do you find these deals? Well, I suggest some strategies in the next two sections, but every city is different; the tour operators I mention may not offer deals convenient to your city. If that's the case, check with a local travel agent: They generally know the most options close to home, and how best to put together things such as escorted tours and airline packages.

Joining an Escorted Tour

You may be one of the many people who love escorted tours. The tour company takes care of all the details, and tells you what to expect at each leg of your journey. You know your costs up front and, in the case of the tame ones, there aren't many surprises. Escorted tours can take you to the maximum number of sights in the minimum amount of time with the least amount of hassle.

If you decide to go with an escorted tour, I strongly recommend purchasing travel insurance, especially if the tour operator asks to you pay up front. But don't buy insurance from the tour operator! If the tour operators don't fulfill their obligation to provide you with the vacation you paid for, there's no reason to think they'll fulfill their insurance obligations either. Get travel insurance through an independent agency. (I give you more about the ins and outs of travel insurance in Chapter 10.)

When choosing an escorted tour, along with finding out whether you have to put down a deposit and when final payment is due, ask a few simple questions before you buy:

- **What is the cancellation policy?** Can they cancel the trip if they don't get enough people? How late can you cancel if you are unable to go? Do you get a refund if you cancel? If *they* cancel?

- **How jam-packed is the schedule?** Does the tour schedule try to fit 25 hours into a 24-hour day, or does it give you ample time to relax by the pool or shop? If getting up at 7 a.m. every day and not returning to your hotel until 6 or 7 p.m. at night sounds like a grind, certain escorted tours may not be for you.

- **How big is the group?** The smaller the group, the less time you spend waiting for people to get on and off the bus. Tour operators may be evasive about this, because they may not know the exact size of the group until everybody has made reservations, but they should be able to give you a rough estimate.

- **Is there a minimum group size?** Some tours have a minimum group size, and may cancel the tour if they don't book enough people. If a quota exists, find out what it is and how close they are to reaching it. Again, tour operators may be evasive in their answers, but the information may help you select a tour that's sure to happen.

- **What exactly is included?** Don't assume anything. You may have to pay to get yourself to and from the airport. A box lunch may be included in an excursion but drinks may be extra. Beer may be included but not wine. How much flexibility do you have? Can you opt out of certain activities, or does the bus leave once a day, with no exceptions? Are all your meals planned in advance? Can you choose your entree at dinner, or does everybody get the same chicken cutlet?

Depending on your recreational passions, I recommend one of the following tour companies:

- **Maupin Tour** (☎800-255-4266; Internet: www.maupintour.com) offers vacations for the general-interest traveler. In business since 1951, Maupin offers an 8-day bus package that includes the Grand Canyon, Monument Valley, Lake Powell, Sedona, several Indian reservations, and a resort in Scottsdale, among other things. The price of $1,580 per person, includes transportation between sights, guides, food, and accommodations, but not airfare.

✔ **GORPtravel** (☎877-440-GORP; Internet: www.gorptravel. gorp.com), on the other hand, specializes in adventure. You can choose anything from a 3-day hiking, walking, mountain biking trip in Northern Arizona ($595, including base-camp accommodations, equipment, transportation, and gourmet camping meals) to an 8-day trip to Indian ruins and archaeological sites ($1,549, including inn accommodations, meals, entrance to national parks, and talks, among other things). Again, airfare is extra. Prices are based on double occupancy; there's usually an extra fee for single occupancy.

You can also check out Chapter 5, which outlines a few special-interest escorted tours.

Picking a Peck of Package Tours

For lots of destinations, package tours can be a smart way to go. In many cases, a package tour that includes airfare, hotel, and transportation to and from the airport costs less than the hotel alone on a tour you book yourself. That's because packages are sold in bulk to tour operators, who resell them to the public. It's kind of like buying your vacation at a buy-in-bulk store — except the tour operator is the one who buys the 1,000-count box of garbage bags and resells them 10 at a time at a cost that undercuts the local supermarket.

Package tours can vary as much as those garbage bags, too. Some offer a better class of hotels than others. Some offer the same hotels for lower prices. Some offer flights on scheduled airlines; others book charters. In some packages, your choice of accommodations and travel days may be limited. Some let you choose between escorted vacations and independent vacations; others allow you to add on just a few excursions or escorted day trips (also at discounted prices) without booking an entirely escorted tour.

For Arizona, the resorts (see Chapter 8) tend to have good package deals, often throwing in activities such as golf and spa treatments with their room rates (especially during the off season). But for packages with more variety, your best options are from airlines: **America West Vacations** (☎800-442-5013; Internet: www.americawest.com/othertravel/vacations) and **American Airlines Vacations** (☎ 800-321-2121; Internet: www.aavacations.com). Both offer a similarly wide range of departure cities and comparable hotel/rental car choices, so you can base your choice on which airline's hub is convenient for you, and from which airline you prefer to acquire frequent flyer miles. Both have deals to the Grand Canyon, Sedona, Tucson, and the Valley of the Sun and offer the widest range of accommodations in Phoenix and Scottsdale. If you're a duffer, check out Chapter 5 for America West's statewide golf vacation packages. If you live in or near Minneapolis, you might also consider packages from **Sun Country** (☎800-752-1218; Internet: www.suncountry.com), a small airline that runs escapes from Minnesota to Phoenix.

Another option is to check the travel section of your local Sunday newspaper and the ads in the back of national travel magazines such as *Travel & Leisure, National Geographic Traveler,* and *Condé Nast Traveler.* **Liberty Travel** (call ☎ **888-271-1584** to find the store nearest you; Internet: www.libertytravel.com) is one of the biggest packagers in the Northeast, and usually boasts a full-page ad in Sunday papers. **American Express Vacations** (☎ **800-346-3607;** Internet: http://travel.americanexpress.com/travel/) offers a few Arizona choices, too.

Making Your Own Arrangements

You may want to be totally independent, whether that's because you're a control freak and can't stand even a single detail being out of your hands; because you're into spontaneity and hate to have anything pre-arranged outside of what's absolutely essential (like, say, your flight); or because you're completely anti-social (warning: Arizona is a very friendly state). Whatever the reason you want to make your own arrangements, I'm happy to supply some basic transportation data.

Finding Out Who Flies Where

You won't have a problem flying into Arizona's capital: **Phoenix Sky Harbor International Airport** (Internet: www.phxskyharbor.com) is served by 18 major airlines and 3 commuter airlines (Table 6-1 lists them all), with nonstop service to and from more than 100 cities in the United States and around the world. Phoenix is a hub for America West Airlines and Southwest Airlines. Nonstop international service is provided by Aeromexico (to and from Mexico), British Airways (to and from London-Gatwick Airport), Air Canada (to and from Toronto), and America West (to and from Vancouver, British Columbia and Mexico).

You have fewer options if you want to go directly to **Tucson International Airport** (Internet: www.tucsonairport.org); its eight U.S. carriers offer nonstop service to only 12 cities (Albuquerque, Chicago, Cincinnati, Dallas, Denver, Houston, Las Vegas, Los Angeles, Minneapolis, Phoenix, Salt Lake City, and San Diego).

Table 6-1	Airlines That Fly into Arizona	
Airline	*Web Site*	*Toll-Free Number*
Air Canada	www.aircanada.ca	**800-776-3000**
Alaska Air*	www.alaskaair.com	**800-426-0333**
America West and America West Express*	www.americawest.com	**800-235-9292**
American*	www.americanair.com	**800-433-7300**

(continued)

Table 6-1 *(continued)*

Airline	Web Site	Toll-Free Number
American Trans Air	www.ata.com	800-225-2995
British Airways	www.british-airways.com	800-247-9297
Continental*	www.flycontinental.com	800-525-0280
Delta*	www.delta.com	800-221-1212
Frontier	www.flyfrontier.com	800-432-1359
Midwest Express	www.midwestexpress.com	800-452-2022
Northwest*	www.nwa.com	800-225-2525
Scenic Air	www.scenic.com	800-634-6801
Southwest*	www.iflyswa.com	800-435-9792
Sun Country	www.suncountry.com	800-752-1218
TWA	www.twa.com	800-221-2000
United Airlines*	www.united.com	800-241-6522
US Airways	www.usairways.com	800-428-4322

Offers service to both Phoenix and Tucson.

Getting the Best Airfare

Competition among the major U.S. airlines is unlike that of any other industry. Every airline offers virtually the same product (a coach seat is a coach seat is a . . .), yet prices can vary by hundreds of dollars.

Business travelers who need the flexibility to buy their tickets at the last minute and change their itinerary at a moment's notice, and whose priority it is to get home before the weekend, pay (or at least their companies do) the premium rate, known as the full fare. But if you can book your ticket long in advance, stay over Saturday night, or are willing to travel on a Tuesday, Wednesday, or Thursday, you can qualify for the least expensive price — usually a fraction of the full fare. On most flights, even the shortest hops within the United States, the full fare is close to $1,000 or more, but a 7- or 14-day advance purchase ticket is closer to $200 or $300. Obviously, it pays to plan ahead.

The airlines also periodically hold sales, in which they lower the prices on their most popular routes. These fares have advance purchase requirements and date-of-travel restrictions, but you can't beat the prices. As you plan your vacation, keep your eyes open for these sales, which tend to take place in seasons of low travel volume. You almost never see a sale around the peak summer vacation months of July and August, or around Thanksgiving or Christmas, when many people fly, regardless of the fare they have to pay.

Consolidators, also known as bucket shops, buy seats in bulk from the airlines and then sell them back to the public. Their prices are much better than the fares available to you from the airlines, and are often even lower than what your travel agent can get you. You see consolidators' ads in the small boxes at the bottom of the page in your Sunday travel section. Some of the most reliable include **Cheap Tickets** (☎ 800-377-1000; Internet: www.cheaptickets.com), which also offers discounts on car rentals and hotel rooms; **Travac Tours & Charters** (☎ 877-872-8221; Internet: www.thetravelsite.com), with useful links to lots of different travel Web sites, though not many Arizona deals per se; and **FlyCheap** (☎ 800-FLY-CHEAP; Internet: www.flycheap.com), which requires you to provide a lot of information about yourself before you can find out very much about them.

Because competition among carriers for Phoenix air space is so much greater than for the sky above Tucson, you're most likely to get the lowest fares if you fly into Phoenix's Sky Harbor airport. If you're pressed for time, it may be worth it to fly directly to Tucson (if, of course, that's your ultimate destination), but keep in mind that there's hourly shuttle service to Tucson from Sky Harbor. The trip takes about 2 hours each way and costs less than $30, round-trip (Chapter 13 has more info on the shuttle).

Booking Your Ticket Online

Another way to find the cheapest fare is to scour the Internet. That's what computers do best — search through millions of pieces of data and return information in rank order. The number of virtual travel agents on the Internet has increased exponentially in recent years.

Frankly, booking tickets online drives me crazy; I'd much rather pick up the phone and discuss my options with a live airline representative, even if I have to wait on hold for a bit. But this is a running argument I have with friends who would much rather click a mouse than a number pad — and here I defer to them.

It would be impossible to go into all the travel booking sites, but a few of the more respected (and more comprehensive) ones are **Travelocity** (www.travelocity.com), **Microsoft Expedia** (www.expedia.com), and **Yahoo! Travel** (http://travel.yahoo.com). Each has its own little quirks, but all provide variations of the same service. Just enter the dates you want to fly and the cities you want to visit, and the computer looks for the lowest fares. Several other features have become standard to these sites: the ability to check flights at different times or dates in hopes of finding a cheaper fare; e-mail alerts when fares drop on a route you specified; and a database of last-minute deals that advertises super-cheap vacation packages or airfares for those who can get away at a moment's notice.

Great last-minute deals are also available directly from the airlines themselves through a free e-mail service called *E-savers.* Each week, the airline sends you a list of discounted flights, usually leaving the upcoming Friday or Saturday, and returning the following Monday or

Tuesday. You can sign up for all the major airlines at once by logging on to **Smarter Living** (www.smarterliving.com) or going to each individual airline's Web site. These sites offer schedules, flight booking, and information on late-breaking bargains.

See the "Finding Out Who Flies Where" section in this chapter for the Web addresses of the airlines that fly into Phoenix and Tucson.

Arriving by Other Means

Though flying is your most likely arrival mode, you have a couple of alternatives to getting airborne. I cover them in the following sections.

By Car

Driving to Arizona is a fine idea if you live in the southern sections of California, Nevada, Utah, or Colorado, or in western New Mexico — or if you have a few weeks to spare for a major road trip. You can save lots of money on car rental fees and throw everything you could possibly need into the trunk, or the back of your SUV. You can definitely make good connections: I-40 runs through the state in the north and I-10 traverses it (going through both Phoenix and Tucson) in the south. Phoenix is 369 miles from Los Angeles, 455 miles from Albuquerque, 660 miles from Salt Lake City, and 287 miles from Las Vegas.

By Train

Two **Amtrak** (☎800-USA-RAIL; Internet: www.amtrak.com) routes service Arizona. The Southwest Chief, which runs between Chicago and Los Angeles, stops in Flagstaff once a day from each direction, while the Sunset Limited from Orlando to Los Angeles stops in Tucson 3 days a week in each direction. Both routes offer shuttle buses to Phoenix, but there's no direct train service to the capital. You can tootle into Tucson or Flagstaff and rent a car there, or even continue on to the Grand Canyon from Flagstaff and explore the region via a bus tour (see Chapter 7). It's not the most time-effective method of travel, nor necessarily the most economical, but it's relaxing (no need to worry about getting lost or about air turbulence) and, for many, loads of fun.

Chapter 7

Getting Around Arizona

● ●

In This Chapter

▶ Exploring the state by car

▶ Getting deals on rented wheels

▶ Considering planes, trains, and buses

● ●

So what's the best way to see Arizona? That depends on your time frame, bank account, and interests. If you want to visit just the Grand Canyon in the north and Tucson in the south and are more strapped for time than funds, you may want to take to the skies. If you're like most people, however, you want to see more, and at eye level, which brings you to the most popular way to get around. . . .

Driving In

Wheels are by far the best way to tool around this large state. There are supplementary and make-do means of transportation, but driving rules — which is why the longest section of this chapter is devoted to road ways and means and the wheelings and dealings of acquiring a rental car.

Navigating Highways and By-Ways

For the most part, Arizona roads are modern and well-maintained — just what you would expect in the wide-open Southwest. I-40 and I-10 are the main east-west thoroughfares, traversing the northern and southern portions of the state, respectively. They're linked between Phoenix and Flagstaff by I-17 which, despite the "I" in its name, isn't an interstate. The speed limit on these three arteries, all 4- to 6-lane divided highways, is 75 miles per hour, except on curvy stretches and around towns and cities.

Be very careful when you're driving in Indian country. Not all the live-stock on the reservations is fenced in, and cows and goats often wander out on the road. Not only is it dangerous and unpleasant (not to mention sad) to hit an animal, you'll also pay a hefty fee to the owner for destroying private property.

 In desert areas, you may be surprised to see signs reading, "Do not enter when flooded." Take them seriously. The area may be bone-dry 99 percent of the time, but flash floods occur, well, in a flash — as do drownings of people who drive into washes that suddenly fill up with water.

Other road hazards include dust storms, kicked up by fast-moving winds. Turn your lights on if you have trouble seeing, and pull over if the visibility is too low.

 Finally, fill'er up often — it can be as many as 60 miles between gas stations in some places — and keep extra water in your car if you're traveling in the desert. You don't know when both you and your car may overheat.

Renting a Car

Unless you drive your own vehicle, you need to rent a car. The good news is that every car rental company you can think of — and some you've probably never heard of — is represented in Arizona, so rates are fairly competitive. Advantage, Alamo, Avis, Budget, Courtesy, Dollar, Enterprise, Hertz, National, and Resort (see the Appendix for toll-free numbers and Web sites) all have rental counters in the termi-nals at Phoenix Sky Harbor Airport and several others are on the air-port's grounds.

Getting the Best Deal

Car rental rates vary even more than airline fares. The price depends on the size of the car, the length of time you keep it, where and when you pick it up and drop it off, where you take it, and a host of other fac-tors. Asking a few key questions may save you hundreds of dollars.

✔ Weekend rates may be lower than weekday rates. If you're keeping the car five or more days, a weekly rate may be cheaper than the daily rate. Ask if the rate is the same for pickup Friday morning as it is Thursday night.

✔ Some companies may assess a drop-off charge if you don't return the car to the same rental location; others, notably National, do not.

✔ Check whether the rate is cheaper if you pick up the car at a loca-tion in town; both Tucson and Phoenix add on a hefty concession recovery fee if you rent at the airport.

✔ Find out whether age is an issue; many car rental companies add on a fee for drivers under 25; some don't rent to them at all.

✔ If you see an advertised price in your local newspaper, be sure to ask for that specific rate; otherwise you may be charged the standard (higher) rate. Don't forget to mention membership in AAA, AARP, and trade unions. These usually entitle you to discounts ranging from 5 percent to 30 percent.

✔ Check your frequent flyer accounts; not only are your favorite (or at least most-used) airlines likely to have sent you discount coupons, but most car rentals add at least 500 miles to your account.

✔ As with other aspects of planning your trip, using the Internet can make comparison shopping for a car rental much easier. All the major booking sites — **Travelocity** (www.travelocity.com), **Expedia** (www.expedia. com), **Yahoo! Travel** (www.travel. yahoo.com), and **Cheap Tickets** (www.cheaptickets.com), for example — have search engines that can dig up discounted car-rental rates. Just enter the size of the car you want, the pickup and return dates, and location, and the server returns a price. You can even make the reservation through any of these sites.

Adding Up the Charges

On top of the standard rental prices, other optional charges apply to most car rentals (and some not-so-optional charges, such as taxes). The Collision Damage Waiver (CDW), which requires you to pay for damage to the car in a collision, is covered by many credit card companies. Check with your credit card company before you go so you can avoid paying this hefty fee (as much as $15 a day). (By the way, CDWs are illegal in some states, but not in Arizona.)

The car rental companies also offer additional liability insurance (if you harm others in an accident), personal accident insurance (if you harm yourself or your passengers), and personal effects insurance (if your luggage is stolen from your car). Your insurance policy on your car at home probably covers most of these unlikely occurrences. However, if your own insurance doesn't cover you for rentals or if you don't have auto insurance, definitely consider the additional coverage (ask your car rental agent for more information). Unless you're toting around the Hope diamond, and you don't want to leave that in your car trunk anyway, you can probably skip the personal effects insurance, but it's never a good idea to drive around without liability or personal accident coverage; even if you're a good driver, other people may not be, and liability claims can be complicated.

Some companies also offer refueling packages, in which you pay for your initial full tank of gas up front, and can return the car with an empty gas tank. The prices can be competitive with local gas prices, but you don't get credit for any gas remaining in the tank. If you reject this option, you pay only for the gas you use, but you have to return it with a full tank or face charges of $3 to $4 a gallon for any shortfall. In my experience, gas prices in the refueling packages are at the high end, plus, I always find myself trying to drive the car in on fumes so I don't pay for an extra drop of fuel. So, I prefer to forego the refueling package and always allow plenty of time for refueling en route to the car rental return. However, if you usually run late and a refueling stop may make you miss your plane, you're a perfect candidate for the fuel-purchase option.

The two most likely places to rent a car are Phoenix Sky Harbor Airport and Tucson International Airport. Added costs include state tax (5 percent); city and county tax (8 to 10 percent in Phoenix, 10 to 12 percent in Tucson); a surcharge that pays for things you probably don't care about, like baseball stadiums ($2.50 in Phoenix, $3.50 in Tucson); and the aforementioned concession recovery fee — the extra charge for renting at the airport (10 to 15 percent in Phoenix, 8 to 10 percent in Tucson).

If you're planning to base yourself in either Phoenix or Tucson, it may make sense to rent a car at your hotel rather than at the airport, if it's an option. The cost of a shuttle or cab to and from the airport may well be less than the extra tax on your rental car.

Comparing Car Costs

I made price-comparison calls to three rental companies for Phoenix and Tucson airports in July 2000. Clearly, it pays to shop around. Sample prices are weekly rates for an economy car with unlimited mileage and without taxes or special discounts.

Budget
- Phoenix: $176
- Tucson: $109

    $5 per day per additional driver, $10 (Tucson) and $20 (Phoenix) daily surcharge for drivers under 25.

Hertz
- Phoenix: $204
- Tucson: $180

    $6 per day per additional driver (maximum $30), no drivers under 25.

Avis
- Phoenix: $204
- Tucson: $180

    $25 per additional driver per day, no drivers under 25.

Surprisingly, when I checked prices for February 2001, they were either the same or only slightly higher.

Flying In

America West Express (☎ **800-235-9292;** Internet: www.americawest.com) offers the most short hops around the state. Of the destinations I cover in this book, America West offers flights from Phoenix's Sky Harbor to Flagstaff, Fort Huachuca/Sierra Vista, Prescott, and Tucson. These flights rarely exceed $180 with a 21 day advance purchase and a Saturday night stayover. **Sunrise Airlines** (☎ **800-347-3962;** Internet: www.sunriseair.net) services Page from Sky Harbor; flights cost roughly $250 round-trip with a 14-day advance purchase. Feeling flush? **Westwind Aviation** (☎**888-869-0866**) runs charters from all Valley airports to anywhere in Arizona and the Southwest.

Flying into Prescott and, especially, Sierra Vista isn't an especially time- and cost-effective option because neither town is a prime touring base. If you make good connections, the half-hour flight to Flagstaff from Phoenix may be useful, but the drive, which is fairly scenic, only takes about 2½ hours. Plus, you don't have the hassle of changing planes. It's a toss-up whether the time you save is sufficient to warrant the extra expense.

If you're more time- than budget-conscious and are primarily interested in touring the Grand Canyon's North Rim and Indian Country, I definitely recommend Sunrise's Phoenix-Page hop.

Riding the Rails

Although arriving by train is fine, it's not a useful way to get around. The exception is the service to the Grand Canyon from Williams on the **Grand Canyon Railway** (☎**800-THE-TRAIN;** Internet: www.thetrain.com), which combines recreation with a very good means of transportation — you get the canyon without the parking hassle. For train schedules and fares, see Chapter 17.

Leaving the Driving to Them

You can get to plenty of places in Arizona by bus — but you end up at a bus station without a car. The most useful buses are the various shuttle buses from the Phoenix airport to places where you can rent wheels, including Tucson, Sedona, and Prescott. In southeast Arizona, taking the bus to Bisbee and Tombstone, two towns you can walk around, is a viable option (see Chapter 15).

Buses are otherwise handy when it comes to tours. A few excursions around southern Arizona are noted in Chapter 13. In addition, the trips run out of Flagstaff by **Nava-Hopi Tours** (☎ **800-892-8687**) cover a wide range of northern Arizona destinations.

Chapter 8

Booking Your Accommodations

• •

In This Chapter:

▶ Choosing an Arizona bunk

▶ Reserving it

▶ Paying as little as possible for it

• •

*1*t would be hard to find a state with as wide a range of accommodations, and in as many different price categories, as Arizona. This chapter sketches your many lodging options, and then suggests ways for you to book them without paying top dollar.

What Color is Your Pillowcase? Finding the Right Room

Not every traveler is alike — which is why Arizona's large range of rooms makes the state such an appealing destination. You may want to concentrate on the scenery and not spend a lot of money on lodgings, in which case, any place you lay your head at night is fine as long as it has the basics (a good bed, air-conditioning/heating, a phone, and — admit it — a TV). But maybe sightseeing — and your budget — are not primary concerns, and you'd like to spend your entire vacation being catered to in ultra-posh digs.

In this chapter, I talk about the features you can expect from each type of accommodation — and about how much you can figure on paying. If you want to see a list of my favorite spots in each category, go back to Chapter 1. If you're looking for a list of accommodations suitable for wheelchair travelers, see Chapter 5. The only type of Arizona accommodation I don't cover in this book is camping; I assume you want a hard roof over your head. If you're interested in details about where to pitch a tent, consult a more comprehensive guide such as *Frommer's Arizona* (IDG Books Worldwide, Inc.).

I arrange the different accommodation types in descending price order, based on their *rack rates,* which is the maximum rate a hotel charges for a room (see "Rack Rates (And Why You Don't Have to Pay Them)" later in this chapter). Here and throughout this book, $ signs give you an idea of prices, which are based on the nightly rack rate for two people in a double room in high season (Chapter 2 gives more details about what I mean when I refer to high or low season, but in general, summer is high season in northern Arizona, while winter is high season in southern Arizona) and represent the following price ranges:

$ Inexpensive: $75 and under

$$ Moderate: $76 – $125

$$$ Expensive: $126 – $175

$$$$ Very Expensive: More than $175

A few top-dollar resorts and destination spas factor taxes and gratuities into the price quote they give you, but they're the exceptions, not the rule. You have to figure out most of these added costs on your own — but with my help. I give you the tax rates on sales, hotels, and car rentals in the "Quick Concierge" sections of the two city chapters, Chapters 11 and 13. (You can find information on the tax rates in the rest of the state in the Appendix.)

Leave Everything (Including Your Inheritance) to Us: Destination Spas

A destination spa is exactly what it sounds like: A healthful retreat where you hole up to have all your needs — mind and body — attended to. No need to rent a car, as there's no reason to leave the premises. Arizona boasts two world-famous lodgings of this type, both in the Tucson area: Canyon Ranch and Miraval (see Chapter 13 for information on both).

Stay at one of them and you don't have to pay for anything beyond what's included in your original room package: all meals and snacks (healthful, of course), fitness classes, guided outdoor activities, stress reduction and nutrition classes, and a certain number of spa treatments and New Age-type activities (everything from tarot readings to climbing wall challenges). You pay extra for additional spa treatments and personalized services and, in the case of Miraval, booze (Canyon Ranch is dry so that's not an option).

Rooms are nice but not especially luxurious. Don't worry — getting away from everyday worries doesn't included being deprived of a TV. In-room amenities at Canyon Ranch and Miraval include hairdryers, irons, ironing boards, dataports, and robes; all Canyon Ranch rooms also have CD and video/cassette players, while Miraval provides coffeemakers, coffee, and small refrigerators stocked with water, juices, and healthy snacks as standard amenities (at Canyon Ranch, these are only in the upgraded quarters).

Both spas run a variety of specials, particularly in low season — for example, mother-and-daughter getaway weekends, with reduced room rates. But that's a reduction from a per person price that's very high to begin with, even off-season: All the rooms at destination spas fall into the Very Expensive ($$$$) category. Because of the included meals and services, it's hard to compare prices precisely with other types of lodgings. Suffice it to say that, although staying at a destination spa is super, any stress-reduction you might experience there could vanish when you get your credit card bill.

Taking Luxury to its Limits: Resorts

Most hotels and motels are designed to keep guests happy for a night or two, but resorts have a more ambitious job description: They want to keep you playing — and paying — on their grounds for more extended periods.

Arizona's top resorts, primarily located in Scottsdale and Tucson, fulfill that role to a tee — literally. You can expect at least one great golf course on the premises (or, barring that, privileges at a few exclusive ones nearby), along with a pool complex, exercise facilities, and tennis courts. Pampering centers are the most recent competitive arena, with resorts adding larger and better spas featuring the latest (and sometimes the farthest out) treatments. But forget about weight control: You can expect great restaurants and watering holes; resorts host some of the best eateries and bars in the state.

But resorts also know that you may want to bring your family, so all have at least some kid-friendly recreational facilities; many have elaborate children's programs as well. If they don't have baby-sitting or daycare facilities on the grounds, they can refer you to a place you can trust — after all, the resort's reputation is on the line.

Your room won't be anything to sneeze at, either: Accommodations and grounds are constantly being refreshed, and you can expect the latest in room decor, whether that happens to be pastels or earth tones, austerity or fussiness. You always get high-quality bath amenities (many resorts put out their own spa brands); other luxurious touches may include a wood-burning fireplace or a TV you can view from an oversize tub. Standard amenities include room service (sometimes 24-hour), laundry/valet service (usually except for Sundays), minibars (sometimes those sneaky ones that I mentioned in Chapter 4), hairdryers, irons/ironing boards, and data ports (often with a separate, dedicated phone line). Robes and in-room wall safes are other semi-frequent features. Less often, you'll have a coffee maker, but sometimes you have to pay extra for the coffee — which is kind of like giving you a free pair of shoes, but making you pay extra for the laces.

At some resorts, room options include a *casita* (literally a "little house"). These free-standing units, which may or may not be larger than a suite or even a standard hotel room, have their own private entrances; you usually won't have to pass through the hotel lobby to reach them, though that depends on the resort's layout. Sometimes a casita building has more than one unit, so you'll still have a next-door neighbor, but quite often, casitas are completely self-contained and thus ideal for light sleepers (unless, of course, you've brought your own personal snorer along with you).

Naturally, none of this comes cheap. Rack rates for most resort rooms start at about $225 in high season — $350 in many Scottsdale places. But almost every resort runs a variety of packages, throwing in spa treatments, golf, a bottle of champagne and breakfast in bed, tennis lessons . . . pretty much any of the resort's services you can think of, if you're willing to spend two nights or more. Some resorts cater to businesspeople, so they're willing to offer weekend specials. And in summer, when the rates are low to begin with, resorts can really get creative: One in Scottsdale, for example, offered to send a house cleaning service, free, to the home of locals who stayed at the resort for the weekend.

How the Tourist West Was Won: Guest Ranches

Once upon a time in the early twentieth century, ranchers had the clever idea of renting out rooms to Easterners who were caught up in the romance of the West. Said entrepreneurs got a bit of extra spending money, and the Easterners got lots of fresh air and family fun. The heyday (or is that hay day?) of Arizona's dude ranches — now called guest ranches — may have passed and many of the original ranches have shut down, but several still remain, primarily around Tucson, southeast Arizona, and Wickenberg. And they're seeing a resurgence, as family fun and fresh air come back in fashion.

That's not to say all guest ranches are as rustic as they used to be. There are phones and TVs in some — but by no means all — quarters. You can expect private baths (though not necessarily with bathtubs, though all have at least a shower) in all and basic bath amenities such as soap and shampoo, but otherwise they vary widely; a few of the fancier ones may include hair-dryers and irons, but they're very much the exceptions, not the rule. Many have retained the old rooms with their wonderful, original furnishings, while building on additional, more modern ones.

A few guest ranches have added amenities like an exercise room or golf course, but far more typical are a swimming pool and low-tech recreation like volleyball, shuffleboard, and, of course, horseshoes. There's always plenty of stuff for kids to do — everything from petting zoos to crafts centers — and there are often special activities geared toward children, such as riding or roping contests. At night, expect cookouts, hayrides, sing-alongs, and other retro-Western activities.

Rates for a guest ranch stay are in the Very Expensive ($$$$) range, but they include three hearty, all-American meals (alcohol extra), two horseback rides a day (in most cases; a few ranches offer unlimited riding, while a few others charge extra for rides), and all other activities. Most charge lower weekly rates, and if you're willing to stay put and relax, you won't have to shell out for a rental car.

There's often a minimum stay, especially in high season, and many of the guest ranches shut down for at least part of the summer, if not for all of June, July, and August (horses need a vacation, too, ya know).

They're History: Hotels, Lodges, & Inns

Arizona doesn't have many modern high-rise hotels, in part because new construction tends to go out (as in sprawling resorts or low-slung motels) rather than up. But in the past, many hotels either tried to pretend they weren't in Arizona, or got into the mood of their locales with a vengeance. As a result, you'll find a wonderful variety of historic lodgings in all shapes and sizes — everything from funky old Victorian mining hotels with no TVs in the rooms and, in some cases, shared baths, to rustic-elegant lodges that may no longer be luxurious but have the basics as well as loads of character, to once-chic hotels and inns with rooms revamped to include amenities matching those of the toniest resorts. Don't worry; you'll be able to distinguish between them from my descriptions in the individual chapters.

I don't include any places that aren't clean, safe, and comfortable, but the number of perks tends to increase with the price. That funky mining hotel is going to be in the Inexpensive ($) category; the rustic, elegant lodge that provides, minimally, a private bath and TV, probably falls into the Moderate ($$) range; and the born-again chic inn or hotel that has been refitted with top-notch room amenities and modern onsite facilities such as a fitness room falls into the Expensive ($$$) or Very Expensive ($$$$) price slots. Make sure to ask about special packages when you call any of these places.

Cozy Does It: B&Bs

If you automatically associate the words "bed & breakfast" with a certain British queen, you won't be entirely disappointed in Arizona B&Bs. In Prescott, for example, Arizona's capital during the height of Queen Victoria's reign, you find gingerbread and turrets to match those of any New England B&B. But you can also find B&Bs far more characteristic of the state: one built of adobe in the Tucson desert, a former bordello that now rents rooms in Williams, even a hogan (traditional Navajo home) near the Canyon de Chelly. B&Bs are scattered throughout the state, but the greatest concentrations are in Tucson and southeast Arizona and around Flagstaff, Prescott, and Sedona in north-central Arizona.The vast majority of Arizona's B&Bs tend to be comfortable but not luxurious. With a few exceptions, I don't recommend places with fewer than three rooms nor ones that share baths (I specify where that's the case). You can expect full breakfasts — as opposed to Continental spreads — at almost all of them, and prices are generally in the Moderate ($$) category. The exception to this rule is Sedona, where the B&Bs tend to resemble small luxury inns. Almost all boast high-tone touches — expensive bath salts, say, hair dryers, individual breakfast menus that you can order entrees from — and rates to match: Most of Sedona's B&Bs fall into the Very Expensive ($$$$) slot.

 In order to have room for the top choices in a variety of lodging categories, I wasn't able to include all the good B&Bs in the state, but if you're particularly interested in this type of lodging, contact the **Arizona Association of Bed & Breakfast Inns** (P.O. Box 22086, Flagstaff, AZ 86002, ☎ **800-284-2589;** Internet: www.bbonline. com/az/aabbi), which has strict membership guidelines, or the

Arizona Trails Bed & Breakfast reservation service (☎ 888-779-4284 or 480-837-4284; E-mail: aztrails@arizonatrails.com; Internet: www.arizona.trails.com), which represents a wide variety of inns of all types (including AABBI members), also vetted for quality.

Linking Up: Franchise Motels

Sometimes — when you pull into town late at night or you're traveling with kids or you just want to economize — nothing fits the bill like a chain motel. And if you're like most people, you've probably got your favorites, perhaps because booking them gets you frequent flyer miles — or because you like their generous breakfast buffets. So you'll be glad to hear that you'll pretty much have your pick of the lodgings throughout Arizona; there's not an area I can think of that doesn't have at least a few links (and I don't mean golf courses); see the Appendix for the toll-free numbers for those represented in the state. Rooms are generally in the inexpensive ($) or, at the most, moderate ($$) price range.

Remember that not all links of a chain are necessarily alike. In Arizona for example, several Best Western hotels (including one in Tucson and one in Wickenburg) have loads of historic character. The granting of a franchise by a corporate office only means the franchisee has to live up to certain standards; it doesn't mean that the rooms have to be boring. That cuts both ways, of course: If the corporate headquarters doesn't impose strict and frequent quality checks on its members, you may love the Hotel X in St. Louis but be disappointed by the one in Phoenix. Bottom line: Always ask to look at the room before you put your John Hancock on a credit card slip.

When — and Whether — You Need to Pin Down a Room

It never hurts to make advance reservations — you can find out about special deals that way, for one thing — so *whether* to make a call to a hotel that you're interested in isn't really at issue. The question is how far in advance you need to call, and how much you need to panic if you forgot — or weren't able — to book ahead for some reason.

Chapter 2 gives you good general guidelines about what is defined as high season — the period when rooms are in most demand — in different parts of the state. Some destinations and accommodation types are busier than others in high season, however. For example, lodgings in Grand Canyon National Park of nearly every kind are at a premium in July (high season), while a room at a Scottsdale resort may be harder to book in February (high season) than, say, one at a nearby chain motel. And although, with the exception of the Gem and Mineral Show in Tucson, few events listed in the calendar of events section in Chapter 2 have a significant impact on room occupancy, you never know when a huge convention is going to descend on a resort that you have your heart set on.

Within the chapters, I alert you to lodgings that need to be booked particularly far in advance — for example, Phantom Ranch at the bottom of the Grand Canyon. In general, it's a good idea to reserve a room as soon as you know exactly when or where you want to stay, especially if you're planning a high season visit. What do you have to lose by phoning even 6 months ahead of time? You usually need to put down a credit card number to secure your room, but few places make you pay a nonrefundable deposit until much closer to the time you're planning to come (usually about a month).

If you haven't made a reservation in low season, don't worry. You still have a wide range of rooms to choose from, even if the specific place you want turns out to be booked (conventions descend on southern Arizona in the summer, too; they're less expensive for the companies). And don't give up if you don't get the room you covet in high season: You may luck into a last minute cancellation. Make alternative plans that don't require a deposit — and just keep trying the lodging you want.

Rack Rates (And Why You Don't Have to Pay Them)

The *rack rate* is the maximum rate a hotel charges for a room. It's the rate you get if you walk in off the street and ask for a room for the night. You sometimes see these rates printed on the fire/emergency exit diagrams posted on the back of your door.

Hotels are happy to charge you the rack rate, but you don't have to pay it. Hardly anybody does. Perhaps the best way to avoid paying the rack rate is surprisingly simple: just ask for a cheaper or discounted rate. You may be pleasantly surprised.

Getting the Best Room at the Best Rate

In all but the smallest accommodations, the rate you pay for a room depends on many factors — chief among them being how you make your reservation. A travel agent may be able to negotiate a better price with certain hotels than you could get by yourself. (That's because the hotel often gives the agent a discount in exchange for steering his or her business toward that hotel.)

Reserving a room through the hotel's toll-free number may also result in a lower rate than calling the hotel directly. On the other hand, the central reservations number may not know about discount rates at specific locations. For example, local franchises may offer a special group rate for a wedding or family reunion, but they may neglect to tell the central booking line. Your best bet is to call both the local number and the toll-free number and see which one gives you a better deal.

As should be clear by now, room rates (even rack rates) change with the season, as occupancy rates rise and fall. But even within a given season, room prices are subject to change without notice, so the rates quoted in this book may be different from the actual rate you receive when you make your reservation. Be sure to mention membership in AAA, AARP, frequent flyer programs, any other corporate rewards programs you can think of — or your Uncle Joe's Elks lodge in which you're an honorary inductee, for that matter — when you call to book. You never know when it may be worth a few dollars off your room rate.

After you make your reservation, asking one or two more pointed questions can go a long way toward making sure you get the best room in the house.

Always ask for a corner room. They're usually larger, quieter, and have more windows and light than standard rooms, and they don't always cost more. Also ask if the hotel is renovating; if it is, request a room away from the renovation work. Inquire, too, about the location of the restaurants, bars, and discos in the hotel — all sources of annoying noise. And if you aren't happy with your room when you arrive, talk to the front desk. If they have another room, they should be happy to accommodate you, within reason.

Surfing the Web for Hotel Deals

Although the major travel booking sites (Travelocity, Expedia, Yahoo! Travel, and Cheap Tickets; see Chapter 6 for details) offer hotel booking, you may be better off using a site devoted primarily to lodging. You can often find properties not listed with more general online travel agencies. Some lodging sites specialize in a particular type of accommodation, such as B&Bs, which you won't find on the more mainstream booking services. Others, such as TravelWeb in the following list, offer weekend deals on major chain properties, which cater to business travelers and have more empty rooms on weekends. A few of the sites worth checking out are:

- **All Hotels on the Web** (www.all-hotels.com): Although the name is something of a misnomer, the site *does* have tens of thousands of listings throughout the world, including Arizona. Bear in mind that each hotel has paid a small fee ($25 and up) to be listed, so it's less an objective list and more like a book of online brochures.

- **hoteldiscount!com** (www.180096hotel.com): This site lists bargain room rates at hotels in more than 50 U.S. and international cities, including Greater Phoenix and Tucson. The cool thing is that hoteldiscount!com prebooks blocks of rooms so sometimes it has rooms — at discount rates — at hotels that are otherwise sold out. Select a city, input your dates and you get a list of the best prices for a selection of hotels. This site is notable for delivering deep discounts in cities where hotel rooms are expensive. The toll-free number is printed all over this site (☎ 800-96-HOTEL); call it if you want more options than are listed online.

✔ **InnSite** (www.innsite.com): InnSite has B&B listings in all 50 U.S. states and more than 50 countries around the globe. Find an inn at your destination, see pictures of the rooms, and check prices and availability. This extensive directory of B&Bs includes listings only if the proprietor submitted one (it's free to get an inn listed). The descriptions are written by the innkeepers and many listings link to the inn's own Web sites. Try also the Bed and Breakfast Channel (www.bedandbreakfast.com).

✔ **TravelWeb** (www.travelweb.com): Listing more than 26,000 hotels in 170 countries, TravelWeb focuses mostly on chains (both upper and lower end), and you can book almost 90 percent of these online. TravelWeb's Click-It Weekends, updated each Monday, offers weekend deals at many leading hotel chains.

Chapter 9

Money Matters

In This Chapter
▶ Figuring out how much money to carry
▶ Deciding how to carry it
▶ Losing it: What to do if that happens

*O*kay. You already have an idea of how much your trip is going to cost. Now you need to work out some logistics — like how much, and with what, you're going to pay as you go — and contemplate some worst-case scenarios, such as losing your credit cards or having them stolen. Not to worry. If you have a plan, you'll be on top of events, even the bad ones.

Cash 'n' Carry

You're the best judge of how much cash you feel comfortable carrying or what alternative form of currency is your favorite. That's not going to change much on your vacation to Arizona. True, you'll probably be moving around more and incurring more expenses than you generally do (unless you happen to eat out every meal when you're at home), and you may let your mind slip into vacation gear and not be as vigilant about your safety as when you're in work mode. But, those factors aside, the only type of payment that won't be quite as available to you away from home is your personal check.

If you generally like to deal with all your day-to-day expenses in cash so as not to rack up credit card debt, there's no need to discontinue that practice, as long as you remember not to do dumb things such as leave your wallet unattended by the pool. If you like to carry smaller amounts of cash, which you can get from ATMs as you go, that's okay too: There's no shortage of cash machines in Arizona. And if you prefer to pay for nearly everything with an airline credit card so you can get your next trip to Arizona with frequent flyer miles — no problem. You're not, I promise, entering a credit-free zone. That said, I tell you about all the drawbacks to those practices in the next section.

The only parts of Arizona where the rules change slightly are on the Indian reservations in the northeast where not all the crafts vendors or tour operators take credit cards, and cash machines are fewer and farther between. If you're traveling to that part of the state, you may want to have more cash with you than in the other parts, especially if you're planning to buy crafts.

Having a Pocketful of Paper and Plastic

So how will you pay for day-to-day expenses on your Arizona adventure? You have several options to consider, each with their own advantages and disadvantages. This section will help you choose the one that's right for you.

Traveling with Traveler's Checks

Traveler's checks are something of an anachronism from the days when people wrote personal checks instead of going to an ATM. Although I haven't used them in ages, even during travels to foreign countries, if traveler's checks make you feel more secure about your funds, by all means buy some. Every institution that offers traveler's checks also offers replacements if they're lost or stolen, and the service charges are fairly low, or even nonexistent if you know where to go.

You can get travelers checks at almost any bank. American Express offers checks in denominations of $20, $50, $100, $500, and $1,000. You'll pay a service charge ranging from 1–4 percent, though AAA members can obtain checks without a fee at most AAA offices. You can also get American Express traveler's checks over the phone by calling ☎ 800-221-7282.

Visa (☎ 800-227-6811) also offers traveler's checks, available at Citibank locations across the country and at several other banks. The service charge ranges between 1.5 and 2 percent; checks come in denominations of $50, $100, $500, and $1,000. **MasterCard** has its hand in the traveler check market, too; call ☎ 800-223-9920 for a location near you.

Automatically Transferring Money with ATMs

These days far more people use ATMs than traveler's checks. Most cities have these handy 24-hour cash machines linked to a national network that almost always includes your bank at home. Cirrus (☎ 800- 424-7787; Internet: www.mastercard.com/atm/) and Plus (☎ 800-843- 7587; Internet: www.visa.com/atms) are the two most popular networks; check the back of your ATM card to see which network your bank belongs to. The toll-free numbers and Web sites will give you specific locations of ATMs where you can withdraw money while on vacation. You can use them to withdraw just the money you need every couple of days, which eliminates the insecurity (and the pickpocketing threat) of carrying around a large green stash. Of course, many ATMs are little money managers (or dictators, depending on how you look at it), imposing limits on your spending by allowing you to withdraw only a certain amount of money — a maximum of $200, say — per day.

I can't think of any state, except maybe California, where the process of acquiring cash has been raised to such an art form as Arizona. It's as safe and easy as can be. In addition to the bank locations, which are everywhere in the big cities, there are ATMs in shopping malls, ATMs in late- or all-night supermarkets, and, in Tucson, even drive-through ATMs. In short, there's no shortage of places to get the green stuff in the Grand Canyon state.

One important reminder before you go ATM crazy, however: Many banks now charge a fee ranging from 50 cents to three dollars whenever a non-account holder uses their ATMs. Your own bank may also assess a fee for using an ATM that's not one of their branch locations. This means in some cases you'll get charged twice just for using your bankcard when you're on vacation. It may just be cheaper (though certainly less convenient) to revert to the traveler's check policy.

How to decide? Call your local bank and find out if they have branches in Arizona; many are represented in the state, especially in Greater Phoenix and Tucson. Bank of America, Bank One, and Wells Fargo are particularly ubiquitous.

Paying with Plastic: Debit and Credit Cards

Another way of working with money you have — as opposed to the theoretical money of credit cards — is by using a debit card (an ATM card with a credit card logo). In many cases, your debit and ATM card are the same piece of plastic. Instead of getting cash, however, the debit card pays for purchases anywhere a credit card is accepted. The advantage? It takes money out of your checking account rather than pushing up against your credit card limit. There's never any charge for using your debit card, no matter where you use it (in that way it's closer to a credit card than to an ATM card), and you have less cash to carry around.

But most people don't have unlimited checking account resources, and credit cards are invaluable when traveling: They're a safe way to carry money and they provide a convenient record of all your travel expenses when you arrive home. Of course, the disadvantage is that they're easy to overuse. Unlike ATM or debit cards, which are directly connected to the money you have in your checking account, credit cards will take you as far as your credit limit — which may not bear much relation to your actual financial resources — can go. Credit cards let you indulge in a lot more impulse buying than any other form of payment.

You can also get cash advances off your credit card at any ATM if you know your Personal Identification Number (PIN). If you've forgotten it or didn't even know you had a PIN, call the phone number on the back of your credit card and ask the bank to send it to you. It usually takes 5–7 business days, though some banks can give you your PIN over the phone if you tell them your mother's maiden name or provide some other security clearance.

I personally would never get a cash advance from my credit card unless it was an emergency and for some reason I didn't have my ATM card with me. Interest rates for cash advances are often significantly higher than rates for credit-card purchases. More importantly, you start paying interest on the advance *the moment you receive the cash*. On an airline-affiliated credit card, a cash advance does not earn frequent-flyer miles.

My personal travel strategy? I put as much money into my checking account as I can spare before I leave and use my ATM/debit card as much as possible. I save my credit card for things like restaurant and hotel bills and for purchases that I've planned for and know I can pay off in full. That way, I avoid incurring interest and having really boring stuff like gas — which it's impossible to reminisce fondly about — turn up on my bill long after I'm back from a trip.

What to Do if You Lose Your Wallet (Besides Cry)

Sometimes, no matter how careful you are, you can lose your wallet. Take a deep breath and get to a phone. Almost every credit card company has an emergency toll-free number you can call if your wallet or purse is stolen or lost. They may be able to wire you a cash advance off your credit card immediately; in many places, they can get you an emergency credit card within a day or two. The issuing bank's toll-free number is usually on the back of the credit card, but that won't help you much if the card is gone. Write down the number on the back of your card before you leave, and keep it in a safe place (um, not your wallet or purse) just in case.

Citicorp Visa's U.S. emergency number is ☎ **800-645-6556.** American Express cardholders and traveler's check holders should call ☎ **800- 221-7282** for all money emergencies. MasterCard holders should call ☎ **800-307-7309.**

If you opt to carry traveler's checks, be sure to keep a record of their serial numbers — in the same, separate place — so you can handle just such an emergency.

Odds are that if your wallet was stolen, you've seen the last of it, and the police aren't likely to recover it for you. However, after you realize it's gone and you cancel your credit cards, call the local constabulary to report it. You're likely to need the police report number for credit card or insurance purposes later.

Chapter 10

Tying Up the Loose Ends

*O*kay, so you've made the big decisions — when and where and how you want to go to Arizona. Now it's time to deal with those last picky details that can make or break your trip.

Placating the Universe: Buying Travel and Medical Insurance

Buying insurance is kind of like carrying around an umbrella; if you have it, you won't need it. But insurance can be expensive. So, should you or shouldn't you?

Of the three primary kinds of travel insurance — trip cancellation, medical, and lost luggage — the only one I recommend is trip cancellation insurance in the event that you have to pay a large portion of your vacation expenses up front. Medical and lost luggage insurance don't make sense for most travelers. Your existing health insurance should cover you if you get sick while on vacation (though if you belong to an HMO, check to see whether you are fully covered when away from home). Homeowner's insurance policies cover stolen luggage if they include off-premises theft. Check your existing policies before you buy any additional coverage. The airlines are responsible for $2,500 on domestic flights (and $9.07 per pound, up to $640, on international flights) if they lose your luggage; if you plan to carry anything more valuable than that, keep it in your carry-on bag.

Some credit cards (American Express and certain gold and platinum Visa and MasterCards, for example) offer automatic flight insurance against death or dismemberment in case of an airplane crash. If you feel you need still more insurance, try one of the companies listed below. But don't pay for more insurance than you need. For example, if you only need trip cancellation insurance, don't buy coverage for lost or stolen property. Trip cancellation insurance costs approximately 6–8 percent of the total value of your vacation. You can get any kind of travel insurance from the reputable travel insurance companies in the following list.

- **Access America,** 6600 W. Broad St., Richmond, VA 23230 (☎ 800- 284-8300; fax: 800-346-9265; Internet: www.accessamerica.com)

- **Travelex Insurance Services,** 11717 Burt St., Ste. 202, Omaha, NE 68154 (☎ 800-228-9792; Internet: www.travelex-insurance.com)

- **Travel Guard International,** 1145 Clark St., Stevens Point, WI 54481 (☎ 800-826-1300; Internet: www.travel-guard.com)

- **Travel Insured International, Inc.,** P.O. Box 280568, 52-S Oakland Ave., East Hartford, CT 06128-0568 (☎ 800-243-3174; Internet: www.travelinsured.com)

Finding Medical Care When You're Away from Home

Not only can getting ill ruin your vacation, but it can be scary. It's not always easy to find a doctor you trust when you're away from home. The best defense against illness is a good offense. Bring all your medications with you, as well as a prescription for more if you worry that you'll run out. Bring an extra pair of contact lenses in case you lose one. It's always good to have Pepto-Bismol on hand for common travelers' ailments like upset stomach or diarrhea (but if you forget, you can also find it in most hotel gift shops or nearby convenience stores).

If you have health insurance, check with your provider to find out the extent of your coverage outside of your home area. Be sure to carry your identification card with you. And if you're concerned that your existing policy won't be sufficient, get medical insurance (see the preceding section) for more comprehensive coverage.

If you suffer from a chronic illness, talk to your doctor before taking the trip. For such conditions as epilepsy, diabetes, or a heart condition, wearing a Medic Alert identification tag immediately alerts any doctor to your condition and gives him or her access to your medical records through Medic Alert's 24-hour hotline. Membership is $35, with a $15 annual renewal fee. Contact the Medic Alert Foundation, 2323 Colorado Ave., Turlock, CA 95382 (☎ 800-432-5378; Internet: www.medicalert.org).

Inventory Your Health

This chapter includes tips about health insurance but it doesn't take your machismo (or machisma) level into account. If you never hiked a day in your life, don't plan on walking to the bottom of the Grand Canyon. And if your health is a problem, going to a remote Indian reservation isn't smart; you aren't near any very contemporary medical facilities. Sticking near Phoenix or Tucson, both chock-a-block with specialty hospitals, is a far better idea.

It's not a good idea to travel to the more remote areas in northeastern Arizona if you fear that your medical condition may flare up. There are few modern hospitals on the Indian reservations and they're not always within easy driving distance.

If you do get sick in Arizona, try contacting your doctor back home to see if he or she can refer you to someone local; Greater Phoenix and Tucson have a large range of excellent medical facilities. A friend of mine had a medical emergency, a detached retina, while she was visiting me in Tucson. When she phoned her eye doctor in Massachusetts, he recommended a physician at a nearby clinic that specialized in retinal surgery. Turned out, she felt she'd received better medical care and more personalized attention than she usually got back home.

If you can't get ahold of your doctor or don't have one you can phone, ask a concierge or manager at your hotel to recommend a local physician — even his or her own if necessary. This is probably a better recommendation than any national consortium of doctors available through a toll-free number.

Finally, if you can't get a doctor to help you right away, try the emergency room at the local hospital. Many hospital emergency rooms have walk-in clinics for emergency cases that are not life-threatening. You may not get immediate attention, but you won't pay the high price of an emergency room visit (usually a minimum of $300 just for signing your name, on top of whatever treatment you receive).

The bottom line: Don't panic; it'll only compound your symptoms.

Making Reservations and Getting Tickets

Good news. Arizona is, for the most part, a play-it-as-it-lays kind of destination (shoot, we cowhands don't like to be fussed makin' plans). There's very little, besides hotel rooms (see Chapter 8) that you'll need to arrange before you go. You may, however, want some advance notice on what's happening when you visit.

I noted two things in the calendar of events section in Chapter 2 that you'll want to prepare for ahead of time: the Fiesta Bowl in Tempe and Jazz on the Rocks in Sedona. In the same chapter, I sketched the top (or most interesting) events, but if you want to find out more about what's going on all around the state, log on to the Arizona Office of Tourism Web site at www.arizonaguide.com, and then click on "Activities" and "Annual Events Snapshot" (or — for more details than you may actually want — click on to the name of the month that you're planning to visit).

If you want to visit Kartchner Caverns State Park (see Chapter 15) or take a mule ride into the Grand Canyon (see Chapter 17), you'll need to do a bit of scheming. I discuss logistics for both — and contingency plans if you can't get the date you want — in the respective chapters.

Taking in a Game and Delving into Museums

There's no need to make special plans for the events at Phoenix's Heard Museum, but if you want something to look forward to, log on to www.heard.org. You can find out if there are any major traveling art shows in town by visiting the Phoenix Art Museum's Web site, www.phxart.org. If you're traveling with kids, get them psyched for the trip by giving them a preview of the fun events they might catch at Phoenix's Arizona Science Center. (For more info, check their Web site: www.azscience.org.)

Sporting events in Phoenix rarely sell out unless they're playoffs, which you can't predict very far in advance (if you could, you'd be rich — or arrested). If you're interested in booking good seats for the Arizona Diamondbacks, log on to www.azdiamondbacks.com or contact Ticketmaster (☎ **480-784-4444;** Internet: www.ticketmaster.com), which also sells tickets to the Phoenix Suns and Coyotes, Arizona Cardinals, Cactus League baseball games, and to various other jock activities detailed in the "Spectator Sports" section of Chapter 11.

You won't have to do much planning for most participant sports, but the best tee times are not always easy to get in high season; see Chapters 11 and 13 for information on places that'll help get you on course in Greater Phoenix and Tucson.

Reserving for Dinner

I'm always joking that I moved to Arizona because I got tired of begging people in New York to eat "early" — that is, at 8 p.m. If you're used to dining at what many would consider a civilized hour, 8:30 or 9 p.m., you shouldn't have a problem getting reservations at even the best restaurants in Greater Phoenix and Tucson (if, on the other hand, you want to dine at 10 p.m. or later, you're out of luck for the most part; the kitchen staff at even the big city eateries are preparing to crawl into bed by then). If, however, you want to eat at prime Arizona time, 7 or 7:30 p.m. in high season, it couldn't hurt to book a week to ten days in advance at Rancho Pinot, Hapa, and T. Cook's in Scottsdale (see Chapter 11) and at Janos or The Dish (because it's tiny) in Tucson (see Chapter 13). In Sedona (Chapter 16), tables at the Yavapai Room in the Enchantment Resort are at a premium and high season isn't as clear-cut as in the other places; as soon as you know when you're going to be in town, give them a holler.

Trip-Planning Resources

Most people don't really to come to Arizona to see Broadway shows or major arts performances, though there are plenty of both in Greater Phoenix and Tucson. If you want to know about Arizona's main cultural (and less cultural) events, check the listings sections of the big cities' free papers, the **Phoenix New Times** (www.phoenixnewtimes.com) and the **Tucson Weekly** (www.tucsonweekly.com). Available solely online, www.phoenix.citysearch.com is another good resource for events in the Valley of the Sun. For seats to the big deal concerts and shows in major venues, contact Ticketmaster.

Packing Tips

Arizona is super casual; unless you attend a board meeting or a funeral, you don't need a suit or fancy dress (see "Dressing Like the Locals," later in this chapter).

Settling on a Suitcase

When choosing your suitcase, think about the kind of traveling you'll be doing. Unless you settle into one city or town for a while, you're likely to be on the road, schlepping your bag in and out of B&Bs or motel rooms. If that's the case, why not leave your extra-large suitcase at home. You don't need an enormous encumbrance, just your traveling essentials.

You probably don't need a fold-over garment bag; this luggage is good for keeping dressy clothes wrinkle-free, but you're not likely to need anything very fancy in Arizona. Garment bags are a nuisance if you pack and unpack a lot.

 Keep in mind that hard-sided luggage may protect breakable items better — you're not going to be packing your best china, are you? — but weighs more than soft-sided bags. Whichever type you chose, if you move around, I suggest several smaller pieces of luggage rather than one or two large ones; that way, if you shift locales — going from cooler high country to the desert, say — you can transfer items that are no longer appropriate (such as sweaters) into a smaller bag. In addition, you don't need to keep dragging something that weighs a ton into your hotel room each night.

Packing Pointers

My first tip is to pack light. Take everything you think you need and lay it out on the bed. Then get rid of half of it. It's not that the airlines won't let you take it all — they will, with some limits — but why would you want to get a hernia from lugging half your house around with you? Suitcase straps can be particularly painful to sunburned shoulders.

So what are the bare essentials? Comfortable walking shoes, a camera, a versatile sweater and/or jacket, a belt, toiletries and medications (pack these in your carry-on bag so you have them if the airline loses your luggage), and something to sleep in.

When packing, start with the biggest, hardest items (usually shoes); then fit smaller items in and around them. Pack breakable items among several layers of clothes or keep them in your carry-on bag. Put things that could leak, such as shampoos and suntan lotions, in sealed plastic bags. Secure your suitcase with a small padlock (available at most luggage stores, if your bag doesn't already have one), don't put anything valuable in an unlocked outside pocket, and, unless your bag is bright purple or yellow or polka dotted, put a distinctive identification tag on the outside so it'll be easy to spot on the carousel.

Carrying On: Meeting Airline Baggage Requirements

If you're flying, keep in mind that you're allowed two pieces of carry-on luggage, both of which must fit in the overhead compartment or under the seat in front of you. These could contain a book; any breakable items you don't want to put in your suitcase; a personal headphone stereo; a snack in case you don't like airline meals (to paraphrase Woody Allen, who was alluding to people complaining about the Catskills hotels: The food is lousy and there isn't enough of it); any vital documents you don't want to lose in your luggage (like your return tickets, wallet, and so on); and some empty space for the sweater or jacket you'll want to wear on the plane, but later shed while you're waiting for your luggage in an overheated terminal.

Because lost-luggage occurrences have reached an all-time high, consumers are trying to avert disaster by bringing their possessions on board. But planes are more crowded than ever and overhead compartment space is at a premium. Some domestic airlines have begun to crack down, limiting you to a single carry-on for crowded flights and imposing size restrictions to the bags you bring on board. The dimensions vary, but the strictest airlines say carry-ons must measure no more than 22 x 14 x 9 inches, including wheels and handles, and weigh no more than 40 pounds. Many airports are already furnished with X-ray machines that literally block any carry-ons bigger than the posted size restriction. It sounds drastic, but keep in mind that many of these regulations are enforced only at the discretion of the gate attendants. However, if you plan to bring more than one bag aboard a crowded flight, be sure your medications, documents, and valuables are consolidated in one bag in case you are forced to check the second one.

Dressing Like the Locals

Not to sound like the snobbish ex-New Yorker that I am, but dressing like the locals in Arizona won't get you into the pages of *Vogue*. It is, on the other hand, going to keep you nice and comfortable.

Forgo the polyester — it has gone out of style again anyway, thank heavens — in favor of porous natural fabrics like cotton. Jeans are fine if you're going to northern Arizona or if you'll be in the south in the height of winter, but they'll be too heavy in the warmer months in the south. Wherever you go, be sure to throw in a pair or two of walking shorts; things tend to heat up quickly in this state. In general, think loose fitting and non-clingy — and, of course, layers. Lots of places are very air-conditioned, so even if it's toasty outside you may want something to throw over your shoulders.

You won't always want to be wearing socks, so a sturdy, comfortable pair of sandals to walk in is a good idea for southern Arizona. But also take along closed shoes like sneakers, as well as light-weight, full-length slacks: You don't want your legs or toes exposed if you're going to get up close and personal with any cacti.

Speaking of which, bring along a pair of tweezers, in case of any too-close encounters; a thin-toothed pocket comb is also a good prickle remover (in Arizona, being spineless is a good thing). A fanny pack with a slot for a water bottle is essential, whether you're heading north or south; it's very easy to get dehydrated in the strong sun and high altitude, even if the air feels coolish.

Some Book and Audiovisual Advice

I don't know about you, but when I'm traveling, I love to read mysteries set in the locales that I'm visiting (I take it on faith that I won't come across any actual bodies). For northeast Arizona, you can't do better than Tony Hillerman, whose fictional detectives, Jim Chee and Joe Leaphorn, are Navajo and whose books are largely set on the "rez." If you're visiting southeast Arizona, try the J.A. Jance series that features Joanna Barnes as the sheriff of Bisbee (for example, *Skeleton Canyon*). Most of Jake Page's books are set in and around Santa Fe, New Mexico, but *The Stolen Gods* uses the Hopi reservation and Tucson as its prime locations.

Alternatively, all these authors are available in audio book versions from either **Books on Tape** (☎ 800-88-BOOKS; www.booksontape.com) or **Recorded Books, Inc.** (☎ 800-638-1304; www.recordedbooks.com). You can borrow them for free from many local libraries or, if you can't find them near you, order them directly from the companies. I especially recommend taking Hillerman tapes along with you if you're going to northeast Arizona. Listening to the books makes the longer legs of the trip zip by — and it's a kick to be actually viewing lots of the places being described.

At night, resort clothes — flowing skirts and tops, nice slacks, and a good sports shirt — are fine for almost every good restaurant. If you think you're going to want to go to a restaurant in the $$$$ category (see Chapter 4), a sports jacket and chic sundress (not worn together, please) should fit the bill. In all, unless you're in Arizona on business, leave that little Prada outfit with matching heels or that Armani suit at home.

Part III
Exploring the Big Cities

The 5th Wave   By Rich Tennant

@RICHTENNANT

"Oh, it's okay if you're into neo-romanticist art. Personally, I prefer the soaring perspectives of David Hockney or the controlled frenzy of Gerhard Richter."

In this part. . .

Meet Arizona's two sprawling major cities, the metroplex known as Greater Phoenix or the Valley of the Sun, and its southern rival, Tucson. In this part, I give you everything you need to know about both of them, from boring nitty-gritty details such as how to get from the airport to your hotel, to the best places to boogie after dark. And when you're ready for some great day (or overnight) escapes from the cities, I have some terrific ones lined up for you, too.

Chapter 11

Phoenix, Scottsdale, and the Valley of the Sun

. . . .

In This Chapter

▶ Getting the scoop on Greater Phoenix

▶ Bunking in the best places in the Valley

▶ Chowing down in the top eateries

▶ Seeing the prime sights and diversions

▶ Shopping till you drop

▶ Kicking up your heels after dark

. . . .

*L*os Angeles without water: Except for its oceans of swimming pools, Phoenix epitomizes the new urban Southwest — leisure bent and car obsessed. This northern Sonoran Desert city is only part, albeit a major one, of a complex of satellites known collectively as the Valley of the Sun, which includes the tourist destinations of Scottsdale and Tempe.

For visitors, it's the Valley of the Fun. Great museums and sports — of both the watching and doing variety — are Phoenix's prime arenas, while Scottsdale specializes in ritzy resorts, lush golf courses, tony boutiques, and posh spas. Tempe, home to Arizona State University, competes for tourist attention with a youthful personality, strollable streets, and a newly acquired town lake. But all the Valley towns share one key asset: Plenty of year-round sunshine and endless ways to play in it.

Flying In

Phoenix is Arizona's prime transportation hub, receiving more flights than anywhere else in the state and linking to all major highways — but you can't get there by train.

More major airlines fly into **Phoenix Sky Harbor International Airport,** 3 miles east of downtown Phoenix (☎ **602-273-3321**), than into any other city in the state (see Chapter 6 for details); almost 12 million visitors pass through here annually. This is the place where you're likely to begin your Arizona trip, even if you're not staying in the Valley. (See the individual chapters for details about the various shuttles that leave from the airport.)

The three terminals (2, 3, 4) and lower level baggage claim areas are easy to negotiate. Because the various bus, taxi, and shuttle services are cloned at each terminal, you won't have a problem if you're only going to collect your luggage and head into Phoenix or out to another part of the state via ground transportation. If, however, you have to switch gates within a terminal, it can be stressful, because the distances between the gates are often great — I always seem to find myself having to get from A-1 to C-35 in 3 minutes — and there's only a moving sidewalk to get you around. Nor is there any indoor inter-terminal transport; you'll have to head outside through baggage claim to catch the free shuttle from one terminal to another. Although these run frequently during the day (every 5 or 10 minutes), the wait can be nail-bitingly long in the evening. If possible, don't cut your connections too close.

Each terminal has its own tourist information desk and rental car facilities, easily located in the baggage claim area. (You'll probably have plenty of time to familiarize yourself with this area; Sky Harbor is one of the busiest airports in the country so luggage arrival is not always swift.) Some hotels and resorts offer free shuttle service; be sure to ask before you touch down if — and precisely where — you can expect to be retrieved.

You have several options when it comes to getting from the airport to wherever you're planning to lay your head, and the following sections let you know what they are.

Renting a Car

Seventeen rental car companies operate out of Sky Harbor, so you're bound to find your favorites here — or at least those for which you have discount coupons; see the appendix for the toll-free numbers. The major players — **Alamo, Avis, Budget, Dollar, Enterprise, Hertz, National,** and **Thrifty** — all have service counters at the individual terminals and return areas within the airport.

If you're headed to downtown Phoenix or Scottsdale, you'll want to leave the airport by the west (24th Street/Squaw Peak Parkway) exit; for Phoenix, continue west on 24th Street to Washington Street; for Scottsdale, take 24th Street to the Squaw Peak Parkway (Highway 51) and go north to the exit most convenient to your resort, generally Indian School Road or Lincoln Drive. To reach Tempe, take the eastern exit, an extension of 44th St., to the Hohokam Expressway (Highway 143), and drive south one exit to University Ave., which goes straight into town.

Hailing a Cab or Hopping on a Shuttle

Outside the baggage claim area, you'll see queues of taxis from the only three companies licensed for airport pickup: **AAA Cab** (☎ 602-437- 4000), **Courier Transportation** (☎ 602-232-2222), and **Yellow Cab** (☎ 602-252-5252). Rates average about $2 per mile, with a flag-drop fee (rate at the start of the meter) of $3 and a $1 airport surcharge. If you're headed to downtown Phoenix, expect to pay between $7 and $15, and from $15 to $30 if you're traveling to an outlying city such as Scottsdale.

The **SuperShuttle** (☎ **800-258-3826** or 602-244-9000) vans provide reliable door-to-door service Valleywide, 24/7. A company agent stationed on the center island outside the baggage claim area will call a van for you when you've retrieved your luggage and are ready to hit the road. Fares are based on the zip code you're traveling to: If you're heading to central or downtown Phoenix, you'll pay about $7 for the first person and (always) $6 for each additional person. Trips to surrounding areas, such as Scottsdale, will cost close to $15 for the first person and, again, $6 for each additional person; children 3 and under ride free. Credit cards are accepted and tips are expected.

The farther from the airport you're headed, the more sense it makes to use the shuttle; if, on the other hand, you're traveling a shorter distance to downtown Phoenix or Tempe, a cab is likely to be quicker (no stops for other passengers) and cost about the same (or less). The shuttle operates on an as-needed basis, so you don't need to make reservations before you arrive in town; when returning to the airport, however, be sure to call a day in advance to arrange a pick up from your hotel.

Taking the Bus

On Monday through Friday, there's direct Valley Metro bus service (see "Getting Around," later in this chapter) from terminals 2, 3, and 4 of Sky Harbor Airport to downtown Phoenix and to central Tempe. On Saturday, it's more complicated to get to Phoenix and there's no service to Tempe; on Sunday, all the buses take a rest. If you don't have much luggage, it's a good deal: For $1.25, you can get to Tempe and downtown Phoenix in about 20 minutes. Although there are free transfers to Scottsdale and other Valley destinations, any savings are not generally worth the chunk of time this form of transit will carve from your vacation (and if you're staying in Scottsdale, you're probably not on a really tight budget).

To reach downtown Phoenix, take the Red Line to the east; buses, which can be found at the eastern end of the upper level of terminals 3 and 4, run from 5:42 a.m. to 10:02 p.m. To reach Tempe, catch the Red Line west; buses can be found on the western end of the upper level of terminals 3 and 4, and they run from 3:43 a.m. to 10:21 p.m. The frequency depends on the time of day — during peak rush hour periods, they may leave as often as every 15 minutes, but off-times they may only run hourly. The Bus Book, which lists schedules, is sometimes available at the airport tourist information desk, but don't count on it; best call ☎ **602-253-5000** to check the times if you're contemplating this form of transport.

Driving In

Two interstates run into and through Phoenix — I-10, which extends from Florida to southern California, and I-17, which, despite its name, isn't really an interstate because it only goes north to Flagstaff, where it turns into Arizona Highway 89. It does, however, hook up at Flagstaff with I-40, a genuine interstate that stretches from North Carolina to California. See "Getting Around" later in this chapter for descriptions of some of the more minor arteries into town.

Riding In (No, not on Horseback)

If you're going **Greyhound** (☎ **800-231-2222**), you can roll into one of several area stations, including Phoenix, Tempe, and Mesa. The main terminal is in Phoenix at 2115 E. Buckeye Rd. (☎ **602-389-4202**), near Sky Harbor Airport.

Amtrak (☎ **800-872-7245** or 602-253-0121) does not provide train service to Phoenix, but runs buses there (specifically to 401 W. Harrison St. at 4th St.) from depots in Tucson and Flagstaff (see Chapters 13 and 17, respectively). Although the bus leaves you downtown, you'll still have to cab it to your hotel — thus gobbling up any money you may save by using this inconvenient-to-Phoenix form of transport.

Here's what helps me. I picture the entire Valley as a donut clock — what can I say? I have a vivid imagination that usually involves food — with Sky Harbor Airport as its more-or-less empty center; aside from the runways and the old railroad tracks, there's not much else in this area. Starting from noon where Phoenix's **Camelback Corridor** district lies, you'll be moving around this junk food timepiece to **Paradise Valley** (1 p.m.), **Scottsdale** (1:30 p.m.), **Mesa** (3 p.m.), **Tempe** (4 p.m.), **South Phoenix** (6 p.m.), and **downtown Phoenix** (9 p.m.). Beyond the more remote sections of Phoenix that run along I-17 from 9 p.m. to midnight is what's called the **West Valley,** a largely suburban and residential region; its best-known towns are **Glendale, Peoria,** and the two **Sun City** planned retirement communities. You're likely to be spending most of your visit in Phoenix and the East Valley where — rough rule of thumb — the farther north and east you go of downtown Phoenix, the ritzier it gets.

Orienting Yourself

The Valley of the Sun is so large — 9,127 square miles if you include all 22 incorporated cities — that, AAA gives you two maps for Greater Phoenix. The one you'll probably be wearing out the folds of is called Phoenix/Central & Eastern suburbs (Central & Western suburbs is the other one). Don't be surprised if you find it all a bit daunting; I still do after years of driving up from Tucson.

The Fabulous Resorts of . . . Pumpkinville?

The Mormons who settled in the Valley of the Sun in the 1860s called Phoenix "Pumpkinville" after the gourds that grew along the canals built by the Hohokam Indians. It was Englishman Darrell Dupa's 1868 proclamation that "a new city will spring phoenix-like upon the ruins of a former civilization" that inspired the state legislature to adopt the city's more romantic, if less colorful (well, at least not orange) monicker.

 In the late 1990s, these geographical divisions were made telephonically official: Phoenix kept its old area code, 602, while the East Valley's prefix was changed to 480 (Paradise Valley, Scottsdale, Mesa, and Tempe), and the West Valley's (Glendale, Peoria, and the Sun Cities) to 623.

Phoenix, Scottsdale, and the Valley of the Sun: A Breakdown by Neighborhood

The Valley is made up of a series of cities and towns — if you can get to know the names of these, you can make getting around a lot easier on yourself. Within these, there are smaller geographical sub-units but, don't forget, you're not in Kansas (or, better for this example, Boston) anymore: With few exceptions, these sprawling new western towns don't divvy up into neighborhoods in the traditional sense of the term.

Phoenix

Most of Phoenix's attractions are in the downtown and Camelback Corridor areas, but South Mountain and the Papago Salado regions have a few tourist hooks, too.

In the throes of a building frenzy, the formerly seedy southern sector of **downtown,** roughly bounded by Fillmore St. (north), Jefferson St. (south), 1st Ave. (west), and 7th St. (east), embraces several high and low-tone tourist zones: the two major sports stadiums — America West Arena and Bank One Ballpark ("BOB") — both directly south of Jefferson; Heritage Square and the adjacent museum complex, including the Arizona Science Center; the glitzy Arizona Center entertainment/dining/office complex; and the nearby cultural hub of the Herberger Theater Center and Phoenix Symphony. Drive about a mile north along Central Avenue, get beyond the I-10 overpass, which is flanked by Margaret T. Hance Park (also known as Deck Park), and you come to the Arizona Historical Society Museum, the Phoenix Art

Museum, and the Heard Museum, in that order. This part of downtown includes mostly older businesses, some newer corporate headquarters, and two actual neighborhoods: the ritzy **Encanto/Palmcroft** enclave near Encanto Park and, to the east, **Willo,** more middle class but artsy, with lots of appealing old bungalows.

The **Camelback Corridor,** extending along Camelback Road through North Central Phoenix towards Scottsdale (roughly from 20th to 44th Streets), has fewer tourist attractions; with gleaming rows of office towers interspersed with upscale shops, hotels, and restaurants, the area is populated mostly by natives. It's abutted by the wealthy residential **Arcadia** (44th to 68th Streets from Camelback to Indian School Roads), which was once swathed with ranches and orange groves.

Papago Salado, named for Phoenix's earliest Native American settlers, is a mostly faceless, freeway-ridden area at the conjunction of Phoenix, Scottsdale, and Tempe. It's home, however, to the Desert Botanical Gardens, Phoenix Zoo, and Papago Park northwest of Highway 202, and to the Pueblo Grande Museum and Cultural Park, sandwiched between highways 143 and 153.

South Phoenix, which is slowly being revitalized, hosts the huge South Mountain Park and, just before its entrance, Mystery Castle. A few resorts and the large Arizona Mills mall are in this area, too.

Scottsdale

Arizona's answer to Palm Springs, **Scottsdale** is a newer, hipper version of the California town that coined the concept of wealthy desert-chic. The long, skinny city of about 200,000 people stretches some 20 miles from Tempe in the south to Carefree in the north. Not very long ago, you could see endless stretches of empty desert along the northern part of Scottsdale Road, the town's main drag, but now you'll be hard pressed to guess where Scottsdale ends and the manicured planned community of Carefree starts (okay, the intersecting Carefree Road is a dead giveaway).

Not surprisingly, the town tends to be divided up into shopping and arts districts (see "Shopping," later in this chapter, for more details). **Downtown Scottsdale,** near Tempe, runs roughly between Osborn Rd. (south), Camelback Rd. (north), 68th St. (west), and Civic Center Boulevard (east); within that area, the four square blocks of now touristy **Old Town** have authentic historic cachet. Scottsdale Road between Indian School Road and Shea Boulevard has been dubbed **Resort Row** because of — you guessed it — its abundance of large, upscale lodgings.

Paradise Valley

Nestled just west of central Scottsdale, **Paradise Valley** may be the most exclusive stretch of real estate in the Valley. It's almost entirely residential, with large, desert-embracing estates. A few hotels and resorts may bring you here if you don't happen to have rich relatives.

Tempe

Home to Arizona State University, **Tempe** comes closest to what is traditionally considered a town: You can stroll along its main drag, Mill Avenue, and actually see other people. Tempe has always had a thriving, student-driven nightlife, but aside from the museums and the Sun Devil Stadium on the ASU campus, there was little to bring tourists here during the day. That changed with the opening in 1999 of the man-made Tempe Town Lake, which flows between the Rio Salado Parkway and Highway 202 along a formerly dry bed of the Salt River. A waterfront scene hasn't developed yet, but chances look good that it will.

Glendale

Of all the West Valley towns, **Glendale** is the one out-of-towners are most likely to visit. Not only is it the closest to downtown and central Phoenix, but it also has a walkable downtown with lots of historic buildings and a plethora of antiques shops. In 1999 it acquired another lure, the charming Bead Museum.

Street Smarts: Where to Get Information After You Arrive

The bilingual — that's Spanish and English — staff at the information booths in each of the airport terminals dispenses tour brochures, city maps, and other introductory information.

The **Phoenix Convention and Visitors Bureau** has two walk-in centers: 50 N. 2nd St. at Adams, downtown (☎ **602-452-6282;** open Mon through Fri 8 a.m. to 5 p.m.), and Biltmore Fashion Park, 24th St. and Camelback Rd. (☎ **602-452-6281;** open Mon through Fri 10 a.m. to 9 p.m., Sat 10 a.m. to 6 p.m., and Sun noon to 6 p.m.). (You'll find the second location between Macy's and Christofle, if you don't get sidetracked.) In addition, the Phoenix CVB-staffed service centers in the lobbies of the Phoenix Civic Plaza buildings, N. Third St., with entrances between Monroe and Jefferson, can book dinner or shows for you (but they can't be held responsible if you don't like what you see or eat).

The **Scottsdale Chamber of Commerce/Convention and Visitors Bureau** (7343 Scottsdale Mall, Old Scottsdale ☎ **480-945-8481**) is open Monday through Friday 8:30 a.m. to 6 p.m., Saturday 10 a.m. to 4 p.m., and Sunday 11 a.m. to 5 p.m. (closed Sunday June through August).

Whoa, There!

Phoenix is the sixth largest city in the United States and still growing. It vies with Las Vegas as America's fastest growing large (population over 1 million) city, boasting a growth rate of 20 percent during the 1990s.

Getting Around

Greater Phoenix practically defines the term urban sprawl, and it's severely public-transportation challenged to boot. Unless you're checking out a concentrated area like downtown Phoenix, Old Scottsdale, or Mill Avenue in Tempe, you'll need wheels if you want to see anything. Interested in exploring with just two of them? See "Keeping Active," later in this chapter, for the best urban and rural biking routes.

Exploring by Car

Because of multiple mergings and name metamorphoses, the many highways that thread through the Valley are not always easy to track. **I-17,** which leads north to Flagstaff, is the Valley's main north-south thoroughfare. Just south of downtown Phoenix, it veers east and merges with **I-10,** at which point it becomes the **Maricopa Freeway.** I-10 snakes through the Valley in a variety of directions, but in the west Valley and downtown Phoenix, where it's called the **Papago Freeway**, it generally runs from east to west. North of the airport, it connects with **Highway 202** (otherwise known as the **Red Mountain Freeway**); if you head east on 202, you'll get to downtown Tempe. Go north at the interchange of I-10 and Highway 202 and you'll be on the ever-expanding **Highway 51/Squaw Peak Freeway,** which is the best route into Scottsdale from the west; from the east it's **Highway 101,** which connects with both Highway 202, and **Highway 60, the Superstition Freeway.** Highway 60 leads east through Tempe and Mesa towards Apache Junction and the Superstition Mountains (see Chapter 12); in the other direction, when it gets beyond I-10, it becomes Grand Avenue and then merges with Highway 89 as it wends its way northwest through Glendale, Peoria, and Sun City toward Wickenburg. Two roads you'll have less need to think about are **Highway 143,** the short Hohokam Expressway, which connects Highway 202 with I-10 on the east side of the airport; and **Highway 87, the Beeline Highway,** which starts in Mesa and heads northeast.

Great Wheel-y Adventures

All the major car rental companies have offices in the Valley, but if you want something a little flashier than a Ford Escort, consider Scottsdale Jeep Rentals (☎ 480-951-2191) or Great Escapes (☎ 602-674-8469). Both rent four-wheelers for about $130 a day (8 a.m. to 5 p.m.), with lower rates the longer you hold on to your Jeep, and both companies help guide you to the best off-roading places. If you've got a motorcycle license but haven't brought your Harley, Western States Motorcycle Tours, 9401 N. Seventh Ave. (☎ 602-943-9030) can help; rates range from $75 to $175 a day ($450 to $750 a week) depending whether a major Hog or something smaller is your speed.

Smile: You're on Candid (Traffic) Camera

In many Valley cities, hidden traffic light cameras are aimed at snagging red light runners or speeders (look closely; you may see the flashing lense). Also keep an eye out for unmarked white trucks set up along the side of the road. If you see one with its back door lifted, chances are it's a police truck with a fancy camera set up inside. And don't assume that just because you've borrowed wheels, you won't be tracked down. The rental car companies like to forward the bills they receive from the city to their scofflaw customers.

Make sure you have your directions planned out before you hit the road; you and your navigator are not going to have much map-consulting time while you're freeway-switching.

Driving the streets is less confusing, if more time consuming: Phoenix, Scottsdale, and Tempe all operate pretty much on grids. The address nexus of the Valley is the intersection of Washington Street and Central Avenue in downtown Phoenix. Running north and south to the west of Washington are numbered *avenues* (they go from 1st Avenue up to 107th Avenue and higher in such West Valley cities as Glendale, Peoria, and Sun City); east of Washington are the numbered *streets*. The east-west thoroughfares have names; Camelback, Indian School, and McDowell roads are major routes across central Phoenix.

In Scottsdale, as opposed to the rest of the Valley, the left-turn arrows appear at the end of the light, not at the beginning. If you don't know the precise boundaries between Scottsdale, Phoenix, and Tempe — and most Valley residents don't — it can be dangerous to assume you can turn left. Always wait until you see the green arrow before moving into an intersection.

Getting around by Taxi

Don't expect to be able to hail a cab on the street, even in downtown Phoenix (the exception is when there's a sports or concert event on there). You'll have to phone for your wheels and not on the spur of the moment, either; if you're on a tight schedule, book at least an hour in advance. There are more than 40 taxi companies in the Greater Phoenix area, but some of the more reliable ones include **Yellow Cab** (☎ 602-252-5252), **Checker Cab** (☎ 602-257-1818), and **Scottsdale Taxi** (☎ 480-994-4567). Keep in mind, however, that you're likely to be going a far stretch and taxi fares are unregulated; always ask ahead of time how much the fare will be and confirm before stepping into the cab. Unless you're on a company expense account or traveling within a very limited area, this is not a great way to get around.

Riding a Bus or Taking the Trolley

The Valley Metro Bus System (☎ 602-253-5000) services Phoenix, Scottsdale, Tempe, Mesa, and Gilbert, but coverage is not exactly comprehensive; most lines stop running by 8 p.m. and there's no service on Sunday (that may be changing soon). You can sometimes find a copy of the Bus Book at the airport, at Central Station on Van Buren Street and Central Avenue, and at any Fry's or Safeway supermarket, but it's far easier to take advantage of the telephone trip-planning service (available through the main number) that will map out your exact route. Fares are $1.25 for adults, 60¢ for ages 6 to 18 and seniors over 65, and free for children under 6 accompanied by an adult. Buses are equipped to accept dollar bills, but you'll need exact change. You can get free transfers between routes — they're good for 60 minutes after your bus reaches its final destination — but you need to ask for one when you pay your fare.

Being Wheeled around by Pedicab

Pedal power to the people. If you're downtown at a concert or sporting event, consider tooling around with the **Arizona Pedal Cab Corp.** (☎ 602-252-1152). You can usually find a few of these open-air, bicycle-powered vehicles waiting around at the Arizona Center, at Bank One Ballpark, and at the America West Arena on game nights. The cyclists work for tips rather than charging a set fee, but it's a good idea to check first before you get a leg on.

Free-for-All

Although bussing it around the Valley is not generally the best way to go, you can't lose by taking advantage of three Valley transit freebies. Ollie the Trolley is a separate entity; call **Valley Metro** (☎ 602-253-5000) for exact schedules of both DASH and FLASH.

✔ **DASH** (Downtown Area Shuttle) runs around downtown Phoenix every 4 to 6 minutes from 6:30 a.m. to 5:30 p.m., Monday through Friday. Look for the DASH stop sign at any one of the 35 stops between 18th Avenue and 5th Street within the boundaries of Jefferson and Van Buren streets.

✔ **FLASH** (Free Local Area Shuttle) loops around the areas surrounding Arizona State University in Tempe. Routes run on Mill Avenue and around Sun Devil Stadium and buses pick up about every 10 minutes.

✔ **Ollie the Trollie** (☎ 480-596-9069) does its free thing in downtown Scottsdale, shuttling around the various shopping areas from Monday through Saturday (except from June through September).

Where to Stay

Hospitality has long been a major industry in Phoenix, and it's growing quickly along with the Valley. It's shape-shifting, too, as the old guest ranches are replaced by (in some cases, converted into) some of this country's most spectacular resorts. These mini-leisure worlds are many people's prime reason to go to Arizona, so I've devoted the first listings sections to them; see Chapter 8 for details on what you can expect for amenities and special packages, which you should always ask about when you call.

The second lodging section covers hotels and inns; the Valley has some dazzlers in the second category, but because of complicated zoning practices, there's a dearth of bed and breakfasts — which explains why I've included only one. The vast majority of listings are for places in Scottsdale and Phoenix, the two most visitor-friendly locations, but I've also included a few in Tempe — not only a nice place to wake up, but also extremely convenient to Sky Harbor Airport. Again, make sure to ask about special packages when you call; many of these places have them.

Because of its appeal as a winter escape, the Valley is one of the most expensive places in the United States for a vacation. A standard room at a resort in Phoenix or Scottsdale will definitely fall into the $$$$ ($175 and up) category, with many rooms starting at $250 and beyond in high season. What's available in the mid-price range tends to be of the chain variety. If you're looking to save a few bucks, you may want to consider one of these. See the appendix for the chains' toll-free numbers. It's hard to predict precisely when there'll be a rush on rooms (major sports events are a factor, as are major snow storms in the rest of the country), but the area is popular from mid-December through March — which is also when (surprise, surprise) the rates are highest. See Chapter 2 for more details on seasonal and monthly happenings.

The Top Resorts

The Arizona Biltmore
$$$$ Phoenix/Camelback Corridor

A local favorite since it opened its Southwest art deco doors — designed, like the rest of the resort, by one of Frank Lloyd Wright's colleagues — in 1929. It's an ageless wonder, staying at the leisure cutting edge with such amenities as electric bike rentals and the latest spa treatments while maintaining its old style gracious service. Rooms are understatedly elegant and the grounds are gorgeous, acres of rolling lawns poised against craggy Camelback Mountain. The Biltmore was the spur for the thriving Camelback (or Biltmore) Corridor of restaurants and shops and remains its anchor, so you couldn't find a better base if you want to be entertained. See also "Nightlife," later in this chapter, for the Biltmore's swank bar.

Phoenix, Scottsdale & The Valley of the Sun Accommodations

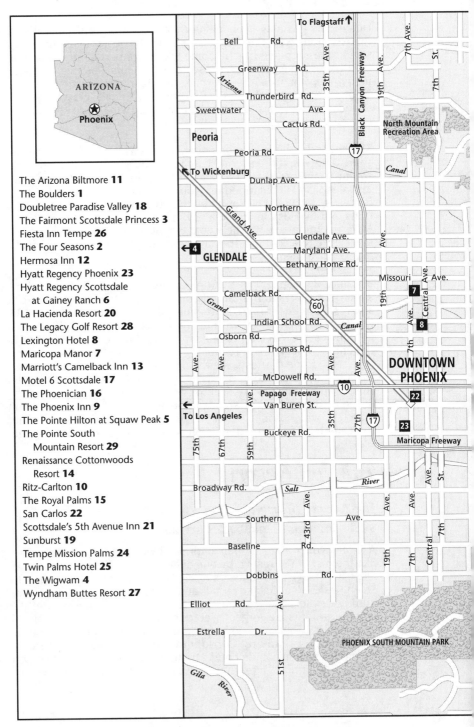

The Arizona Biltmore **11**
The Boulders **1**
Doubletree Paradise Valley **18**
The Fairmont Scottsdale Princess **3**
Fiesta Inn Tempe **26**
The Four Seasons **2**
Hermosa Inn **12**
Hyatt Regency Phoenix **23**
Hyatt Regency Scottsdale
    at Gainey Ranch **6**
La Hacienda Resort **20**
The Legacy Golf Resort **28**
Lexington Hotel **8**
Maricopa Manor **7**
Marriott's Camelback Inn **13**
Motel 6 Scottsdale **17**
The Phoenician **16**
The Phoenix Inn **9**
The Pointe Hilton at Squaw Peak **5**
The Pointe South
    Mountain Resort **29**
Renaissance Cottonwoods
    Resort **14**
Ritz-Carlton **10**
The Royal Palms **15**
San Carlos **22**
Scottsdale's 5th Avenue Inn **21**
Sunburst **19**
Tempe Mission Palms **24**
Twin Palms Hotel **25**
The Wigwam **4**
Wyndham Buttes Resort **27**

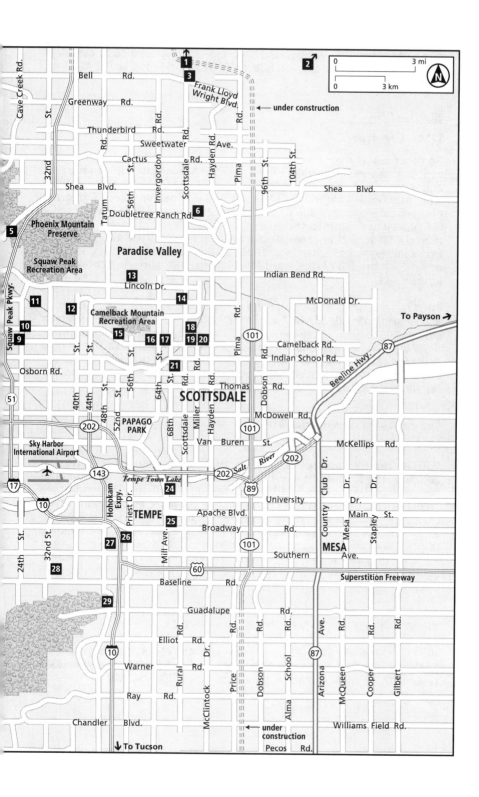

24th St. and Missouri. ☎ *800-950-0086 or 602-955-6600. Fax: 602-954-2571. E-mail:* azbres@arizonabiltmore.com. *Internet:* www.arizonabiltmore.com. *Self-parking free; $15 valet. Rack rates: Jan–mid-May $380–$535; mid-May– mid-June $275–$355; mid-June–mid-Sept $165–$250; mid-Sept–Dec $320–$445. AE, CB, DC, DISC, MC, V.*

The Boulders

$$$$ Carefree

No other resort even came close to maximizing a rugged desert setting as stunningly as the Boulders until the Four Seasons debuted in the new millenium. But the Boulders will up the ante again in September 2001, when the Golden Door spa, a branch of the famed southern California pamper palace, is scheduled to open. Until then, you'll just have to settle for superlative Southwest-design casitas; gorgeous grounds, including two excellent golf courses; top-notch dining facilities; the on-site El Pedregal shopping center (see "Getting (Boutique) Mall'd," in this chapter), with a branch of the Heard Museum, no less; and a not-too-shabby interim spa.

34631 N. Tom Darlington Dr. (just north of the Scottsdale Rd./Carefree Highway intersection). ☎ *800-553-1717 or 480-488-9009. Fax: 480-488-4118. Internet:* www.grandbay.com. *Free self-parking. Rack rates: Jan–May 25 and Sept 10– Dec 9 from $450; May 26–Sept 9 from $185; Dec 10–25 from $265; Christmas–New Year's Eve call for rates. One-, two-, and three-bedroom units available. A $20 per casita service charge is added per night (so no tips are accepted except in the restaurants). Kids under 16 stay free with adult. AE, CB, DC, DISC, MC, V.*

The Fairmont Scottsdale Princess

$$$$ North Scottsdale

With its red-tile roof casitas and hacienda-style dining and recreation complex, the Fairmont takes full advantage of its place in the Sonoran Desert sun. Dining rooms like the Marquesa and the Hacienda (see "Where to Dine" later in this chapter) are a tad more formal than is typical for the Valley, but then the guests here tend to be a tad older. The full array of resort facility suspects — great tennis, an excellent spa, tee-time priority at the adjacent Tournament Players Club of Scottsdale — keeps all ages playing happily together, however. Rooms are as elegantly Southwest as you may expect but the grounds are spread out, and they're not always easy to locate.

7575 E. Princess Drive (off Scottsdale Road, north of Frank Lloyd Wright Boulevard). ☎ *800-344-4758 or 480-585-4848. Fax: 480-585-0086. E-mail:* scottsdale@ fairmont.com. *Internet:* www.fairmont.com. *Free self-parking; valet $15. Rack rates: Jan–Mar $409–$489, suites from $489; Apr–May $359–$489, suites from $439; June–Aug $199–$389, suites from $259; Sept–Dec $309–$489, suites from $389. Children 17 and under stay free with parents. AE, CB, DC, DISC, MC, V.*

The Four Seasons

$$$$ Northeast Scottsdale

The tony Four Seasons chain has pulled out all the stops with its first Arizona link, nabbing a beautiful, still more-or-less remote location, taking advantage of its unusual rock formations, and creating stunning, quintessential Southwest rooms and public areas. The two adjacent Troon North golf courses are as challenging as they come and the views of the Valley from the Acacia dining room are awesome (its New Southwest menu is nothing to sneeze at either). Scenery look familiar? The Coen brothers filmed *Raising Arizona* on this site (pre-Four Seasons).

10600 E. Crescent Moon Dr. (from N. Scottsdale or N. Pima take Happy Valley Rd. east to Alma School Pkwy. and go north [left]; turn west [left] onto E. Crescent Moon Dr.). ☎ **800-819-5053** *or 480-515-5700. Fax: 480-515-5599. Internet:* www.fourseasons.com. *Parking: $15 per night. Rack rates: Dec 25–May 13 $475–$625, suites and casitas from $850; May 14–June 17 and Sept 15–Dec 21 $395–$495, suites and casitas from $850; June 18–Sept 14 $250–$300, suites and casitas from $475. One-, two-, and three-bedroom suites available. Two kids under 17 per room stay free with adult. AE, DC, DISC, MC, V.*

Hyatt Regency Scottsdale at Gainey Ranch

$$$$ North Scottsdale

Water, water everywhere. You'd hardly know you were in arid Arizona what with the ten pools, waterslides, waterfalls, koi ponds . . .even lagoons serviced by gondolas. All this moisture — not to mention a good kids camp — makes the Hyatt wildly popular with families. Besides, you've got the unique Hopi Learning Center and the nouvelle Southwest menu at the Golden Swan Restaurant (see "The Runner-Up Restaurants," later in this chapter) to remind you of where you are. Rooms are well-equipped and comfortable, but try to get one as far from the central lobby's bustle as possible.

7500 E. Doubletree Ranch Rd. (east at Scottsdale Rd; you're 8 miles north of McDonald Drive). ☎ **800-233-1234** *or 480-991-3388. Fax: 480-483-5550. Internet:* www.hyatt.com. *Free self-parking; valet is gratuities only. Rack rates: Jan–mid-May $350–$515, suites and casitas from $800; mid-May–Sept $155–$310, suites and casitas from $240; Sept–Dec $330–$460, suites and casitas from $450. Kids under 18 stay free with adult, excluding some packages. AE, CB, DC, DISC, MC, V.*

Marriot's Camelback Inn

$$$$ Scottsdale

J.W. Marriot, who had been vacationing here with his family since the 1940s, liked this place so well that he decided to buy it as his first resort. It's still easy to see the appeal. The Camelback Inn is as laid-back as it ever was, the newer casitas blend in beautifully with the original adobe units, and kids still happily graduate from the Hopalong College of fun. But such gradually added pleasure-enchancers as the golf courses, a huge spa, and splashy pool complex take up space, so you may have a tough time finding parking near your stylish, home-away-from-home casita.

5402 E. Lincoln Dr. (at Tatum Boulevard). ☎ **800-24-CAMEL** *or 480- 948-1700. Fax: 602-951-8469. E-mail:* packages@camelbackinn.com. *Internet:* www.camelbackinn. com. *Free self-parking; valet is gratuities only. Rack rates: Jan–June 11 $389–$490, suites from $670; June 12–Sept 10 $125–$200, suites from $300; Sept 11–Dec 31 $295–$380, suites from $495. AE, CB, DC, DISC, MC, V.*

The Phoenician

$$$$ Scottsdale

The Phoenicians's formal French Provincial trappings, underground parking, and other attempts to pretend it's not in Arizona have always irritated me — especially because the hotel snagged such a nice swathe of desert — but most guests don't seem to mind. They're too busy enjoying the 27 great holes of golf, state-of-the-art Centre for Well Being, and dazzling array of eateries (see "Dining in the Top Restaurants," later in this chapter, for Mary Elaine's). The airy, light-filled rooms are less stuffy than the public areas. Attentive service wins the resort top rankings in all the glossy travel mag polls, and for a posh place, it's surprisingly kid-friendly, with a super water slide and the Funicians Club supervised activies program (ages 5 to 12).

600 E. Camelback Rd. (between 44th Street and Scottsdale Road). ☎ **800-888-8234** *or 480-941-8200. Fax: 480-947-4311. Internet:* www.thephoenician.com. *Free self-parking; $18 valet. Rack rates: Mid-Dec–mid-June $470–$655, suites from $1,075; mid-June–Sept $195–$245, suites from $500; Sept–mid-Dec $425–$485, suites from $1,075. Children under 17 stay free with adults. AE, CB, DC, DISC, MC, V.*

Pointe South Mountain Resort

$$$$ South Phoenix

The ultimate jock retreat. We're talking two 18-hole golf courses, ten tennis courts, five racquetball courts, two volleyball courts (one sand, one water), one basketball court, six pools, a fitness center the size of an airport hangar with a sports medicine clinic, horseback riding, . . . and that's just on the premises. You're also next door to the endless hiking trails of the huge South Mountain Park. You'll enjoy your attractive Southwest-chic room — should you ever find yourself in it. There's health food to nibble at the fitness center, and a dress-up Continental restaurant and a more casual dining spot — the Wild West Rustler's Roost, the prime magnet for the play-hard, party-harder guests.

7777 S. Pointe Pkwy. (south of Baseline Road, between S. 48th Street and I-10). ☎ **800-947-9784** *or 602-438-9000. Fax: 602-870-8181. Internet:* www. pointehilton.com. *Free parking. Rack rates: Mid-Dec–mid-May $239–$345; mid-May–mid-Sept $99–$129; mid-Sept–mid-Dec $199–$289. Children under 18 stay free with adult. AE, CB, DC, DISC, MC, V.*

Wyndham Buttes Resort

$$$$ **Tempe**

The good news is that this resort is perched atop a mountain overlooking Phoenix and the Valley. The bad news is that its great views are fronted by a freeway. Similarly, the resort's dramatic design and landscaping — the lobby incorporates a cliff — are undercut by the motel-like guest rooms. Still, you've got all the leisure facilities (except on-site golf) you could want, and you can't beat the convenience to Sky Harbor Airport.

2000 Westcourt Way (north of Alameda Drive, west of I-10). ☎ *800-WYNDHAM or 602-225-9000. Fax: 602-438-8622. Internet:* www.wyndham.com. *Free parking. Rack rates: Jan–mid-May $225–$345, suites from $585; mid-May–mid-Sept $99–$215, suites from $475; mid-Sept–Dec $180 – $300, suites from $585. Children 12 and under stay free with adult. AE, DC, DISC, MC, V.*

The Runner-Up Resorts

Doubletree Paradise Valley

$$$$ **Scottsdale**   This resort threw $9.5 million into upgrading its rooms and expanding its sports and business facilities in the late 1990s, but kept the wonderful towering palms and gracious Spanish fountains. *5401 N. Scottsdale Rd. (south of Jackrabbit Rd.).* ☎ *800-222-TREE or 480-947-5400. Fax: 480-481-0209. Internet:* www.doubletreehotels.com.

The Legacy Golf Resort

$$$$ **Phoenix**   Opened in 1999, Phoenix's first new duffer-digs in 10 years counts spacious, attractive suites and proximity to the airport and Arizona Mills mall among its assets. *6808 S. 32nd St. (north of Baseline Road, near South Mountain).* ☎ *888-828-FORE or 602-305-5500. Fax: 602-305-5501. Internet:* www.legacygolfresort.com.

The Pointe Hilton at Squaw Peak

$$$$ **Phoenix**   As family-friendly as they come, this resort has a huge water slide, Coyote Kids camp, and two-level suites that let your kids stay close — but not too close. *7677 N. 16th St. (south of Northern Avenue).* ☎ *800-947-9784 or 602-997-2626. Fax: 602-997-2391. Internet:* www.hilton.com/hotels/PHXSPPR.

Renaissance Cottonwoods Resort

$$$$ **Scottsdale**   This spot doesn't have quite as many amenities as some of the larger resorts — no on-site health club, no golf course — but compensations include spacious all-suite quarters, many with hot tubs on private patios, plus proximity to the posh Borgata shopping complex. *6160 N. Scottsdale Rd. (between Lincoln Drive and McDonald Drive).* ☎ *800-HOTELS-1 or 480-991-1414. Fax: 480-951-3350. Internet:* www.renaissancehotels.com.

Finding Bargain Rooms

The complimentary _Affordable Accommodations/Summer Rates_ brochure, put out by the Greater Phoenix Convention and Visitors Bureau (see "Quick Concierge" at the end of this chapter), lists hotels and resorts that cost less than $100 — some of them even in high season. You can order a copy in advance of your trip over the phone or pick one up at their office once you get into town.

The Wigwam

$$$$ **Litchfield Park** Here you'll find attractive rooms, three golf courses, and tons of other on-site activities. It's a great golfer's getaway, but the remote West Valley location puts you pretty far from all the major sights. _300 Wigwam Boulevard._ ☎ _800-327-0396 or 623-935-3811. Fax: 623-935-3737. Internet:_ www.wigwamresort.com.

The Top Hotels and Inns

Fiesta Inn

$$$ Tempe

In this college town, where the open wallets of separation anxiety-prone parents with kids at Arizona State University tends to jack up the rates for everything, this is the best deal in Tempe. Surprising extras at this link in the Southwest-flavored chain include tennis courts, a putting green, and a driving range; the in-room refrigerators, coffeemakers, and hairdryers, and the comp local phone calls and airport transfers aren't totally expected either. You'll be as close as you want to be to your ASU progeny or to the Mill Avenue action and the airport.

2100 S. Priest Dr. (SW corner of Priest Drive and Broadway). ☎ _800-501-7590 or 480-967-1441. Fax: 480-967-0224. E-mail:_ info@fiestainnresort.com _or_ reservations@fiestainnresort.com. _Internet:_ www.fiestainnresort.com. _Free parking. Rack rates: Jan–May $155, minisuites $165 ; June–Sept $85, minisuites $95; Oct–Dec $132, minisuites $142. AE, CB, DC, DISC, MC, V._

Hermosa Inn

$$$$ Paradise Valley

Built by cowboy artist Lon Megargee as a home and studio in 1930 and later run by him as an inn, this boutique lodging speaks far more of the artist than of the cowboy. True, it's as Western as all get out, with stuccoed adobe walls and rough-hewn beams, but the lush gardens are lovely and the rooms were gussied up, designer style, when the inn was refurbished in the late 1980s. Lon's (see the section on dining in Phoenix later in this chapter) is hugely popular Valley-wide, but guests get first dibs on tables.

5532 North Palo Cristi Rd. (east of 32nd Street at Stanford). ☎ *800-241-1210 or 602-955-8614. Fax: 602-955-8299. E-mail:* info@hermosainn.com. *Internet:* www.hermosainn.com. *Free parking. Rack rates: Jan–April $260–$330, suites $435–$635; May $170–$210, suites $330–$525; June–Sept $95–$140, suites $300–$450; Oct–Dec $220–$275, suites $400–$550. Specials include discounts for reservations made online. AE, CB, DC, DISC, MC, V.*

La Hacienda Resort

$$–$$$ Downtown Scottsdale

Hardly a resort and hardly hacienda style — unless you count the typical motel arrangement of rooms around a central pool — La Hacienda is L.A. retro chic, with etched glass and 1950s-style phones in the rooms, swinging deck chairs outside, and a postmodern look-at-my-cool-decor lobby with a tiny cappucino bar. Some suites have kitchens and microwaves, but you're really here for the (relatively) low rates plus proximity to the prime Scottsdale shopping, clubbing, and eating action.

7320 E. Camelback Rd. (one block east of Scottsdale Road). ☎ *480-994-4170. Fax: 480-994-7387. Internet:* www.suitedreamsaz.com. *Free parking. Rack rates: Nov–May 15 $149–$159; May 16–Oct $89–$99. Children 12 and under stay free with adults. AE, MC, V.*

Maricopa Manor

$$$–$$$$ Central Phoenix

More like an inn than a B&B, the Maricopa Manor draws business types and allergic-to-bonding-with-stranger vacationers with such amenities as in-suite refrigerators, microwaves, and coffeemakers, private entrances and decks, and baskets of breakfast goodies delivered directly to your door. Good desks, portable phones with modem jacks, and free local calls are nice if-you-gotta-work perks. You can happily hang around the pool and hot tub of the pretty Spanish Colonial-style estate (built in 1928), but you're also a hop from all of Phoenix's and Scottsdale's main attractions.

15 West Pasadena Ave. (one block north of Camelback Road, and one block west of Central Avenue). ☎ *800-292-6403 or 602-274-6302. Fax: 602-266-3904. E-mail:* mmanor@getnet.com. *Internet:* www.maricopamanor.com. *Free off-street parking. Rack rates: Jan–May $144–$189; June–Aug $79–$129; Sept–Dec $149–$189 (holiday rates vary). AE, DISC, MC, V.*

The Phoenix Inn

$$–$$$ Phoenix/Camelback Corridor

Location, location, location — in this case, right near the Camelback Corridor — and reasonable rates draw those in the know to this friendly all-suites property, part of a small western chain. Other pluses: Free airport transport, free local phone calls, in-room coffee makers, microwaves, refrigerators, an outdoor pool and Jacuzzi, a fitness center, and guest laundry. All in all, a great deal for families as well as for business travelers.

2310 E. Highland Ave. (west of 24th Street and south of Camelback Road). ☎ 800-956-5221 or 602-956-5221. Fax: 602-468-7220. Internet: www.phoenixinn. com. Rack rates: Sept–April $99–$209; May–Sept $59–$99. Continental breakfast buffet included in room rates. Children under 17 stay free with parents.

Ritz-Carlton

$$$$ Phoenix/Camelback Corridor

You feel like you should be wearing Chanel or Armani rather than resortwear in this hotel, with its crystal-dripping lobby and dark wood-oozing rooms — but you don't have to. True, the Ritz Carlton draws lots of upscale business travelers, but they're not all buttoned-down types; Members of the NFL and other road-tripping teams, as well as high-profile entertainers, also hole up here. They come for the impeccable, discreet service and such perks as proximity to Biltmore Fashion Park — cross the street and you're there — and all the Camelback Corridor restaurants, plus the great rooftop pool and fitness center.

2401 E. Camelback Rd. (at 24th Street, the Camelback Esplanade). ☎ 800-241-3333 or 602-468-0700. Fax: 602-553-0685. Internet: www.ritzcarlton.com. $18 valet parking. Rack rates: Sept–May $315–$375, suites $475–$555; June–Aug $165–$210, suites $245–$285; $99 per night special for the last weeks in April and May, for June–Sept 9, and for Thanksgiving and Christmas weeks. AE, CB, DC, DISC, MC, V.

The Royal Palms

$$$$ Phoenix, between the Camelback Corridor and Scottsdale

The late-1990s return of the Royal Palms, a 1926 Spanish Colonial Revival mansion turned posh getaway (Groucho Marx and Helena Rubenstein were among the early guests — though they didn't travel together) was a major Phoenix lodging event. This place is a knockout, with gorgeous landscaping, including the Egyptian palms for which it's named, vying with the stunning Southwest-meets-country French rooms for your attention. T Cook's (see "Dining in the Top Restaurants," in this chapter) has some of the hottest tables in town — as does the adjacent lounge (see "Nightlife," in this chapter).

5200 E. Camelback Rd. (between 56th Street and Arcadia Drive). ☎ 800-672-6011 or 602-840-3610. Fax: 602-840-6927. Internet: www.royalpalmshotel.com. Free self-parking; valet is gratuities only. Rack rates: Jan–May $325–$495, suites from $385; June–mid-Sept $149–$179, suites from $200; mid-Sept–Dec $295–$425, suites from $325. Children 17 and under stay free with adult. AE, CB, DC, DISC, MC, V.

San Carlos

$$–$$$ Downtown Phoenix

Resurging right along with downtown, this 1928 high-rise got a millennial makeover that lightened up its rooms and added amenities like coffeemakers, hidden mini-fridges, irons, and hairdryers, while holding on to the cool octogonal-tile bath floors. The gorgeously opulent lobby was spiffed up too, as was the (less historic) exercise room. Things aren't quite there yet, but the friendly management is always open to suggestions for improvement, and the location and price are definitely right.

202 N. Central Ave. at Monroe Street. ☎ *800-528-5446 or 602-253-4121. Fax: 602-253-6668. Internet:* www.hotelsancarlos.com. *Self-parking $8 day; valet $12. Rack rates: Jan–April $149, suite $199; May–Sept $99, suite $135; Oct–Dec $125, suite $189. Rates include a Continental breakfast from the on-premises bakery/café, Art of Coffee. AE, DC, DISC, MC, V.*

Scottsdale's 5th Avenue Inn

$$ Scottsdale

If you'd rather blow your budget on portable goods than on lodging, you've found your home away from home a few blocks from Scottsdale's Fifth Avenue shopping district. You were expecting fancy for these prices? Get real. But the rooms are comfortable enough and you've got the requisite motel pool and hot tub.

6935 5th Ave. (north of Indian School Road and west of Goldwater Boulevard). ☎ *800-528-7396 or 480-994-9461. Fax: 480-947-1695. Free parking. Rack rates: Oct–April $49–$99; May–Sept $44–$49. Kids under 12 stay free with parents.*

Sunburst

$$$ Scottsdale

This mini-resort says Southwest from its soaring-ceiling lobby with its native stone fireplace to the nouveau cowboy rooms, featuring vibrant colors and faux-cowhide settees, to the menu of the cheerful Rancho Saguaro restaurant (the fish tacos are super). The only style exception: The lush, tropically landscaped grounds, where you can lounge around a sandy lagoon in the inviting Gilligan's island-style pool complex.

4925 Scottsdale Rd. (4 blocks north of Camelback Road at N. Goldwater Boulevard). ☎ *800-431-8593 or 480-945-7666. Fax: 480-946-4056. Internet:* www.sunburstresort.com. *Free parking. Rack rates: Jan–mid-April $235–$285, suites $635; mid-April–mid-May $215–$255, suites $575; mid-May–mid-Sept $95–$135, suites $300; mid-Sept–Dec 31 $185–$225, suites $500. AE, CB, DC, MC, V.*

The Runner-Up Hotels and Inns

Every hotel and motel chain you can imagine — and some you proba-bly can't — is represented in the Valley (see the appendix for a listing of telephone numbers). And see Chapter 8 for a referral service that can help you locate some of the other rare B&Bs in this area.

Some chain standouts and independents worth checking include:

Hyatt Regency Phoenix

$$$$ Downtown Phoenix   Although a bit large and impersonal, it has a central downtown location and decent amenities — not to mention Arizona's only rotating rooftop restaurant, for better or worse. *122 N. 2nd St. (at Washington Street).* ☎ *800-233-1234 or 602-252-1234. Fax: 602-256-0801. Internet:* www.hyatt.com.

Lexington Hotel

$$ Central Phoenix The Lexington caters to visiting sports teams and their athlete-wannabe fans with a health club so large it has a full-size basketball court. *100 W. Clarendon Ave. (at Central Avenue).* ☎ *800-537-8483 or 602-279-9811. Fax: 602-285-2932. Internet:* www.phxihc.com.

Motel 6 Scottsdale

$ Scottsdale So the name's a dead giveaway — a Motel 6, but it has a great location near Scottsdale's 5th Avenue shopping district and views of Camelback Mountain that usually cost far more. *6848 E. Camelback Rd. at 69th Street.* ☎ *800-4-MOTELS6 or 480-946-2280. Fax: 480-949-7583. Internet:* www.motel6.com.

Tempe Mission Palms

$$$$ Tempe The Palms has loads of sports facilities (pool, tennis, sauna, whirlpool, fitness room) and it couldn't be closer to ASU and Mill Avenue (Tempe's main drag), but rooms, while attractive, are lighting- and mirror-challenged. Free airport transport is the only real bargain. *60 E. 5th St. at Mill Avenue.* ☎ *800-547-8705 or 480-894-1400. Fax: 480-968-7677. Internet:* www.missionpalms.com.

Twin Palms Hotel

$$$ Tempe This standard hotel has more character than you'd expect — resident macaws, striking gem-and-fossil exhibits, poolside tropics — but that doesn't compensate for the higher-than-standard rates. Free guest passes to the nearby ASU Recreation Complex help. *225 E. Apache Blvd. at S. College Avenue.* ☎ *800-367-0835 or 480-967-9431. Fax: 480-303-6602. Internet:* www.arizonaguide.com/twinpalms.

Where to Dine

The Valley dining scene is far too large and complex for a visitor — even one from nearby Tucson — to master, so I turned this section over to **Nikki Buchanan,** *Phoenix Magazine* restaurant critic extraordinaire.

Phoenix has grown both up and out in recent years, making this former cow town a now town, replete with trendy restaurants of every stripe and watering holes for bucks-up tourists, local glitterati, and nationally known celebrities, who — like us average folk — can't get enough of the golf courses and great weather. As you may expect from a community that relies on winter visitors, many of the resort restaurants are top notch, and the chefs who rule these culinary roosts have, in many cases, achieved a kind of cult following and star status.

However, the real glamour pusses of the Valley restaurant scene own their own establishments (most of them eponymously named), and legions of ga-ga locals delight in referring to them by first name only. Like Madonna or Cher, they are simply Chris, Robert, and Michael — don't worry, I'll give you their last names, too.

As you may suspect, a gourmet meal in Phoenix isn't exactly cheap. On the other hand, it represents a real bargain compared to similar restaurants in other major cities, and you can get just about everything here that you can there — except late night hours. Prime table time is about 7:30 p.m. If you want to eat at 8:30 or 9 p.m., you should have no trouble getting a reservation, but most restaurants are shuttered by 10:30 p.m. (see the "Better Late Than . . . Early" sidebar, later in this chapter, for some suggestions of places that aren't).

Dining in the Top Restaurants

Christopher's Fermier Brasserie

$$$–$$$$ **Phoenix (Camelback Corridor)** **Contemporary French/American**

When one of Phoenix's most famous classical chefs decided to ditch the la-de-da shtick, this was the result — a casual, come-as-you-are brasserie offering boutique wines, pâtés, imported cheeses, wood-fired pizzas, and earthy, satisfying bistro food. Luckily for loyalists, the occasional elegant entree from days past shows up as well. Good place to smoke a cigar and make like the power players who hang out here.

2584 E. Camelback Rd. in Biltmore Fashion Park (24th Street and Camelback Road). ☎ *602-522-2344. Reservations recommended for dinner. Main courses: $9–$13 lunch, $17–$30 dinner. AE, DC, DISC, MC, V. Open: Lunch and dinner daily.*

Convivo

$$$ **North Phoenix** **New American**

To say that this upscale but unpretentious place is a mom-and-pop in a strip mall is to do both the owners and their potential customers a gross disservice. Here you find a small but well-thought-out wine list, imaginative food with an occasional Italian tweak, and the kind of attention to detail you'd expect at a pricier restaurant. Begin with the Mediterranean-inspired Convivo Collection appetizer, then move on to something like Niman Ranch grilled pork chops served with herb gremolata. Olive aficionados take note: the complimentary pre-dinner nibbles offered here are fabulous.

7000 N. 16th St. (at Glendale Avenue). ☎ *602-997-7676. Reservations recommended. Main courses: $16–$20. AE, DC, DISC, MC, V. Open: Dinner Tues–Sun.*

Cowboy Ciao

$$$ **Scottsdale** **Southwestern/Italian**

Goofily decorated with Mardi Gras beads and a bright blue star-spangled ceiling, this former art gallery is now Scottsdale's hippest (and friendliest) downtown retreat. Locals drop by for wine flights, entertainment by singing servers, and a winsome menu that successfully pairs Southwestern ingredients with Italian specialties. Try the carpaccio and absolutely do not miss either the sinfully good mushroom pan fry or the praline-sauced bread pudding.

Phoenix, Scottsdale & The Valley of the Sun Dining

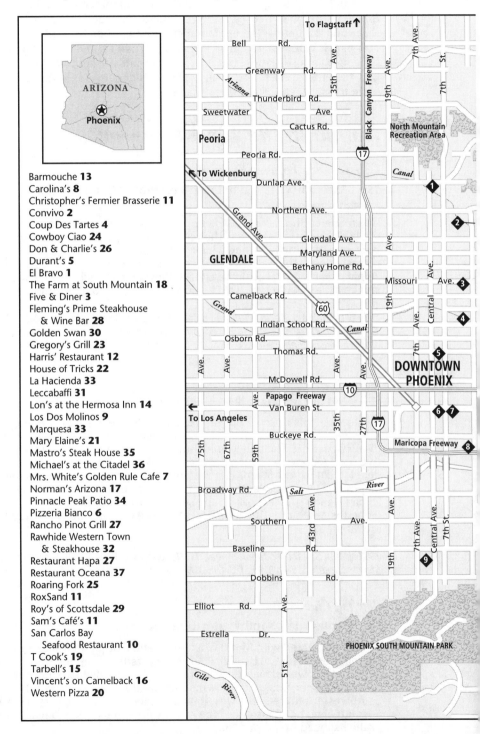

Barmouche **13**
Carolina's **8**
Christopher's Fermier Brasserie **11**
Convivo **2**
Coup Des Tartes **4**
Cowboy Ciao **24**
Don & Charlie's **26**
Durant's **5**
El Bravo **1**
The Farm at South Mountain **18**
Five & Diner **3**
Fleming's Prime Steakhouse
    & Wine Bar **28**
Golden Swan **30**
Gregory's Grill **23**
Harris' Restaurant **12**
House of Tricks **22**
La Hacienda **33**
Leccabaffi **31**
Lon's at the Hermosa Inn **14**
Los Dos Molinos **9**
Marquesa **33**
Mary Elaine's **21**
Mastro's Steak House **35**
Michael's at the Citadel **36**
Mrs. White's Golden Rule Cafe **7**
Norman's Arizona **17**
Pinnacle Peak Patio **34**
Pizzeria Bianco **6**
Rancho Pinot Grill **27**
Rawhide Western Town
    & Steakhouse **32**
Restaurant Hapa **27**
Restaurant Oceana **37**
Roaring Fork **25**
RoxSand **11**
Roy's of Scottsdale **29**
Sam's Café's **11**
San Carlos Bay
    Seafood Restaurant **10**
T Cook's **19**
Tarbell's **15**
Vincent's on Camelback **16**
Western Pizza **20**

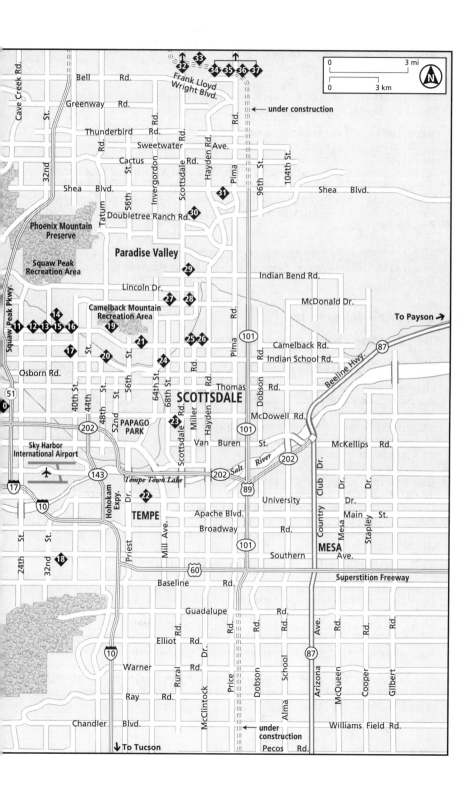

7133 E. Stetson Dr. (north of the Fifth Avenue shops). ☎ *480-946-3111. Reservations recommended. Main courses: $6–$12 lunch, $16–$24 dinner. AE, DC, DISC, MC, V. Open: Lunch Tue–Sat; dinner nightly.*

Leccabaffi

$$–$$$ **North Scottsdale** **Italian**

"Leccabaffi," an Italian colloquialism that roughly translates to "mustache-lickin' good," describes this colorful trattoria's authentic, not-found-elsewhere Italian specialties to a T. Look for the *verdura di campagna* (grilled, olive-oil drizzled appetizers laid out on an antique sideboard), the *seppie* (a Tuscan seafood stew), or the *gnocchetti* (fat semolina dumplings ladled with cheese fondue). Customers consistently complain about service lapses, but when this quirky place is running at top speed, it rocks like no other.

9719 N. Hayden Rd. (at Mountainview, south of Shea). ☎ *480-609-0429. Reservations recommended. Main courses: $13–$25. AE, MC, V. Open: Dinner Tues–Sun.*

Lon's at the Hermosa Inn

$$$ **Paradise Valley** **New American**

Named for cowboy artist Lon Megargee, who built an adobe ranch house on this spot in the 1930s (see "The Top Hotels and Inns," earlier in this chapter), this low-ceilinged, Southwestern artifact–furnished restaurant is a perfect example of rustic Arizona charm. However, the sophisticated menu, boasting everything from signature smoked pork chops to sesame-seared ahi, wasn't designed with the cowboy set in mind. Leave your Stetson at home and snag a table on one of two fabulous patios for lunch or a Sunday brunch.

Hermosa Inn, 5532 N. Palo Cristi Rd. (east of 32nd Street at Stanford). ☎ *602-955-7878. Reservations recommended. Main courses: $8–$15 lunch; $18–$26 dinner. AE, DC, MC, V. Open: Lunch Mon–Fri; dinner nightly; breakfast Sun.*

Mary Elaine's

$$$$ **Scottsdale** **Contemporary French/American**

A sumptuous decor, elegant service, and twinkling views of the city lights by night make this high-up haute spot tops for a money-is-no-object special occasion. Chef de Cuisine James Boyce is a wizard with foie gras and white truffles (the latter of which he puts in everything, including dessert), so expect to spend a small fortune but leave completely wowed. Incredible wine list, too, thanks to a $6 million inventory.

The Phoenician Resort, 6000 E. Camelback Rd. (at 60th Street). ☎ *480-423-2530. Reservations required. Main courses: $34–$45. AE, DC, DISC, MC, V. Open: Dinner nightly.*

A Mexican Lexicon

Phoenix has more Mexican restaurants than you can shake a taco at, which makes finding a great one harder to find than you may think. My best advice? Skip the corporate operations geared toward gringos and zero in on the old-fashioned Sonoran standbys that have kept locals fat and happy for years. (Sonora, by the way, is Mexico's northernmost state, which borders Arizona.) Favorites include:

- **Carolina's,** 1202 E. Mohave St. at 12th Street (South Phoenix) (☎ **602-252-1503**), has locals lining up by 11:30 on any weekday morning, waiting patiently for a crack at the simple Sonoran food. Ambiance is nonexistent, but who cares when there are homemade tortillas still warm from the griddle? $ — a bargain!

- **El Bravo,** 8338 N. 7th St. at Butler Avenue (North Phoenix) (☎ **602-943-9753**), is a sweet, family-run operation, consistently garners awards for its chili Colorado and green corn tamales, but the homemade tortillas, machaca burros, and Navajo fry bread are winners as well. $

- **La Hacienda,** Scottsdale Princess Resort, 7575 E. Princess Dr., north of Bell Road, east of Scottsdale Road (North Scottsdale)(☎ **480-585-4848**), is sumptuously decorated and decidedly expensive, but you won't find its regional Mexican specialties anywhere else. Roast suckling pig (carved tableside) and appetizers filled with glistening huitlacoche (the Mexican equivalent of truffles) are just two exotic examples. $$$

- **Los Dos Molinos,** 8646 S. Central Ave., one block north of E. Euclid, South Phoenix (☎ **602-243-9113**), housed in the former stable of cowboy star Tom Mix, dishes up delicious but hot, hot, hot New Mexican–style fare that'll have you grabbing for the cold brews advertised on its funky neon signs. $

- **San Carlos Bay Seafood Restaurant,** 1901 E. McDowell Rd, West of the 51 freeway (Central Phoenix) (☎ **602-340-0892**), is the place for cool seafood cocktails, incendiary shrimp endiablados (named for the devil himself), whole crisp snapper served Veracruz-style . . . it's all here and it's all good, including great chips, addictive salsa, and creamy refrieds. $–$$

Michael's at the Citadel

$$$ North Scottsdale   New American

It's worth the drive to this lovely restaurant, which boasts a romantic patio and a spectacular indoor waterfall, not to mention memorable food prepared by chef/owner Michael DeMaria. Customers ooh and ahh over the edible spoon hors' doeuvres (the spoon is made of puff pastry) as well as menu favorites such as lobster-stuffed rigatoni and mint-wrapped lamb loin. Private parties of six to ten can reserve the chef's table, located in a private room overlooking the kitchen.

*8700 E. Pinnacle Peak Rd. (at Pima Road).☎ **480-515-2575.** Reservations recommended. Main courses: $5–$16, lunch; $15–$25 dinner. AE, DC, MC, V. Open: Lunch Mon–Sat; dinner nightly; great Sunday brunch menu.*

Norman's Arizona

$$$ **Phoenix, near the Camelback Corridor**
Southwestern/Mexican

Hard surfaced and edgy, this art-filled restaurant is where budget-minded hipsters go for great food that's both Hispanic and Southwestern in feeling. Norman calls his chile mash (a roasted poblano stuffed with mashed spuds), chorizo-marinated rabbit, halibut with cilantro pesto, and famous chocolate chimichangas Nueva Mexicana Cuisine, but the rest of us just call it delicious.

4410 N. 40th St. (S. of Camelback at Campbell Avenue) ☎ *602-956-2288. Reservations recommended. Main courses: $5–$12.50 lunch, $13–$22 dinner. AE, DC, DISC, MC, V. Open: Lunch Tues–Fri; dinner Tues–Sun.*

Rancho Pinot Grill

$$$ **Scottsdale   New American**

What do you get when you cross funky cowboy-kitsch decor with a menu that's hip but homey? The answer is this warm and inviting place, which is booked solid in the winter months for good reason. Chef/owner Chrysa Kaufman's mesquite-grilled shrimp with Thai slaw and mango relish is exotic and justifiably famous, but soothing Nonni's Sunday Chicken is equally delicious. Check out the great wine list and don't skip dessert.

6208 N. Scottsdale Rd. in Lincoln Village (south of Lincoln Drive). ☎ *480-468-9463. Reservations recommended. Main courses: $17–$29. DISC, M, V. Open: Dinner Tues–Sat.*

Restaurant Hapa

$$$–$$$$ **Scottsdale   Asian American**

Small and low-key, Hapa (Hawaiian slang for "half") puts most of the Valley's other Pacific Rim restaurants to shame. That's because chef/owner James McDevitt (who's half Japanese, half American) and his pastry chef wife, Stacey, go about everything — from imaginative but grounded menu design to gorgeous presentation — whole hog. Order his skillet-roasted mussels and crispy whole fish, or her fruit crisps with homemade Saigon cinnamon ice cream, and you'll see why this talented couple wins accolades from every quarter.

6204 N. Scottsdale Rd. in Lincoln Village (south of Lincoln Drive). ☎ *480-998-8220. Reservations recommended. Main courses: $16–$29. AE, MC, V. Open: Dinner Mon–Sat.*

Restaurant Oceana

$$$$ **North Scottsdale   Seafood**

When you're in the mood for serious seafood, take a drive to this whimsically decorated but upscale outpost, dedicated to edibles from the deep. Here's where you come for fresh sardines, sea urchin, smelt, skate — in short, artfully prepared seafood you can't find anywhere else in Greater

Phoenix. Try the signature crabcakes, seared Maine diver scallops with Hudson Valley foie gras, and miso-marinated seabass. And now there's a sushi bar for fishophiles who go the raw route.

9800 E. Pinnacle Peak Rd. in the The Courtyard at La Mirada (Pima Road). ☎ *480-515-2277. Reservations recommended. Main courses: $24–$32. AE, DC, DISC, MC, V. Open: Dinner daily, (summer Tues–Sat).*

Roaring Fork

$$$ Scottsdale Western American

Chef/owner and ex-Texan Robert McGrath dishes up his own brand of hearty but haute Western American cuisine at this handsomely furnished home to the urbane cowboy. Patrons come for house-made beef jerky and a great burger at the bar or sugar and chile-cured duck, excellent pork dishes, and a dandy steak (served with chipotle-bacon cheese grits) in the soft, leathery-looking restaurant proper. A quiet covered patio defies the roar of Camelback Road.

7242 E. Camelback Rd. (E. of Scottsdale Road). ☎ *480-947-0795. Reservations recommended. Main courses: $16–$25. AE, DC, DISC, MC, V. Open: Dinner Mon–Sat.*

RoxSand

$$$–$$$$ Phoenix, Camelback Corridor Fusion

Furnished with huge pieces of contemporary art, this sleek two-story restaurant, which sports a silver staircase and upper dining loft, is nothing if not dramatic. In fact, dramatic may also be the best way to describe chef RoxSand Scocos's transcontinental menu, which includes ingredients and preparations from such far-flung places as Africa and the Middle East. Standouts include the piri piri, b'astilla, and air-dried duck. Good patio for people watching.

2594 E. Camelback Rd. in Biltmore Fashion Park (at 24th Street). ☎ *602-381-0444. Reservations recommended. Main courses: $6–$12 lunch; $18–36 dinner. AE, DC, MC, V. Open: Lunch and dinner daily.*

T Cook's

$$$–$$$$ Phoenix, Camelback Corridor Mediterranean

For both comfort and elegance, nobody does it better than T. Cook's, a lush hideaway with a Mediterranean touch. Try the signature mussels in Chardonnay-thyme broth, the roasted duck breast with foie gras, and one of the insanely ornate desserts, then retire to one of the coziest lounges in town for port and piano music (see "Nightlife," later in this chapter).

5200 E. Camelback Rd. at The Royal Palms Resort (between 56th Street and Arcadia Drive). ☎ *602-808-0766. Reservations recommended. Main courses: $11–$18 lunch, $17–$32 dinner. AE, DC, DISC, MC, V. Open: Lunch Mon–Sat, dinner daily, Sunday brunch.*

Tarbell's

$$$–$$$$ **Phoenix, Camelback Corridor** **New American**

Go here for martinis and appetizers at the beautifully designed bar, a full-blown dinner in the busy, buzzy dining room, or après-cinema dessert (preferably something made with Kea'au Hawaiian Estate chocolate) at the cafe tables near the door. Grilled salmon with molasses-lime glaze, wood oven–roasted half chicken, and an organic vegetable plate prove there's something for everyone at this trendy but likeable hangout for the see-and-be-seen set.

3213 E. Camelback Rd. in Camelback East shops (at 32nd Street). ☎ *602-955-8100. Reservations recommended. Main courses: $14–$33. AE, DC, DISC, MC, V. Open: Dinner nightly.*

The Runner-Up Restaurants

Phoenicians live in their cars, so unless you're shopping at Biltmore Fashion Park on the Camelback Corridor, cruising downtown Tempe, or hanging around Scottsdale's Old Town, don't expect to walk to a nearby restaurant. In Phoenix, we drive for our supper. A few additional places worth the trip include:

Barmouche

$$$ **Camelback Corridor** As much sultry bar and hip hangout as it is an eclectic restaurant, Barmouche offers everything from addictive Belgian frites and $21 tartare-like burgers to mussels in wine sauce and croque madame. *3131 E. Camelback Rd. at 32nd Street.* ☎ *602-956-6900.*

Coup Des Tartes

$$ **Central Phoenix** This cozy, wood-floored BYOB bungalow serves up user-friendly French food with New American overtones. Dessert tarts are the pièce de resistance. *4626 N. 16th St. south of Highland Avenue.* ☎ *602-212-1082.*

Better Late Than . . . Early

Late-night dining is an oxymoron around here, but if you've been to the movies or the theater and you come out hungry, here are a few possibilities to consider: **Barmouche** (see "The Runner-Up Restaurants," in this chapter) serves until midnight every night; **Five & Diner,** at 5220 N. 16th St., north of Camelback, Central (☎ 602-264-5220), dishes up burgers, shakes, sandwiches, and blue plate specials 24/7; **Western Pizza,** 4801 E. Indian School Rd. at 48th Street, between Phoenix and Scottsdale (☎ 602-954-1333), offers plain or fancy pizzas, salads, and snacky stuff to satisfy your late-night cravings until midnight Sunday, 1 a.m. Monday through Wednesday, and 3 a.m. Friday and Saturday.

The Farm at South Mountain

$ and $$$ South Phoenix   This culinary cornucopia has two restaurants. When it's light out, head to **The Farm Kitchen** ($) (☎ 602-276-6360), almost as famous for its healthy salads and sandwiches as for its bucolic lunches at picnic tables under pecan trees. After dark, cozy up at **Quiessence** ($$$) (☎ 602-305-8192), where the fresh produce-laden prix-fixe dinners are prepared in the open kitchen of the wonderful old farm house. BYOB for both places. *6106 S. 32nd St.*

Golden Swan

$$$$ Scottsdale   The Golden Swan takes Southwestern cuisine to elegant heights in a deco-dramatic setting that is nicely offset by a lush outdoor garden with a gazebo and koi pond. Great Sunday brunch. *7500 E. Doubletree Ranch Rd. in the Hyatt Regency Scottsdale at Gainey Ranch.* ☎ **480-991-3388.**

Gregory's Grill

$$$ Scottsdale   Here's proof that Fusion food, when it's beautiful and reality-based, can be deliciously fun, even if prices seem steep for this strip-mall setting. One of the Valley's best BYOB's. *7049 E. McDowell Rd., in Papago Plaza at McDowell and Scottsdale Roads.* ☎ **480-946-8700.**

House of Tricks

$$$ Tempe   House of Tricks is only crafty in the best sense, serving artfully prepared New American fare — ancho chile–glazed salmon, eggplant lasagne with goat cheese — in two charming converted houses and on a knockout outdoor terrace. *114 E. 7th St., two blocks east of Mill Avenue.* ☎ **480-968-1114.**

Marquesa

$$$$ Scottsdale   A great place to get dressed up and blow a wad on Spanish/Mediterranean food, Marquesa offers one of the Valley's most sumptuous settings. Excellent market-style Sunday brunch. *7575 E. Princess Drive at the Fairmont Scottsdale Princess east of Scottsdale Road, north of Bell Road.* ☎ **480-585-4848.**

Mrs. White's Golden Rule Cafe

$ Phoenix   This down-home downtown staple serves satisfying soul food selections such as fried chicken, smothered pork chops, greens, red beans and rice, and peach cobbler. Don't be surprised if you spot some of the Phoenix Suns players here. *808 E. Jefferson St. east of Seventh St. on one-way, east-bound Jefferson.* ☎ *602- 262-9256.*

Pizzeria Bianco

$ Downtown Phoenix   Nestled in the heart of the historic district, this is the place to come for the town's best wood-fired pizzas (all made with top-notch ingredients). Great salads and sandwiches too — some layered with house-made mozzarella. *623 E. Adams Ave. in Heritage Square just west of 7th Street and north of Washington.* ☎ *602-258-8300.*

Roy's of Scottsdale

$$$$ Scottsdale This see-and-be-seen scene is irresistible to star-struck tourists and locals alike who love the imaginatively prepared Pan-Asian food, but come here, first and foremost, for celebrity-scouting. *7001 N. Scottsdale Rd. in the Scottsdale Seville at Indian Bend Road.* ☎ *480-905-1155.*

A Reputation at Steak

Back in the old days, when you could smell the stockyards from the airport, Phoenix was — literally and figuratively — a cow town. Residents still love their meat and potatoes, which explains why the high-end steakhouse trend has taken hold here. Besides corporate favorites such as Ruth's Chris Steakhouse and Morton's of Chicago, the Valley has a fair number of independents capable of properly aging, cutting, and cooking USDA prime. But we haven't lost our fondness for cowboy steaks either, grilled over a mesquite fire and arriving with nothing fancier than a foil-wrapped baker and an iceberg lettuce salad. A few meaty offerings in both categories follow:

✔ **Don & Charlie's,** 7501 E. Camelback Rd. east of Scottsdale Road, Scottsdale (☎ 480-990-0900), is one of the city's most popular restaurants for all sorts of good reasons, one of them being the prime steaks, grilled until they've got a good char around the edges. $$$$

✔ **Durant's,** 2611 N. Central Ave. just south of Thomas, Central Phoenix (☎ 602-264-5967), is Phoenix's favorite old-timer, where local movers and shakers come for martinis, great steaks, and a look at each other. $$$$

✔ **Fleming's Prime Steakhouse & Wine Bar,** 6333 N. Scottsdale Rd. at Lincoln in the Scottsdale Hilton (☎ 480-596-8265), offers prime steaks and great spuds remarkably similar to but slightly less expensive than matching selections at Ruth's Chris. $$$$

✔ **Harris' Restaurant,** 3101 E. Camelback Rd., west of 32nd Street, Phoenix's Camelback Corridor (☎ 602-508-8888), sets out to prove that great steaks don't require a macho setting. Come for the USDA prime; stay for the piano, the patio, and the peacefulness. $$$$

✔ **Mastro's Steak House,** 8852 E. Pinnacle Peak Rd. at Pima, north Phoenix (☎ 480-585-9500), may serve great prime beef, but this party-central spot, featuring a piano bar and a jumpin' dance floor, is also a genteel meat/meet market. $$$$

✔ **Pinnacle Peak Patio,** 10426 E. Jomax Road, way up in north Scottsdale (☎ 480-585-1599), is, after 50 years, still the number one tourist destination for greenhorns hungry for mesquite-grilled steak and a taste of the cowboy life. Wear boots and dance to country bands; wear a necktie and the staff will cut it off and hang it on the wall with your business card. And don't hesitate to bring the kids. $$ – $$$

✔ **Rawhide Western Town & Steakhouse,** 23023 N. Scottsdale Rd. at Pinnacle Peak Road, north Scottsdale (☎ 480-502-1880), is a rootin' tootin' replica of a western town, chock full of storefronts and activities (gold panning, cow petting, and shoot-outs) to keep the kids occupied. If the steak isn't all that memorable, your experience certainly will be. $$–$$$

Sam's Café's

$$ Phoenix and Scottsdale Sam's offers a great introduction to new Southwest cuisine, dishing up good, reasonably priced versions in three colorful, convenient locations. Don't miss the tequila chicken pasta. *455 N. Third St., Arizona Center (downtown Phoenix),* ☎ *602-252-3545; 2566 E. Camelback Rd., Biltmore Fashion Park (Phoenix),* ☎ *602-954-7100; 10010 North Scottsdale Rd. south of Shea Boulevard (Scottsdale),* ☎ *480-368-2800.*

Vincent's on Camelback

$$$ Phoenix Here country French decor complements Southwestern cuisine prepared by Vincent Guerithault — the guy who put Phoenix on the culinary map in the '80s. Quiet spot for a business lunch. *3930 E. Camelback Rd. just west of 40th Street.* ☎ *602-224-0225.*

Seeing the Sights

The Valley generally enjoys such nice weather that many of the best ways to spend your days are listed in this chapter's "Keeping Active" section. What follows here are the top indoor diversions and ways to play outdoors that don't (deliberately) involve sweat.

Arizona Science Center

Downtown Phoenix

The ultimate kids' playscape, with two floors of supercool exhibits including a giant sneezing nose and a Fab Lab where you can shoot paper airplanes. You'll also find a state-of-the-art planetarium and a large-screen Iwerks theater. But you don't have to be pint-size — or a geek — to get a kick out of this place. Valley grown ups liked it so much that they demanded — and got — their own evening here (the first Wednesday of every month). If you're doing the whole shebang — planetarium + film + exhibits — allot a full morning or afternoon. If not, allow at least 2 hours anyway; this is a tough place to tear your kids (and yourself) away from.

Instead of trolling around for parking, pull into the Heritage and Science Park garage on the corner of Fifth and Monroe Streets, where fees are discounted if you get your ticket validated at the science center.

600 E. Washington St. at 7th Street. ☎ **602-716-2000.** *Internet:* www. azscience.org. *Open: 10 a.m.–5 p.m. daily; closed Thanksgiving and Christmas. Admission: $8 adults, $6 ages 4–12 and seniors over 65. Admission to the exhibits plus the film: $10 adults, $8 children and seniors; exhibits, film, and planetarium show: $11 adults, $9 children and seniors.*

Phoenix, Scottsdale & The Valley of the Sun Attractions

The Arizona Doll and Toy Museum **11**
Arizona Mining & Mineral Museum **9**
Arizona Science Center **10**
Arizona State University Art Museum **20**
The Bead Museum **4**
Buffalo Museum of America **2**
Cosanti **3**
Desert Botanical Garden **15**
Grady Gammage
   Memorial Auditorium **19**
Hall of Flame Firefighting Museum **18**
Heard Museum **7**
Heritage Square **11**
McCormick Stillman Railroad Park **6**
Mesa Southwest Museum **21**
Mystery Castle **23**
Old Town Scottsdale **12**
Out of Africa Wildlife Park **14**
Phoenix Art Museum **8**
Phoenix Museum of History **10**
Phoenix Zoo **16**
Pueblo Grande Museum
   and Cultural Park **17**
Scottsdale Museum
   of Contemporary Art **13**
Taliesen West **1**
Tempe Historical Museum **22**
Wrigley Mansion **5**

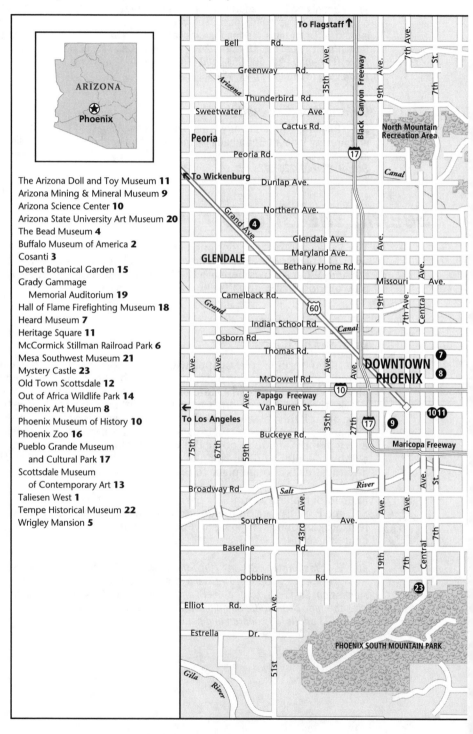

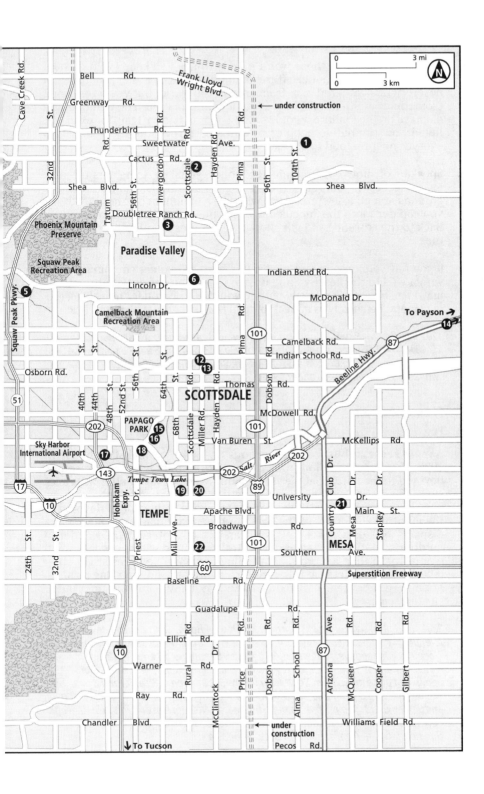

Desert Botanical Garden
Phoenix (Papago Park)

Wondering about all those weird prickly things you keep seeing? You'll still be filled with wonder after examining some of the 20,000 types of desert plants gathered here from around the world, but you'll be armed (sometimes multi-armed) with a lot more information. The ethnobotany displays on the Plants & People of the Sonoran Desert Trail, for example, detail how the native peoples of this area turned the local flora into everything from food to shoes.

Speaking of shoes, wear comfortable ones; you'll be doing a lot of walking, especially if you want to cover the two side trails. Wandering the grounds at a nice, leisurely pace will take a minimum of 2 hours, but you can duck into the Succulent House and Cactus House and loop back to the entrance and gift shop in 45 minutes if you're pressed for time.

If you have children in tow, pack a lunch or — if you're combining this with a visit to the nearby Phoenix Zoo — plan on eating with the animals. The Patio Café is lovely but too gourmet frou frou for most kids; the only menu item likely to appeal to them is an expensive pb&j sandwich.

1201 N. Galvin Pkwy. (south of McDowell Road, west of Scottsdale Road). ☎ 480-941-1225. Internet: www.dbg.org. *Open: Oct–April 8 a.m.–8 p.m., May–Sept 7 a.m.–8 p.m.; closed Christmas. Admission: $7.50 adults, $6.50 seniors, $4 students with I.D., $1.50 ages 5–12, under 5 free.*

Heard Museum
Downtown Phoenix

A must see. Established in a gracious Spanish Colonial-style house in 1929, the Heard has long been one of the country's best museums devoted to the native peoples of the Southwest, and it's better than ever since its late-1990s expansion. No dusty pot shards here: Contemporary, sometimes provocative, Indian art shares space with exhibits devoted to the cultures and crafts of the past, and there are hands-on, interactive displays for kids. On fine days, you can take advantage of the wonderful outdoor sculpture garden and a central courtyard with a casual café. If you factor in time for browsing the huge, impossible-to-resist gift shop (see "Shopping," later in this chapter), figure on a full morning or afternoon here. The Heard Museum North is equally terrific, if on a much smaller scale.

2301 N. Central Ave. (4 blocks north of McDowell Road, on the east side of Central Avenue). ☎ 602-252-8848. Internet: www.heard.org. *Open: daily 9:30 a.m.–5 p.m.; closed major holidays. Admission: $7 general, $6 seniors, $3 ages 4–12, under 4 and Native Americans free. Guided Native Peoples of the Southwest tours included in admission price given from Sept–May (Mon–Sat at noon, 1:30 p.m., and 3 p.m.; Sun. at 1:30 p.m. and 3 p.m.) and June–Aug (Mon–Fri at 1:30 p.m.; Sat 11 a.m., 1:30 p.m., and 3 p.m.; Sun 1:30 p.m. and 3 p.m.). The Heard Museum North is in the El Pedregal complex, 32505 N. Scottsdale Rd., Scottsdale. Open: Mon–Sat 10 a.m.–5:30 p.m., Sun noon–5 p.m. Admission: $2 adults, $1 ages 4–12.*

Phoenix Art Museum
Downtown Phoenix (North)

One of the Southwest's largest art museums, this is the venue for major international traveling shows. The two low-slung boxes that, with a connecting patio, comprise the museum complex are open and attractive, and the permanent collection is especially strong in modern and Western art; the miniatures are a particular treat. To be honest, though, major shows and special events aside, there's no compelling reason to come unless you're visiting from an art-deprived city or experiencing culture shock. Still, you'll find plenty here to hold your attention for a few hours or more.

1625 N. Central Ave. at Coronado Rd. ☎ *602-257-1222. Internet:* www.phxart. org. *Open: Tues, Wed, Sat, and Sun 10 a.m.–5 p.m.; Thurs and Fri 10 a.m.–9 p.m.; closed Mon and major holidays. Admission: $7 adults, $5 students and seniors, $2 ages 6–18, under 6 free. Free admission on Thursdays.*

Pueblo Grande Museum and Cultural Park
Phoenix (Papago Salado area)

This prehistoric Hohokam village and associated museum, sandwiched between several freeways and in full view of Sky Harbor Airport, may not be Arizona's most impressive Native American site, but you won't find a more graphic contrast between the city's past and its present. Materials uncovered during Phoenix's various excavations — many done in order to build highways — are displayed here, so you get a fascinating record of the city's early dwellers, as well as some rare insight into the archaeological process. The real draw, however, is the ruins, which include an ancient ball court.

The ⅔-mile trail through the Hohokam village is not a loop; if it's a hot day or you're tired, you don't need to go beyond the platform mound to see the ball court at the far end of the complex (the perspective is better from on high anyway). The museum is small and the ruin trail relatively short; you should be able to cover both in about an hour.

4619 E. Washington St. (at 44th Street). ☎ *877-706-4408 or 602-495-0901. Internet:* www.ci.phoenix.az.us/PARKS/pueblo.html. *Open: Mon–Sat 9 a.m.–4:45 p.m., Sun 1–4:45 p.m. Admission: $2 adults, $1.50 seniors 55+, $1 ages 6–17, under 6 free. Free admission on Sundays.*

Scottsdale Museum of Contemporary Art
Scottsdale (near Old Town)

It's not easy for an "outpost" art museum to impress an ex-Manhattanite like me, but I'm crazy about this place. It's fun, it's provocative, and it has a great venue, a former discount movie theater creatively converted into an art space by Will Bruder (see the "Architect Trek: The Next Generation(s)" sidebar in this chapter). Rotating exhibits highlight architecture and design along with painting, sculpture, and things less classifiable — for example, an Art Guys exhibit that invited visitors to stick their ABC ("already been chewed") gum on a chair. The museum isn't all that large; you can see everything in an hour or so. If you have time, walk across the plaza to the Scottsdale Center of the Arts (see "The Arts," later in this chapter), a performance venue that also has rotating art exhibits.

7374 E 2nd St. (at Civic Center Boulevard). ☎ *480-994-2787. Internet:* www. scottsdalearts.org/smoca. *Open: Tues, Wed, Fri, Sat 10 a.m.–5 p.m., Thur 10 a.m.–9 p.m., Sun noon–5 p.m.; closed Mondays. Admission: $5 adults, $3 students, under 15 free. Free admission on Thursdays.*

Taliesen West
North Scottsdale

You don't have to be an architecture buff to want to head out to the winter home, studio, and architectural "laboratory" that were the domain of America's master builder, Frank Lloyd Wright, from 1937 until his death in 1959; often considered Wright's best work, Taliesen West is now a National Historic Landmark. From the early days, showing the public around the grounds was part of the training program for the apprentices at the (still operating) Frank Lloyd Wright School of Architecture. The students mostly stick to their studies these days (they do give a 2-hour tour of their own work on Saturdays in high season) and the desert may not be as pristine as it was when Wright ruled here, but as the excellent architectural tours and the Wright-o-bilia sold at the gift shop attest, the architect's work and principles are as vital as ever.

Architect Trek: The Next Generation(s)

Frank Lloyd Wright not only put his mark on the Valley at **Taliesen West** (see "Seeing the Sights," in this chapter) in Scottsdale, the **Arizona Biltmore Hotel** (see "The Top Resorts," in this chapter) in Phoenix (he was a consultant on its design), and the **Gammage Auditorium** at Arizona State University in Tempe (see "More Cool Things to See and Do," in this chapter), to name his best-known local projects; he also inspired two more generations of Greater Phoenix building-space pioneers.

You can see the famed desert community of Wright protege Paolo Solieri at **Arcosanti** (see Chapter 12) and its smaller, Scottsdale prototype, **Cosanti** (see "The Tintinnabulation of the Bells, Bells, Bells" sidebar in this chapter). And Solieri student Will Bruder not only created the **Scottsdale Museum of Contemporary Art** (see "Seeing the Sights," in this chapter), he's also responsible for downtown Phoenix's Burton **Barr Central Library,** 1221 N. Central Ave. south of Culver Street (☎ 602-262-4636), a five-story cube partially covered in copper that's a real dazzler at sunset. For a closer look at some of its more unusual features — for example, the suspended ceiling in the huge reading room — stop at the directions desk at the foot of the stairs when you enter and ask for the self-guided tour pamphlet (there aren't many around, so be prepared to leave your driver's license as hostage).

What's in a (Brand) Name?

A couple of America's best-known products yielded other things besides money. The **Phoenix Zoo** (see "More Cool Things to See and Do," in this chapter), largely endowed by appliance-company magnate Robert E. Maytag, opened in 1962 as the Maytag Zoo (the name was changed at his heirs' request to reflect the community's great involvement). And the **Wrigley Mansion**, 2501 E. Telawa Tr., Camelback Corridor (☎ 602-955-4079), a huge Italianate residence built between 1929 and 1931 by chewing-gum king William Wrigley Jr., can be toured Tuesday and Thursday 10 a.m. and 3 p.m. for $10.70 per person; it's also open for lunch. (To find Telawa, turn into the Arizona Biltmore Circle, off 24th Street, between Missouri and Lincoln.)

12621 Frank Lloyd Wright Boulevard (approximately 114th Street) at Cactus Rd. ☎ *480-860-8810 (tour information) or 480-860-2700 (general information and directions). Internet:* www.franklloydwright.org. *Admission: There are five different guided tours (the only way to see the grounds), which vary depending on the season: They range from the 1-hour standard ("Panorama") tours, offered year-round (Oct–May $14.50 adults, $12 seniors and students, $3 ages 4–12; June–Sept $10 adults, $8 seniors/students, $3 ages 4–12) to a 3-hour "Behind the Scenes" tour ($35 per person in winter; $25, in summer). Don't miss the 2-hour "Night Lights on the Desert" tour ($20) if you're in town on Friday night in summer (the only time it's offered). Open: The visitor's center/gift shop is open Oct–May daily 8:30 a.m.–5:30 p.m., June–Sept daily 8:30 a.m.–5 p.m. Tour times and frequency depend on the season — call ahead — but you can expect something every day starting at 9 a.m.*

More Cool Things to See and Do

✔ **Explore Phoenix's heritage: Heritage Square,** 115 N. 6th St. at Monroe, downtown Phoenix (☎ 602-262-5029, ext. 1 or 602-262-5071), a complex of Victorian-era structures listed on the National Register of Historic Places, gives a glimpse of an architectural style not generally associated with Arizona. The Rosson House is furnished with period antiques, the Silva House (free, Thu–Fri 10 a.m.–4 p.m.) has changing historical exhibits, and the Stevens House hosts the Arizona Doll and Toy Museum (see "The Kids' Corner" sidebar, in this chapter); a tearoom, café, gift shop, and Pizzeria Bianco (see "The Runner-up Restaurants," in this chapter) are also in the complex. Most of the buildings do not charge admission; Rosson House 30-minute tours offered Wed–Sat 10 a.m.–4 p.m. and Sun noon–4 p.m.; last tour at 3:30 p.m.; shorter summer hours. Admission: $4 adults, $3 seniors, $1 ages 6–12, 5 and under free; call ☎ 602-261-8948 to reserve.

✔ **Talk to the animals:** The 125-acre **Phoenix Zoo,** 455 Galvin Parkway in Papago Park (☎ 602-273-1341), stars the usual animal suspects in their usual re-created habitats. Kids can get up close and personal with chickens, goats, sheep, and mules at the four-acre Harmony Farm. It's a fine zoo; just not distinctive enough to put it on top of a Phoenix tour list. Open: May–Labor Day daily 7 a.m.–4 p.m. ; rest of the year daily 9 a.m.–5 p.m. Admission: $8.50 adults, $7.50 seniors, $4.25 ages 3–12, 2 and under free.

✔ **Get historical:** Right next to the Arizona Science Center, the **Phoenix Museum of History,** 105 N. 5th St., between Monroe and Washington Streets (☎ **602-253-2734**), gives a far from fusty peek into the city's past. Exhibits include everything from a replica of the beer-bottle sidewalk that fronted one of the city's saloons to the ultimate cheap hoosegow (a knee-high rock to which prisoners were chained). Open Mon–Sat 10 a.m.–5 p.m., Sun noon–5 p.m. Admission $5 adults, $3.50 seniors and AAA cardholders, $2.50 ages 7–12, 6 and under free.

✔ **Be tempted by Tempe:** There's a lot to do in this pleasant town just east of Phoenix, home to Arizona State University. In addition to strolling the shops of Mill Avenue, taking a Rio Salado tour, or doing your own river cruising (see the sections on shopping, guided tours, and keeping active in this chapter), you can also visit the **Tempe Historical Museum,** 809 E. Southern Ave. at Rural Road (☎ **602-350-5100**), where hands-on activities include diverting the Salt River into canals and fields (open Mon–Thurs and Sat 10 a.m.–5 p.m., Sun 1–5 p.m.; closed Fri and major holidays; admission $2.50 adults, $2 seniors and students with I.D., $1 ages 6–12); or check out the **Arizona State University Art Museum,** Nelson Fine Arts Center on the ASU campus (☎ **480-965-ARTS;** call for directions and parking information), where striking, subterranean galleries display contemporary and Latin American art and some modern American masters (open Tues 10 a.m.–9 p.m., Wed–Sat 10 a.m.–5 p.m., Sun 1–5 p.m.; free). Free half-hour tours of the nearby **Grady Gammage Memorial Auditorium** (☎ **480-965- 4050**), one of Frank Lloyd Wright's last creations, are offered weekdays from 1–3:30 p.m. during the school year. The Tempe Convention and Visitors Bureau, 51 W. 3rd St., #105 (☎ **480-894- 8158;** Internet: www.tempecvb.com), open Mon–Fri 8 a.m.–5 p.m., can give you additional information, such as how to pronounce the town's name (okay, okay, I'll tell you myself: It's tem-PEE).

✔ **See Scottsdale B.C.C. (Before Conspicuous Consumption):** True, its storefronts and wooden sidewalks are chock-a-block with curio shops, but **Old Town Scottsdale,** four square blocks bounded by Indian School Road and 2nd Street, Brown Avenue, and Scottsdale Road, is not all phoney Western baloney. The intersection of Brown and Main Street marks the spot where the general store and post office of the original 1894 Scottsdale townsite stood. Stop in at the 1910 schoolhouse, now home to the Scottsdale Historical Society Museum, 7333 Scottsdale Mall (☎ **480-945-4499**), to pick up a map for a self-guided walking tour highlighting 13 historic sites. Open Wed–Sat 10 a.m.–5 p.m., Sun noon–5 p.m., closed July–Aug. Free.

✔ **Mine the state's history:** The early adventurers and investors who came to Arizona in droves learned the hard way that all that glitters isn't gold; you'll get a far less stressful version of that lesson at the small **Arizona Mining and Mineral Museum,** 1502 W.

Washington St. at 15th Avenue (☎ **602-255-3791**). No matter if you're interested in mines or mining; these rocks and gemstones are mighty pretty — and the admission price is right. Open Mon–Fri 8 a.m.–5 p.m., Sat 11 a.m.–4 p.m. Closed state holidays. Free.

The Kids' Corner

In addition to the Desert Botanical Garden and the Heard Museum, detailed in "Seeing the Sights," earlier in this chapter, and the Phoenix Museum of History and the Phoenix Zoo in "More Cool Things to See and Do," the following are likely to appeal to the prepubescent set:

✔ **The Arizona Doll and Toy Museum**, 602 E. Adams St., Heritage Square, downtown Phoenix (☎ **602-253-9337**), has something for all ages and genders, including an antique, miniature millinery store and dress shop; an elaborate Barbie wedding; and an action-figure exhibit starring GI Joe. Open: Tues–Sat 10 a.m.–4 p.m., Sun noon–4 p.m., closed Aug. Admission $2.50 adults, $1 children.

✔ **Hall of Flame Firefighting Museum**, 6101 E. Van Buren St. in Papago Park, Phoenix (☎ **602-275-3473**), features more than 90 gleaming pieces of fire equipment dating back to 1725. Retired firefighters regale visitors with gripping tales of rescue, and kids get to climb on some of the equipment and (yikes!) even ring alarm bells. Open: Mon–Sat 9 a.m.–5 p.m., Sun noon–4 p.m.; closed New Years Day, Thanksgiving, and Christmas. Admission: $5 adults, $4 seniors, $3.50 ages 6–17, $1.50 ages 3–5, 2 and under free.

✔ **Mesa Southwest Museum**, 53 N. MacDonald St. at 1st Street, Mesa (☎ **480-644-2230**), wraps its learning in a very entertaining package, using everything from animated dinosaurs to hands-on gold panning to teach kids the history of the Southwest. Adults are catered to with rotating exhibits on history and art. All in all, worth the trip out to Mesa, especially since its expansion in 2000. Open: Tues–Sat 10 a.m.–5 p.m., Sun 1–5 p.m., closed Mon and major holidays. Admission: $6 adults, $5 seniors and students with ID, $3 ages 3–12, 2 and under free.

✔ **McCormick Stillman Railroad Park**, 7301 E. Indian Bend Rd. at Scottsdale Road, Scottsdale (☎ **480-312-2312**), is a kick for both kids and adult rail buffs, who can tootle around the park on a 5/12 scale model train. Two railroad depots and lots of model trains add to the fun. There's also a 1929 carousel. Hours vary with the season; call for schedules. $1 for train and carousel rides.

✔ **Out of Africa Wildlife Park**, Fort McDowell Rd., Fountain Springs (take AZ 87 north; 2 miles past Shea Boulevard, turn right on Fort McDowell Road) (☎ **480-837-7779**), is no hideout for hangabout animals; here, everyone's expected to put on a show. Tigers and bears happily cavort in the water, exotic birds prove the air is their element, and the lizards, well, crawl on their bellies like reptiles. Open: Oct–May Tues–Sun 9:30 a.m.–5 p.m.; Memorial Day–Sept Wed–Fri 4 p.m.–9:30 p.m., Sat 9:30 a.m.–9:30 p.m., Sun 9:30 a.m.–5 p.m. $13.95 adults, $12.95 seniors, $4.95 ages 3–12, 2 and under free.

Some Offbeat — and Slightly Off the Beaten Path — Attractions

Up for some delightful oddities? Consider:

✔ **Mystery Castle,** 800 E. Mineral Road (take Central Avenue south to the entrance to South Mountain Park) (☎ **602-268-1581**), created by Boyce Gulley in the 1930s and 1940s from local stones and unusual materials from all around Arizona, is part medieval fortress, part Old West town. Gulley's daughter, for whom the castle was built, still conducts tours of this folk-art phantasmagoria. Open: Thurs–Sun 11 a.m.– 4 p.m. Admission: $5 adults, $3 seniors, $2 ages 6–15, ages 5 and under free.

✔ **Buffalo Museum of America,** 10261 N. Scottsdale Rd., south of Shea Boulevard, Scottsdale (☎ **480-951-1022**), pays tribute to this symbol of the western plains in a strip shopping center. This little two-level museum is packed to the gills with buffalo-related items — everything from the original guns used by Buffalo Bill in his Wild West show to a faux-bloody, faux-buffalo skin featured in *Dances with Wolves*. Open: Mon–Fri 9 a.m.–5 p.m., Sun by appointment. Closed Sat and holidays. Admission: $3 adults, $2.50 seniors, $2 ages 6–17, 5 and under free.

✔ **The Bead Museum,** 5754 W. Glenn Dr. at 58th Avenue, Glendale (☎ **623-931-2737**), is no mere ode to adornment. Beads had — and still have — commercial, ceremonial, and religious purposes, detailed here through a variety of beautiful objects from around the world; you'll see everything from elaborate headdresses to beads that were traded for slaves. Crafters can learn the latest techniques here, too. Open: Mon–Sat 10 a.m.–5 p.m., Thu 10 a.m.–8 p.m., Sun 11 a.m.–4 p.m. Admission: $3, under 12 free; free on Sun.

Keeping Active

From serene golfing greens to extreme biking terrain, Greater Phoenix has the means to keep you happily playing outside. But, in case you hadn't noticed, it's a desert out there. Bring plenty of water and keep on drinking it, even if you don't think you're thirsty, even if you don't realize you're sweating: water evaporates quickly in this dry air. That holds for any sport you're taking part in, but it's especially crucial for the more strenuous ones like hiking and biking.

Biking

Thanks in good part to a large student population, Tempe has more than 140 miles of urban bike paths, making it the Valley's best — really the only — in-city biking territory. In addition, a paved off-street bike path surrounds Tempe Town Lake. You can pick up a bikeway map at the City of Tempe Transit office, 20 E. Sixth St. at Mill Avenue, 3rd floor (☎ 480-350-2739) or at any bike shop in Tempe, including **Tempe Bicycle,** 330 W. University and Farmer, 4 blocks west of Mill Avenue (☎ 480-966-6896), which has a great selection of road and mountain bikes for rent. Rates range between $20 and $50 for 1 day, $30 and $60 for 2 to 3 days, $50 and $80 for a week. In Scottsdale, the Indian Bend Wash Greenbelt, covering more than 12 miles along Hayden Road from

Indian Bend Road to Washington Street, is popular with pavement-happy bicyclists, as well as with joggers and in-line skaters. You can enter the path from several spots off Hayden Road.

Desert-bound mountain bikers have their pick of dramatic Valley trails. **Fat Tire: Tales and Trails, Arizona Mountain Bike Trail Guide,** published by Cosmic Ray in Flagstaff, has the lowdown on the best ones. Get a copy in advance by writing the company at 3960 N. Zurich St., Flagstaff, AZ 86004 or order one online at www.thecanyon.com/cosmicray; they're also available in Scottsdale at **REI,** 12634 N. Paradise Village Parkway W. (☎ **602-996-5400**). Beginners often dust their wheels on the trail starting at Dynamite Road and Pima, 8 miles north of Bell Road in Scottsdale; it's gorgeous with desert blooms in spring. South Mountain Park, 10919 S. Central Ave. (☎ **602-495-5078**), and Papago Park, 625 N. Galvin Pkwy. (☎ **602-256-3220**), in south and central Phoenix, respectively, have plenty of trails to keep all levels happily shifting gears.

Want some company and guidance? **Arizona Outback Adventures,** 7607 E. McDowell Rd., between N. Miller Road and N. 77th Street, Scottsdale (☎ 480-945-2881; Internet: www.azoutbackadventures.com), a full-service bicycle shop and outfitter, offers 4-hour downhill mountain bike tours for $78, including helmet, gloves, water, snacks, and coordination staff who shuttle vehicles from the start to the end points. Feeling extreme? Book a custom tour for $125. You can also contact the Phoenix chapter of the **Arizona Bicycle Club** (☎ 602- 264-5478) to see if you can get in on one of their (not extreme) group rides, for free.

Boating

Kayak, canoe, pedal, or row away a sunny afternoon on the **Tempe Town Lake.** Rent your favorite water toy — it's $15 for the first hour, $9 for each additional half hour — at the kiosk near the Mill Avenue bridge at Tempe Beach Park, 80 W. Rio Salado Pkwy. (☎ **480-517-4050**); be prepared to leave a driver's license and credit card as a deposit. This brand new 220-acre lake is next to the highway and under the airport flight path, so it's not exactly idyllic, but Tempe's Rio Salado project is a work in progress; a lushly landscaped waterfront entertainment complex, with restaurants, shops, nightclubs, is in the works.

Golfing

No doubt about it: In the Valley, golf rules. With more than 180 courses, Greater Phoenix constantly ranks among America's top five golf destinations; you're never much more than a putt away from some major greens action. The *Greater Phoenix Golf Guide,* available from Madden Publishing, 3295 N. Civic Center Boulevard, Scottsdale, AZ 85733 (☎ **480-946-4499**) for $5 in advance, or free locally at most Valley visitor's bureaus (see "Street Smarts . . .," earlier in this chapter), hotels, and resorts, gives a good general wrap up of the local courses. See also Chapter 5 to find out about golf schools and golf-vacation packages.

Careful of Those Cacti: Some Tips for Desert Golfers

If you're used to teeing off onto wide, rolling greens, desert golf — also known as target golf — can be an entirely new ball game. To master these prickly courses:

✔ Concentrate on aim rather than distance. Fairways are narrow and frequently broken up by desert, so you have to hit the ball straight off the tee to get to the greens, even if that means not using a driver right away. (Get it? That's why they call it "target" golf.)

✔ Bring lots of balls. On desert courses, the rough is really rough — as in prickly and spiney. You're not going to want to go poking around in that stuff.

✔ If you do go searching for a ball, take a club with you so you can clobber the rattlesnakes (just kidding about the clobbering — slow but steady retreat is a much better strategy — but not about snakes. Use the club to make sure any underbrush where your ball is hiding out is critter-clear).

✔ Bring lots of water and keep drinking it, even if you don't think you're thirsty. You won't always realize when you're getting dehydrated.

✔ Don't forget sunscreen and a hat.

✔ If you see wildlife about to carry your ball off the fairway, yell loudly — or take a mulligan.

Want to try some different courses but don't feel like juggling tee times? Get **Par-Tee-Time Golf** (☎ 800-827-2223 or 602-230-7223) to do it for you. **Stand-by Golf** (☎ 480-874-3133) is a good, well, standby for last-minute reservations.

Unless I say otherwise, green fees for the following recommended courses — arranged roughly in ascending budget-destroying order — include a cart. You'll find the best deals on weekday summer afternoons, and that's usually what the lowest price in the price range that follows the course description represents.

✔ **Municipal:** You can pay through the nose to play the Valley in high season — which is why people actually camp out for tee times at **Papago Golf Course,** 5595 E. Moreland St., south of McDowell and 52nd Street, Phoenix (☎ 602-275-8428), surrounded by stunning red rock buttes and costing just $8 to $28 (it's another $22 for a cart). The scenery isn't as dramatic but, then, the wait isn't nearly as long at pleasant **Encanto Park,** 2775 N. 15th Ave., two blocks south of Thomas, Phoenix (☎ 602-253-3963) ($9 to $28, plus $18 for a cart).

✔ **Public:** Arizona State alum Phil Mickelson studied his swing at the challenging Pete Dye-designed **ASU-Karsten Golf Course,** 1125 East Rio Salado Parkway at Rural Rd., Tempe (☎ 480-921-8070) ($25–$88). Tom Fazio's Raptor course at **Grayhawk Golf Club,**

8620 E. Thompson Peak Parkway, 3 miles north of Frank Lloyd Wright Boulevard, Scottsdale (☎ 480-502-1800), is one of the toughest — and most gorgeous — in the Valley, with thick desert, deep fairway bunkers, and a two-degree slope that can make your ball do funny things ($50–$195). **McCormick Ranch Golf Club,** 7505 E. McCormick Pkwy. at Scottsdale Road, Scottsdale (☎ 480-948-0260), is older but impeccably maintained; it was designed in an age that encouraged water and trees, restricted on the newer, desert-conscious courses ($40–$110). The mostly flat **Scottsdale Country Club,** 7702 E. Shea Boulevard at 77th Street, Scottsdale (☎ 480-948-6911), is another appealing throwback, thick with eucalyptus, pine, and cottonwood trees, and featuring water hazards on 13 holes ($27–$85). Dramatic elevation changes and deep sand bunkers challenge players at the **Superstition Springs Golf Course,** 6542 E. Baseline Rd. at Power Road, Mesa (☎ 480-985-5555), a PGA Tour Qualifying Site for 2 years ($15–$125). The Scottish-style links laid out by Ben Crenshaw and Bill Coore at the **Talking Stick Golf Club,** 9998 E. Indian Bend Rd., 1 mile east of Loop 101, Scottsdale (☎ 480-860-2221), are some of the best bunkered in Arizona ($40–$125). Always in impeccable condition, **Wildfire Golf Club,** 5225 E. Pathfinder at Tatum Road, Phoenix (☎ 480-473-0205), is desert style but user friendly, with wide fairways and big, multi-level greens ($50–$125).

✔ **Resort:** The perks of staying at a resort include discounted green fees and first dibs on tee times at their golf courses, which consistently rank among the Valley's best — the better to lure guests. The rates listed here assume you won't have these resorts' room keys among your possessions. All the resort courses have different reservation policies for non-guests; ask how far in advance you'll need to reserve (requirements range from 1 to 30 days).

Jay Moorish incorporated the astonishing scenery at **The Boulders,** 3641 N. Tom Darlington Dr., Carefree (☎ 480-488-9009) into the two courses he designed, with eye-popping effect; if you have to choose one, go South ($75–$225). The 27 beautifully landscaped holes at **The Phoenician,** 6000 E. Camelback Rd. at 64th Street, Scottsdale (☎ 480-423-2449), mix traditional and target styles. Camelback Mountain serves as a major distraction ($50–$180). If you've watched the Phoenix Open, you've already eyeballed the **Tournament Players Club (TPC) of Scottsdale,** 17020 N. Hayden Rd. at Bell Road (☎ 480-585-3939), the Scottsdale Fairmont's fairways. The TPC's Stadium course is longer ($77–$182), but the tighter, shorter Desert is a bargain municipal course ($26–$46). The Tom Weiskopf-designed Monument course at **Troon North Golf Club,** 10320 E. Dynamite Boulevard, north Scottsdale (☎ 480-585-5300) — the new Four Seasons' green stomping grounds — is peerless for dramatic desert beauty and, according to many, difficulty; the sister Pinnacle course, which Jay Moorish had a hand in, is no slouch in either category ($75–$240).

Mercury Up, Golf Prices Down

They practically give away golf in the Valley in summer. If you're willing to hit the links in the hot months — and especially during the week after 2 p.m. — you can get great deals on some of the Valley's most exclusive courses. And while they don't have scantily clad maidens and lads with fans following you around, resorts like the Boulders and Marriot's Camelback Inn do the next best thing: They give you golf carts with built-in misters.

Hiking

There are almost as many places to hike in the Valley as there are cacti, and some of the best trails and views are just minutes from the asphalt. Get the big picture from *Day Hikes and Trail Rides in and around Phoenix,* by Roger and Ethel Freeman, available in most Valley sporting goods stores; you can order a copy in advance by sending a check for $14.95 (plus $3 for shipping) to PMPC, P.O. Box 26121, Phoenix, AZ 85068.

 Straddling the border between Phoenix and Scottsdale, **Camelback Mountain** has a 2-mile roundtrip trail guaranteed to work your legs and your heart. It's nearly all uphill and pretty rocky in places — you'll see lots of rock climbers hanging out (and off) here — but the payoff is amazing views from the top. The trail, which begins at the Echo Canyon parking lot east of McDonald Drive and Tatum, is busiest in the morning and early evening — for a good reason: Don't even think about trying this hike in the midday heat.

Also challenging and popular because it leads to one of the best panoramas of the city is the 1.2 mile **Squaw Peak Summit Trail** in the Phoenix Mountains Preserve (☎ **602-262-7901**); look out for lots of switchbacks towards the top. Take Lincoln Drive between 22nd and 23rd Streets to Squaw Peak Drive.

The largest municipal park in the country, **South Mountain Park,** South Phoenix (☎ **602-495-0222**), is honeycombed with dramatic desert-and-mountain trails; to get here, take Central Avenue south until you can't go any farther (about 2 miles past Baseline). Weekdays from 9 a.m. to 5 p.m., you can pick up a trail map at the visitor's center; on the week-end, get one from the ranger station at the park's entrance. **The Summit Trail,** a 15-mile workout (for the very fit only, please), takes you past Indian petroglyphs as well as lots of amazing scenery; follow the signs to the end of San Juan Road inside the park.

Want to know precisely what prickly plants you're coming up against — I hope not literally — on the trail? See the "Ecotours" section, later in this chapter, for naturalist-led hikes.

Horseback Riding

Saddle up in South Mountain Park with **Ponderosa Stables,** 10215 S. Central Ave., south of Baseline (☎ 602-268-1261). Prices start at $17 an hour for scenic trail rides; an early morning breakfast trot will set you back $25. For $100, **Trail Horse Adventures** (☎ 800-SADDLE-UP) will lead you into Phoenix's dramatic North Mountain Preserve on a half-day lunch ride, with a short hike out to look at Indian petroglyphs. The same per person price will buy you a place on a cattle drive — if you (or they) can round up a group of eight or more. **Don Donnelly Stables,** 6010 S. Kings Ranch Rd., Gold Canyon (☎ 480-982-7822), about 20 minutes southeast of Phoenix via Highway 60, offers 2-hour ($32), 4-hour ($53), and full-day ($85) rides into the Superstition Mountains; they've got dinner and breakfast rides, too. See also the "Horsing Around" sidebar in this chapter, for an equine instruction source (the training's for you, not the horse, silly).

River Rafting and Tubing

It's as reliable as the weather — that is, not very — but in a good year, the section of the Salt River that runs northeast of Phoenix can get pretty wet 'n' wild. If there's enough snowmelt from the nearby White Mountains, you can ride class III and IV rapids through starkly dramatic, ancient granite gorges from late February to late May. Outfitters running Salt River raft trips include **Far Flung Adventures** (☎ 800-231- 7238 or 520-425-7272; Internet: www.farflung.com), with prices ranging from $89 per person (including permit) for a 5-hour trip to $650 for a 5-day adventure; and **Mild to Wild Rafting** (☎ 800-567-6745; Internet: www.mild2wildrafting.com), where you'll pay $98 for a full day on the river, $275 for a 2-day/1-night trip.

Of a kinder, gentler piscean persuasion? From May to September, **Salt River Tubing,** Ellsworth and Power Roads, Mesa (take the Power Road exit north from Highway 60 to Ellsworth) (☎ 480-984-3305), will rent you an inner tube and take you to the river (back, too) for $10. The nearby **Saguaro Lake Ranch,** Bush Highway (continue along Power Road until it turns in Bush Highway; you'll see the ranch sign) (☎ 480- 984-2194), has a similar river delivery system, and rents kayaks ($25 half day, $40 full day) as well as tubes ($5 a day). In addition, **Arizona Outback Adventures** (see "Biking," earlier in this chapter) offers half-day guided rafting ($75) and Funyak ($105) — that's an inflatable kayak (sometimes called a "rubber duckie") — trips on easy class I rapids.

Tennis

If you don't want to blow your net worth at a resort (not many are open to outsiders, anyway), you still have a few options to court. It'll cost you only $4.50 before 7 p.m., $6 afterward, to play on one of the 15 courts of the **Kiwanis Park Recreation Center,** 6111 S. All America Way at Mill Avenue, Tempe (☎ 480-350-5201); call the day before to reserve a place. At **Scottsdale Ranch Park,** 10400 E. Via Linda at 104th Street, Scottsdale (☎ 480-312-7774), the fees for the 12 courts in this lovely residential area range from $3 to $6 for 1½ hours, depending on the time of day.

It's a New (Spa) Age

The desert has long been considered a healing — as well as skin-drying — place, so don't be surprised to find Phoenix and Scottsdale at the forefront of the latest spiritual-sybarite trends. Forget Swedish massage. These days, Far Eastern rituals are meeting Native American remedies in aromatherapy-scented rooms presided over by bodyworkers who can unblock your chakras faster than you can say Deepak Chopra. At the Valley's poshest spas, expect everything from rubdowns with heated stones that have been "re-charged" in the moonlight to treatments that involve soothing oils being dripped onto your back — or your third eye.

The resorts generally have the best-equipped pleasure centers. Those at the Boulders, the Phoenician, the Arizona Biltmore, The Fairmont Scottsdale Princess, and Marriot's Camelback Inn, all detailed in "Where to Stay in Phoenix . . .," earlier in this chapter, happily accept day guests. Prices start from around $75 for a 50-minute treatment and go up to about $300 for a full day of indulgence, including the use of the resort's fitness facilities and, sometimes, lunch. Sure it's pricey but, hey, where else can you find bliss in a dimly lit room with a stranger — guilt free?

Spectator Sports

When the Arizona Diamondbacks slithered onto the sports scene in 1998, Phoenix entered the big leagues: It's now one of the few U.S. cities that has professional baseball, basketball, hockey, and football teams. And the high-quality action at Bank One Ballpark, built for the D-backs, and at the America West Arena, where the Phoenix Suns go up and down the court, have breathed life back into downtown Phoenix. Sports bars and restaurants are always packed on game days and the streets buzz with excitement.

Downtown's streets get gridlocked on game nights, so build in plenty of sitting-motionless-in-car and/or hiking-down-from-the-nosebleed-level-of-the-garage time before any sports event you attend there. Most of the garages, which run you between $6 and $10 an evening, are within an 8- to 10-minute walk of the ball parks.

You can buy tickets directly from the sports venue or team; they're also available through **Ticketmaster** (☎ **480-784-4444;** Internet: www.ticketmaster.com).

Baseball

The Arizona Diamondbacks may be the main event, but you can watch America's favorite pastime being played at arenas Valley-wide.

The **Arizona Diamondbacks** go to bat at Bank One Ballpark, 401. E. Jefferson St. at 7th Street (☎ **602-514-8400;** Internet: www. azdiamondbacks.com for online schedules and tickets), an attraction in itself (see "And on Your Left . . .," later in this chapter). Although the D-backs have developed a following since their 1998 debut — it didn't hurt that they made the National League playoffs in 1999 — tickets, which range from $1 to $55, are still easy to score, especially if you don't mind cheering from the second or third levels (all the arena's sightlines are excellent).

Many out-of-towners who visit the Valley from late February to early April can still root, root, root for the home team at one of Arizona's Cactus League spring training games. Tickets cost from $3 to $18 and usually sell out pronto.

- ✔ **Anaheim Angels:** Tempe Diablo Stadium, 2200 W. Alameda Drive, 3 blocks south of Broadway Rd. and east of 48th Street, Tempe (☎ **480-350-5205**)

- ✔ **Chicago Cubs:** HoHoKam Park, 1235 N. Center St. at Brown Street, Mesa (☎ **480-964-4467**)

- ✔ **Milwaukee Brewers:** Maryvale Sports Complex, 3600 N. 51st Ave., south of Indian School, Phoenix (☎ **602-245-5500**)

- ✔ **Oakland A's:** Phoenix Municipal Stadium, 5999 E. Van Buren St./Stadium Way (☎ **602-495-7239**)

- ✔ **San Francisco Giants:** Scottsdale Stadium, 7408 E. Osborn, two blocks east of Scottsdale Road (☎ **480-312-2580**)

- ✔ **Seattle Mariners** and **San Diego Padres:** (they share) Peoria Stadium, 16101 N. 83rd Ave., south of Bell Road, Peoria (☎ **623-878-4337**)

Basketball

Downtown's streets are a sea of purple and orange on nights when the NBA's **Phoenix Suns** (☎ **602-379-7867**) hold court at the America West Arena, 201 E. Jefferson St. between 1st and 3rd Streets; good seats go fast, so plan ahead. Prices range from $11 to $75. The Women's National Basketball Association's **Phoenix Mercury** (☎ **602-252-9622**), who take over the arena between June and August, also have die-hard devotees. Mercury team members meet and greet their fans whenever possible and the club has one of the WNBA's highest attendance rates. Tickets cost between $8 and $35.

Ouch — That Ticket Price Hurts!

If you can't score any seats through the usual means, you have another option: Phoenix is one of the few cities where scalping is legal. Just be sure to check your tickets carefully before handing over the cash and make your deal off the venue's grounds, where scalping is illegal — even a few yards away is okay.

Horsing Around

Come out West to see a horse, of course? The 400-acre **Westworld Equestrian Center,** 16601 N. Pima Rd., Scottsdale (☎ 480-312-6801), hosts a variety of equine-related events — everything from rodeos and polo matches to Arabian horse shows. If you want to mount your own steed, you can get lessons here, too. Call to hear a recorded schedule of events and directions to the center.

Football

Catch the **Arizona Cardinals'** (☎ 800-999-1402 or 602-379-0102) kick-off at Arizona State University's Sun Devil Stadium, 5th Street at Stadium Drive in Tempe; tickets run $20 to $200. The only NFL team still playing in a college stadium, the Cardinals don't have the win-ningest reputation, but they're hoping that'll change if voters approve a new state-of-the-art stadium for them. When the Cardinals aren't play-ing, the ASU Sun Devils (☎ 480-965-2382) usually are.

Hockey

Okay, so they're not the Montreal Canadiens — hey, those kids don't get a lot of ice to practice on in the desert — but the NHL's **Phoenix Coyotes** (☎ 888-255-PUCK or 480-563-PUCK) have a lot of clout in the Valley, where they share the America West Arena with the Phoenix Suns and the Phoenix Mercury. Ticket prices range from $10.50 to $215.

And on Your Left, the Heard Museum: Seeing the Valley by Guided Tour

In addition to the tours listing here, see also the biking and river rafting sections of "Keeping Active," earlier in this chapter.

General Bus Tours

Gray Line Tours of Phoenix (☎ 800-732-0327 or 602-495-9100; Internet: www.graylinearizona.com) traces the city's history from its Hohokam Indian past during a 3½-hour tour ($30 per person). Stops include the state capitol, celebrity homes in Paradise Valley, and the Arizona State University campus in Tempe. The more intimate **Vaughan's Southwest Custom Tours, Inc.** (☎ 800-513-1381 or 602-971-1381) are an hour longer and have smaller groups (11 people maximum), which cost $38 per adult and cover roughly the same ter-rain. Both companies provide hotel pickups in Phoenix and Scottsdale.

Ecotours

Walk Softly (☎ 480-473-1148; Internet: www.walksoftlytours.com) gives a deliberately hands-off introduction to the flora and fauna of the Sonoran Desert. The naturalist-led hikes range from a 3-hour walk around the McDowell Mountain Preserve ($50 per person) to an 8- to 9-hour trek into the Cañon Caminar Despacio, a remote desert canyon with breathtaking rock formations and desert springs ($105; not available in summer). Other options include customized half-day trips to the Gila River Indian Cultural Center, including crafts demonstrations and traditional dancing by Akimel O'odham school children ($70), and an Apache Trail tour (see Chapter 12).

Jeep Tours

Climb aboard the most powerful 4x4 for a 4-hour excursion with **Desert Storm Hummer Tours** (☎ 480-922-0020; Internet: www.dshummer.com) ($90 per person). You're likely to see lots of desert wildlife on your ride — and short nature hike — which includes the Tonto National Forest and Four Peaks, Goldfield Mountain, Superstition Mountain, and Saguaro Lake. Take off with the offbeat but savvy guides at **Wild West Jeep Tours, Inc.**, 7127 E. Becker Lane, Scottsdale (☎ 480- 941-8355; Internet: www.wildwestjeeptours.com), and you'll have a blast — literally. You'll explore 1,000-year-old Indian ruins, get acquainted with the Sonoran desert (in the summer, tasting prickly pear cactus fruit is on the menu), and try your hand (well, just your trigger finger) at shooting a six-gun. Tours cost $60 for adults, $35 for ages 12 and under.

Photo Tours

Don't know how to adjust for the harsh desert light or get an angle on adobe? Shutterbugs of all levels might consider going on one of professional photographer Pam Singleton's 4-hour **Photo Excursions** (☎ 602- 946-3246; Internet: www.photoexcursions.com). The architectural tour focuses on two uniquely Southwestern structures, and the landscape tour focuses on desert plants and critters ($80 and $60, respectively, assuming at least 10 people sign on). Come spring, **Walk Softly** (see "Ecotours," in this section) and its affiliate jeep-tour operator **Rattlesnake Roundup Inc.** (☎ 480-473-1148) will four-wheel you or trek you out to take your best shot at the desert's amazing blooms ($65 per person on either of these 4-hour excursions).

River Tours

Float down Tempe Town Lake on a half-hour **RioLago Cruise** (☎ 480- 517-4050) and you'll be regaled with amusing tales of Tempe's past. The tours ($5.75 for adults, $4.75 seniors 65 and older and ages 6–12, $3.50 ages 5 and under) run regularly from Sunday through Thursday from 9 a.m. to 9 p.m., and Friday and Saturday from 9 a.m. to 10 p.m.; buy your tickets from the same kiosk that rents the lake's water toys (see "Boating," under "Keeping Active" in this chapter).

The lakeshore isn't especially scenic during the day; until the planned landscaping kicks in, do this tour after dark, when the lights illuminating the overhead archways are lovely.

Some BOB Stats

Bank One Ballpark, known as BOB, was the world's first sports facility to combine a retractable roof, air-conditioning, *and* a natural turf playing field.

The roof is made up of 9 million pounds of structural steel. Using the technology found in drawbridges and cranes, a pair of 200-horsepower motors can zip it open or closed in under 5 minutes.

Because grass gets confused when it's subjected to both sun and air-conditioning, a whole new strain had to be developed for BOB. Steve Cockerham, one of the nation's leading turf agronomists — bet you didn't even know that was a job description — and head of the Department of Agricultural Operations at the University of California at Riverside, eventually came up with the hardy DeAnza hybrid.

Stadium Tour

Want to get up close and personal with BOB — as **Bank One Ballpark,** 401 E. Jefferson St. at 7th St. (☎ **602-462-6799**), is affectionately known — without lots of other people around or any Diamondback action to distract you? Terrific behind-the-scenes tours take you to see everything from the private pool area near third base to the National Baseball Hall of Fame memorabilia. (Sorry, they won't retract the famous ceiling for you). Outside of baseball season, tours are given Tuesday through Saturday at 10:30 a.m., noon, 1:30 p.m., and 3 p.m.; Sun at noon, 1:30 p.m., and 3 p.m. In season — but when the D-backs aren't playing — they're offered Monday through Saturday 10:30 a.m., noon, 1:30 p.m., and 3 p.m. There are no tours during holidays or special events. Tickets, sold at the Tour Window at the main box office, cost $6 for adults, $4 ages 7-12 and seniors over 60, $2 ages 4-6, 3 and under free.

Suggested 1-, 2-, and 3-day Sightseeing Itineraries

I have plenty of ideas about the best ways for you to arrange your days (and, unlike my family and friends, you may even pay attention to them), but the Valley is very spread out. If you're sequestered away in a north Scottsdale resort, you'll be doing a lot more driving on these itineraries than if, say, you're holed up in central Phoenix. Similarly, lots of the best things to do involve the great outdoors. I'm assuming that you're visiting when most people do — in winter, when the outdoors are great. If you're in town between May and October (and especially June, July, and August), it's not too smart to be wandering around outside in the middle of the day, when the heat can be unbearable. (For details on the attractions, restaurants, and activities mentioned in these itineraries, see the corresponding sections earlier in this chapter.)

1-Day Itinerary

If you have only 1 day in the Valley, concentrate your time in downtown and central Phoenix, where you can get in a good dose of nature and Native American culture — as well as a little retailing. Start out at the **Pueblo Grand Museum and Cultural Center,** easy to reach by freeway from pretty much anywhere, and then head over to the **Desert Botanical Gardens;** both are in the Papago Salado part of town. The Botanical Gardens has a lovely, if slightly pricey, outdoor café for lunch. If you'd like something a bit more exotic, wait to eat at your next stop, the **Heard Museum,** where you can sample a Navajo taco or lamb stew in the court-yard café. Spend the afternoon perusing the exhibits and great gift shop, then head a short way north to the beautiful art deco **Arizona Biltmore** resort, and kick back with a cocktail on the terrace. If you haven't satis-fied your acquisitive urges at the Heard, you're right near **Biltmore Fashion Park,** where you could drop some more dollars and then have dinner at **Sam's Café, RoxSand,** or **Christopher's Fermier Brasserie** (be sure to book the last two in advance). Not completely done in? Boogey over to Old Town Scottsdale. Unless you've gone back to your hotel to change into something drop dead, you'll probably feel out of place in one of the see-and-be seen clubs, but you can still ogle the Valley glit-terati before ducking in to one of the more casual watering holes such as the **Rusty Spur Saloon.** (*Note:* If you think this itinerary will send you into overdrive, cut out the Pueblo Grand Museum; it's a great place but the Heard Museum covers some of the same cultural territory.)

2-Day Itinerary

If you have 2 days, you can take a more leisurely approach to the sights covered on the 1-day itinerary and add a few more. Have a quick swim at your hotel, then spend the morning at the Heard Museum. In the afternoon, head over to downtown Scottsdale. If you haven't already had lunch at the Heard, chow down at **Cowboy Ciao** before browsing the Fifth Avenue shops and Main Street galleries. The nearby **Scottsdale Museum of Contemporary Art** and the boutiques and gal-leries of **Old Scottsdale** should keep you happy the rest of the after-noon. If you want to stick around for the nightlife, you might save Cowboy Ciao for dinner.

On day 2, visit the **Pueblo Grand Museum and Cultural Park** and the **Desert Botanical Gardens** in the morning; in the afternoon, head to northern Scottsdale to tour **Taliesen West** and visit **Cosanti.** If you haven't eaten at the Desert Botanical gardens, have lunch at the Scottsdale branch of **Sam's Café.** For dinner, both the upscale **Oceana** and the more casual **Pinnacle Peak** steakhouse will take you just a bit farther north.

If you're traveling with kids (or want to get in touch with your inner child), skip Taliesen West and Cosanti, and instead add the **Arizona Science Center** and either the **Phoenix Museum of History** and the **Arizona Doll and Toy Museum** or a tour of the **Bank One Ball Park,** all close to the science center. You can also substitute the **Phoenix Zoo** for the Pueblo Grande Museum and Cultural Park.

3-Day Itinerary

Follow the 2-day itinerary until the afternoon of the second day, then head over from the Papago Salado area (where the Pueblo Grand Museum and the Desert Botanical Gardens are) to nearby **Tempe.** Spend the afternoon kayaking, lake touring, strolling along Mill Avenue, checking out the sights on the Arizona State University Campus, or any combination thereof — and be sure to book a table in advance for dinner at the **House of Tricks.** On day 3, head up to Cosanti first thing so you can watch the bronze bells being cast, then go over to Taliesen West. It's not a very far drive north along Scottsdale Road to the towns of Carefree and Cave Creek (see Chapter 12). Either have a Southwest-chic lunch at the **Palo Verde Room** at the Boulders and then hit the ritzy boutiques and the Heard Museum's northern branch at **El Pedregal,** or go the wilder west route with chili beer at **Crazy Ed's Satisfied Frog** and the more down home shops of Cave Creek.

Shopping

Shopping in the Valley tends to be an all-mall affair — with several notable exceptions, which, of course, I'll tell you about. That's not to say you won't find highly original, individual stores, just that you shouldn't be surprised if you sometimes find them in faceless retail strips.

Best Shopping Areas

You can drop your dough at plenty of places throughout the Valley, but downtown Scottsdale is a shopper's nirvana, with the most concentrated doses of retail bliss per square block. The main indulgence districts here include, from north to south: **5th Avenue,** angling diagonally between Indian School and Scottsdale roads, where Native American arts and jewelry shops and western galleries number among the one-of-a-kind boutiques; the intersecting **Marshall Way Arts District,** roughly between Indian School Road and 3rd Avenue, lined with contemporary art galleries; **Old Town Scottsdale** (see "More Cool Things to See and Do," in this chapter), featuring lots of Old West curio shops; and the adjacent **Main Street Arts & Antiques** district, Main Street and 1st Avenue between Scottsdale Road and Goldwater Boulevard, where the galleries tend towards the traditional and the Western, and boutiques sell a wide range of stuff that's been around long enough to get expensive.

It's best to park your car at the free lot on the corner of 2nd Street and Wells Fargo Avenue near Old Scottsdale and explore the shopping areas by foot or trolley (see the "Free-for-All" sidebar, near the beginning of this chapter). There's a strictly enforced 3-hour limit on the lower levels, but no time restrictions upstairs.

In Tempe, the upbeat, young **Mill Avenue,** from University Drive near the Arizona State University campus to Rio Salado Parkway, is great for trendy, cheap clothing shops; independent bookstores; and people watching.

Antiques Freak Alert

If you have a fondness for remembrances of things past, check out the Midwest-meets-the-desert town of **Glendale**, about 20 minutes west of Sky Harbor Airport, with more than 90 antiques emporiums. The best pickings are in Old Towne Glendale, on Glendale Avenue between 57th Avenue and 58th Drive, but be sure to meander a few blocks to the north to the beautiful converted bungalows in the historic Catlin Court district. The **Glendale Tourism Division**, 5850 W Glendale Ave. at 58th Avenue (☎ **877-800-2601** or 623-930-2957; Internet: www.tour.glendaleaz.org), open 8 a.m. to 5 p.m. Monday through Friday, has maps of both areas and details about the free trolley that'll take you through them.

Getting Mall'd

The **Arizona Center,** Van Buren between 3rd and 5th Streets, downtown Phoenix (☎ **602-271-4000**), is more outdoor entertainment complex than mall, with lushly landscaped courtyards, restaurants (including Sam's Café; see "The Runner-Up Restaurants," in this chapter), bars and nightclubs, a 24-screen movie theater, and some 50 small shops and retail carts. Come here to pick up anything you can think of that bears a Phoenix sports team logo or, at the Arizona Highways store, a great state-themed gift that's not jock related. In nice weather, Native American musicians often play in the center courtyard at lunchtime.

Arizona Mills, 500 Arizona Mills Circle, Tempe (southeast quadrant of I-10 and US Highway 60) (☎ **480-491-9700**), is bargain and big-store central, featuring leading discount outlets like Last Call Neiman Marcus, Marshall's, and Burlington Coat Factory, and oversized retailers such as Virgin Megastore and Oshman's Supersports USA; the smaller stores tend towards the lower end of the retail spectrum. An IMAX theater, a 24-plex cinema, a branch of Stephen Spielberg's super high-tech GameWorks play center (☎ **480-839-4263**; Internet: www.gameworks.com); and theme eateries such as the Rainforest Café mean you won't have any problem dragging the kids along (although getting them out may be difficult).

Biltmore Fashion Park, Camelback and 24th Street, Phoenix (☎ **602- 955-1963**), is the Camelback Corridor's retail and restaurant hub, where seriously upscale shops — we're talking Saks, Williams Sonoma, Gucci — mingle among bricked paths and lush greenery with middle-of-the-roaders such as Macy's and Pottery Barn. Suffering from shopper's fatigue? Stop in at Elizabeth Arden's Red Door Salon for a pedicure or refuel at RoxSand, Christopher's Fermier Brasserie, or Sam's Café (see " The Runner-Up Restaurants," in this chapter).

Scottsdale Fashion Square, Camelback and Scottsdale Roads (☎ **480- 941-2140**), is the undisputed queen of upscale Arizona malls, with 1.8 million square feet of retail space, retractable skylights, and the likes of Nordstrom, Neiman Marcus, Nicole Miller, and Tiffany & Co. singing siren songs to your credit cards. When you're ready to give the plastic a break — or at least a change of pace — a movie theater and panoply of restaurants await (I think there must be a state law mandating a minimum number of movie screens and feeding stations per mall).

In Chapter 12, see also Day Trip #1 for Prime Outlets at New River Anthem, and Day Trip #2 for the Factory Stores of America and Tanger Factory Outlet Center, both at Casa Grande.

Getting (Boutique) Mall'd

The Borgata of Scottsdale, 6166 N. Scottsdale Rd. between Lincoln and McDonald Drives (☎ 480-998-1822), looks like a Tuscan village, replete with courtyards, fountains, and (maybe not so Tuscan) upscale specialty shops, selling everything from Southwest art to silver jewelry and resort apparel. If you're in town on Friday between October and March, don't miss the farmer's market, with gorgeous produce, fresh baked breads, and exotic Southwest products (prickly pear jam anyone?).

El Pedregal Festival Marketplace at the Boulders, 34505 North Scottsdale Rd., just north of Carefree Highway (☎ 480-488-1072), may just be Arizona's most scenic place to shop, its low-slung Pueblo architecture blending (almost) organically with the surrounding desert and rocks. It would be cynical of me to suggest that a setting so soothing might inspire you to spend more money than you intended at all those art galleries and boutique specialty shops, including the gift shop of the Heard Museum north (hey, you know what they say: You can take the girl out of New York, but you can't take New York out of the girl).

What to Look for and Where to Find It

Whether your tastes run to golf gear or high art, you can find something to satisfy them down in the Valley.

At the (Art) Hop

On Thursday nights from 7 to 9 p.m. year-round (except Thanksgiving), take part in the Scottsdale Gallery Association's self-guided **ArtWalks** (☎ 480-990-3939), with cocktail receptions and artist appearances designed to put you in an art-buying mood. Phoenix gets into the art action each month between October and June with **First Fridays** (☎ 602-256-7539); I don't have to tell you which day of the week and which part of the month they take place, do I? Park downtown in the lot of the Burton Barr Central Library, 1221 N. Central Ave., south of Culver Street, and, from 7 to 10 p.m., hop an ArtLink shuttle that loops around the 20 participating galleries (check the art listings in the local papers).

Art

True, the Valley may have one of the highest rates per capita of can-vasses filled with lonesome cowboys, but there's a whole lot more in town than Western art. In fact, Scottsdale is second only to Santa Fe as a Southwest art destination. With more than 100 galleries and studios to choose from, you'll find everything from hand-blown glass and Native American abstracts to contemporary mixed-media pieces — and even plenty of non-cliché Western art.

✔ **Eclectic: Art One,** 4120 N. Marshall Way, Scottsdale (☎ 480-946- 5076), is the place to see the up-and-comers and maybe get some art bargains; the works by the young Arizona art students represented here never run higher than $1,000. One of the most dynamic galleries in the Valley, the 5,000-square-foot **gallerymateria,** 4222 N. Marshall Way, Scottsdale (☎ 480-949-1262), showcases some 95 artists from the Americas, Asias, and Europe; media range from the traditional to fiber and wood, and much of the art is wearable. There's also a beautiful courtyard sculpture garden. About the only type of work you won't find at the **Work of Artists Gallery,** 10835 N. Tatum Boulevard, Suite 101, Phoenix (☎ 480-596-0304), is contemporary. Wood carvings, paintings, pottery, furniture, and Native crafts by more than 200 artists cost anywhere from $1 to $5,000.

✔ **Contemporary: Mind's Eye Gallery,** 4200 N. Marshall Way, Scottsdale (☎ 480-941-2494), runs the cutting-edge gamut from sculpture, photography, art furniture, and ceramics to glass and jewelry. This space is best known for its kaleidoscopes — includ-ing a kaleidoscope bar. The pricier **Lisa Sette Gallery,** 4142 N. Marshall Way, Scottsdale (☎ 480-990-7342), represents more established but still nontraditional artists.

✔ **Regional/Western: Suzanne Brown Gallery,** 7160 Main St., Scottsdale (☎ 480-945-8475), helped jump-start Scottsdale's art scene in 1962. It originally had a French focus, but the gallery is now about 60 percent regional (and 100 percent expensive, with prices starting at about $6,000). Also open for more than 30 years, the **Meyer Gallery,** 7173 E. Main St., Scottsdale (☎ 480-947-6372), sells high-quality Western and Native American art in the realist/impressionist tradition. Another Scottsdale veteran, the **Joan Cawley Gallery Ltd.,** 7135 E. Main St., Scottsdale (☎ 480- 947-3548), includes Native American artist R.C. Gorman among its top-notch talent. **Trailside Galleries,** 7330 Scottsdale Mall (☎ 480-945-0195), showcases several members of the Cowboy Artists of America, including founder Joe Beeler, as well as other high-end Western painters. **Riva Yares,** 3625 N. Bishop Lane (☎ 480-947-3251), is renowned for its contemporary Mexican, South American, and Native American collection, though aesthetically compatible Anglos such as Milton Avery turn up here, too. The work tends to be exciting, but not inaccessible (except maybe in price).

The Tintinnabulation of the Bells, Bells, Bells

You can tour **Cosanti**, 64333 Doubletree Ranch Rd. at Invergorden, Paradise Valley (☎ 480-948-6145), the architectural prototype for Arcosanti (see Chapter 12) and an Arizona State Historic Site, if you book ahead. Most people, though, just come for the wonderful ceramic and bronze Soleri windbells (prices start at about $20 and $50, respectively); get here early, and you can watch them being cast. The majority of the proceeds go to support the Arcosanti project, but if you buy a bell from the "Cause" collection, you can contribute to your favorite participating non-profit. Open daily from 8 a.m. to 5 p.m.

Golf Supplies

The Valley definitely has the golf goods — everything from antique clubs to discounted state-of-the-art carts. You'll like the putting green, the personalized service, and Knuckles, the friendly bulldog, at **Hornacek's House of Golf,** 23359 N. Pima Rd., south of Pinnacle Peak Rd., Scottsdale (☎ 480-502-0555), owned by the brother of former Phoenix Sun Jeff Hornacek. A duffer's fantasy, **In Celebration of Golf,** 7001 N. Scottsdale Rd. at E. Indian Bend Road, Scottsdale (☎ 480-951- 4444), is part golf museum, part golf-art gallery (the country's largest), part upscale golf retail store. Play (virtually) 18 holes at Pebble Beach in a simulation room, browse 1,000 pairs of shoes, or just munch free cookies while watching the Golf Channel. The two **Golfsmith** superstores, at 8026 W. Bell Rd., Glendale (☎ 623-412-9901), and 880 N. 54th St., Chandler (☎ 480-705-6771), are a bit off the beaten tourist turf, but these two stores warehouse a mind-boggling amount of golf supplies while catering to your every golf quirk.

Native American Crafts

Street vendors may try to sell you Native American jewelry and other crafts. Don't bite; it's the Arizona version of the Rolex watch scam. Only buy from reputable dealers who can guarantee the goods (see Chapter 19).

For the best one-stop Native American crafts shopping, head straight to the gift shop at the **Heard Museum** (see "Seeing the Sights," in this chapter). Here, you can get high-quality weavings, rugs, jewelry, pottery, baskets, katsinas, fetishes — you name it — at fair prices. Better yet, unlike in many places, the profits go to the people who create the crafts rather than to store owners, traders, or other middlepeople. The downtown Phoenix store has the best variety, but there's also a decent selection in the El Pedregal branch at the Boulders Resort in Carefree (see "Getting (Boutique) Mall'd," in this chapter).

Western Wear

Az-Tex Hat Company, 3903 N. Scottsdale Rd. between Main and 1st Streets, Old Scottsdale (☎ **480-481-9900**), goes to the head of the tailoring class, carefully suiting their headgear to your cranium; buy a hatband or get your old Stetson reblocked here. **Buckaroo Babes,** 7001 N. Scottsdale Rd. at E. Indian Bend Road, Scottsdale (☎ **877-232-1884** or 480-483-9392), outfits aspiring rhinestone cowgirls in upscale Southwestern duds. **Saba's Western Wear,** 7254 Main St. at Brown Ave., Old Town Scottsdale (☎ **480-949-7404**), has catered to the Valley's cowpokes and cowpoke wannabes since 1927. Still in the same family, they've expanded to nine stores around the Valley, including another in Old Scottsdale (3965 N. Brown Ave. at First Avenue, ☎ **480-947-7664**).

Nightlife and the Arts

You won't have a hard time finding something to do in the Valley after dark, but unless — and it's pretty unlikely — you're staying within walking distance of the areas where the clubs and concert halls are concentrated, you're going to have to drive in order to do it. If you're hitting any watering holes but aren't likely to restrict yourself to water, have a designated driver in tow — or just bite the bullet and shell out for a cab both ways.

The best source of listings for clubs and alternative arts events is the free *Phoenix New Times,* which comes out on Wednesday. *The Rep* weekend entertainment guide, included with the *Arizona Republic* on Thursday, but also available for free around town, is good for the more mainstream arts and nightlife listings.

Nightlife

Old Town Scottsdale is the prime destination for see-and-be-seen partyers. Expect to dispense a little cash in this neck of the night owls' woods — both for covers and for valet parking, as regular parking is hard to come by and you can club hop by foot (if your heels aren't too high) around here. Similarly, the pubs and dance clubs on **Mill Avenue,** near Arizona State University in Tempe, are generally just a Birkenstock trot away from one another.

Phoenix's clubs, which tend to be a bit more sophisticated than those in Tempe, but less pretentious than those in Old Town Scottsdale, aren't conveniently clustered. The exception is the **Arizona Center** (see "Getting Mall'd," in this chapter), which has several sports bars and dance clubs, as well as a cadre of casual restaurants; it's within walking distance of Bank One Ballpark, America West Arena, the Phoenix Convention Center, and downtown arts venues such as Phoenix Symphony Hall and the Herberger Theater.

Smoke Gets in My Eyes

There's no rule against smoking in bars or nightclubs, so be prepared for the possibility of a smokescreen wherever you go. The good news for the smoke-sensitive, however, is that most places in the Valley have breezy open-air patios that are just as happening as the dance floors inside.

Country and Western

Two-step to live sounds any night of the week at **Handlebar-J,** 7116 E. Becker Lane, Scottsdale (☎ 480-948-0110), but come on Wednesday, Thursday, and Sundays if you want to learn how (for free). Vince Gill and Willie Nelson have dropped in to the **Rusty Spur Saloon,** 7245 E. Main St., Old Scottsdale (☎ 480-941-2628), where a band gets the crowd boot scootin' six nights a week. It opened its doors in 1922 as Scottsdale's first bank; the safe now serves as a walk-in cooler. The history of **Toolies Country Saloon and Dance Hall,** 4231 W. Thomas Rd. at 43rd Ave., Phoenix (☎ 602-272-3100), isn't quite as colorful — it's a converted Safeway supermarket — but the country action is; this place has a knack for booking acts like Clint Black and Garth Brooks before they hit it big.

Rock/R&B

For a taste of Mardi Gras, check out the **Cajun House,** 7117 E. Third Ave., Scottsdale (☎ 480-945-5150); the huge dance floor is lined with New Orleans–style balconies and the live rock and funk acts guarantee a good time (Tuesday nights are especially popular). **Long Wong's,** 701 S. Mill Ave., Tempe (☎ 480-966-3147), is a tiny club with a big sound; the best local rock bands do their original thing here. Don't let the name of the **Martini Ranch,** 7295 E. Stetson Dr. (☎ 480-970-0500), an Old Town Scottsdale staple, fool you; it's better known for its live rock acts and frat-type crowd than for its Manhattans. The intimate, candlelit **Nita's Hideaway,** 1816 E. Rio Salado Parkway, Tempe (☎ 480-966-7715), was a "dive" bar about 25 years ago, but now books some of the best rock bands in town.

Jazz/Blues

Char's Has The Blues, 4631 N. 7th Ave., Phoenix (☎ 602-230-0205), has been voted Arizona's best blues club 7 years in a row by the Phoenix *New Times* and *The Arizona Republic.* Keep an eye (and ear) out for all-female rockers Sistah Blue. Enjoy fine cigars and martinis at **The Famous Door,** 7419 E. Indian Plaza, Scottsdale (☎ 480-970-1945), while listening to oh-so-smooth riffs; some nights there's an open microphone, others a Latin mix-it-up. At the distinctively non-glitzy, non-glamorous **Rhythm Room,** 1019 E Indian School Rd., Phoenix (☎ 602-265-4842), some of the country's best jazz and blues musicians bring the real thing back home.

For a complete listing of blues events, call the **Phoenix Blues Society** (☎ 602-252-0599) or log on to www.phoenixblues.org.

Dance

George Clooney, Rod Stewart, and Michael Jordan have all made the scene at the wildly stylish sister clubs **Axis** and **Radius,** 7340 E. Indian Plaza, Scottsdale (☎ **480-970-1112**). Most of the footwork action is at Radius, where the bands range from house and techno to salsa. Calling all Lindy hoppers: The **Bash On Ash,** 230 W. 5th St., Tempe (☎ 480- 966-8200), is the place to be Tuesdays and Thursdays, when you can take an hour-long class before heading into a serious swing session. **Pepin,** 7363 Scottsdale Mall, Scottsdale (☎ 480-990-9026), a small Spanish restaurant, has some of the steamiest Latin dancing in the Valley; it's especially incendiary on Saturdays. Over-the-top and a bit pretentious — you'll recognize it by its dramatic fire-laced facade — **Sanctuary,** 7340 E. Shoeman Lane, Scottsdale (☎ 480-970-5088), which packs in the see-and-be-seeners nightly. Highlights (or lowlights, depending on how you feel about this five-room, seven bar club) of this hip spot: The intimate Divine Lounge and elaborately themed Moroccan Room.

Pubs and Sports Bars

Can't get tickets to the big game? Eight large screen TVs and 40 brands of bottled beer at **America's Original Sports Bar,** 455 N. 3rd St., Phoenix (☎ 602-252-2502), can help you cope. The Hofbrau Hefeweizen, handcrafted by the **Arizona Roadhouse & Brewery,** 1120 E. Apache Boulevard, Tempe (☎ 480-929-9940), recently grabbed the gold at the Great American Beer Festival. Shoulder up (but not too close) to the local soccer and rugby players who party down after a big game at **The Blarney Stone,** 4341 N. 75th St., Scottsdale (☎ 480-424- 7100); if you're lucky, the Clare Voyants will be performing. Profs and undergrads alike come to the **Bandersnatch Brew Pub,** 125 E. 5th St., Tempe (☎ 480-966-4438), for its good beer, kicked-back patio, and, on Wednesday night, Irish bands. The only suds served at **Hops! Bistro & Brewery,** 7014 E. Camelback Rd., Phoenix (☎ 602-468-0500), are the eight brewed here, but the pale ale, stout, and the raspberry ale keep everyone hoppy.

Lounges and Cocktail-Sipping Spots

You'll have to push through the rock-steady crowd at Martini Ranch to get to the **Shaker Room,** 7295 E. Stetson Dr., downtown Scottsdale (☎ 480-970-0500) — which, with its sleek leopard-print couches and hardwood floors, is a far better place to sip the drinks for which its sibling is named. An open patio looking out on the park, romantic red loveseats, and chairs well positioned for conversation all make **AZ88,** 7353 Scottsdale Mall, Old Scottsdale (☎ 480-994-5576), ideal for discussing what you've just seen — or are planning to see — at the nearby Scottsdale Center for the Arts. Enjoy intimate conversation over a kir royale at the ultra romantic **T. Cook's Lounge,** Royal Palms Hotel, 5200 E. Camelback Rd., Phoenix (☎ 602-808-0766), decked out with fresh flowers and plushy Mediterranean-style fittings. Luxe leather chairs and a fireplace make the adjoining cigar room cozily clubby (now if only they would can those stogies). If the chic desert-deco Squaw Peak patio bar at the **Arizona Biltmore** (see "The Top Resorts," in this chapter) looks familiar, that's because Angela Bassett and her gal pals did some serious bonding here in *Waiting to Exhale.*

A Great Way Tequila Hour — or Several

About 120 kinds of tequila go down at the gazebo-bar of the **Old Town Tortilla Factory**, 6910 E. Main St., Scottsdale (☎ 480-945-4567) and almost as many types of margaritas. Perch on the patio and gaze out at the orange trees, night-lit fountain, and, in winter, a blazing firepit; you'll soon be channeling Jimmy Buffett.

The Arts

Most Broadway road shows and national concert tours swing through the Valley. For tickets to almost any event or for a recorded listing of what's on in town, phone **Ticketmaster** (☎ 480-784-4444); you can also make reservations through the Web site at www.ticketmaster.com. If your chosen event is sold out, try calling **Tickets Unlimited** (☎ 602- 840-2340), **Western States Ticket Service** (☎ 602-254-3300), or **The Ticket Company** (☎ 602-279-4444); one of them may have the coveted tickets tucked away.

Top Arts Venues

Phoenix Symphony Hall, 225 E. Adams St., downtown (☎ 800-AT-CIVIC or 602-262-7272), home to the Phoenix Symphony, also hosts performances by Ballet Arizona, the Arizona Opera Company, Broadway touring shows, and more. The box office, at the entrance to the adjacent Phoenix Convention Center in Lobby 2, also sells tickets for events at the **Orpheum Theater,** 203 W. Adams St. at Second Avenue (☎ 602-262-7272), an elegant 1929 structure with a colorful, wonderfully ornate facade.

The Arizona Theater Company, the Actors Theater of Phoenix, and the Arizona Jewish Theater Company all share the **Herberger Theater Center,** 222 E. Monroe St. (☎ 602-252-8497), a Spanish-style complex that stages more than 600 performances a year.

The lobby of the **Scottsdale Center for the Arts,** 7390 E. Second St. in the Scottsdale Mall (☎ 480-994-2787; Internet: www.ScottsdaleArts.org), doubles as an art gallery. Some of the best modern dance, jazz, and theater in town take place here; this is also where the Scottsdale Symphony Orchestra performs. When the weather is nice, part of the action moves outside to the Scottsdale Amphitheater.

The **Grady Gammage Memorial Auditorium** in Tempe, Mill Ave. and Apache Boulevard (☎ 480-965-3434), will not only wow you with the quality of its Broadway performances, but also with its Frank Lloyd Wright design (see "More Cool Things to See and Do," in this chapter).

Classical Music

The **Arizona Opera Company,** 4600 N. 12 St., Phoenix (☎ 602-266- 7464), shared by Phoenix and Tucson, hits the high notes at Symphony Hall about five times a year from October through March (ticket prices range from $20 to $70). Members of the top-ranked **Phoenix Symphony Orchestra,** 455 N. 3rd St., Suite 390, Phoenix (☎ 602-495-1999), arguably the best strings and brass in the Southwest, make beautiful music together at Phoenix Symphony Hall when they're not doing outdoor pops ($15 to $40).

Dance

Ballet Arizona, 3645 E. Indian School Rd., Phoenix (☎ 602-381-1096), pliés at the Orpheum and Phoenix Symphony Hall (when they're not making their graceful moves in Tucson); tickets range from $16 to $48. The **Center Dance Ensemble** (☎ 602-252-8497), take a turn in another direction, staging contemporary dance at the Herberger ($8 to $20).

Theater

Almost two dozen professional and nonprofessional theater companies perform in the Valley. The major players include the **Actors Theater of Phoenix,** the resident troupe at the Herberger Theater (☎ 602-252- 8497), putting on a full range of drama, comedy, and musicals, and the **Arizona Theater Company,** 502 W. Roosevelt, Phoenix (☎ 602-256- 6995), which does its dramatic thing at the Herberger Theater and the Orpheum when they're not shuttling off to Tucson. Tickets for both range from $22 to $36.

Out-Going Entertainment

It doesn't get much better than an outdoor concert on one of the Valley's balmy nights. Between September and March, the **Desert Botanical Garden** (see "Seeing the Sights," in this chapter) stays open late for its "Music in the Garden" series on Sunday nights at 7 p.m. (there's a buffet at 5:30) between September and March; the program changes but you can expect the sounds to be mellow. Tickets cost $13.50. The **El Pedregal Festival Marketplace** (see "Getting (Boutique) Mall'd," in this chapter) takes up the outdoor music slack from April through June and in September with the "Music by Moonlight" jazz, blues, and rock series on Thursday nights. All shows begin at 7 p.m. and tickets run between $5 and $10. Check what's happening, too, at the amphitheater of the Scottsdale Center of the Arts (see "The Arts," in this chapter).

Baby Bards

Childsplay, Tempe Performing Arts Center, 132 E. 6th St., Tempe (☎ 480-350-8112), puts on performances that range from the classic (the "Wind in the Willows") to the thought-provoking (the Holocaust-themed "And Then They Came for Me"). Venues include the Herberger Theater Center, Scottsdale Center of the Arts, and Tempe Performing Arts Center. The **Great Arizona Puppet Theater,** 302 W. Latham St. at 3rd Ave., Phoenix (☎ 602-262-2050) pulls lots of strings in a historic theater; call ahead to check if any puppet classes are being offered while you visit.

Quick Concierge: Phoenix

American Express: 2508 E. Camelback Road, Phoenix (☎ 602-468-1199); or 6900 E. Camelback Road at Scottsdale Fashion Square, Scottsdale (☎ 480-949-7000), both open 10 a.m. to 6 p.m. Monday through Friday, 10 a.m.–3:30 p.m. on Saturday.

Area Code: Greater Phoenix is divided into three area codes that require 10-digit dialing (that is, the number and area code *not* preceded by a 1); there's no long-distance charge when dialing between Valley area codes. Phoenix's area code is **602;** that for East Valley cities such as Scottsdale, Tempe, and Mesa is **480;** and for the West Valley towns such as Glendale and Peoria, dial **623.**

Doctors: To find a local doctor, call the Physician Referral and Resource Line (☎ 602-230-2273). Also try the American Board of Medical Specialties (☎ 800-776-2378) or the Maricopa County Medical Society (☎ 602-252-2844).

Emergencies: For fire, police, or medical emergencies, dial ☎ **911.** Phoenix Police (☎ 602-262-6151); Phoenix Fire (☎ 602-253-1191); Rural Metro Fire (☎ 602-994-3886).

Hospitals: The reputable St. Luke's has locations in Phoenix, 1800 E. Van Buren at 18th Avenue (☎ 602-251-8100), and in Tempe, 1500 S. Mill Ave. south of E. Parkway Boulevard (☎ 480-968-9411). There are two branches of the Scottsdale Healthcare system, at 9003 E. Shea Boulevard (☎ 480-860-3000) and 7400 E. Osborn Rd. (☎ 480-675-4000). For kids, Phoenix Children's Hospital, 1111 E. McDowell Rd. at 10th St. (☎ 602-239-2400), is the best. There's also a branch of the famous Mayo Clinic in Scottsdale at 13400 E. Shea Boulevard (☎ 480-301-8000).

Information: The Phoenix Convention and Visitors Bureau has two locations: 50 N. 2nd St. at Adams (☎ 602-452-6282), open Mon–Fri 8 a.m.–5 p.m.; and Biltmore Fashion Park, 24th St. and Camelback Rd. (☎ 602-452-6281), open Mon–Fri 10 a.m.–9 p.m., Sat 10 a.m.–6 p.m., and Sun noon–6 p.m.. The Scottsdale Chamber of Commerce/Convention and Visitors Bureau, 7343 Scottsdale Mall, Old Scottsdale (☎ 480-945-8481), is open Mon–Fri 8:30 a.m.–6 p.m., Sat 10 a.m.–4 p.m., and Sun 11 a.m.–5 p.m. (closed Sun June–Aug). The Tempe Convention and Visitors Bureau, 51 W. 3rd St., #105 (☎ 480-894-8158; Internet: www.tempecvb.com), is open Mon–Fri

8 a.m.–5 p.m. And, finally, the Glendale Tourism Division, 5850 W. Glendale Ave. at 58th Avenue (☎ 877-800-2601 or 623-930-2957; Internet: www.tour.glendaleaz.org), is open 8a.m.–5p.m. Mon–Fri.

Internet Access and Cyber Cafes: Cyber cafes include Gypsy Java, 3321 E. Bell Rd., Phoenix (☎ 602-404-9779, www.gypsy-java.com), and Innhouse Video & Cybercafe, 160a Coffee Pot Dr., Sedona (☎ 520-282-7368, www.inhouse video.com). Kinko's provides high-speed Internet access in eight cities throughout the Valley. Three of the most convenient locations are: in downtown Phoenix, 4801 N. Central Ave. (☎ 602-241-9440); in Scottsdale, 4000 N. Scottsdale Rd. (☎ 480-946-0500); in Tempe, 933 E. University Dr. (☎ 480-894-1797).

Mail: The Phoenix main post office is at 4949 E. Van Buren St., east of N. 48th Street (☎ **602-407-2076**).

Maps: Because Greater Phoenix is so spread out, any single map is either going to be sketchy or unwieldy. That's why I'd suggest having two: one to put the Valley in geographical perspective — get this from any car rental company or tourist bureau — and another with real detail. The H.M. Gousha map, sold at most gas stations, supermarkets, and convenience stores, is as good as any in the latter category. If you're a AAA member, you can ask for the double-your-fun Phoenix maps in advance or pick one up in Phoenix at 3144 N. 7th Ave. (☎ 602-276-1116) or in Scottsdale at 701 N. Scottsdale Rd. (☎ 480-949-7993). Whatever you get, make sure it's current; the streets in the Valley shift far faster than its weather.

Newspapers/Magazines: *The Arizona Republic* is Phoenix's largest daily newspaper, with the *Tribune* coming in second in Scottsdale and Tempe. You can find the excellent free alternative weekly, the Phoenix *New Times,* at corner dispensers,

coffeehouses, supermarkets, and many other places around the Valley. The monthly *Phoenix Magazine* covers Valley-wide topics of interest and carries restaurant reviews by this chapter's dining critic, Nikki Buchanan. The glossy *Valley Guide*, published quarterly, is another good source of visitor-friendly articles and information.

Pharmacies: Walgreens has 21 Valley pharmacies that never close; call ☎ 800-WALGREENS for the location nearest you. Two Phoenix branches of Fry's Pharmacy are also open 24 hours a day: at 30th St. and Thomas (☎ 602-468-9188) and at Tatum and Bell (☎ 602-867-4060).

Police: Call ☎ **911.**

Restrooms: In downtown Scottsdale, where merchants want to be sure that shoppers are comfortable, there are four nice, clean public restrooms: off Marshall Way, between 1st and 2nd Streets; on the east and west ends in the Scottsdale Civic Center, north of 2nd Street, between Brown and Civic Center Boulevard, and at 5th Avenue, between Marshall Way and Craftsman Court. Otherwise, you'll have to do what you have to do everywhere else in Arizona: duck into a restaurant, hotel, or shopping mall.

Safety: Counter to the statistical trend in the rest of the country, Phoenix's violent crime rate is rising slightly (but it lagged behind the rest of the country to begin with so it's just catching up a bit). Stick to crowded public areas at night, especially in downtown Phoenix; on the nights of sports events or concerts, stay with the rest of the crowd when walking to and from your parking spot. There's also a high rate of car break-ins, even in the more established areas, so it's a good idea to leave valuables in your hotel safe (and never on your front or back seat).

Smoking: Several Greater Phoenix cities passed ordinances in the1980s and 1990s that outlawed smoking in designated public places and in all areas of government buildings. Private businesses, however, can set their own rules. The great majority — including malls, sports facilities, and cultural venues — don't allow indoor smoking, but many restaurants, especially those with bars, still have designated smoking and nonsmoking sections.The only exception is the city of Mesa, which outlawed puffing in all public places, including restaurants, in 1996.

Taxes: State sales tax plus the sales tax in Maricopa County — where Greater Phoenix is located — adds up to 5.7 percent, but there are also variable local taxes. You can expect to be taxed a total of 7.5 percent on purchases and restaurant tabs in Phoenix, 7.1 percent in Scottsdale. Hotel room tariffs add up to 9.97 percent in Tempe, 10.67 percent in Scottsdale and Paradise Valley, and 11.07 percent in Phoenix. See Chapter 7 for information on car rental taxes at Sky Harbor airport.

Taxis: AAA Cab (☎ 602-437-4000), Checker Cab (☎ 602-257-1818), Courier Transportation (☎ 602-232-2222), Scottsdale Taxi (☎ 480-994-4567), and Yellow Cab (☎ 602-252-5252).

Time Zone: Mountain Time Zone. (Note: The state does not observe daylight saving time.)

Transit Info: Phoenix Transit (☎ 602-253-5000).

Weather Updates: (☎ 602-379-4000) or Internet: www.phx.noaa.gov.

Chapter 12

Side Trips from Greater Phoenix

•••

In This Chapter

▶ Traveling I-17 north

▶ Exploring along the Apache Trail

▶ Visiting old houses and big houses (prisons, that is)

•••

*Y*ou can go back to the future on these side trips from the Valley, with sights that include everything from Casa Grande, impressive Native American ruins dating to the 1200s (Day Trip #3), to Arcosanti, a vision — or is that mirage? — in the desert of cities to come (Day Trip #1). All these trips are a mixed bag, combining a variety of attractions from which you can pick and choose, so you may want to base your decision on direction as much as on diversion. If, for example, after your stay in the Valley, you head north to Sedona via I-17, you may want to cover the attractions in Day Trip #1 en route. Day trips #2 and 3, on the other hand, both take you east. In the individual itineraries, I explain how you may combine elements of each.

Day Trip #1: From Rock Art to Arcosanti

You don't leave the Valley to begin this tour north along I-17, which starts at the Deer Valley Rock Art Center, continues north to Cave Creek and the Pioneer Arizona Living History Museum, and finishes at Arcosanti, some 65 miles from central Phoenix. If you travel with kids, you may want to skip Arcosanti, an experimental desert community, which is probably of limited interest to them.

Getting There

I-17 intersects I-10 in central Phoenix. Just take I-17 north and keep veering off to the various exits as directed (maybe I'd better rephrase that . . .). Sorry, no back roads or convenient loops connect the sights on this trip; you must return to the freeway to move on to the next location. The good news is, that for a major highway, I-17 is fairly scenic and definitely quick (75 mph speed limit).

The Mother of Outlet Malls

Need a shopping fix? Stop off on your way back from Arcosanti at the crème de la crème of Arizona's outlet malls: **Prime Outlets at New River Anthem,** 4250 W. Anthem Way (exit 229 off the southbound side of I-17; ☎ **623-465-9500**). Barney's, London Fog, and Donna Karan are among the 90 retailers, many of them upscale and rare to the outlet scene. If you travel from Phoenix, the trip takes about 15 minutes from north of the Bell Road exit of I-17 (generally considered by locals as the northern boundary of the Valley).

Seeing the Sights

Close to the city — about 15 miles north of downtown Phoenix — and to the freeway is the **Deer Valley Rock Art Center,** 3711 W. Deer Valley Rd. (2 miles west of I-17 via exit 217B; ☎ **623-582-8007**). The center isn't especially rustic but it has a large concentration of *petroglyphs* (rock paintings) that transport you to an era that was. Some of the 1,500 images made by the region's earliest settlers may date back as far as 10,000 years. Kid-friendly activities include identifying petroglyphs. If your kids want to create rock art on clay disks, they may take their creations home. Open: Oct–Apr Tues–Sat 9 a.m.–5 p.m., Sun noon–5 p.m.; May–Sept Tues–Fri 8 a.m.–2 p.m., Sat 9 a.m.–5 p.m., Sun noon–5 p.m. Admission: $4 adults, $2 seniors and students, $1 ages 6–12, 5 and under free.

Return to I-17 and take exit 223 east to reach **Cave Creek,** founded as a mining camp in the 1870s and still capitalizing on its Old West roots — as well as on the striking volcanic rock formations in the area. You may wander around and browse the crafts, souvenir, and antiques shops, or soak in the atmosphere at one of the Western saloons (see "Where to Eat," for this day trip). However, you aren't charged anything (except a voluntary donation) for admission to the **Cave Creek Museum,** 6140 E. Skyline Dr. and Basin Road (☎ **480-488-2764**). The museum includes a small historic complex with the town's first church, a tuberculosis quarantine cabin, and a mill (open Wed–Sun 1–4:30 p.m. Oct–May). Head east on Cave Creek Rd., and you soon come to the manicured community of **Carefree,** home to the Boulders Resort and the El Pedregal shopping center (see Chapter 11 for both), which hosts an offspring of the Heard Museum (the mother museum is one of Phoenix's don't-miss attractions).

Another 2 miles north on I-17, the Williamsburg-gone-West **Pioneer Arizona Living History Museum,** 3901 W. Pioneer Rd. (just off exit 225; ☎ **623-465-1052**), has 28 original and reconstructed buildings — everything from a sheriff's office to a Victorian mansion. The costumed staff demonstrates typical frontier activities such as blacksmithing and you can see a medicine show at 11 a.m. (Wed–Fri), plus two staged shoot-'em-ups a day. Open: Wed–Sun 9 a.m.–5 p.m. Admission: $5.75 adults, $5.25 seniors, $4.25 students and ages 6–12, 5 and under free.

Side Trips from Greater Phoenix

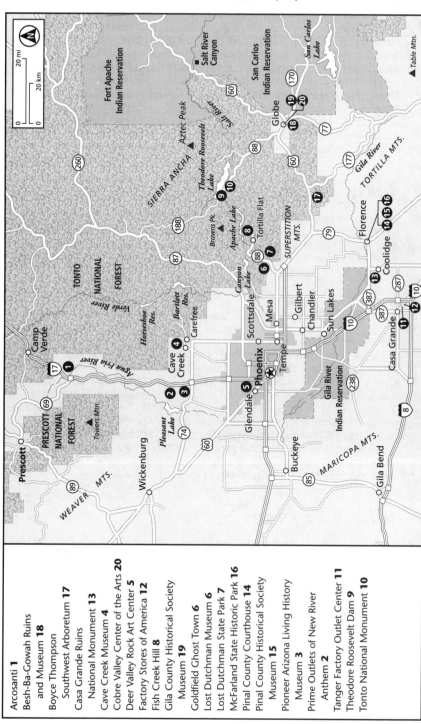

Arcosanti **1**
Besh-Ba-Gowah Ruins
    and Museum **18**
Boyce Thompson
    Southwest Arboretum **17**
Casa Grande Ruins
    National Monument **13**
Cave Creek Museum **4**
Cobre Valley Center of the Arts **20**
Deer Valley Rock Art Center **5**
Factory Stores of America **12**
Fish Creek Hill **8**
Gila County Historical Society
    Museum **19**
Goldfield Ghost Town **6**
Lost Dutchman Museum **6**
Lost Dutchman State Park **7**
McFarland State Historic Park **16**
Pinal County Courthouse **14**
Pinal County Historical Society
    Museum **15**
Pioneer Arizona Living History
    Museum **3**
Prime Outlets of New River
    Anthem **2**
Tanger Factory Outlet Center **11**
Theodore Roosevelt Dam **9**
Tonto National Monument **10**

From the Pioneer museum along I-17 to exit 262 (follow the signs), the distance is 37 miles to **Arcosanti** (☎ **520-632-6217;** www.arcosanti. org). This drive involves about a mile and a half on a dusty, bumpy dirt road; close your windows and go slow. Arcosanti started in 1970 and is far from completed; this desert community embodies architect Paolo Solieri's vision of a world without suburban sprawl. Whether you come away convinced that you've seen the future and that Solieri's vision could in fact work, or think Arcosanti is New Age hokum, the guided tours give you food for thought. Get more substantial fare at Arcosanti's excellent bakery/café; then browse among the Soleri windbells and other crafts created on site — these crafts make good gifts. Open: 9 a.m.–5 p.m. daily except Thanksgiving and Christmas; tours run every hour on the hour from 10 a.m.–4 p.m. Admission: $5.

Taking a Tour

You can't wander freely around Arcosanti; aside from the bakery and the bell shop, most of the site is accessible only by guided tour. However, you're on your own for the rest of these attractions I list. If you want to see Cave Creek from the back of a horse, contact **Cave Creek Outfitters** (☎ **480-471-4635**) for a 2-hour ride for $55.

Where to Stay

You may return to the Valley on this easy day trip. If you want a change of venue, a couple of interesting options are available to you. Occupying four hillside acres near Cave Creek's historic center, **Gotland's Inn Cave Creek** ($$–$$$$), 38555 N. Schoolhouse Rd. (☎ **888-488-2865** or 480-488-9636; Fax 480-488-6879; E-mail: gotlands@inficad.com; Internet: www.unleash.com/gotlands), is the height of rustic Southwest elegance. You may want to bed down in the city of the future for the prices of the past; **Arcosanti** (click on "Overnight Visits" at www.arcosanti. org) offers basic rooms that range from $20 for a single with shared bath to $30 for a double (two single beds) with a private bath. A two-bedroom suite with stellar views ($75) is also available.

Where to Dine

In Cave Creek, **Crazy Ed's Satisfied Frog** ($$), 6245 E. Cave Creek Rd. (☎ **480-488-4742**), is renowned for its barbecued chicken and ribs — and for the incendiary beer that's brewed on the premises. Perch on the patio of the **Palo Verde Room** ($$$) at the Boulders Resort (see Chapter 11) for Southwest-chic dishes and wonderful desert vistas. My favorite lunch stop en route north from Tucson is the **Rock Springs Café and Bakery** ($–$$) (☎ **623-374-5794**), a funky former stagecoach stop; take exit 242 of I-17, between the Pioneer Living Museum and Arcosanti, and follow the signs. Just two words of menu advice: "barbecue" and "pie."

Day Trip #2: Around the Apache Trail

The Apache Trail's 120-mile loop starts and ends at Apache Junction and passes through one of the country's most awe-inspiring landscapes. The loop's beginning stretch is a 48-mile trail created between 1906 and 1911 to haul construction materials to the site of the Theodore Roosevelt Dam. The dam's namesake said of the trail that it "combines the grandeur of the Alps, the glory of the Rockies [and] the magnificence of the Grand Canyon" — even before they named the dam after him.

There *is* a catch: Part of the road (along Fish Creek Canyon) is unpaved and narrow and even the paved sections are two-lane and, in many spots, loaded with switchbacks. In short, the trail isn't for the faint of heart or the afeard of heights. Consider taking a tour if you fit into either category — or if you just want to sit back and enjoy the scenery.

The route offers loads to do and its beauty may inspire you to linger overnight. However, you may be pressed for time. Don't worry; you can fit this tour into one very full day.

Getting There

Take Hwy. 60 east from Phoenix to Apache Junction; then get on Hwy. 88 east. Hwy. 88 east loops north and back south; follow it until you reach Hwy. 60 (near Globe/Miami). Hwy. 60 takes you west, back to Apache Junction.

Seeing the Sights

This trip begins some 3.5 miles northeast of Apache Junction on Hwy. 88 at the **Goldfield Ghost Town** (☎ 480-983-0333), a reconstruction of the 1890s mining boomtown that once stood on the site. Admission to the town complex (open daily 10 a.m. to 5 p.m.) is free. However, you must pay to descend into a replica gold mine ($5 adults, $3 ages 6–12); ride on Arizona's only narrow-gauge railroad ($4 adults, $2 ages 5–12); and gawk at live rattle-snakes, gila monsters, and scorpions ($3 adults, $2 children). The less touristy **Superstition Mountain/Lost Dutchman Museum** (☎ 480-983-4888) details the area's Native American and mining history; exhibits include 23 maps of the Lost Dutchman mine (10–4 daily; $3 adults, $2.50 seniors, $1 students grades 1–12).

These days, the **Lost Dutchman State Park,** 1 mile past Goldfield (☎ 480-982-4485), generally attracts people more interested in hiking them thar hills — that is, the volcanically formed Superstition Mountains — than in finding the gold reputed to be in them. Open: Sunrise to 10 p.m. year-round. Admission: $5 per vehicle ($10 to camp).

Not Dutch, but Definitely Lost

Full of greed, gold, and rugged desert terrain, the story of the Lost Dutchman mine is the stuff of Hollywood scripts. In fact, *Lust for Gold,* starring Henry Ford and Ida Lupino, was among the Westerns roughly based on this legend. The truth is tough to pin down, but folks widely believe that two German ("Deutsch" — which got garbled to "Dutch") miners, Jacob Waltz and Jacob Weiser, found a fabulously rich gold lode in the Superstition Mountains in the 1870s. Waltz supposedly passed along the secret of its location to a Phoenix woman while on his deathbed, but neither she nor her relatives, who spent 40 years looking, ever found the gold mine. Today, some folks doubt that the mine ever existed — and some hopeful explorers still try to locate it.

As you leave the park and enter Tonto National Forest, you're officially on the **Apache Trail.** The trail was designated as Arizona's first historic and scenic highway in 1988. Drive 11 of those miles to get to **Canyon Lake,** popular for fishing and swimming and boarding the **Dolly** steamboat (☎ **480-827-9144**), a replica of a 100-foot double-deck sternwheeler. The 90-minute narrated nature cruise runs daily at noon and 2 p.m. and costs $14 adults, $8 ages 6–12, 5 and under free; twilight dinner cruises run on the weekends.

Two miles farther down the road, **Tortilla Flat** (☎ **480-984-1776**) looks like a Western film set. This 1904 stagecoach stop, largely destroyed in a 1987 fire, consists of a post office, general store, ice cream shop (renowned for its fruity and not at all spiny prickly pear ice cream), and saloon; all are generally open from 10 a.m. to 5 p.m. Who knows? The town may have been called Pancake Stack if the person observing the thin boulders nearby had been hungry for flapjacks rather than for Mexican food.

The pavement ends after about 5 miles as you begin a precarious (1,500 feet in 3 miles) descent down **Fish Creek Hill** — one of the most literally breathtaking rides you're likely to ever take. By the time you reach the marina at **Apache Lake,** some 9 miles away, you may be ready to spend the afternoon decompressing on the water. Windsurfing, pontoon boating, and fishing (if you pick up an Arizona fishing license) are all possibilities.

You get a gander at the impressive **Theodore Roosevelt Dam,** the world's highest masonry dam, in another 14 miles. You may also look at it from the 1,080-foot-long steel arch bridge that sits about ¼ mile upstream from the dam or from the back patio of the Roosevelt Lake Visitor Center, another mile up the road (☎ **520-467-3200**). Lake Roosevelt, the largest body of water contained within the state borders — don't you love these carefully qualified statistics? — is another get-wet-in-the-desert mecca.

The Apache Trail ends at the dam, returning you to paved road for the 5-mile trip to **Tonto National Monument** (☎ 520-467-2240), a well-preserved complex of cliff dwellings built by the Salado people between 1100 and 1400 B.C. You can hike ½ mile up the hill to the Lower Room on your own, but you should call a few weeks in advance if you want a place on the (free) 3-hour ranger-led hikes to the more extensive Upper Ruin. Open: Daily 8 a.m.–5 p.m. (Lower Ruin trail closes at 4 p.m.). Admission: $4 per car.

As you drive the 25 miles from Tonto National Monument to the Hwy. 60 junction, you know you're in mining country by the vast mesas of *tailings* — bleached-out remains of extracted rock — which you begin to see. From the junction, head east on Hwy 60 for 3 miles to the Greater Globe-Miami Chamber of Commerce, 1360 N. Broad St. (☎ 800-804-5623 or 520-425-4495), where you may pick up a walking tour map of historic downtown **Globe.** Next door, the **Gila County Historical Society Museum,** 1330 N. Broad St. (☎ 520-425-7385), gives you the lowdown on the area's mines. For a more elevating perspective, stop downtown at the **Cobre Valley Center of the Arts,** 101 N. Broad St. (☎ 520-425-0884), an artist's co-op housed in the 1906 Gila County Courthouse. On the southeast side of town, the excellent **Besh-Ba-Gowah Ruins and Museum,** 150 Pine St. (☎ 520-425-0320), makes the ancient Salado Indian culture come alive. Kids like climbing the ladders into the upper stories of the ancient pueblos, where pottery and tools excavated at the site are laid out to look like they're waiting to be used. Open: Daily 9 a.m.–5 p.m. Admission: $3 adults, $2 seniors, under 12 free.

As you head west on Hwy. 60 toward Apache Junction, you wind your way through the magnificent Devil's and Queen Creek Canyons (not nearly as white-knuckled as the Fish Creek Hill descent, but not exactly relaxing, either). In contrast, the **Boyce Thompson Southwestern Arboretum,** 37615 E. Hwy 60 (☎ 520-689-2811), created between 1923 and 1929, is a picture of tranquility. If you think you're cactus-ed out by now, think again. You see rare desert specimens from around the world here, including the bizarre Boojum tree featured in Lewis Carroll's poem, "The Hunting of the Snark." The beautifully manicured grounds are a soothing reminder that nature may — occasionally — be tamed. Open: Daily (except Christmas) 8 a.m.–5 p.m. Admission: $5 adults, $2 ages 5–12, under 5 free.

Taking a Tour

True to its name, **Apache Trail Tours & Superstition Mountain Adventures** (☎ 480-982-7661; Internet: www.apachetrailtours. com) specializes in this area. An 8-hour jeep jaunt begins at Goldfield (where the company is located) and includes stops at Tortilla Flat, lunch at Apache Lake, and a hike through Tonto National Monument ($125). The company also offers half-day off-road trips into the Lost Dutchman mine terrain ($60), guided hikes into the Superstitions ($10 per person per hour), and a variety of other hike/jeep combinations.

Want to horse around in the mountains? Rides offered by **Apache Lake Ranch,** Hwy. 88 at mile marker 227 (☎ **520-467-2822;** Internet: www.apachelakeranch.com), go into the spectacular northern Superstition Wilderness ($20 for the first hour, $10 for each additional hour). See Chapter 11 for info on **Don Donnelly Stables,** which also offers rides into the southern Superstitions.

Superstition Mountain Helicopter Tours (☎480-491-0758) whirlybird you over the area's lakes, canyons, and peaks. Flights run from $360 (for four people, the maximum permitted) for 35 minutes to $480 for 45 minutes.

Once a month in winter, on the Saturday night closest to the full moon, the rangers at **Lost Dutchman State Park** lead 2-hour-long moonlit hikes. These hikes have become very popular. The park has not set up a reservation system or hiker quota yet, but stay tuned.

Where to Stay

Whether your interests tend toward the nautical, historical, or golfical, the Apache Trail has a place for you. The motel-like rooms at the **Apache Lake Marina and Resort** ($), Apache Lake (☎ **520-467-2511;** Fax: 520-467-2338; Internet: www.apachelake.com), aren't particularly exciting, but their proximity to great water sports and to the surrounding rugged wilderness is. With sweeping views of the Pinal Mountains from the windows, kids must have found it harder than usual to pay attention at the North Globe Schoolhouse, now the **Noftsger Hill Inn** ($), 425 North St. (☎ 520-425-2260). Other pluses: mining-era antiques and huge breakfasts. At **Gold Canyon Golf Resort** ($$$–$$$$), 6100 S. Kings Ranch Rd., Gold Canyon (☎ **800-624-6445** or 480-982-9449; Internet: www.gcgr.com), you can bunk in an upscale Southwestern-style casita and tee off on two gorgeous mountainside courses. Gold Canyon is only about 20 minutes from Phoenix but the canyon is still very desert-ed.

Where to Dine

The **Mammoth Steak House & Saloon** ($$) (☎ 480-983-6402) at the Goldfield Ghost Town is fine for a meaty lunch — if you don't mind Bambi's mother staring down from the wall at you. The **Superstition Saloon** ($) at Tortilla Flat is as well known for its wallpaper — business cards and dollar bills lining every available inch of space — as for its chili. The restaurant at the **Apache Lake Resort** ($$) (see the preceding section) serves up good American food and an even better view of Apache Lake. Globe's **Blue Ribbon Cafe** ($–$$), 474 N. Broad St. (☎ 520-425-4423), housed in a turn-of-the-century building, features Cornish pasties — traditional miners' meat-and-potato-filled pastries imported from the British Isles.

Day Trip #3: Casa Grande and Florence

This quick foray from the Valley — about 60 miles — takes you to southern Arizona's most interesting archaeological site and to a town that time — but not the state prison system — forgot. On this day trip, you may return via the scenic or the shopping route.

Getting There

To reach Casa Grande Ruins National Monument, take I-10 south to exit 185 and head east on Hwy. 387, which turns into Hwy. 87/287. After exploring the site, continue 9 miles east to Florence on Hwy. 287. If you want to take the same basic return route but stop off to shop, go back to I-10 and head about 10 miles south to the Casa Grande outlets at exits 194 and 198. For a longer but more scenic loop return, go north on Hwy. 79 from Florence to Florence Junction and Hwy. 60. Hwy 60 west returns you to I-10 and to various other Valley freeways. If you can take the time, detour east 12 miles on Hwy. 60 to the Boyce Thompson Arboretum (see Day Trip #2, in this chapter).

Seeing the Sights

Although **Casa Grande Ruins National Monument,** 1100 Ruins Drive, Coolidge (☎ 520-723-3172), became the nation's first prehistoric cultural site in 1892, the monument remains somewhat of a mystery. Archaeologists are fairly certain that the four-story "big house," or *casa grande* — named by the Spanish missionaries who stumbled across it in the late seventeenth century — was built by the Hohokam people in the thirteenth or fourteenth century but no one is exactly sure why. Some signs, for example, seem to indicate astronomical practices — walls that face the compass points, openings that align with heavenly bodies — but no real evidence proves that the structure was an observatory. The remains of 25 ovens, recently found near one of the site's ball courts, are equally elusive. Archaeologists think they were used to cook ceremonial mescal roots (rather than, say, Nathan's hot dogs). Open: Daily 8 a.m.–5 p.m., except Christmas Day. Admission: $2 per adult, ages 16 and under free.

The nearby town of **Florence,** founded in 1866, is home to another big house: the state prison. The prison moved here from Yuma in 1909 and still is the site of all Arizona's executions. The **Pinal County Historical Society Museum,** 715 S. Main St. (☎ 520-868-4382), has a collection of death-house paraphernalia, including hangman's nooses and the wooden chairs on which the condemned sat in the gas chamber (Open: Wed–Sat 11 a.m.–4 p.m., Sun noon–4 p.m., closed mid-July through Aug; admission by donation). The **McFarland State Historic Park,** Main and Ruggles (☎ 520-868-5216), a striking adobe that served as the town's first (1878) courthouse, displays some scary antique medical instruments and screens videos of World War II's largest POW camp, located near Florence (Open: Thu–Mon 8 a.m.–5 p.m.; Admission: $2 adults, $1 ages 7–13, 6 and under free). The early, clean-lined courthouse was replaced in 1891 by the ornate Victorian-style **Pinal County Courthouse,** at Pinal and 11th Street, the oldest public building still in daily use in Arizona. The courthouse is impressive, but chronometrically challenged: To save money on repairs, four clocks, all perpetually reading 11:44 or 8:58, were painted on the tower.

Take exit 198 off I-10 to reach the **Tanger Factory Outlet Center** (☎ **800-4TANGER** or 520-836-0897), with more than 50 stores, including Liz Claiborne, Guess, Reebok, and Carol Little. If the outlet doesn't offer enough shopping for you, join Shopper's Anonymous or stop at the **Factory Stores of America** (☎ **800-SHOP-USA** or 520-421-0112); its 30-odd outlets aren't especially exciting, but the mall houses a decent discount bookstore.

Taking a Tour

From November through April, rangers give 30-minute guided tours of the Casa Grande Ruins at regular intervals during the day. A tour of some of the 139 buildings in Florence listed on the National Register of Historic Places is offered only on the first Saturday in February. However, you can pick up a map from the **Florence Chamber of Commerce,** 291 N. Bailey St. (☎ **800-437-9433;** Internet: www.florenceaz.org; Open: 10 a.m.–4 p.m. Mon–Fri), and tour the homes on your own.

Where to Stay

Plenty of motels are available in Casa Grande (the town, not the ruin) but the area's only real sleeping standout is Florence's **Rancho Sonora Inn** ($–$$), 9198 North Hwy. 79 (☎ **800-205-6817**; Fax: 520-868-8000, E-mail: rancho@c2i2.com; Internet: www.florenceaz.org/ranchosonora). This inn is a converted 1930s adobe guest ranch with a walled courtyard; cottages with kitchenettes are available too. If you take the scenic Hwy. 60 route, consider bunking at the Gold Canyon Golf Resort (see Day Trip #2, in this chapter).

Where to Dine

The Sicilian-born owners of **A&M Pizza** ($–$$), 445 W. Hwy 287 (☎ **520- 868-0170**), just outside Florence on the Casa Grande Ruins approach, guarantee their pies' authenticity. **Murphy's Soup & Salad** ($), 310 N. Main St. in downtown Florence (☎ **520-868-0027**), had its 15 minutes of fame in 1985, when it doubled as a drugstore in the movie *Murphy's Romance.* Enjoy good, fresh versions of the light dishes for which this place is named while watching James Garner and Sally Field reprise their roles on video. Lunch only.

Chapter 13

Tucson

· ·

In This Chapter

▶ Getting the lowdown on Tucson

▶ Scoping out the best Tucson bunks

▶ Chowing down on the city's top grub — Southwestern, Mexican, and more

▶ Checking out Tucson's prime attractions and activities

▶ Shopping for crafts, Western gear, and more

▶ Finding the prime after-dark diversions

· ·

*A*rizona's second-largest city — far older than Phoenix, it was only outpaced by its more development-happy rival after World War II — Tucson combines New West urban savvy with Old West kicked-back attitudes. You've got natural attractions: The city is sandwiched between two sections of Saguaro National Park (how weird is that?), ringed by craggy mountain ranges, and shot through with swathes of pristine desert. But you've also got thriving dining, shopping, and cultural scenes, sparked by University of Arizona–inspired energy and anchored by rich Native American and Hispanic heritages. Add Sun Belt leisure staples like have-it-all resorts, world-class spas, and manicured golf courses, and we're talking a major crowd-pleaser of a metropolis.

Author bias alert: Tucson has been my home since 1992, when I moved here from Manhattan.

Getting There

Chapter 6 gives you the lowdown on the airlines that fly into Tucson. As I mention there, more carriers serve Phoenix, so, depending on where you're coming from, it may be cheaper for you to land in the capital and then drive or shuttle down to Tucson (see "Riding In," in this chapter). Railing and bussing it into town are other possibilities, though if you don't eventually get your own wheels, sightseeing isn't easy.

Cancel That Camel — Hump(h)

Tucson sits smack in the middle of the Sonoran Desert, which also sweeps across Northern Mexico, but don't start thinking *Lawrence of Arabia*. This high desert region, as it's technically known, gets 11 to 12 inches of rain a year and is lush with flora and fauna. But it does occasionally get very hot (up to 105 degrees in summer) — and it is a dry heat.

Flying In

The **Tucson International Airport,** 8½ miles south of downtown (☎ **520-573-8000**), is small and easy to negotiate. It has just one main terminal; the baggage carousels on the lower level are few in number, so even if your flight number isn't posted (it happens) it's pretty obvious which revolving luggage was just tossed off your plane. The baggage area is also where you find the tourist information desk.

You have several options when it comes to getting from the airport to wherever you plan to lay your head.

✔ **Renting a car:** You need a car in Tucson so — except for the slightly higher taxes you incur by renting at the airport — there's no reason to put off the inevitable. It's always a good idea to have your car reserved in advance, and in the busy winter season it's essential. The major car rental companies line up in the baggage area. The nearby courtesy phones, across from the tourist information desk, connect you to agencies without booths in the airport. (See Chapter 7 for tips on renting a car.)

✔ **Hailing a taxi or hopping a shuttle:** Many of the airport area hotels run free shuttles — you can contact them via courtesy phones in the baggage area — but as far as the majority of Tucson's far-flung lodgings are concerned, you're on your own. Head for the taxi queue across the street from the main airport terminal exit. Cab rates aren't regulated, but they're competitive, varying from around $1.25 to $1.50 flagdrop (the cost at the start of the meter) and $1.10 to $1.50 per mile. You may also get an unmetered cab with a driver who just quotes you a fare to your hotel (assume it's without tip included) which is often slightly cheaper than a metered taxi. Ballpark figures are $15 to $20 for central Tucson, and from $28 to $38 for an outlying ranch or resort.

✔ **Boarding the Arizona Stagecoach:** The shuttle booth for the van service (☎ **520-889-1000**) is next to the Hertz stand on the lower airport level. For most of the downtown and central Tucson hotels, rates are $14 per person, $18 per couple one way, or $24 per person round-trip. To get to the hinterlands (where many of the resorts are), you pay $25 per person one way, $43 round-trip, or $34 per couple each way. Kids under 12 ride free when traveling with an adult (or a reasonable facsimile thereof). You don't have to reserve in advance when you arrive, but you need to call at least 24 hours ahead to get a van back to the airport.

If two or more of you are heading to central Tucson together, it generally makes sense to take a taxi rather than the shuttle. Prices are comparable when you add up the cost of the individual shuttle fares, and a cab takes you straight to your destination — do not pass go, do not drop anyone else off.

✔ **Taking the bus:** If you're traveling light and have lots of time (but not much money) to spare, catch the city Sun Tran (☎ 520- 792-9222) bus number 11; the stop is just to the left of the lower level as you leave the terminal. Buses run every half hour from about 6 a.m. to 7 p.m. Monday through Friday, from 8 a.m. to 6:30 p.m. on Saturday, and from 9 a.m. to 6:15 p.m. on Sunday, heading north on Alvernon Way, one of the town's main north-south thoroughfares. From this route, you can transfer to most east-west bus lines; if you ask the driver nicely, he or she will tell you which bus gets you closest to where you're staying. You can also transfer to a variety of lines via bus number 25, which leaves less frequently from the same airport location and heads to the Roy Laos transportation center south of town. To find out about fares and transfers, see "Getting around Tucson," later in this chapter.

Driving In

I-10 is the main entryway into Tucson from practically everywhere. It snakes around town, so find out in advance what exit is closest to your hotel. (Another freeway, I-19, connects with I-10 in Tucson, but it only goes to Nogales, Arizona, just across the border from Nogales, Mexico.) Most people who drive down from Phoenix take the quick I-10 route. Unless you hit traffic (or stop at the discount outlets in Casa Grande; see Chapter 12), it shouldn't take you more than 1½ hours to drive the 111 miles from Phoenix's Sky Harbor airport to Tucson — the speed limit is 75 miles per hour most of the way. It is, however, a pretty boring and deceptively ugly ride; I'd hate for you to think it's a preview of what Tucson looks like. If you have time (about 2½ hours), and especially if you're staying in one of the resorts on the far north side of town, take Highway 60 from Phoenix to Highway 79 to Highway 77, both scenic; the latter turns into Oracle Road, a major north-south thoroughfare.

North or West?

Signs on freeway entrances in Tucson read "West-Phoenix" — which is confusing, if you assume (rightly) that Phoenix is north. In fact, Phoenix is due northwest of Tucson. If you keep driving on I-10 past Arizona's capital, you eventually hit the beach at Santa Monica, California.

Riding In

Although most people fly or drive to Tucson, some choose other means, one of which may appeal to you.

- **Shuttling in from Phoenix:** Phone **Arizona Shuttle** (☎ **800- 888-2479** or 520-795-6771) at least 24 hours in advance and tell them what flight you're taking into Phoenix's Sky Harbor Airport so they save you a seat. Shuttles leave from the terminal (ask where, exactly, when you book your seat) every hour on the half hour from 6:30 a.m. until 11:30 p.m. (fare: $22 one way, $40 if you book a return). The vans drop you off at (and depart to Phoenix from) three convenient Tucson locations. **Tucson Phoenix Shuttle** (☎ **888-584-6116** or 520-584-0000) does a less expensive version of this service ($18 one-way, $30 round trip, with discounts for students, seniors, and military personnel), departing Sky Harbor every hour on the hour, with a drop-off at three different — but also convenient — Tucson locations. You need to book a day in advance. The only catch (you knew there had to be one, didn't you?): Because the company doesn't have its own booth in the baggage claim area, you have to phone again and arrange for a later shuttle if your plane is delayed.

- **Riding the rails:** Amtrak's (☎ **800-872-7245** or 520-623-4442) Sunset Limited tootles into the terminal at 400 E. Toole Ave. four times a week on its Orlando/Los Angeles run. If downtown were still Tucson's hub, this would be convenient. As it is, you need to take a taxi (there are always some around when the trains arrive) to your new home away from home.

- **Taking the bus:** If you decide to go Greyhound (☎ **800-231-2222** or 520-792-3475), you arrive in downtown Tucson at 2 S. 4th Ave. — just across from the Hotel Congress — a good place to bunk if you're traveling on a tight budget (see "The Top Hotels and B&Bs," in this chapter).

Orienting Yourself

Some parts of this large city are easy to figure out, others less so. This section gives you the lowdown on Tucson's main geographical areas and directs you to a few additional places to seek help.

Tucson by Neighborhood

Like many auto-dependent western cities, Tucson is divided into geographical areas rather than neighborhoods. Well, okay, some neighborhoods do exist, but they're mostly in the older areas; the newer parts (the majority) of town are larger and definitely not strollable, and have uninspiring designations like Northwest and Eastside.

Address-ing a Few Issues

Central Tucson runs pretty much on a grid system, with Stone (north-south) and Broadway (east-west) as ground zero. Addresses on these streets and those parallel to them theoretically increase by 100 for every block you go from the Stone/Broadway intersection, so that 1820 E. Speedway is 18 blocks east of Stone — you get the idea. In theory, too, the odd addresses are on the north side of the street and the even numbers on the south — but sometimes (on Grant Road, for example) they switch when you cross Stone. And when you get to downtown, the Foothills, or any of the other outlying areas, all address-predicting bets are off.

And then there's the matter of the invisible addresses: It's really hard to see the numbers on most Tucson houses and businesses, especially when you're zipping by in a car; that goes double at night. If you're heading into unfamiliar territory — and you probably are — call ahead or ask at your hotel for helpful landmarks.

Downtown

It's not the city's commercial hub any more, but the area where the Spanish soldiers planted their flag in 1775 still oozes character. Many of the city's architectural treasures are concentrated in three downtown historic districts. **El Presidio,** site of the city's original walled fortress, has some of the city's most opulent early homes, as well as the Tucson Museum of Art and Historic Block and the gorgeous mosaic Pima County Courthouse. The Tucson Convention Center complex is a bridge to **Barrio Historico,** where many of the city's more modest early adobes still stand. It borders **Armory Park,** home to the ornate Temple of Music and Art and the Tucson Children's Museum. Downtown's boundaries are — very roughly — I-10 on the west, Toole (which curves around the railroad tracks and turns into 3rd Avenue) to the north and east, and Kennedy/E. 16th Street (they switch names at Stone) on the south.

The University of Arizona/4th Avenue

The **West University Historic District** developed just east of El Presidio after the University of Arizona was established in 1891. Bounded to the north and south by Speedway Blvd. and Sixth Street, respectively, and east and west by Euclid and Stone Avenues, it includes lots of beautiful turn-of-the-century homes as well as the northern section of the **4th Avenue shopping district** (which extends roughly from University to 9th Street). The University of Arizona campus adjoins the historic district on the east side of Euclid.

So Why Isn't It O'Tucson?

Tucson was founded by an Irishman, Hugo O'Conor, who served as a captain in the Spanish army — which explains why St. Patrick's Day is a big deal here. But the name Tucson comes from the Indian word *stjukshon (stuck-shahn),* "spring at the foot of a black mountain." The city often calls itself the "Old Pueblo," referring to the adobe barricades, or *presidio,* built on O'Conor's watch.

Central

Most real estate agents consider central Tucson's boundaries to be 22nd Street on the south, Oracle Road on the west, Wilmot Road on the east, and Fort Lowell Road or (pushing it) Prince Road on the north. Most of the town's business is conducted here, and many of the hotels and restaurants — but not most of the tourist attractions — are located in this area. You come across older, ritzy neighborhoods like **Sam Hughes,** east of the UA; **El Encanto,** near El Con Mall; and **Winterhaven,** on north Tucson Blvd. (renowned for its elaborate displays of Christmas lights), but strip malls, fast food restaurants, and low-key homes and apartment complexes predominate. Be on the lookout for some great old neon signs between bouts of golden arches. (See also "Exploring by Car" in this chapter, for the main streets that run through central Tucson.)

Eastside

After central Tucson was settled, much of the city's development moved east towards Colossal Cave and the Rincon district of Saguaro National Park. The majority of the housing complexes here are nothing to write home about, but the size of the lots — and the homes — begins expanding as you get beyond Pantano Road, where the desert starts to reassert itself.

Foothills

East of First Avenue and north of Ina/Skyline, the lower reaches of the Santa Catalina Mountains are dotted with expensive homes and upscale restaurants (saying people live in the Foothills is code for "they're loaded"). Lots of tony resorts have staked a claim to this territory, too. Sabino Canyon and Mount Lemmon are the main outdoor visitor magnets, but locals hike other parts of them thar hills, too.

Education — Second Only to Incarceration

When the thirteenth Territorial Legislature voted to fund a university in Tucson in 1891, much of the local populace was annoyed. They wanted an insane asylum and prison, the more lucrative institutions that rival Phoenix nabbed.

"The Ugliest Road in America" — or Tucson's soul?

A 1970 photoessay in *Life* magazine called Speedway Boulevard "the ugliest road in America." In 1994, *Arizona Highways* magazine defended the 23-mile-long drag as Tucson's real downtown, "a low-rise, linear strip devoted to the car culture . . . exhibiting the city's charms, eccentricities, and warts."

Northwest

New development is rampant in this part of town, which extends to the northern reaches of Saguaro National Park West and the Tucson and Tortolita mountain ranges; its eastern sections are often considered the Foothills. Two of Tucson's most popular malls, Tucson Mall and Foothills Mall (which, name notwithstanding, is not even close to the Foothills), are in the Northwest, as are several resorts and guest ranches.

Westside

The once-pristine patch of desert you pass en route to Saguaro National Park West, Old Tucson, and the Arizona-Sonora Desert Museum is slated for the next building frenzy. In 2001, a huge Marriott resort is scheduled to open at the east end of Tucson Mountain Park near Starr Pass, which already has a golf course and smaller resort and is in the throes of creating a large residential development.

South Tucson

This separately incorporated, largely Mexican-American city doesn't get much Chamber of Commerce hype, but it's a magnet for Mexican food lovers, who flock to the down-home restaurants that line 4th Avenue south of 12th Street, and to shoppers who frequent "the Lost Barrio" strip (see the "Decorator Fever: The Other South Park" sidebar in this chapter).

The Northern Satellites

Catalina, Marana, Casas Adobes, and Oro Valley, strung out along Highway 77 near Catalina State Park, Biosphere 2, and such far north-west resorts as Miraval and the Sheraton El Conquistador, are constantly battling Tucson and each other about their legal status (they want their own services and governments; Tucson wants their tax dollars). Part of Tucson or not, they're here to stay and expanding, as leisure and residential growth creeps northward. A Ritz-Carlton is slated for this area soon.

Street Smarts: Where to Get Information after You Arrive

The **Welcome Newcomers** organization runs a booth near the airport's baggage claim area from 7 a.m. to 11 p.m. (☎ **520-573-8100**). In addition to paging people and helping with directions around the airport, the volunteers answer questions about Tucson and distribute tourist brochures; if you haven't booked a room (bad! bad! — except in summer), they'll call around and make reservations for you.

The **Metropolitan Tucson Convention and Visitors Bureau,** Open Monday through Friday 8 a.m. to 5 p.m., Saturday and Sunday 9 a.m. to 4 p.m., is located downtown in La Placita Plaza, 110 S. Church St. (corner of Broad-way), Suite 7199 (☎ **520-624-1817**; Internet: www.visittucson.org).

Getting Around

Tucson is v-e-r-y s-p-r-e-a-d o-u-t (we're talking a metropolitan area of almost 500 square miles) and its public transportation system is limited. Unless you can afford a private chauffeur or want to rely on tour companies, you need to drive to the city's prime attractions.

Some Tucson Driving Oddities — and Tips

Come winter, tourists, UA students, and snowbirds (northern retirees down for the season), all converge (well, with luck, not literally) on Tucson's roads, which makes for some, er, interesting traffic interactions. Other quirks to watch out for:

✔ The left-turn arrow appears at the end of the green light, not the beginning.

✔ The center turn lanes of Grant Road and Broadway are transformed into traffic lanes during rush hour (heading west from 7 to 9 a.m., east from 4 to 6 p.m.) No left turns are allowed on the marked portions of those roads during this time. Confusing? You bet. That's why Tucsonans call these "suicide lanes."

✔ To find north, look for the Santa Catalina Mountains, the largest and most looming of the ranges that surround the city; they're visible from almost everywhere in central Tucson. Of course, you're out of luck at night, unless you know how to navigate by the constellations — which, as it happens, are terrifically visible most evenings (see the "Who's Calling Whom a Dim Bulb" sidebar, in this chapter).

And, be aware that no matter how ludicrous the "Do Not Enter When Flooded" signs look most of the year, when it rains, it pours, and Tucson has no real drainage system. Take those signs seriously; every year at least one person who ignored them makes the 10 o'clock news — as a drowning victim.

Who's Calling Whom a Dim Bulb?

If you think Tucson's streets seem darker than those in most other cities, you're not imagining it. The many astronomical observatories in and around the city — more in a 50-mile radius than anywhere else in the world (see Chapter 14) — have inspired ordinances to help prevent light pollution. For example, lights have to be aimed downwards, rather than up beyond the horizon, and athletic fields have to call lights-out by 10:30 p.m. The International Dark-Sky Association (www.darksky.org) is headquartered in Tucson; check out the site if you want to find out how good being kept in the dark can be.

Exploring by Car

If the bad news is that you need to rent a car in Tucson, the good news is that driving around town is relatively low stress. Unlike Phoenix and the Valley of the Sun, which are loop de loop with raised asphalt, Tucson has only I-10 as a freeway and, because it runs on the west side of a town that's spreading east, it's used more as an escape route than as a way of getting around. As a result, you actually get to see the city when you drive here (okay, maybe more slowly than you might want to at times). And, except in downtown, where they tend towards the one-way and narrow, Tucson's streets are generally wide, well marked, and dual-direction; on the largest of them, center turn lanes help ease the traffic flow. The main east-west thoroughfares in central Tucson are, from north to south: River, Ft. Lowell, Grant, Speedway, Broadway, and 22nd St. Popular north-south streets (from the west) are Oracle, Stone, Campbell, Alvernon, Swan, Craycroft, Wilmot/Tanque Verde, and Kolb.

Getting around by Taxi

Don't even think about trying to hail a cab on the street; if you want a ride, phone ahead for one. And because the town is so spread out, you're not likely to get away cheap. Taxi rates vary, so ask in advance what it costs to get where you're going. A few of the more reliable cab companies include **Allstate** (☎ 520-798-1111), **ABC** (☎ 520-623-7979), and **Yellow Cab** (☎ 520-624-6611). The drivers of **Fiesta Taxi** (☎ 520- 622-7777) speak both English and Spanish.

Riding the Bus

Tucson's public bus system, **Sun Tran** (☎ 520-792-9222), is clean and pleasant, but its hours of operation and routes don't cut it for most tourist purposes (for example, many lines stop running after 6:30 or 7 p.m.). The system gets you around central Tucson, though, which includes several of the sights and shops detailed in this chapter. Fares run $1 for adults, 40¢ for seniors; 5 and under are free. You need exact change and to request a (free) transfer as soon as you board the bus.

Hoofing It

The downtown historic neighborhoods and the University of Arizona/ 4th Avenue areas are really the only desirable strolling spots. Most of the other walking you can do is around malls or in the desert — where it's called hiking.

Where to Stay

Tucson has been in the hospitality business for a long time — dudes started coming to the ranches in the 1920s — and it shows. These days the city has something to suit every lodging taste and budget, from inexpensive chain motels to some of the country's ritziest resorts and spas (in fact, Tucson also has two, world-famous, destination spas, Canyon Ranch and Miraval). Because you may have a clue as to whether you want to stay in a spa, resort, guest ranch, hotel, or B&B (see Chapter 8 for more about these different lodging types), I divided this section into those categories.

Christmas to mid-March is called high season for a reason — the room rates go through the roof. Still, prices for resorts and hotels in Tucson are generally lower than those in other leisure-bent Southwest cities — Scottsdale, for example — and, in the general scheme of things, are a deal. Don't be surprised if you have a hard time finding a room, at whatever price, during the Tucson Gem and Mineral Show in the first two weeks of February (see Chapter 2); You may not have heard of it, but dealers and buyers from all over the world have. The events are held downtown, so during those weeks, your best shot at finding a place to stay is in the Foothills or other resort-filled outskirts, rather than in the central area.

In addition to the rack rates, each lodging has a price category shown in $ signs — see Chapter 8 for an explanation of both, and for details of resort features. When calling the resorts and hotels, don't forget to inquire about package deals — too numerous to include here. Finally, you don't have to shell out for parking in any of the places listed, unless you want to leave your Jag for the valet guy to test drive — and even then, that privilege is generally free (those fellows work for tips and that chance to drive your cool car); I note that in the listings, too.

Summer Sizzlers

Room prices in Tucson dip drastically when the mercury rises. Summer rates are sometimes as much as 70 percent lower than winter ones.

The Top Spas

Canyon Ranch

$$$$ **Foothills**

A branch in the Berkshires and a day spa in Las Vegas now share this high-cachet name, but this is the original, opened in 1979 on the site of the historic Double U Guest Ranch. The city has grown up around the facility in the last two decades. The grounds aren't as isolated as they used to be, but this is still a darned pretty desert getaway. And it's hot, hot, hot (and I don't mean the weather) with the latest equipment and programs — everything from tarot card readings to state-of-the-art body-fat measuring techniques (me, I prefer that info on a "need to know" basis — and that urge has never come up). It's also dry, dry, dry: They do not serve alcohol. If you want to be prodded into making a major life change, this is still the place to come.

8600 E. Rockcliff Rd. (take Sabino Canyon Road to Snyder, turn right, then look out for Rockcliff on the right; you'll see the signs for the resort). ☎ ***800-742-9000*** *or 520-749-9000. Fax: 520-749-1646. Internet:* www.canyonranch.com. *Rack rates: Prices based on 4-,7-, or 10-day stay. Sept 18–June 10 $2,905–$6,380 single, $2,360–$5,150 per person (double occupancy); June 11–Sept 17 $1,991–$4,427 single, $1,788–3,957 per person (double occupancy). Rates include all meals, 4–8 spa and sports services, $100–$210 allowance for health and healing services, round-trip airport transfers, tax, and a mandatory 18 percent service charge for tips. 4-night minimum stay (7 during Dec 25–Jan 2). AE, DISC, MC, V.*

Miraval

$$$$ **Catalina**

The new (healthy) kid on the block, Miraval was voted the world's top spa in 2000 by the readers of *Condé Nast Traveler.* It's easy to see why. The food is so good that it's hard to believe it's healthy (but it is). The remote desert setting is spectacular; and the Zen-style be-in-the-moment programs are less regimented than those at Canyon Ranch. There's no Prohibition here, either (in fact, the bar has a good single-malt scotch list). You can be as New Age as you wanna be, but you don't have to go in for the more offbeat things like equine therapy (that's for you, not the horse); you can just kick back and get pampered, head to toe. This spa introduced the supremely soothing hot stone massage; don't miss it.

5000 East Via Estancia Miraval (take Oracle/Highway 77 20 miles north of Tucson to Golden Ranch Rd., turn left, go 2 miles to Lago de Oro, turn right; you see the gates in another 2 miles on your right). ☎ ***800-825-4000*** *or 520-825-4000. Fax: 520-792-5870. Internet:* www.miravalresort.com. *Rack rates: June 13–Sept $350–$520 single, $295–$570 per person (double occupancy); Oct–June 12 $495–$645 single, $395–$520 per person (double occupancy). Rates include all meals and activities, one spa treatment per night/or round of golf, and round-trip airport transfers (does not include tax or 17.5 percent service charge added to all bills). AE, DC, DISC, MC, V.*

Tucson Accommodations

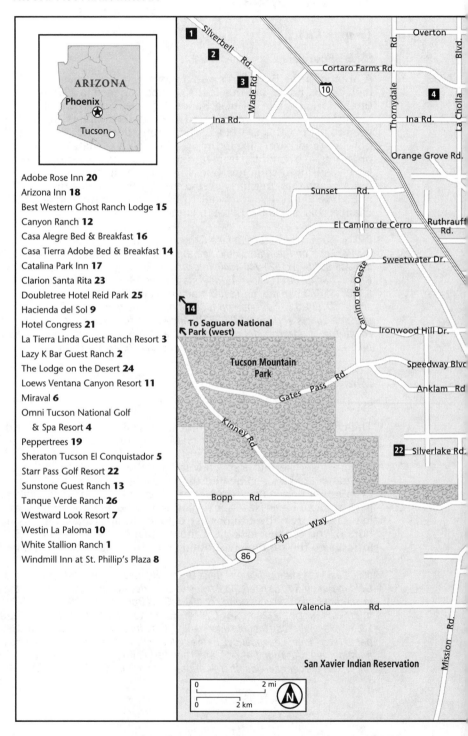

Adobe Rose Inn **20**
Arizona Inn **18**
Best Western Ghost Ranch Lodge **15**
Canyon Ranch **12**
Casa Alegre Bed & Breakfast **16**
Casa Tierra Adobe Bed & Breakfast **14**
Catalina Park Inn **17**
Clarion Santa Rita **23**
Doubletree Hotel Reid Park **25**
Hacienda del Sol **9**
Hotel Congress **21**
La Tierra Linda Guest Ranch Resort **3**
Lazy K Bar Guest Ranch **2**
The Lodge on the Desert **24**
Loews Ventana Canyon Resort **11**
Miraval **6**
Omni Tucson National Golf
    & Spa Resort **4**
Peppertrees **19**
Sheraton Tucson El Conquistador **5**
Starr Pass Golf Resort **22**
Sunstone Guest Ranch **13**
Tanque Verde Ranch **26**
Westward Look Resort **7**
Westin La Paloma **10**
White Stallion Ranch **1**
Windmill Inn at St. Phillip's Plaza **8**

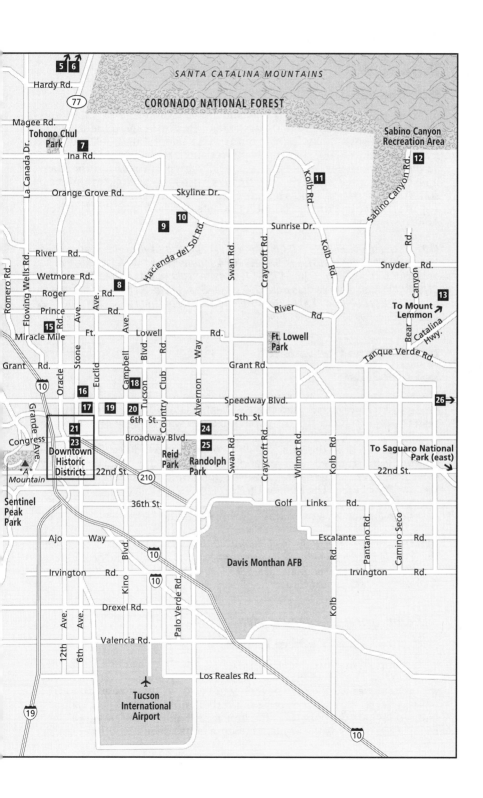

The Top Resorts

Hacienda del Sol

$$$$ **Foothills**

A movie-star magnet in the 1940s and 1950s (Katherine Hepburn and Spencer Tracy were among its devotees), this one-time dude ranch is now more resort-y than horsey, but with an understated, relaxed tone rather than the glitz of some of the newer and larger places in town. The 32 old-growth desert acres in the foothills are gorgeous, and the main house rooms are done in rich, deep tones, with Mexican folk-art touches; some of the separate casitas have fireplaces. The romantic Grill (see "The Top Restaurants," in this chapter) boasts a cool bar and a hot New American menu.

5601 N. Hacienda del Sol Rd. (between River Rd. and Skyline Rd., just east of Campbell). ☎ **520-299-1501.** *Fax: 520-299-5554. Internet:* www.haciendadelsol. com. *Rack rates: Jan 3–Apr $135–$190, suite $290, casitas from $325; May $115–$130, suites $200, casitas from $250; June–Sept 13 $75–90, suites $140, casitas from $170; Sept 14–Dec 17 $115–$140, suites $200, casitas from $250; Dec 18–Jan 2 $145–$195, suites $290, casitas from $325. AE, MC, V.*

Loews Ventana Canyon Resort

$$$$ **Foothills**

The most architecturally dramatic of Tucson's resorts — it's a low-slung modernist tribute to sand and stone — Ventana Canyon is also a bit stuffier than the others. But it has the goods: 93-acres with an eye-popping Santa Catalina backdrop, including two top-rated golf courses — plus a place where you can drop the kids off guilt-free, while you indulge. Oh-so-tasteful, subtly desert tone rooms are about the size of a small apartment; they even have TVs in the marble baths. Dining options include the swank Ventana Room (see "The Runner-Up Restaurants," in this chapter), and the Flying V, where you can sample the chef's creative Southwest/Latin American cuisine on a patio while gazing out at the 18th hole.

7000 N. Resort Dr. (at N. Kolb and E. Sunrise Dr.) ☎ **800-234-5117** *or 520-299-2020. Fax: 520-299-6832. Internet:* www.loewshotels.com. *Complimentary valet parking. Rack rates: Jan–mid-May $355–$385, mid-May–Aug $110–$150, Sept–Dec $320–$345. AE, DC, DISC, MC, V.*

Sheraton Tucson El Conquistador

$$$$ **Oro Valley (Northern satellite)**

With a spread up north near Biosphere 2, the Sheraton is a bit farther from the center of town than Tucson's other top resorts — but, then, why would you ever want to leave when you've got 45 holes of great golf, 31 tennis courts, 2 exercise rooms, basketball, horseback riding, racquetball, volleyball, 3 pools . . . plus knockout Santa Catalina views? The rooms (separate casitas or main building units) define "southwest chic" and the staff is super friendly. Among the multiple feeding and watering holes, the star is the pigout Sunday brunch buffet, with a make-your-own sundae dessert bar.

10000 N. Oracle Rd. (about 10 miles north of Tucson; turn east off Oracle onto El Conquistador Way). ☎ 800-325-7832 or 520-544-5000. Fax: 520-544-1222. Internet: www.sheratonelconquistador.com. *Complimentary valet parking. Rack rates: Jan–May 24 $319–$488, May 25–Sept 9 $129–$320, Sept 10–Dec $254–$460. AE, DC, DISC, MC, V.*

Westward Look Resort

$$$$ **Northwest**

The New Age meets the Old West at Westward Look. Built as a private residence in 1912, turned guest ranch in the 1920s, and morphed into a resort in 1943, it opened a wellness center in the mid-1990s. Other on-site stress-reducers include the usual resort suspects — pretty much everything except golf — and soothing earth-tone rooms, with Mexican tile and (on the upper floor) beamed ceilings. You can tell that the Westward Look was a guest ranch because, in most cases, you can drive right up to your door — a nice perk. The Gold Room is excellent (see "The Runner-Up Restaurants," in this chapter) and you're also very close to a lot of great Northwest restaurants.

245 E. Ina Rd. (between Oracle Road and First Avenue). ☎ 800-722-2500 or 520-297-1151. Fax: 520-742-1573. Internet: www.westwardlook.com. *Complimentary valet parking. Rack rates: Jan 2–May $199–$239, June–Aug $99–$129, Sept $109–$149, Oct–Nov $229–$269, Dec–Jan $159–199. AE, DC, DISC, MC, V.*

Westin La Paloma

$$$$ **Foothills**

A conventioneer magnet (most of Tucson's resorts are), this sprawling pink Westin also gets lots of repeat family business, with Arizona's longest resort water slide and a separate children's lounge. Grown-ups don't mind the extra time to relax by the adults-only pool, play a few sets of tennis, tee off, and (starting in early 2001) get pampered in the resort's posh new Red Door spa by Elizabeth Arden. The copper-accented rooms all have private balconies that look out on the city lights, the golf course, or the lush grounds. The usual array of on-site eateries are okay, but Janos and J Bar — on the property, but not part of the resort — kick culinary butt (see "The Top Restaurants," in this chapter). The Westin's service consistently gets raves, too.

3800 E. Sunrise Dr. (at Swan). ☎ 800-228-3000 or 520-742-6000. Fax: 520-577-5878. Internet: www.westin.com. *Valet parking $10. Rack rates: Jan–mid-May $289–$379, mid-May–mid-Sept $129–$199, mid-Sept–Dec $229–$319. Holiday rates vary. AE, DC, DISC, MC, V.*

The Top Bunks for Cowpoke-Wannabes

They're no longer called "dude" ranches (hey, should we blame the surfers for that, man?), but by any name, guest ranches are a ton of fun, with hayrides, cookouts, singalongs . . . if it's corny and Western, they've got it. Expect other low-tech activities like tennis, basketball, shuffleboard, volleyball, billiards, and, of course, swimming. At the following top horsy hangouts, all meals and two rides per day are included in the rates, which are per person, per night, based on double occupancy, unless noted otherwise.

Lazy K Bar Guest Ranch

$$$$ Northwest   A major revamp in 1999 upgraded the facilities of the Lazy K without cutting back on any of its considerable color. Organized activities include cantering among the cacti in Saguaro National Park West and bi-weekly cattle drives, along with more tenderfoot stuff like tennis, mountain climbing/rappelling, and guided nature walks. *8401 N. Scenic Dr. (16 miles northwest of Tucson; from I-10, take W. Cortaro to N. Silverbell, then take W. Pima Farms Rd.).* ☎ **800-321-7018** or 520-744-3050. Fax: 520-744-7628. Internet: www.lazykbar.com. *Rack rates: Dec 20–Apr $152–$194, May–Sept $115–$161, Oct–Dec 19 $136–$180. Kids camp mid-June to mid-July (closed to adults); closed mid-July–Aug. Three-night minimum stay (holiday minimums vary). AE, DISC, MC, V.*

Tanque Verde Ranch

$$$$ Eastside   Opened in the 1880s and one of the country's oldest guest ranches, the Tanque Verde has gone upscale, with an exercise room, sauna, relatively posh accommodations, and seriously good food. But with 600 acres between Saguaro National Park East and Coronado National Forest (Paul and Linda McCartney had an adjacent spread, so you gotta know it's mighty purty land), this is definitely still the real deal. *14301 E. Speedway Blvd. (far east end of Speedway).* ☎ **800-234-3833** or 520-296-6275. Fax: 520-721-9426. Internet: www.tanqueverderanch.com. *Rack rates: Dec 16–Apr $160–$240, May–Sept $130–$190, Oct–Dec 15 $135–$195. AE, DISC, MC, V.*

White Stallion Ranch

$$$$ Northwest   This spectacular 3,000-acre spread has been owned and run by the same family for more than 30 years. If you actually know what you're doing on a horse, this is your place, though greenhorns are equally happy, and kids are crazy for the petting zoo. Rooms are frill free — no phones or TV — but comfortable. *9251 W. Twin Peaks Rd. (from I-10 take W. Cortaro to N. Silverbell, which turns into W. Twin Peaks Rd.).* ☎ **888-977-2624** or 520-297-0252. Fax: 520-744-2786. Internet: www.wsranch.com. *Rack rates: Oct–Dec 18 $112–$148, $749–$980 (per person per week); Dec 19–May $122–$175, $812–$1,176 (per person per week). Closed June–Sept. No credit cards.*

The Runner-Up Resorts

Omni Tucson National Golf & Spa Resort

$$$$ **Northwest** With great golf and a huge spa, this resort lives up to its name. It doesn't have the character of some of the other resorts, but all the amenities, plus proximity to Foothills Mall, where you can shop, eat, and watch movies 'til you drop. *2727 W. Club Dr.* ☎ *800-528-4856 or 520-297-2271. Fax: 520-297-7544. Internet:* www.tucsonnational.com.

Starr Pass Golf Resort

$$$ **West** In the middle of what will be a huge hotel/residential complex (scheduled to be finished in 2002), this spot is currently a relatively low-key place to hike, swim, work out, and tee off on an excellent course. Plus, you're near prime westside sights such as the Arizona Sonora Desert Museum. Rooms are large, kitchenequipped, and attractive — and still a lot less pricey than those at comparable resorts. *3645 W. Starr Pass Blvd.* ☎ *800-503-2898 or 520-670-0300. Fax: 520-670-0427. Internet:* www.starrpasstucson.com.

The Top Hotels and B&Bs

Adobe Rose Inn

$$ **Central**

No howling coyotes (thank heaven), but you can't get much more Southwest. This centrally located B&B consists of a 1933 main house, two poolside cottages, and two suites around the corner, all done in tasteful Santa Fe style; my favorites — in the main house — have the original tilework and stained glass. There are coffeemakers, robes, irons, hairdryers, and TVs in all the units; two also have fireplaces. Other pluses: A bougainvillea-draped ramada overlooking an inviting pool and hot tub.

940 N. Olsen Ave. (at 2nd St., two blocks east of Campbell). ☎ *800-328-4122 or 520-318-4644. Fax: 520-325-0055. E-mail:* aroseinn@aol.com. *Internet:* www.arizonaguide.com/premier. *Rack rates: $105 fall and winter, $45–$55 off season (spring and summer); rates include full breakfast. DISC, MC, V.*

Arizona Inn

$$$–$$$$ **Central**

High tea, anyone? Croquet? Such civilized rituals plus the superb service of an earlier era have kept the Arizona Inn Tucson's lodging darling since its 1930 debut. Some of the rooms, arranged in pink stucco casitas around a perfectly manicured lawn, have gotten bland with frequent upgrades, but the tradeoff is a state-of-the-art exercise room. The fine dining room (see "The Runner-Up Restaurants," in this chapter) is worth visiting for all those massive wood beams alone, and the swank piano lounge is a local favorite for a romantic aperitif.

2200 E. Elm St. (between Campbell and Tucson Blvd.; you can't miss the low-slung pink building). ☎ ***800-933-1093*** *or 520-325-1541. Fax: 520-881-5830. Rack rates: Jan 15–May $210–$320, June–Sept 15 $89–$150 (including breakfast and nightly ice cream), Sept 16–Dec 15 $130–$140. Lowest rates are on weekdays; holiday rates vary. AE, MC, V.*

Best Western Ghost Ranch Lodge

$$ **Central**

This is not your average chain hotel: The logo was designed by Georgia O'Keeffe in 1936 as a wedding gift for the property's original owner (see "A Ghostly Connection" sidebar, in this chapter). The grounds include an orange grove and lovely cactus garden. The red-tile-roof guest units ooze old Tucson charm — and go for an old Tucson price. The once-rural area is now a semi-seedy motel row bridging I-10 and Oracle Road, which turns into Highway 77 — convenient, if not exactly scenic — but get a room as far from the road as possible and you can almost think you're still in the country (or the desert equivalent thereof).

801 W. Miracle Mile (just off the I-10 Miracle Mile exit, and west of Oracle between Glenn and Fort Lowell). ☎ ***800-456-7565*** *or 520-791-7565. Fax: 520-791-3898. Rack rates: Jan–Apr 17 $86, April 18–July 1 $54, July 2–Oct 1 $42, Oct 2–Dec 31 $42–$52; suites from $60–$124. Room rates include Continental breakfast. AE, DC, DISC, MC, V.*

Catalina Park Inn

$$ **4th Ave/University of Arizona**

You get the best of several worlds at this romantic B&B: It's close to the University of Arizona and 4th Avenue's shops but also near a quiet city park, and it's high-tone without being stuffy. You can ogle all the details of the gorgeously restored 1927 neoclassical home, including the original Art Nouveau tilework in several rooms. Views of the park and of lovely back gardens from the many balconies and porches compensate for the lack of a pool. And talk about deluxe: All six rooms have robes, irons, and hairdryers, and breakfast is served on fine china, dahling.

309 E. 1st St. (at N. 5th Ave.). ☎ ***800-792-4885*** *or 520-792-4541. E-mail:* cpinn@ flash.net. *Internet:* www.catalinaparkinn.com. *Rack rates: Dec–May $104–$124, June–Aug $75, Sept–Nov $84–$104. Rates for holidays and special events are different from those listed. Rates include a full (and deliciously gourmet) breakfast. AE, DISC, MC, V.*

A Ghostly Connection

Tucson's Ghost Ranch Lodge was an offshoot of the original Ghost Ranch in Abiquiu, New Mexico, famous because a section of it was sold to Georgia O'Keeffe. The ranch's owner, Arthur Pack, is better known here as one of the founders of the Arizona-Sonora Desert Museum (see "The Top Sights," in this chapter).

Hotel Congress

$ Downtown

Fun and funky, with its Western art-deco decor and gunslinger history (outlaw John Dillinger holed up here for a while), the Congress is definitely not for everyone; it helps to be under 30 and a heavy sleeper. The rooms are pretty basic and the rocking Club Congress is a literal blast, especially on the weekends. But the price is right, the location is public transport-friendly (you're right near the Greyhound and Amtrak stations and the main Sun Tran terminal), and who can resist a place with both its original 1919 switchboard and a cyber cafe? The hotel's Cup restaurant is the hip downtown hangout (the food's good, too).

311 E. Congress St. (between Toole and 6th streets). ☎ *800-722-8848 or 520-622-8848. E-mail:* hotel@hotcong.com. *Internet:* www.hotcong.com. *Rack rates: Feb–Apr $65–$75, May and Sept–Nov $48–60, Jun–Aug $32–42, Dec–Jan $58–$70. AE, MC, V.*

The Lodge on the Desert

$$$–$$$$ Central

The Mexican hacienda-style Lodge, built in 1931, has lots of mature citrus, winding paths, a central location — easy access to the airport and freeway as well as to restaurants on both the east and west sides of town — and (relatively) reasonable rates. A late 1990s revamp stripped the rooms of some character, but they still have beehive fireplaces and wood-beamed ceilings. Ask for one as far away from the main road, Alvernon, as possible; the walls are not especially thick. The on-premises Cielos restaurant serves good Continental/Mediterranean cuisine — but often a bit slowly.

306 N. Alvernon Way (north of Broadway). ☎ *800-456-5634 or 520-325-3366. Fax: 520-327-5834. Internet:* www.lodgeonthedesert.com. *Rack rates: Mid-Jan–mid-April $169–$249, mid-April–May $99–$159, June–Sept $69–$129, Oct–Dec $109–$215. Weekend and weekday rates may vary. AE, DC, DISC, MC, V.*

Sunstone Guest Ranch

$$$ Foothills

Name notwithstanding, this place is tough to typecast. Even if it had horses (which it doesn't), it's far too cushy and manicured to be a guest ranch, but it's also too sprawlingly hacienda-ish to fit into the B&B niche. Whatever you call it, Sunstone is wonderfully serene, with burbling fountains, winding flagstone paths, and huge, shade-giving mesquite trees. The rooms are spacious — they were designed in the 1920s for people who used to hole up in them for the whole winter — and, with their tony antiques as well as rustic touches, they have a Ralph Lauren-meets-the-Marlboro-Man appeal.

2545 North Woodland Road (off Tanque Verde Rd.). ☎ *520-749-1928. Fax: 520-749-2456. Internet:* www.azstarnet.com/~sunston. *Rack rates: Sept–May $145, June–Aug $95. MC, V.*

Windmill Inn at St. Phillip's Plaza

$$$ Central

A surprisingly good deal, especially for the location — a ritzy shopping complex near the Foothills neighborhood. The suites look good and work even better: Each has a separate sitting area with fold-out couch, microwave, wet bar, two TVs, and three telephones. The extras — free local calls and complimentary continental breakfast and newspaper delivered to your door — don't hurt either. And the guest laundry is a boon, especially if you bring the kids.

4250 N. Campbell Ave. (just south of River Road on the east side of Campbell). ☎ *800-547-4747 or 520-577-0007. Fax: 520-577-0045. Internet:* www.windmillinns.com. *Rack rates: Jan–April 21 $135–$145, April 22–mid-June $99–$120, mid-June–Aug $65–$85, Sept–Dec $99–$120. AAA discount available. AE, DC, DISC, MC, V.*

The Runner-Up Hotels and B&Bs

You don't need me to direct you to the dozens of chain hotels in town — you can find a link in your favorite (or at least the one that gives you frequent flyer miles) by phoning the toll-free numbers listed in the appendix — but these are a few that I like. I've also included some close-to-the-top-cut B&Bs, most of them centrally located; see Chapter 8 for additional resources.

Casa Alegre Bed & Breakfast

$$ Central   This conveniently located B&B is right near the UA, Fourth Avenue, and downtown, and just a straight shot west from Saguaro National Park and the Arizona-Sonora Desert Museum. Other assets: lots of beautiful antiques, a pool, hot tub, great breakfasts, and Phyllis Florek, the always helpful and friendly owner/innkeeper. *316 E. Speedway Blvd.* ☎ *800- 628-5654 or 520-628-1800. Fax: 520-792-1880. E-mail:* alegre123@aol.com. *Internet:* www.bbonline.com/az/alegre.

Casa Tierra Adobe Bed & Breakfast

$$ West   Unless you're a coyote, this is about the closest you can come to sleeping near Saguaro National Park West. This pretty hacienda-style house, made of adobe brick and located down a dirt road, does not have a pool, but rooms include kitchenettes and private entrances and the stars look mighty nice from the hot tub. Closed July and Aug. *11155 W. Calle Pima.* ☎ *520-578-3058. Fax: 520-578-3058. Internet:* www.bbonline.com/ az/casatierra.

Clarion Santa Rita

$$ Downtown   Today, this place gives little hint of its venerable history (the mosaic tile pool is a clue), but in-room coffeemakers, irons, microwaves, and hairdryers — not to mention the terrific Cafe Poca Cosa (see "The Top Restaurants," in this chapter) — go far to compensate. *88 E. Broadway at Scott Street.* ☎ *800-252-7466 or 520-622-4000. Fax: 520-620-0376. Internet:* www.presidiohotels.com.

Doubletree Hotel Reid Park

$$$$ Central This spot is pricey for a non-resort, but you're paying for a super-central location; large, comfortable rooms; lots of on-site recreation; and the bargain-price Randolph Park municipal golf course across the road (you can make up for the high price of your room in saved green fees). *445 S. Alvernon Way (just south of Broadway).* ☎ *800-222-8733 or 520-881-4200. Fax: 520-323-5225. Internet:* www.doubletree.com.

La Tierra Linda Guest Ranch Resort

$$$ Northwest Here you find a gorgeous desert spread near the northern part of Saguaro National Park West. Don't take the name too seriously: This revamped historic property is more of a B&B than a guest ranch (horseback riding and all meals except breakfast are a la carte) or resort (not enough activities, though a pool, spa, and a few tennis courts are on-site). *7501 N. Wade Rd.* ☎ *888-872-6241 or 520-744-7700. Fax: 520-579-9742. E-mail* ranch@tierralinda.com. *Internet:* www.latierralinda.com.

Peppertrees

$$ University of Arizona/4th Ave. Practically on the University of Arizona campus, Peppertrees has pretty, antiques-filled rooms in a Victorian main house as well as more contemporary units (some with kitchens and washer/dryers) in a separate building. Everyone gets to eat the wonderful breakfasts prepared by innkeeper (and cookbook author) Marjorie Martin. *724 E. University Blvd.* ☎ *800-348-5763 or 520-622-7167 (tel and fax). Internet:* www.bbonline.com/az/peppertrees.

Where to Dine

Dining out in my adopted home town has taught me two things: You can eat seafood in the desert — as one of my new friends put it when I balked at first, "So I suppose all the fish you ate in New York came out of the Hudson River?" — and you can find great food in a strip mall. Tucson has a surprising number of top-rate places to eat for a city of its size and chain orientation. But that's a fairly recent development. When I moved here from Manhattan in the early 1990s, modest Mexican *tacquerias* (loose translation: taco joints) and cowboy steakhouses were the local mainstays. Happily, they're still thriving, but they've also been joined in the last decade by far more sophisticated eateries, including many in the resorts.

Although the cuisine may be more sophisticated now, Tucson is still a cow town in many ways — that is, it shuts down seriously early. Prime dining time is 7 p.m. If you like to eat after 8 p.m. — but not too much later, as most restaurants shut their doors by 9:30 or 10 p.m. — you won't have trouble getting a table (even a good one) at the most popular spots.

Don't forget — lots of Tucson's top dining rooms shut their doors on Sundays. To avoid driving around, ready to eat your arm, call ahead. The resort restaurants and the ethnic eateries are your best bets.

Tucson Dining

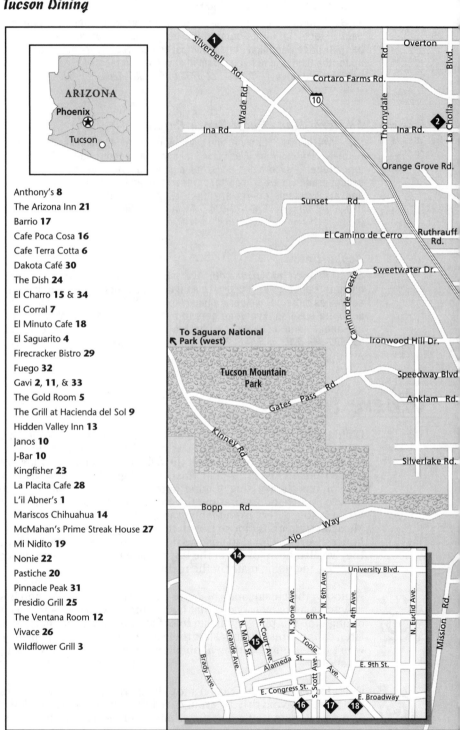

Anthony's **8**
The Arizona Inn **21**
Barrio **17**
Cafe Poca Cosa **16**
Cafe Terra Cotta **6**
Dakota Café **30**
The Dish **24**
El Charro **15** & **34**
El Corral **7**
El Minuto Cafe **18**
El Saguarito **4**
Firecracker Bistro **29**
Fuego **32**
Gavi **2, 11,** & **33**
The Gold Room **5**
The Grill at Hacienda del Sol **9**
Hidden Valley Inn **13**
Janos **10**
J-Bar **10**
Kingfisher **23**
La Placita Cafe **28**
L'il Abner's **1**
Mariscos Chihuahua **14**
McMahan's Prime Streak House **27**
Mi Nidito **19**
Nonie **22**
Pastiche **20**
Pinnacle Peak **31**
Presidio Grill **25**
The Ventana Room **12**
Vivace **26**
Wildflower Grill **3**

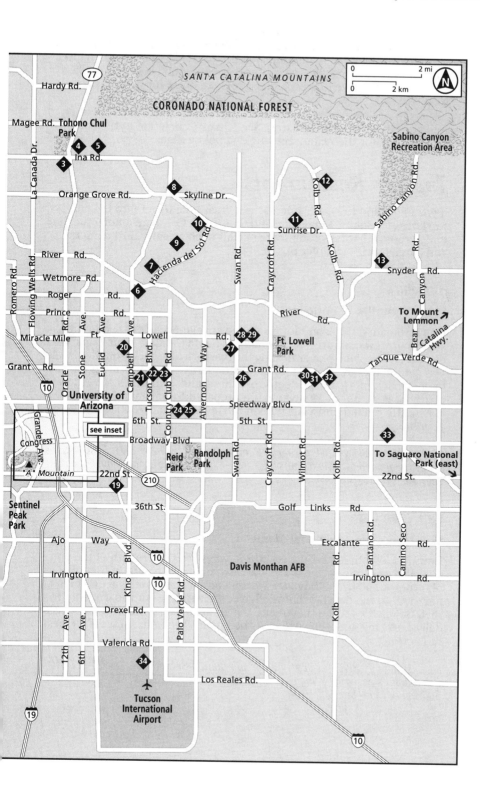

A couple of other things: Dark clothing is not required in Tucson after dark and some people dress very casually for even the nicest dining rooms. My rule: If the restaurant is in the $$$–$$$$ range (see Chapter 4 for the key to the dollar signs after the restaurant's name), I get fairly duded up, but I save that little black cocktail dress for trips back to New York.

And stuff those smokes (mostly): See "Quick Concierge" at the end of this chapter, for the restaurant smoking policy saga.

The Top Restaurants

If you can stand the heat, summer is a great time to get into the city's top kitchens. Janos, Kingfisher, and Cafe Terra Cotta are among the fine dining rooms that hawk summer specials such as early bird dinners and bargain-price sampler plates.

Anthony's

$$$$ Foothills   Continental

Isn't it romantic? Tucson's longstanding special-occasion restaurant has sweeping views of both the city and the Santa Catalina mountains; candlelit tables, a piano player tickling the ivories in the background . . . well, you get the picture. The Continental standards — lamb Wellington, say, or filet mignon — are perfectly prepared and Anthony's always gets plenty of *Wine Spectator* awards. Be prepared to have your water glass constantly refilled and your napkin retrieved should you let it slide off your lap.

6440 N. Campbell Ave. (NE corner of Sunrise Dr.). ☎ *520-299-1771. Reservations highly recommended. Main courses: $19.95–$29.95. Open: Lunch Mon–Fri, dinner daily. AE, CB, DC, DISC, MC, V.*

Cafe Poca Cosa

$$ Downtown   Regional Mexican

How do I love thee? Let me count the ways: To the breadth of the complex flavors of the regional Mexican dishes; to the height of friendliness of owner/chef Suzana Dávila, a walking ad for the beneficial qualities of her food; to the depth of knowledge of the servers, who so expertly roll their Spanish r's when they recite the chalkboard menu, which changes daily. I take my out-of-town visitors here when I want to show off the best of Tucson.

88 E. Broadway Blvd. (at Scott Ave. in the Clarion Santa Rita). ☎ *520-622-6400. Reservations essential in high season. Main courses: $11.50–$17.50. Open: Lunch and dinner Mon–Sat. MC, V.*

Café Terra Cotta

$$–$$$ **Foothills** **Southwestern**

Southwest chef extraordinaire Donna Nordin was still creating a new venue for her talents when we went to press (it's scheduled to open on Jan. 1, 2001), so I can't describe the setting. No matter: The food's the thing. Don't miss the macadamia nut–laden, garlic custard appetizer, served with salsa and hot crusty French bread; shrimp stuffed with goat cheese on a tomato coulis; and any one of the designer pizzas. A nice by-the-glass wine list and a loyal clientele is bound to keep things lively.

4310 N. Campbell Ave, St. Phillips Plaza; beginning Jan 2001, 3500 E. Sunrise, between 1st Ave. and Campbell. ☎ _520-577-8100. Reservations recommended. Main courses: $11.95–$23.95. Open: Lunch and dinner daily. AE, DC, DISC, MC, V._

Firecracker Bistro

$$ **Foothills** **Pacific Rim**

Straddling the Far Eastern fence between standard Cantonese/Szechuan and cutting-edge Pacific Rim, Firecracker strikes a nice culinary balance. The crowd is hip, the decor tongue-in-cheek — tiki torches outside and harlequin-pattern banquettes amidst a birch grove inside. I usually start with the spicy chicken in crispy lettuce, a kind of do-it-yourself eggroll, move on to the sesame seared ahi or five-flavor duck, and (always) finish with the coconut creme brûlée. Unfortunately, a reservation doesn't always guarantee that you won't have to wait for your table.

2990 N. Swan Rd. at Ft. Lowell in Plaza Palomino. ☎ _520-318-1118. Reservations essential on weekends. Main courses: $8–$15. Open: Dinner daily. AE, DC, DISC, MC, V._

The Grill at Hacienda del Sol

$$$–$$$$ **Foothills** **New American**

I have a hard time deciding what moves me most about this place, the dining room, the views, or the food (it's not — sorry to report — the consistent service). Enjoy the likes of lobster and wild mushroom risotto followed by a perfectly grilled pork tenderloin in one of the rustic-elegant dining rooms, or book a seat on the enclosed patio and watch the blinking lights in the city below. A mesquite-fired rotisserie in the open kitchen gives the meat and seafood its distinct but subtle smoked taste.

5601 N. Hacienda del Sol Rd. ☎ _520-529-3500. Reservations highly recommended. Main courses: $18–$36, $25 Sunday brunch. Open: Dinner nightly; terrific brunch. AE, DC, DISC, MC, V._

Janos

$$$$ **Foothills** **Southwestern**

Chef Janos Wilder was downtown's culinary star for years; now he reigns from on high in the Foothills as Tucson's blue corn king. The elegant soaring-ceiling dining rooms are a fitting setting for Wilder's dazzling

French-inspired Southwest cuisine. A la carte menus change seasonally and the prix-fixe menu changes weekly. Options may include a chile stuffed with mushrooms and brie served on a tomato coulis for an appetizer and grilled quail marinated in rosemary and served with a potato/corn risotto as an entree. The wine list is stellar — and where else can you find chocolate jalapeño ice cream (trust me, it's amazing).

3770 E. Sunrise Rd. at The Westin La Paloma. ☎ **520-615-6100.** *Reser- vations strongly recommended. Main courses: $26–$34; nightly prix-fixe dinners $65, with matching wine $100. Open: Dinner Mon–Sat. AE, DC, DISC, MC, V.*

A Taste of Mexico

A top ten list of Mexican restaurants in Tucson? No way, Jose! Locals all have favorites that they would defend to the death (at least of their appetites), many of them on South Fourth Avenue in South Tucson. This is just a sampler, with a wide geographical sweep. Expect the bustle level and the friendliness quotients to be high, the prices low (in the $–$$ range).

- **El Charro**, 311 N. Court Ave. between Franklin and Washington streets (Downtown)(☎ 520-622-1922), was opened in 1922 by the current owner's great aunt, who lays claim to the invention of the chimichanga. Don't miss the carne seca, made with meat smoked on the roof, and the great margaritas. A time (and tummy) filling bonus — there's a branch at the airport (central terminal, ☎ 520- 573-8222).

- **El Minuto Cafe**, 354 S. Main Ave. at Cushing Street (Downtown) (☎ 520- 290-9591), near the Tucson Convention Center, has a gringo-friendly staff who serve up barrio-authentic food. Other pluses: Late hours and a great beer selection.

- **El Saguarito**, 7216 N. Oracle Rd. just north of Ina (Northwest)(☎ 520-297-1264), lets you be as bad — or as good — as you wanna be: a "Corazon Contento" (Happy Heart) menu includes delicious low-fat dishes like bean-and-nopalito (cactus-pad) burritos and baked chicken tostadas.

- **La Placita Cafe**, 2950 N. Swan Rd. in Plaza Palomino at Fort Lowell (Central) (☎ 520-881-1150), is as upmarket as its tony shopping center home, but the excellent food and soothing atmosphere are worth the (slight) extra expense.

- **Mariscos Chihuahua**, 1009 N. Grande Ave. at Speedway (Westside) (☎ 520- 623-3563), is plain and simple, but serves up some of the best Mexican seafood in town.

- **Mi Nidito**, 1813 S. 4th Ave., at 28th St. (South Tucson) (☎ 520-622-5081), is where the local politicos brought President Clinton when they wanted to show him some down-home South Tucson cooking.

J-Bar

$$ **Foothills** **Southwest-Mex**

Janos Wilder has set up a more casual, kicked-back bar and dining room right across the reception area from his fine dining room. Come here to enjoy the chef's high-class cooking without the high-class prices. You'll never want to eat nachos any other way once you try them here: heaped with chorizo, chili con queso, smoked poblano chiles, and salsa fresca. Can't decide on an entree? Get the combination plate, including the terrific spicy jerked pork and the soft-fish tacos made with cabrilla.

3770 E. Sunrise Rd. at The Westin La Paloma. ☎ *520-615-6100. Reservations strongly recommended. Main courses: $9.50–$16. Open: Dinner Mon–Sat. AE, DC, DISC, MC, V.*

Kingfisher

$$$ **Central** **New American/Seafood**

Tucson's hippest roadhouse, with large, cushy booths, lots of neon, brick, and contemporary art, a terrific bar — and atypically late hours. The seasonally changing menu is a map of the current state of American regional cooking, with an emphasis on the two coasts; Kingfisher spearheaded (as it were) the drive to bring good fish to the desert. The fresh oyster selection is always awesome but use your excess-calorie allotment on the warm cabbage salad with bacon and bleu cheese; the desserts don't cut it.

2564 E. Grant Rd. one block east of Tucson Boulevard (Central). ☎ *520-323-7739. Reservations recommended. Main courses: $12.50–$18.50. Open: Lunch Mon–Fri, dinner and late-night menu nightly. AE, CB, DC, DISC, MC, V.*

Vivace

$$$ **Central Northern** **Italian**

Viva Vivace! It was here, in Tucson's best upscale Italian eatery, that I discovered you can find bliss in a strip shopping center. Among my favorite entrees from Daniel Scordato's open kitchen: grilled shrimp with wild mushrooms in a phyllo cup and a terrific polenta with eggplant and roasted peppers. Get your greens from a side of sautéed spinach with garlic, then reward yourself with some house-made tiramisu. I wish that the noise level in the sleek, stylish room were a bit lower, though.

Crossroads Festival Shopping Center, 4811 E. Grant Rd., #155 (NE corner of Swan). ☎ *520-795-7221. Reservations essential on high season weekends. Main courses: $12.50–$22.50. Open: Lunch and dinner Mon–Sat. AE, DC, MC, V.*

Wildflower Grill

$$$ **Northwest** **New American**

Everything's coming up roses for Wildflower, a chic contemporary dining room that looks more California than Arizona (check out the clever trompe l'oeil ceiling). Standouts include the spinach, stilton, and apple salad; the smoked salmon on a potato gallette; and the grilled ahi with bok choy and wasabi mashed potatoes (be careful: they bite back). Save room for divine desserts like the three-chocolate mousse, served in a martini glass. Snag a seat on the outdoor patio for great lunchtime views of the Santa Catalinas.

7037 N. Oracle Rd., Casas Adobes shopping center (off the SW corner of Ina Rd). ☎ *520-219-4230. Reservations highly recommended. Main courses: $10.50–$19.50. Open: Lunch and dinner daily. AE, DC, DISC, MC, V.*

The Runner-Up Restaurants

Fourth Avenue and University Avenue, near the University of Arizona, are really the only two areas where you can find good food (mostly of the casual, college-budget persuasion) just by strolling around. Most of the time you're driving toward a restaurant goal, but if you're on dinner patrol, a couple of stretches of road are particularly fruitful (also vegetable-ful). Tanque Verde, between Grant and Sabino Canyon roads is considered Tucson's Restaurant Row; Jonathan's Cork, City Grill, Yuki's Sushi, Sakkoro, Dakota Café (see below), and Fuego (see below) are all good bets. Campbell Avenue, between Grant and Fort Lowell, has an equally high culinary stock. It's near (though not within walking distance of) the university, so you can find low-key restaurants like the Native Café; the Blue Willow; Coffee, Etc.; and Beyond Bread along with more upscale spots such as Pastiche (see below).

Others that came close to the top of my roster include:

The Arizona Inn

$$$ **Central** Although it serves less than dazzling American/ Continental fare, you'll be more than sufficiently stimulated by the beautiful Masterpiece Theatre-meets-Bonanza dining room. Go for the steamed fish with ginger and leeks for dinner, and anything that catches your fancy at Sunday brunch. *2200 E. Elm St. (between Campbell and Tucson Blvd.).* ☎ *520-325-1541.*

Barrio

$$–$$$ **Downtown** This spot is cool to the core, with a stylish Southwest menu (the chicken quesadilla with roasted garlic, cheddar, and peppers . . . mmm), sleek Western deco decor, and a great bar. *135 S. 6th Ave. (just south of Broadway).* ☎ *520-629-0191.*

Dakota Café

$$ **Central** A hip, unlikely tenant of touristy Trail Dust Town, this cafe dishes up delicious designer quesadillas, spicy chilled scallop salad, and terrific chunky fries in two witty postmodern dining rooms and on a relaxing outdoor terrace. *6541 E. Tanque Verde Rd. (between Wilmot and Kolb/Grant).* ☎ *520-298-7188.*

Yo! Go for Topopo (Salad, That Is)

No one's exactly sure where the name came from and how it turned up in Tucson — or why you won't find it anywhere else. But everyone agrees that the topopo salad is a treat. It comes in many varieties but, basically, it's a crispy corn tortilla spread with refried beans and topped with lettuce, tomato, chicken, cheese, and, often, sour cream (hey, I didn't say it was lo-cal). Most of the South Fourth Avenue Mexican places and several of those listed in the "Taste of Mexico" sidebar (in this chapter) include a version of it on their menu.

The Dish

$$$ Central   The closest thing in Tucson to an intimate summer club, The Dish is the deserved darling of Tucson food and wine aficionados. The listings on the New American menu — "fancy salad," "big dishes" — may be playful, but items like the fontina tart and pork chop with cashews are seriously good. *3200 E. Speedway Blvd. (behind the Rumrunner wine shop, 1 block east of Country Club).* ☎ **520-326-1714.**

Fuego

$$$ Central   Fuego may be cozily elegant, but Southwest cuisine maven Alan Zeman knows how to wield a mean chipotle. If you don't mind being the center of attention while your food is being immolated, try the flaming Fuego! shrimp-and-sausage appetizer. *6958 E. Tanque Verde Rd. (between Kolb and Sabino Canyon).* ☎ **520-886-1745.**

Gavi

$$ Three locations   Gavi has cloned itself from its original Broadway location but remains true to the elements that drew the crowds in the first place: Reasonably priced, well-prepared Italian food — and lots of it — in a friendly atmosphere. The "no reservations" policy means you can expect lines at prime times in all three locations. *7865 E. Broadway Blvd., between Kolb and Pantano (Eastside)* (☎ **520-290-8380**); *7401 N. La Cholla Blvd., at the Foothills Mall (Northwest)* (☎ **520- 219-9200**); *and 6960 E. Sunrise Dr., between Kolb and the Ventana Canyon Wash (Foothills)* (☎ **520-615-1900**).

The Gold Room

$$$–$$$$ Northwest   The menu, divided between traditional Continental classics and more adventurous regional specialties, showcases chef Jason Jonilonis's considerable talents. Nab a window or terrace table for breathtaking city views. *245 E. Ina Rd. (in the Westward Look Resort).* ☎ **520-297-0134, ext. 413 or 418.**

Keep Them Dogies . . . Cookin': A Cowboy Steakhouse Sampler

Hankering after big meat in a down-home setting? Tucson's got your number. Your steak isn't always gonna be lean, your dropped knife may go unnoticed — but you're not gonna have to refinance your mortgage to eat here, either. You walk out of these places stuffed, relaxed, and financially sound. All these places are in the $$–$$$ price range.

- ✔ **El Corral,** 2201 E. River Rd., just east of Campbell Ave. (Foothills) (☎ 520- 299-6092) has been roping Tucsonans in since 1936; as the town grew, so did the original adobe ranch house. If you're primed for prime rib, don't miss it.

- ✔ **Hidden Valley Inn,** 4825 N. Sabino Canyon Rd. at Snyder Rd. (Foothills) (☎ 520- 299-4941), piles busloads of tourists into its fake, Old West saloon — and they always have a blast. Expect your basic steak and cowboy beans.

- ✔ **L'il Abner's,** 8501 N. Silverbell Rd., between Cortaro and W. Ina (Northwest) (☎ 520-744-2800), a former Butterfield stagecoach stop, has great mesquite-grilled steaks (or chicken, if you insist) and gen-u-ine cowboy cachet going for it. This place is so untrendy it still serves 32-ounce cuts of beef.

- ✔ **Pinnacle Peak,** 6541 E. Tanque Verde Rd. in Trail Dust Town (Central) (☎ 520- 296-0911), is renowned as much for its tie-clipping ways — the crowd just waits for a city slicker to come in wearing one — as it is for its large cuts of steaks and generous sides.

McMahon's Prime Steak House

$$$$ Central Tucson's swankiest big-meat palace — and the most expensive — serves surf (terrific Alaskan King crab legs) as good as the turf, and the wine list is massive. *2959 N. Swan Rd. (south of Ft. Lowell Rd.).* ☎ *520-327-7463.*

Nonie

$$ Central Not only does Nonie cook up kickin' Cajun and Creole dishes (fried pickles plus crawfish etouffe plus Black Voodoo beer equals heaven), but it also has literary cachet: The owner's father is mystery writer Elmore Leonard. *2526 E. Grant Rd. (just east of Tucson Blvd).* ☎ *520-319-1965.*

Pastiche

$$–$$$ Central Because Pastiche knows that not everyone wants to hold back at lunch or pig out at dinner, the same sophisticated but not overpriced New American menu turns up at both meals; half portions of several dishes are available, too. *3025 N. Campbell Ave. (just south of Fort Lowell).* ☎ *520-325-3333.*

Presidio Grill

$$$ Central   One of Tucson's first innovative dining rooms, the Presidio has a great bar, techno-chic decor, and interesting, well-prepared food going (and going and going) for it. Added bonus: The Loft, the city's main art cinema, is right across the street. *3352 E. Speedway Blvd. (east of Country Club Road in El Rancho Shopping Center).* ☎ *520-327-4667.*

The Ventana Room

$$$$ Foothills   This pricy place moves way up my list when someone else is picking up the tab for the excellent Continental food, harp-soothed fine dining room, and lovely views. *Loews Ventana Canyon Resort, 7000 N. Resort Dr. (at N. Kolb and E. Sunrise Dr.).* ☎ *520-299-2020.*

Exploring Tucson

East side, west side, all around the town . . . Tucson's attractions are as spread out as the city itself — more so, in fact, because some of the top spots to tour lie beyond the city's borders. Check out "Suggested 1-, 2-, and 3-Day Sightseeing Itineraries," later in this chapter, for ideas on how to arrange your days so as to minimize what can otherwise be major road time. And remember, it can get really hot around noon; if you're in town from mid-March to mid-October, try to be outdoors only in the early morning and late afternoon, and save the indoor, air-conditioned stuff for midday.

The Top Sights

Arizona-Sonora Desert Museum

Westside

My top pick for Tucson. Don't let the name scare you; this isn't a museum, but a terrific zoo and desert botanical garden. I love coming here with visiting friends' kids to watch them check out all the strange desert critters, from gila monsters to stinky javalinas (okay, so I'm usually the one that has to be pulled away from the adorable prairie dogs). The museum is mostly an outdoor attraction but a great mineral/geological display, creepy snake and bug house, and good gift shop can keep you indoors for a while. All in all, this place is BIG: Wear comfortable shoes and plan on spending an entire morning or afternoon here; at the minimum, allot two hours.

The general advice to come early applies double here: This place gets very crowded and parking spots fill up fast. Call in advance to see whether the Ocotillo Cafe is open; it has limited hours (high season, Thursday through Sunday, lunch only), but it's worth planning your day around having lunch on its terrace. The salads use herbs grown at the Desert Museum — and where else are you going to find prickly pear sorbet?

Tucson Attractions

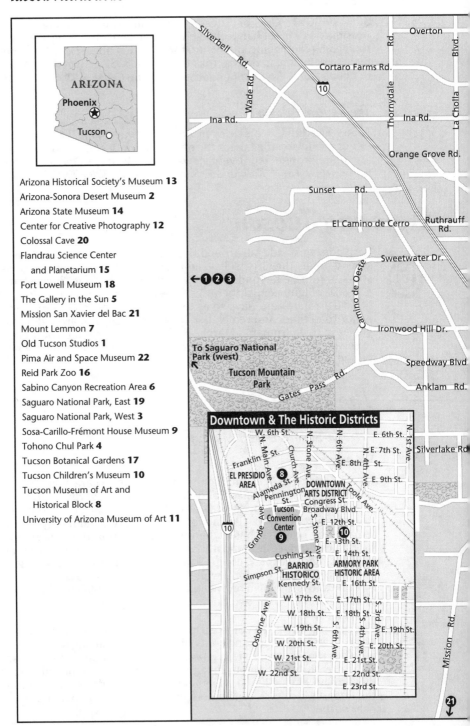

Arizona Historical Society's Museum **13**

Arizona-Sonora Desert Museum **2**

Arizona State Museum **14**

Center for Creative Photography **12**

Colossal Cave **20**

Flandrau Science Center
   and Planetarium **15**

Fort Lowell Museum **18**

The Gallery in the Sun **5**

Mission San Xavier del Bac **21**

Mount Lemmon **7**

Old Tucson Studios **1**

Pima Air and Space Museum **22**

Reid Park Zoo **16**

Sabino Canyon Recreation Area **6**

Saguaro National Park, East **19**

Saguaro National Park, West **3**

Sosa-Carillo-Frémont House Museum **9**

Tohono Chul Park **4**

Tucson Botanical Gardens **17**

Tucson Children's Museum **10**

Tucson Museum of Art and
   Historical Block **8**

University of Arizona Museum of Art **11**

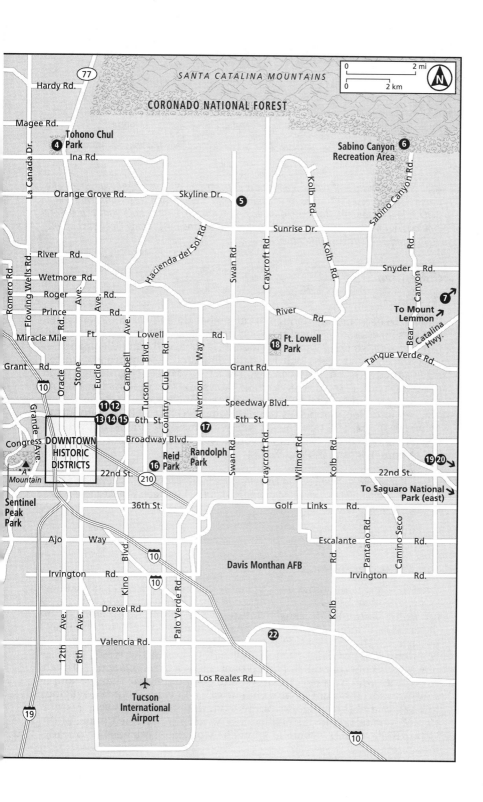

SANTA CATALINA MOUNTAINS

CORONADO NATIONAL FOREST

0   2 mi
0   2 km

Hardy Rd.

Magee Rd.

Tohono Chul Park **4**

Ina Rd.

Sabino Canyon **6**
Recreation Area

La Canada Dr.

Orange Grove Rd.

Skyline Dr.

5

Kolb Rd.

Sunrise Dr.

Romero Wells Rd.

Flowing Wells Rd.

River   Rd.

Wetmore Rd.

Roger   Ave.   Rd.

Prince   Rd.   Ave.

Miracle Mile   Ft.

Lowell

Hacienda del Sol Rd.

Swan Rd.

Craycroft Rd.

Kolb   Rd.

Snyder   Rd.

Bear   Canyon   Rd.

To Mount Lemmon **7**

Catalina Hwy.

River   Rd.

Ft. Lowell **18**
Park

Tanque Verde Rd.

Grant   Rd.

Grant Rd.

Oracle

Stone

Euclid

Campbell

Tucson

Country   Club

Alvernon

Blvd.   Rd.

Way

Blvd.

10

Speedway Blvd.

11 12

13 14 15   6th St.

5th   St.

17

Craycroft Rd.

Wilmot Rd.

Kolb Rd.

19 20

Grande Ave.

Congress

**DOWNTOWN
HISTORIC
DISTRICTS**

Broadway Blvd.

Reid **16**
Park

Randolph
Park

22nd St.

22nd St.

To Saguaro National
Park (east)

"A"
Mountain

22nd St.

210

Swan Rd.

Golf   Links   Rd.

Escalante   Rd.

Sentinel
Peak
Park

36th St.

Ajo   Way

Kino Blvd.

10

Palo Verde Rd.

Davis Monthan AFB

Pantano Rd.

Camino Seco   Rd.

Irvington   Rd.

Kolb   Rd.

Irvington   Rd.

10

Drexel Rd.

12th   Ave.

6th   Ave.

Valencia Rd.

Kolb

22

19

Los Reales Rd.

Tucson
International
Airport

10

The Roving Padre

In the late seventeenth century, Father Eusebio Francisco Kino established 22 missions in northern Mexico and southern Arizona; he is to Arizona schoolkids what Juniperro Serra is to California third graders, and what the Puritan founding fathers are to youngsters nodding off (er, learning history) in East Coast classrooms.

2021 N. Kinney Rd., 14 miles west of downtown Tucson via Speedway Blvd. and Gates Pass Rd. (you see signs as you head west). ☎ **520-883-2702.** *Open: Mar–Sept, daily 7:30 a.m.–5 p.m.; Oct–Feb, daily 8:30 a.m.–5 p.m. Last tickets sold 1 hr before closing. Admission: Nov–Apr $9.90 adults, $1.75 ages 6–12; May–Oct $8.95 adults, $1.75 ages 6–12, free 5 and under.*

Old Tucson Studios

Westside

It helps to be either old enough to remember the movies shot here when this was an operating film studio — it was built in 1939 for the motion picture *Arizona,* starring William Holden, Rita Hayworth, and Glenn Ford — or young enough to get a kick out of the simulated shootouts and assorted rides added later on. But even if you're an in–betweener and don't mind corny, you may enjoy the production shows, the (very interactive) actors strolling around in Western gear, and the film clips of classic westerns. You run into plenty of places to put on the feed bag, and lots and lots of souvenir shops. The ticket price gets you tons of activities and you can take advantage of many extras. If you're with kids, don't figure on getting out of here in less than three hours.

201 S. Kinney Rd, inside Tucson Mountain Park. ☎ **520-883-0100.** *Open: daily 10 a.m.–6 p.m., sometimes extended operating hours. Admission: $14.95 adults, $9.45 ages 4–11, free 3 and under.*

Mission San Xavier del Bac

San Xavier Reservation

Even if religious buildings aren't usually your thing, don't miss this one. One of the most beautifully preserved of the Spanish missions, this graceful white Moorish/Spanish structure is set dramatically against the desert. The Tohono O'odham Indians, for whom it was founded in 1692 by Jesuit father Eusebio Francisco Kino, still worship here, and the wooden statue of Saint Francis Xavier that lies in the west chapel is pinned with photographs of loved ones and small tin *milagros* (literally "miracles," which represent parts of the body or psyche that the supplicant prays to the saint to heal). It's worth coming just for the religious folk art; one of the members of the team that finished a 5-year restoration of the mission in 1997 called San Xavier the "Sistine Chapel of the United States" (and he should know) he worked on Michelangelo's original in Rome.

Lunch with a Mission

The **Wa:k [sic] Snack Shop** (☎ 520-573-9191) at the back of San Xavier Plaza is a great place to try Indian fry bread — fresh hot dough topped with anything from honey or powdered sugar to meat, lettuce, and cheese. Just looking at the stuff raises your cholesterol 20 points — but it's worth every point.

San Xavier Rd., 9 miles southwest of Tucson (take the Mission Road exit 92 on I-19 south). ☎ 520-294-2624. Open: daily 7 a.m.–5 p.m.; gift shop 8 a.m.–5 p.m. No admission. Three masses celebrated on Sunday, one mass each day Mon–Sat; if you'd like to attend, phone ahead for a schedule.

Mount Lemmon

Foothills (sort of; this is one of the hills that the town sits at the foot of)

Rarely is there enough white stuff on the ground for you to schuss down Mount Lemmon (see "Skiing," later in this chapter), but driving to the top is a peak experience any time. As you wind your way 8 miles to the summit of the 9,157 foot mountain, the terrain changes from desert to pine forest and the temperature drops about 20 degrees. There are plenty of places to picnic and hike (ask at milepost 19.9, the Palisades Ranger Station) and, at the top, you can hop on the ski resort's chair lift ($6 adult, $3 for kids) for spectacular views. Also at the summit is the tiny alpine village of Summerhaven, with several cutesy shops and restaurants (don't miss The Mt. Lemmon Café — fruit pie heaven).

Because of a $16.5 million road widening, Mt. Lemmon Highway will be closed every Tuesday and Thursday from 9 a.m. to 3 p.m. until early 2002. You can also expect significant road delays on Mondays, Wednesdays, and Fridays during that time — so weekends are your best bet. Phone the Federal Highway Administrations's Mount Lemmon Hotline at ☎520-751-9405 for the latest details.

Take Tanque Verde Rd. to the Catalina Highway, which becomes Mt. Lemmon Highway as you head north. ☎ 520-749-3329 (road conditions); 520-749-8700 (Coronado National Forest). Open: Palisades Ranger Station, Sat–Tues 8:30 a.m.– 4 p.m. in winter, 8:30 a.m.–5 p.m. daily from Apr 12–Labor Day. There's a $5 toll per vehicle per day for those not going all the way up, no toll for those going to Summerhaven or Ski Valley.

Sabino Canyon Recreation Area

Foothills

This is both a local favorite — hikers, bikers, and swimmers come here to take advantage of a terrain that mixes forest and (usually) water with desert — and a prime visitor stop, because of the fun Desert 101 narrated tram rides. The trams go directly (if not straight) to the top of Sabino

Canyon; you can walk the entire way back — it's all downhill — or design a stroll of whatever length you like and catch another tram back at one of nine stops. Another (talk-free) tram heads out to Bear Canyon, where a popular trek leads to Seven Falls. The narrated tram ride takes 45 minutes, round-trip; if you just want a quick zip through nature, you can stay on all the way. If, however, you want to hike (see "Keeping Active," in this chapter), you can spend anything from a few hours to the entire day (bring your own food, though — there are no concessions). In high season, volunteer naturalists lead free nature and geological walks through the canyon; call ☎520-749-8700 for details.

Sabino Canyon Rd. (drive 4 miles north of Tanque Verde Rd.). ☎ *520-749-8700 (Coronado National Forest visitor's center) or 520-749-2861 (tram information). Canyon admission free. Sabino Canyon trams $6; Bear Canyon trams $3, $2.50 ages 3–12. Visitor's center open Mon–Fri 8 a.m.–4:30 p.m., Sat–Sun 8:30 a.m.–4:30 p.m.; call for daily tram schedules. Call* ☎ *520-749-2327 to find out about—and book— moonlight tram tours.*

Saguaro National Park

Eastside and Westside

Strange but true: This national park, which has the world's largest concentration of saguaro cactus, is divided into two parts by the city of Tucson — which means you can pick and choose the side you want to visit, depending on where you're staying. The western section, or Tucson Mountain District, is smaller (24,000 acres) and more visited, in part because it adjoins the Arizona Sonora Desert Museum (in this section); combining the two is a great way to spend the day. It also has the newer visitor's center, which gives a great introduction to the desert, and easily visited Hohokam petroglyphs (rock art) at Signal Hill. The eastern Rincon Mountain District looks a little less dramatic at first, but its 67,000 acres cross five climate zones; it's also the only section where you can mountain bike on the dirt hiking trails. You can pick up hiking/driving maps in the visitor's centers in both districts, along with lots of excellent literature on the desert. It's hard to say how long you're going to want to stay here; you can do a loop drive in an hour or spend all day hiking or biking around. There are no snack bars or restaurants in either park section, though, so come prepared to picnic.

Western District: 2700 N. Kinney Rd. (15 miles west of Tucson via Speedway Blvd. and Gates Pass Rd.). ☎ *520-733-5158. Internet:* www.nps.gov/sagu/. *Open: Visitor's center daily 8:30 a.m.–5 p.m.; park roads 6 a.m.–sunset. Admission: Free. Eastern District. Old Spanish Trail (take Speedway Blvd. or 22nd St. east)* ☎ *520-733-5153. Open: Visitor's center daily 8:30 a.m.–5 p.m.; park roads 7 a.m.–sunset. Admission: $4 per vehicle, $2 individuals entering by bicycle or on foot.*

Tucson Museum of Art and Historic Block

Downtown

The Tucson Museum of Art itself is nothing to write home about (though it has decent visiting shows), but it's on the site of the town's original 1775 *presidio* and part of a fascinating art and historic complex. The modern building is adjoined via a courtyard to the John K. Goodman Pavilion of Western Art, housed in an 1868 adobe home. Connected to it by a breezeway, another nineteenth-century adobe displays the museum's excellent world folk art, pre-Columbian, and Spanish Colonial holdings. The Spanish Mediterranean–style J. Knox Corbett House, to the north, is a showcase for the Arts and Crafts period, and across the Plaza of the Pioneers, on the east side of the complex, La Casa Cordova's two small rooms show how Tucsonans lived before the railroad — not to mention air conditioning — arrived (don't miss them). Depending on your artistic tastes and historic interests, you may want to linger in some galleries and houses longer than others, but allow at least 1½ hours to do the whole complex justice.

140 N. Main Ave. (between Alameda and Washington). ☎ *520-624-2333. Open: Mon–Sat 10 a.m.–4 p.m., Sun noon–4 p.m. Closed: Major holidays, Mon, June, Jul, and Aug. Admission: $2 adults, $1 students and seniors, 12 and under free; Sun free. Free docent-led tours of the historic block are given Wed and Sat at 11 a.m. (Oct–May); you can also arrange for a tour on other days by phoning in advance.*

University of Arizona Museums

University of Arizona/4th Avenue

Okay, I know, this isn't a single sight, but I always think of it collectively because visiting the UA museums is one of my favorite things to do when I'm not spending time outdoors. All are interesting and, except for the Flandrau, free, but if I had to choose only two I'd go for the Center for Creative Photography and the Arizona State Museum (newer north building); the Flandrau would top my list if I was traveling with kids. The Center for Creative Photography and the University of Arizona Museum of Art are right across from one another, and the Arizona Historical Society's Museum isn't far from the Arizona State Museum; if you've eaten your Wheaties, you could visit all four on foot. The Flandrau, however, is on the other side of the campus; you'd really have to be an atypically fit museum buff to trek over there and back.

You're best off visiting the museums on weekends or during the summer (for a heat escape), when the students aren't on campus and parking's not a problem. The most convenient garage to the Arizona Historical Society's Museum and the Arizona State Museum is at Euclid and 2nd St.; the one most convenient to the Center for Creative Photography and to the Museum of Art is at Park and Speedway (an underpass leads from here to the campus). There's a visitor parking lot just south of the Flandrau building. The garage charge is $2 for the first hour, $1 for each additional hour; get validated at the Arizona Historical Society's Museum and the parking is free.

Arizona Historical Society's Museum, 949 E. 2nd St. at Park Ave. (☎ 520- 628-5774), explores the state's past beginning with the Hohokam Indians. This is pretty much an adult-oriented museum, but kids like the replica of a mine shaft. My favorites here are the library's historical photographs; you can get reprints of many of them for a small fee. Open: Mon–Sat 10 a.m.–4 p.m., Sun noon–4 p.m. Free, donations gratefully accepted.

Saguaro Savvy

It's pronounced *suh-wah-roh*. Say the "g" and everyone will instantly peg you as a tourist.

It grows only in the western Sonoran Desert, that is, northern Mexico and Arizona. Don't be taken in by those saguaro shots in films supposedly set in Texas or Wyoming.

It's supported by an interior skeleton. Its woody "ribs" were used by the Spanish to make furniture and roof cross beams.

It grows v-e-r-y slowly — only about an inch a year.

Those holes you see in it aren't potshots taken by drunken rednecks; they're pecked out by birds, especially gila woodpeckers, who call the cacti home. When the holes are large enough, they harden into cactus boots (not to be confused with cowboy boots, which are usually a little bigger).

It's the country's largest cactus, sometimes growing to 60 feet or higher. Saguaros can weigh 5 tons or more, sprout more than 50 arms, and live more than 150 years.

It blossoms once a year, usually in June. The white saguaro blossom is Arizona's state flower.

It's illegal to damage or steal a saguaro. Plow into one or stick one in your suitcase and you could get fined $250 or more.

The **Arizona State Museum,** just inside the main gate, near Park Ave. at University Blvd. (☎ 520-621-6302), first opened its doors in 1893, making it the state's oldest museum. The south building focuses on fossils and dendrochronology (that's tree-ring dating to most of us); the displays are interesting, but the multimedia exhibits on native Arizonans and northern Mexicans in the newer north building are even better. Open: Mon–Sat 10 a.m.– 5 p.m., Sun noon–5 p.m. Free.

Center for Creative Photography, 1030 N. Olive Rd., on campus, just south of Speedway Blvd. north of 2nd St. (☎ 520-621-7968), is a must-see for fans of modern and contemporary photography in general and of Ansel Adams, who first conceived of this place and is well represented here, in particular. Open: Mon–Fri 9 a.m.–5 p.m., Sat and Sun noon–5 p.m. $2 suggested donation.

Flandrau Science Center and Planetarium, Cherry Ave. and University Blvd. (☎ 520-621-STAR [recorded information]), is a terrific introduction to astronomy and more earthly sciences. The Flandrau has all kinds of cool stuff — a great collection of gems and minerals, some of which glow in the dark; an exploding asteroid exhibit that teaches all about space debris (and you thought you had trash!); big-screen science films; laser and planetarium shows; and a 16-inch telescope through which visitors can take pictures of the stars in the early evening. Open daily 9–5 and Wed–Sat evenings 7–9 p.m. Telescope open clear nights Wed–Sat mid-May–mid-Aug 7:30–10 p.m., Wed–Sat mid-Aug–mid-May 6:45–10 p.m. Admission: $3 for exhibits for adults, $2 for ages 13 and under; exhibits' admission free with tickets to laser shows and planetarium shows (prices range from about $5 to $7 for adults; call ahead).

University of Arizona Museum of Art, Fine Arts Complex, Bldg. 2, southeast corner of Speedway Blvd. and Park Ave. (☎ **520-621-7567**), makes up in quality what it lacks in size. Highlights include Fernando Gallego's 1488 Ciudad Rodrigo altarpiece and the world's second-largest collection of Jacques Lipschitz's sculptures. Open: Sept–mid-May, weekdays 9 a.m.–5 p.m., Sun noon–4 p.m.; mid-May–Aug, weekdays 10 a.m.–3:30 p.m., Sun noon–4 p.m. Free.

More Cool Things to See and Do

✔ **Get flighty:** You don't have to be aviation crazy to be riveted by the **Pima Air and Space Museum,** 6000 E. Valencia Rd. (I-10 exit 267), Southside (☎ **520- 625-7736**), where one of the world's largest private collections of historic aircraft are displayed in 75 outdoor acres and five indoor hangars. The more than 250 flying machines include the surprisingly low-key Air Force One plane used by presidents John F. Kennedy and Lyndon Johnson and NASA's Super Guppy. See the guided tour section ("And on Your Left . . .") of this chapter for information about the Davis Monthan Air Force tours that leave from this facility, and Chapter 15 for details of the Titan Missile Museum, also operated by the Arizona Aerospace Foundation. Open: Daily 9 a.m.–5 p.m. (last admission at 4). Admission: $7.50 adults, $6.50 seniors and active military, $4 ages 7–12, 6 and under free.

✔ **Go underground: Colossal Cave,** Colossal Cave Rd. and Old Spanish Trail Rd., 20 miles east of Tucson (take Broadway Blvd. or East 22nd St. to Old Spanish Trail, turn right to Colossal Cave Road or take I-10 to the Vail-Wentworth exit, # 279, and follow signs) (☎ **520-647-7275**), is the world's largest dry cavern; it's so big that parts of it still haven't been explored. Tour guides regale you with cave facts and romantic legends — like the one about the stagecoach robbery booty that's reputedly hidden here. Note: Colossal Cave may be large, but ceilings are often quite low; this is not the good bet if you're claustrophobic. Open: Oct–mid-Mar Mon–Sat 9 a.m.–5 p.m., Sun and holidays 9 a.m.–6 p.m.; mid-Mar–Sept, Mon–Sat 8 a.m.–6 p.m., Sun and holidays 8 a.m.–7 p.m. Admission: $7.50 adults, $4 ages 6–12, 5 and under free.

✔ **Explore more of Tucson's past:** In addition to the **Arizona Historical Society's** museum/headquarters at the UA (see "The Top Sights," in this chapter), two more branches should appeal to history buffs. The **Fort Lowell Museum,** Fort Lowell Park, 2900 N. Craycroft Rd., Central (☎**520-885-3832**), once the digs of the commanding officer of a military installation built to protect Tucson from Apache attacks, highlights life on the base from 1873–1891.

Artifacts from the Hohokam Indian village that predate the fortress are also on view in Fort Lowell Park. Civilian life — and attempts to live civilly on the frontier — are the focus of the **Sosa-Carillo-Frémont House Museum,** 151 S. Granada Ave., downtown (☎ 520-622-0956). The Sonoran-style adobe home, built in 1858 with saguaro-rib ceiling crossbeams, was rented out to territorial Governor John Fremont in 1878. Admission to both museums is free, and both are open Wed–Sat 10 a.m.–4 p.m.

✔ **Get artsy:** The somewhat sentimental depictions of Native American and Mexican life by Arizona artist Ted De Grazia at **The Gallery in the Sun,** 6300 N. Swan Rd., 1 mile north of Sunrise (Foothills) (☎ 520-299-9191), may not be to your taste, but the artist's former home, gallery, and gravesite, built of materials from the surrounding desert — and especially the small mission-style church where De Grazia is buried — are impressive. No original artwork is for sale, but you can get good reproductions in the gift shop. Free. Open daily 10 a.m.–4 p.m.

✔ **Check out some more cacti:** When it comes to prickly plants, Saguaro National Park isn't the only cactus patch in town. You can stroll along nature trails and wander through demonstration gardens at **Tohono Chul Park,** 7366 N. Paseo del Norte, 1 block west of Ina Rd., Northwest (☎ 520-742-6455). The lovely 48-acre desert preserve also includes a greenhouse, a small art gallery, two excellent gift shops, and a tearoom/restaurant (☎ 520- 797-1222). Sunday brunch is especially big; come early to avoid waits of an hour or more. $2 suggested donation. Park open daily 7 a.m.– sunset; buildings daily 9:30 a.m.–5 p.m. The **Tucson Botanical Gardens,** 2150 N. Alvernon Way just south of Grant (☎ 520-326-9686), smack in the center of town, has plantings that date back to the 1930s. A garden designed to attract birds and an area for carefully touching plants are part of the instruction — and fun. Bird and gardening tours are given at 9 a.m. every Tuesday, and docent-led botanical garden tours begin at 10 a.m. Wed–Fri. Call to find out about additional garden talks and classes. Open: Daily 8:30–4:30. Admission: $4 adults, $3 seniors, children free.

✔ **Put some spring (training) into your step:** Tucson is the only city in the country to host three major-league baseball teams for spring training. The **Chicago White Sox** and the **Arizona Diamondbacks** go to bat during the month of March at the new Tucson Electric Park, 2500 E. Ajo Way, near the airport (☎ 520-434-1367; Internet: www.tucsonbaseball.com). Ticket prices run from $3 to $14. The Cactus Leaguers turn over the mound from April through August to the **Tucson Sidewinders** (☎ 520-434-1021), the Diamondbacks' AAA team (clearly, this franchise assumes that reptilian names won't rattle the fans). Tickets are $4.50 to $8, with discounts for seniors, active military, and children under 16. Vying for fans of America's favorite pastime in March, the **Colorado Rockies** (☎ 520-327-9467 in season, or 303-ROCKIES otherwise) perfect their pitch(es) at Hi-Corbett Field, 3400 E. Camino Campestre in Reid Park (S. Country Club and E. 22nd St.). Prices for their games range from $4 to $12.

✔ **Spa down:** The desert can do a number on your skin, but it's also often considered a spiritual place (hey, if you're going to look like an alligator, you better have an attractive soul); the area's many spas tend to both body and soul with a panoply of soothing — and sometimes far out — treatments. Most of the spas at Tucson's resorts have day-visit options; my top picks are those at **Miraval, Omni Tucson National,** and **Westward Look** (all listed in "Where to Stay in Tucson," in this chapter). (But they're about to get a run for their money from the Westin La Paloma, which is debuting a Red Door Spa by Elizabeth Arden in early 2001.) Of the independent day spas, **Gadabout** has the most facilities and locations (five). The one in St. Phillips Plaza, 1990 E. River Rd. at Campbell (☎ **520-577-2000**), is the largest of those in central Tucson, but other branches may be more convenient to your hotel; check the Yellow Pages. Treatments start anywhere from $20 for a pedicure at Gadabout and go all the way up to $1000 for a full day — including hot stone massage, Dead Sea salt scrub, marine facial, scalp treatment, hair cut, signature bathrobe, and more — at Miraval.

Keeping Active

Ways to play in Tucson's balmy weather abound — but don't play too long or too hard without the proper precautions.

Biking

The best of Tucson's many bicycle-friendly areas include **Sabino Canyon** with a paved path to the top — uphill, but very scenic (it's open to bicyclists only from dawn to 9 a.m. and from 5 p.m. to dusk), and **Saguaro National Park East,** where hikers share several trails with mountain bikers. See "The Top Sights," in this chapter for both locations. Another option is **Rillito River Park,** a level, 4-mile trail that runs parallel to River Road between Campbell Avenue and La Cholla Blvd. along a (usually dry) river bed. The Tucson Transportation Department (☎ **520-791-4372**) will mail you a city bike map; you can also pick one up at the downtown office of the Pima Association of Governments, 177 N. Church St., Suite 405 (☎ **520-792-1093**).

Neophyte Neck Kneaders

One of the most prestigious massage schools in the country, Tucson's Desert Institute of the Healing Arts (125 E. 5th St., ☎ **792-1191**) offers hour-long Swedish massages for $20 to those willing to serve as its students' guinea pigs, er, subjects. These cut-rate pummeling sessions are available on Tuesdays at 1:15 and 2:30 p.m. during the school semester.

Also Getting Kudos from Kids. . .

Along with the other kid-friendly spots noted in this chapter, families have two more options.

Ideal for a central city afternoon outing, **Reid Park Zoo,** Reid Park, Lake Shore La., entrance off 22nd St. just east of Country Club Rd., Central (☎ 520-791-4022), is just big enough to keep kids occupied for an hour or two, but not too large to tire them (or you). The baby animal displays always score major points. Open: Daily 9 a.m.– 4 p.m., until 6 p.m. Mar–May. Closed Christmas. Admission: $4 adults, $3 seniors, 75c ages 5–14 accompanied by an adult, 4 and under free.

At the **Tucson Children's Museum,** 200 S. 6th Ave. at 13th St., Downtown (☎ 520- 792-9985), your energetic offspring can work off excess juice while learning about everything from the human body to electricity. The "Take a Hike" program lets kids explore gender-bending career choices. Open: Tues and Thur 9 a.m.–5 p.m., Wed and Fri 9:30 a.m.–5 p.m., Sat 10 a.m.–5 p.m., Sun noon–5 p.m. Closed Jan 1, Easter, Thanksgiving, Christmas day. Admission: $5.50 adults, $4.50 seniors, $3.50 ages 2–16; $14 for four family members on Sun; free for everyone third Sun of each month.

Reliable, centrally located bike stores include **University Bikes,** 940 E. University Ave. at Park (☎ 520-624-3663), which will loan you a regular bike for $10 a day, $20 for 24 hours; and **Full Cycle,** 3232 E. Speedway Blvd. (☎ 520-327-3232), where you can rent mountain bikes ($25 a day for front suspension, $45 a day for full suspension) as well as street bikes ($35/day). Full Cycle is also headquarters for the Southern Arizona Mountain Biking Association, which sometimes organizes group rides.

Bird-watching

Southern Arizona is a bird-lover's mecca. Although the greatest concentrations of birds flock to areas southeast of Tucson (see Chapter 15), the feathered ones also take to more citified spots. The best source for local birding information is the **Tucson Audubon Society,** which has an office and nature shop near the UA at 300 E. University Blvd., Suite 120 (☎ 520-629-0150). The society's publication, *Finding Birds in Southeast Arizona,* includes two chapters on urban bird hangouts and, during high season, members run field trips in and around Tucson and southeastern Arizona.

Golfing

Desert, traditional, resort, municipal — Tucson has golf courses to satisfy every duffer's taste and pocketbook. To get the lowdown on the local courses, write or phone **Madden Publishing Inc.** (2730 East Broadway, Suite 250, Tucson 85716; ☎ 520-322-0896) for a copy of *The Tucson & Southern Arizona Golf Guide* ($5). Another good resource is **Tee Time Arrangers** (6286 E. Grant Rd.; ☎ 520-296-4800 or 800-742-9939), which can tailor Tucson golf packages to your interests, budget, and skills.

Biking Tips

Despite being rated one of America's top-five bike-friendly cities by *Bicycling* magazine, and despite its many designated bike lanes, drivers in busy central Tucson aren't always as friendly to their two-wheeled road companions as you may expect. For hassle-free biking, stick to the recreational areas or the outskirts of town.

If you plan to go green(s) for at least a week or more, consider the **Tucson Resort Golf Card** (6286 E. Grant Rd.; ☎ 520-886-8800), which buys you discounts to ten of the area's top courses. If you're an early riser or don't mind teeing off in the late afternoon, consider coming to Tucson in summer when greens fees and room rates at the golf resorts dip drastically. I give you brief rundowns of the types of courses in the following list. (See also tips for desert golfing in Chapter 11.)

✔ **Municipal courses:** Tucson's five municipal courses are far-from-seedy (though they're often seeded) city greens. In fact, the flagship of these bargain courses, **Randolph North,** hosts the annual LPGA tours, while **Fred Enke** stands out for being an urban target course. For locations, greens fees (which ranged from $32 to $37 in high season 2000, without cart), and reservations, contact the Tucson Parks and Recreation Department (☎ 520-791-4336). To avoid disappointment, book the municipal courses at least a week in advance.

As if the municipal courses weren't cheap enough, if you play after 3 p.m., for as many holes as you can see until it gets dark (generally about 7 or 7:30 p.m. — Arizona doesn't go on daylight savings time), it runs you only $16.

✔ **Public courses:** Three of Tucson's newest non-resort courses, all desert track and extremely scenic, are already among its most popular public places to get teed off. No one ever says "nevermore" about the **Raven Golf Club at Sabino Springs** (9777 E. Sabino Greens Dr., Foothills; ☎ 520-749-3636), designed by Robert Trent Jones, the closest to town of the three. The **Golf Club at Vistoso** (955 W. Vistoso Highlands Dr., Oro Valley, north of Tucson; ☎ 520-797-7900) a Tom Weiskopf creation, was selected as Number 1 in Tucson by *Golf Digest* in 1999. Also in the north, at the foothills of the Tortolita Mountains in Marana, **Heritage Highlands** (5400 W. Tangerine Rd.; ☎ 520-579-7000), shows Arthur Hill's touch in a championship course that's very playable for all levels. Greens fees range from $99–$125 in winter, $40–$55 in summer.

✔ **Resort courses:** The Westin La Paloma has a guests-only policy for its greens, but you can play at all the other resorts even if you're not staying there — keeping in mind, however, that guests get first dibs on the prime tee times. The two Tom Fazio-designed **Ventana Canyon** courses (6200 N. Clubhouse Lane, Foothills; ☎ 520- 577-4015), renowned for their spectacular scenery, are the most popular of the resort desert target courses. Prefer traditional midwestern links? Go for the greens at **Omni Tucson National Golf Resort and Spa** (2727 W. Club Drive, Northwest; ☎ **520-297-2271**), site of the annual Tucson Chrysler classic. This resort, as well as Loew's (next to Ventana Canyon), Sheraton Tucson El Conquistador, and Starr Pass, are all detailed in this chapter's "Where to Stay in Tucson" section.

Hiking

Saguaro National Park, Sabino Canyon, and Mount Lemmon (see "The Top Sights," in this chapter, for all) are Tucson trekker favorites; if you're seeking (relative) solitude, the Eastern district of the national park is your best bet. Other options include **Catalina State Park** (11570 N. Oracle Rd., 9 miles north of the city; ☎ **520-628-5798**; admission $4) and **Tucson Mountain Park** (☎ **520-740-2690**). The latter has no visitor's center (or fee); you see signs for it just before you come to Saguaro National Park West. You can usually hitch a hike with the local chapter of the **Sierra Club** (☎ **520-620-6401**), which tends to head for the (foot)hills most weekends in high season. The best all-around trail resource is the *Tucson Hiking Guide* by Betty Leavengood, which rates hikes by difficulty and discusses details such as terrain. You can pick up a copy at the **Summit Hut** (5045 E. Speedway Blvd.; ☎ **520-325-1554**), which is also a good place to buy or rent hiking equipment.

Tucson's super dry air is deceptive; just because you're not sweating doesn't mean you're not getting dehydrated. Take plenty of water with you — about 2 to 4 quarts for a standard day hike, double that when it's really hot — and keep on drinking, even when you don't think you're thirsty. Try to down about 20 ounces of fluids — nothing carbonated, caffeinated, or alcoholic, please — two hours before you get started and then take a hearty swig from your water bottle every 15 minutes.

Horseback Riding

No matter if the closest you've come to a horse is watching *Mr. Ed* on Nickelodeon, this town has a mount with your brand on it. **Pusch Ridge Stables** (13700 N. Oracle Rd.; ☎ **520-825-1664**), backed dramatically up against the Santa Catalinas north of Tucson, offers everything from advanced private rides ($35/hour) to easy group trots through the desert ($20 for 1 hour, $35 for two hours, $30 for 1½-hour sunset rides). You can find your bliss — or at least have fun — at **Cocaraque Ranch** (6255 Diamond Hills Lane; ☎ **520-682-8594**), a working cattle ranch on the west side of town near Old Tucson. You have to gather together a group of at least ten if you want to take part in a cattle drive ($90 per person; Sept–May), but you can ride around with a guide until the cows come home — or until your money runs out (trail rides cost $15 an hour, $20 1½ hours, $25 2 hours).

Skiing

Yes, Virginia, there is snow in southern Arizona — sometimes. But because the **Mt. Lemmon Ski Valley,** at the top of Mt. Lemmon (see "The Top Sights," in this chapter) (☎ **520-576-1321** or 520-576-1400 for a recorded snow report), has no machines to help Mother Nature along

with the white stuff, chances are good that you may not be able to do
any schussing during your visit. When the ski area is open, lift tickets
cost $28 for an all-day pass, adult ($32 on the weekend), $23 for a half
day (starting at 1 p.m.; $27 on the weekend); children 12 and under ski
for $14 ($12 after 1 p.m.). Instruction starts at $50 an hour for private
lessons, $30 for semi-private, $18 for a 2-hour group lesson. A $49 first-
time skier's package ($26 for under 12) includes equipment rental, a
lesson, and a lift pass upon completion of the lesson. The Valley offers
18 runs, ranging from beginner to advanced. And this is not a snow-
board-free zone; you can rent them here as well as use them.

Mount Lemmon is not the place for serious skiers; you'll be disappointed if you want expert slopes. If you just want a quick downhill fix,
however, you can't beat going swimming in the morning and then hitting the slopes in the afternoon.

Tennis

Although the resort courts are restricted to hotel guests — Loews
Ventana Canyon, Sheraton Tucson El Conquistador, Westin La Paloma,
Westward Look, and Canyon Ranch (see "Where to Stay in Tucson," in
this chapter) have the most — good public netscapes abound. The
king of the city park tennis scene is **Randolph Tennis Center** (50 S.
Alvernon Way; ☎ 520-791-4896), with 25 courts, 11 of them night lit.
Fort Lowell Park (2900 N. Craycroft Rd.; ☎ 520-791-2584) and **Himmel
Park** (1000 N. Tucson Blvd.; ☎ 520-791-3276) have eight lighted courts
each. All are in central Tucson and all charge ridiculously reasonable
fees: $2 per adult per 1½ hour, plus $6 per court for night lighting. Ft.
Lowell reduces the fees to $1 for ages 17 and under and seniors;
Himmel's cost for seniors is $1, too, and the courts are free (but not
always unoccupied) from about 11 a.m. to 5:30 p.m. No reservations
are taken: First come, first served (or serving). The least crowded
times to play are from about 10 a.m. to 3 p.m., which is, of course,
when it's the most uncomfortably warm.

And on Your Left, Mission San Xavier del Bac: Seeing Tucson by Guided Tour

If you don't drive or just don't want the hassle of trying to find your
way around a large, new city, you have some good general sightseeing
options. Want to focus on some special interests? In addition to the
tours covered here, you can find more in this chapter's listings for
Sabino Canyon and Tucson Museum of Art (both in "The Top Sights),
Tucson Botanical Gardens (in "More Cool Things to See and Do"), and
Tucson Audubon Society (in "Keeping Active").

General Tours

Great Western Tours (☎ 520-572-1660; Internet: www.
greatwesterntours.com) has the largest menu of Tucson
excursions, ranging from 3-hour city tours for $30 per person to
all-day trips to Tombstone and Bisbee (see Chapter 15) for $85.
You're picked up at your hotel and transported to your destination(s)
of choice.

Desert Tours

Sunshine Jeep Tours, 9040 N. Oracle Rd., Ste. D (☎ **520-742-1943;** Internet: www.sunshinejeeptours.com), gives you a great introduction to the desert in the Tortolita Mountains northwest of Tucson. You're off-roaded to an archaeological site with ancient petroglyphs (rock art) and you get the dirt on all the local flora and fauna (snake handling optional). A 3½-hour tour costs $48 for adults, $36 ages 11–15, $24 6–10, 5 and under free. **High Desert Convoys, Inc.,** 16200 N. Columbus Blvd. (☎ **800-93-TOURS** or 520-818-1848; Internet: www.arizonaguide.com/highdesertconvoys) uses World War II jeeps for a similar desert jaunt, but adds a riparian (near water) habitat to its nature stops. Prices are $47.25 for adults, $25 12 and under. In the slow but not too hot months of September, October, and November, the company adds a full-day tour of nearby ghost towns ($65 adults).

Archaeology Tours

Enjoy channeling ancient civilizations (if only on the Discovery channel)? Dig it! The nonprofit **Center for Desert Archaeology** (☎ **520- 885-6283**) offers three tours, including prehistoric Hohokam ball courts in Santa Catalina State Park, petroglyphs in Saguaro National Park, and stone circles near A Mountain. Prices for a 4½-hour tour begin at $65 for one person, $47 each for two people, and go down from there as the number of participants increases; it's cheaper, too, if you're willing to follow the guide in your own car. Rates include a year's membership in the society. **Old Pueblo Archaeology Center** (☎ **520-798-1201;** Internet: www.azstarnet.com/nonprofit/oldpueblo) has a regular schedule of 2-hour tours of a Hohokam ruin in Sabino Canyon on Saturdays from September through April from 9 a.m. to 11 a.m.; it's $10 for adults, $2 for 12 and under. You can also book private tours with the group.

Aviation Tours

Get on a higher plane with a bus tour of **AMARC** (Aerospace Maintenance and Regeneration Center), a 2,700-acre facility at the Davis Monthan Air Force base, which hosts more than 5,000 aircraft. They (the tours, not the planes) leave every 90 minutes from the Pima Air & Space Museum (see "More Cool Things to See and Do," in this chapter), starting at 9:30 a.m. Monday through Friday, and take about an hour. It's $5 for adults; with picture ID, discount rate available for seniors and military ($3.50) and ages 16 and under ($3). Reservations (☎ **520-574-0462**) are required at least a day in advance.

History Tours

Arrange for walking tours of the historic **El Presidio** district by calling the Arizona Historical Society at ☎ **520-622-0956** ($5 per person; Nov–Mar only). You can get a free self-guided tour map of the district from the Tucson Museum of Art (see "The Top Sights," in this chapter) or the Metropolitan Tucson Convention & Visitors Bureau (see "Quick Concierge," at the end of this chapter).

Suggested 1-, 2-, and 3-Day Sightseeing Itineraries

When planning your perfect Tucson itinerary, factor in two variables: the weather and the location of your hotel. Because many of Tucson's attractions are outdoors and because the city is so spread out, if you visit in summer (or during one of our brief winter rainy bouts) and stay in an outlying resort, you may not be able to follow these itineraries as well as, say, someone who bunks in central Tucson on sunshiny winter days. These are rough sketches, then, not directions set in stone or — in local lingo — petroglyphs. For details on all the sights and restaurants mentioned in these itineraries, see the relevant sections of this chapter.

1-Day Itinerary

If you have just a single day in Tucson, start out early and hit the **Arizona-Sonora Desert Museum** as soon as it opens. Spend a few hours there, then drive over to the visitor's center of **Saguaro National Park West,** about 10 minutes away. Look out at the amazing vistas, maybe view the introductory film, and browse the bookstore; you don't have time for much else before you head downtown to the **Tucson Museum of Art and Historic Block.** It's lunchtime by now so grab a sandwich or salad at the museum's Café á la C'Art (if you have a sweet tooth, order dessert first — they sell out fast), and then wander through the various galleries and historic houses. The museum's gift shop is good, but if you want a larger selection of things Southwestern, head for the 1850s **Old Town Artisans** complex, just a few blocks away. You aren't far from I-10. Drive a few exits east to I-19 and zip down to the **Mission San Xavier del Bac.** When you get your fill of all the wonderful religious folk art, walk across the courtyard to **San Xavier Plaza,** where you can (again) satisfy your more material urges with Native American arts and crafts (check out the friendship bowls made by the Tohono O'odham people). I'm not going to tell you to resist the Indian fry bread (I hardly ever can myself), but unless you share, you'll ruin your appetite for dinner (book a table at a restaurant near your hotel). If, after all that running around, you're revived by food, go for some live country & western sounds at **Maverick: King of Clubs.**

2-Day Itinerary

On Day 1, take a more kicked-back approach to the morning part of the 1-day itinerary: You still want to arrive early at the **Arizona-Sonora Desert Museum** to avoid taking your first Tucson hike in its large parking lot, but when you get there, spend a little more time hanging out with the snakes and the hummingbirds (no, they're not in the same enclosure). If you're visiting from Thursday through Sunday in high season, have lunch in the Ocotillo Café; if not, or if you're traveling with kids, the Ironwood Cafeteria is fine for a midday meal. Then head over to **Saguaro National Park West** and get directions to Signal Hill, where you can take a short hike to some Hohokam petroglyphs. Pack lunch in a cooler before you head out in the morning and you can picnic here. Head back to your hotel and relax by the pool before dinner — an essential part of the Tucson experience, too. (If you're traveling with kids, substitute **Old Tucson Studios** for Saguaro National Park West, and expect to spend the entire afternoon there.) Unless you spend the afternoon at Old Tucson, you should have energy for a night out at the **Maverick** after dinner.

On Day 2, go to the **Tucson Museum of Art and Historic Block** and **Old Town Artisans** in the morning; afterward you may want to wander over to the ornate Spanish-Moorish style **Pima County Courthouse** (on Church, between Alameda and Pennington), then continue south on Church to Congress and east to Fifth Avenue, where you can get lunch at the hip Cup Café in the historic **Hotel Congress** (if that looks like your scene, check out the Club Congress schedule and come back at night). Alternatively, after looking at the Pima County Courthouse, you can eat at **Café Poca Cosa,** my favorite Mexican restaurant (take Church to Broadway, then head east 2½ blocks). Gallery hopping in this area is another post–Tucson Museum of Art possibility: **Etherton Gallery** and **Barrio,** which share the same building, make a good art-lunch combo. In the afternoon, drive down to the **San Xavier Mission** and **San Xavier Plaza.** Who knows? You may be able to put in some more swim time before dinner.

3-Day Itinerary

For the first two days, follow the 2-day itinerary. Start your third day at **Sabino Canyon,** catching the tram tour up, and taking a nice, easy walk down. Have lunch in one of the restaurants on Tanque Verde's restaurant row — maybe on the terrace of the **Dakota Café.** Interested in Western art? **El Presidio** gallery and **Venture Fine Arts** are in this area. In the afternoon, head over to the **University of Arizona Museums,** where you can further your education in photography, history, ethnology, fine art, astronomy — or any combination thereof. After the museums, you can browse on nearby **Fourth Avenue** and then have dinner in one of the low-key restaurants there, or head for the restaurant strip on Campbell north of Grant. Don't worry if you haven't changed your clothes from the morning walk through Sabino Canyon (unless you're smelly from hiking — in which case go back to your hotel and shower immediately!); casual is fine for any of the restaurants around here.

Shopping

The shopping scene, which runs the gamut from Western kitsch-carrying thrift stores to sky's-the-limit native crafts boutiques, mirrors Tucson's ethnic and economic diversity. As in most western cities, mall-sprawl is more characteristic than eastern urban-style retail concentrations, but there are several good the-buck-drops-here enclaves.

Tucson's malls tend to be open from 10 a.m. to 9 p.m. Monday through Saturday, 11 a.m. to 6 p.m. on Sunday, with longer hours around the winter holidays. Shops in other areas — well, that's anyone's guess. Many open at 8 or 9 a.m. and shut their doors at 6 p.m. Monday through Saturday, while others don't close until much later. You can expect Sunday hours to be shorter (say, 11 a.m. to 5 p.m.) or nonexistent.

Music to Downtown's Ears

Opened in 1919 and still in the same family, the **Chicago Music Store**, 130 W. Congress St., at 6th Ave. (☎ **520-622-3341**), strikes the right note with nearly every musician who blows through Tucson; Johnny Cash, ZZ Top's Billy Gibbons, and Jackson Browne have all dropped in. The place claims the largest selection of new and used musical instruments and sheet music in the Southwest; it also has a great neon storefront.

Best Shopping Areas

Much of Tucson's retail is conducted in the strip malls along Speedway, Broadway, Grant, and Ina roads (east/west), and Oracle, Campbell, and Tanque Verde (north/south). Two of the best shopping stops, Tubac and Nogales, Mexico, lie just south of Tucson along I-19; see Chapter 15 for details. Interesting shopping areas in town include:

Fourth Avenue

Baby boomer alert: You may have flashbacks on this neo-hippie drag between University Avenue and 9th Street, lined with second-hand clothing stores and bead-boutiques, along with some more upscale Southwestern wear shops and galleries. This is really Tucson's only shop 'n' stroll strip, with a few cafes to rev you up and some good bars to wind you down.

Downtown

Formerly Tucson's retail center, downtown no longer has prime shopping cachet — in fact, several of the more interesting independents have shut their doors in recent years — although some good galleries and a few unique shops are still left. Congress Street between Toole and Scott is the best stretch to try. Old Town Artisans (see "What to Look for and Where to Find It," in this chapter), near the Tucson Museum of Art, is a downtown standout, as is the museum's gift shop.

Getting Mall'd

The most popular shopping complex in town is the **Tucson Mall,** 4500 Oracle Rd. at Wetmore, Northwest (☎ **520-293-7330**), with more than 200 stores, including Dillards, Macy's, Robinson-May, and Sears department stores; the Arizona Avenue section specializes in things Southwestern. One of the city's oldest retail centers, **El Con,** 3601 Broadway Blvd. at Dodge, Central (☎ **520-327-8767**), is undergoing a major updating, though exactly what form it will take is anybody's guess. With luck it'll do as well as the **Foothills Mall,** 7401 North La Cholla at Ina, Northwest (☎ **520-219-0650**), a once languishing collection of shops that was resuscitated by the addition of various upscale outlets (including Off-Saks Fifth Avenue) as well as a Barnes & Noble Superstore and several good refreshment stops (see Gavi in "The Runner-Up Restaurants" and Thunder Canyon Brewery in "Nightlife and the Arts," both in this chapter).

Spiny Souvenirs

You won't want to stuff any cacti in your suitcase, but you can get them shipped by **B&B Cactus** Farms, 11550 E. Speedway Blvd., 1.5 miles past Houghton Rd., Eastside (☎ 520-721-4687), the town's top prickly plant connection. It's far out on the eastside, but it's a beautiful drive and, if you're going to Saguaro National Park East or Colossal Cave, not out of the way.

Getting (Boutique) Mall'd

For the arty and upscale, try **St. Phillips Plaza,** 4280 N. Campbell Ave. at River, Foothills (☎ 520-529-2775), which includes several galleries, a number of high-end eateries, and lots of tony clothing stores. There's a farmer's market every Sunday and, often, outdoor concerts. **Plaza Palomino,** 2970 North Swan at Fort Lowell, Central (☎ 520-795-1177), is similarly decked out in neo-Spanish hacienda style and also has lots of expensive galleries and home-furnishing and clothing boutiques; among the restaurants here are Firecracker and La Placita (see "The Top Restaurants" and the "A Taste of Mexico" sidebar, respectively, in this chapter).

What to Look for and Where to Find It

As you may have guessed, things Southwest — everything from western wear to Native American crafts — should top your Tucson shopping list. The good news: Although Tucson gets its fair share of tourists, it's a big city that caters to local pocketbooks — which means you can often get better deals on Southwest goods here than you can in more high-rent towns like $cottsdale, $edona, or $anta Fe.

Art Galleries

The clarity of light, the beauty of the desert, and, no doubt, the relatively low cost of living have all made Tucson an artist magnet; if you want to invest in an as-yet undiscovered Picasso, this may just be the place. On Thursday evenings from September through May, you can survey the downtown/Fourth Avenue scene by taking a free **ArtWalk;** call the Tucson Arts District Partnership (☎ 520-624-9977) for details. **ArtLife Southern Arizona,** found in the lobbies of major hotels, resorts, and home decorating stores around town, covers the entire city, with an emphasis on the more established galleries; if you can't find a copy, phone the publisher at ☎520-747-1271.

Dinnerware Contemporary Art Gallery, 135 E. Congress St., Downtown (☎520-792-4503), veering strongly toward the avant garde, is a good starting point for a budding art star search. Also in the heart of downtown, **Etherton,** 135 S. 6th Ave., ½ block south of Broadway (☎ 520-624-7370), focuses on photography, historic as well as contemporary, although painting has a strong presence, too. Just south of downtown **Philabaum,** 711 S. 6th Ave., north of 18th St.

(☎ 520- 884-7404), features the work of world-renowned glass artist Tom Philabaum and other outstanding practitioners of the fragile art; don't miss this one, even if you can't afford to buy anything. **Eleanor Jeck,** 4280 N. Campbell Ave., St. Phillips Plaza (☎ 520-299-2139), specializes in contemporary painting, much of it boldly colored and unconventional. The more traditional **El Presidio**, with branches at 3001 E. Skyline Dr. at Campbell, Foothills (☎ 520-299-1414) and at 7000 E. Tanque Verde Rd. at Sabino Canyon Rd., Central (☎ 520-733-0388), is a prime source for Western painting and bronze sculpture, as is the nearby **Venture Fine Arts,** 6541 E. Tanque Verde Rd. between, Kolb and Wilmot (☎ 520-298-2258).

Clothing

If your tastes tend toward the colorful and flowing, **Maya Palace,** in Plaza Palamino (☎ 520-325-6411), should suit you. **Del Sol,** 435 N. 4th Ave. at 6th St., 4th Ave./UA (☎ 520-628-8765), sells similarly attractive, unconstructed clothing. (Just a coincidence that many of the styles have elastic waists and this is a city where large quantities of Mexican food are consumed? I think not.) Sorry, guys, women only for both stores — see the "Western Wear" section, later, for men's fashions.

Crafts

Tucson is a prime gathering ground for Native American crafts, including Navajo rugs, Hopi katsinas, Zuni fetishes, and Tohono O'odham baskets, and for artistic items from neighboring Mexico (see Chapter 19). Anglo crafters in the Southwest tend to be influenced by both Indian and Mexican designs; expect to find many interesting interpretations thereof in Tucson's galleries.

Bahti Indian Arts, in St. Phillips Plaza, #20 (☎ 520-577-0290), is a great place to buy — and learn about — Navajo rugs and other crafts; owner Mark Bahti has been a trader for a long time and is the author of several books on the Southwest. The **Kaibab Shops,** 2837-41 N. Campbell Ave. just north of Glenn, Central (☎ 520-795-6905), which have been around since the 1940s, offer a wide-ranging, high-quality selection of Native American crafts. The two gift shops at Tohono Chul Park (see "More Cool Stuff to See and Do," in this chapter) sell an outstanding array of contemporary Mexican and Southwestern crafts at very reasonable prices (If you're traveling with kids, I dare you to try to leave without buying a stuffed javalina or other cool Southwest nature toy.) You can phone the shop next to the tearoom at ☎ 520-297-3169; the slightly smaller one next to the main house is at ☎ 520-297-4999. A little on the pricier side but of consistently high quality, the shops at **Old Town Artisans,** 201 N. Court at Alameda, in downtown's El Presidio Historic District (☎ 800-782-8072 or 520-623-6024), sell the works of some 100 regional crafters as well as Latin American imports. Justify the excursion — if you need to — on the grounds of historic and horticultural research: This hacienda-style adobe complex was built in the 1850s and has a lovely courtyard garden.

Decorator Fever: The Other South Park

South Park Avenue between 12th Street and 13th Street in South Tucson, known as "The Lost Barrio," boasts a row of stores specializing in ethnic home decoration and furnishings. At ¡**Aquí Esta**!, 204 S. Park Ave. (☎ 520-798-3605), you can buy the Mexican goods ready made or tailor the tilework, fabrics, and woodwork to your tastes. **Rústica,** 200 S. Park Ave. (☎ 520-623-4435), also goes beyond the border for its vibrantly colored wares. Prices at both stores are probably the best you find north of Nogales — and you don't have to bargain here. Try **Garden Arts,** 299 S. Park Ave. (☎ 520-624-6163), for outdoor decor; Dante Fraboni's whimsical wrought-iron bugs are plant enhancers, not destroyers.

If you head south on Park from central Tucson, you get stuck in the middle of the University of Arizona campus; instead, take Euclid Avenue south to 12th street (one block beyond Broadway) and go left two blocks.

Jewelry

The crafts stores and art galleries already described should satisfy most of your adornment urges, particularly of the silver sort; look out especially for Beth Friedman's gorgeous inlay work at Old Town Artisans. Another gem of a place, for lapis, opals, diamonds, as well as the blue stuff, is the **Turquoise Door** in St. Phillips Plaza, Suite #73, across from Gadabout (☎ 520-299-7787).

Western Wear

Rarin' to dress Western? Take it from the top with **Arizona Hatters,** 3600 N. 1st Ave. at Prince, Central (☎ 520-292-1320), with a huge selection of wrangler headgear, both ready-to-ride and customized. **Corral Western Wear,** 4525 E. Broadway between Swan and Colombus, Central (☎ 520- 322-6001), which first opened its doors in 1945, carries everything the style-conscious cowboy or girl could want, from tight-fitting jeans and gaudily embroidered shirts to spur-stud earrings. The goods at **Western Warehouse** aren't quite as exciting, but the selection is huge and you're bound to find a branch near you; central Tucson stores are located on 3030 E. Speedway Blvd. at Country Club (☎ 520-327-8005); 3719 N. Oracle Rd., one block north of Prince (☎ 520-293-1808); and 6701 E. Broadway Blvd. between Wilmot and Kolb (☎ 520- 885-4385). Corral and Western Warehouse both carry footwear, but if you're not a perfectionist, head for **Stewart Boot Mfg. Co.,** 30 W. 28th St. between S. 6th and 7th streets, South Tucson (☎ 520-622-2706); only you and your pocketbook will know your boots are slightly factory flawed.

Nightlife and the Arts

You probably didn't come to Tucson to attend the opera, but it's nice to know it's there should you get a diva urge. In fact, this former desert outpost is one of only 14 U.S. cities that has opera, symphony, theater, and ballet companies (okay, it shares a couple of them with Phoenix). As for its low places . . . well, Tucson doesn't exactly rock after dark, but you can choose from a decent number of spots to hit when the sun sets — and some pretty exciting sunsets.

Consult the *Arizona Daily Star's* "Caliente" section, published with the paper on Friday, for arts events; it also has club listings, but the free alternative *Weekly,* distributed Thursday, is better in that department.

Nightlife

Although most major music acts that tour this part of the Southwest tend to bypass Tucson for Phoenix or Las Vegas, the city draws top-notch country talent to the Tucson Convention Center (see "Making the Arts Scene," later in this section) or, sometimes, the Pima County Fairgrounds, 11300 S. Houghton Rd., east of town (☎ **520-792-3930**). Tex-Mex-inspired tejano and Tohono O'odham waila ("chicken scratch") bands also turn up in the Old Pueblo, and the annual Tucson International Mariachi Conference (see Chapter 2) often gets home-town girl Linda Ronstadt up on stage in April.

Up-and-coming indie bands regularly mosey down to Tucson, too, usually stopping first at **Club Congress,** 311 E. Congress at 5th Ave., Hotel Congress (☎ **520-622-8848**). The alternative venue is the **Rialto Theatre,** 318 E. Congress St. between S. 4th and 5th Sts. (☎ **520-740-0126**), which also presents good mid-range pop, jazz, Latin, and blues acts.

Bars

Unlike in many cities, Tucson's watering holes aren't all age segregated; sure, college hangouts exist, but lots of bars get a surprising inter-generational mix. Bars close at 1 a.m. (last call's usually at 12:30), and covers typically range from nonexistent to about $4.

Good bars are all around Tucson, but downtown stands out for its local color, the Foothills for its views. In between, the hip crowd drinks at the **Presidio Grill** and **The Dish,** both near The Loft, Tucson's main art cinema; see "The Runner-Up Restaurants," in this chapter.

The colorful ¡**Toma!,** 311 North Court Ave. at Franklin (☎ **520-622-1922**), joined at the hip with El Charro Mexican restaurant, has the best margarita list in town and, possibly, the liveliest crowd. A bit more sophisticated, the **Cushing St. Bar and Restaurant,** 3433 S. Meyer Ave. at Cushing St. (☎ **520-622-7984**), has a gorgeous wooden bar that dates back to the nineteenth century. Tony **Barrio,** 135 S. 6th Ave. just south of Broadway (☎ **520-629-0191**), can't claim the same historic cachet, but the delicious flavored vodkas made by the barkeep go far to compensate.

Some Lofty Perches

You can catch the sun dipping down beyond the horizon at **The Flying V Bar and Grill,** Loew's Ventana Canyon Resort, 7000 N. Resort Dr. (☎ **520-299-2020**); the **Cascade Lounge** at the same resort doesn't have the knockout views, but you clink glasses here to the tinkling of piano keys. Its name lays no false claims: **The Lookout Lounge,** Westward Look Resort, 245 W. Ina Rd. west of 1st Ave. (☎ **520-297-1151**), has forever views of the sunset and the city lights. And it doesn't get much mellower than seeing the clouds turn pink and purple against the Santa Catalinas while sipping a cocktail at **The Desert Garden Lounge,** Westin La Paloma, 3800 E. Sunrise between Campbell and 1st Ave. (☎ **520-742-6000**).

Blues, Rock, and Reggae

Berky's, 5769 E. Speedway Blvd., between Craycroft and Wilmot, Central (☎ **520-296-1981**) lays on live R&B, blues, or retro rock nightly. The large Chianti bottle that lets you know you've arrived at **The Boondocks,** 3306 N. 1st Ave. just north of Fort Lowell, Central (☎ **520-690-0991**), may be fake, but the blues are for real. The **Chicago Bar,** 5954 E. Speedway Blvd. between Craycroft and Wilmot, Central (☎ **520-748-8169**), has eclectic tastes (er, sounds), but you can expect whatever bands are brought in to rock. Named for a song by Jimi Hendrix and with signed guitars by B.B. King and Buddy Guy over the bar, **Third Stone,** 500 N. Fourth Ave. at N. 6th St. (☎ **520-628-8844**), is R&B to the bone (except on Wednesday when jazz takes over). Calling all Bob Marley fans: Look out for Neon Prophet, a good local reggae band that usually turns up at one local venue or another.

Country and Western

The most kick-butt of the country & western bars — musically, not literally — **Maverick, King of Clubs,** 4702 E. 22nd St. at Swan (☎ **520- 748-0456**), gets the crowds two-stepping to live bands from Tuesday through Saturday. The **Cactus Moon Cafe,** 5470 E. Broadway Blvd. at Craycroft (☎ **520-748-0049**), is a little more yuppified, but who cares when you can get free dance lessons, frequent drink specials, and bargain buffets. Although it has changed its name and owners more times than a C&W songster loses lovers, **The New West,** 4385 W. Ina Rd., east of I-10 and west of Thornydale (☎ **520-744-7744**), still draws big-name live talent, though most nights it's a DJ mix.

Jazz and Swing

One of Tucson's longest standing jazz venues, **Cafe Sweetwater,** 340 E. 6th St. at N. 6th Ave., 4th Ave/UA (☎ **520-622-6464**), can be depended on for the quality of its music — and of its food, for that matter. The **lounge at the Arizona Inn,** 2200 E. Elm St. between Campbell and Tucson Blvd. (☎ **520-325-1541**), is the genuine item when it comes to cool piano riffs, and why not — it dates back almost to the Jazz Age.

They've Got Game: Indian Casinos

Don't expect Las Vegas. No booze is sold or permitted on the premises, and scantily clad servers are in short supply. But if Indian gaming attracts you, try **Casino of the Sun,** 7406 S. Camino de Oeste, 15 miles southwest of Tucson (☎ **800-344-9435** or 520-883-1700), operated by the Pascua Yaquis, who have a small reservation in central Tucson and another near the San Xavier Mission; or **Desert Diamond Bingo and Casino,** 7350 S. Old Nogales Highway, near the airport (☎ **520-294-7777**), a Tohono O'odham enterprise; call for directions. Both have the usual array of one-armed bandits, video and live poker, keno, and bingo, and both are open 24–7. Desert Diamond will soon be superseded by the as-yet unnamed $52 million 180,000-square-foot casino being built by the Tohono O'odham about 10 miles south of Tucson. Slated to open in 2002, it'll have shops, a restaurant, and an open plaza where native artisans will sell their work.

Microbreweries

The shining vats at **Thunder Canyon Brewery,** Ina and La Cholla, at the Foothills Mall, Northwest (☎ **520-797-2652**), produce some mean ales and lagers; the place always bustles but especially on prime movie nights (it's near the mall multiplex). **Nimbus Brewing Co.,** 3850 E. 44th St. at Palo Verde, South Tucson (☎ **520-745-9175**), is the hippest place for hops, a funky warehouse with terrific home brews and live music Thursday to Saturday. If you like Belgian-style white beer, this is the place.

The Arts

Most of the major companies perform at **the Tucson Convention Center Music Hall,** 260 S. Church Ave. at Cushing St., downtown (☎ **520-791-2246**).

Centennial Hall, University of Arizona campus at University Blvd. and Park Ave. (☎ **520-621-3341**), hosts the hard-to-typecast but always top-rate UApresents series (see http://uapresents.arizona.edu for an advance schedule); the 2000/01 roster includes Rent, Salerno-Sonnenberg, the Martha Graham Dance Company, and lots of international talent (now if only the hall's acoustics were better . . .). Tickets range from $14 to $60. When box offices are closed, you can get tickets for the more mainstream performances by phoning Ticketmaster (☎ **520-321-1000**); tickets for UApresents events are also available online.

The Great (Arty) Outdoors

Don't want to be an art shut-in? The **Tucson Parks and Recreation Department** airs out an excellent (free!) cultural program most weekends from late February through late June. The Tucson Pops Orchestra and the Orts Theatre of Dance put in regular appearances at the De Meester Outdoor Performance Center in Reid Park, Country Club Rd. and E. 22nd St.; the season ends with a weekend of Shakespeare under the stars. The Arizona Symphonic Winds breeze over to Morris K. Udall Park, at Tanque Verde and Sabino Canyon roads. Call Event and Theater Services (☎ 520-791-4079) for schedules and directions or check the newspaper entertainment listings sections. The **Tucson Jazz Society** (☎ 520-743-3399) often takes their cool sounds outside, too, most regularly to St. Phillips Plaza, Campbell Avenue and River Road.

Classical Music

Tuning up successfully since 1929, the **Tucson Symphony Orchestra** (☎ 520-882-8585) divides its time between the Tucson Convention Center Music Hall and the Pima Community College Center for the Arts, 2202 W. Anklam Rd., Westside (☎ 520-206-6988). Tickets range from $10.75 to $33. You can get your opera fix with **The Arizona Opera Company** (☎ 520-293-4336) at the Tucson Convention Center Music Hall between November and March — when they're not in Phoenix (tickets from $19 to $69).

Dance

When **Ballet Arizona** (☎ 888-322-5538) isn't pliéing or pas de deuxing in Phoenix, they're toeing the line at the Music Hall in the Tucson Convention Center (tickets from $16–$38, 12 and under half-price, 10 percent senior discount). For more contemporary movement, try the **Orts Theatre of Dance,** 930 N. Stone Ave. at 6th St., downtown (☎ 520- 624-3799) ($6–$12).

Theater

Not only is the **Arizona Theatre Company** (☎ 520-622-2823) a class act, but they strut their stuff — everything from Shakespeare to Stoppard — at downtown's Temple of Music and Art, 330 S. Scott Ave. at Broadway (☎ 520-622-2823). When you're not focused on the stage of the gorgeously restored Spanish colonial/Moorish theater, browse the theatrical arts shop and the upstairs art gallery. Tickets run from $19 to $28. For less traditional — and often less expensive ($12 and up) — fare, try the **Invisible Theatre,** 1400 N. 1st Ave. at Drachman, Central (☎ 520- 882-9721).

Cheer the heroes and boo the bad guys at the Gaslight Theatre, 7010 E. Broadway, just west of Kolb (☎ 520-886-9428), equally popular with kids and adults who need to blow off steam. Ticket prices ($6 for children 12 and under, $13.95 for adults) include free popcorn, but pizza, wine, beer, and soft drinks cost extra.

Quick Concierge: Tucson

American Express: 3573 E. Sunrise Dr., between Campbell and Swan (☎ 520-577-0550).

Area Code: Tucson's area code is **520.**

ATMs: You can cash out all over town: supermarkets, bank branches (Bank One and Bank of America are ubiquitous), and even at drive-through ATMs. . . .

Doctors: Check your health insurance carrier before you leave for recommended — and covered — doctors in town. Or phone ☎ 520-324-2000 for local referrals.

Emergencies: Call ☎ **911** for fire, police, or ambulance.

Hospitals: Options include Tucson Medical Center, 5301 E. Grant Rd. at Craycroft, Central (☎ 520-327-5461), and University Medical Center, 1501 N. Campbell Ave. at Elm, Central (☎ 520-694-0111), known for its advanced heart and cancer research.

Information: Contact the Metropolitan Tucson Convention and Visitors Bureau (☎ 800- 638-8350, www.visittucson.org).

Internet Access & Cyber Cafes: Get connected at the Library of Congress in the Hotel Congress, 323 Congress St., downtown (☎ 520-622-2708; Internet: www.hotcong.com/litcong/); it's $3 per half hour for Internet access. You can also retrieve your e-mail at Kinko's for $12 an hour or 20¢ a minute. The most centrally located of the four Tucson locations is at 2607 E. Speedway at Tucson Blvd., Central (☎ 520-795-7796).

Mail: Call ☎ 800-275-8777 and punch in the zip code of where you're staying to locate the post office nearest you. The main post office is at 1501 S. Cherry near Kino Parkway.

Maps: The Gousha map of Tucson, available in every convenience store, supermarket, or gas station, will do you just fine. For more map options, visit Tucson Map & Flag Center, 3239 N. 1st Ave., just north of Ft. Lowell, Central (☎ 520- 887-4234), tops in Mexico and Southwest cartography.

Newspapers/Magazines: The *Arizona Daily Star* is the morning bringer of tidings; the *Tucson Citizen* comes out Monday through Saturday afternoons (on Sunday, the ad-stuffed *Star* is the only game in town). The *Star's* Friday entertainment supplement, *Caliente,* has an "Outside" section that details hikes and other fresh-air activities along with arts and nightlife listings. The free, alternative *Tucson Weekly*, which turns up in supermarkets, bookstores, and various publication racks around town on Thursday, has the best club listings. The glossy *Tucson Guide Quarterly,* found on the newsstands and, often, in hotel rooms, has useful tourist-oriented listings as well as articles of local interest (sometimes written by yours truly).

Pharmacies: Several Walgreens (☎ 800-925-4733) and Osco (☎ 800-654-6726) drugstores operate 24-hour pharmacies. Type in your hotel's zip code when you phone and get the location nearest to you.

Police: Call ☎ 911 for emergencies; the non-emergency number is ☎ 520-791-4452.

Restrooms: Sorry. You only find public restrooms in parks and malls. Alternatively, your best bet is to duck into a hotel or restaurant; I've never been turned down yet when I've asked to use the facilities.

Safety: For a large metropolitan area, Tucson is relatively safe. Most of the crime involves car theft rather than mugging. Be careful in large, poorly lit parking lots after dark: When leaving a movie theater or a mall late at night, know where your car is and have your keys ready so you're not wandering around, looking clueless. It's not a good idea to stroll around downtown after attending a theater or other arts performance, either; unfortunately, the streets there are usually fairly empty after dark (except when the bimonthly Downtown Saturday Night street fairs are held; check listings).

Smoking: Tucson imposed a full ban on restaurant smoking in 1999, making it the only city in the state besides Mesa and Flagstaff to stuff puffing. But the confusing laws are still being contested — smoking is allowed in bars and, if a restaurant gets more than 50 percent of its revenue from alcohol, it can be classified as one. In addition, smoking is permitted on restaurant terraces, if they're far enough from the restaurant's interior.

Taxes: The sales tax in Tucson is 7 percent; hotels add 9.5 percent to your tab, plus $1 per room per night. The car rental excises are 12 percent if you pick up your car in the city; if you get it from a counter in the airport — as most people do — add on a 10 percent concession fee, for a whopping total of 22 percent. An additional $3.50 per car rental is added on wherever you get your wheels (your contribution to repaying the baseball stadium bonds).

Taxis: A few of the more reliable cab companies include Allstate (☎ 520-798-1111), ABC (☎ 520-623-7979), and Yellow Cab (☎ 520- 624-6611). The drivers of Fiesta Taxi (☎ 520- 622-7777) speak both English and Spanish.

Time Zone: Tucson is in the Mountain time zone, but because Arizona doesn't observe daylight savings time, the city is in the Pacific time zone when the rest of the country changes their clocks in the spring.

Transit Info: Call ☎ 520-792-9222.

Weather: Call ☎ 520-881-3333 or check www.noaa.gov/Tucson.

Chapter 14

Side Trips from Tucson

In This Chapter

▶ Checking out the cacti in Organ Pipe National Monument

▶ Getting celestial at Kitt Peak National Observatory

▶ Exploring under the dome of Biosphere 2

*T*hese day trips from Tucson take you to some mighty otherworldly places, from Organ Pipe National Monument, with its arrays of strange, multi-armed cacti; to Kitt Peak National Observatory, where peering at different galaxies is on the nightly agenda; to Biosphere 2, originally conceived as an experiment in living away from Earth. You can also visit many of the attractions in southeastern Arizona — particularly the sights along I-19. However, this area has so many things to offer that I devote an entire chapter to it (see Chapter 15), in addition to the day trip here.

Day Trip #1: West to Organ Pipe National Monument

On this trip, reach for the stars — but not, I hope, for the cactus. This excursion takes you through some of the most pristine stretches of desert in Arizona, much of it belonging to the Tohono O'odham people. **Kitt Peak National Observatory** and **Organ Pipe Cactus National Monument** are the high points of this trip (Kitt Peak, literally), but the old mining town of **Ajo,** near Organ Pipe, has a certain appeal, too. You can easily visit Kitt Peak and return to Tucson the same day; in fact, **Mission San Xavier del Bac** (see Chapter 13) is en route, so you can tour both (and should, if you haven't already seen the mission). Including the mission and observatory in your journey makes the day more interesting. After all, if you just want to see more cactus, you can stick around Tucson.

Side Trips from Tucson

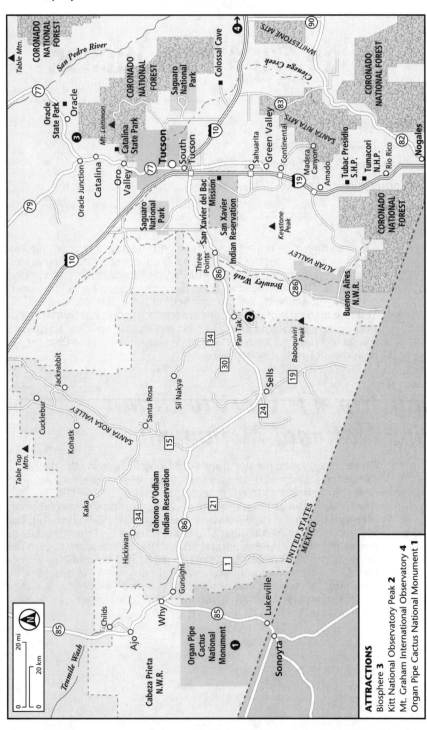

ATTRACTIONS
Biosphere **3**
Kitt National Observatory Peak **2**
Mt. Graham International Observatory **4**
Organ Pipe Cactus National Monument **1**

Getting There

To reach Kitt Peak, take I-10 to I-19 south; then get on Highway 86 (Ajo Way) west for 44 miles to Highway 386, where signs lead you to the 12 winding miles up to the observatory. To continue on to Ajo, return to Highway 86 and keep driving west to the junction of Highway 85 at Why (don't ask why, see "The Answer to Why" sidebar). From here you can either go north on Highway 85 to Ajo or south on Highway 86 to Organ Pipe Cactus National Monument.

Seeing the Sights

As you head west from an ugly industrial section on Tucson's south side, vacant lots, warehouses, and fast food strips soon begin to give way to hills and open desert. You know you're approaching the eastern border of the Tohono O'odham reservation when you see a mountain dotted with white bumps (the observatories). Nearby, you see a striking thumb-shaped peak — that's Baboquiviri (say *baa-buh-key-vuh-ree*). This peak is sacred to the Tohono O'odham Indians from whom the astronomers lease their 200 lofty acres.

Funded by the National Science Foundation and managed by a consortium of more than 20 major universities, **Kitt National Observatory Peak** (☎ **520-318-8726** [visitor's center] or 520-318-7200 [recorded information]; Internet: www.tuc.noao.edu/kpno/pubpamph/pub. html) has the world's greatest concentration of optical telescopes. The collection includes the world's largest solar telescope and the world's largest asteroid hunter (if a huge chunk of space debris is due to crash into Earth, these folks are the first to know). In order to keep human body heat from interfering with its data, one of the sensitive telescopes has its own separate building. The drive to the top of the 6,882-foot mountain and the free guided tours make this a great place to visit during the day. In addition, the nighttime dinner and astronomy program, which must be booked in advance (see "Where to Dine," in this section), is *really* out of this world. The gift shop carries astronomy-related books, T-shirts, and toys. You also find a good selection of Tohono O'odham baskets — they're pricey, but remember, these baskets take a long time to create. Bring a picnic; the picnic tables offer wonderful views, but no food concessions are available. Open: 9 a.m. to 4 p.m. daily except Thanksgiving Day, New Year's Day, and Christmas Day. Admission: free ($2 donation requested).

Just northwest of Why, **Ajo** owes its growth to copper — as you can see when you pass the mountains of *tailings* (rock waste from mining) on your way in. Strolling the palm-lined Spanish Colonial Revival town square, laid out in 1917, is pretty much what there is to do after you visit the small **Ajo Historical Society Museum,** 160 Mission St. (☎ 520- 387-7195). You may drive up to the New Cornelia Mine lookout, at the end of Indian Village Road, and gaze at the gaping pit that once produced the town's wealth. For details on both, stop in at the Ajo Chamber of Commerce, 321 Taladro (just south of the Plaza; ☎ 520- 387-7742); it's open Monday through Saturday 9 a.m. to 4 p.m. most of the year, sporadically during the summer. To find out about the

860,000-acre **Cabeza Prieta Wildlife Refuge,** a bighorn sheep preserve about 10 minutes east of Ajo, go to the refuge office, 1611 N. 2nd Ave. (☎ 520-387-6483). You need a high-clearance, four-wheel-drive vehicle and a permit to enter.

Some 24 miles south of Why, you see a sign for the turnoff to **Organ Pipe Cactus National Monument,** Route 1 (☎520-387-6849), where the multi-armed cousins of the saguaro congregate. The organ pipe cactus, which does sort of resemble a pipe organ (so why isn't this Pipe Organ park?), doesn't grow as high as the saguaro and doesn't live as long. In fact, you see more saguaros here than organ pipes. Lusher stands of these cacti grow south of the border, but let's not get picky (or prickly): This is a beautiful desert park and much more serene than its Tucson kin.

 In addition to several hiking trails (the visitor's center has details), two graded dirt drives wind through the park. If you only have time for one, take the 21-mile Ajo Mountain loop drive with thicker vegetation and taller peaks as a backdrop. The somewhat flatter 53-mile Puerto Blanco loop has one key draw: the beautiful **Quitobaquito Springs oasis.** The oasis provides a great bird-watching spot, but don't go wandering off too far for too long: The parking lot isn't far from a road that parallels the border and car break-ins are common. The park visitor's center is open daily from 9 a.m. to 5 p.m. Admission is $4 per car.

The Lukeville, Arizona/Sonoyta, Mexico border is only 5 miles from the park exit. This border crossing is popular with Arizonans headed to Rocky Point, the closest Mexican beach. **Sonoyta** isn't seedy like some border towns, but not much happens here. If you want to say you visited Mexico (no passport required), you can visit a few curio shops and sit outside at a pleasant patio restaurant. Lots of people drive down to Lukeville, buy cigarettes and perfume in the duty-free shop, and perform the strange ritual of walking across the border and back in order to retrieve their discount booty.

Taking a Tour

Great Western Tours (☎ 520-572-1660; Internet: www.greatwesterntours.com) offers a 5-hour (round-trip) tour of Kitt Peak from Tucson for $60 per person. If you travel on your own, you can take one of Kitt Peak's three free, hour-long guided tours, led by docents who are often amateur astronomers. The 10 a.m. tour visits the **McMath-Pierce solar telescope;** the 11:30 a.m. visits the (nameless) 2.1-meter telescope, a pioneer in photographic astronomy; the 1:30 p.m. visit the 4-meter **Mayall telescope,** the second largest telescope in the world when it was built and instrumental in discovering dark matter. If you can't stay around for all three tours, come early to see the McMath — it's not only the largest telescope of its kind in the world, but it also collects data in the daytime. On occasion, the scientists let visitors come in to see what they're up to.

All the tours of Organ Pipe Cactus National Monument are self-guided; the next section details your two driving loop options.

The Answer to Why

Not much more than a gas station and a general store at a "Y"-shaped crossroad, the town of Why got its querulous moniker in 1950 when the postal service was handing out zip codes: Every place that wanted a zip code had to have a minimum of three letters in its name (at least that's the most plausible explanation I heard of why Why is Why).

Where to Stay

There are three modest motels in Ajo. I stayed at the **Marine Resort Motel** ($), 1966 N. 2nd Ave. (Highway 85) (☎ **520-387-7626**), and had no complaints (other than that it's not a marine and not a resort). The town has two B&Bs; the 1919 **Mine Manager's House** ($$), 601 West Greenway Dr. (☎ **520-387-6505**, fax 520-387-6508), sits on the top of a hill overlooking town. Mine Manager's House is larger and more dramatically sited, but I like the nice theme rooms and the friendly owners of the **Guest House Inn** ($$), 700 Guest House Road (☎ **520-387-6133**).

Where to Dine

The food is fine at Kitt Peak's nighttime program. The fare is a cold box dinner, but the sandwiches are fresh and the cookies are baked on site (but you're there for the astronomy, not the gastronomy). You get lessons on how to use a planisphere, are regaled with ancient star myths, peer through a 16-inch telescope, and maybe even operate the observatory's retractable dome. Programs, which start half an hour before sunset and last about three hours, are offered nightly year-round but are restricted to 20 people; book as far in advance as you can (at least a month, maybe more, from November through April, at least a week the rest of the year). Cost: $35 adults, $25 for seniors, students, and children under 18.

If you attend Kitt Peak's dinner program, not only do you drive down a winding, mountain road at night but, for the first $\frac{7}{10}$ of a mile or so, you are only allowed to use parking lights (so as not to interfere with the telescopes). Still, you follow a guide car so you aren't completely in the dark and the road is wide and fully paved.

If you visit Kitt Peak in the daytime, you can buy picnic fixings at Basha's supermarket, Topawa Rd. (☎ **383-2800**). Basha's is located in the main shopping center of Sells, the Tohono O'odham reservation's tribal capital.

Ajo isn't fine-dining terrain, but a couple of options are available to you. The Mexican combination plates dished up at **Señor Sancho** ($),

663 N. 2nd Ave. (☎ **520-387-6226**), are far less gringoized than the restaurant's name — though they're definitely American-sized. The **Copper Kettle** ($–$$), 23 Plaza (☎ **520-387-7000**), is fine for a burger or a home-style breakfast on the town square.

Day Trip #2: Biosphere 2

Visiting Biosphere 2 takes up a good chunk of the day, but you may want to squeeze in a stop at **Catalina State Park,** which is en route. You walk a good bit at Biosphere 2, so you probably won't want to go for a long trek at the state park. As an alternative to walking, you can contact Pusch Ridge Stables (see Chapter 13) to get a friendly equine to take you around.

Getting There

Oracle Road, one of Tucson's main north-streets, turns into Highway 77 (take the road's right fork at Oracle Junction). Just keep heading north on Highway 77; you see signs for Biosphere 2 at mile marker 96.5, about 45 minutes from central Tucson.

Seeing the Sights

The **Biosphere 2 Center** (☎ **520-825-1289** or 800-828-2462; Internet: www.bio2.edu) isn't as press sexy as it was in the early 1990s. During that time, eight people of opposite genders holed up together for two years in the desert terrarium in a controversial experiment in self-contained (potentially extraterrestrial) living. After Columbia University took over Biosphere 2's management in 1995, the experiment went completely legit; now you settle for learning about science (with a little gossip about the good — or bad — old days thrown in). Guided tours are included in the admission price. These tours take you to the visitor's center, where there's an introductory film and a model of Biosphere 2, and through the demonstration labs, where you experience scaled-down versions of the rain forest (you only occasionally get rained on) and coastal fog *biomes* (ecological units). Then you walk around the big glass dome and into the famed peek-through apartments where the Biosphere 2 "crew" used to live (these apartments now house scientific displays). The tour, which takes approximately an hour and 45 minutes, ends at the viewing gallery of the ocean biome.

For an extra $10, you can enter through the Biosphere's massive airlock doors. These 45-minute "Under the Glass" tours take you to see the operating systems in the basement and onto the savanna, which overlooks the Biosphere's ocean (sorry, no swimming allowed). When no research is being conducted, you can enter other biomes, too.

Colonizing Mars may no longer be a Biosphere goal, but peering at the red planet is still on the agenda. An observatory with a state-of-the-art 24-inch telescope was recently added to Columbia's research facilities and, in 2000, opened to the public. Astronomy-related lectures — the

2000 program included one by David Levy — followed by stargazing sessions are given bi-monthly when viewing conditions permit (that is, *not* during the July through September rainy season). Call or check the Web site for events and schedules.

The visitor's center is open daily from 8:30 a.m. to 6 p.m. (5 p.m. in winter) except Christmas; guided tours begin every hour on the hour daily, with the first tour at 9 a.m. If you want to see everything, don't arrive later than 3 p.m. Stargazing programs begin at 7 or 8 p.m., depending on the time of year. No reservations are needed for the general tours, but it's a good idea to make them for the "Under the Glass" tours (limited to 20 people) and for the observatory programs. Admission: $12.95 adults, $8.95 ages 13–17, $6 ages 6–12, 5 and under free; AAA, AARP, student, and military discounts available with valid ID. Tickets for the lectures and night-viewing programs range from $15 to $20 for adults, $8.95 for 17 and under.

Taking a Tour

The price of admission to Biosphere 2 ($50 per person) includes a tour of the grounds; it's $10 extra for an "Under the Glass" interior tour (see the next section for details). The 5-hour excursions to Biosphere run by Great Western Tours (☎ **520-572-1660;** Internet: www.greatwesterntours.com) cover the general admission tour in their cost, but not the interior tour.

Where to Stay

Biosphere 2 isn't very far from Tucson, or especially from the northern resorts in Tucson, so sleeping at the center isn't really necessary. If you attend one of the stargazing evenings, however, you may want to hit the pillow rather than get back on the road. Biosphere 2's hotel and conference center ($$), which was on the grounds even before the big terrarium, has nice rooms with desert views for reasonable rates; ticket and meal packages are available too. For reservations call ☎ **800-828-2462** or 520-896-6200.

Where to Dine

On Biosphere 2's grounds, the **Cañada del Oro** ($$–$$$) restaurant serves good Southwestern and American fare; it's open for breakfast, lunch, and dinner (until 7 p.m.) because it services the hotel on the premises. On the way to Biosphere 2, **Cibaria** ($$), 12985 N. Oracle, at Rancho Vistoso Blvd. (in the Abco/Walgreens shopping center; ☎ **520- 825-2900**), features fine light northern Italian cuisine; stop in for lunch or plan on a terrace dinner, when you can watch the sun turn the Santa Catalinas a deep pink.

Star Trek Southern Arizona

Southern Arizona is heaven for anyone with even the slightest interest in astronomy. In addition to Kitt Peak and the observatory at Biosphere 2 (both described previously), stargazers also find bliss at the University of Arizona's Flandrau Science Center (Chapter 13); the Fred Whipple Observatory on Mt. Hopkins and the Skywatcher's Inn (both in Chapter 15); and the UA's astronomy camps (Chapter 5).

And there's still more. Two other astro-tour possibilities include:

Mt. Graham International Observatory, perched on a 10,477-foot peak some 75 miles northeast of Tucson (☎ **520-428-6260;** Internet: www.discoverypark.com), hosts some of the world's newest, most advanced telescopes. Most Saturdays from mid-March to mid-November (when snow is unlikely to close the roads), the observatory runs day-long (10 a.m. to 4 p.m.) tours. The price, $30, includes a sack lunch and admission to the Gov Aker Observatory's fun, interactive science center. At the science center, you can listen to noises from outer space, watch lightening strike Earth, or (for an extra charge) take a virtual tour of the solar system on a high-tech flight simulator. In spring and summer, peer at the sun through a 5-inch solar refractor telescope and at any time of year, return after dark to gaze at the night sky through a 20-inch reflecting telescope. Attendance on the Mt. Graham tours is limited to 15 and you need to reserve at least two weeks in advance (that gives them time to make sure you're not an eco-terrorist; an endangered squirrel species on Mt. Graham made building the telescopes controversial).

The University of Arizona has some BMOC (Big Mirrors on Campus). Beneath the east wing of the UA's football stadium, the **Steward Observatory Mirror Laboratory** houses some of the largest, lightest mirrors in the world — ideal for collecting light from faint astronomical objects. The mirrors include several created for NASA projects as well as the two 8.4-meter mirrors for Mt. Graham's Large Binocular Telescope (how many years of bad luck do you suppose you'd have if you broke one of those?). The university offers free tours of the mirror lab with 10 days' advance notice Monday through Friday from 9:30 a.m. to 3:30 p.m.; contact Ann Klocko at ☎ **520-621-1022.** Maximum group size of 15 (no minimum) and participants need to be at least high school age.

Part IV
Exploring the Regions

The 5th Wave   By Rich Tennant

"I think we should arrange to be there for Garlic-Anchovy-Chili Bean Week, and then shoot over to the Breathmint-Antacid Festival."

In this part. . .

Ladies and gentlemen, start your engines: You're going on a major road trip. This part takes you here, there, and (almost) everywhere in Arizona, from the little cowboy towns of the south to the great — okay, grand — canyons of the north. Please, don't forget to buckle your seat belts.

Chapter 15

Southeast Arizona

● ●

In This Chapter

▶ Meandering along the Santa Cruz River and dipping into Mexico

▶ Discovering the grasslands and vineyards of eastern Santa Cruz

▶ Exploring the Old (and New) West in southern Cochise County

▶ Traveling above ground and below in northern Cochise County

● ●

*1*f you're looking for the Old West of Spanish missions and *presidios,*
fierce Indian battles, go-for-broke mines, and rough 'n' tumble boomtowns, you're hard pressed to find a better stretch of Arizona to
explore than the southeast. All that history sound like a yawn? Don't
cross this region off your list yet. Nature lovers, wine connoisseurs,
folk-art aficionados . . . even die-hard duffers find something here. All in
all, the region fits those who prefer the simple pleasures of a pretty
and, in parts, surprisingly green rural region to glamour and glitz.

You can cover a lot of this area in day trips from Tucson, but one day
doesn't really give southeast Arizona its due. You should spend more
than a single day here because the area has loads of terrific places to
stay. A more or less leisurely three days should be enough, though,
because the region isn't nearly as spread out as other areas in the
state. You may settle into a local ranch, tour on scouting missions, or
hop around the historic hotels and colorful B&Bs that dot the area.
Although the town of Bisbee has the most varied lodging options,
where you lay your head depends largely on your interests: Stargazers
may seek an aerie in an astronomy-oriented B&B near Benson, while
birders may want to nest near the Patagonia or Ramsey Canyon nature
preserves.

Because much of this area sits at a higher elevation, it's great for escap-
ing the southern Arizona desert heat in summer. The summer is also
the season when many local business people go on vacation, however,
especially around Patagonia and Sonoita. Expect to find some restaurants, lodgings, and shops closed, sometimes without advance notice.

What's Where? Southeast Arizona and Its Major Attractions

I divide this chapter into four regions, each with its own highlights, which are previewed in the following sections.

Along the Santa Cruz River

At the end of the seventeenth century, Jesuit missionary Eusebio Kino followed the route north from Nogales, Mexico to Tucson. Later, conquistador Juan Bautista de Anza used the same route. Neither traveler would recognize it today — it's now I-19 — but it's still scenic and full of interesting stops, natural, historical, and scientific. These sights include:

✔ **The Asarco Mineral Discovery Center,** a working copper mine. Whatever you think about strip mining, this is a rare chance to see it in action.

✔ **The Titan Missile Museum,** which has as its centerpiece the only one of the country's 54 Titan II missiles that wasn't destroyed by a treaty with the Soviet Union.

✔ **Tubac,** the oldest European settlement in Arizona and now a state park, adjoins a thriving artisans colony. Tubac and nearby Amado are good jumping off points for **Madera Canyon,** a hikers' and birders' mecca; the Smithsonian Institution's **Fred Whipple Observatory;** and **Tumacácori National Historical Park,** which includes the ruins of one of two missions that Tubac was established to protect.

✔ **Nogales,** a bustling Mexican border town, where you find great shopping and, naturally, authentic Mexican food.

Nogales, Arizona and Nogales, Mexico are sister towns in two separate countries. Unless I say otherwise, when I refer to Nogales, I'm talking about the one in Mexico (its U.S. sibling doesn't have a whole lot of tourist appeal).

That's One Weird Road

Although the "I" in "I-19" stands for interstate, the Tucson-Nogales road never leaves southern Arizona. I-19 is also one of the few U.S. highways marked in kilometers, not miles — the result of a failed attempt to get America to go metric. (It's 1.6 kilometers to the mile, by the way, or 6.2 miles for every 10 kilometers.)

Southeast Arizona

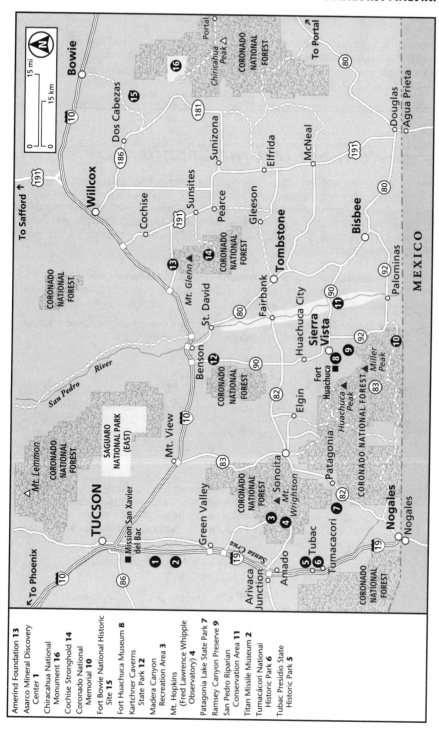

15 mi

15 km

To Safford ↑

To Phoenix

To Portal

Bowie

Dos Cabezas

Willcox

Cochise

Sunsites

Pearce

Gleeson

Sunizona

Elfrida

McNeal

Portal

Chiricahua Peak △

CORONADO NATIONAL FOREST

Douglas

Agua Prieta

MEXICO

Palominas

Bisbee

Tombstone

Fairbank

Huachuca City

Sierra Vista

Fort Huachuca

Miller Peak ▲

Huachuca Peak ▲

Benson

St. David

Mt. Glenn ▲

CORONADO NATIONAL FOREST

Elgin

Sonoita

Mt. Wrightson ▲

Patagonia

CORONADO NATIONAL FOREST

Nogales

Nogales

Tumacacori

Tubac

Amado

Arivaca Junction

Green Valley

Mt. View

SAGUARO NATIONAL PARK (EAST)

TUCSON

Mission San Xavier del Bac

Mt. Lemmon △

CORONADO NATIONAL FOREST

San Pedro River

Santa Cruz

CORONADO NATIONAL FOREST

Amerind Foundation **13**
Asarco Mineral Discovery
    Center **1**
Chiricahua National
    Monument **16**
Cochise Stronghold **14**
Coronado National
    Memorial **10**
Fort Bowie National Historic
    Site **15**
Fort Huachuca Museum **8**
Kartchner Caverns
    State Park **12**
Madera Canyon
    Recreation Area **3**
Mt. Hopkins
    (Fred Lawrence Whipple
    Observatory) **4**
Patagonia Lake State Park **7**
Ramsey Canyon Preserve **9**
San Pedro Riparian
    Conservation Area **11**
Titan Missile Museum **2**
Tumacácori National
    Historic Park **6**
Tubac Presidio State
    Historic Park **5**

High Chaparral Chic

Chaparral is the official name for the habitat found at elevations of 3,500 to 6,000 feet that gets between 13 and 23 inches of rain per year. The leggings that cowboys wear when traveling through the chaparral are named "chaps" after this name for the dense, scruffy habitat.

Eastern Santa Cruz County

Its lush river valleys, oak-dotted peaks, and golden grasslands make the high-elevation area east of the Santa Cruz River a lovely anomaly in southern Arizona. Missionaries, ranchers, miners, and more recently, wine makers have all been drawn to this fertile patch southeast of Tucson (as have migrating birds). Two noteworthy towns dot the map in this region:

- ✔ **Sonoita:** More of a crossroads than a town but a good gateway into wine country, has several surprisingly good restaurants and some interesting lodgings.
- ✔ **Patagonia:** An old railroad and mining town, has become a haven for crafts folks and bird-watchers in recent years.

Southern Cochise County

Even the name "Cochise County" sends Western history buffs into raptures, invoking some of the most famous — and most romanticized — events in our country's past. It's the southern section of the county that carries most of the big tourist guns. Again, historical sites mingle with natural attractions in:

- ✔ **Sierra Vista:** A military and retirement community where Fort **Huachuca,** an active army post with history museums, operates. The adjoining San Pedro Valley encompasses **Coronado National Memorial,** the **Arizona Folklore Preserve,** and **Ramsey Canyon,** a birder's paradise.
- ✔ **Bisbee:** A once and — maybe — future mining town with a Victorian flavor, perched high on a hill.
- ✔ **Tombstone:** Yep. Doc Holliday, the Earps, the Clantons, the OK Corral . . . this is the place.

Northern Cochise County

The rugged high plains where Cochise and his Apache troops evaded capture — now bordered on the north by I-10 — is relatively undeveloped, making it ideal for hiking or backroad driving. You can hide out on a ranch or tour from a couple of small towns:

> ✔ **Benson:** A one-time railroad crossroads, back on the map because of the debut of nearby **Kartchner Caverns State Park;** the **Amerind Foundation Museum,** an American Indian museum, is an oldie-but-a-goodie detour from here, too.

> ✔ **Willcox:** Kicked-back hometown of cowboy star Rex Allen and a good base for exploring **Chiracahua State Park, Cochise Stronghold,** and **Fort Bowie.**

Along the Santa Cruz River

Because the Santa Cruz River straddles a major road and is usually dry, this area is hard to picture as the conquistador and missionary route that gave rise to its settlements — until you venture a little way from the freeway. In a relatively short span (only 65 miles separates Tucson from Nogales, Mexico), you get a terrific sweep of Arizona history from its Mexican roots and earliest settlements to its most recent major industries.

Of all the areas I detail in this chapter, this stretch is the easiest to cover in a day trip from Tucson. If you're pressed for time, you can squeeze in the sights that interest you most, eat in Nogales, and drive back. You may decide to spend the night in one of several fine lodgings in the area; you get a slower, more authentic experience (remember, those padres and conquistadors only traveled on foot or horseback).

Getting There

I-19 intersects with I-10 in Tucson. Keep in mind that the road is marked in kilometers, but the speed limit — 75 for the most part — is in miles per hour. This metric/English system mix-it-up gives the illusion that you're traveling from one place to the next really, really fast.

No rail service is available to this area, but **Greyhound** (☎ 800-231-2222) runs buses among Phoenix, Tucson, and Nogales, Arizona. To get to Nogales, Mexico from the Greyhound station is a hassle, though: The distance from the station is too far to walk and buses run from the depot into Mexico only about once an hour.

Getting Around

You need wheels to get around most of this area because good public transportation is not available; you want to tour Tubac and Nogales by foot once you get to those towns, however.

Where to Stay

Some chain motels populate this route, but if you're not going to hole up in one of the more interesting places, you may as well stay in Tucson where you have bigger pickin's. Spending the night in Nogales has little advantage, too; best to soak up south-of-the-border color during the day then return to sleep in the good ol' U.S. of A. (See Chapter 8 for a key to the $ sign price rating system.)

Amado Territory Inn

$$ Amado

A mid-1990s reconstruction of a late 1800 ranch house, this B&B gives you the best of both worlds: old Southwest color and new Southwest plumbing. Some of the attractive, nouveau-ranch guest rooms have decks with mountain vistas; downstairs, a sunny breakfast nook adjoins a lobby with a soaring ceiling and huge fireplace. Because it's part of a beautifully landscaped complex, practically as big as postage stamp–sized Amado across the highway, you don't feel as close to the highway as you actually are.

3001 E. Frontage Rd. (exit 48 from I-19). ☎ *888-398-8684 or 520-398-8684. Fax: 520-398-8186. E-mail:* info@amado-territory.inn.com. *Internet:* www.amado-territory-inn.com. *Rack rates: July–Oct $90–$105, Nov–June $105–$135. AE, DISC, MC, V.*

Rex Ranch

$$–$$$ Near Amado

The journey itself is worth the price of a room: To get here, you drive across the (usually almost dry) Santa Cruz River, winding past trees that date back to the days when this was a royal Spanish land grant. The Rex no longer functions as a guest ranch, but you can still book a horseback ride. A stress reduction program is scheduled, but just lounging around this desert oasis should lower your blood pressure by several points. The old ranch buildings are lovely and the generic motel cabins are being redone in vibrant Arizona-Mex style. (See also Cantina Romantica in "Where to Dine," in this chapter.)

131 Amado Montosa Rd. (exit 48 from I-19, follow signs for the ranch). ☎ *888-REX RANCH or 520-398-2914. Fax: 520-398-8229. E-mail:* info@ rexranch.com. *Internet:* www.rexranch.com. *Rack rates: Oct–May $120–$135, $225 casitas; June–Sept $105, $205 casitas. AE, DC, DISC, MC, V.*

Tubac Golf Resort

$$$ Tubac

You don't have to be a duffer to want to stay at this golf resort, part of Arizona's first Spanish land grant (issued in 1789) and loaded with Old West charm. In fact, resort guests don't get discounts on green fees (don't whine; the charge is low enough; see "Exploring along the Santa Cruz River"). When nearby Tubac sends you into retail overdrive, just kick back on the deck of your red tile roof casita — some have full kitchens, others separate bedrooms — splash around the palm-flanked pool, hit a few tennis balls around, or sink into one of the lobby's deep leather couches.

1 Otero Rd. (exit 40 from I-19; the resort is just west of Tubac). ☎ *800-848-7893 or 520-398-2211. Fax: 520-398-9261. Internet:* www.arizonaguide.com/tubac. *Rack rates: May 15–Sept $85, $125 casita; Apr 17–May 14 $105, $150 casita; Jan 17–Apr 6 $145, $190 casita; Oct–Jan 16 $95, $140 casita; rates lower Mon–Thurs. AE, MC, V.*

Rio Rico Resort & Country Club

$$$–$$$$ Rio Rico

Although the Rio Rico lacks character compared to the other lodgings in this area — despite several multi-million-dollar touch-ups, its late 1960s roots still show — this conference-oriented resort has a terrific location in the mountains near Nogales, and is ideal for those who like their accommodations thoroughly modern. Perks include a golf course designed by Robert Trent Jones, Sr., horseback riding, an Olympic-size pool, tennis courts, sauna, Jacuzzi, and a small exercise room.

1069 Camino Caralampi (exit 29 from I-19; follow the signs). ☎ *800-288-4746 or 520-281-1901. Fax: 520-281-7132. Internet:* www.rioricoresort.com. *Rack rates: Jan–Mar $165–$185; Apr–May and Sept–Dec $135–$175; Jun–Aug $100–$150. AE, DISC, DC, MC, V.*

Where to Dine

With a few notable exceptions, this area isn't gourmet territory, but it is Mexican-food heaven and fine for down-home American tastes. Cantina Romantica aside, all the restaurants listed here are on or near the I-19 frontage road or within walking distance of recommended sights.

Some clichés are based on fact: Drinking the water in Mexico is not a good idea. In Nogales restaurants, stick to the bottled stuff *(agua pura),* beer, or drinks without ice; on the streets, go for bottled soft drinks rather than the tempting fresh fruit drinks, often blended with ice. (For a key to the $ signs, see Chapter 4.)

Amado Café

$$ Amado   Southwest/Mediterranean

The Southwest meets the Greek isles in this cheerful light-wood dining room. Well-prepared, generously portioned dishes such as mesquite-grilled steak and Greek chicken always taste fresh; the atmosphere is as warm as the regions that inspire the multicultural menu.

3001 E. Frontage Rd. (exit 48 from I-19). ☎ *520-398-9211. Reservations recommended. Main courses: $10–$17. AE, DISC, MC, V. Open: Dinner Tues–Sun.*

Clueless in Nogales?

Most places in Nogales, Mexico, are pretty easy to locate, but if you find yourself in need of directions, don't hesitate to ask a shopkeeper or a man or boy on the street (women tend to be shyer about talking to strangers). To ask for directions in Spanish say, "Dónde está (*dohn*-day ess-*tah*) [fill in the blank] . . . ." Usually, you'll get instructions in English, but if the person you ask actually leads you to the place you're seeking, don't forget to tip him or her a dollar or so.

Cantina Romantica

$$$ Amado Continental

The menu and restaurant both are small and cozy — seven entrees and 13 tables. However, the dining at this spot in gracious Rex Ranch is grand. Sit on wrought-iron chairs under the sun or stars or on (more comfortable) banquettes in a rustic elegant room and enjoy such appetizers as baked artichokes with brie and entrees such as pecan-crusted pork. The dinner menu is Continental with a few Southwest touches; the influences are reversed for the more casual lunches. And true to its name, this upscale cantina is *muy romantica.*

131 Amado Montosa Rd. (exit 48 from I-19, follow signs to Rex Ranch). ☎ *520-398-2914. Reservations required for lunch and dinner. Main courses: $19–$23.50; Sunset Supper, a choice of one of three entrees plus soup or salad and soft drink costs $17. Open: Lunch daily; Sunset Supper Sun and Mon (4–7 p.m.); dinner Tues–Sat. AE, DC, DISC, MC, V.*

Cow Palace

$–$$ Amado American/Tex-Mex

The kitschy rooftop steer is a magnet for fans of truck-stop food. If you're one, this dark, sprawling bar/restaurant doesn't disappoint. A variety of salads and sandwiches fill out the huge menu, but hearty Mexican breakfasts, burgers, and Trail Driver steak dinners are the real reasons to come here.

28802 South Nogales Highway (exit 48 off I-19 south; cross to the Frontage Road on the other side). ☎ *520-398-2201. Reservations recommended for dinner, though this place is BIG, so I'd give it a shot even if you haven't booked. Breakfast: $3–$7.50, lunches: $4–$6, Dinners: $6–$17. Open: Breakfast, lunch, and dinner daily. DISC, MC, V.*

Molina's Pete Kitchen Outpost

$ Nogales, Arizona Mexican

If you don't feel like crossing the border, you can still get the real thing here, and in a historic setting to boot. This brick-walled, wood-beamed restaurant was built in the mid-1960s to resemble the ranch house belonging to Pete Kitchen, an early pioneer. Business people from both sides of the divide come for the generous combination plates — everything from top sirloin with a cheese enchilada, tortillas, and beans to Guaymas shrimp prepared in one of three traditional Mexican styles.

555 E. Frontage Road (exit 8 off I-19 south; go left over the freeway, take the first right and drive for about 1½ miles on the Frontage Road). ☎ *520-281-1852 or 520-281-9946. No reservations needed except for large groups. Combination plates: $6.35–$13.80. Open: Lunch and dinner daily. AE, DC, DISC, MC, V.*

La Roca

$$ Nogales, Mexico Mexican

Savvy Tucsonans know about this delightful cliffside restaurant; you aren't the only ones habla-ing Ingles here, but you're definitely off the beaten tourist track. The small but killer margaritas go well with whatever you choose — *carne tampiqueña* (assorted grilled meats served with a chile relleno and enchilada), or large, succulent Guaymas shrimp. Unlike other restaurants, many of the dishes are served a la carte; your tab can add up if you don't watch it. The folk art and rough stone walls lend an informal feel during the day and candlelight and white-jacket service make the room lovey dovey at night.

Calle Elias 91 (from the border, cross the railroad tracks and walk east [left] several blocks). ☎ *888-527-0220, toll free from the U.S., or (52) 631-2-08-91. No reservations needed except for large groups. Main courses: $8–$16. Open: Lunch and dinner (until midnight!) daily. AE, DC, MC, V.*

Elvira

$ Nogales, Mexico Mexican

A wall made out of crockery and an airy patio are two of the reasons tourists troop into Elvira's. The restaurant also boasts good, inexpensive food (try the chicken mole or the chile rellenos); a location practically across the street from the border; and free shots of tequila as soon as you sit down. Incidentally, the restaurant's name is not pronounced like that of the well-endowed TV ghoul queen — say *el-vee-ruh*.

Av. Obregón 1 (cross the road after you pass through the international border and walk two blocks west [right]). Or follow the crowds; it's at the top of Nogales's most popular shopping street. ☎ *(52) 631-2-47-73. Reservations not accepted. Main courses: $5–$12. Open lunch and dinner daily. MC, V.*

Exploring along the Santa Cruz River

Two of the top attractions in this area include the artisans colony of Tubac and the city of Nogales. Both are magnets for the same activity: producing friction on your plastic (skip ahead to "Shopping along the Santa Cruz River," if that's your thing). Except for golf, this area's other prime draws shouldn't have a negative impact on your wallet.

The Top Things to See and Do

Asarco Mineral Discovery Center

Sahuarita

Wondering about the strange, defoliated slopes you see on the west side of I-19 south of Tucson? You get the dirt (or at least see how it's moved around) on this tour, operated by the American Smelting and Refining Company. Take the PR spiels about the importance of mining and its born-again environmental friendliness for what they're worth and enjoy the rare opportunity to see copper mining, one of Arizona's formative industries, in action. The tours take about an hour, but you're likely to spend another 20 minutes or so at the gift shop and exhibits in the Discovery Center, which is also where you buy the tour tickets. Unless you find the ore-extraction process endlessly fascinating, skip the free half-hour film.

1421 W. Pima Mine Rd. (15 miles south of Tucson; take I-19 exit 80 and go west [right] from the exit ramp; you see the copper roof buildings 100 feet away on the south side of Pima Mine Road). ☎ *520-625-7513. Open: Tues–Sat 9 a.m.–5 p.m. Tours of the Mission Mine open pit leave the Discovery Center at 9:30 a.m., 10 a.m., 11 a.m., 11:30 a.m., 12:30 p.m., 1 p.m., 2 p.m., 2:30 p.m., and 3:30 p.m. Admission $6 adults, $5 seniors (62+), $4 ages 5–12, children under 5 free.*

Titan Missile Museum

Sahuarita

Both hawks and doves are fascinated by this Cold War relic, the only one of 54 Titan II missiles in the United States — including the 18 that ringed the city of Tucson — allowed to stay intact under the terms of the Salt II treaty with the Soviet Union. In fact, this museum offers the only such exhibition of missiles in the world. Tours, which last an hour, take you down into the control center where the ground crew lived and prepared, if necessary, to fire a 165-ton rocket that held a nuclear payload 214 times as powerful as the bomb that destroyed Hiroshima. This museum is operated by the Arizona Aerospace Foundation, which also runs the Pima Air & Space Museum (PASM) and the Aerospace Maintainence and Regeneration Center (AMARC) tours; see Chapter 13 for details on both.

The four men who lived and worked in the cramped mission control area weren't claustrophobes (I hope!). If you are uncomfortable in somewhat small, enclosed spaces, you may want to pass on this tour. If you experience mobility problems, on the other hand, special elevator tours can be arranged; you aren't expected to tread the 55 steps that are involved.

1580 W. Duval Mine Rd. (about 25 miles south of Tucson; take I-19 exit 69 west ¹⁄₁₀ mile past La Cañada to entrance). ☎ *520-625-7736. Open: Nov–Apr, daily 9 a.m.–5 p.m. (except Thanksgiving and Christmas); May–Oct, Wed–Sun 9 a.m.– 5 p.m. Tours given every half hour; last tour at 4 p.m.; walking shoes (i.e., no heels) required. Admission $7.50 adults; $6.50 seniors, active military; $4 ages 7–12; 6 and under free. Combination PASM/Titan Missile Museum (TMM) $13; combination TMM/AMARC $12; combination PASM/TMM/AMARC $18.*

I Left My Heart in . . . Tubac?

Juan Bautista de Anza led 240 colonists across the desert from Tubac, an expedition that resulted in the founding of San Francisco in 1776. In 1859, Arizona's first newspaper was printed in Tubac and in 1860 the town was reckoned to be the largest one in Arizona.

Tubac Presidio State Historic Park and Museum

Old Tubac

Litte remains of the first European settlement in Arizona or of the *presidio* (garrison or fortress) set up to protect it — just a portion of the original 1752 fort and an 1885 schoolhouse. You need to stop at the small museum adjoining the visitor's center to get an idea of this former Spanish colony's importance. A tour of the entire complex shouldn't take you more than an hour, unless you picnic in the pleasant park.

For more action, come on Sunday from 1 to 4 p.m. October through March, when living history presentations let you chat up a frontier friar, a señora preparing tortillas, or soldiers garrisoned at the fort. Kids may be bored here the rest of the week but they definitely like this part.

1 Burruel St. (take exit 40 or 34 off I-19 and follow Tubac Road into the large parking lot at the back of Old Tubac). ☎ *520-398-2252. Open: Daily 8 a.m.–5 p.m. Admission $2 adults, $1 children 7–13, 6 and under free.*

Tumacácori National Historical Park

Tumacácori

Nearby San Xavier del Bac (see Chapter 13) may be Arizona's most impressive Spanish mission, but moody, ruined San Jose de Tumacácori is my favorite, both for the isolated beauty of its setting and the simplicity of the Franciscan structure. The visitor's center/history museum shouldn't take more than 45 minutes to tour; the timing of the rest of your visit depends on how contemplative you feel when you stroll around the mission grounds. On most Wednesday afternoons (1–5 p.m.), from September through April, free van tours explore Calabazas and Guevavi, two other ruined missions in the historical park. The van holds only 14 people; reserve as far in advance as you can.

The courtyard of this mission was a stand-in for Tucson in the movie *Boys on the Side*. The mission isn't usually as lively as it is in the film, but the Christmas festivals are pretty great. (Find more on the festivals in Chapter 2.)

1891 E. Frontage Rd. (take exit 34 off I-19 south and turn right on the frontage road; you see the mission in about 3 miles). ☎ *520-398-2341. Open: Daily 8 a.m.–5 p.m. except Thanksgiving and Christmas. Admission $4 carload (of any ages and number — fill up that Humvee!); $2 adults; 16 and under free; 62 and older with Golden Age Pass free.*

More Cool Things to See and Do

If you like to hike or ride across the landscape, tee off from it, or even leave it behind for the stars, this region has more options for you.

- ✔ **Follow in the footsteps of the conquistadors:** The flat 4½-mile stretch along the Santa Cruz River from Tumacácori to Tubac, popular with hikers and birders, is part of the **Juan Batista de Anza National Historic Trail.** Get a route map from the visitor's center of either historical park. (See "Exploring along the Santa Cruz River," in this chapter.)

- ✔ **Tee off:** Several golf courses in this area are open to the public. The **Rio Rico Resort & Country Club,** 1069 Camino Carampi (☎ 520-281-8567), was voted among the top 25 best in the state and is the site of many qualifying events for USGA and PGA tournaments (green fees $50 before 1 p.m., $30 after). The Spanish-style archways of the **Tubac Golf Resort,** 1 Otero Rd., Tubac (☎ 520-398-2211), starred with Kevin Costner and Rene Russo in *Tin Cup;* and in fact, the lake on the 16th hole was created for the film (green fees $66 before 12:30, $40 after). **Kino Springs,** 187 Kino Springs Dr., Nogales, AZ (☎ 520-287-8701), is on the site of a working cattle ranch once owned by married film stars Stewart Granger and Jean Simmons (green fees: Mon–Fri $35 before 1 p.m., $25 after; Sat–Sun $40 before 1 p.m., $25 after). The green fees in all three cases include a cart but not tax.

- ✔ **Hit the hiking or birding trail:** The Coronado National Forest and the Santa Rita Mountains meet at the **Madera Canyon Recreation Area,** featuring about 200 miles of scenic trails and almost 400 types of birds. To get there, take exit 63 off I-19 and go east on White House Canyon Rd. for 12.5 miles (it turns into Madera Canyon Rd.). Call ☎ 520-670-5464 in Tucson for information; the small, volunteer-run visitor's center in Madera Canyon is only open on weekends.

- ✔ **Horse around:** Even if you don't stay there, you can mount a steed at **Rex Ranch** (☎ 520-398-2914; see "Where to Stay," in this chapter) from mid-October to mid-May. Rates range from $15 for 1 hour to $50 for a half day. **Rio Rico Stables** (☎ 520-394-2701) also offers tours in this area; see the "Horsing around Santa Cruz County" sidebar, in this chapter.

- ✔ **Go on a star search:** Full day (9 a.m.–3 p.m.) tours of the **Fred Lawrence Whipple Observatory** on Mt. Hopkins are offered for $7 on Monday, Wednesday, and Friday from mid-March through November (weather and attendance permitting). You don't actually see any stars (this is a daytime tour, remember?), but the work that is done here is fascinating. And you don't get these great mountaintop views at night. Tour sizes are limited; call ☎ 520-670-5707 for reservations and directions to the visitor's center.

That's One Hot Tamale

The small, spice-redolent **Santa Cruz Chili & Spice Co.**, 1868 E. Frontage Rd. (just south of Tumacácori National Monument; ☎ 520-398-2591), is salsa and chili powder central. Prices are reasonable and you can watch many of the products being made on the premises, as they have been for the past half century.

Shopping

Some people — okay, me included — have been known to skip all the historical sights and just make a beeline for the shops in Tubac and Nogales. You find some similar goods in both places, especially ceramics. Prices are better in Mexico, but the schlep across the border is more of a hassle. In either place, avert your eyes from all those great terra cotta planters and ceramic pots; the cost of shipping them is prohibitive, especially if you want them to arrive in one piece.

Tubac

Forget hostile Pima Indians. The biggest obstacle to reaching the old Tubac Presidio these days is getting past scores of friendly shopkeepers. The town of Tubac is adjacent to the historic park and chock-a-block with more than 80 shops and galleries selling arts and crafts, many staffed by the artisans who created them. No one area is better for shops than another; excellent quality and schlock know no geographical boundaries. Park where you can — things can get pretty crowded on winter weekends — and just roam around.

Check out the wonderful floral metal fountains created by the artisans at **Lee Blackwell Studios,** 18 Plaza Rd. (☎ 520-398-2268), everything from yuccas to irises and roses; and browse the lacquered tables and hand-carved mesquite armoires sold at **Rogoway Gallery,** 1 Calle Baca (☎ 520-398-2913). Take the pulse of the local art scene at the **Tubac Center of the Arts,** 9 Plaza Rd. (☎ 520-398-2371), which hosts high-quality juried shows. Most of the work is for sale.

Nogales

As soon as you cross the border, you start seeing rows of colorful stalls and hear vendors calling out to you, "Come take a look, everything's on sale today." If you're not used to this sort of atmosphere, the sensory input may be overwhelming. Relax. Don't stop because you're being addressed, just smile and keep walking west (right) with the rest of the crowd. You soon reach Avenida Obregón, the main shopping street, where stores with doors line the street and you browse without being hassled (much). (See the "Nogales Shopping Tips" sidebar, in this chapter.)

Nogales Shopping Tips

Shopping in Nogales, Mexico is easy enough; however, to get the best prices, you should keep a few points in mind:

✔ **You don't need to change your dollars into pesos.** The Nogales merchants are happy to have greenbacks and you lose money on the exchange rate if you don't end up spending all your Mexican moolah.

✔ **You may pay a bit more for the privilege of using plastic.** Shopkeepers pass on the hefty charges they incur from the credit card companies. Cash is a good bargaining tool.

✔ **Know when to haggle.** If the store has a door, you may not be able to bargain in it. In a stall, anything goes.

Price tags on an item may or may not be an indicator of a fixed price. A merchant willing to bargain may offer you a better price if you stand around looking undecided. It doesn't hurt to ask, "Is that your final price?" Don't be rude if the shop owner says "Yes."

When bargaining, start out by offering 50 percent of the vendor's asking price. You've done well if you end up meeting the seller halfway between the 50 percent you offer and the original selling price.

Although you can happily walk back and forth along Obregón, maxing out your credit card, good shops exist off the beaten path as well (some of which are detailed later). In particular, Calle Elias (turn east [left] of the tracks rather than right as you cross the border) is fertile shopping ground.

Driving into Mexico is a hassle; the customs line for cars is long and slow and it's hard to find a place — safe or otherwise — to park your car. You're much better off parking on the Arizona side and walking over. When you get close to the border, you see guarded lots that cost about $4 or $5 per day. Practically all the good shopping is within easy strolling distance of the border, anyway.

Serapes and onyx chess sets abound, but you can also find high-quality crafts from all over Mexico in Nogales. Everything from cactus-stem margarita glasses and tinwork mirrors to leather-and-wood *equipale* chairs and Spanish colonial-style wood-and-iron chandeliers are for sale. For portability's sake, brightly patterned rugs and wall hangings, tinwork candlesticks, and papier-mâché fruit are a good bet. The following shops all offer good selections — but no bargaining.

Tearing yourself away from the endless rooms of new and antique home furnishings may be tough at **El Changarro** (Calle Elias 93, just next door to la Roca; see "Where to Dine," earlier in this chapter). Embroidered clothing for women and sterling silver jewelry from Taxco are the specialties at **El Sarape** (Av. Obregón 161). **The Lazy Frog** (Calle Campillo 57; you see it before you get to Obregón) has one of the best selections of crafts from all over Mexico — very high quality and not very low priced. I always ogle the wrought-iron-and-leather barstools and other made-to-order furnishings at **Rusticos de Mexico** (Av. Obregon 182, upstairs) and fantasize about redoing my house. Telephone numbers are difficult to find for the shops — but you probably don't want to hassle with calling them anyway.

Quick Concierge: Santa Cruz River

Area code: 520.

Emergencies: Call ☎ **911.**

Hospitals: In case of an emergency, return to Tucson (see Chapter 13).

Information: To get information by mail, contact the Tubac Chamber of Commerce (☎ 520-398-2704; Internet: www.tubacaz.com); it has no physical address, however, so visit the state historic park for a map of the town and other information. The Nogales-Santa Cruz County Chamber of Commerce, 123 W. Kino Park, Nogales, AZ (☎ 520-287-3685), doesn't have much information about Nogales, Mexico, but can direct you there and answer questions about the rest of the towns and attractions in the area. Nogales, Mexico has a tourist information office on International Street (left of the border crossing; ☎ [011-52] 631-20-203).

Pharmacies: Nogales is known for its pharmacies; practically every corner has one. Arizonans make regular forays south of the border to buy discounted drugs. You may not be arrested if you sneak back a tube of Retin A, but you're supposed to have prescriptions for all drugs, including antibiotics, that you buy in Mexico. Don't even think about trying to smuggle back pharmaceuticals that are illegal or controlled (again, unless you have a prescription) in the United States.

Police: Call ☎ **911** in the United States and try not to get in trouble in Mexico. If you do, you can find the American Embassy on Calle San Jose in the Los Alamos district (☎ [011-52] 631-348-20).

Post Office: Tubac: 2261D Frontage Road (☎ 520-398-0164). Tumacácori: 1910 E. Frontage Road (☎ 520-398-2580).

Eastern Santa Cruz County

With its fields of high golden grass waving in valleys of oak-dotted mountains, this section of Arizona falls far outside the state's scenery stereotypes. (In fact, the area doubled for prairie in the film *Oklahoma.*) Eastern Santa Cruz County is nevertheless rich in Arizona history, with mining and cattle shipping key industries in its past and ranching still important to its present. The (hoped for) future, however, is a product of the unusual geography: Lots of wineries crop up in this area.

Aside from a few shops, Sonoita has little to see; it's primarily a place to eat and sleep. However, you may easily spend a morning or afternoon poking around Patagonia, stopping into funky boutiques, and just strolling around absorbing the small town western flavor. If you want to tour the area's wineries, devote at least half a day. And if you're a birder — well, you're the best judge of how long you want to hang around the Patagonia-Sonoita Creek Preserve and other avian haunts waiting for that Elegant Trogon to put in an appearance.

Getting There

I-10 east intersects with Highway 83 east of Tucson; take it south to reach Sonoita, which sits at the junction of Highway 82. If you come from I-19, take Highway 82 east from Nogales, Arizona, to Patagonia. No rail or bus service is available to this area.

Getting Around

No public transportation is available in either Sonoita or Patagonia; these towns are 12 miles from each other via Highway 82. Central Patagonia is nice to tour on foot, but you need a car for any other explorations. Both towns pretty much consist of main streets that are easy to spot because highways change into them. In Sonoita, the highway keeps its name, Highway 82; in Patagonia, it's called Naugle Avenue and the street that runs parallel to it is McKeown Avenue. Most of what happens in Patagonia — which isn't much — happens on Naugle and McKoewn between Third and Fourth Avenues.

Where to Stay

Fans of chain hotels are out of luck here. Stay in this area and you settle for character rather than consistency. That doesn't mean giving up creature comforts by any means, but this *is* a rural area. Even the places that offer cable TV don't necessarily get good reception. (See Chapter 8 for a key to the $ sign rating system.)

Sonoita Inn

$$ Sonoita

This unusual Kentucky-inspired A-frame once belonged to Secretariat's owner and housed the famed racehorse's triple crown — which explains all the photographs of horses and area ranches inside. Guest rooms, recent (1999) additions to the soaring-ceiling structure, are individually decorated in attractive western country style. The upstairs rooms are worth the extra charge — they're larger and offer superb views (you overlook the road if you stay in the front on either floor).

3243 Highway 82 (just east of the Highway 82/83 intersection). ☎ *520-455-5935. Fax: 520-455-5069. E-mail:* info@sonoitainn.com. *Internet:* www.sonoitainn. com. *Rack rates: $99 (downstairs), $125 (upstairs). Rates include Continental breakfast. AE, DC, DISC, MC, V.*

The Vineyard Bed &Breakfast

$$ Sonoita

This delightful, 20-acre rural retreat comes with spreading oak tree and hammock, two burros, two black labs, a parrot, hens who provide eggs for the generous country breakfasts, and of course, a vineyard. Three of the rooms, in a 1916 adobe, are country cozy; the fourth, in a separate casita, is more Southwestern.

92 Los Encinos Rd. (from the Highway 82/83 intersection, take 83 south to Los Encinos and turn left). ☎ *520-455-4749. Internet:* www.virtualcities.com/ arizona/sonoita. *Rack rates: $85–$95. Rates include full breakfast. No credit cards. No children under 12. Closed July 4–end of July.*

Circle Z Ranch

$$$ Patagonia

Sonoita Creek runs through this 5000-acre spread in the foothills of the Santa Rita Mountains, abutting Coronado National Forest. This idyllic setting, along with cheery rooms and friendly service, explains why generations of guests come back to Arizona's oldest continuously operating dude ranch (started 1926) year after year. No organized programs for kids, but they ride and eat dinner separately (and well supervised) from the adults — fun for them, even more fun for the grownups.

4 miles southwest of Patagonia. (Look for the ranch sign between the 14- and 15-mile markers on the west side of Highway 82.) ☎ *888-854-2525 or 520-394-2525. Fax: 520-394-2058. E-mail:* info@circlez.com. *Internet:* www.circlez.com. *Rack rates: $945–$990 per adult in double room per week high season (Nov 21–27, Dec 19–Jan 1, Feb 20–Apr 29); $750–$796 low season (Oct 31–Nov 20; Nov 28– Dec 18; Jan 2–Feb 19, Apr 30–May 14). Ages 14–17 $750 high season, $570 low season; ages 5–13 $570 high season, $468 low season; under 5 $300 high season, $240 low season. Rates higher for stays under a week, 3 night minimum. Cottages, family rates available. Rates include all meals, 2 trail rides a day (except Sun). No credit cards; personal checks accepted. Closed mid-May through Oct.*

The Duquesne House

$ Patagonia

Patagonia personified, this B&B is historical, artsy, and a bit funky. Built as a miner's boarding house at the turn of the last century, it abounds in the creative touches of owner Regina Medley (see "Shopping," for her Mesquite Grove gallery). This comfortable and charming spot may not cut it with the Starbucks crowd, though.

357 Dusquesne Ave. (on the south side of town, between Third and Fourth Avenues). ☎ *520-394-2732 or 520-394-0054. Rack rates: $75 double. Rates include full break-fast. No credit cards.*

The Stage Stop Inn

$ Patagonia

Don't let the lobby and the hotel name fool you: All western character here begins and ends with those two features. Rooms are standard motel issue, with no higher aspirations, but they're reasonably priced and include TVs. Convenience — it's smack in the center of town — and a swimming pool are other pluses.

303 W. McKeown Ave. (on the town's main street, near Third Ave.). ☎ *800-923-2211 (in AZ) or 520-394-2211. Rack rates: $69. AE, D, DC, MC, V.*

Where to Dine

The good news is that this area has some surprisingly sophisticated restaurants. You find dining quality equal to that of the big cities without big-city prices. The bad news is that the hours are still small town. Some places don't open every night and many stop serving dinner at 8 p.m. In summer . . . well, all bets are off about when most of the restaurants decide to operate.

Finding most of the following Sonoita and Patagonia restaurants is not a problem. With the exception of Grasslands, every place I recommend is on the towns' main streets (see "Getting Around," at the beginning of this section). Although Sonoita and Patagonia are only 12 miles from each other, they're dark miles that you don't want to drive at night — especially if you take advantage of the fact that this is wine country. If possible, plan to eat near where you stay. (For a key to the $ signs, see Chapter 4.)

Café Sonoita

$$ Sonoita American

Come to these small, unassuming dining rooms for comfort food — especially if you find solace in the likes of fresh pan-seared salmon, sauteed sea scallops with tortellini, or (for brunch) Blackforest ham, cheddar, and onion omelets. More traditional mood-soothers, such as meatloaf and prime rib with mashed potatoes, are regulars on the ever-changing chalkboard menu. In addition, you can get homemade soups and desserts. Sandwiches and burgers are the lunchtime staples, but smaller portions of the nightly specials may turn up, too.

3280 Highway 82 (½ mile east of the Highway 82/83 intersection on the north side of the road). ☎ *520-455-5278. Reservations recommended for 5 or more at dinner. Main courses: $6.95–$15.75. Open: Lunch Thur–Sat, dinner (5 p.m.–8 p.m.) Wed–Sat, Sun brunch (11 a.m.–3 p.m.).*

The Grasslands

$ Sonoita Bakery/Cafe

If you're around Sonoita at breakfast or lunchtime, seek out this bakery/cafe, serving homey fare with a slight German accent. Organic ingredients are used whenever possible in the excellent quiches, pastas, and sandwiches, the latter made with bread baked on the premises. There's also a full bar (in case you were feeling far too pure). Don't leave without trying — or at least taking away — some of the terrific cinnamon rolls.

3119 S. Highway 83 (½ mile south of Highway 82 intersection). ☎ *520-455-4770. Reservations not needed. Sandwiches, platters, and pastas: $7.95–$9.95. Open: Wed–Sun 8 a.m.–3 p.m. AE, MC. V.*

Karen's Wine Country Cafe

$$–$$$ Sonoita   Continental/New American

More Sonoma than Arizona, save for the Mexican tile floor and Spanish-style ceiling beams, this small, country-cute dining room has a wonderful grassland vista and a small but well-chosen menu. The menu always includes beef, pork, chicken, and fish dishes — perhaps beef tenderloin with bleu cheese or chicken with Asiago cream sauce. The lighter options include grilled vegetables and the wonderful Wine Country salad: organic greens with dried fruit, glazed pecans, and three types of cheeses. However, the wine country represented by the bottle and glass is not, for the most part, the one you admire from the restaurant's large windows — the selection of local wines is extremely small.

3266 Highway 82 (about ½ mile east of the Highway 83 intersection, north side of the street). ☎ *520-455-5282. Reservations strongly recommended. Main courses: $12.95–$19.95; four-course wine dinner $39.95. Open: Daily for lunch, Thurs–Sat dinner (5 –8 p.m.). Closed first 2 weeks of July. MC, V.*

The Steak Out

$$–$$$ Sonoita   Steak/American

Well prepared simple fare in a barnlike setting is the winning formula for this cowboy steakhouse. In the large wood-paneled room, you watch mesquite-grilled steaks, ribs, and chicken emerge from the open kitchen, while a few antlered heads stare down at you from the rafters. Good country and western bands play on Friday, Saturday, and Sunday nights. Sundays bring a captive audience: This restaurant is the only place open in town that night.

3235 Highway 82 (just east of the intersection with Highway 83, next to the Sonoita Inn). ☎ *520-455-5205. Reservations suggested on the weekends. Dinners: $15–$22 (including salad, beans, roll); burgers: $6.95–$15.95. Open: Lunch Sat and Sun, dinner nightly. AE, DC, DISC, MC, V.*

Cose Buone

$$ Patagonia   Italian

Here in the middle of nowhere, you find some of the best food in southern Arizona (or northern Arizona, for that matter) at extremely reasonable prices. Twenty dollars gets you a choice of soup or antipasto, pasta or risotto, plus an entree. The menu changes every 2 weeks. The risotto may come with gorgonzola and toasted walnuts (good vegetarian options are always available); the entree choices could include pork tenderloin stuffed with fontina, fresh sage, and prosciutto. Don't agonize: You won't be disappointed, whatever you decide on. Shelling out extra for desserts such as chocolate and amaretto semifreddo or for one of the reasonably priced bottles of Italian wine is well worth the bucks.

436 Naugle Ave. ☎ *520-394-2366. Reservations highly recommended. Main courses: $20 for a three-course, prix-fixe dinner. Open: Dinner 5:30–8 p.m. Fri–Tues. MC, V. Closed mid-June–early Sept.*

Marie's

$$–$$$ **Patagonia Mediterranean**

The food and the setting vie for your attention at Marie's, where creative Mediterranean food is served in the cozy, colorful rooms of a charming old house. Whatever you go for — maybe the chicken and pistachio pâté followed by moussaka — save room for the signature chocolate hazelnut torte.

340 Naugle Avenue. ☎ *520-394-2812. Reservations strongly advised. Main courses: $9.95–$13.95. MC, V. Open: Dinner Wed–Sat, Sun 1–7 p.m. Closed September.*

Velvet Elvis

$ **Patagonia Pizza**

This combination art gallery/pizza place is as hip as its name, but the food doesn't have attitude (unless you count the fact that it's super fresh). Come here for creative, hot-from-the-oven calzone and pizza, as well as for interesting salads. And yes, there is a velvet Elvis (say that three times fast!) prominently displayed up front.

292 Naugle Ave. ☎ *520-394-2102. Reservations not accepted. Calzones $6.50–$8.25; pizzas $11.95 (extra for toppings), around $2.25 by the slice. Open: Thur 5–8 p.m., Fri–Sun noon–8 p.m. MC, V.*

Exploring Eastern Santa Cruz County

I'm almost tempted to say about eastern Santa Cruz County that there is no there there. Except for Patagonia, this region doesn't really have a tourist center; you'll spend much of your time in this region roaming about.

The Top Things to See and Do

A one-time shipping center for cattle and silver, Patagonia manages to maintain its western flavor. I observed ranch hands on horseback trotting alongside traffic on the town's main drag (which flanks Highway 82). Conversely, Patagonia draws a variety of artsy types. Strolling around the streets, looking at the old railroad depot — now the town hall — and browsing the crafts stores (see " Shopping") are pleasant activities. Other things to do around here include:

> ✔ **Go birding and hiking:** The 1400-acre **Nature Conservancy's Patagonia-Sonoita Creek Preserve** (☎ 520-394-2400) protects a rare waterside habitat. Nearly 300 types of birds have been spotted here (some of them are even spotted), along with plenty of less flighty creatures — everything from desert tortoises to deer. To get here, make a right on Fourth Ave., which comes to a dead end; then make a left. The paved road soon becomes dirt; take it

¾ of a mile to the preserve. Open Wed–Sun 7:30 a.m.–3:30 p.m.; guided walks are offered Saturday at 9 a.m. (call ahead to check). Suggested donation: $5 for nonmembers.

✔ **Check some more birds off your list:** The roadside rest located 4.2 miles south of Patagonia on Highway 82 is famed for sightings of the rare violet-crowned hummingbird and rose-throated becard. The **Empire-Cienaga Resource Conservation Area,** with entrances 7 miles north of Sonoita on the east side of Highway 83 and 5 miles north of Sonoita on the north side of Highway 82 (☎ **520-722-4289**), is another avian haven; you may spot a grey hawk here.

✔ **Check out the bar scene, western style:** For some real local color — including the occasional bar brawl — mosey over to the **Big Steer Saloon/Dance Hall,** 339 McKoewn Ave. (☎ **520-394-2500**), and the **Wagon Wheel Saloon,** 400 W. Naugle Ave. (☎ **520-394-2433**); both stay open until 1 a.m.

More Cool Things to See and Do

If you have a bit more time in Patagonia, you may want to consider one of the attractions listed below. If you're a horse fan, check out the "Horsing around Santa Cruz County" sidebar, in this chapter.

✔ **Get splashy:** A large reservoir formed by the damming of Sonoita Creek, and subsequently stocked with fish, is the centerpiece of **Patagonia Lake State Park** (☎ **520-287-6965**). Rowboats, paddle-boats, canoes, and fishing supplies and licenses are available at the marina store (☎**520-287-6063**). You can swim at a sandy beach and water-ski on the western part of the lake daily off season, weekdays in summer. This spot is not as tranquil on week-ends or in the summer, but it is fun. To get here, take Highway 82 7 miles south from Patagonia; then make a right at Lake Patagonia Road and drive 4 miles.

Horsing around Santa Cruz County

What's ranching country without equines? **The Sonoita Fairgrounds** (☎ **520-455-553**) hosts several horsy events including the Grass Ridge Horse Trials in mid-October; the Santa Cruz County Horse Races on the last weekend in April/first weekend in May; and the Sonoita Quarter Horse show, billed as the oldest quarter horse show in the nation, during the first weekend in June. In addition, the fairgrounds holds the Sonoita Rodeo on Labor Day weekend, which includes a Sunday night steak fry and dance.

If you want to do your own horsey thing, contact **Sonoita Stables** (☎ **520-455-9266**) or **Arizona Trail Tours/Rio Rico Stables** (☎ **520-394-2701**; Internet: www.aztrailtours.com). Options range from $20 for an hour-long ride to $750 for a 3-night pack trip.

✔ **Wine around:** See the "Great Grapes! Southern Arizona's Surprising Wineries" sidebar, in this chapter, for the area's loop to get looped.

✔ **Give up the ghost (Not):** Looking for some prime real estate in the beautiful San Rafael Valley? The abandoned mining town of **Duquesne** — which now consists of about five vandalized but still intact buildings southeast of Patagonia — may be for sale. If you want to check the town out, don't go without consulting a good Forest Service map, obtainable at the visitor's center in Patagonia. A high-clearance vehicle is also an excellent idea. (I punctured a hole in my oil pan while driving the rough roads en route to the elusive town — that definitely dampened my buying enthusiasm.)

Shopping

In Sonoita, a few good shops dot the strip center on Highway 82 where Karen's Wine Country Cafe (see "Where to Dine," in this chapter) is located; I especially like the upscale western duds at **Cowboy's Sweetheart,** 3266 Highway 82 (☎ 520-455-4652).

Great Grapes! Southern Arizona's Surprising Wineries

Who wudda thunk it? Vinifera grapes seem to like the high elevation (4,100 feet plus) valleys in Santa Cruz County. The area has lots of warm, sunny days and a lush topsoil that has been compared to the (pay) dirt in Burgundy, France. Although grape growing and fermenting in this region date back centuries, scientifically based wine making is a much more recent phenomenon.

True, Sonoma doesn't have to start sweating just yet; most of the wine makers in the area are not quite ready for prime time. The exception is Kent Callaghan, whose **Callaghan Vineyards** (3 miles southeast of Elgin, ☎ 520-455-5650) and **Dos Cabezas Wineworks** (near Willcox, ☎ 520-455-5285) produce top-notch bottles. But tooling around this beautiful area, stopping and sipping along the way is still fun; you find some decent wines — or at least good souvenir labels — at reasonable prices.

In addition to Callaghan, which is only open on Sunday afternoons, the best bets in the immediate area are **Sonoita Vineyards,** 3 miles southeast of Elgin (☎ 520-455-5893), whose founder, Dr. Gordon Dutt, reintroduced winemaking to the area; and **The Village of Elgin Winery,** in Elgin (☎ 520-455-9309), occupying a former (1985) bordello building and selling bottles with names such as Tombstone Red. If you're near Tucson, stop off at the **Dark Mountain Brewery and Winery,** 13605 E. Benson Highway, Vail (exit 279 off I-10; ☎ 520-762-5777). Arizona's oldest winery, Dark Mountain is also the only one in the Southwest that incorporates a microbrewery. Tasting days and times vary and change seasonally; call ahead.

But Patagonia is definitely the place for serious retail patrols — just walk up and down the two main streets, McKoewn and Naugle. These roads flank Highway 82 between Third and Fourth Avenues. My favorites for local crafts are **Mesquite Grove Gallery**, 371 McKoewn Ave. (☎ 520-394-2358) and **Global Arts Gallery**, 315 McKoewn Ave. (☎520-394-0077), where I bought a pair of great horse earrings and a Carmen Miranda cookie jar (sorry, no more left). **Kazzam Nature Center**, 348 Naugle Ave. (☎ 520-394-2823), is a terrific resource for gardeners and, especially, birders.

Quick Concierge: Eastern Santa Cruz County

Information: Sonoita-Elgin Chamber of Commerce, 3123 Highway 83, unit C (in Carnevale Travel), (☎ 520-455-5498). Patagonia Visitors Center, 305 McKoewn Ave. (in Mariposa Books), (☎ 888-794-0060 or 520-394-0060; Internet: www.theriver.com/Public/patagoniaaz).

Post Office: Sonoita: Intersection of Hwys. 82 and 83 (☎ 520-455-5500). Patagonia: 100 Taylor Ave., just off Highway 82 (☎ 520-394-2950).

Medical: The only medical facility in Sonoita is a pharmacy: Old Pueblo United Drugs, 3272 Highway 82, ☎ 520-455-0058. Patagonia does not have a pharmacy, but it does have a medical center: Family Health Center, 101 Taylor St. (just off Highway 82; ☎ 520-394-2262), open Mon–Fri 9 a.m.– 5 p.m. As you may guess, you want to head for Tucson or Sierra Vista (see "Southern Cochise County") in the event of a medical emergency.

Southern Cochise County

The lower portion of Cochise County has the greatest concentration of attractions in southeastern Arizona, largely of the historical sort but also of the green variety. This area also has the widest range of places to stay; it's a good base for side trips to the rest of the region.

In a time crunch, plan to devote at least half a day to Tombstone and another half to Bisbee. (Tombstone gets all the press, but Bisbee is equally interesting and far more scenic.) If you're not in a rush, spend a full day in each of these two towns. Military history buffs should allot a few hours to Fort Huachuca in Sierra Vista, while nature lovers should schedule some time for Ramsey Canyon and Coronado Monument, both near Sierra Vista.

Getting There

To reach **Sierra Vista** from Tucson, take I-10 east to Highway 90 and drive south some 35 miles to the junction with Highway 92. **Tombstone** is 28 miles northeast of Sierra Vista via Highway 90 or 24 miles south of

Benson via Highway 80, and **Bisbee** is 24 miles south of Tombstone on Highway 80.

Regular flights are scheduled to Fort Huachuca Airport (Sierra Vista) via **America West/Mesa** (☎ 800-235-9292), and several major car rental companies are available at the airport. Unless you or a member of your family is in the military (Fort Huachuca is a major military base), though, you may find it far more convenient to fly into — and drive from — Tucson.

The Douglas Shuttle (☎ 520-388-9896 in Tucson) runs vans eight times a day from Tucson to Benson, Tombstone, and Bisbee, finishing its route in Douglas (near Mexico); the charge is about $15 to go from Tucson to Bisbee. The larger **Golden State** (☎ 520-624-9434) buses go four times daily from Tucson to Sierra Vista and Bisbee ($16), ending in Agua Prieta, Mexico, across the border from Douglas. You need wheels in Sierra Vista. But if you've got more time than money and don't care about touring the rest of the region, you can visit both Tombstone and Bisbee by bus. See also Chapter 13 for information on a day trip to both towns.

Getting Around

A wide-ranging public bus system serves **Sierra Vista;** call ☎ 520-459-0595 for schedules and stops. You may prefer motoring yourself; the city is sufficiently spread out (and the attractions sufficiently limited) that driving is the way to go.

On the other hand, wheels are not necessarily an asset in **Bisbee.** A San Francisco in miniature, it has narrow streets, many of which veer sharply uphill, and off-street parking is a rare commodity. Unless you stay or eat in the suburb of Warren, you can cover most of what you want to see on foot. And if you're hill weary and nowhere near your car or your hotel, the 60¢ public transit provided by Catholic Community Services of Cochise County (☎ 520-432-2285 or 459-0595; 800-352-8161TDD) every day except Sunday can be an, er, godsend.

You either have to hoof it in **Tombstone,** which is fairly compact anyway, or drive. In this somewhat parking spot–challenged town (at least in the major tourist areas), it's a good idea to leave your car at your lodging if you sleep anywhere near Allen Street, Tombstone's main drag. If you're in reasonably good shape, you should be able to walk to most of the town's tourist attractions (though not to Boot Hill, which is too far).

Where to Stay

Except for Sierra Vista, this territory isn't prime with chain hotels, which can make your stay difficult if you travel with kids. This area is, however, great for those looking for something entirely different — everything from a bordello-style B&B to a place where you can rent a vintage RV. (See Chapter 4 for a key to the $ sign rating system.)

The Top Hotels in and around Sierra Vista

Casa de San Pedro

$$–$$$ Hereford

This B&B is for the birds — and for their human fans who can hike out the back door to the nearby San Pedro Riparian Conservation Area. When you return to your nest, you can check any sightings on the Robert Tory Peterson software installed on the common room computer. A hacienda-style complex with Southwest modern rooms, this B&B was custom-designed in the mid-1990s for those who like creatures but also enjoy creature comforts. Birding tours and courses are often offered (for an extra fee) on many weekends.

8933 S. Yell Ln. (from the Highway 90/92 intersection in Sierra Vista, go south on 92 [18.5 miles], north on Palominas Rd. [2.0 miles], and east on Waters Rd. [1.0 mile]). ☎ **800-588-6468** *or 520-366-1300. Fax: 520-366-0701. E-mail:* casadesanpedro@ naturesinn.com. *Internet:* www.naturesinn.com. *Rack rates: $100–$139; rates include full breakfast (and all the fresh pie you can eat); discounts on long-term stays off-season. DISC, MC, V.*

Ramsey Canyon Inn Bed & Breakfast

$$–$$$ Hereford

Hummingbirds, a nature preserve, a historic home, and fresh-baked pies: Now that's a winning lodging combination. When the Nature Conservancy, which manages the adjacent Ramsey Canyon Preserve, took over the native-wood-and-stone inn in 1999, they toned down the Victorian frills a bit but kept the former owner's two-fresh-pies-a-day tradition intact. Even if you're not a birder, you'll be charmed by the hummingbirds feeding outside the window of the breakfast nook where B&B guests do some heavy-duty feeding of their own.

29 Ramsey Canyon Rd. (from Sierra Vista, take Highway 92 south to Ramsey Canyon Rd, turn right [west] and drive 4 miles). ☎ **520-378-3010.** *Fax: 520-378-0487. E-mail:* lodging@theriver.com. *Internet:* www.tnc.org/ramseycanyon/ ramseycanyoninn. *Rack rates: $110–$132 (inn rooms); $132 self-contained apart-ment units. Two-night mininum stay. Inn rates include full breakfast, apartment rates don't. MC, V.*

San Pedro River Inn

$$ Hereford

The stuff of escapist fantasies is here: fishing on the pond of an old dairy farm; sitting out on a front porch, just staring at a blue, cloudless sky; and barbecuing some burgers to fortify yourself for another day of doing exactly the same. The four fully equipped cottages on this lush spread next to the San Pedro Riparian Conservation Area aren't fancy, but if you want a laid-back place to bring the kids (and dog and horse), you found yourself the perfect getaway.

8326 S. Hereford Rd. (from Sierra Vista, take Highway 92 south two miles to Hereford and go east over the one-way bridge; follow the signs from there). ☎ and fax: 520-366-5532. Internet: www.sanpedroriverinn.com. Rack rates: $95 for two guests in a cottage, but three of the cottages are large enough for four to six people, which lowers rates; rates include Continental breakfast brought to your door the night before. For $5 each, pets are boarded in an outdoor pen, horses in corrals. No credit cards.

Runner-Up Hotels in and around Sierra Vista

The Sierra Vista Convention and Visitors Bureau (see "Quick Concierge: Southern Cochise County," in this chapter) has listings of the various motels and hotels in town, including links to the **Budget Inn, Motel 6,** and **Super 8 chains** (see the appendix for 800 numbers). For a similar but slightly more upscale accommodation consider the **Windermere Hotel & Conference Center** ($), 2047 S. Highway 92, Sierra Vista (☎ 800-825-4656 or 520-459-5900; Fax 520-458-1347). Although business-oriented and bland, it's good for families because of the reasonable rates (including full breakfast) and amenities such as a pool and in-room refrigerators. The Windermere is also convenient to Ramsey Canyon.

The Top Hotels in Bisbee

The Bisbee Grand

$–$$ Old Bisbee

Over-the-top and verging on kinky, this converted copper miners' roost has some of the most gorgeous, opulent rooms in town. (I spotted a riding crop on the bed of the equestrian suite and the flocked red wallpaper in the hallway is high-bordello style.) All are on the second floor above a historic saloon (where you collect your key) and some look out onto bustling Main Street, so serenity isn't one of this B&B's strong points.

61 Main St. ☎ 800-421-1909 or 520-432-5900. Rack rates: $55–$78; $95–$110 suite; rates include full breakfast. AE, CB, DC, DISC, MC, V.

Calumet & Arizona Guest House

$ Warren

Architect Henry Trost was ahead of his time: The wonderfully clean-lined, pretty-in-pink confection he created for a Bisbee mining executive in 1906 could be straight out of the pages of this month's *Architectural Digest*. Rooms inside the B&B, located in a quiet Bisbee suburb, are as lovely as the house and its grounds — which makes the fact that pets and children are welcome all the more surprising. Some adjoining rooms share a bath, but that works fine for families.

608 Powell St. (in the Bisbee suburb of Warren; call for directions). ☎ 520-432-4845. Rack rates: $60–$70, including full, order-from-a-menu breakfast. MC, V.

Copper Queen

$$ Old Bisbee

Host to the likes of John Wayne and Teddy Roosevelt for decades after it opened in 1902, Bisbee's only full-service (three-meal restaurant, pool, bar) hotel isn't posh enough to be a celebrity magnet anymore, but it's great for local color. Although the rooms lost some Victorian charm with the addition of such amenities as private baths, phones, and color TVs, the public areas are so Old West authentic that you feel as if you should pull up in a horse-drawn carriage.

11 Howell Ave. ☎ *800-247-5829 or 520-432-2216. Fax: 520-432-4298. Rack rates: $70–136. AE, D, DC, MC, V*

High Desert Inn

$–$$ Old Bisbee

A long way from its days as the Cochise County lockup, this inn is the most comfortable and up-to-date place to stay in Bisbee — hands down. The oddly attractive neoclassical jailhouse was gutted to install pared-down but lovely rooms that are cable TV and modem friendly. The excellent restaurant downstairs (see "The Top Restaurants," in this chapter) is another key asset.

8 Naco Rd. (take the Old Bisbee exit from Highway 80 and take a right at the stop sign; you see the inn on the left). ☎ *800-281-0510 or 520-432-1442. E-mail:* highdesert@theriver.com. *Internet:* www.highdesertinn.com. *Rack rates: $70–$95. DISC, MC, V. Closed first 3 weeks in June.*

The Runner-Up Hotels in Bisbee

My top picks just skim the surface; Bisbee can be mined more deeply for rooms that may suit your personal quirks. Check with the Chamber of Commerce (see "Quick Concierge: Southern Cochise County," in this chapter) in person or online if the above are full. And also consider the following lodgings.

The Hotel La More/The Bisbee Inn

$ **Bisbee** This spot has small baths and limited parking but the historic restoration is beautiful and you can't find a better breakfast (especially gratis!) in town. 45 OK St. ☎ 888-432-5131 or 520-432-5131. Fax: 520-432-5343. E-mail: bisbeeinn@aol.com. Internet: www.bisbeeinn.com.

The Inn at Castle Rock

$–$$ **Old Bisbee** This 1890s miners' boarding house perched on a hillside is lush (gardens and flowers galore), funky (a flooded mine shaft in the dining room), and well located. 112 Tombstone Canyon Rd. ☎ 800-566-4449 or 520-432-4449. Fax: 520-432-7868. E-mail: mail@theinn.org. Internet: www.theinn.org.

Stay in the Ultimate of '50s Style

You may expect to see Wally and the Beaver emerging from one of the **Shady Dell Vintage Trailers**, 1 Douglas Rd. (near the Highway 80 traffic circle; ☎ **520-432-3567**). For retro freaks who don't mind close quarters — and a cemetery across the road — the period-furnished 1940s and 1950s Airstreams and Spartenettes are a kick. Rates range from $30 to $70, double occupancy. The owner also operates the adajacent Dot's Diner, equally retro and equally fun.

The Schoolhouse Inn

$–$$ **Bisbee** This inn in a former schoolhouse is a good choice if you don't mind third-grade flashbacks. The subject-themed rooms — for example, arithmetic and writing — are amusing and you don't have to worry about getting held back. 818 Tombstone Canyon Rd. ☎ **800-537-4333** or 520-432-2996.

The Top Hotels in Tombstone

The Best Western Look-Out Lodge

$–$$ **Tombstone**

The only chain lodging in Tombstone, this Best Western has rooms with all the advantages of its genre including your own personal TV and a heated pool. In addition, you can expect terrific mountain and desert views and such nice (and nongeneric) touches as handcrafted wood clocks. The only drawback is that it's not within, uh, shooting distance of Allen Street, the town's main drag.

Highway 80 W (just beyond Boot Hill Cemetery, if you're coming from town). ☎ ***800-528-1234** or 520-457-2223. Fax: 520-457-3870. E-mail:* bwlookoutlodge@ tombstone1880.com. *Rates: $69–$79. Continental breakfast included. AE, D, DC, MC, V.*

Tombstone Boarding House

$ **Tombstone**

Historic character plus a private bath in every antiques-filled room makes these two joined-at-the-hip 1880s adobes my top Tombstone B&B pick. Another plus for B&B-phobes: Although guests eat breakfast next door in the owner's house, all the rooms have private entrances, so you have less of a sense that you're intruding on someone else's space (or vice versa).

108 N. Fourth St. (between Safford and Bruce, two blocks from Allen). ☎ ***520-457-3716.** Fax: 520-457-3038. Rack rates: $60–$80, including full breakfast. AE, MC, V.*

Victoria's Bed and Breakfast

$ **Tombstone**

At Victoria's, guests look through rose-colored glasses — 1880 rose-design etched-glass panes, to be precise. Rooms are romantic and a wedding chapel is on the premises in case you want to tie the knot at the former Emily Morton's Boarding and Pleasure House.

211 Toughnut (next door to the Tombstone Courthouse Historic Park). ☎ *800-952-8216 or 520-457-3677. E-mail:* vsbb@primenet.com. *Internet:* www.tombstone1880.com/vsbb. *Rack rates: $65–$75, higher on holiday weekends; full breakfast included.*

The Runner-Up Hotels in Tombstone

The room supply is somewhat short in Tombstone, but the Chamber of Commerce (see "Quick Concierge: Southern Cochise County," in this chapter) lists additional places to stay. Two others you might try are

Marie's Bed and Breakfast

$ **Tombstone**   This 1906 Victorian adobe has only two rooms with a shared bath, but they're nicely decorated. The owner, who volunteers at the Chamber of Commerce, is a great source of insider tourism tips (don't worry, tourism tips are legal). 101 N. Fourth St. ☎ 520-457-3831. Fax: 520-457-9016. E-mail: maries@theriver.com. Internet: www.theriver.com/maries.

Priscilla's Bed and Breakfast

$ **Tombstone**   A beautifully restored two-story clapboard, this spot is for those who like the words "B&B" and "Victorian" to be synonymous. The three upstairs bedrooms share a bath; the one downstairs has its own. 101 N. Third St. ☎ 520-457-3844. E-mail: prisc@theriver.com. Internet: www.tombstone1880.com/priscilla.

Where to Dine

Southern Cochise County has good sleeps, not so great eats. The only three places you should drive out of your way for are in Bisbee and these restaurants limit their hours. I list them in the next section and relegate the others — which are convenient to tourist sights and fine, just not worth a detour — to the runners-up category. (For a key to the $ signs, see Chapter 4.)

The Top Restaurants

Café Roka

$$ **Old Bisbee   Italian-New American**

Totally out of character for hippyish Bisbee when it opened in the mid-1990s, Cafe Roka proved that Cochise County was ready for a sorbet palate freshener between courses. An open dining room with exposed brick walls and the original tinwork ceiling is the retro chic setting for such dishes as portobello mushroom ravioli, pine nut risotto cakes, and roasted half duck, served with a lovely salad, fresh soup of the day — and the aforementioned sorbet.

35 Main St. ☎ *520-432-5153. Reservations essential; this is the region's foodie magnet. Main courses: $10.50–$17.50 (including soup, salad, sorbet). Open: Dinner Wed–Sat. AE, MC, V.*

High Desert Inn Dining Room

$$–$$$ **Old Bisbee   French/Continental**

As high-tone as you may expect from a Cordon Bleu-trained chef but with prices adjusted for small-town wallets, the menu in this intimate dining room-cum-art gallery is to drool over (but please don't; that would be terribly uncouth). A meal here may start with a warm terrine of fresh chevre with roasted pepper, followed by a Provençal-braised chicken breast with cous cous. Desserts never disappoint, and Sunday's champagne brunch is wonderful, too.

8 Naco Road. ☎ *520-432-1442. Reservations essential (this is Cochise County's other gourmet roost and it's smaller than Cafe Roka). Main courses: $13.50–$18.50. Open: Dinner Thur–Sat, Sunday brunch 10 a.m.–2 p.m. DISC, MC, V.*

Rosa's Little Italy

$$ **Warren   Italian**

A something-for-everyone menu, generous portions, and reasonable prices make this restaurant well worth the short drive from Old Bisbee, especially on fine days when you can dine outside on the wisteria-draped patio. Other pluses include a mean antipasto, superb veal scallopini, and a full page devoted to vegetarian pastas. But Rosa's deserved popularity makes the no reservations policy a drag; if you don't come before opening time (5 p.m.) or after 8 p.m., expect a wait.

7 Bisbee Road, Warren Plaza (across from the Bisbee Hospital). ☎ *520-432-1331. No reservations accepted (see gripe, above). Main courses: $10.50–$14.95 (served with soup, salad, and unlimited pasta of the day); pastas: $7.75–$14.95; bring your own wine. Open: Dinner Tues–Sat. DISC, MC, V.*

The Runner-Up Restaurants

The Brewery Restaurant & Stock Exchange Bar

$$ **Old Bisbee**   This family-casual spot has lots of options for picky eaters of all ages. When you're rarin' for a good steak or burger, this is the place. *15 Brewery Gulch.* ☎ *520-432-3317.*

Copper Queen

$$ **Old Bisbee**   Despite playing musical chefs in recent years, the Copper Queen serves fine American/Continental fare three meals a day. A Victorian-pretty dining room, an outstanding outdoor terrace, and a

special kiddie menu with dinosaur-shaped chicken nuggets also make this a good choice. *11 Howell Ave.* ☎ *520-432-2216.*

Don Teodoro's

$–$$ **Tombstone** The Mexican food here is far better than the service. Drink enough margaritas or come to hear live flamenco guitar and you won't care. *Fourth Street between Allen and Fremont.* ☎ *520-457-3647.*

The Longhorn Grill

$–$$ **Tombstone** Kids eat happy here with hot dogs, tacos, and the like; for adults, there's Big Nose Kate's, a reincarnation of the site's original Bucket of Blood Saloon. *Fifth and Allen Streets.* ☎ *520-457-3405.*

The Mesquite Tree

$$ **Near Ramsey Canyon** This spot's convenience to Ramsey Canyon and cozy atmosphere are as noteworthy as its steaks and seafood (don't stray too far from American menu items, though). *Corner of S. Highway 92 and Carr Canyon Rd.* ☎ *520-378-2758.*

The Peacock

$$ **Sierra Vista** The Peacock stands out among Sierra Vista's many Asian restaurants for its excellent and reasonably priced Vietnamese food. *80 S. Carmichael St.* ☎ *520-459-0095.*

Exploring Southern Cochise County

Some of the best tourist stompin' grounds in the state are here with loads of stuff to do and relatively short driving distances between attractions. Enjoy, but don't try to fit too much in. Running from attraction to attraction only makes you ornery.

The Top Things to See and Do

Tombstone

Don't blame Tombstone for being touristy. Hollywood glamorized the "Town Too Tough to Die" so much that many visitors are disappointed if they don't get a little showmanship. Don't worry; crass commercialism (silver speculating, tourism, what's the difference?) is an old Tombstone tradition. Just relax and enjoy the Old West costume dramas.

Besides, plenty of genuine history was made here. The town's main drag and most of the town's attractions are either on or within walking distance of Allen Street; it may be lined with tacky tourist shops but if you look closely you can still see bullet holes in some of the buildings. The following activities are a mix of the real thing and a past that has been, shall we say, embellished:

Some Straight Shooting about the OK Corral

The OK Corral, on Allen St. between Third and Fourth streets (☎ 520-457-3456), has three sections: The Historama, which screens a short background film; a room with the printing press and other equipment from the Tombstone *Epitaph;* and the corral where you-know-what occurred, plus C.S. Fly's photo gallery. The Historama and the corral/photo gallery cost $2.50 each; the *Epitaph* room is free. Although the fake gunfighter figures could use a makeover by Madame Tussaud, you can't leave town without seeing the world's most famous horse pen (the much-reproduced photographs of Geronimo by C.S. Fly are themselves worth the admission price). But, unless it's real quiet in Tombstone, don't try to schedule your day around the over-packed 2 p.m. re-enactment of the shootout (another $2). And save yourself $2.50 and 26 minutes by skipping the Historama; the fact that the late Vincent Price narrates it is an, er, dead giveaway of the film's vintage and historical subtlety. All are open daily 9 a.m.–5 p.m.

✔ **Get the lowdown:** Definitely the real thing. Among the many fascinating displays at the **Tombstone Courthouse State Historic Park,** Toughnut and Third Sts. (☎ 520-457-3311), are two diagrammed scenarios of what actually may have happened at the famous shootout between the Earps and Clantons at the OK Corral. Make this stop your first if you want some perspective on the other, more duded up attractions. Admission $2.50 per adult, $1 ages 7–13, 6 and under free; open daily 8 a.m.–5 p.m. except Christmas.

✔ **Go with Guinness:** The **Rose Tree Inn Museum,** Toughnut and Fourth Sts. (☎ 520-457-3326), holds the Guinness World Record for having the largest rose tree in the world (it's 8,600 square feet, give or take a few thorns). The 1880s period rooms also give a window on a much more genteel Tombstone than the one generally seen on the silver screen. Admission $2 adults, free 14 and under; open daily 9 a.m.–5 p.m., closed Christmas.

✔ **Witness a shootout:** Although the re-enactment of the gunfight at the OK Corral (see "Some Straight Shooting about the OK Corral" sidebar in this chapter) is the best known, it's not the only showdown in town. Both the **Six-Gun City Wild West Show** (☎ 520-457-3646), held at Fifth and Toughnut every day at 11:30 a.m., 1 p.m., and 3:30 p.m. and the **Tombstone Cowboys** (☎ 520-457-2203), who perform at the Helldorado Amphitheater, near Fifth and Toughnut daily at 11:30 a.m., 1 p.m., and 3 p.m., use professional stuntmen. Prices are $3 adults, $1 children for Six-Gun; $4 adults, $3 seniors, 12 and under are free for the Cowboys. Don't sit near the front if you're shy; these shows are big on audience participation. In addition, every second, fourth, and fifth Sunday of the month at 1 p.m., the non-profit **Tombstone Vigilantes** (☎ 520-457-3434) rabble rouse along Allen Street for free. Hangings by appointment only.

✔ **Take to the stage:** The horse-drawn stagecoach excursions run by **Old Tombstone Historical Tours,** Allen St. (next to Big Nose Kate's; ☎ 520-457-3018), from 9 a.m. to 5 p.m. every day, are a fun way to pick up some information (to be swallowed with a grain of salt). Admission: $3.

✔ **Get theatrical:** The **Bird Cage Theater,** Sixth and Allen Sts. (☎ 520-457-3421), looks as if it hasn't been dusted since it was abandoned in 1889. The theater's treasures include the gold-trimmed Black Moriah hearse that transported the losing team at the OK Corral shootout to Boot Hill cemetery as well as the velvet-draped "cages" where the ladies of the night plied their trade above the dance hall and casino. It's also the site of the longest poker game on record (eight years, five months, and three days). Open daily 8 a.m.–6 or 6:30 p.m.; admission $4.50 adults, $4 seniors, $3 ages 8–18, under 8 free; $12.50 family rate (for 2 adults, 2 kids age 8–18).

✔ **Drink in some history:** The ornate mahogany bar at the **Crystal Palace,** corner of Fifth and Allen (☎ 520-457-3611), was moved from its original location but it's still the genuine item. This place is great for sipping a few beers and, on occasion, listening to the live country and western sounds of pre-Garth/Dixie Chicks vintage.

✔ **Boot up:** You must walk through a huge souvenir shop to enter the **Boot Hill Graveyard,** on Highway 80 (just northwest of town; ☎ 800-457-9344 or 520-457-9344), and most of the grave markers are reproductions. Nonetheless, you can't leave without visiting the town's famed nineteenth-century boneyard. Get the "Essential Guide" tour pamphlet for 50¢ to find out who's buried where and why (James Hickey, for example, was "shot in the left temple by Wm. Clayborne for his over-insistence that they drink together"). No charge; open daily 7:30 a.m.–dusk.

The Truth about Tombstone

The town's name was a nose-thumbing by prospector Ed Schieffelin to all the people who warned him that if he ventured into what was then dangerous Apache territory, all he would find was his tombstone. Instead, in 1877, he struck one of the West's richest silver veins.

Tombstone earned its "town too tough to die" nickname because it survived two major fires, an earthquake, and the rising of its water table — which caused the silver mine to literally go under.

In its silver mining heyday, Tombstone was larger than San Francisco.

The town wasn't all bar brawls; it was also a major cultural center. Enrico Caruso, Sarah Bernhardt, and Lillian Russell were among those who trod the boards at the Bird Cage Theatre.

Bisbee

More of a success story than Tombstone in many ways, Bisbee is much less well known, in part because its outlaws were of the corporate sort: Phelps, Dodge & Co. was the main beneficiary of the multibillion dollar copper lode that gave rise to this thriving mountainside town. The last mining operation didn't shut down until 1975 and if the price of copper ever goes up, Bisbee's mine may reopen. In the meantime, this one-time hippie enclave is being prospected by an increasing number of tourism-savvy entrepreneurs.

When you drive into town, take the Old Bisbee exit off Highway 80 and slot your car into the first (hopefully legal) spot you find. Below and west of Main Street is a large lot that fills up fast. From here you can walk to the town's major attractions — although it's literally uphill from here.

Bisbee sits at a mile-high elevation in the Mule Mountains; you may find yourself especially short of breath when you walk uphill. If you experience respiratory problems, take it slow, please.

Stroll around **Main Street,** with its well-preserved Victorian buildings and interesting boutiques (see "Shopping," in this chapter); check out the copper-trimmed Bank of America, at the foot of the street (no, you don't have to go in). Other historic attractions include the **Copper Queen** hotel (see "The Top Hotels in Bisbee," in this chapter) and the nearby **Muheim Heritage House,** 207 Youngblood Hill (☎ 520-432-7071), an unusual Swiss-built structure with period furnishings. Heritage House is located at the top of **Brewery Gulch,** which used to be lined with saloons and literally flowed with beer. In addition, you can

- ✔ **Get down:** Actually, the **Copper Queen Mine Tour,** 478 N. Dart Rd. (☎ 520-432-2071), takes you *up* a 30 degree grade into the mine's shaft; it just feels like you're descending. These fascinating inter-earth journeys, which depart daily at 9 a.m., 10:30 a.m., noon, 2 p.m., and 3:30 p.m., are led by miners who once worked the Copper Queen. This tour is Bisbee's most fun thing to do. (In addition to everything else, you get to put on a yellow slicker and a hard hat.) Be aware that the tour isn't for claustrophobics; however, they're not left out because a surface tour goes around Old Bisbee and to the perimeter of the Lavender Pit Mine. The surface tour operates at the same times as the other tours (except for the 9 a.m. one). Mine tour: $10 adults, $3.50 ages 7 to 15, $2 ages 3 to 6, under 3 free; surface tours $7 for all ages.

- ✔ **Mine more of the town's history:** The small **Mining and Historical Museum,** No. 5 Copper Queen Plaza (☎ 520-432-7071; open daily 10 a.m.–4 p.m.; admission $3), gives a great overview of Bisbee's early years. You can't miss the **Lavender Pit Mine;** it's that huge, multi-colored hole off Highway 80 en route into town from the west. Something that produced 94 million tons of copper is worth more than a drive by. Go beyond town to the intersection of Hwys. 80 and 92 for an overlook that has a typewritten history of the mine (hey, they're not real formal in Bisbee).

Buffalo Braves

The 9th Cavalry, 10th Cavalry, 24th Infantry, and 25th Infantry — all four of America's all-black regiments — trained at Fort Huachuca. These regiments were given the respectful name Buffalo Soldiers by the Chiricahua Apaches, who were among the groups the 9th Cavalry was commissioned to fight in 1877. The outstanding record of these African American units is detailed throughout the Fort Huachuca Museum; a special section devoted to the black military experience in the American West includes a rare description of Estevanico de Dorante, the African slave-turned-conquistador who took part in the earliest European exploration of Arizona.

Fort Huachuca Museum
Sierra Vista

Fort Huachuca is the last of the famous western forts to remain operational. (Today, it is maintained as an active military base.) Many of the barracks from the 1800s are still used as offices or, in this case, as exhibition space. The main museum highlights the African American role in the U.S. military (see the "Buffalo Braves" sidebar, in this chapter) among other historical displays. Although the main museum is the most interesting, you may stroll over to the annex and military intelligence museum while you're here. To do all (or both) of the museums takes about an hour or so, a little longer to check out the sculptures in the surrounding complex (what's with that gold sphinx, anyway?). A scenic overlook at Reservoir Hill and hiking trails at Garden Canyon are also sites you may visit.

The main gate to Fort Huachuca is southwest of the intersection of Hwys. 90 and 92. Call ahead for directions; ☎ *520-533-5736. Open: Main museum and annex Mon–Fri 9 a.m.–4 p.m., weekends 1–4 p.m.; Military Intelligence Museum Mon, Wed, Fri 10 a.m.–2 p.m. Admission Free.*

Ramsey Canyon Preserve
Hereford

You can learn all about the unusual biodiversity of Ramsey Canyon, part of the Upper San Pedro River ecosystem in Hereford, at the Nature Conservancy visitor's center or you can just grab a trail map and stroll around this remarkably pretty, tranquil preserve. Fourteen species of hummingbirds — more than anywhere else in the United States — stop off here. When the hummers aren't flitting around, you still see plenty of other creatures to ooh and aah over. The Miller Peak Wilderness Area in the Huachuca Mountains is honeycombed with trails, so serious hikers can spend all day in this area. For the rest of us, the easy 1-mile walk from the preserve headquarters to a scenic overlook makes a good couch potato goal.

27 Ramsey Canyon Rd. (about 6 miles from Sierra Vista; go south on Highway 92 and take a right on Ramsey Canyon Rd). ☎ *520-378-2785. Open: Daily 8 a.m.–5 p.m. Admission $5 suggested donation.*

More Cool Things to See and Do

If you enjoy the outdoors, this region offers more ways to take in the local scenery and culture, in addition to some sunshine (don't forget the sunscreen!).

- ✔ **Reconquer new Spain:** You can see for miles and miles at the **Coronado National Memorial,** 4101 E. Montezuma Canyon Rd., Hereford (☎ 520-366-5515). The memorial is a preserve dedicated to Spanish conquistador Francisco Vasquez de Coronado, who passed through here in 1540. For the best views, drive the 3-mile dirt road from the visitor's center to Montezuma Pass; then walk up another ½ mile to the top of Coronado Peak (almost 7,000 feet high). A sign for the memorial is 16 miles south of Sierra Vista on Highway 92 and just across the Mexican border; the visitor's center, open daily from 8 a.m.–5 p.m., is 5 miles from the turnoff.

- ✔ **Get folksy:** I can't think of a more perfect way to spend the day than strolling around Ramsey Canyon in the morning and seeing a performance at the nearby Arizona Folklore Center in the afternoon. See the "Pick a Peck of Pickers and Poets" sidebar in this chapter.

- ✔ **Go borderline:** Straddling Mexico to the east of Bisbee, **Douglas** was a ranching center and smelter for many of the area's most successful mines. A typical border town now, it still has a few lures. You might recognize the **Gadsden Hotel,** 1046 G. Ave. (on the town's main street; ☎ 520-364-4481), from the Paul Newman movie *The Life and Times of Judge Roy Bean;* the stained glass window of a Southwest landscape and a western saloon decked with rancher's brands are highlights. The **Slaughter Ranch Museum** (☎ 520-558-2474), a National Historic Landmark, re-creates the area's ranching heyday in a remote, rural setting (bring a picnic lunch). Take 15th Street east to Geronimo Trail and follow the signs; it's 15 miles down a gravel road to the site, open Wed—Sun 10 a.m.–3 p.m. Admission: $3 adults, children under 14 free.

Pick a Peck of Pickers and Poets

Just before you come to Ramsey Canyon you see a sign for the **Arizona Folklore Preserve,** 44 Ramsey Canyon Rd. (☎ 520-378-6165; Internet: www.arizonafolklore.com). This unique performance space, research center, and bookstore was founded by Doolan Ellis, an original member of the 1960s folk group, the New Christy Minstrels. Ellis is also Arizona's official state balladeer (bet you didn't know Arizona had one). Jury-selected folk artists — from cowboy poets to storytellers, fiddlers, and bluegrass guitarists — perform each Saturday and Sunday at 2 p.m. The preserve's new (opened fall 2000) space and performance venue is larger than the original one across the road, but tickets ($8) can sell out quickly. Call as far ahead in advance as you can to book a seat.

A Fly-By-Night (And Day) Region

This is the place for those just following the flock. Southeast Arizona, where almost 500 migrating species use several ecologically diverse "sky islands" for migrational rest stops, is considered one of this country's top five bird-watching spots. In addition to the many places already listed in this chapter, the avian-oriented should visit the San Pedro Riparian National Conservation Area, near Sierra Vista; the Willcox Playa, near Willcox; and Cave Creek Canyon, near Chiricahua National Monument. The Sierra Vista Convention and Vistors Bureau (see "Quick Concierge: Southern Cochise County" in this chapter) can direct birders to all these preserves as well as supply the CVB's "Birder's Guide" pamphlet and the Arizona Department of Tourism Southeastern Arizona Birding Trail map.

Want more guidance? The nonprofit **Southeastern Arizona Bird Observatory,** based in Bisbee (☎ 520-432-1388; E-mail: sabo@sabo.org; Internet: www.sabo.org), offers year-round walks and workshops as well as seasonal banding programs. For more extended birding excursions, see Chapter 5.

Birding is usually a low-key kind of activity, but "Wings over Willcox: A Sandhill Crane Celebration" involves tours, seminars, and lots of food vendors (for humans). The event is held in mid-January when the big, graceful birds blow into the Willcox Playa. Call the Willcox Chamber of Commerce (☎ 800-200-2272) for details.

Shopping

In **Tombstone,** beyond touristy Allen Street, you find several high-quality crafts shops. **William Brown Holster Co.**, 600 E. Fremont St. (☎ 520-457-9208), specializes in hand-tooled reproductions of nineteenth-century holsters and also designs belts, saddlebags, and chaps. If it's western-style, leather, and silver studded, Brown does it. The **Tombstone Smithy,** 302 E. Fremont St. (☎ 520-457-2326), is the place to find everything from custom-made horseshoe candlesticks to a life-sized cow sculpture for your backyard. **Earthwalkers,** 204 E. Fremont St. (☎ 520-457-2448), crosses boots with moccasins to get attractive, extremely comfortable footwear; be prepared to plaster cast your feet. The jewelry at the **Wizard's Workshop,** 800 E. Fremont (☎ 520-457-3152), is as magical as the shop's name, with settings that do justice to the region's stones — Bisbee turquoise, azurite, and fire agate, to name a few.

In **Bisbee,** many of the best shops are on Main Street. Tom Selleck and Faye Dunaway had themselves custom fitted for Panama hats at **Optimo,** 47 Main St. (☎ 520-432-4544). It's easy to go ceramics crazy at **Poco Loco,** 81 Main St. (☎ 520-432-7020), purveyors of wonderfully colorful dishes and other covetable housewares. **Primitives,** 41 Main St. (☎ 520-432-2903), stands out among the many antiques shops along the road; the owner does amazing things with gourds. **Jane Hamilton Fine Art,** 29 Main St. (☎ 800-555-3051), is probably the largest, most central showcase for local talent. In the Copper Queen Plaza, at the foot of Main Street, **Sala del Cobre** (☎ **520-432-3379**), sells jewelry and ornaments made of the town's favorite metal (*cobre* is Spanish for copper). Need some energy for all that acquisition? Check out the homemade fudge, peanut brittle, and chocolate nut clusters at the adjacent **This and That** (☎ **520-432-3500**).

Quick Concierge: Southern Cochise County

Hospitals: Sierra Vista Regional Health Center, 300 El Camino Real (☎ 800-880-0088; 520-458-2300 or 4641) and the Copper Queen Community Hospital in Bisbee, 101 Cole Ave. (☎ 520-432-5383), offer 24-hour emergency service. In **Tombstone:** Dr. Young's Medical Clinic, 14 Penn at Fremont Frontage Rd. (☎ 520-457-9104), is open Mon–Fri 8 a.m.– 6 p.m., Sat 9 a.m.–1 p.m.

Information: Sierra Vista Convention and Visitors Bureau, 21 E. Wilcox Dr. (☎ 800-288-3861, 520-458-6940, or 520-459- EVNT [special events hotline]; Internet: www.visitsierravista.com), open Mon–Fri 8 a.m.–5 p.m., Sat 8 a.m.–noon. The Tombstone Chamber of Commerce, Fourth and Allen (☎ 888-457-3929 or 520-457-9317; Internet: www.tombstone.org), open Mon–Fri 9 a.m.–1 p.m.; the city-operated Visitors Information Center, just behind the Chamber on Allen Street (☎ 520-457-3929; Internet: www.cityoftombstone.com), open daily 10 a.m.–4 p.m. The Bisbee Chamber of Commerce, 31 Subway St.

(☎ 520-432-5421; Internet: www.azguide. com/bisbee), open Mon–Fri 9 a.m.–5p.m., Sat and Sun 10 a.m.–4 p.m.

Internet Access: The Quartermoon Coffeehouse in Bisbee, 1 OK St. (☎ 520-432-9088), can get you plugged in and wired up.

Pharmacies: Sierra Vista: Walgreens, 1950 E. Fry Blvd. (☎ 520-458-5638), open Mon–Fri 8 a.m.–10 p.m., Sat 9 a.m.–7 p.m., Sun 10 a.m.–6 p.m. Tombstone Pharmacy, 512 Allen St. (☎ 520-457-3542), open Mon– Fri 9 a.m.–6 p.m., Sat 9 a.m.–1 p.m.; Bisbee: Safeway Pharmacy, 101 Naco Highway (☎ 520-432-2918), open Mon–Fri 9 a.m.– 8 p.m., Sat 9 a.m.–6 p.m., Sun 10 a.m.–4 p.m.

Police: Call ☎ 911 for emergency.

Post Office: Sierra Vista: 2300 E. Fry Blvd. (☎ 520-458-2540). Tombstone: 516 E. Allen St. (☎ 520-457-3479). Bisbee: 6 Main St. (☎ 520-432-2052).

Northern Cochise County

The long-awaited debut of **Kartchner Caverns State Park** in late 1999 is changing the face of an area that time — and tourists — forgot. Among other things, chain motels and fast food restaurants are cropping up in this region, which spreads south of I-10 to the east of Tucson. **Benson,** the town closest to the caverns, probably hasn't had this much press since the late 1880s, when it was a crossroads for three rail lines.

Benson may eventually become as convenient a base as Sierra Vista for forays into southern Cochise County but at the moment, you won't find much reason to spend the night there. (With one notable exception, which I tell you about in the lodging section.) **Willcox,** the other small town along I-10, has more Old West flavor but no good reason for bedding down there, either. Unless you plan to retreat to one of the area's guest ranches or explore the great outdoors, you can cover Northern Cochise County's main attractions in a very full day trip from Tucson.

Getting There

Benson is 45 miles southeast of Tucson via I-10; continue another 38 miles on the freeway to reach Willcox. **Amtrak (☎ 800-872-7245)** runs trains from Tucson to Benson three times a week. The **Douglas Shuttle** (see "Getting There" in the Southern Cochise County section of this chapter) stops in Benson, and **Greyhound (☎ 800-231-2222)** has regular service to both Benson and Willcox, but you need a car to get around either town.

Getting Around

Sorry, you're pretty much stuck if you don't have wheels around here. The good news is that finding your way around Benson and Willcox is easy — just get off the first freeway exits you see to these two towns. You'll be tooling along their main streets in no time.

Where to Stay

Benson has a **Best Western** and **Days Inn;** in **Willcox,** you find links in both of those chains as well as a **Motel 6** and **Super 8.** (See the Appendix for the 800 numbers.) The two towns also offer a few low-key, non-chain motels; choose your favorite neon sign and ask to look at a room if you want to take a chance. The limited number of more interesting places to stay in the area follows.

Grapevine Canyon Ranch

$$$ **Pearce**

This is the real deal, a guest ranch in a western-purty setting with a working cattle ranch next door. This ranch is hog heaven for cowgirl and cowboy wannabes who can ride to their hearts content and take part in round-ups and other ranching activities (May, July, October, and January only). Tenderfoots can choose to hike, swim, or soak in a hot tub. The cabins are fairly ordinary, the casitas more Southwest chic, and both types of rooms have kick-back porches or decks along with city slicker amenities such as refrigerators, coffee makers, and hairdryers.

Highland Rd. (beyond Sunsites, off Highway 191; call for directions). ☎ 800-245-9202 or 520-826-3185. Fax: 520-826-3636. Internet: www.gcranch.com. *Rack rates: March–May and Sept–Dec (per person, based on double occupancy) casitas $180 nightly, $2,268 for two weeks; cabins $160/$2016; Jan–Feb and June–Aug,* *casitas $140/$1,764, cabins $120/$1512. Rates include three meals and most activities. See the Web site for information on their online auction of off-season rooms. AE, DISC, MC, V. 3-night minimum. Ages 12 and over only.*

Muleshoe Ranch

$$ Muleshoe Ranch Cooperative Management Area

How does holing up in a cabin near a natural hot spring in a nature preserve in the middle of nowhere sound to you? Yep, I'm about ready, too. Clawfoot tubs, Mexican tile, and woodstoves are among the appealing details of these Nature Conservancy–run casitas, some of which date back to the late 1800s. All the units have kitchens or kitchenettes — crucial in this fast food–barren wilderness. The ranch is co-managed by the Nature Conservancy, the Bureau of Land Management, and the U.S. Forest Service.

30 miles northwest of Willcox (call for directions). ☎ **520-586-7072** *or 520-622-3861. Rack rates: $85–$125. AE, MC, V. Closed June, July, August.*

Skywatcher's Inn

$$ Benson

It's stellar. What other B&B do you know that has a private observatory and a rent-an-astronomer service? This place abounds in techno-gismos, including a classroom with mineral displays and science videos. Rooms are by no means geeky and the daylight-inclined can look out at lovely rural vistas from the wrap-around porch. This place is great for a family vacation, catering to those seeking earthly comforts as well as to those with their head in the clouds.

Astronomers Road (2 miles southeast of I-10 at exit 306; call for directions). ☎ *and fax: 520-615-3886. E-mail:* vegasky@azstarnet.com. *Internet:* www.communiverse.com/skywatcher. *Rack rates: $75–$110; rates include full breakfast. Observation programs from $85–$150 for up to 5 people; telescope rental available. MC, V.*

Sunglow Guest Ranch

$$ Pearce

What a concept — guest ranching a la carte — a mix-and-match menu of meals, rooms, and activities. You can come by for a single riding lesson or a ranch tour in a stagecoach or choose among settling in for a week to fish in a nearby lake, hiking, birding, or hanging out with the emus that are bred here. The setting is beautiful and the ranch site is rich in history; the girlfriend of outlaw Johnny Ringo is said to have lived in the 1879 building that's now the ranch dining room. The extra charges for meals (book at least a day in advance if you want to eat here) and riding add up, but room rates are reasonable and you can't beat the flexibility.

Turkey Creek Rd. (call for directions). ☎ **520-824-3334.** *Fax: 520-824-3176. E-mail:* sunglow@vtc.net. *Internet:* www.sunglowranch.com. *Rack rates: $89, $534 weekly; two-bedroom casitas that sleep up to 12 available. Children under 10 free. MC, V.*

Where to Dine

These ain't no gourmet stompin' grounds; chain restaurants and modest cafes are pretty much all the area has to offer when it comes to chow. The Old West diner atmosphere of the Horseshoe Café always gets me to stop in Benson; I've driven even farther out of my way for an apple pie from Stout's Cider Mill in Willcox (see "Exploring Northern Cochise County" in this chapter). You can't beat a meal at the Sunglow Ranch (see "Where to Stay," in this chapter). Other than these three suggestions, I can't think of any other detour-worthy spots. The following is a (very) short list of recommended restaurants if you need to eat in the area, both on Benson's main drag:

Horseshoe Café

$–$$ **Benson**

The cafe duded up its menu a bit for tourists but the green chili burgers and fries are as good as ever, and they can never take the neon horseshoe off the ceiling — not if they don't want to change the restaurant's name, anyway.

154 E. Fourth St. ☎ *520-586-3303.*

Ruiz Restaurant

$ **Benson**

This is fine for a down-home Mexican meal in an unpretentious setting.

687 W. Fourth St. ☎ *520-586-2707.*

Exploring Northern Cochise County

Life existed in northern Cochise County before the Caverns, but you'd never know it these days; most of the tourist action seems to have gone underground. The area's more remote natural attractions, particularly Chiricahua National Monument, are equally striking — not to mention less pricey — and Willcox hides a good bit of western color behind its I-10 sprawl.

The Top Things to See and Do

Amerind Foundation Museum

Dragoon

A stark Texas Canyon setting, a lovely Spanish colonial–style building, and a wide ranging collection of American Indian (thus the name) artifacts make a visit to this middle-of-nowhere museum in Dragoon a wonderfully unique experience. The historical materials contributed by founder William Fulton, an amateur archaelogist, are complemented by contemporary work in the same tradition. The museum is small, but allow 45 minutes to do it justice; if pressed for time, you can zip through the nice, but fairly traditional, Southwest art gallery next door.

What Season Is It, Anyway?

Boulders aren't the only things doing a strange balancing act in Chiricahua National Monument. Most years, a mix of sun and rain keeps the brown, yellow, and red fall foliage around until April or May, when the leaves intermingle with the green spring growth.

Dragoon Rd., 1 mile southeast of I-10 (Exit 318). ☎ *520-586-3666. Open: Sept–May daily 10 a.m.–4 p.m., June–Aug Wed–Sun 10 a.m.–4 p.m. Admission $3 adults, $2 seniors and ages 12–18, 11 and under free.*

Kartchner Caverns State Park

Near Benson

A quarter of a century, secrecy to match the CIA's (on its good days), and about as much effort as was devoted to preserving Egypt's pyramids led to the public opening of this state park. The caverns were discovered by two Tucson cavers in 1974. The fascinating story is detailed in the visitors center. Despite the hype, don't get your expectations up too high: The sections of Kartchner that you can walk through aren't nearly as large as those in other cave systems and — call me a cynic — I thought the sound-and-light show at the end of the tour was tacky (others tell me it has moved them to tears).

Kartchner is still a work in progress. Not all the areas are open to visitors yet because scientific studies on tourism impact are still being conducted to determine, for example, whether the Big Room should be closed in summer when the resident bats are most active. Cave tours last an hour and you may want to spend another half hour or so in the visitors center; the 20 minute introductory film is definitely worth viewing. (The park's hiking trails are being touted, but you're far better off heading for the more interesting Chiricahua National Monument instead.)

Rex Redux

Rex Allen Days, held the first weekend of October, continue despite the fact that Rex Allen, Sr., isn't around any longer to attend the festival that bears his name. For details about these 4 days of western style whoop-de-do, including everything from turtle races and all-you-can-eat pancake breakfasts to a rip roarin' rodeo, call the Willcox Chamber of Commerce (see "Quick Concierge: Northern Cochise County" in this chapter).

As a result of big publicity for relatively small-capacity cave tours, Kartchner Caverns books up well in advance. If you don't want to be disappointed, MAKE RESERVATIONS (yes, I'm shouting at you, but it's for your own good). Call Mon–Fri from 8 a.m.–5 p.m., but be prepared to be patient; the line is constantly busy. 100 tickets are set aside each day for people who haven't reserved; they go on sale at 7:30 a.m. and are usually sold out within 45 minutes. Because these tickets are for staggered tour times, you may have to wait around or come back much later for your assigned tour.

9 miles south of I-10, exit 305 via Highway 90. ☎ *520-586-CAVE (reservations). Open: Daily 7:30 a.m.–6 p.m.; cave tours run from 8:30 a.m.–4:30 p.m. Closed Christmas. Admission for access to park grounds and Discovery Center (cave exhibits and visitor's center): $10 per car for up to four people per vehicle; additional fee of $1 per person above 4. Cave tour (and you can't go underground without one): $14 adults, $6 ages 7–13, 6 and under free.*

Chiricahua National Monument

Dos Cabezas Route

This natural monument is one of my favorites in Arizona. The volcanic rock outcroppings impossibly balanced against each other define the term "rugged western terrain." The Chiricahua Apaches, who spent a lot of time trying to keep white settlers out of it, called this site the Land of the Standing-Up Rocks. But eroded boulders are not the whole story; a huge variety of plant and animal species, many of them more typically found in Mexico's Sierra Madres, make this a great place to hike and bird-watch. An 8:30 a.m. shuttle goes to a trailhead where you have a choice of descending via a 4-mile or 7½-mile route. If you're interested in history, try to arrive before 10 a.m to catch the daily ranger-led tours of Faraway Ranch that give a glimpse of life in the homesteading and early guest-ranch days. The park has no services; gas up and stock up on picnic supplies in Willcox.

Take I-10 to the first Willcox exit and drive through town to Highway 186, where signs will direct you to the visitor center. ☎ *520-824-3560. Internet:* www. nps.gov/chir. *Open: Daily 8 a.m.–5 p.m. except Christmas. Admission $6 per car, $3 for hikers or bicyclists; hiker's shuttle $2 per person; Faraway Ranch tour $2 per person.*

Go Offroad (In Another Sense)

The most scenic rest stop in the state may well be the one in **Texas Canyon,** along I-10 between Benson and Willcox. You can see the precariously balanced boulders, similar to those in Chiricahua National Monument, from the freeway while you whiz by in your car. (You may view them in more comfort after, er, just whizzing.)

Ghost Riding in Southeast Arizona

When no more booty was left in the many small (and not so small) mines that once dotted southeast Arizona or when the wells that supported them ran dry, the surrounding towns were eventually abandoned. Most of these towns can only be identified by a few boarded up mine shafts and foundations of adobe homes long returned to dust. However, three of the best preserved — and most accessible — lie southeast of Willcox.

From I-10, take Highway 191 29 miles south of Willcox; soon after Sunsites, you come to Pearce Road. Follow it west a short way to reach what's left of the gold mining camp of **Pearce,** the most alive of the three ghost towns. In addition to the 100-year-old general store, a post office, and several ruined adobe houses, a few retailing residents still live here; you can buy soap made from goat's milk at Udder Delight and sundries at the Old Pearce Apothecary. From here, the Gleeson-Pearce Road leads south to **Courtland,** once a respectable settlement with a motion picture theater, though you'd never know it. The jailhouse is one of the only upright structures in the now completely abandoned town. You find a nearly identical lockup at **Gleeson,** just a short way down the same road. However, here the cemetery and wood-frame homes with bullet holes are even more interesting — as is the street's sole business, the Gleeson Saloon. If you want to circle back to the freeway rather than retracing your route, take Gleeson Road 15 miles west to Tombstone, where you can pick up Highway 80 to I-10.

Be careful when you tread around these towns; many of the old mine shafts and ruined houses are unstable. And don't ignore the "no trespassing" signs; some of the owners may be unstable too — and armed.

Willcox

These days more trucks than trains stop at Willcox, formerly one of the country's major cattle shippers. However, the town still has some Old West kick left, especially in the Railroad Historic District. You can see the recently restored Southern Pacific Willcox Historical Depot and the Commercial Company, Arizona's oldest department store in the Railroad Historic District. In addition to ducking into those two Railroad Avenue icons, you may also want to:

 ✔ **Get some cowboy glitter:** Willcox's favorite son, singing cowboy star Rex Allen, died in Tucson in 1999. The **Rex Allen Arizona Cowboy Museum and Theater,** 155 N. Railroad Ave. (☎ 520-384-4583), displays the spangly costumes and other memorabilia from the many films its namesake made in the 1940s and 1950s. The Willcox Cowboy Hall of Fame, in the museum's back room, pays tribute to the area's less melodic ranchers and rodeo stars. Admission to both, $2 per person, $3 per couple, $5 per family (talk about family values!); open daily 10 a.m.–4 p.m., except Thanksgiving, Christmas, and New Year's Day.

✔ **Learn the cider house rules:** Strange, but true: At an elevation of nearly 4,200 feet, Willcox is Arizona's apple center. And of the many local places to apple polish your trip, **Stout's Cider Mill** rules (☎ **800-871-PIES** or 520-384-2272). The mill is located across the parking lot from the Chamber of Commerce (see "Quick Concierge: Northern Cochise County" in this chapter). Don't try to pretend you're there for anything else but the famous pie, with a crust about 5 inches high and — the baker boasts — more apple-packed than any other (but who's gonna weigh all those pies to check?).

✔ **Find out why Willcox is named Willcox:** The town's historical museum is on the move; it's scheduled to open in a new building in fall, 2001. Check with the Willcox Chamber of Commerce (see "Quick Concierge: Northern Cochise County," in this chapter) for its location and hours.

More Cool Things to See and Do

From ancient rock art to nineteenth-century battlegrounds and current Arizona literature, you can learn about the state's past and present in this region.

✔ **Get fortified:** You drive down a graded dirt road and trek 1½ miles to reach **Fort Bowie National Historical Site.** Little of the 1862 fort or of the Butterfield Stage Station it guarded is left and no evidence remains of the many skirmishes between the Chiricahua Apaches and the U.S. Cavalry that took place here. Markers along the route and a serene setting render this a good way to combine a little exercise — the hike's easy — with some history. The grounds are open from dawn to dusk; a visitor's center and book-store are open daily 8 a.m.–5 p.m. To get here, take any of the I-10 Willcox exits to Highway 186; 22 miles south, signs point you to the site.

✔ **Go offroad:** Benson-based **High Desert Adventures** (☎ **520-586-9309**, Internet: `www.highdesertadventures.com`) offers a variety of excellent jeep tours. Destinations include such hard-to-reach ghost towns as Charleston, Millville, and Fairbank. In addition, you can visit several *petroglyph* (Indian rock art) sites in the Dragoon Mountains. Rates start at $45 per adult for (a minimum of) two people on a 3½-hour adventure to $65 per adult for 6½ hours on the road. Prices go down slightly as the number of passengers goes up. The tours are private and personalized, so you never ride with someone who wants to go shopping in Tombstone when you want to be looking at birds.

✔ **Find a hideaway:** At **Cochise Stronghold** you see why it took so long for the U.S. Cavalry to capture Cochise and Geronimo. This natural granite fortress south of Dragoon is in a remote, rugged rock region that's great for hiking. To find it, take exit 331 from I-10 to Highway 191; look for the sign for Cochise Stronghold at Ironwood Drive, near Sunsites. Drive nearly 10 miles on a fairly rough dirt road; you know you arrived at the right place when you see some picnic tables, campsites, and restrooms.

✔ **Get bookish:** A top-rate selection of books about Arizona plus a unique ranch setting make the **Singing Wind Bookshop,** Ocotillo Ave. (☎ **520-586-2425**), worth the search. Take I-10 exit 304, just beyond Benson, and turn left; in about 2¼ miles, you see a signpost at the bookstore turnoff. Prepare to stop and open the large green gate.

Quick Concierge: Northern Cochise County

Hospitals: Benson Hospital, 450 S. Ocotillo (☎ 520-586-2261); Northern Cochise Community Hospital in Willcox, 901 Rex Allen Drive (☎ 800-696-3541 or 520-384-3541).

Information: Benson Visitors Center, 249 E. Fourth St. (☎ 520-586-4293, Internet: www.bensonchamberaz.com), open Mon–Sat 9 a.m.–5 p.m., Sun 1–5 p.m. Willcox Chamber of Commerce and Agriculture, 1500 N. Circle I Rd. (☎ 800-200-2272 or 520-384-2272, Internet: www.willcoxchamber.com), open Mon–Sat 9 a.m.–5 p.m., Sun 9 a.m.– 1 p.m.

Pharmacies: The pharmacies at the Safeway supermarkets in both Benson (559 W. Fourth St.; ☎ 520-586-7323) and Willcox (670 N. Bisbee; ☎ 520-384-4612) stay open the longest in town.

Post Office: Benson: 150 W. Fifth St. (☎ 520-586-3422). Willcox: 200 South Curtis St. (☎ 520-384-2689).

Chapter 16

Central Arizona

● ●

In This Chapter

▶ Taking in Sedona and the Verde Valley: Red rocks, good vibes, and ancient sites

▶ Exploring Prescott: From Victorian row houses to Whiskey Row

▶ Going out Wickenburg Way: Dudes, upside down rivers, and bola ties

● ●

Central Arizona has its ups and downs; like much of the rest of the state, it's on a geological roller coaster. Sedona, perched at 4,400 feet, and Prescott, nearly a mile high, are prime summer retreats for Phoenicians who, along with out-of-staters, are also drawn year-round by the stunning red-rock vistas and charming Victorian neighborhoods, respectively. Wickenburg, Arizona's self-proclaimed dude-ranch capital, nestles at about 2,000 feet in the Hassayampa Valley; it's nice and warm in winter, spring, and fall, but perhaps a bit too hot to handle in summer. The towns in central Arizona are as different in personality as they are in elevation, but each offers loads of Western color and eye-catching vistas.

With its no-holds-barred scenery and upscale lodging, dining, and shopping, Sedona has the highest profile in this generally low-key region. You can base yourself here for three or four nights, making trips to the Grand Canyon, Prescott, and Verde Valley, but you'd have to be feeling pretty flush. Sedona is not only the most expensive place to stay in central Arizona; it's up there with Scottsdale as the priciest in the state. Prescott is much more economical, though it is a slightly less central base: The Grand Canyon is about 40 miles (round-trip) farther from here than it is from Sedona. Wickenburg is fine for hops to Prescott and Phoenix, but lots of folks just like to settle in for a spell with a three-meal-a-day-plus-all-the-Western-relaxation-you-can-take guest-ranch package.

 The distances between Prescott, Sedona, and Wickenburg aren't great, but the roads between them aren't straight. The Highway 89A/89 route from Sedona to Prescott to Wickenburg has long stretches of mountain road switchbacks. Much of the scenery is spectacular, but if you find this kind of driving as stressful as I do, you probably won't be able to enjoy the view.

Central Arizona

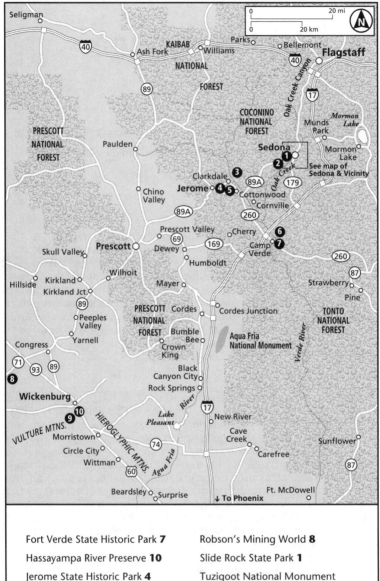

Fort Verde State Historic Park **7**

Hassayampa River Preserve **10**

Jerome State Historic Park **4**

Montezuma Castle
   National Monument **6**

Red Rock State Park **2**

Robson's Mining World **8**

Slide Rock State Park **1**

Tuzigoot National Monument
   & Dead Horse Ranch State Park **5**

Verde Canyon Railroad Depot **3**

Vulture Mine **9**

What's Where? Central Arizona and Its Major Attractions

A few interesting sights are scattered throughout central Arizona, but most of the area's attractions are concentrated in and around its three main towns. That's true especially of Wickenburg and Prescott; the Verde Valley, on the other hand, gives neighboring Sedona a bit of tourism competition.

Sedona and the Verde Valley

In Sedona and the Verde Valley, starving artists and hippie spiritual seekers have been replaced by their more established (or at least richer) reincarnations, and the red rocks are hardly a state secret these days. No matter. Sedona's stunning geological formations, millions of years in the making, are seemingly impervious to human incursions. In addition to the town itself, where shopping and rock gazing are the main activities, the surrounding area offers other attractions:

  ✔ **Slide Rock State Park,** a natural water wonderland just outside Sedona.

  ✔ **Montezuma's Castle, Montezuma's Lake,** and **Tuzigoot State Parks,** three related Native American sites operated by the state park system.

  ✔ **Jerome,** a hillside "ghost" town that's still alive and retailing.

  ✔ **The Verde Canyon Railroad,** a scenic ride into the past.

Prescott

Prescott was Arizona's territorial capital — in other words, its capital before Arizona became a state. Prescott boasts a large, leafy town square that looks back to its sometimes rowdy glory days. You can follow a day of shopping for antiques and crafts by bar-hopping along Whiskey Row. (Of course, some folks just skip the shopping and cut straight to the chasers.) Along with golf, hiking, and horseback riding, Prescott's lures include:

Great Scott! (Not)

Named for William Hickling Prescott, an East Coast historian, Prescott is pronounced *PRESK-it,* the second syllable rhyming with "biscuit." Why? According to local historian Melissa Ruffner, Prescott came from Boston, which was big on renouncing its colonial English roots — pronunciations included. Whatever the derivation, if you pronounce the "Scott," you're announcing loud and clear that you're an out-of-towner.

> ✔ **The Phippen Museum,** highlighting cowboy artists in a western setting.
>
> ✔ **Sharlot Hall,** a museum complex focusing on frontier life.
>
> ✔ **The Smoki Museum,** as striking for its architecture as for its Native American artifacts.

Wickenburg

Established in 1863, making it a year older than Prescott, Wickenburg has a small but appealing historic downtown. Most people come here for a chance to play cowpoke at a dude ranch. However, when city slickers get saddle sore, they head to:

> ✔ **The Desert Caballeros Museum,** where Western art and Wickenburg history get together.
>
> ✔ **Hassayampa River Preserve,** a Nature Conservancy property that gives you a glimpse of the town's strange hidden river.
>
> ✔ **Robson's Mining World,** a re-created mining town, replete with drilling equipment, watering holes, and lots of shops.

Sedona and the Verde Valley

John Wayne meets the New Age in Sedona, a much-filmed Western landscape where, some people believe, powerful energy centers called *vortexes* enhance your well being and creativity (in other words, your basic good vibes). The area definitely attracts lots of artists, and visitors do tend to feel mellow, but that could also be because they're eye-balling incredible red rock scenery and downing good margaritas. Stretching out below Sedona, the Verde Valley gets far less press; most people come to the valley to see the Indian ruins and Jerome, a funky and far-from-moribund ghost town.

Sedona is an end, not a means, to other places, as its abundance of rooms, restaurants, and shops attest. But again, it's not cheap. Nor is it especially peaceful: In high season, the town can get annoyingly crowded with tourists (not you — all those other people). But Sedona has the best restaurants in the region — even some of the best in the state — and I can see why you'd want to spend as much time in this gorgeous setting as possible.

Getting There

From Phoenix, take I-17 to Highway 179; from the airport, the drive is about 119 miles, most of them on the freeway. I-17 is curvy for stretches, but it's wide enough that you can drive the right lane at your own pace, letting the NASCAR racers zoom past.

Sedona & Vicinity

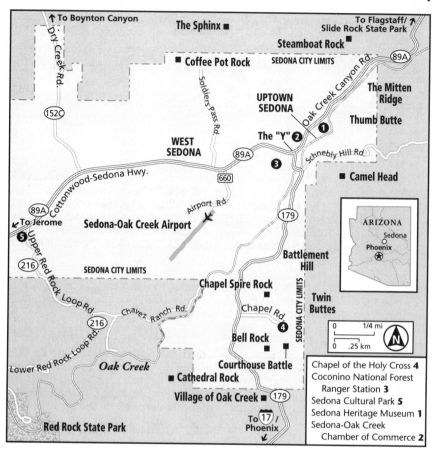

↑ To Boynton Canyon

Dry Creek Rd.

The Sphinx ■

To Flagstaff/ ↗
Slide Rock State Park

Steamboat Rock ■

■ Coffee Pot Rock

SEDONA CITY LIMITS

89A

Soldiers Pass Rd.

Oak Creek Canyon Rd.

152C

UPTOWN
SEDONA

The Mitten
Ridge

Thumb Butte

WEST
SEDONA

The "Y" ❷

❶

89A

❸

Schnebly Hill Rd.

Cottonwood-Sedona Hwy.

660

■ Camel Head

89A

← To Jerome

Cottonwood

Upper Red Rock Loop Rd.

Sedona-Oak Creek Airport

Airport Rd.

179

Battlement
Hill

❺

216

SEDONA CITY LIMITS

ARIZONA

Sedona
○
Phoenix
⊛

Chapel Spire Rock
■

Twin
Buttes

Chavez Ranch Rd.

216

Chapel Rd.

❹

SEDONA CITY LIMITS

0   1/4 mi

0   .25 km

Lower Red Rock Loop Rd.

Oak Creek

Courthouse Battle

Bell Rock
■

■ Cathedral Rock

Village of Oak Creek ■ 179

To 17 /
Phoenix
↙

Red Rock State Park

Chapel of the Holy Cross **4**
Coconino National Forest
 Ranger Station **3**
Sedona Cultural Park **5**
Sedona Heritage Museum **1**
Sedona-Oak Creek
 Chamber of Commerce **2**

TIP

Sedona doesn't have commercial air service from Phoenix, but you can pick up the **Sedona-Phoenix Shuttle** (☎ **800-448-7988** in Arizona or 520-282-2066) at each of the baggage claim areas at Phoenix Sky Harbor International Airport. Seven of these shuttle runs operate from 10 a.m. to 8 p.m. during the week, about one every hour and a half, and six run on the weekend. The cost is $35 one-way and $60 round-trip. However, you may want to skip the shuttle and head straight for the car rental agency. Although several car rental agencies operate in Sedona, you'll have more flexibility — and probably save some money — if you rent a car at the Phoenix airport.

The **Switchback Shuttle** (☎ **520-774-2200**) makes daily runs from the Flagstaff visitor's center (see Chapter 17) to uptown Sedona or to anywhere reasonable in town, which excludes, say, remote canyons. Buses leave at 9 a.m. and 3 p.m. every day, and the cost is $15 each way. No need to reserve; just show up.

A Tasty Detour

Are you flying into Phoenix and driving towards Sedona around feeding time? Don't hassle with trying to find a place to eat in the big city. Get on I-17 and then stop in at the Rock Springs Café and Bakery, about a half hour north of the airport.

Getting Around

Sedona does not have public transportation. You can get an overview of the town via the **Sedona Trolley** (☎ **520-282-5400** or 520-282-6826) or you can have **Bob's Sedona Taxi** (☎ **520-282-1234**) take you around, but that's about it for anything other than transporting yourself. **Enterprise** (☎ **800-325-8007** or 520-282-2052), **Practical** (☎ **800-464-8697** or 520-282-6702), and **Sedona Car Rentals** (☎ **520-282-2227**) can all lend you wheels.

Before you set out on your own, you need to learn the lay of the land, and it's not as simple as you might think. The town known as Sedona really consists of four distinct areas.

Coming in from Phoenix on Highway 179, you first encounter the **Village of Oak Creek,** which has a designer outlet mall with an IMAX theater; a few decent, reasonably priced restaurants; and several lodgings, mostly of the motel variety. Continuing north past a rapidly shrinking stretch of undeveloped land, you see a sign for Sedona and several upscale strip shopping centers on your left. When you spot the shopping village of Tlaquepaque on your right, you know you're near the "Y," as the usually crowded intersection with Highway 89A is known.

Take a right on Highway 89A to get to the visitor's center and the touristy drag called **Uptown Sedona,** where you have to wade through a lot of schlock to find the gems. Several restaurants, hotels, and galleries do fall into the latter category. Beyond Uptown Sedona is **Oak Creek Canyon.** Woodsy lodges and a few laid-back restaurants dot this extremely scenic route to Flagstaff.

If you go left at the "Y," you encounter **West Sedona** — the real people's town, with amenities such as supermarkets, drugstores, and movie theaters. Most of Sedona's top restaurants and several of its best places to stay are here as well. Boynton Canyon is off to the right and, as you continue along 89A toward Prescott, you pass the new arts complex and Red Rock State Park.

The stretch of Highway 179 between the Village of Oak Creek and the Y has some of the worst traffic in the state. This winding, two-lane road is lined with businesses (maybe including your hotel) but has few turn lanes. Moreover, lots of people spend the afternoon or evening sipping margaritas on outdoor decks along this route. During the day, the road is usually too congested for much harm to be done, but watch out at night, when both the traffic flow and the booze flow accelerate.

Where to Stay

Sedona is chock-a-block with rooms with a view and rooms that ooze character; economical lodgings, on the other hand, are as rare as traffic-free crossings at the "Y" intersection. In this section, I give you a wide range of choices in the top hotel and runner-up categories, as well as in the "Inns (but no outs) of Sedona" sidebar. The town has several chain hotels and — who knows? — maybe even places I haven't unearthed. Contact the Sedona–Oak Creek Chamber of Commerce (see "Quick Concierge: Sedona and the Verde Valley," in this chapter) for a complete listing of lodgings and reservation services. See Chapter 4 for a key to the dollar sign ratings used in this section.

You may want to consider Flagstaff (see Chapter 17), which is silly with economical rooms and sadly lacking in those with character, as a base for a visit to Sedona; it's only 28 miles away via Oak Creek Canyon. Cottonwood, even closer — about 15 miles from Sedona on Highway 89A — is another possibility. Its many chain hotels — the Cottonwood Chamber of Commerce (see "Quick Concierge: Sedona and the Verde Valley") can direct you to them — and its central location make it a particularly good base for exploring the region. On the opposite end of the spectrum, the ghost town of Jerome has lodgings with nothing if not personality. See the Jerome listing in "Chewing, Snoozing, and Boozing in Jerome" sidebar in this chapter for my hotel suggestions. They're not as luxurious as those in Sedona but not as pricey either.

The Top Hotels

Enchantment Resort
$$$$ West Sedona

A knockout Boynton Canyon setting, rooms done in the height of Southwest chic, and a stellar array of facilities have always put Enchantment on the top of my Sedona lodging list. (It's one of my favorites in the entire world, actually.) And with the opening of a huge state-of-the-art spa in late 2000, it has gotten even better. I admit that I love the envy factor: Other people have to travel to reach the spectacular hiking trails at your doorstep here; you have dibs on the coveted tables in the Yavapai dining room (see "Where to Dine" in this chapter); and now you've got the edge on the hottest spa treatments in town, too.

525 Boynton Canyon Rd. ☎ *800-826-4180 or 520-282-2900. Fax: 520-282-9249. E-mail:* info@enchantmentresort.com. *Internet:* www.enchantmentresort. com. *Rack rates: Feb 11–June 24 and Sept–Dec $325; Jan 3–Feb 10 and June 25–Aug $275; suites from $390 in low season. Kids camp and tennis clinics available. AE, DC, DISC, MC, V.*

Getting Creek-y

Keep in mind that there are two Oak Creeks in central Arizona. (Well, actually there's just one body of water but two areas near Sedona with that name.) The Village of Oak Creek on Hwy. 179 is a rather nondescript town. Oak Creek Canyon is the lovely gorge that Hwy. 89A winds through en route to Flagstaff. If you don't distinguish between the two when you ask for directions, you could be . . . well, up a creek.

Garland's Oak Creek Lodge

$$$$ Oak Creek Canyon

It's tough to get into this 1930s creekside lodge set on 17 acres — literally as well as figuratively. You have to drive across Oak Creek to get here, and the lodge is only open part of the year, so the 16 cabins book up far, far in advance. But all the repeat guests come back for good reasons: Great food, made with ingredients grown on the grounds; an idyllic leafy setting; and all the relaxation (including fishing) you can stand. People do cancel at the last minute, so it's worth giving this place a holler.

Highway 89A, 8 miles north of Uptown Sedona. ☎ 520-282-3343. Rack rates: $198. Rates include breakfast, afternoon tea, and dinner; 15% tip is added to the bill. Closed mid-Nov–March and Sun all year. MC, V.

L'Auberge de Sedona Resort

$$$$ Uptown Sedona

So what if this hillside resort feels more European than Southwest? When you cozy up in the canopy bed, listening to the babbling of Oak Creek, you are in Romance World, anyway. There are three types of accommodations: A motel-flavored structure called The Orchards, where rooms have some Southwest touches but not a whole lot of charm; appealing Country French–style quarters in a main lodge building; and brookside cabins, all with jetted tubs and wood-burning fireplaces. Although L'Auberge seems tucked away, you are within walking distance of all the Uptown Sedona tour operators and shops — not to mention the resort's excellent French restaurant (see "Where to Dine" in this chapter).

301 L'Auberge La. (½ mile west of the "Y," off Highway 89A). ☎ 800-272-6777 or 520-282-1661. Fax: 520-282-2885. E-mail: info@uberge.com. *Internet:* www.lauberge.com. *Rack rates: The Orchards: Jan–Feb 27, Nov 27–Dec 21 $160–$180; Feb 28–Nov 26, Dec 22–Dec 31 $175–$195. The Lodge: $190–$210/$230–$240. Cottages: $245–$275/$315–$345. AE, DISC, DC, MC, V.*

Los Abrigados

$$/$$$$ Near the "Y"

This resort has gone 85 percent time share, but it still has plenty to offer its temporary guests, including a great spa and exercise facilities, in-your-pocket proximity to Sedona's famed Tlaquepaque shopping village, and suites comfortable enough for long-term stays. Three lively restaurants add to the mix; Joey Bistro is always hopping, and the Rocks Bar and Grill often has live music. Nine hotel rooms next to the tennis courts are a real deal: Although smaller, they have coffeemakers, microwaves, and minifridges as well as a quieter location.

160 Portal Lane (next to Tlaquepaque shopping village; south of the "Y"). ☎ *800-521-3131 or 520-282-1777. Fax: 520-282-2614. E-mail:* webmaster@ ilexresorts.com. *Internet:* www.ilxinc.com. *Rack rates: $110; $225–$285 suites. AE, DISC, DC, MC, V.*

Sedona Real

$$–$$$ West Sedona

Practically brand new, with airy, well-equipped suites (that feature TVs, VCRs, refigerators, and microwaves), this place is reasonably priced. Best of all, you don't have to fight traffic to get into your room. Family harmony extra: Some suites have two TVs, and you can get microwave popcorn and movies at the front desk.

Highway 89A West at Arroyo Piñon Drive (across from the movie theater). ☎ *877-299-6016 or 520-282-1414. Fax: 520-282-0900. E-mail:* info@sedonareal.com. *Internet:* www.sedonareal.com. *Rack rates: Mar 10–Nov 25, Dec 25–Jan 2 $120–$195 1-bedroom suites; Jan 3–Mar 9, Nov 26–Dec 24 $89–$169. Children under 12 stay free. Internet specials. AE, DISC, MC, V.*

Sky Ranch Lodge

$$–$$$ West Sedona

I can't vouch for the existence of the vortex that's purportedly on Airport Mesa, this hotel's perch, but I can guarantee you a feeling of great well-being if you book a room here. The grounds, with their old-growth trees and gardens, are lovely; the rooms, while simple, have touches that add character (some offer decks and/or fireplaces); and you get some of the most spectacular red rock views in town for some of the most reasonable rates.

Airport Road (take Airport Road, off Highway 89A, almost to the top). ☎ *888-708-6400 or 520-282-6400. Fax: 520-282-7682. E-mail:* info@skyranchlodge.com. *Internet:* www.skyranchlodge.com. *Rack rates: $75–$149. AE, MC, V.*

The Runner-Up Hotels

Doubletree Resort

$$$ Village of Oak Creek   This resort has nice nouveau Southwest rooms and upscale facilities; it's next to Sedona's best golf course and a fine new spa. But it's a bit too far from the Sedona action — and not far enough from the Sedona traffic. 90 Ridge Trail Drive. ☎ *800-222-8733 or 520-284-4040. Fax: 520-284-6940. Internet:* www.doubletreehotels.com.

Junipine Resort

$$$–$$$$ **Oak Creek Canyon** Choose from an assortment of family-friendly one and two-bedroom condos, most with creekside views. Room service and a good on-site restaurant save you from having to drive through the canyon into Sedona at night. *8351 N. Highway 89A.* ☎ *800-742-PINE or 520-282-3375. Fax: 520-282-7402. Internet:* www.junipine.com.

The Inns (No Outs) of Sedona

When it comes to some of Sedona's more intimate lodgings, the "bed and break-fast" label is misleading. True, they offer personalized service and a morning meal, but the following accommodations bear a much stronger resemblance to boutique inns than they do to host homes. (All except the Wishing Well have at least eight guest units.) There's no enforced communal dining at any of them, either, so you can be as friendly — or as antisocial — as you wanna be in the a.m.

Briar Patch Inn, 3190 N. Highway 89A, Oak Creek Canyon (☎ **888-809-3030** or 520-282-2342; Fax: 520-282-2399; E-mail: briarpatch@sedona.net; Internet: www.briarpatchinn.com), features lovely 1930s cottages with spiffy Southwestern facelifts. During summer, be soothed at breakfast by live classical music, along with the rushing waters of Oak Creek. $$$–$$$$.

Casa Sedona, 55 Hozoni Dr., West Sedona (☎ **800-525-3756** or 520-282-2938; Internet: www.casasedona.com), has an attractive room to suit your personal-ity, whether you like cowboys or lace, and an outdoor hot tub with red-rock views. $$$–$$$$.

The Graham, 155 Canyon Circle Dr., Village of Oak Creek (☎ **800-228-1425** or 520-284-1425; Fax: 520-284-0767; Internet: www.sedonasfinest.com), offers attractive, standard B&B lodgings. The four drop-dead-gorgeous casitas, in a Spanish village–style complex, are the reason to stay here. $$$–$$$$ (B&B rooms), $$$$ (casitas).

The Inn on Oak Creek, 556 Highway 179, south of the "Y" (☎ **800-499-7896** or 520-282-7896; Fax: 520-282-0696; Internet: www.sedona-inn.com), counts a pri-vate creekside park, striking Southwestern rooms, and afternoon h'ors doeuvres among its many luxurious perks. $$$–$$$$.

The Lodge at Sedona, 125 Kallof Place, West Sedona (☎ **800-619-4467** or 520-204-1942; Fax: 520-204-2128; E-mail: lodge@sedona.net; Internet: www.lodgeatsedona.com), boasts a woodsy setting, gourmet breakfasts served on lace-covered tables, and a labyrinth in the backyard. $$$–$$$$.

The Wishing Well, 995 N. Highway 89A, at the beginning of Oak Creek Canyon (☎ **800-728-WISH** or 520-282-4914; E-mail: wishwell@sedona.net; Internet: www.sedona.net/bb/wishwell), may be the most romantic inn in Sedona. All the Victorian-pretty rooms have private decks and hot-tubs, and breakfast is deliv-ered to your door. $$$.

Poco Diablo

$$–$$$ **Between the Village of Oak Creek and the "Y"** This is one of the town's older properties. Regular revamps haven't eliminated the rooms' motel-like look, but a nice nine-hole golf course, several tennis courts, and some terrific rate deals definitely help compensate. *1752 S. Highway 179* ☎ *800-528-4275 or 520-282-7333. E-mail:* info@pocodiablo.com. *Internet:* www.pocodiablo.com.

Where to Dine

Sedona has fewer dining choices than lodging options, but with a population of only 16,000, it definitely outdoes most towns its size, culinary-wise. It doesn't hurt (except in the pocketbook) that many of Sedona's transplanted residents have the sophisticated palates that often come along with high-priced real estate. Because restaurants cater more to the upscale visitors than to the New Age kind (the owners know what side their bruschetta is buttered on), hippie health food dives are in short supply. However, most places please chic non-meat eaters with a variety of vegetarian choices. For a key to the dollar signs used in this section, see Chapter 4.

The Cowboy Club

$$–$$$ **Uptown Sedona** **American/Southwestern**

Who wudda figured a place called the Cowboy Club in the touristy hub of Uptown Sedona would dish up sophisticated Southwest fare? But the kitchen of one of Sedona's only historical structures turns out such trendy appetizers as buffalo brochettes (less fat than beef, don't 'ya know?) and entrees such as pistachio-crusted halibut; even the fried chicken comes with cumin gravy. Unless you really need to go home and say you've eaten reptile, skip the novelty items such as the rattlesnake bites.

241 Highway 89A (on main street). ☎ *520-282-4200. Reservations suggested on weekends. Main courses: $12.95–$23.95. Open: Daily lunch and dinner. AE, MC, V.*

Dahl & Di Luca

$$$ **West Sedona** **Italian**

A taste of Roma in Sedona. A cozy candlelit room with hand-decorated walls is the setting for such starters as mushrooms stuffed with mozzarella and fresh basil, followed, perhaps, by linguini in pomodora vodka sauce with prawns, all expertly turned out by Rome-born chef Andrea diLuca. Soft jazz or live blues enhance the romantic atmosphere (though the liberal use of garlic doesn't).

2321 W. Highway 89A. ☎ *520-282-5219. Reservations suggested. Main courses: $9.95–$23.95. Open: Dinner nightly. AE, DC, DISC, MC, V.*

Heartline Café

$$$ West Sedona New American

A friendly (but not obnoxiously so) staff serves some of the freshest, most interesting dishes in town in a cheery dark-wood dining room with flowers on every table. The cultural mix-it-up menu may include such appetizers as chicken dumplings with spicy peanut sauce, entrees such as grilled salmon with tequila lime glaze, or one of the always good vegetarian selections. A casual late night menu featuring pizza, salads, and sandwiches is a nice recent addition.

1610 W. Highway 89A. ☎ 520-282-0785. Reservations suggested. Main courses: Lunch $6–$12; dinner $14–$26. Open: Lunch Fri–Mon, dinner nightly; late night menu with entertainment Fri and Sat. AE, DISC, MC, V.

Javalina Cantina

$$ South of the "Y" Mexican

This is one of Sedona's most popular — and rowdiest — eateries. The specialty margaritas flow like water in this sprawling, oh-so-Southwest dining room; seats on the redwood deck with red-rock views are naturally the most coveted. Food of the Americanized Mexican persuasian — tacos, tamales, enchilada combos, huge tortilla-base salads — is the name of the game here. Kids have a separate menu; and, with all the hubbub, most whining should go unnoticed.

671 Highway 179 (in the Hillside shopping center). ☎ 520-203-9514. Reservations suggested. Main courses: $9.25–$13.95 (a few dishes higher). Open: Daily 11:30 a.m.–9:30 p.m. AE, DC, MC, V.

L'Auberge de Sedona

$$$$ Uptown Sedona French

L'Auberge is definitely a special occasion restaurant, both because of its priciness and its formality; this is one of the few places in Arizona where men have to wear jackets. But the occasion will definitely be special if you dine here. The room is country French pretty, the service precise, and the cuisine seriously haute, with a wine and liqueur list to match. You can order a la carte, but the five-course prix-fixe menu is the way to go. Try to snag a window seat for a view of Oak Creek.

L'Auberge Resort, 301 L'Auberge La. (½ mile west of the "Y," off Highway 89A). ☎ 520-282-1661. Dinner reservations essential. Main courses: $31.50–$39.50; prix-fixe $65; add $40 for matching wines; $30 for the elaborate Sunday champagne brunch. Open: Daily lunch and dinner; Sun brunch. AE, CB, DC, DISC, MC, V.

Oaxaca

$$ Uptown Sedona Mexican

It doesn't get much better than sitting on the outdoor deck of Oaxaca at sunset with a killer margarita in tow. Although this friendly Mexican restaurant caters to the Uptown Sedona crowds, it never goes for the lowest common denominator. A multi-page menu lists exotic items such as grilled cactus pads (deprickled) with zesty romesco sauce — which also happens to be one of several heart-healthy selections. Said healthy choices are counterbalanced by desserts such as the incredible fried ice cream. The presentations are attractive, too. And did I mention the margaritas?

321 N. Highway 89A (on main street). ☎ *520-282-4179. Reservations needed for parties of more than 6. Directions: Smack in the middle of the main Uptown Sedona drag. Main Courses: $15.95–$21.95; most all-day Mexican specialties: $9.25–13.95; all-you-can-eat breakfast and fruit bar: $6.50 adults, $3.95 children. Open: Daily breakfast, lunch, dinner; happy hour Mon–Fri 3–6 p.m. AE, DISC, MC, V.*

Pietro's

$$$ West Sedona   Northern Italian

Forget marinara and meatballs (except on the early-bird menu). Along with typical Northern Italian menu items — the veal piccata, say, or the spaghetti puttanesca — Pietro's menu includes dishes rare in cities far larger than Sedona. For example, you can try a starter of crépes with mushrooms and proscuitto in bechamel sauce, or an entree of fettucine with duck, shiitake mushrooms, and figs cooked in port wine. The service is as sophisticated as the cuisine. The lively atmosphere draws a hip Gen Xer-and-up crowd after 6:30 p.m.

2445 W. Highway 89A. ☎ *520-282-2525. Reservations highly recommended. Main courses: $14.50–$18.50 pasta, $16–$23.50 entrees; early-bird entrees, Sun–Wed until 6:30 p.m., $9.50–$12.50. Open: Dinner nightly. AE, DC, DISC, MC, V.*

The Prime Cut

$$–$$$ West Sedona   Steakhouse

You'd expect to find a good steakhouse in Sedona — this is, after all, the West — but a reasonably priced one is a nice surprise. Unlike the big, fancy meat chains where everything besides a naked slab of steak costs extra, here you get soup or salad and potatoes or vegetables with your handcut, certified Angus beef (and that's no slouch of a cow slice!). Steak averse? The "surf" is as good as the "turf" here. The dining rooms are more comfy lounge-casual than fancy.

A Million Dollar Cobbler

The phone at the Sedona Chamber of Commerce started ringing off the hook after Regis Philbin raved on national TV about the great peach cobbler he had in Sedona. Everyone wanted to know where to find it. And our final answer is: **Robert's Creekside Cafe**, Creekside Plaza, 251 Highway 179, south of the "Y" (☎ 520-282-3671), which also has excellent sandwiches, salads, seafood, fresh-baked bread, and more. It's open for lunch and dinner daily ($$–$$$).

The Red Rocks of . . . Schnebly?

When Theodore Schnebly, a Pennsylvania Dutch settler who bought 80 acres near Oak Creek in 1901, applied for a post office permit, he was told that his proposed name, "Schnebly Station," was too long. Luckily, his wife had a nice, short name: Sedona.

2250 W. Highway 89A (between Rodeo Dr. and Coffee Pot Rd.). ☎ *520-282-2943. Reservations recommended. Main courses: $8.95–$21.95. Open: Lunch Mon–Fri, dinner nightly, brunch and dinner menu both available from 11:30 a.m. Sunday. AE, DISC, MC, V.*

Rene's

$$$$ Just south of the "Y"   Continental

For a less formal setting than L'Auberge and a more traditional menu than those at the Yavapai Room, the Cowboy Club, or Heartline Café, try this pretty lace-curtain dining room in the Tlaquepaque shopping village. True, you can order seitan tofu Wellington, but the signature rack of lamb and the roast duck with sun-dried cherry sauce are much more typical. The French onion soup makes a fine starter, and if you don't mind calling attention to yourself while the server immolates your dessert, finish with the flamboyant bananas foster.

Tlaquepaque, B-118, 336 Highway 179. ☎ *520-282-9225. Reservations recommended. Main Courses: $17.95 – $29.95. Open: Lunch and dinner daily. MC, V.*

The Yavapai Room

$$$$ West Sedona   New American

Is it the 180-degree views of Boyton Canyon or the regional American cuisine that puts the tables at Enchantment's fine dining room at such a premium? Well, the former no doubt play a major role, but that wouldn't explain all those people who look perfectly pleased with their food (smoked trout tostada followed by grilled deer loin, perhaps) after dark. Don't think about showing up without a reservation, even at lunchtime; you won't get past the guard station on the property.

Enchantment Resort, 525 Boynton Canyon Rd. ☎ *520-282-2900. Reservations essential for all meals. Main courses: $21–$35.95; $28.50 for the elaborate champagne brunch. Open: Breakfast, lunch, and dinner daily; Sun brunch. AE, DC, DISC, MC, V.*

The Runner-Up Restaurants

The Hideaway

$$ South of the "Y"   This spot serves up spectacular red rock views and decent Southern Italian food at prices below most of those in Sedona. *Country Square, Highway 179.* ☎ *520-282-4204.*

Sedona Swiss

$$$ Uptown Sedona   Come here for Alpine comfort food par excellence; the French-style pastries are especially soothing after a long, hard day of shopping. Avoid this place at lunchtime, however, when the tour buses descend for the low-priced buffet. *350 Jordan Rd.* ☎ *520-282-7959.*

Takashi

$$–$$ Uptown Sedona   This Japanese garden of tranquility (with red rocks replacing the usual gray pebbles) sits in a generally frenetic part of town. Delicate tempura, spicy sushi tuna salad, and green tea ice cream are among the menu high-lights. *465 Jordan Rd.* ☎ *520-282-2334.*

Exploring Sedona and the Verde Valley

Sedona is strong on splendor and sports, but not so strong on history. If you want to explore the area's rich mining and Native American past, tour the Verde Valley (which is no slouch in the scenery department, though not as showy).

If you drive up from Phoenix during daylight hours and aren't too tired from your flight, detour off I-17 en route to Sedona to visit Montezuma's Castle and — if you're a military history buff — Fort Verde. You can enjoy Jerome, Tuzigoot, and the Verde Valley Railroad when you're red-rock sated. Keep in mind, too, that Jerome is about halfway between Sedona and Prescott on Highway 89A. If you want to visit Prescott from Sedona, be sure to build some extra time into your schedule for Jerome.

The Top Sights

Jerome

Jerome was a bustling, rough 'n' tumble mining camp in the early 1900s. The population rose and fell with the price of copper, climbing up to about 15,000 in the late 1920s. Jerome earned its "ghost town" label after the last mine was shut down in 1953 and only 50 people stuck around the mountain. The town had a hippie and biker resurgence in the 1960s, and now some 450 folks — many of them artsy and crafty — call Jerome home. Despite interesting shopping (see "Shopping" in this chapter) and fascinating history, another reason to wind your way some 2,000 feet up the side of Cleopatra Hill is for the views. On a clear day, you really can see forever: The Verde Valley spreads out below you, flanked by Sedona, the multi-hued Mogollon Rim, and the San Francisco Peaks, Arizona's highest mountains.

Chewing, Snoozing, and Boozing in Jerome

For a ghost town, Jerome lays on lots of corporeal comforts. Here are my top picks for the best sleeps, eats, and drinks.

Lodging: The **Jerome Grand Hotel ($–$$)**, 200 Hill St., (☎ **888-817-6788** or 520-634-8200; Internet: www.jeromegrandhotel.net) used to be the town's hospital. The views from the hill are still super, and you no longer have to be laid up to enjoy them. The vistas from the nearby **Surgeon's House ($$–$$$)**, 101 Hill St., (☎ **800-639-1452** or 520-639-1452) are also therepeutic, and the generous breakfasts included in the room rate will cure whatever ails you.

Dining: The **Flatiron Cafe ($)**, 416 Main St., (☎ **520-634-2733**) is the place to come for your morning latte or mid-day smoked salmon quesadilla. You can wash down the more basic American fare served at the **Jerome Brewery ($–$$)**, 111 Main St., ☎ **520-639-8477,** with one of several good microbrews. The name of **Apizza Heaven ($–$$)**, near the corner of Main and Hull Sts., (☎ **520-649-1843**) isn't just pie in the sky; the pizzas and other casual Italian dishes are stellar. The **House of Joy,** Hull Ave. just off Main Street, (☎ **520-634-5339**) is only open for dinner on Saturday and Sunday, so if you want to dine Continental-y in a former bordello (prix-fixe three-course meals $23 and up), book far in advance.

Nightlife: Jerome's rowdy days are far from over. Bikers, hippies, and yuppies all pile into the **Spirit Room,** Main Street and Highway 89A (☎ **520-634-8809**) and **Paul and Jerry's Saloon,** just down Main Street (☎ **520-634-2603**), especially on live music nights.

Jerome is about 25 miles southwest of Sedona via Highway 89A en route to Prescott; if you want to stay in town for a while, see the "Chewing, Snoozing, and Boozing in Jerome" sidebar in this chapter. I list the hours for the town's few formal sights in this section, but don't hold me to them (except in the case of the state park). The attitude toward time in Jerome is, shall we say, relaxed.

In addition to strolling the town's Main Street, you can:

✔ **See how the other half lived:** The mansion that's the centerpiece of **Jerome State Historic Park,** off U.S. 89A on Douglas Road (☎ **520-634-5381**), used to belong to Little Daisy mine owner "Rawhide Jimmy" Douglas. His original furniture sits among the displays, which include ore samples and mining equipment. The introductory film has a corny ghost narrator, but it's worth sitting through for the historical overview. Open daily 8 a.m.–5 p.m., except Christmas; admission $2.50 adults, $1 children 7–13, free for ages 6 and under. *Note:* This is also the town's unofficial visitor center. You pass it on the way up, so stop in if you have any questions.

✔ **Mine more of the town's history:** Among its many documents and artifacts, the **Jerome Historical Society and Mine Museum,** 200 Main St. (☎ **520-634-5477**), includes stock certificates in mind-boggling amounts. (And you thought your shares of Amazon.com were worth something!) Open daily 9 a.m.–4:30 p.m., admission $1. The displays at the **Gold King Mine and Ghost Town,** Perkinsville Road (follow the signs about 1 mile from the center of town; ☎ 520-635-0053), mix history with hype, but it's fun to poke around the ruins of the town's once hugely wealthy gold mine. Open daily 9 a.m.–5 p.m., admission $3.

Montezuma Castle National Monument

Near the town of Camp Verde

There may be larger remains of early Native American living quarters in the Southwest, including some in more dramatic settings, but few are as well preserved and as easily viewed as these two twelfth-century Sinagua cliff dwellings. Beaver Creek flows through this tree-shaded area — which explains why the Sinagua built homes here and why you'll especially enjoy your visit. A leisurely stroll around the guided loop path shouldn't take more than a half hour; devote another 15 minutes or so to the small visitor's center museum, which traces the history of the Sinaguas in the Verde Valley.

If you have time, get back on I-17 heading toward Flagstaff and take the next (McGuireville) turnoff; signs will direct you to **Montezuma Well,** which is part of the national monument (same hours; no fee). There you will see a huge, strikingly blue spring-fed pond, some 368 feet across and 65 feet deep. Another easy side trip from Montezuma's Castle is to Fort Verde (see "More Cool Things to See and Do" later in this section). If you need to choose between these two because of time constraints, I'd vote for Montezuma Well.

Exit 289 from Highway 17 and follow the signs. ☎ *520-567-3322. Open: Memorial Day to Labor Day, daily 8 a.m.–7 p.m.; 8 a.m.–5 p.m. the rest of the year. Admission: $2; 16 and under free. Golden Age/Golden Eagle passes accepted for free admission.*

Sedona/Oak Creek Canyon

Few activities in or near Sedona involve taxing your brain cells — except maybe calculating how close you are to maxing out your credit cards. This town is mainly about gazing at stunning scenery. This section lists numerous ways to do that, starting with activities you can do on your own — without expending too much energy.

Wondering what gives Sedona's rosy rocks their color? The brightest red of the three layers of sandstone around here got its distinct hue when iron minerals mixed with oxygen to form iron oxide — in other words, rust.

✔ **See some stately rocks:** No, the rusty sandstone cliffs that fall under the aegis of **Red Rock State Park,** 4050 Red Rock Loop Rd. (☎ 520-282-6907), are no more exciting than any of the others in this area. This is, however, a good spot to walk along some gentle trails near Oak Creek and to take one of the daily ranger-led nature walks (10 a.m.). Call ahead, too, for the seasonally changing schedules of birdwatching excursions. The turnoff for the park, open daily from 8 a.m.–5 p.m., is 2 miles beyond West Sedona on Highway 89A. Cost: $5 per car with up to four people.

✔ **Go slip-sliding away:** The natural water slide in Oak Creek gives **Slide Rock State Park,** 7 miles north of Sedona on Highway 89A, Oak Creek Canyon (☎ 520-282-3034), its name. The water slide — along with a volleyball net, BBQ grills, the pizza-providing Slide Rock Market, and picnic tables — makes this a major summer party place and family gathering ground. After the warm weather sets in, hardly a parking spot can be found after 10 a.m. Several trailheads are in this area, too. The park is open daily 8 a.m.– 7 p.m. summer; until 5 p.m. winter; until 6 p.m. fall and spring. Admission: $5 per vehicle up to 4 people; $1 each additional person; under 12 free.

✔ **Get religious:** You don't have to subscribe to any particular belief system to want to visit the **Chapel of the Holy Cross** (☎ 520-282- 4069), built in 1956 by a protegé of Frank Lloyd Wright. Like her mentor, Marguerite Brunwige Staude knew the importance of working with your surroundings, and this simple, clean-lined house of worship seems to have sprung from the red cliffs that surround it. Look for the cross on the right side of Highway 179 as you head north towards the "Y" from Oak Creek Village, and turn right on Chapel Road. Open daily 9 a.m.–5 p.m.

✔ **Soothe body and soul:** Myofascial release is a stretch/pressure point treatment designed to eliminate tension and pain. At **Therapy on the Rocks,** 676 North Highway 89A in Uptown Sedona (☎ 520-282-3002), prices start at $60 for a neck and face treatment. A combination myofascial release/Swedish massage, including a hot tub soak on a red rock–view deck, runs $95 per hour. The spas at Los Abrigados and Enchantment (see "Where to Stay") offer more traditional treatments; those given at the **Center for New Age** (see the "What Color Is Your Aura?" sidebar) are even farther out.

✔ **Soak up some history:** Okay, so I lied. A few attractions in this area do cater to people who like to revisit the past. You have to plan ahead, however; touring hours are limited at the first two. At Red Rock State Park (described earlier in this section), rangers lead tours of **House of Apache Fire,** formerly the home of Jack and Helen Fry, at 10 a.m. on Wednesday and Sunday. (Jack Fry used to be president of TWA, and the Frys owned the park property.) Each Saturday at 9 a.m. in summer, 1 p.m. in winter, you can be guided through the **Pendley Homestead** at Slide Rock State Park (described earlier in this section). Both the Pendley Homestead and the **Sedona Heritage Museum,** 735 Jordan Rd., Uptown Sedona (☎ 520-282-7038), give a feel (or is that a peel?) for an era when apple-growing was a major source of income in this region. Check out the 45-foot-long apple-sorting machine located inside the museum. The museum is the most comprehensive of these three historical sites and features a room devoted to film — dozens of Westerns have used Sedona as a backdrop. Open daily 10 a.m.–4 p.m., except major holidays; admission $3, under 12 free.

What Color Is Your Aura?

Chakras blocked? Past lives eluding you? Not to worry. **The Center for the New Age,** 341 Highway 179, across from Tlaquepaque (☎ 520-282-2085), can address your every psychic or spiritual need. This one-stop New Age shopping center is the place to come for crystals, astronomical charts, healing vitamins, regressions, energy releases, and more. Even if you're a complete skeptic, it's worth getting a massage from Rhonda Gerard — her body work is out of this world. (And yes, you can get a snapshot that will show you precisely where your aura falls on the chromatic scale.)

Tuzigoot National Monument

Just outside Clarkdale

The group of Sinagua Indians who lived in Montezuma Castle (described earlier in this section) went for the creekside real estate. Their kin who settled at Tuzigoot between the years 1125 and 1400 liked the hilltop property, prime both for protection purposes (enemies approaching from anywhere around the Verde Valley could be spotted from up here) and for the adjacent fertile farmland that the Hohokam Indians had left behind. These days, some of the views are spoiled by a slag field left over from the mines at nearby Jerome, but this is still a scenic spot to soak in some local history. It should take you about a half hour to do the slightly hilly loop around the pueblo complex; add another 10 minutes for the museum/visitor center. Broadway Road (off Highway 89A, between Old Town Cottonwood and Clarkdale). ☎ *520-634-5564.* Open: Daily 8 a.m.–7 p.m. Memorial Day to Labor Day, 8 a.m.–5 p.m. the rest of the year. Admission: $2; 16 and under free. Golden Age/Golden Eagle passes accepted for free admission.

More Cool Things to See and Do

Here you have more options to spend time outdoors, whether you want to explore an old fort, look for bald eagles, or play cowboy.

✔ **Get fortified:** A museum and several reconstructed officers quarters in **Fort Verde State Historic Park,** 125 E. Hollamon St., Camp Verde (☎ 520-567-3275), tell the story of this fairly short-lived (1871–1891) military installation. Established to protect Verde Valley from Indian raids, it supervised the forced displacement of the Yavapai and Tonto Apaches to reservations in Eastern Arizona. Open daily 8 a.m.–5 p.m., except Christmas; $2 adults, $1 ages 7–13, 6 and under free. To get here, follow the signs from any of the three Camp Verde exits on I-17. (Only the first, if you're coming from Phoenix, is marked "Fort Verde," but all three lead to downtown, where the park is located.)

✔ **Find out what's in a name:** While away an afternoon at **Dead Horse Ranch State Park,** 675 Dead Horse Ranch Rd., Cottonwood (☎ 520-634-5283). You can bird watch — say, for bald eagles in winter — picnic in a shady spot, or hike some gentle trails along the Verde River. The strange moniker? When the former owner of the property asked his little boy which ranch he should buy of several they'd surveyed, his son picked the one where they'd seen a dead horse. The park is a mile north of Cottonwood; take Main Street (Highway 89A) to 10th Street and follow the signs. Open daily 8 a.m.–6 p.m.; admission $4 per car.

✔ **Go country:** The **Blazin' M Ranch,** off 10th Street in Cottonwood (☎ 800-WEST-643 or 520-634-0344), is a replica of an Old West town. It has pony rides, a shooting gallery, a mechanical horse, and souvenir shops, but most people come for the chuck-wagon suppers and Western stage shows, held nightly Wed–Sun (closed Jan and Aug). For $18.95 adults, $8.95 children 10 and under, you get a good homespun dinner and good, clean Country & Western entertainment. Kids who think they're hip don't necessarily cotton to the old cowboy ballads and Hee Haw-style comedy routines, but they do tend to like the big barn setting — not to mention eating food off a tin plate. To get here, follow the signs to Dead Horse Ranch State Park (see previous listing) and turn left just past the entrance.

Guided Tours

All the following tours are given in Sedona. See also the "Take the Last Train from Clarkdale" sidebar for excursions on the Verde Canyon Railroad.

✔ **General tours:** If you want to survey the lay of the land, board the **Sedona Trolley** (☎ 520-282-5400 or 520-282-6826). Two 55-minute tours depart from the Chamber of Commerce (see "Quick Concierge: Sedona and The Verde Valley"). One (10 a.m., noon, 2 p.m., 4 p.m.) goes along Highway 179 to Tlaquepaque, the Chapel of the Holy Cross, and gallery row. The other (11 a.m., 1 p.m., 3 p.m., 5 p.m.) visits West Sedona, some scenic canyons, and Enchantment Resort. Cost: $7 adults, $2 children 12 and under, both tours $11.

✔ **Air tours:** Feeling a bit too grounded? Tour operators in Sedona cater to every lofty inclination. If you go for a hot-air ballon ride, you'll be picked up at your hotel; if you're up for a helicopter or small plane jaunt, drive to the Sedona Airport (turn off 89A west of the "Y" onto Airport Road and keep going up to the top of the hill).

A helicopter may be the best bet if you're a bit afraid of heights like me: It's more enclosed than the hot air-balloon, and those big, whirling blades make it feel more stable than a small plane. (That's a purely personal, totally nonaerodynamically informed opinion.)

- **By hot air balloon:** What could be more heavenly than float-ing above the red rocks at sunrise in a hot air balloon? (Well, maybe floating above the red rocks at sunset, so you don't have to get up before dawn, but that's just my opinion.) Wind conditions permitting, **Red Rock Balloon Adventures** (☎ 800-258-3754 or 520-284-0040) will take you up, up, and away for a minimum of an hour, then reward you with a champagne picnic and proof-of-flight certificate. The $145 per person fee also includes one free video of your trip per reservation.

- **By helicopter:** There's nothing like a whirlybird for getting up close and personal with the landscape. Prices for a 10-minute tour of Cathedral Rock, Bell Rock, and other Sedona landmarks start at $36 per person at **Sky Dance Helicopters** (☎ **800-882-1651** or 520-282-1651) and top off at $140 per person for a 40-minute buzz through various dramatic canyons. If you shell out $300 to $400 per person, you can be transported to the top of a secluded mesa and served a gourmet meal on a white tablecloth. A personalized video-tape costs extra for the shorter flights but is included in the price of the mesa-top dining deal.

- **By plane:** Widen your horizons on a **Red Rock Bi-Plane** (☎ **888-866-7433** or 520-204-3939) with an open cockpit that lets you indulge your Red Baron fantasies. Prices start at $36 per person for a 10-minute tour; travel as far as Jerome on the 45-minute $139 per person tour. Interested in a (literally) hands-on ride? For $185 you get 30 minutes of stick shift time (under the pilot's supervision, of course).

✔ **Jeep tours: Pink Jeep,** 204 N. Highway 89A, Uptown Sedona (☎ **800-873-3662** or 520-282-5000), is the largest and most blushingly conspicuous of Sedona's off-road tour operators. You can choose adventures ranging from a 1½-hour Canyon West jaunt ($32 per person) to a 3½-hour Sugarloaf tour ($75); the 2-hour Broken Arrow tours ($60) into the Coconino National Forest are the most popular. **Earth Wisdom,** 293 N. Highway 89A, Uptown Sedona (☎ **800-482-4714** or 520-282–4714), can take you on a magical mystery tour of Sedona's vortexes that lasts about 2½ hours and costs $50 per person. Earth Wisdom also offers guided "walkabouts."

It's a Material World: Psychic Scammers

It may be a New Age, but lots of hucksters in Sedona are running old scams, playing on visitors' vulnerabilities to part them from their money. Anita Dalton of the Center for the New Age has some suggestions to avoid being duped:

✔ Don't trust anyone who diagnoses your "problem" and starts discussing money without having spent much time talking to you.

✔ Go with your gut. If someone makes you feel uncomfortable or some treatment doesn't feel right to you, don't proceed any further.

✔ Be careful of anyone who claims the psychic power to heal you of an illness — for a fee.

Take the Last Train from Clarkdale

Tootle through some of the most interesting scenery in Arizona on the **Verde Canyon Railroad**, 300 N. Broadway, Clarkdale (☎ 800-293-7245 or 520-639-0010; Internet: www.verdecanyonrr.com). You'll be riding rails that once transported tons of ore from Jerome's United Verde Copper Mine. The four-hour round-trip ride through a protected wilderness area in a red-rock canyon has some historical constants — the ghost town of Perkinsville and a few Indian cliff dwellings, for example — but nature puts on a different show each season. The bald eagle watch from December through March is the most renowned, but fall foliage, spring wildflowers, and summer waterfalls are pretty impressive, too. Schedules vary, but trains always depart Wednesday through Sunday at 1 p.m. In peak times, especially March, April, October, and November, a Monday ride is added, and double trains run on Saturday from March to mid-May and October to mid-November. Rates are $32.95 adult, $32.95 senior (65+), and $20.95 (ages 2–12) in coach, $54.95 for all in first class. Call to ask about the summer starlight trains.

Keeping Active

If you're looking for even more ways to get some fresh air in Sedona, here y'go:

- ✔ **Biking:** In recent years, Sedona has become a mountain-biker's mecca. You can get wired up and wheeled out at the **Sedona Bike & Bean Shop,** 376 Jordan Road, Uptown Sedona (☎ 520-282-3515), a coffee bar that rents bikes (half day $24, full day $39) and runs guided rides ($65 per person). **Mountain Bike Heaven,** 1695 W. Highway 89A, West Sedona (☎ 520-282-1312) offers rentals by the hour ($7.50 for a full suspension bicycle, including helmet and water bottle), with a 2-hour minimum.

- ✔ **Fishing:** Anglers of all ages have fun at the stocked **Rainbow Trout Farm,** 3500 N. Highway 89A, 3 miles north of Sedona in Oak Creek Canyon (☎ 520-282-5799). For a buck — what a bargain! — you get a pole with a hook and bait. After that, you pay according to the size of your catch from $3.25 to $6.25 per fish (fish under 8 inches are free). It costs another 50¢ each if you want to take them back clean. Open weather permitting year-round; Mon–Fri 9 a.m.–5 p.m., Sat–Sun 9 a.m.–7 p.m. most of the year; Mon–Fri 8 a.m.–5 p.m., Sat–Sun 8 a.m.–7 p.m. in summer.

- ✔ **Golfing:** There are only two 18-hole championship golf courses in the Sedona area. Green fees at the new Gary Panks–designed course at the **Sedona Golf Resort,** 35 Ridge Trail Drive, off Highway 179, near the Village of Oak Creek (☎ 520-284-9355), run $87 Mon–Thu and $97 Fri–Sun. You pay $75 every day to play the **Oak Creek Country Club,** 690 Bell Rock Blvd., also off Highway 179 near the Village of Oak Creek (☎ 520-284-1660), where Robert Trent Jones put his hand to the grass arrangement. A quick game at the 9-hole course at **Poco Diablo** (see "Where to Stay" in this chapter) sets you back only $12; it's $18 for an all-day pass. There's no extra charge for the red rock distractions at all three.

✔ **Hiking:** There are more trailheads than vortexes in this primo trekking region. Some of the most popular hiking spots are Boynton Canyon and Loy Canyon in West Sedona, the trails leading to Bell Rock along Highway 179, and the West Fork Trail in Oak Creek Canyon. But you're the only one who knows your stamina and experience. Check with the **Coconino National Forest Ranger Station,** 250 Brewer Rd., south of the "Y" (☎ 520-282-4119), open Mon–Fri 7:30 a.m.–4:30 p.m., Sat 7:30 a.m.–4 p.m., regarding the length and difficulty of the various trails. (To find the station if you come from the south on Highway 179, take a left on Ranger Road just past Tlaquepaque, and another left on Brewer Road.) For other hiking suggestions, see "Exploring Sedona and the Verde Valley" earlier in this chapter.

✔ **Horseback riding:** At **Trail Horse Adventures,** Lower Red Rock Loop Road, 2 miles west of Sedona on Highway 89A near Red Rock State Park (☎ **800-SADDLE-UP** or 520-282-7252), rates start at $30 per person for a 1-hour guided ride. The $50 2-hour excursions across Oak Creek give you more of a back-in-the saddle experience. **Sedona Red Rock Jeep Tours,** 217 N. 89A, Uptown Sedona (☎ **800-848-7728** or 520-282-6826), combine engine and equine back-road adventures. Prices start at $42 for a combination 1-hour trot around Boynton Canyon and about a 1½-hour drive in a Jeep. **A Day in the West,** 252 Highway 89A (☎ **800-973-3662** or 520-282-4340), does a similar Jeep/horse combo but rides through the Bradshaw Ranch and adds a cowboy cookout to the mix. It's $74.95 per person for a 3½-hour adventure (ages 7 or older only; same price for all).

Shopping

Both Sedona and Jerome offer great shopping, particularly if you want to buy art and Southwestern crafts. This section will help you find your way to the area's best stores.

Where to Look in Sedona

Shoppers practice conspicuous consumption on almost every square foot of (paved) Sedona, but it's most concentrated in two areas: Uptown Sedona and the stretch along Highway 179 from the town limit sign north to the "Y". The east side of Highway 179 hosts several shopping strips, the best known and most upscale of which are **Hillside Courtyard,** 671 Highway 179 (☎ **520-282-4500**) and **Hozho Center,** 431 Highway 179 (☎ **520-204-2257**). On the west side of the road as you approach the "Y" is the jewel in Sedona's shopping crown, **Tlaquepaque Arts & Crafts Village,** Highway 179 at the bridge (☎ **520-282-4838**), a replica of the shopping town outside of Guadalajara, Mexico (except you won't find bargaining — or bargains — here). Even if you don't want to buy anything, drop in to stroll around the two charming plazas of this red-tile roof complex; it even has its own small wedding chapel.

Large parking lots adjoin Tlaquepaque, but the places to leave your car at Hillside and Hozho are more limited; you may have to drive around for a while in a rather tight area before a space opens up.

In addition to the storefronts lining Highway 89A and the galleries along Jordan Road, Uptown Sedona has two shopping complexes: **Sinagua Plaza,** 320 N. Highway 89A (☎ 520-282-0641) and **Sacagawea Plaza,** 301 N. Highway 89A (☎ 520-284-1110) — a much easier name to remember since the $1 coin with the image of Lewis and Clark's young Shoshone guide was issued in 2000. The shopping plaza predates the currency, though; look for John Soderberg's powerful bronze statue of Sacagawea and her child inside.

Don't bother cruising congested Highway 89A for a spot in Uptown Sedona; leave your car in the lot behind the Chamber of Commerce (see "Quick Concierge: Sedona and the Verde Valley" in this chapter) or in the larger, two-level one in the back of Sinagua Plaza.

What to Buy in Sedona

Art galleries and Southwest crafts boutiques dominate all of the previously mentioned complexes; Hozho is particularly strong on art, Tlaquepaque on crafts. The best of them? I could devote another entire book to Sedona shopping; take these as just a few starter suggestions, ranging over a wide area of interests. Serious shoppers can plumb the town's retail well far more deeply.

One of Arizona's (and possibly the world's) best places to buy Native American weavings and other crafts is **Garland's Navajo Rugs,** 411 AZ 179 at Schnebly Hill Road (☎ 520-282-4079). For personal decoration, visit Garland's **Indian Jewelry Inc.,** Highway 89A, 4 miles north of Uptown Sedona at Indian Gardens in Oak Creek Canyon (☎ 520-282- 6632).

Two of the biggest guns in the fine-art collecting game are **Exposures Gallery of the West** in Hillside (☎ 800-526-7668 or 520-282-1125) and **Lanning Gallery** in Hozho (☎ 520-282-6865). **James Ratliff Gallery,** also in Hozho (☎ 520-282-1404), carries more fanciful — and sometimes less expensive — pieces by less established artists. The **Sedona Arts Center Gallery Shop,** Highway 89A and Art Barn Rd., Uptown Sedona (☎ 520-282-3865), is the place to find out what the local art gang is up to.

For women's western wear, check out **Looking West,** 245 W. Highway 89A (☎ 520-282-4877), and **Cowboy Corral,** 219 W. Highway 89A (☎ 800-457-2279 or 520-282-2040), both in Uptown Sedona. If I could afford it, I'd make a big dent in the inventory of hand-woven scarves and hand-stitched jackets at **Isadora,** No. 120, Bldg. A, Tlaquepaque (☎ 520-282-6232).

If you like to give picture-perfect dinner parties — and aren't as klutzy as I am — browse the beautifully designed vases and stemware at **Kuivato Glass Gallery,** Patio Azul, Tlaquepaque (☎ 800-282-4312 or 520-282-1212), and the vibrantly patterned ceramic dishes at the **Clay Pigeon,** Hillside (☎ 520-282-2845). It's hard to know how to categorize

Mother Nature's Gallery, B-218, Tlaquepaque (☎ 520-282-5932) — it's kind of Sharper Image meets Fred Flintstone — but if you think a dinosaur sculpture or trilobite bas-relief would look good in your living room, this is the place to come. (You can find lots of fun science toys, too.)

In addition to the Center for the New Age (see the "What Color Is Your Aura?" sidebar earlier in the chapter), **Crystal Magic,** 2978 W. Highway 89A (☎ 520-282-1622), and **Eye of the Vortex Book Center,** 1405 Highway 89A (☎ 520-282-5614), both in West Sedona, are one-stop spiritual need shops.

The relatively small **Prime Outlets at Sedona,** 6601 S. Highway 179, Village of Oak Creek (☎ 888-545-7227 or 520-284-2150), includes the usual suspects — Mikasa, Corning/Revere, Bass, and more.

Where to Look and What to Buy in Jerome

Shopping in Jerome is easier than Sedona: Jerome's shops are on one main street — usefully called Main Street — with some additional shops on Hull Avenue, just around the bend. The **Jerome Artist's Cooperative,** 502 Main St. (☎ 520-639-4276), is a good spot for a general survey of some of the town's best crafts. If you want to zoom in on jewelry, head straight for my favorite store, **Aurum,** 369 Main St. (☎ 520-634-3330), where you find unique designs by artists from all over the state; semi-precious stones and silver dominate. I've also put in a fair share of time trying on floppy hats and colorful Southwestern clothes next door at **Designs on You,** 233 Main St. (☎ 520-634-7879) — don't expect the street numbering to make sense in Jerome. Other shops on my regular check-in list include **Nelly Bly,** 136 Main St. (☎ 520-634-0255), with an unusual collection of kaleidoscopes; **Jerome Gallery,** 240 Hull Ave. (☎ 520-634-7033), featuring beautiful handcrafted furnishings and home-decor tchotchkes; and **Raku Gallery,** 250 Hull Ave. (☎ 520-639-0239), shimmering with the distinctive shiny-glaze ceramics that give the shop its name.

Nightlife and the Arts

Sophisticated by day, Sedona is surprisingly provincial at night. If you've already seen the few first-run movies in town, your night will probably end with dinner. A few live music options include the following:

- ✔ The **Oak Creek Brewing Co.,** 2050 Yavapai Dr., off Highway 89A in West Sedona (☎ 520-204-1300), where good suds and a cool courtyard with a fire pit draw a party-hearty crowd.

- ✔ The **Lizard Head Lounge,** 2375 W. Highway 89A, West Sedona (☎ 520-282-1808), with music ranging from jazz to calypso and dancing on a tiny, always-packed floor.

- ✔ The **Rainbows End Steakhouse & Saloon,** 3235 W. Highway 89A, West Sedona (☎ 520-282-1593), boot scootin' and hootin' since the 1940s, when the Duke and other Western legends of the silver screen wet their whistles here.

- ✔ **Casa Rincon & Tapas Cantina,** 2620 W. Highway 89A, West Sedona (☎ **520-282-4849**), often featuring classical Spanish guitar but sometimes sizzling with Latin dance lessons.

- ✔ **Shugrue's Hillside,** 671 Highway 179, south of the "Y" (☎ **520- 282-5300**), where a mellow bass, guitar, and piano ensemble can soothe you after a hard day on the red rocks.

 Jerome's nightlife has more life (see the "Chewing, Snoozing, and Boozing in Jerome" sidebar earlier in the chapter) — but you definitely shouldn't drive down that mountain after you've had a few, or even one.

Sedona's a little better in the arts department, especially since the 50-acre **Sedona Cultural Park,** 250 Cultural Park Place, West Sedona, (☎ **800-780-2787** or 520-282-0747), opened at the western edge of town in the summer of 2000. This outdoor amphitheater in an 80-foot-deep natural bowl has become a summer retreat for several of the state's performing arts organizations, including the Phoenix Symphony. It also hosts annual local festivals such as the Sedona Chamber Music Festival (late May) and Jazz on the Rocks (fourth Saturday of September). The park is also a venue for folk, jazz, country, and pop concerts (but don't expect any gangsta rap or heavy metal). Check the listings in the free *Red Rock Review,* available at your hotel or at the Chamber of Commerce office, to find out what's on the schedule during your visit.

Quick Concierge: Sedona and the Verde Valley

Area Code: The area code in Sedona and the Verde Valley is **520.**

Emergency: For police, ambulance, or fire emergencies, call ☎**911.** In Sedona, the nonemergency number for the police is ☎ 520-282-3100.

Hospitals/Clinics: The Sedona Medical Center, 3700 W. Highway 89A, West Sedona (☎ 520-204-3000) has 24-hour emergency service. Sedona Urgent Care, 2530 W. Highway 89A, West Sedona (☎ 520-203-4813) is open for drop-ins Mon–Fri 8 a.m.–8 p.m., Sat–Sun 10 a.m.–6 p.m.

Information: Sedona-Oak Creek Chamber of Commerce, 331 Forest Rd. at Highway 89A, Uptown Sedona (☎ 800-288-7336 or 520-282-7722; Internet: www.sedonachamber.com), is open Mon–Sat 9 a.m.–5 p.m., Sun 9 a.m.– 3 p.m. The far less frenetic Cottonwood Chamber of Commerce, 1010 S.

Main St, junction of Hwys. 89A and 260 (☎ 520- 634-7593; Internet: www.chamber.verdevalley.com) is open 9 a.m.–5 p.m. daily. Jerome Chamber of Commerce (☎ 520-634-2900 for recorded information; Internet: www.jeromechamber.com).

On-line Access: Sedona doesn't have any cyber cafés, but there's a local access number for both Earthlink and AOL.

Pharmacies: Walgreens, 1995 Highway 89A, West Sedona (☎ 520-282-3903) is open Mon–Fri 8 a.m.–10 p.m., Sat 8 a.m.–6 p.m., and Sun 9 a.m.–6 p.m.

Post Office: Sedona's main post office is at 190 West Highway 89A, Uptown Sedona (☎ 520-282-3511).

Weather: Call ☎ 520-774-3301 or log on to www.sedonabest.com for 24-hour weather and road conditions.

Prescott

Lots of resident college students and retirees, plus waves of heat-escaping Phoenicians, have given Prescott an orientation toward pleasure (not to mention an iffy mix of drivers). It's the hub of north-central Arizona and much more of a real-people place than Sedona. However, with its oak-shaded central square, Victorian houses, and temperate climate, Prescott feels almost Midwestern; if you're looking for a Southwest stereotype, you won't find it here. That said, the rugged rocks of the nearby Granite Dells could come straight out of a John Ford film, and there are plenty of places to saddle up. If you like the outdoors, antiques, and history, you could easily spend a few days relaxing here. Prescott is also a relatively inexpensive base for exploring the Verde Valley; a day trip to the Grand Canyon from here is doable, too.

Getting There

If you drive in from Phoenix, take I-17 north to Highway 69 west (at exit 262, Cordes Junction); it's a quick 96 miles. From Sedona, take Highway 89A southwest (it'll merge with Highway 89 5 miles north of town); this 60-mile route has some very curvy stretches. An alternative would be to take Highway 179 south from Sedona to I-17 south, then head west on Highway 169 and 69 — less scenic, and you miss Jerome, but you may save your nails and cuticles by going this way.

The **Prescott Airport Shuttle** (☎ 800-445-7978 or 520-445-5470) makes nine daily runs from Phoenix's Sky Harbor Airport and the Phoenix Greyhound station to the Prescott Greyhound station; the cost is $21 each way or $32 round-trip. **America West** (☎ 800-235-9292) flies to Prescott three times a day from Sky Harbor. Prescott isn't likely to be your sole Arizona destination, however, so renting a car in Phoenix may make more sense than these two options.

As you may have figured from the stops that the shuttle from Sky Harbor makes, **Greyhound,** 820 E. Sheldon (☎ 800-231-2222 or 520-774-4573), has a presence in Prescott.

Getting Around

Prescott has a public bus system, but it's not something you really want to bother with as a tourist. Much of the town is strollable, and you need wheels for the rest. Budget, Enterprise, and Hertz all have offices in town; see the appendix for the 800 numbers.

When they enter town, Hwys. 69 and 89 merge into Gurley Street, Prescott's main thoroughfare. Gurley meets Montezuma and Cortez in the town's center; add Goodwin Street, which runs parallel to Gurley, and you've got **Courthouse Plaza.** Almost all the action in Prescott takes place on or near this large, eminently strollable town square.

High and Hilly (Gasp!)

Not only does Prescott sit at 5,347 feet, but the town is also subtly hilly. Don't worry if you find yourself breathing heavily on your return to your hotel, when heading out seemed like a breeze — you may have just hit an upslope. But do take it easy if you arrive direct from sea level, especially if you have respiratory problems.

Where to Stay

If you like your rooms with a bit of history, you'll be in heaven here, whether you want to cozy up with a painted lady, stay in Arizona's first car-friendly hotel, or get pleasantly spooked by a resident ghost. And you won't pay an arm and a leg for the privilege, either. Couldn't give a hoot about haunts or the past? Prescott's got plenty of up-to-date lodgings, including one with a casino.

Highway 69 and, as you get closer to town, its Gurley Street continuation are lined with modest motels, several with classic 1950s kitsch appeal. It's a good place to cruise if you're not looking for anything special or don't feel like planning ahead. Chains represented in town include **Best Western, Comfort Inn, Days Inn, Holiday Inn Express, Ramada Resort,** and **Super 8** (see the appendix for the toll-free numbers). See Chapter 4 for a key to the dollar sign ratings used in the following listings.

Hassayampa Inn

$$ **Prescott**

Hassayampa is Prescott's premier historic hotel — it has a great Western art deco lobby and introduced porte cocheres to the state in 1929. It's also a good deal, especially when you consider that cocktails in a lovely lounge and a generous order-from-the-menu breakfast at one of the town's best restaurants are included in the rate. (See The Peacock Room in the "Where to Dine" section.) Not all the rooms are large, and they can be a little noisy — you're near the main square and the walls are thin — but loads of character and a prime location are the tradeoffs.

122 Gurley St. (one block east of Courthouse Plaza). ☎ ***800-322-1927** or 520-778-9434. Fax: 520-445-8590. E-mail:* inn@primenet.com. *Internet:* www.hassayampainn.com. *Rack rates: Jan–Mar & Nov–Dec, $99–$109 Sun–Thur, $109–$129 weekends, holidays, and special events; Apr–Oct, $111–$121/$125–$141; suites from $155–$195 year-round. Rates include full breakfast and complimentary cocktail. AE, CB, DC, DISC, MC, V.*

Hotel St. Michael

$ Prescott

This hotel, built in 1900 on Whiskey Row, is a great base for a bar crawl, but if you need quiet to sleep off your hangover, you're not going to get it here. And the rooms are more funky than they are functional. On the plus side, you're in the heart of the shopping district — the lobby has a boutiques-filled arcade — the Caffé St. Michael is the hippest spot to sip a latte on the plaza, and you won't find lower rates in the center of town.

205 W. Gurley St. (on Courthouse Plaza). ☎ *800-678-3757 or 520-776-1999. Fax: 520-776-7318. Rack rates: Mon–Fri $42–$54, Sat–Sun $52–$68; $75/$85 suites. Rates include Continental breakfast at Caffé St. Michael. AE, DISC, MC, V.*

Hotel Vendome–Clarion Carriage House Inn

$$–$$$ Prescott

A cross between a hotel and a B&B, the Vendome has the privacy of the former (including your own bath and remote-control TV) and the character of the latter (including a ghost). A wine bar, convenience to Courthouse Plaza, and a cheerful verandah on each floor are other pluses. This pleasant, reasonably priced place was built in 1917 but extensively revamped in the mid-1990s.

230 S. Cortez St. (1½ blocks south of Courthouse Plaza). ☎ *888-468-3583 or 520-776-0900. Fax: 520-771-0395. Internet:* www.vendomehotel.com. *Rack rates: Sun–Thu $79, Sat–Sun and holidays $99–$139; suites from $99–$189. Rates include Continental breakfast. AE, DC, DISC, MC, V.*

The Marks House

$$ Prescott

Hail Brittania. Victorian B&Bs abound in this town, but with its proximity to Courthouse Plaza and its meticulous attention to period detail, this one rules. The suite in the circular turret will fulfill your every princess- (or prince-)in-the-castle fantasy. If you wouldn't dream of such imperial leanings, just revel in the spectacular Thumb Butte views.

203 E. Union St. (1 block east of Courthouse Plaza). ☎ *800-370-MARK or 520-778-4632. E-mail:* markshouse@cableone.net. *Internet:* www.virtualcities.com/ons/az. *Rack rates: $85–$95, $110–$125 suites. Rates include full, formal breakfast. DISC, MC, V.*

Prescott Resort Conference Center and Casino

$$$ Prescott

Although not historic and nowhere near Courthouse Plaza, this Prescott Resort has one unique feature: A casino. It also has more clean living-type facilities than the town's other hotels, including tennis and racquetball courts, a health club, and a spa. Rooms are fully loaded with amenities too, and because this resort sits on a hill, the vistas from the balconies are unbeatable.

Love on the Rocks — But That's a Good Thing

Some of the state's most civilized quarters meet some of its most ruggedly beautiful scenery at **Rocamadour**, 3386 N. Highway 89, 4 miles north of Prescott (☎ **888-771-1933** or 520-771-1933). Furnishings from the owners' former inn in Burgundy, France, have been transported to the Granite Dells, a region of huge, strangely eroded boulders just outside Prescott. All the individually decorated rooms feature beautiful antiques and artwork. Plush robes, fresh flowers, TV/VCR, and private entrances — and in two cases, a private deck with a spa — complete the romantic picture. $95–$195 doubles, no credit cards.

1500 Highway 69 (on the eastern edge of town). ☎ ***800-967-4637*** *or 520-776-1666. Fax: 520-776-8544. E-mail:* info@prescottresort.com. *Internet:* www.prescottresort.com. *Rack rates: Apr–Oct $139–$159, Nov–Mar $119–$139. AE, DC, DISC, MC, V.*

SpringHill Suites by Marriott

$$ **Prescott**

This all-suites property isn't especially charming, but it compensates with a location near Courthouse Plaza and great on-site amenities such as an exercise room, pool, whirlpool, and guest laundry. Fold-out couches and kitchenettes in the large, comfortable rooms make them family-friendly. Guests suffering from work (or e-mail) separation anxiety will appreciate the dual phone jacks, free local phone calls, and good desks.

200 E. Sheldon St. (about 5 blocks northeast of Courthouse Plaza). ☎ ***888-287-9400*** *or 520-776-0998. Fax: 520-776-0998. Internet:* www.springhillsuites.com. *Rack rates: Spring Sun–Thurs $79, Fri & Sat $109, summer $84/$129, fall & winter $79/$99. Rates include Continental breakfast buffet and (really good) afternoon cookies. AE, DC, MC, V.*

Where to Dine

Prescott College, Yavapai Community College, and Embry-Riddle Aeronautical University are all in this area, which means that Prescott has a nice, college-casual dining scene. But although lots of restaurants cater to student budgets and tastes, there are enough places to satisfy sophisticated professorial and postgraduate palates. Most of the top choices are on or near Courthouse Plaza. In addition to the restaurants listed here, all open for dinner, **The Plaza Cafe,** 106 W. Gurley St. (☎ **520-445-3234**), is great for a country-comfort breakfast, a healthy salad, or a hearty sandwich at lunchtime. Portions are huge — plan on a few post-prandial turns around the square. If it's chopped meat on a bun that you want, **Kendall's Famous Burgers & Ice Cream,** 113 S. Cortez (☎ **520-778-3658**), has earned its name. For a key to the dollar signs used in this section, see Chapter 4.

The Dry Gulch Steakhouse

\$\$–\$\$\$ Prescott   Steakhouse/American

This is the real, more or less ungussied-up, item — a cowboy steakhouse to remind you that you're out west. The drive here is worth it for the great steaks, chicken, or prime rib (Friday and Saturday only). Dinners — everything except the sandwiches, burgers, and salads — come with soup or salad, cowboy beans, or (mmmm) steak fries.

1630 Adams St. (between Vyne and Shoupe streets, northwest of downtown). ☎ *520-778-9693. Reservations not needed. Main courses: \$8.45–\$15.95. Open: Lunch and dinner Tues–Fri, dinner only Sat and Sun. MC, V.*

Gurley St. Grill

\$\$ Prescott   American/Italian

This place is nice for families, because it's busy and has plenty of kid-friendly stuff on the menu. It's good for singles, because of the central dining station where business-types perch for a quick lunch. And it's great for everyone who likes haute hippie cuisine — generous, reasonably priced food that's creative without being frou frou. (I especially like the grilled veggie salad with feta cheese and prickly pear vinaigrette.) Basic burgers, steaks, pizzas, salads, and sandwiches keep food conservatives happy, too.

230 W. Gurley St. (one block west of Courthouse Plaza). ☎ *520-445-3388. Reservations only for parties of 5 or more at dinner. Main courses: \$8.99–\$13.99. Open: Lunch and dinner daily; late night menu nightly 10–midnight. AE, DISC, MC, V.*

Murphy's

\$\$\$ Prescott   American/Continental

I've never found the food at this local favorite particularly exciting, but the setting — an 1890s building with lots of its original fittings — the 60-item beer list, and the extras that come with dinner help explain Murphy's continued popularity. The mesquite grill does a nice job with beef, chicken, and pork; the seafood is dependable; and the desserts often shine.

201 N. Cortez. (one block north of Courthouse Plaza). ☎ *520-445-4044. Reservations recommended for large groups. Main courses: \$12.95–\$26.95. Open: Lunch and dinner daily, Sun brunch. AE, DISC, MC, V.*

The Peacock Room

\$\$\$–\$\$\$\$ Prescott   Continental

In a slump for a while after longtime chef Linda Rose left to start her own place (see The Rose, later in this section), the Hassayampa Inn's restaurant is now definitely ascendant. Standouts include the moist but crispy crab cakes and the classic filet mignon with Bordelaise sauce. Prescott's a pretty casual town, but all the etched-glass and sparkling crystal — not to mention the sorbet palate cleanser — may make you feel like putting on the ritz here.

Hassayampa Inn, 122 Gurley St. (one block east of Courthouse Plaza). ☎ 800-322-1927 or 520-778-9434. Reservatons strongly suggested on weekends. Main courses: $15.95–$27.95. Open: Breakfast, lunch, and dinner daily. AE, CB, DC, DISC, MC, V.

Prescott Brewing Company

$–$$ Prescott   American/Pub

There may be fancier places in town, but I love kicking back here with a Prescott Pale Ale, some hot beer pretzels (the horseradish dipping sauce is killer), and a grilled salmon salad. It's pub grub raised to a higher level: Everything's made from fresh ingredients and nicely spiced, and there are lots of veggie and white-meat selections. And who could resist a place that has northern Arizona's largest single malt scotch selection *and* a kids menu with dinosaur nuggets?

130 W. Gurley St. (Bashford Shopping Center on Courthouse Plaza). ☎ 520-771-2795. Main courses: $6.50–$12.95. Open: Sun–Thu 11 a.m.–10 p.m., Fri– Sat 11 a.m.–11 p.m. AE, DC, DISC, MC, V.

The Rose

$$$ Prescott   Continental

The main fine-dining competitor of The Peacock Room (see listing earlier in this section), The Rose has a similarly gourmet menu and a similarly well-selected wine list. The chicken limone, veal marsala, and anything with seafood are stars. Prices are lower than The Peacock Room, but the tradeoff is privacy and comfort: The placement of the tables in the small dining rooms verges on personal space invasion. If it's nice out, go for the covered porch or front patio (great for people watching, too).

234 S. Cortez St. (one block south of Courthouse Plaza). ☎ 520-777-8308. Reservations strongly recommended. Main courses. $13.95–$26.95. Open: Dinner Wed–Sun. AE, DISC, MC, V.

Zuma's Woodfire Café

$$ Prescott   Southwest/New American

It's hard to say which are the bigger crowd pleasers — the designer pizzas, pastas, and grilled dishes or the two outdoor patios with blazing fire pits. The tapanade (chopped olive spread) that comes with all the main courses — coconut fried shrimp, say, or Southwest lasagna made with green chiles — is easy to load up on, but try to save room for a dessert of wood-fired S'mores. (Where else are you going to find that?) Live music and a huge selection of beer and tequila add to the always-festive atmosphere.

124 N. Montezuma (½ block north of Courthhouse Plaza). ☎ 520-541-1400. Reservations recommended on weekends for four or more, on weekdays for six or more. Main courses: Individual pizzas $6.95–$7.95, dinners $8.50– $17.95. Open: Daily lunch and dinner, Sun brunch. AE, DISC, MC, V.

Exploring Prescott

You're likely to spend much of your time in Prescott on Courthouse Plaza, the downtown square bounded by Goodwin and Gurley Street to the north and Montezuma and Cortez to the east and west, respectively. Two of the town's most popular activities, shopping and bar hopping (see "Shopping" and "Nightlife in Prescott," later in this chapter), dovetail on Montezuma Street, the town's historic Whiskey Row.

While you're here, you can also:

✔ **Step back in time:** If you want to explore the city's many beautifully restored Queen Anne–style houses (some 525 buildings are listed on the National Register of Historic Places), take Goodwin Street east of Courthouse Plaza to Mount Vernon Street and stroll north. The three blocks between Goodwin and Sheldon streets brim with turrets, shingles, and gingerbread trim. For some more rough-hewn historic sites, see the hiking suggestions in "Keeping Active" later in this section.

✔ **Go one-stop history shopping:** I've spent hours poking around the **Sharlot Hall Museum,** 415 W. Gurley St., two blocks west of Courthouse Plaza (☎ 520-445-3122), a complex of buildings and gardens named for protofeminist, poet, and historian Sharlot Hall. Its centerpiece is the rustic pine cabin that served as the first territorial governor's mansion, but 15 other stations lead you through Prescott's past. Displays include everything from a mummified mouse, found during the mansion's excavation, to a small Wells Fargo stagecoach that squeezed some 31 people in with its bundles of mail. Open: Apr–Oct Mon–Sat 10 a.m.–5 p.m., Sun 1–5 p.m.; Nov–Mar Mon–Sat 10 a.m.–4 p.m., Sun 1–5 p.m. Free; suggested donation $5 per family.

✔ **Find out about the region's Native American past:** The striking **Smoki Museum,** 147 N. Arizona St., about ¾ mile east of Courthouse Plaza via Gurley Street (☎ 520-445-1230), was built in 1935 in the shape of a pueblo and houses a high-quality collection of Native American artifacts. Open: Apr 17–Sept Mon–Sat 10 a.m.–4 p.m., Sun. 1–4 p.m.; and Oct Fri–Sat 10 a.m.–4 p.m., Sun 1–4 p.m. Open by appointment only the rest of the year. Admission: $4 adults, 12 and under free.

✔ **Get artsy:** Perched on a hill near the Granite Dells, the small **Phippen Museum,** 4701 Highway 89, about 7 miles north of downtown (☎ 520-778-1385), isn't only for Western art fans. The work (including that of George Phippen, a member of the Cowboy Artists of America) does tend toward the traditional and representational, but you never know what you'll see here. During my last visit, a painting by Native American abstractionist Fritz Scholder was on display. There's a good gift shop, too. Open: Mon, Wed–Sat 10 a.m.–4 p.m., Sun 1–4 p.m. (closed Tues). Admission: $3 adults, $2 seniors, ages 11 and under free.

Guided Tours

Melissa Ruffner takes her **Prescott Historical Tours** (☎ 520-445-4567) very personally — she's descended from some of the town's pioneers. Ruffner's excursions through the town's past, done in Territorial-era costume, cost $7 per person if a minimum of 10 people sign on. Two people can book a $40 tour package that includes an autographed copy of Ruffner's *Prescott: A Pictorial History.*

Keeping Active

Want to spend your time here out of doors? Prescott offers you a few ways to keep active while doing so. These include:

✔ **Golfing:** Prescott always ranks high in the surveys of America's best retirement towns, which may explain why it's getting to be a golfer's destination.

The city-owned **Antelope Hills,** 1 Perkins Dr., 7 miles east of downtown near where Hwys. 69 and 89 split (☎ **520-776-7888** or 800-972-6818 in AZ), has panoramic views of the Granite Dells and the Mogollon Rim on its two 18-hole courses. One course is a Gary Panks creation. Green fees are $36; add $12 for cart rental.

A dramatic Bradshaw Mountain backdrop and a major revamp in 1999 make the 18-hole **Prescott Golf & Country Club,** 1030 Prescott Country Club Blvd., 13 miles southeast of Prescott off Highway 69 (☎ **520-772-8984**), a duffer's dream. Green fees for nonmembers range from $24 (after noon, from Nov–Apr) to $48 (before 1 p.m. Fri–Sun, May–Oct); a cart runs another $14 year-round.

The semi-private **Prescott Lakes Community Golf Course,** 315 E. Smoke Tree Lane, 3 miles north of downtown (☎ **520-717-2300**), opened in June 2000. The course boasts brand new greens and state-of-the-art clubhouse facilities — not to mention 15 acres of lakes. It costs $40 (with cart) to tee off at this Hale Irwin–designed course in winter, $80 in summer.

Tom Weiskopf laid out a course among the pines, mountain streams, and rocky outcroppings near Thumb Butte for the posh **Hassayampa Country Club,** 2060 Golf Club Lane, less than a mile west of downtown (☎ **520-445-0009**). The course is private, but if you want to experience these 18 holes, you can rent one of the three beautifully furnished golf lodges and get full course membership privileges. Rates start at $150 a night for a one-bedroom suite.

Come summer, lots of hotels run "Stay and Play" packages, which may throw in a golf game for two at Antelope Hills or Prescott Golf and Country Club with the price of a room.

✔ **Hiking:** Some 450 miles of trails, covering a wide range of landscapes, crisscross Prescott National Forest. The hike up to **Thumb Butte,** Prescott's best-known landmark, is fairly steep, but you are rewarded with spectacular vistas of the entire region, including (on clear days) the San Francisco Peaks. It's much easier to reach two historic sites in the piney **Lynx Lake area:** the Lynx Creek Indian ruins, where you can wander among the remains of a prehistoric Indian pueblo; and Charcoal Kiln, a large brick dome used to create charcoal from wood in the 1800s. The dramatic boulders of the **Granite Dells** near Watson Lake Park attract rock climbers as well as hikers.

The **Bradshaw Ranger District** of the **Prescott National Forest,** 2230 E. Highway 69, east of downtown (☎ 520-445-7253), is the best place to get information on these and other trails. It's only open Monday through Friday from 8 a.m. to 4:30 p.m., so if you want to hike on the weekend, plan ahead. You can also stop into the Chamber of Commerce (see "Quick Concierge: Prescott," in this chapter) for information on the less complicated hikes.

✔ **Horseback riding:** The daily guided rides given by **Granite Mountain Stables,** 2400 W. Shane Dr., some 7 miles northeast of Prescott (☎ 520-771-9551), start at $35 an hour. Rates go down the longer you stay on your horse, and there are overnight pack trips, too. Along with its regular trail rides (which cost $25 an hour or $35 for 2 hours), **Rafter 6 Outdoor Adventures,** Chino Valley, 30 miles north of Prescott (☎ 520-636-5007), also offers chuck-wagon dinner trots. For $65 per person (with a minimum of four people), you can follow two hours of saddle time with victuals like cobbler and biscuits cooked in a Dutch oven.

Shopping

Prescott's many antiques shops sell everything from top-notch (but not notched) Victorian cabinets to cowboy kitsch pitchers, and at pretty good prices. That's one reason why Phoenicians like to weekend here. Of course, if you fly into Arizona, the shipping costs on large pieces may wipe out any savings, but who knows? You may find something portable — or worth the shipping expense. Antique shops are scattered around town, but the best pickings are on Cortez Street, just north of Courthouse Plaza between Gurley and Sheldon. Ask at the Chamber of Commerce (see "Quick Concierge: Prescott" in this chapter) for the "Antique Shops Guide" pamphlet.

Crafts and Western tchotchke shops line Courthouse Plaza, particularly Montezuma and Gurley streets. You can concentrate your retail search in two good arcades, **Bashford Courts,** 130 W. Gurley St. (☎ 520- 445-9798), and **St. Michael's Plaza,** 205 W. Gurley St. (☎ 520-776- 1999). My favorite boutique, though, is slightly off the square, tucked among all the antiques shops on Cortez Street: **Ogg's Hogan** and **Maggie Manygoats,** which share a space and phone number — 111 N. Cortez, ☎ 520-443-9856 — are a two-fer treat. Ogg's concentrates on exquisite Native American crafts and Old West collectibles, while Maggie carries creative Western-style clothing (including high-quality vintage) and fun home furnishings.

Nightlife

Not as exciting as it once was in the early 1900s, when some 20 saloons and brothels lined Whiskey Row (Montezuma St.), Prescott's nightlife still thrives, thanks in part to Prescott's many higher drinking (er, learning) institutions.

They Had Their Priorities Straight (If Not Sober)

Talk about fiddling while Rome burned. On July 14, 1900, when a fire engulfed Whiskey Row, its resident souses roused themselves to haul the 24-foot-long, 12-foot-high mahogany bar from the Palace Bar across the road to the relative safety of Courthouse Plaza. They then continued to drink while watching the rest of the block go up in flames.

✔ The ornate mahogany bar at **The Palace,** 120 S. Montezuma St. (☎ 520-541-1996), is a huge tourist magnet — see the "They Had Their Priorities Straight (If Not Sober)" sidebar.

✔ **Matt's Saloon,** 112 S. Montezuma St. (☎ 520-778-9914), is a genuine cowboy bar, with lots of two-steppin' to live country and western sounds.

✔ Next door at the **Birdcage,** 148 S. Montezuma (☎ 520-778-9921), the music is rock-ier and the crowd more collegiate.

✔ A block north of Courthouse Plaza, **Lyzzard's Lounge,** 120 N. Cortez St. (☎ 520-778-2244), books good alternative bands. Drop by to see the bar, manufactured in the 1880s in Chicago, shipped down the Mississippi and around Cape Horn to San Francisco, and transported to Prescott by covered wagon. Now that's a long, thirsty journey!

One of Prescott's most popular nightspots, **Bucky's Casino** in the Prescott Resort and Conference Center (see "Where to Stay" earlier in this chapter), is far from Whiskey Row. But who needs history when you've got lots o' slots?

Highbrow highlights include performances by the **Prescott Jazz Society** (☎ 520-445-0000). Find out what's happening at all kinds of venues in town from *The Daily Courier* (Internet: www.prescottaz. com/pdc/courier.htm) on Thursday and Friday.

Quick Concierge: Prescott

Area Code: Prescott's area code is **520**.

Emergency: For police, ambulance, or fire emergencies, call ☎ **911;** the nonemergency police number is ☎ 520-778-1444.

Hospitals/Clinic: Prescott's hospital is Yavapai Regional Medical Center, 1003 Willow Creek Rd. ☎ 520-445-2700.

Information: Prescott Chamber of Commerce, 117 W. Goodwin St. (☎ 800-266-7534 or 520-445-2000; Internet: www.prescott.org),

is open Mon–Fri 9 a.m.–5 p.m., weekends 10 a.m.–2 p.m.

Online Access: Prescott has a local access number to both AOL and Earthlink.

Pharmacies: Walgreens, 178 E. Sheldon St. (☎ 520-776- 1936), is open Mon–Fri 8 a.m.–9 p.m., Sat 9 a.m.–6 p.m., and Sun 10 a.m.–6 p.m.

Post Office: The post office is located at 101 W. Goodwin Street (☎ 520-778-7411).

Wickenburg

Located on the northwestern edge of the Sonoran Desert, Wickenburg resembles Phoenix and Tucson more than higher elevation towns such as Prescott and Sedona. Like Tucson, it sits at approximately 2,000 feet. When you visit this sleepy town, you get a glimpse of what Arizona's two largest cities may have been like a century ago — give or take a few cars and a Spanish fortress or two.

Wickenburg, incorporated in 1863, is the oldest town north of Tucson and the fifth oldest in the state. It was named for Henry Wickenburg, a Prussian prospector who discovered gold in them thar hills. The town began mining a widespread interest in warm winters and the Old West during the 1920s and 1930s, when it became known as "The Dude Ranch Capital of the World." Most of the dude ranches have been shuttered, and the "dudes" are now called "guests," but the ranches that remain are still the town's main draw. So, although it doesn't take more than a day to explore little Wickenburg, the average visitor stays around for about five days, determined to relax.

Getting There

Wickenburg is 53 miles northwest of Phoenix via Highway 60, a straight but wonderfully scenic route, lush with thick stands of saguaro cactus and other high-desert vegetation. The town is 61 miles south of Prescott via Highway 89 which connects to Highway 93 just outside of town — a more dramatic but also more harrowing drive through the mountains.

Wee Drive Shuttle (☎ 800-842-2070) goes from the Phoenix airport to town in about 1½ hours; the cost is $50 per person each way from 6 a.m.–6 p.m., and the cost increases in the evening. But unless you plan to hunker down and never leave your dude ranch of choice, rent a car in Phoenix; there's only one car rental company in Wickenburg, **Jones Ford** (☎ 520-684-5481), so the rates aren't likely to be very competitive.

Getting Around

Walking around Wickenburg's compact historical downtown is one of the highlights of any visit, but you need wheels to get there and anywhere else you want to tour. When Highway 60 enters town, it's called Wickenburg Way. When Highway 93 comes through, it becomes Tegner St. These two main thoroughfares cross in the old historic downtown district; the stoplight where they meet is often used as a directional reference. (The town has a few more stoplights, but when people tell you that something is "two blocks east of the stoplight," this is the one they mean.)

Du-du-dudeo

From December through April, the four guest ranches take turns hosting monthly "Dudeos." These friendly inter-ranch duke outs do not have bull-riding, calf-roping, or other dangerous activities — just a lot of good clean (okay, good dusty) fun. Mostly kids take part in events like the horseback relay races, but if enough qualified older riders are interested, the grown ups get to play, too.

Where to Stay

Most people come to Wickenburg to relax at one of the town's four remaining guest ranches. They all have different personalities — and accordingly different rates. All include meals but not booze in their room rates, and only the Wickenburg Inn and the Kay El Bar include riding; the other two offer equine time a la carte or as part of a package. All four are great for family vacations, though only the Wickenburg Inn and Rancho de los Caballeros have special activities and programs for kids. And though they all, by definition, have loads of Southwest character, the Kay El Bar really shines in that department.

The town has plenty of other places to bunk. Low-key motels, including a Super 8 (see the appendix for the chain's toll-free number), line the main drags, Tegner Street and Wickenburg Way. See the description of Robson's Mining World in "Exploring Wickenburg" in this chapter; it's an offbeat (and definitely off the beaten path) place to stay.

Remember, come summer, it can get mighty toasty in town. Of all the guest ranches listed, only Merv Griffin's Wickenburg Inn is open year-round.

Guest Ranches

Flying E
$$$$ **Wickenburg**

Families and friends come back year after year to the Flying E, the only working cattle ranch of the lot (though guests can't get involved with any of the round-up related activities, which take place in summer while the ranch is closed). The views of the Bradshaw mountains from the ranch's Yarnell Hill perch are spectacular, and the place has a nice down-home feeling. However, it isn't as luxurious as Rancho de Los Caballeros or the Wickenberg Inn, and it doesn't have as much character as the Kay El Bar. Still, rooms are comfortably rustic, and fun stuff abounds, including a guest "branding" with traffic line paint at every cookout.

2801 W. Wickenburg Way (4 miles west of town, via Highway 60). ☎ **888-864-2650** *or 520-684-2690. Fax: 520-684-5304. E-mail:* Flyinge@primenet.com. *Internet:*

www.flyingeranch.com. *Rack rates: Jan–Apr $220–$240 double occupancy, 3-night minimum; Nov–Dec 2-night minimum; 4-night minimum all holidays. Rates include all meals for two people. No credit cards. Closed May 2–Oct. 31.*

Kay El Bar Ranch

$$$$ Wickenburg

Ceiling planks taken from a gold mine, antique Monterey furniture, a hot tub made of old adobe brick . . . talk about soaking in Old West history! If you want to experience what dude ranching must have been like in its hey(hay?)day, this 12-room ranch, opened to guests in 1926 and listed on the National Register for Historic Places, is for you. It's also the place for serious riders. All riders are evaluated and matched with an appropriate horse and trail pardners so you're never going to go faster or slower than you'd like. The gorgeous grounds have lots of old-growth tamarisk and eucalyptus along with lush stands of saguaro.

Rincon Road (take Highway 93 2 miles past the junction with Highway 60, turn right onto Rincon Rd. and drive 1½ miles). ☎ ***800-684-7583** or 520-684-7593. Fax: 520-684-4497. E-mail:* kayelbar@w3az.net. *Internet:* www.kayelbar.com. *Rack rates: Year-round $275–$300 double occupancy, $1,000 weekly rate. 10% discount on rack rates Dec 1–17 and Jan 15–31. Rates include all meals and horseback riding; children must be at least 7 to ride. Two-day mimimum stay Oct 12–Feb 14; four-day minimum stay all holidays and Feb 15–May 1. Closed May 2–Oct 11. MC, V.*

Merv Griffin's Wickenburg Inn and Dude Ranch

$$$$ Wickenburg

This large guest ranch strikes a nice balance. Rooms combine creature comforts and character, and the (relatively) remote location is compensated for by loads of on-site facilities. Because you have to drive two miles on a graded dirt road to get to this 4,700-acre compound, you feel like you're away from it all — all, that is, except a huge swimming pool, rodeo grounds, a nature center, an arts and crafts room, and an excellent restaurant. Kids choose from activities such as gold panning, roping lessons, and barrel racing.

34801 N. Highway 89 (8 miles north of Wickenberg, off Highway 89). ☎ ***800-942-5362** or 520-684-4225. Fax: 520-684-2981. E-mail:* wickinn@primenet.com. *Internet:* www.merv.com. *Rack rates: Feb–May and holidays $325–$430 double occupancy rooms and studio casitas; June–mid-Sept $215–$255; late-Sept–Jan $275–$325; one- and two-bedroom casitas available. Rates include all meals and horseback riding (except all-day rides and private lessons) for two people. 16% gratuity added to all bills. AE, DC, DISC, MC,V.*

Rancho de Los Caballeros

$$$$ Wickenburg

Los Cab, as it's known locally, is the poshest of the horse resorts: Lots of spiffy new suites and an excellent golf course cater to corporate retreaters. But the original dining room and lobby ooze Old West charm, as do the rooms in the original ranch house, which even cost a bit less (they'd be my first pick). The ranch has been in the same family since 1948, so the owners have a continued personal stake in making guests feel welcome and well cared for. A free kids program for ages 5–12 keeps the young'uns happily playing together from 8 a.m. to 1:30 p.m. and from 6 to 9 p.m.

1551 S. Vulture Mine Rd. (off Highway 60 on the west side of town, 1½ miles from the Vulture Mine turnoff). ☎ *800-684-5030 or 520-684-5484. Fax: 520-684-2267. E-mail:* home@SunC.com. *Internet:* www.SunC.com. *rack Rates: Oct–Jan, May $289–$339 double occupancy, $399 suites; Feb–Apr $339–$399/$499. Rates include all meals for two people; ask about lower weekday rates. 15% gratuity added to all bills. No credit cards. Closed June–Sept.*

The Runner-Up Hotels

The Best Western Rancho Grande

$–$$ Wickenburg   The same family that helped create the original Best Western hotel association in 1946 still operates this old hacienda-style lodging. Features include in-room refrigerators, coffee makers, and microwaves, and a spa adjoining one of the town's first heated pools. *293 E. Wickenburg Way.* ☎ *800-854-7235 or 520-684-5445. Fax: 520-684-7380. Internet:* www.bwranchogrande.com.

The Rincon Ranch Lodge

$$ Wickenburg   This former guest ranch now rents out five one- and two-bedroom cabins. The grounds are beautiful, a full breakfast is included in the room rate, and you can book a horseback ride on the premises (see "Exploring Wickenburg" in this chapter). Closed summer. *Rincon Rd. (just beyond the turnoff to the Kay El Bar — see previous section).* ☎ *888-684-2338 or 520-684-2328.*

Where to Dine

Most people who come to Wickenburg don't do much dining out, because many guest ranch rates include meals, but several good independent restaurants cater to day-trippers or to dudes who want to branch out from the ranch. And two of the ranches open their doors to nonguests: You can book a meal at the Rancho de Los Caballeros dining room (the all-you-can-eat lunch buffets are justly renowned) or at Griff's at the Wickenberg Inn, where the à la carte menu matches those of many big city fine dining rooms. I also have lots of good reports about a German restaurant, **House Berlin,** 169 E. Wickenburg Way (☎ 520-684-5044), but I just never find myself feeling sufficiently schnitzel-y to try it when I'm in town.

When I talk about making reservations during "high season" in the following listings, I mean February through April, the busiest tourist months. For a key to the dollar signs used in this section, see Chapter 4.

Homestead Restaurant
$$ Wickenburg   American

Owned by the same family as the Best Western across the road (see the previous section), this sprawling restaurant with a Victorian gay-90s theme is great for American comfort food. You can get everything from liver and onions or chicken fried steak with country gravy to Yankee pot roast, all served with lots of sides. Choose from lighter fish selections — if you must — but those big shrimp really taste great when fried.

222 E. Wickenburg Way (in the historic downtown district). ☎ *520-684-0648. Dinner reservations recommended in high season. Main courses: $4.25–$9.95 breakfast, $4.25–$7.95 lunch, $9.95–$18.95 dinner. Open: Daily breakfast, lunch, and dinner. AE, CB, DC, DISC, MC, V.*

Santa Fe Grill
$$ Wickenburg   American/Southwest

Bernaise and bar-b-que sauce share space on Santa Fe Grill's menu, but the French influence is slight — except when it comes to things such as fresh ingredients and attractive presentations. Creatively prepared steaks, chicken, and prime rib dishes dominate the short bill of fare. The two small dining rooms are Southwest attractive, but try for a seat on the pretty back patio, weather permitting.

681 West Wickenburg Way (½ mile west of the stoplight at the Highway 89/93 junction). ☎ *520-684-3113. Dinner reservations recommended. Main courses: $10.95–$18.95. Open: Mon–Sat lunch and dinner. AE, MC, V.*

Rancho Bar 7
$$ Wickenburg   American/Mexican

At lunchtime, come to this dimly lit local favorite, which hasn't changed much since it opened in 1937, if you want a great steak sandwich or a cheese-smothered Mexican combination plate. You can even get a soda served in a glass cowboy boot. For dinner, you can't go wrong with the prime rib, roast pork, fried chicken, or any of the nightly specials. The crispy onion rings are great any time of day; there's also a homemade soup and salad bar.

111 E. Wickenburg Way. ☎ *520-684-5484. Dinner reservations suggested in high season. Main courses: $8.95–$15.95; great lunch and dinner specials. No credit cards. Open: Lunch and dinner nightly; closed Sun in summer.*

Exploring Wickenburg

Wickenburg's small historic district is more or less bounded by Tegner Street on the north, Frontier Street on the south, Yavapai Street on the east, and Highway 60/Wickenburg Way on the west. It looks like a set for a Western flick (especially Frontier Street), but it's the genuine item, with several buildings dating back to the 1890s. Stop in at the Old Santa Fe depot on Frontier Street, now home to the Chamber of Commerce (see "Quick Concierge: Wickenburg"), for a self-guided walking tour map.

Other things to see and do in the area include:

✔ **Get some Western culture: The Desert Caballeros Western Museum,** 21 N. Frontier St. (☎ **520-684-2272**), has it all — Remingtons, Russells, antique cowboy gear (the terrific "Spirit of the Cowboy" collection will be on display through 2002), Native American pottery, glowing minerals, and period rooms that re-create several of the town's businesses down to the last dry goods details. The special exhibits, covering topics from the town's dude ranch history to bola ties (see Chapter 19), are always top-rate, too. The museum is small enough to hold kids' interest, and they can sit on Rusty, the plaster horse, and try on cowpoke stuff. There's also a good gift shop. Open: Mon–Sat 10 a.m.–5 p.m., Sun noon–4 p.m. Admission: $5 adults, $4 seniors, $1 ages 6–16, 5 and under free.

✔ **Mine Wickenburg's mining past:** Although a bit contrived, all the artifacts gathered in **Robson's Mining World,** 27 miles northwest of Wickenburg (take Highway 93 to Highway 81 and follow the signs, ☎ **520-685-2609**), are real. This re-creation of an old Arizona mining town, replete with chapel, saloon, ice cream parlor, and trusty burros, is well done. Open: Mon–Fri 10 a.m.–4 p.m., Sat and Sun 10 a.m.–6 p.m.. Admission: $5 adults, $4.50 seniors over 55, children under 10 free; gold panning $8 per person with instruction. A B&B ($$) done in the style of a timbered frontier hotel is on the premises. Rooms aren't fancy, but they're attractively decorated in Southwest style.

For a look at the ununduded up item, drive out to the ruins of the historic **Vulture Mine,** the most profitable gold and silver mine in Arizona in its day. Stop at the Chamber of Commerce (see "Quick Concierge: Wickenburg") for a map to the site.

✔ **Go natural:** The Nature Conservancy runs the **Hassayampa River Preserve,** 49614 Highway 60, 3 miles southeast of town near mile marker 114 (☎ **520-684-2772**), which is one of the few places where the Hassayampa River puts in an above-ground appearance. The water attracts some 230 species of birds, as well as salamanders, lizards, and other local wildlife. A desert garden outside the visitor's center, which is a converted 1860s ranch, identifies the more typical local plants, and you often see hummingbirds flitting around the feeders. Open: Sept 16–May 14 Wed–Sun 8 a.m.–5 p.m., summer 6 a.m.–noon. $5 suggested donation for those who aren't Nature Conservancy members.

Guided Tours

The four trips run by **Wickenburg Jeep Tours** (☎ **800-596-JEEP** or 520-684-0438) do justice to the area's rough but beautiful desert terrain and rich history. The off-road adventures range from a two-hour nature excursion along the Hassayampa River ($50 per person, $25 ages 12 and under) to a four-hour jaunt around the region's old mines ($70 per person, $35 ages 12 and under).

A Leafy Jail and a Tall Tale

Two of Wickenburg's strangest, most colorful attractions are quick takes. Stop by Tegner and Wickenburg Way, right next to the Circle K, to see the 200-year-old mesquite called the **Jail Tree**. From 1863–1890, outlaws were chained to it instead of being locked up. In the late 1800s, Wickenburg residents used to exaggerate the town's wealth to the point that the word "Hassayamper" was coined to describe people who had a tendency to play fast and loose with the facts. From there came the legend that anyone who drank from the waters of the Hassayampa River would never utter a word of truth again. A plaque next to the **Old Wishing Well**, on the north side of the Highway 60/93 bridge across the Hassayampa River (just past Apache Street if you come from downtown), tells the tale — all true — in verse.

Keeping Active

Just because you're not duding doesn't mean you can't saddle up. Horseback rides with **Rincon Ranch Lodge** (☎ **888-684-2338**) cost $45 for two hours, $75 for a half day with lunch, and $100 for a full day with lunch. Feeling stubborn? Consider finding a kindred spirit at **Big Corral**, 520 N. Tegner (☎ **520-684-2317**), which offers a variety of mule rides. These large creatures (a cross between a female horse and a male donkey) are better on hillsides than horses, so you can go on narrow canyon trails and into mining areas where your ride's ancestors may have worked grinding ore. (Guess they didn't have mule labor laws in those days.) The cost is $35 for a three-hour ride and $60 for a five-hour excursion including lunch.

Shopping

The historic downtown area can keep you happily browsing for several hours. **Ben's Saddlery & Shoe Repair**, 174 N. Tegner (☎ **520-684- 2863**), deals in tack (in the horse sense of the term); come here to watch saddles being made or to buy a Western belt or boots. Give **Salsa**, 124 N. Tegner (☎ **520-684-7262**), your measurements and they'll create a Western outfit for you during your stay; compliment-drawing accessories might include a necklace made of blue corn. It would be worth visiting **The Gold Nugget Gallery**, 274 E. Wickenburg Way (☎ **520-684-5849**), for its historic 1863 adobe building alone, but the excellent selection of paintings, pottery, jewelry, and furniture — everything from traditional Western landscapes to contemporary glass mouse pads — is what you're really here for.

Two stores worth a short drive are **Double D,** 955 W. Wickenburg Way (☎ **520-684-7987**), with a huge selection of both men's and women's Western wear, and **Renderings**, 30220 Highway 60 (☎ **520-684-0112**), which features antique and contemporary Western and Mexican furniture and collectibles.

Nightlife

Not much happens in Wickenburg after dark — besides the sky filling up with stars. However, a couple of watering holes will take you back to the Old West. **The Rancher Bar,** 910 W. Wickenburg Way (☎ **520-684- 5957**), owned by former rodeo cowboy Stubb Hill, brings in live Country and Western bands on the weekends. **Rancho Bar 7** has — count 'em — two historic bars where you can kick back with a longneck.

Quick Concierge: Wickenburg

Area Code: Wickenburg's area code is **520.**

Emergency: For police, ambulance, or fire emergencies, call ☎ **911.**

Hospitals/Clinics: Wickenburg Regional Medical Center, 520 Rose Lane, ☎ 520-684-5421.

Information: Wickenburg Chamber of Commerce, 216 N. Frontier St. (☎ 800-942-5242, 520-684-5479, or 520-684-0977; Internet: www. wickenburgchamber.com), is open Mon–Fri 9 a.m.–5 p.m., Sat 9 a.m.–4 p.m.,

Sun noon–4 p.m., with shorter hours on the weekends during the summer; call ahead to check.

Pharmacies: Osco Drug, 2033 W. Wickenburg Way (☎ 520-684-7841), is open Mon–Fri 8 a.m.–8 p.m., Sat 8 a.m.–7 p.m., Sun 9 a.m.–5 p.m.

Post Office: The main post office is located at 2029 W. Wickenburg Way (☎ 520-684-2138), but there's also a small mail depot in the historic district at 190 N. Tegner St. (☎ 520-684-0729).

Chapter 17

The Grand Canyon and Northwest Arizona

*P*robably more purple prose has been devoted to the Grand Canyon than to any of the country's other natural attractions. It's a fact: Gazing (or better yet, walking) into the famous abyss is an unforgettable experience. But you're not the only one who wants to enjoy the canyon, which means you need to plan your visit. I can't come over to do your packing, but I can help with just about everything else. And — more good news — the rest of northwest Arizona doesn't just exist to deliver tourists into the vast maws of the canyon god. This part of the state has plenty of other interesting (and less crowded) things to do, especially in and around Flagstaff, northern Arizona's largest town.

The length of your stay in this area is going to depend on the part of the canyon you visit and what you want to do. If, like most visitors, you just straddle the edge of the South Rim, a full day at the national park should be enough. If, however, you dip in — say, by hiking, river rafting, or mule riding (and I definitely recommend that you do) — plan on at least two days; add another two to do the rest of the region justice. The more remote North Rim, a destination rather than a drop in, requires more of a time commitment, no matter what you do when you get there; you need to allot at least a day of traveling each way.

Where you bunk also depends on your touring style. If you want to be Johnny or Jane on the spot, by all means spend a night or two in the national park or as close to it as possible (that's more of a given if you're going to the North Rim). Me, I like staying in Flagstaff when I visit the South Rim; the drive to the canyon is easy and the town has many more places to stay, eat, and play after dark. Flagstaff makes a great base for travel to other places, including central Arizona (see Chapter 16) and northeastern Arizona (see Chapter 18).

The Grand Canyon & Northern Arizona

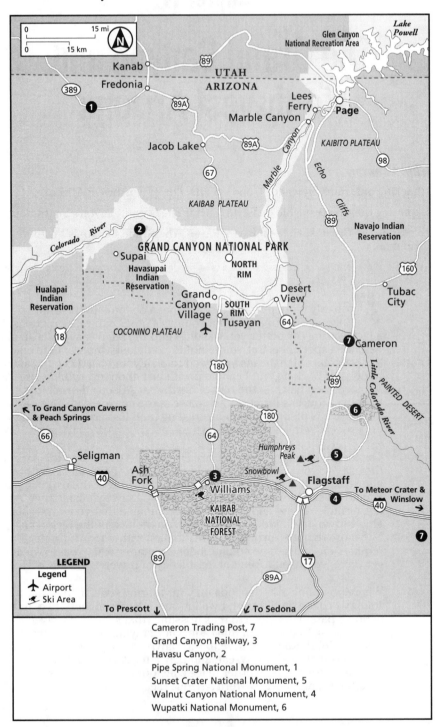

Cameron Trading Post, 7
Grand Canyon Railway, 3
Havasu Canyon, 2
Pipe Spring National Monument, 1
Sunset Crater National Monument, 5
Walnut Canyon National Monument, 4
Wupatki National Monument, 6

Next Time, Arizona Will Claim the Rockies

In spite of the fact that Arizona bills itself as "The Grand Canyon State," when the U.S. Postal Service issued a series of commemorative American landmark stamps in early 1999, the caption placed the famed natural wonder in Colorado. After a National Park Service ranger pointed out the mistake, the entire printing of 100,000 stamps was destroyed (now, if only I had a sheet of those to retire on!). The stamp's reissue, the following year, had only a minor error: The photograph, of Lipan Point on the South Rim, is backwards, so you get a mirror image instead of the actual view. Third time's the charm?

Major Attractions in the Grand Canyon and Northwest Arizona

From Old Route 66 and former lumber towns to the grandest canyon of them all, this region boasts some of Arizona's best-known attractions.

The South Rim Approach: Lower Northwest Arizona

The woodsy region below the Grand Canyon's south rim, once traversed by Route 66 and now bulleted by I-40, is home to Arizona's third largest city as well as to an appealing smaller town, several Native American sites, and a number of natural attractions. Highlights include:

✔ **Flagstaff:** A one-time railway and lumber center now better known as the home of Northern Arizona University and, of course, the gateway to the Grand Canyon. Prime draws are a historic downtown oozing Route 66 color; Riordan Mansion State Park, once ruled by two lumber baron brothers; Northern Arizona Museum, top-notch for both art and natural history; the Lowell Observatory, where Pluto (the planet, not the Disney dog) was discovered; and Snowbowl, the state's top ski spot.

✔ **Williams:** Another town that once banked on its trees but has lately turned to the Grand Canyon — in this case the railway — for its fortunes. More old Route 66 kicks — or at least the memory of them.

✔ **Walnut Canyon:** A pretty wooded area east of Flagstaff where the Sinagua people once built their homes in cliffs.

✔ **Sunset Crater and Wupatki:** A twofer national monument — extinct volcanos and Native American dwellings — in the 2,000-square-mile San Francisco Volcanic Field north of Flagstaff.

✔ **Havasu Canyon:** Part of the Grand Canyon that's home to the Havasupai people and to amazingly turquoise pools below awesome waterfalls.

The Grand Canyon's South Rim

The South Rim is Arizona's big tourism cheese and the source of a not-so-small cottage (pine, of course) industry of hotels, restaurants, and tours, tours, tours. Among the ways you may approach the South Rim, both literally and metaphysically (you haven't seen my latest title, "Zen and the Art of Visiting the Grand Canyon?"):

  ✔ **Along the rim:** By automotive means, self-driven or guided.

  ✔ **Above the rim:** By small plane or helicopter.

  ✔ **Into the depths:** By foot, mule, or raft.

The North Rim (And More)

Go the extra mile — 210 miles from the South Rim, to be precise — and you have the Grand Canyon to yourself, comparatively speaking (only from mid-May to mid-October, though; it's closed the rest of the year). As for the "(and more)" bit:

  ✔ **En route:** Rafters and fisherfolk gather at Lees Ferry, Navajo Bridge spans the canyon, and buffalo feel at home to roam.

  ✔ **The Arizona Strip:** To the west, the Strip is as remote as it gets. A restored Mormon fort and ranch reminds you that some folks still practice multiple marriages around here; you can also view an ancient rock art gallery.

The South Rim Approach: Lower Northwest Arizona

A pretty, piney region financed by lumber and railways before the Grand Canyon became a growth industry, lower northwest Arizona has a whole (though not a hole) lot going for it. The San Francisco Peaks, the state's highest mountains, were uplifted by a not-so-ancient volcano, which also left behind soil so fertile that several Indian civilizations were drawn to this area — the proof is in Walnut Canyon and Wupatki National monuments. Route 66, which helped speed tourists toward the abyss, left a legacy of cool neon signs, while the establishment of Northern Arizona University gave Flagstaff a youth boost. Snowbowl, on one of the San Francisco Peaks, boasts the best skiing in the state — though I admit that's not saying all that much.

You may initially think that Flagstaff never met a hotel or restaurant chain it didn't like. Don't be put off by first impressions. Behind all the fast food and hotel strips sits a friendly, alpine (altitude: 6,902 feet) college town with the best nightlife in the area (okay, so maybe that's not saying a whole lot, either). Inexpensive hotel rooms, abundant restaurants, and a central location make Flagstaff a great base for visiting the Grand Canyon and all the other area attractions, the city itself

Flagstaff

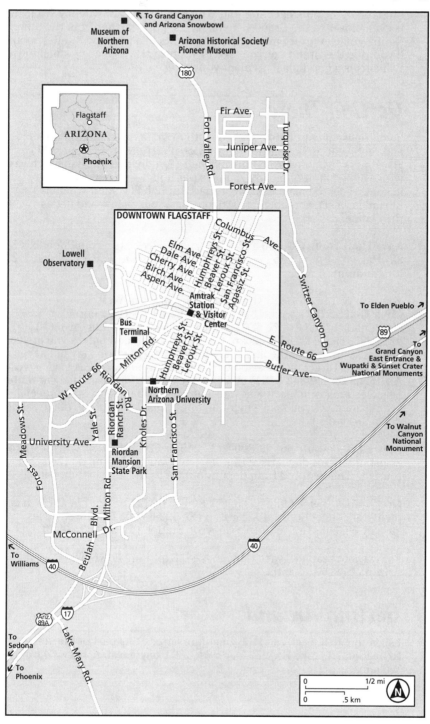

To Grand Canyon
and Arizona Snowbowl

Museum of
Northern
Arizona

Arizona Historical Society/
Pioneer Museum

180

Flagstaff
ARIZONA
Phoenix

Fort Valley Rd.

Fir Ave.

Juniper Ave.

Turquoise Dr.

Forest Ave.

DOWNTOWN FLAGSTAFF

Columbus Ave.

Lowell
Observatory

Elm Ave.
Dale Ave.
Cherry Ave.
Birch Ave.
Aspen Ave.

Humphreys St.
Beaver St.
Leroux St.
San Francisco St.
Agassiz St.

Amtrak
Station
& Visitor
Center

Switzer Canyon Dr.

To Elden Pueblo

Bus
Terminal

Milton Rd.

Humphreys St.
Beaver St.
Leroux St.

E. Route 66

89

To
Grand Canyon
East Entrance &
Wupatki & Sunset Crater
National Monuments

W. Route 66

Riordan Rd.

Ranch St.

Riordan

Knoles Dr.

Northern
Arizona University

Butler Ave.

To Walnut
Canyon
National
Monument

Meadows St.

Yale St.

University Ave.

Forest

Riordan
Mansion
State Park

San Francisco St.

McConnell

Beulah Blvd.

Dr. Milton Rd.

To
Williams

40

40

Ariz.
89A

17

To
Sedona

To
Phoenix

Lake Mary Rd.

0   1/2 mi
0   .5 km

N

also deserves some attention — at least a day. Devote another one to Walnut Canyon, en route to the Petrified Forest National Park (see Chapter 18) or Sunset Crater and Wupatki, if you can. Woodsy Williams is even closer to the Grand Canyon, but slightly farther from the other sights; you can pretty much cover its sights in a morning or afternoon. If you ride the Grand Canyon rails or want to stay in a cozy, small town, Williams is a good place to plant yourself for a bit.

Getting There

If you're like most people who come to Arizona, you fly into Phoenix and rent a car at Sky Harbor International Airport (see Chapter 11). Flagstaff is 134 miles from Phoenix via I-17, a divided four-lane highway with a speed limit of mostly 75 miles per hour — somewhat curvy in spots. I-40, the main east/west road through Flagstaff, Williams (30 miles west), and northern Arizona, is about as fast and flat as they come.

Nava-Hopi Tours (☎ 800-892-8687) runs daily buses from Phoenix's Sky Harbor airport into Flagstaff. Fares are $24 one way for adults, $12 for children.

You can fly from Phoenix to Flagstaff via **America West** (☎ 800-235-9292), which has frequent nonstops daily into Flagstaff Pullium Airport (☎ 520-556-1234), 3 miles south of town (I-17 exit 337). These short hops are pricey, however, and unless you arrive before 2 p.m. (when the flights are most frequent), you may not save much time. Direct flights also fly to Flagstaff from Las Vegas via **Farwest Airlines** (☎ 800-843-8724). Avis, Budget, Hertz, and National car rental agencies are available at Flagstaff's airport. You need to make special arrangements if you take a night flight because most of the offices shut down around 6 p.m.

Amtrak, 1 E. Route 66 (☎ 800-872-7245 or 520-774-8679), whistles into Flagstaff twice a day. Arrive this way and you get a jump on the other tourists: The restored train depot doubles as the information center.

Greyhound, 399 S. Malpais La. (☎ 800-231-2222 or 520-774-4573), has plenty of connections into Flagstaff (☎ 520-635-0870); fewer buses stop in Williams at the town's Chevron Station (☎ 520-635-0870).

For ways to reach Havasu Canyon, see "Exploring Lower Northwest Arizona," in this chapter.

Getting Around

I-40 is the main east/west thoroughfare across this part of the state; to head north, take Hwy. 89A or Hwy. 180 from Flagstaff, Hwy. 64 from Williams.

Flagstaff

I-17 and 89A merge south of Flagstaff and, heading north, turn into Milton Road, Humphreys Road, and Fort Valley Road (also known as Hwy. 180), which leads to the Grand Canyon. Business Route 40, which parallels I-40 and runs east-west, reverts to its old name, Route 66, for a while in town but also does a brief stint through the town center under the alias Santa Fe Avenue. Leroux Street, in the heart of downtown — the roughly four-square-block area surrounding the old railroad depot at Old Route 66 and Beaver Street — marks the divide between the east and west sides of town. When locals refer to the east side, however, they generally mean the section beyond Fourth Street. Northern Arizona University, which you pass if you come in on I-17, is on Flagstaff's south side.

Because of name changes and lack of a grid, Flagstaff's streets can be really confusing. Unless you stop at a gas station, asking for directions won't generally do you much good, either; half the people you encounter are also from out of town. Pick up a good map at the visitors center or from the front desk of your hotel (call your hotel for directions if finding your destination becomes difficult).

Pine Country Transit (☎ **520-779-6624**) is fine for getting you around town during the week (fare: 75¢) if you have time, but on Saturday, service drops from three lines to two and on Sunday it's nonexistent.

Williams

Williams's main streets are Railroad Avenue and Bill Williams Avenue/Route 66, which run one-way through town before merging at both ends into the historic Route 66. The town does not have public transportation, but most of the sights are within walking distance of the hotels anyway.

Where to Stay

This area has every kind of place to bunk — resort-type motels, historic hotels, interesting B&Bs, and lodges — except full-scale luxury resorts (head south to Sedona for more upscale lodgings; see Chapter 16 for more details). A glut of rooms means you can pick and chose and get some real bargains to boot during the off season. The closer you get to summer, when the hordes descend on the Grand Canyon, rooms are more difficult to find and pricier. Spring break is also a busy time, in Williams as well as in Flagstaff. If your heart is set on a particular place, chain hotels included, book as far in advance as possible. (See Chapter 4 for a key to the $ sign ratings.)

The Top Hotels in Flagstaff

Comfi Cottages

$$ Near downtown

Great for a family or group of friends traveling together. These six rental cottages near downtown Flagstaff give you that warm, homey feeling in addition to privacy. All are country cute but with modern facilities; even if you're not big on antiques or frills, you appreciate the fully equipped (and stocked) kitchens, cable TVs, picnic tables, and backyard barbecues. The term "cottages" is a bit misleading for these spacious units, especially the one with three bedrooms; they're all definitely "comfi," though.

1612 N. Aztec (reservations office). ☎ **888-774-0731** *or 520-774-0731. Internet:* www.virtualflagstaff.com/comfi. *Rack rates: $105–$140 for 2 people, depending on the size of the house (larger houses for up to 8 people available), to $195 for 6 people. AE, DISC, MC, V.*

The Inn at 410 Bed and Breakfast

$$$ Downtown

The classiest lodging act in Flagstaff, hands down — so it's no surprise that it's also the priciest. Each room and suite of this restored 1907 banker's house gets its chosen theme down to the last detail — a hand-painted French impressionist screen in the Monet's Garden room, say, or clean-lined Craftsman pieces, such as those found in historic lodges, in the Canyon Memories room. The lovely decor plus such details as whirlpool tubs and/or fireplaces in several units make this a great romantic getaway.

410 N. Leroux St. at Dale. ☎ **800-774-2008** *or 520-774-0088. Fax: 520-774-6354. E-mail:* info@inn410.com. *Internet:* www.inn410.com. *Rack rates: $125–$175. 2-night minimum on weekends Apr–Oct, 3-night minimum some holidays. MC, V.*

The Inn at NAU

$$ South side

Northern Arizona University has one of the best hotel and restaurant management training programs in the country. Stay at this on-campus inn and be part of the educational process. These rooms are great guinea pig digs. The campus is leafy and quiet (at least at night and in summer); the building used to be the university president's home; and the large, well-designed rooms come equipped with all the goods: hairdryers, refrigerators, coffeemakers, large desks, and safes. And such a deal when it comes to meals — not only is breakfast free, but the seven-course gourmet dinners served Friday nights at the Garden Terrace dining room cost $19.99 (no tipping allowed). Don't worry, the students are carefully supervised and graded on how well they treat you.

San Francisco St., on the NAU campus (call for directions). ☎ **520-523-1616.** *Fax: 520-523-1625. Internet:* www.nau.edu/~hrm. *Rack rates: June–Sept Sun–Thu $89, Fri–Sat $99; Oct–May $69/$79; rates include breakfast. AE, DC, MC, V.*

Little America Flagstaff

$$ Eastside

My all-time favorite motel. This link in a smallish western chain is near I-40 but shrouded by pine trees. Who can resist the 24-hour deli; a great gift shop (open until 11 p.m.); a 1970s-style coffee shop with phones at the tables (they're for the truckers, not the international financiers); a retro-swank cocktail lounge; a laundry room; 2-mile hiking trail, exercise room, large pool . . . even a gas station? Rooms are huge and, oddly, French Provincial style (too pretty to be kitsch, though), with large-screen TVs.

2515 E. Butler Ave. (at I-40 exit 198). ☎ *800-FLAG-FUN or 520-779-7900. Fax: 520-779-7983. Internet:* www.littleamerica.com. *Rack Rates: Jan–Nov and major holidays, $119–$129; Dec $89–$99. AE, DC, DISC, MC, V.*

Radisson Woodlands Hotel Flagstaff

$$ Westside

The closest thing in Flagstaff to a fancy hotel, the Radisson is slightly schizy, with its Euro-tony lobby, Southwestern style rooms, and a Japanese restaurant, Sakura. But who cares? The rates are modest, Sakura has great sushi, and the quarters are very comfortable. An exercise room, steam room, heated pool, and spa are on the premises, and this hotel is one of the few places in town with business perks such as room service, valet service, and complimentary airport transfers.

1175 Rte. 66 (at Milton Ave.). ☎ *800-333-3333 or 520-773-8888. Fax: 520-773-0597. Internet:* www.radisson.com/flagstaffaz. *Rack Rates: Mid-June–mid-Aug $99, from $89 rest of the year (except Nov 15–Dec, when rates are higher). AE, DC, DISC, MC, V.*

The Top Dog of Flagstaff Inns

A rustic and elegant B&B is not a novelty, but add a team of adorable Siberian huskies — in Arizona, yet — and you have something to write home about. At the **Sled Dog Inn,** 10155 Mountainaire Rd. (6 miles south of Flagstaff; ☎ **800-754-0664** or 520-525-6212; E-mail: sleddog@infomagic.com; Internet: www.sleddoginn.com), the pups are essential personnel (poochnel?). Snow — and you — permitting, these pooches take you sledding, carting, and skijoring (like water-skiing, only with dog, not outboard, power) under their owners' expert guidance. You can also indulge in canine-free sports such as rock climbing, hiking in the surrounding Coconino Forest, and snowshoeing as part of the inn's adventure du jour packages. Or just kick back in the sauna and stare out at the stars from a hot tub. All the rooms have private baths but no phones or TVs. Rates: $119–$129; adventure du jour add-ons start at $15 per guest with a minimum 2-night stay. AE, DISC, MC, V.

Snowbowl Skilift Lodge

$$ North of Flagstaff

Flagstaff's last call for lodging en route to the Grand Canyon via Hwy. 180. Located at the foot of Snowbowl ski resort, near the Flagstaff Nordic Center, the lodge has nothing but miles of undeveloped land to its north. In summer, guided horseback rides and cowboy cookouts take up the activity slack. Originally part of a 1930s western set, dismantled and trucked here from Sedona, this motel (sorry — surrounding trees do not a lodge make) has rooms with gas-burning log stoves, pine walls, and little front porches. All rooms are equipped with TVs, but no phones.

6355 Hwy. 180 (7 miles north of Flagstaff). ☎ *800-472-3599 (in AZ & CA) or 520-774-0729. Fax: 520-779-3019. Rack Rates: Sun–Thu $75, Fri–Sat $85. Downhill and cross-country ski packages available, snow permitting. AE, DC, MC, V.*

The Runner-Up Hotels in Flagstaff

Flagstaff has long been the most popular sleepover en route to the Grand Canyon. You shouldn't have any trouble finding a link in your favorite hotel chain here (see the appendix for the toll-free numbers). If you want something with a little more personality, try one of the following:

Birch Tree Inn

$$ Near Downtown Antiques-filled but homey, this inn has a pool table, huge breakfasts, and an outdoor hot tub. Two rooms share a bathroom; the other three rooms each have their own bathroom. *824 W. Birch Ave. (at Aztec).* ☎ *888-774-1042 or 520-774-1042. Fax: 520-774-8462. E-mail: birch@flagstaff.az.us. Internet: www.birchtreeinn.com.*

Jeanette's B&B

$$ Eastside This B&B should appeal to art deco devotees. Although new, the style captures the flapper era to a (Model) tee. *3380 E. Lockett Rd. (at N. Fanning Dr.).* ☎ *800-752-1912 or 520-527-1912. Fax: 520-527-1713. E-mail: jbb@infomagic.com. Internet: www.bbonline.com/az.*

Hotel Monte Vista

$-$$ Downtown When it was built in 1926, this was *the* place to stay. (Check out the names of visiting celebrities on the guest room doors.) Although a tad shabby now, it's cheap and in the heart of downtown. *100 N. San Francisco St. (at E. Birch).* ☎ *800-545-3068 or 520-779-6971. Fax: 520-779-2904.*

Where to Stay in Williams

In recent years, more and more interesting bunks compete with the row of chain hotels lining Williams' main streets for the Grand Canyon shut-eye trade.

The Best Little Whorehouse in Arizona

A former bordello that served railroad roughs and their pals, the **Red Garter**, 137 Railroad Ave. (☎ **800-328-1484** or 520-635-1484, Internet: www.redgarter.com), now caters to the (theoretically) more respectable B&B crowd. Owner/innkeeper John Holst is happy to talk about his terrific restoration of the house — he kept the original graffiti in one of the "girls'" rooms, for example, but added private baths. You have to walk up a flight of stairs to get to your room; the exercise is good for you because the free Continental breakfast includes your pick of pastries made in the connecting bakery — anything from piña colada Danishes to Scottish scones. Rack Rates: $65–$105. AE, DISC, MC, V.

Fray Marcos

$$ Williams

A 1990s tribute to the original 1908 Williams depot, this hotel is part of the Grand Canyon Railway complex, which includes a gift shop, Max & Thelma's fine dining room (see "Where to Dine in Williams," in this chapter), Spenser's bar/casual restaurant, and a railway museum. The Southwest contemporary-style rooms don't have as much character as the grand public areas, but — great expectations aside — they're perfectly pleasant and comfortable.

235 Grand Canyon Blvd. (at the railway station; just follow the tracks). ☎ *800-843-8724 or 520-635-4010. Fax: 520-773-1610. Internet:* www.thetrain.com. *Rack rates: Jan–Mar 15 $87, Mar 16–Oct 14 $119, Oct 15–Dec $69. A variety of train packages, most including buffet breakfast, available. AE, DISC, MC, V.*

Norris Motel

$ Williams

The Union Jack flying out front of this motel, next to Old Glory, makes this place stand out from its row of competitors, as does the friendly welcome you get from the British owners. The rooms are pretty nondescript, but many have refrigerators; a hot tub and pool are on the premises.

1001 Rte. 66/I-40 (at S. 9th St.). ☎ *800-341-8000 or 520-635-2202. Fax: 520-635-9202. Rack rates: Sept 8–Oct and April–May 14 $44–$54; Nov–Feb $28–$36; Mar $30–$40; May 15–Sept 7, $55–$67. AE, DISC, MC, V.*

Sheridan House Inn

$$–$$$ Williams

A tough act to top: This inn has the hominess of a B&B, the privacy and (many) amenities of a hotel, and great food served in large quantities. Rooms in the main and adjoining house all have cable TVs, VCRs, and

CD stereo systems. A guest laundry, hot tub, pool table, and wooded decks are on-site. Best of all, the owner, who used to cook for a cruise line, lays out huge breakfasts and gigantic happy-hour buffets (with open bar!). Not quite cruise-ship luxury, but these are not quite cruise-ship prices.

460 E. Sheridan Ave. (at the end, off Grand Canyon Blvd.). ☎ *888-635-9345 or 520-635-9441. Fax: 520-635-1005. E-mail:* SheridanHouse@thegrandcanyon. com. *Internet:* www.thegrandcanyon.com/sheridan. *Rack rates: $110–$175, suites/family units $155–$225. Rates include breakfast. AE, DISC, MC, V.*

Terry Ranch

$$$ **Williams**

Built expressly as a B&B, this is your basic Victorian inn — except that it's a two-story log cabin. The four airy rooms are country pretty, with claw-foot tubs/showers and high-quality antiques; one room has a TV/VCR, another a two-person whirlpool tub, and all have access to a wrap-around verandah. The smell of fresh-baked breads lures guests to the large wooden table in the morning for a huge breakfast.

701 Quarterhorse (at Rodeo Dr.). ☎ *800-210-5908 or 520-635-4171. E-mail:* terryranch@ workmail.com. *Internet:* www.bbonline.com/az/terryranch. *Rack Rates: Apr–Sept $125–$155, Oct–Mar $115–$145. Rates include breakfast. AE, DISC, MC, V.*

Where to Dine

Students, as much as tourists, drive the dining scene in Flagstaff. Fast food rules, but a few fine dining options and plenty of good ethnic and down-home restaurants exist, too. (You didn't really come here to dress up for dinner, did you?) As you may expect, smaller Williams offers proportionately fewer places to refuel. (See Chapter 4 for a key to the $ sign ratings.)

Where to Dine in Flagstaff

Beaver St. Brewery

$–$$ **Downtown**   **Brew Pub/American**

The sprawling, ever-popular Beaver Street Brewery isn't just hopping because of its hops. Creative salads, wood-fired designer pizzas, and big, meaty burgers also draw the hungry hordes. The raspberry beer gets raves; I prefer my fruit in a bowl but can definitely recommend the pale ale.

115 Beaver St. (at Cottage St.). ☎ *520-779-0079. Reservations not accepted. Individual pizzas $7.50–$8.75, salads $6.50–$7.95, sandwiches $7.50–$8.65. Open: Daily lunch and dinner. AE, DISC, MC, V.*

Cafe Espress

$–$$ Downtown   Vegetarian/American/Tex-Mex

Your quintessential college chow house: political flyers, local art, a menu heavy on tofu and veggies. But Tex-Mex dishes such as the super quesadilla are far from bland, and the bakery turns out some tasty pastry; the student budget-geared prices are pretty sweet, too.

16 N. San Francisco St. (at E. Aspen Ave.). ☎ 520-774-0541. Reservations not accepted. Main courses: $4.75–$8.95. Open: Daily breakfast, lunch, and dinner. MC, V.

Cafe Olé

$–$$ Downtown   Mexican

This colorful little family-run restaurant is a magnet for politicos, NAU professors, and everyone else in town with a guacamole-and-fresh-made-tortilla-chip jones. If one of the combination plates on the chalkboard menu includes green chile-and-cheese tamales, go for it.

119 S. San Francisco St. (north of Butler). ☎ 520-774-8272. Reservations not accepted. Main courses: $5–$8.95. No credit cards. Open: Mon dinner, Tues–Fri lunch and dinner (closes 8 p.m.), closed Sat and Sun.

Cottage Place

$$$ Between downtown and NAU   Continental

A cozy, candlelit classic, Cottage Place has perfectly prepared Continental fare, an award-winning wine list, and service that's attentive without being in your face. Veal marsala and beef tournedos are typical of the specialties, but vegetarians are never ignored — nor bored.

126 W. Cottage Ave. (2 blocks north of Humphries). ☎ 520-774-8431. Reservations suggested in high season, essential weekends. Main courses: $16.50–$22.95. Open: Tues–Sun dinner. AE, MC, V.

Down Under

$$$ Downtown   New Zealand/Continental

Not just the kick of occasionally seeing kangaroo on the menu (I'm told it's lean and tastes nothing like chicken) has the locals flocking to this sleek but friendly New Zealand dining room. Less exotic dishes such as fresh salmon and rack of lamb are also done to a dream here. Don't pass up the melt-in-your mouth Pavlova meringue dessert.

6 E. Aspen St. (at Leroux, in Heritage Square). ☎ 520-774-6677. Dinner reservations suggested. Main courses: $15.95–$23.95. Open: Daily lunch and dinner (closed Mon night in winter). AE, MC, V.

Pasto

$$ Downtown   Italian

This intimate Italian bistro draws a slightly-more-sophisticated-than-student crowd, with its slightly more sophisticated (and slightly more expensive) menu. Fare is pretty traditional — spaghetti marinara, salmon piccatta — but dishes such as the Southwestern black bean ravioli definitely didn't debut in Italy. A pretty urban back patio opens up in summer. Romantic, yes, but beware — they go really heavy on the garlic here.

19 E. Aspen (at N. Leroux St.). ☎ **520-779-1937.** *Reservations strongly suggested on weekends. Main courses: $7.95–$12.95 (pastas); $11.95–$15.95. Open: Dinner nightly. AE, MC, V.*

Strombolli's

$–$$ Southwest   Pizza/Italian

This kicked-back place is super popular with parents and their children for its build-your-own pizzas (you know you're in Arizona when jalapeño is an optional topping) and cheese-rich calzones. The garlic bread is baked in the pizza oven; you can make a meal out of it and the creamy artichoke/spinach dip.

1435 S. Milton Ave. (at Butler). ☎ **520-773-1960.** *No reservations, but you can call ahead when you're ready to leave to put your name on a waiting list. Pizza: $8.95–$14.95, pastas/main courses: $6.25–$10.95. Open: Daily lunch and dinner. MC, V.*

Where to Dine in Williams

Max & Thelma

$$–$$$ Williams   American

During the day, all-you-can-eat buffets hustle the railway crowd in and out, and a miniature train chugs around a trestle. At night, this depot dining room is pretty and candlelit. The oysters are super fresh, the steak and seafood are good, and desserts such as coffee mousse are worth blowing a diet for. (In case you were wondering, Max and Thelma own the Grand Canyon Railway — and the restaurant.)

235 Grand Canyon Blvd. (at the railway station; just follow the tracks). ☎ **520-635-4010.** *Main courses: $11.75–$20.75; breakfast buffet: $6.95, lunch buffet: $7.95, dinner buffet: $9.95. Open: Daily breakfast, lunch, and dinner. AE, DC, MC, V.*

Pancho McGillicuddy's Mexican Cantina

$$ Williams   Tex-Mex/American

Okay, so it ain't authentic (what did you expect with a name like Pancho McGillicuddy?), but the chimichangas are filling, the patio is pretty, and it's fun to down a cold one in an 1893 saloon. Live music available some nights, too.

141 Railroad Ave. (at Grand Canyon Blvd.). ☎ *520-635-4150. Main courses: $4–$12.95. Open: Lunch and dinner in summer, dinner (from 3 p.m.) in winter. AE, DISC, MC, V.*

Pine Country Restaurant

$ Williams American

Locals pile into this blue-curtained dining room for huge slices of home-baked pies, gravy-smothered biscuits, hefty burgers, and crispy fried chicken (prepared in canola oil, the menu says; now can't you just feel your cholesterol count dropping?).

107 N. Grand Canyon Blvd. (at Railroad Ave.). ☎ *520-635-9718. Main courses: $5.95–$6.95 (sandwiches $2.95–$5.75, breakfasts $2.50 to $5.75). Open: Daily breakfast, lunch, dinner. AE, DISC, MC, V.*

Bean There, Done That

What's a college town without coffeehouses? The fact that Flag hasn't achieved Starbucks status is more than compensated for by:

✔ **Campus Coffee Bean,** 1800 Milton Rd. (in a strip shopping center near NAU; ☎ 520-556-0660). This coffeehouse has live music or poetry readings most nights. The menu stretches beyond coffees, *chais* (an Indian cold tea drink), and Italian sodas to include some sandwiches and sweets.

✔ **Jitters,** 3504 E. Route 66, one block west of Milton Rd., eastside (☎ 520-774-2466), serves freshly made soups, gourmet sandwiches, and a tempting array of cakes and pies. Great selection of offbeat greeting cards, too.

✔ **Late for the Train,** 107 N. San Francisco St. at Aspen, downtown (☎ 520-779-5975), features the requisite black-clad *barristas* (a fancy name for the workers who brew your coffee) with attitude preparing requisitely strong espresso. Possibly the hippest of the bunch.

✔ **Macy's European Coffeehouse and Bakery,** 14 S. Beaver St. (just south of the railroad tracks/Santa Fe Ave; ☎ 520-774-2243), is far more Californian than European (what self-respecting cafe on the Continent would serve tempeh veggie lasagne?) and terrifically hippie chic with its bright-red coffee roasters and infinite java riffs.

✔ **Tea and Sympathy,** 409 N. Humphreys St. (between Dale and Elm, near downtown; ☎ 520-779-2171), only has caffeine in common with the other spots, but I can't resist telling you about this veddy civilized lace-curtained hideaway with sink-down chairs and darling flowered tea tins.

Dynasty, Northern Arizona-Style

Lots of downtown's buildings bear the Babbitt name, after the five brothers who arrived in 1886 and made it big in the mercantile business. Bruce Babbitt, Secretary of the Interior in the Clinton administration and a former governor of Arizona, is just the latest of this Flagstaff pioneer family's overachievers.

Rod's Steak House

$$–$$$ Williams Steakhouse/American

The kitschy red Fiberglas steer on Rod's roof has heralded good corn-fed, mesquite-broiled beef since 1946. The atmosphere is low-key, but the meat is high profile, with a house specialty prime rib that weighs in from the 9-ounce "ladies' lite" to a 16-ounce "cattleman's hefty."

301 E. Route 66 (at Flagel, east end of town). ☎ *520-635-2671. Main courses: $8–$25. Open: Daily lunch and dinner (closed Jan 4–20, Sun Nov–Mar). MC, V.*

Exploring the Lower Northwest

You may be surprised at how many different, as in both varied and strange, things you see around here — from volcanic fields to observatories to mansions made of logs. Many of the following attractions involve being outdoors, but I put the activities primarily designed to keep you moving — as opposed to these, where moving is just a necessary adjunct — into the "Keeping Active" section. (You don't even have to look at that section if you feel lazy, honest.)

The Top Things to See and Do

Flagstaff

Beyond its motel and fast food–frenzied facade, Flagstaff has sights that track back to its roots as a railroad and lumber center and to its Route 66 glory days. Stop in at the visitors center at the old Santa Fe depot (see "Quick Concierge: Lower Northwest Arizona," in this chapter) to pick up a self-guided map of the many turn-of-the century masonry buildings in the Downtown Historic Railroad District. Or just wander around on your own, reading the brass historic plaques. In addition you can:

✔ **Plateau out: The Museum of Northern Arizona,** 3101 N. Fort Valley Road (Hwy. 180 north, 3 miles north of Flagstaff) (☎ 520-774-5213 or Internet: www.musna.org), which highlights the arts, culture, and geology of Colorado Plateau, would be a standout anywhere, but it's a must-see if you're in this area; the 1928 native stone building is worth the trip alone. Greatest hits include the Navajo rug collection and, in a terrific new Western-design wing, ceramics and paintings (look for the work of Mary-Russell Colton). Kids especially like the life-sized Dilophosaurus, a dino-carnivore that stomped this region when it was a swamp. Museum films can be deadly, but the half-hour *Sacred Lands of the Southwest* isn't; don't miss it if you have time. (See also "Shopping in Flagstaff," in this chapter.) Open: Daily 9 a.m.–5 p.m., closed Thanksgiving, Christmas, New Year's Day, and Easter. Admission: $5 adults, $4 seniors, $3 students with ID, $2 ages 7–17, 6 and under free.

✔ **Check out the lifestyles of the timber rich and famous:** Tour the **Riordan Mansion State Historic Park,** 1300 Riordan Ranch St., on the NAU campus, off S. Milton Rd. (☎ **520-779-4395**), to see what you get when you mix a lot of tree money and a little eccentricity. The 40-room native log-and-stone mansion, built in 1904, was the domain of two lumber baron brothers who married two sisters. Along with the more typical rich people trappings are one of the best collections of Craftsman furniture in the country and photo transparencies of the Grand Canyon that double as window panes. You can also see Paul Bunyan's baby shoes (it's a long — and tall — story). Open: May–Sept daily 8 a.m.–5 p.m., Oct–Apr daily 11 a.m.–5 p.m.; closed Christmas. Guided tours hourly from 9 a.m. in summer (reservations recommended), hourly from noon in winter; last tour 4 p.m. year-round. Admission: $4 adults, $2.50 ages 7–13, 6 and under free.

✔ **Do some pioneering research:** The Arizona Historical Society's small **Pioneer Museum,** 2340 N. Fort Valley Rd. (Hwy. 180, north of W. Fir Ave.; ☎ **520-774-6272**), housed in Coconino County's first (1908) hospital for the poor, has a few grim displays such as an old iron lung, but the museum is generally upbeat about Flagstaff's early days. A "Playthings of the Past" exhibit opens every winter and a couple of railroad cars always sit out front. Open: Mon–Sat 9 a.m.–5 p.m.; closed Christmas, New Year's Day, Easter, and Thanksgiving. Admission: Free (donations appreciated).

✔ **Get cosmic:** Interactive astronomy exhibits and slide shows make the **Lowell Observatory,** 1400 West Mars Hill Rd. (☎ **520-774-3358** or 520-774-2096 (after hours); Internet: www.lowell.edu), interesting enough during the day, but peak science geek time is after dark when you can peer through the facility's telescopes. Schedules depend on weather and planetary alliances; no stargazing available in January and February, but about four viewings a week in summer. The telescopes are in an open dome, so dress for an evening outdoors. Open: Nov–Mar daily noon–5 p.m., Apr–Oct daily 9 a.m.–5 p.m.; call for directions and night-viewing program schedule. Admission: $4 adults, $3.50 seniors and AAA members, $2 ages 5–17; 4 and under free.

A Plutonic Affair

The Lowell Observatory was founded in 1894 and the planet Pluto was discovered there in 1930, after a decades-long search started by Percival Lowell (that's just one of the many reasons they named the place after him).

✔ **Get a (ski) lift:** Even with no chance of snow on Mt. Agassiz, one of the San Francisco Peaks, you can get lofted to the top via the **Arizona Snowbowl chairlift,** Snowbowl Road, off Hwy. 180, about 15 miles north of town (☎ **520-779-1951**). This is the high point of a Flagstaff visit — 11,500 feet, to be precise and, on a clear day, you can see forever (well, at least to the North Rim of the Grand Canyon). Open: Memorial Day–Labor Day daily 10 a.m.– 4 p.m., after Labor Day–mid-Oct Fri–Sun. Admission: $9 adults, $6.50 seniors, $5 ages 6–12 (5 and under ride free with adults).

✔ **Find some guidance:** Nava-Hopi, 114 W. Route 66 (☎ **800-892-8687** or 520-774-5003; Internet: www.navahopitours.com), runs a 3½-hour tour of Flagstaff, covering the Museum of Northern Arizona, the Riordan Mansion State Historic Park, and the Pioneer Historical Museum ($19.50 adults, $9.50 ages 5–15). In summer, free 90-minute walking tours of downtown are led by local historians dressed in turn-of-the-century costumes. These tours depart from the Flagstaff Visitors Center. For dates and additional information, call ☎ **520-774-8800.**

Havasu Canyon

If you want to see some of the state's most spectacular scenery *and* visit an Indian reservation, this canyon, south of the central part of the national park, fits the bill. Home to some 500 Havasupai people, Havasu Canyon is famous for its astonishingly turquoise water and for the 200-foot waterfalls that cascade down vivid red sandstone cliffs into limpid pools. Swimming in said pools — and for some people, hiking into and out of the canyon — is pretty much what there is to do here; the village, such as it is, consists of fairly run-down homes. If you can stand being forced to relax in a beautiful spot, though, this may just be your place. Keep in mind that the Havasu Canyon is a little more than off the beaten path; you must hike, ride, or book a helicopter flight to enter.

From Williams, take I-40 west 44 miles to Seligman, where the road splits; continue on Hwy. 66 west for 26 miles and turn north on Indian Route 18 (if you reach Peach Springs, you drove 6 miles too far). It's 60 miles to Haulupai Hilltop, where the 8-mile-long Hualapai Trail, a fairly precipitous, winding route (at least for the first mile; it levels off after that) descends into Supai, Havasu Canyon's only settlement and home to the **Havasupai Tourist Enterprise** (☎ **520-448-2141**).

If you don't want to hike down, contact the tourist enterprise and arrange for a horse or mule to take you (round-trip rates are $110 from Hualupai Hilltop to the campground, $80 from the hilltop to Supai Village, and $40 from Supai Village to the campground). The Havasupai Tourist Enterprise isn't always easy to reach by phone. If you're not in a rush, writing (Supai, AZ 86435) is often the best way to get information.

Alternatively, **Papillon Grand Canyon Helicopters** (☎ **800-528-2418** or 520-638-2419) runs two excursions to Havasu Canyon from the Grand Canyon Airport in Tusayan. For $440 per adult, you get a round-trip helicopter ride plus a guided horseback ride to Havasu Falls (but no meals), returning the same day. If you want to stay overnight at Havasupai Lodge, the package will run you $482 (more or less — depending on how many share a room); the price again includes the helicopter and a horse but no food.

The cost is $15 (Apr–Oct) or $12 (Nov–Mar) to enter the tribal lands; the fee is payable in advance by phone or mail or at the Havasupai Tourist Enterprise when you arrive. MC and V are the only credit cards accepted.

The **Havasupai Lodge** in Supai (☎ 520-448-2111) has comfortable rooms, but no TVs or phones (Apr–Oct $75–$96, Nov–Mar $45–$66).

Sunset Crater Volcano and Wupatki National Monuments

A double header. When Sunset Crater erupted in A.D. 1064–65 (that's just about the time William the Conquerer was taking over Europe), the Sinagua Indians abandoned their fields and fled — only to return a few decades after the action cooled down because the eruption had enriched the soil and improved farming conditions. Sunset Crater and Wupatki national monuments, connected by a 36-mile loop road, not only give you a chance to witness the aftermath of a fiery natural phenomenon, but also to take a look at the ancient civilizations directly affected by it.

You can take a mile-long, self-guided walk around the base of the 1,000-foot-high Sunset Crater, a study in red and black dotted by pines, but the cone itself is off limits; if climbing is your thing, ask at the visitors center about climbing Lenox Crater or Doney (in Wupatki) instead. Wupatki is interesting enough for its well-preserved structures, but what makes it really unusual is that three different native cultures — the Kayenta and the Cohonina peoples, along with the Sinagua — coexisted here. Don't miss the high-rise pueblo for which the national monument is named (take the short trail from the back of the Wupatki visitors center) and the Maya-like ball court with its barometer-like blow hole.

Sunset Crater visitors center, 19 miles northeast of Flagstaff, off U.S. 89, ☎ 520-526-0502. Wupatki visitors center, 20 miles north of the Sunset Crater visitors center along Sunset Loop Rd., ☎ 520-679-2365. Open (visitors centers): summer 8 a.m.–6 p.m., winter 8 a.m.–5 p.m., closed Christmas; gates open year-round sunrise to sunset. Admission (to both but collected at Sunset Crater): $3 per person over age 17.

Pseudo Sunset, Pseudo Moon

When the iron and sulfur in the lava that flowed from Sunset Crater during its last eruption (around A. D.1250) oxidized, it gave the rim of the volcano a red and yellow "sunset" glow — and a perpetually molten, about-to-blow look. Fast forwarding ahead some seven centuries, the lava flow at Sunset Crater looked so much like the moon's surface that NASA sent Neil Armstrong and other astronauts over to practice their rock specimen collecting (Armstrong must have passed the rock test; he was the first man to walk on the moon).

Walnut Canyon National Monument

Move this spot to the top of your must-see list. This beautiful canyon would be worth visiting for its lush ponderosa pine, juniper, and Douglas fir forest alone, but you can also see — and even enter — some wonderfully well-preserved cliff dwellings here, built by the Sinagua people between 1125 and 1250. No one is exactly sure why these dwellings were left behind by 1300. They were protected over the years by limestone overhangs and by the area's dry climate.

If you're in good shape, the 185-foot Island Trail down to the ruins from the visitors center shouldn't be a problem. Remember, you're at 6,690 feet — which makes breathing hard to begin with. If you suffer from respiratory problems, go for the easier ½-mile Rim Trail; you can still look out at the cliff dwellings, and explore prehistoric pit houses.

10 miles southeast of Flagstaff (take I-40 7.5 miles east to exit 204, then drive 3 miles south on Walnut Canyon Road). ☎ *520-526-3367. Open: Mar–May, Sept–Nov daily 8 a.m.–5 p.m.; June–Aug 8 a.m.–6 p.m.; Dec–Feb 9 a.m.–5 p.m. The Island Trail closes 1 hour before the park closes; the Rim Trail closes ½ hour before the park closes. Admission: $3 adults, 16 and under free.*

Williams

A town entry sign and the tourist brochures all hail Williams as the "Gateway to the Grand Canyon," but the town also has a life, thank you — or at least a past. In its logging and railroad heydey, this alpine outpost bustled with brothels, bars, and opium dens. The population (around 3,000) is about the same now as it was then, but not nearly as wild. At one time the town became a popular Route 66 stopover. Along with hiking the woods or strolling the streets, some things that may get you to stick around before or after you ride the Grand Canyon rails include:

✔ **Getting railroaded:** Even if you're not too-too-tootling away, the **Grand Canyon Railway** depot (just west of Grand Canyon Blvd., north of the tracks) is the most happening place in town. The entertainment includes staged cowboy hijinks at 9 a.m. (before the train departs). A free museum is open the rest of the day; it is devoted to Grand Canyon hospitality and includes a steam locomotive and coach car display, and a great gift shop (see "Shopping in Williams," later in this chapter).

✔ **Play George of the forest:** The Grand Canyon Deer Farm, 8 miles east of Williams (exit 171 of I-40; ☎ 520-635-4073), is a great place for kids to get up-close-and-personal with Bambi — as well as with llamas, miniature horses, pygmy goats, wallabies, turkeys, buffalo, and more. Open: Nov–Feb daily 10 a.m.–5 p.m. (weather permitting), Mar–May 9 a.m.–6 p.m., Jun–Aug 8 a.m.–7 p.m.; $5 adults, $4 seniors, $2.75 ages 3–13; the corn-and-pellet feed mixture costs extra.

Double Billing

Williams was named for Mountain Man Bill Williams (1787–1849), a fur trapper and pathfinder famed for his survival skills (the result of being saddled with the same first and last names?).

Keeping Active

Home to Northern Arizona University's High Altitude Sports Training Complex for Olympic athletes, surrounded by forest, and flanked by the highest mountains in the state, Flagstaff is outdoor adventure central for northern Arizona. Williams is no slouch either, when it comes to getting you to play outside.

- ✔ **Climbing:** If you're not repelled by rappelling, **Flagstaff Mountain Guides,** P.O. Box 2383 (☎ 520-635-0145; Internet: NAZCLIMB@ aol.com), can help you scale the heights. Classes range from full-day beginner instruction ($150) to advanced 5-day tours ($750). Canyoneering and mountaineering classes are also available. You can also prepare for on-the-rocks action at **Vertical Relief Rock Gym,** 205 S. San Francisco St. (☎ 520-556-9909), which claims to have the tallest indoor walls in the Southwest (who measures these things, anyway?). Costs run $14 to play for a day, $8 to rent equipment.

- ✔ **Golfing:** Elephant Rocks, 2200 Country Club Dr. (3 miles west of downtown Williams; ☎ 520-635-4935), had to give up its title as the self-proclaimed "#1 9-hole golf course in Arizona," when Gary Panks, the original course architect, made it into an 18-holer recently. But the course has other lures to compensate — a pretty ponderosa pine setting and low green fees ($39 weekends, $34 during the week, $22 after 4 p.m., all including cart). This well-maintained municipal course is open from mid-April to mid-November.

- ✔ **Hiking:** Locals head for glen and dale (whatever a dale is) in the San Francisco Peaks and Coconino National Forest when the white stuff isn't covering up the trails; it's especially fun to take the Arizona Snowbowl ski lift up Mt. Agassiz (see "The Top Things to See and Do," earlier in this section) and hike back down. Get trail maps and advice about the best trekking spots from the **Peaks Ranger District office,** 5075 N. Hwy. 89 (☎ 520-526-0866), open Sun–Fri 7:30 a.m.–6 p.m., or the **Coconino National Forest office,** 2323 Greenlaw La. (☎ 520-527-3600), open Mon–Fri 7:30 a.m.–4:30am.

- ✔ **Horseback Riding: Hitchin' Post Stables,** 4848 Lake Mary Rd. (☎ 520-774-7131), has assorted horseplay options, ranging from 1-hour guided rides ($25) to 6-hour excursions to Walnut Canyon ($90; see "The Top Things to See and Do," earlier in this section). You can also ride in a wagon to a steak barbecue at sunset or (from December through April) snuggle with your honey in a horse-drawn sleigh.

Hollywood Horses

Hitchin' Post Stables' equines have starred in countless films and commercials — everything from *Wanda Nevada* with Brooke Shields and Peter Fonda to *Wild Horses*, a made-for-TV movie with Kenny Rogers and Pam Dauber, to ads for Marlboro and for Hubba Bubba Bubble Gum.

✔ **River rafting:** If you don't have time for a weeklong Grand Canyon rafting trip but want to get your toes into the chilly Colorado River, consider a 1- or 2-day excursion with the **Hualapai River Runners** (☎ 800-622-4409 or 520-769-2210). All trips, which depart from Peach Springs (see Havasu Canyon in "The Top Things to See and Do," earlier in this section) on the Hualapai reservation, cover the same wet territory; the 2-day excursion just takes it more slowly and includes a camp-out on the river bank. Expect a combination of white and calm waters and lots of wonderful scenery along the way. It's $160 for a half day, $250 for a full day, $500 for 2 days; all bookings get you discounted rates at the tribe's good Hualapai Lodge, 900 Rte. 66 (☎ 888-255-9550 or 520-769-2230) in Peach Springs.

✔ **Skiing:** It's all downhill at the **Arizona Snowbowl** (☎ 520-779-4577 for a snow report, Internet: www.arizonasnowbowl.com), where you can rent anything snow-oriented, including snowboards and the latest in parabolic skis. The 32 slopes (2,300 vertical feet, total) have a nice mix of beginner, intermediate, and advanced runs. Lift tickets range from $20 for a half-day midweek pass to $37 for a weekend all-day pass (adults); ages 8 to 12 pay $15 for a half day, $20 full day, no matter what day of the week. Because Mt. Agassiz is an extinct volcano, no groundwater for snow making is available; for this reason, tracking the weather is more important than usual if you're thinking about coming.

At 30 acres, the **Williams Ski Area,** 10 minutes south of town (take Fourth St. to the Kaibab National Forest) (☎ 520-635-9330), may be the smallest in the state, but the area's fun for snow-bonding families who can also rent sleds and inner tubes for a sledding hill. When enough white stuff falls (usually starting in December), the ski area stays open Thurs–Mon 9:30 a.m.–4:30 p.m. (also open Christmas week, except Christmas day). Lift tickets: $21 adults all day weekends and holidays, $16 adults all day weekdays; $16 12 and under and seniors 60 and over all day for weekends and holidays, $13 12 and under and seniors 60 and over all day weekdays. Lower half-day (1 p.m. and after) and beginner rates available.

The altitude averse have a couple of cross-country options. The **Flagstaff Nordic Center,** operated by Snowbowl, 15 miles north of Flagstaff on 18400 N. Hwy. 180 (☎ 520-779-1951), has 40 kilometers of groomed track. All-day trail passes cost $10. Other options include skijoring (you can rent the skis but it's BYOD — bring your own dog — to haul you along on them). The **Mormon Lake Ski Center,** 28 miles south of Flagstaff on Lake Mary Rd. (☎ 520-354-2240), has more than 21 miles of groomed ski trails; $5 buys you an all-day trail pass. Snowmobiles as well as ski rentals are available at both.

Don't want to restrict your skiing action to the daylight? The Arizona Snowbowl/Flagstaff Nordic Center (☎ 520-779-1951 for both) can indulge you. On snowy winter weekends, moonlight crosscountry ski tours are followed by hot drinks in a *yurt* (a ski hut) and, perhaps, a bout of stargazing. In summer, you can enjoy a romantic candlelight dinner after a sunset ride on the Mt. Agassiz skilift. Call for the latest details.

At Arizona Snowbowl and Mormon Lake Ski Center, those 7 and under and 70 and over ski free.

Shopping in Flagstaff

In this region, you find Native American jewelry and crafts and lots of Route 66 memorabilia, among other things.

Downtown is by far Flagstaff's most fertile retail ground; sporting goods, crafts, and nostalgia are among the best-sellers. A 1920s bowling alley turned bookstore, **McGaugh's Newsstand,** 24 N. San Francisco (☎ 520-774-2131), is *the* place for out-of-town papers, smokes of all sorts, and books on the area. The excellent **Four Winds Traders,** 118 W. Route 66 (☎ 520-774-1067), sells both new and pawn Native American jewelry; lots of Navajo crafters come here for supplies. The creative home furnishings and gifts sold at **Zani,** 9 N. Leroux (☎ 520-774-9409), are entirely up-to-date, but the long-dead owner of the building, a 1911 brick house, apparently likes to come back and browse. **The Artists Gallery,** 17 North San Francisco St. (☎ 520-773-0958), represents more than 40 locals who work in genres ranging from stained glass and calligraphy to sculpture; some of the jewelry is outstanding.

The Mother Road Mother Lode

Williams was the last Route 66 town to be bypassed by the freeway: Not until 1984 was the stretch of I-40 that replaced the famous road completed here. As a result, it's hard to find a store on Williams' main streets that *doesn't* hawk Route 66-o-bilia. The best place to find it en masse, however, is the **headquarters of Route 66 Magazine,** 326 W. Route 66 (☎ 520-635-4322), where, in addition to the glossy publication that examines America's most nostalgia-inducing stretch of macadam from every imaginable angle, you can buy books and mementos that run the gamut from hot car models and neon signs to Burma Shave soap sets and Route 66 brand bath gel.

Celestial Strings

Edward Bowell, an astronomer at Flagstaff's Lowell Observatory, is a huge classical music booster. In honor of the local orchestra's 50th anniversary in 2000, he renamed Asteroid 6582, which he had discovered decades earlier, "Flagsymphony."

From late May through September, Zuni, Navajo, and Hopi artisans come from all over the Southwest to show — and sell — their work at the huge annual Celebration of Native American Art at the Museum of Northern Arizona (see "Exploring Lower Northwest Arizona," in this chapter). Other times of the year, you can make do with the extensive selection at the museum gift shop.

Shopping in Williams

In addition to its Route 66 stuff (see "The Mother Road Mother Lode" sidebar in this chapter), Williams is big on train- and forestry-theme things; head over to the Grand Canyon Railway depot to find everything from wind chimes hung with leather-jacketed Harley bikers to train clocks and stuffed Smokey Bear dolls.

Nightlife and the Arts in Flagstaff

Whether you're looking for an evening of high-brow entertainment or just a place to quench your thirst, you have several options from which to choose.

Flagstaff offers both an arts and a nightlife scene, and they're not half bad either. Summer's the high culture pinnacle, with the various Native American festivals, marketplaces, exhibits, and lectures at the **Museum of Northern Arizona** (see "Exploring Lower Northwest Arizona," in this chapter, and check the Internet address at www.musnaz.org for a schedule), and the June through July Summer Arts theater and music extravaganza co-sponsored by **Northern Arizona University** (☎ 520-523-5111 [ticket office]; Internet: www.nau.edu) and the **Flagstaff Symphony Orchestra**, 113A E. Aspen Ave. (☎ 520-774-5107; Internet: www.flagstaffsymphony.org), which kicked off in 2000; check NAU's Web site for the current schedule, and call ☎ 888-520-7214 for tickets to this and other events in Flagstaff.

But the Flagstaff Symphony, a fine regional orchestra that has been around since 1949, doesn't just stay tuned in summer. In addition, **Theatrikos**, Flagstaff Playhouse, 11 W. Cherry St. (☎ 520-774-1662), will satisfy your basic thespian needs year-round.

The club scene changes constantly but **Monsoons**, 22 E. Santa Fe Ave. (☎ 520-774-7929), has been bringing in a mix of live sounds for a long time. The historic **Weatherford Hotel**, 23 N. Leroux, ☎ 520-779-1919,

---

Two-Steppin' and Taxidermy on Route 66

Never mind the name: The **Museum Club**, 3404 E. Route 66 (☎ 520-526-9434) is anything but stuffy (although lots of things that look down from the walls at you are stuffed). Nicknamed the Zoo because it was built in 1931 to house a taxidermy collection, this huge log cabin does attract the usual bar stiffs, but comes to life each night with the best country and western sounds in town. If you can't get here after dark, check it out during the day.

---

has two good venues: Charley's, mostly rock, and the Zane Grey Ballroom right above it, a surprisingly swanky spot to hear jazz and, sometimes, poetry. Handcrafted-beer lovers find their bliss in downtown Flagstaff: In addition to the fairly ferny **Beaver Street Brewery** (see "Where to Dine in Flagstaff," in this chapter), there's the funky **Mogollon Brewing Company,** 15 N. Agassiz St. (☎ 520-773-8950), where a chain saw hangs over the pool table and the pale ale wins accolades. Somewhere in between the two, the **Flagstaff Brewing Company,** 16 E. Route 66 (☎ 520-773-1442), compensates for a lack of strong suds personality with an impressive array of single malts and small batch bourbons; some townies swear by its pale ale, too. You can try many local beers on tap at the **Pay 'n' Take,** 12 W. Aspen (☎ 520-226-8595), an unlikely convenience store-cum-wine bar that's one of the town's hottest hangouts.

Nightlife and the Arts in Williams

If you're not into biker bars and nothing's happening at Pancho McGillicuddy's (see "Where to Dine in Williams" in this chapter), Williams does not have a whole lot to do after dark, but it's worth wandering over for a drink at Spenser's Lounge in the Fray Marcos hotel (see "Where to Stay in Williams" in this chapter): The gorgeous carved wood 19th-century bar was shipped over to the hotel from Ireland where, the story has it, the architect agreed to build it in exchange for free drinks for the rest of his life. Because he was still putting them away well into his 80s, it turned out not to be a bad deal — for him.

Quick Concierge: Lower Northwest Arizona

Area Code: The area code for this entire region is **520.**

Emergency: For police, ambulance, or in case of fire call ☎ **911.**

Hospitals-Clinics: Flagstaff Medical Center, 1200 N. Beaver St. (☎ 520-770-3366). There's nothing in Williams; patients head over to Flag.

Information: You can't miss the Flagstaff Visitors Center, One East Route 66, at the corner of Beaver Street (☎800-842-7293 or 520-774-9541; Internet: www.flagstaffarizona.org); just follow the tracks to the train depot. It's a great source of area information — as well as a prime people-watching spot because it's always bustling with hapless Grand Canyon-bound travelers, many from other countries. Hours are Mon–Sat 7 a.m.–6 p.m. and Sun 7 a.m.–5 p.m. Another former railroad depot, the Williams-Grand Canyon Chamber of Commerce/Kaibab National Forest Visitors Center, 200 W. Railroad Ave (☎ 800-863-0546, 520-635-4704, or 520-635-4061), is also an excellent resource, dispensing information, as its weighty monicker implies, on the town, the forest, and the great gorge; lots of excellent books on the region are avaible here. Open daily from 8 a.m.–6:30 p.m. in high season, closing earlier in winter.

Newspapers/Magazines: *The Arizona Daily Sun,* published daily in Flagstaff and sold throughout northern Arizona, is the best source of local news and events. Its weekend nightlife/arts insert, *The Flare,* gets some competition from the free *Live!* listings tabloid.

Pharmacies: In Flagstaff, Walgreens, 1500 E Cedar Ave (☎ 520-773-1155), stays open the latest in town (Mon– Fri 9 a.m.–10 p.m., Sat 9 a.m.–6 p.m., Sun 10 a.m.–6 p.m.). In Williams, Harker's Professional Pharmacy, 301 S. 7th St. (☎ 520-635-2222), open Mon–Fri 9 a.m.–6 p.m. is about it; you're out of luck on the weekends.

Post Office: In Flagstaff, 2400 N. Postal Blvd. (☎ 520-714-9302); in Williams, 115 S. 1st St. (☎ 520-635-4572)

Road Conditions: Call ☎ 888-411-7623.

Weather: Call ☎ 520-774-3301.

The Grand Canyon's South Rim

Even if seeing the Grand Canyon is not the sole reason you go to Arizona, you probably still have to visit it. If you don't, you spend more time explaining why you didn't go than the time it takes to get there. (I'm exhausted even thinking about it.) But that's fine. The Grand Canyon doesn't disappoint; it deserves all the press it gets. (One of the most amazing things about the canyon is that it seems to appear out of nowhere: You drive around this nice but fairly ordinary pine forest and — whammo!)

The commercialism and crowds that surround the South Rim may, on the other hand, put you off; they've done the same to me. Which is why I show you how to get the most out of your experience, whether you just go for the day or make a bigger time commitment.

I'm going to beg of you (ain't too proud) to please, please, come in the off season if you can. Summer, spring, and fall are the busiest months; you're much happier here from November through February (the crowds are minimal, and if it snows, the bonus of seeing the Grand Canyon dusted by all that pretty white stuff is worth the trip). But if you can't — and I forgive you — be sure to book hotel rooms and popular tours such as river rafting and mule rides well in advance (more on that later). Reserving in advance means you get to do everything that

Grand Canyon Village

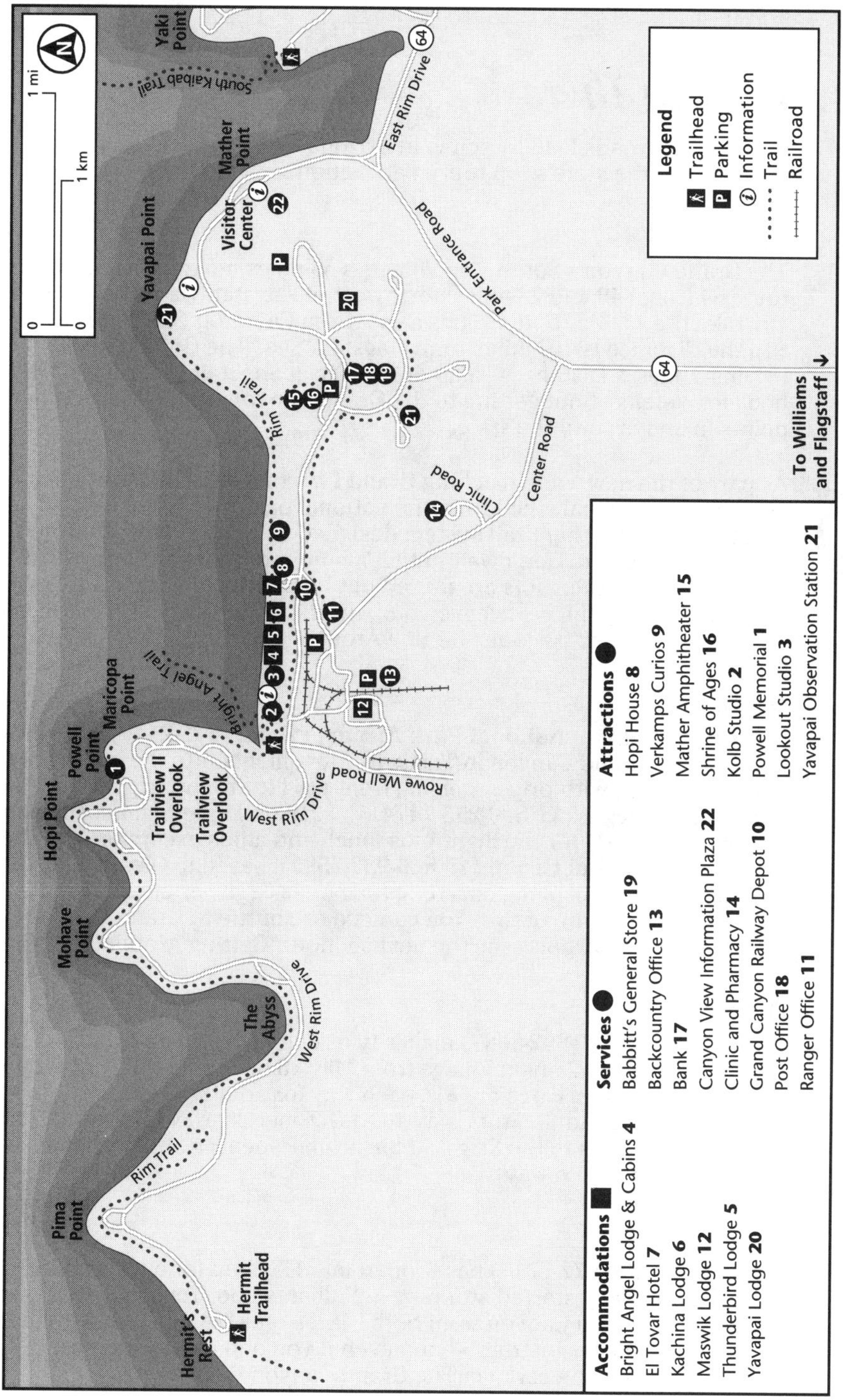
0
0
1 km
1 mi
N
Yaki Point
South Kaibab Trail
Mather Point
East Rim Drive
64
Yavapai Point
Visitor Center
Park Entrance Road
Rim Trail
Center Road
Clinic Road
To Williams and Flagstaff →
Bright Angel Trail
Maricopa Point
Powell Point
Hopi Point
Trailview II Overlook
Trailview Overlook
West Rim Drive
Rowe Well Road
Mohave Point
The Abyss
Pima Point
Hermit Trailhead
Hermit's Rest
Legend
Trailhead
Parking
Information
Trail
Railroad
Accommodations ■
Bright Angel Lodge & Cabins 4
El Tovar Hotel 7
Kachina Lodge 6
Maswik Lodge 12
Thunderbird Lodge 5
Yavapai Lodge 20
Services ●
Babbitt's General Store 19
Backcountry Office 13
Bank 17
Canyon View Information Plaza 22
Clinic and Pharmacy 14
Grand Canyon Railway Depot 10
Post Office 18
Ranger Office 11
Attractions ●
Hopi House 8
Verkamps Curios 9
Mather Amphitheater 15
Shrine of Ages 16
Kolb Studio 2
Powell Memorial 1
Lookout Studio 3
Yavapai Observation Station 21

you really want to do. Reserving some things in advance during the quieter months is also important; I let you know which reservations to secure.

Getting There

In Europe all roads lead to Rome; in Arizona every type of transport takes you to the state's top tourist attraction.

By Car

The Grand Canyon's South Rim Village is 59 miles north of Williams via route 64 from I-40 and 78 miles northwest of Flagstaff via route 180. If you take the scenic route from the east from Cameron (US 80 to Hwy. 64), the distance is 107 miles from Flagstaff. See "The Grand Canyon Driving Times & Distances" map on the Cheat Sheet at the front of the book for details about getting to the Grand Canyon from other popular points in and around the state.

As part of the new, wide-reaching Grand Canyon General Management Plan, cars will be banished from the national park by 2005 or 2006 — whenever the new light rail system designed to bring visitors in from Tusayan is finished. Don't wait until it's required, though: During high season, when parking lots are maxed out but all the in-park transit systems are running full gear, leave your wheels in Tusayan and shuttle or taxi in (see the next section "Getting Around").

By Plane

The **Grand Canyon National Park Airport** (☎ 520-638-2446) is 6 miles south of the Grand Canyon in Tusayan. Most flights into the airport are from Las Vegas, with prices ranging from $164 for round-trip airfare alone on **Air Vegas** (☎ 800-255-7474) to $218 on **Eagle/Scenic Airlines** (☎ 800-634-6801) for the flight plus lunch and a bus excursion into the canyon. The **Global Group** (☎ 800-933-7590), based in Glendale, near Phoenix, runs small plane charters; the fare is $212 per person round-trip, with a minimum of two. You can taxi or shuttle to Grand Canyon Village from the airport (see the next section, "Getting Around").

By Bus

Nava-Hopi (☎ 800-892-8687) makes two round-trips a day from Flagstaff to Grand Canyon Village from May 16 to October 30, one a day the rest of the year. Fares are $14 each way for adults, $7 ages 5 to 15 traveling with an adult. From May 16 to October 30, Nava-Hopi also offers connections to the Flagstaff bus from Phoenix's Sky Harbor Airport ($22/$12 one way).

By Train

Amtrak (☎ 800-872-7245) has tootled into Flagstaff for ages, and in 1999 the company started stopping in Williams, too. You can catch the bus into the Grand Canyon from both places (see "By Bus", above), but if you come this far by train — and even if you don't — by all means continue on into the park via The Grand Canyon Railway.

Riding the Grand Canyon Rails

Train travel to the Grand Canyon was hot, hot, hot when it was introduced in 1901, but by 1927 it was already passé: Automobile fever had taken hold of the country and more people wanted to drive than to ride the rails. In 1968, rail service was suspended for lack of interest; only three passengers rattled around the train on the last national park run.

But that was then. In the last couple of decades, after people began to realize that car exhaust probably wasn't all that good for the canyon, the **Grand Canyon Railway** (☎ **800-THE-TRAIN**; Internet: www.thetrain.com) came back by popular demand — and in close to its original form. From Memorial Day weekend through September, it steams into the national park with a restored 1923 engine on a 2¼-hour (each way) sentimental journey. Passengers ride refurbished Pullman cars, cowboy balladeers and "outlaws" entertain, and the food concessions even sell soda in glass bottles.

Every day (except December 24 and 25) the train leaves from the Williams depot at 10:00 a.m., departing the Grand Canyon depot at 3:30 p.m. The five classes of service range from Coach ($49.95 adult round-trip, $24.95 16 and under round-trip) to Deluxe Observation (add $70 per person). (I suggest you pass on paying extra to get a better view of the scenery; until you actually get into the national park, it's no big deal). All kinds of packages, most of them involving a stay at the Fray Marcos hotel (see "Where to Stay in Williams," in this chapter), are available; call for details or click on to the "packages" box of the train's Web site.

Getting Around

If, like most people, you approach the Grand Canyon from the south, the first place you come to is **Tusayan,** a national park feeder (and sleeper) town with a glut of mostly chain motels, fast food restaurants, and tour operators. Another mile north on Hwy. 64 you find the park entryway/fee station, and an additional 6 miles from the entryway you see the park's visitor hub, **Grand Canyon Village** (which is not, however, where the visitors center is — more on that on in a minute).

If you arrive via Cameron and Hwy. 64 east, you pay your fee 25 miles back and take the scenic **East Rim Drive** before reaching Grand Canyon Village. The other main route within the park is the West Rim Drive; both are described in more detail in "Exploring the South Rim," later in this chapter.

By Shuttle

The **Tusayan-Grand Canyon Shuttle** (☎ **520-638-0821**) goes between the Grand Canyon Airport in Tusayan and the Maswik Transportation Center in Grand Canyon Village, making three other stops in Tusayan and one just outside the park, at the Moqui Lodge. Buses start at about 9:30 a.m. and leave once an hour on the half hour from April through

September, returning from about 5 to 7 p.m., depending on the month; October through March has a more limited schedule. The fare is $4 each way, plus $6 for the park-entrance fee. Any 6th ride is free — and that applies to friends — so one of you catches a break if you're with five other people (okay, just split the difference).

From mid-March to mid-October (the dates vary a little each year), three free park shuttles operate. The **Village Loop bus** circles through Grand Canyon Village, making stops at the visitors center, hotels, campgrounds, and the Yavapai Observation Center; the **West Rim Loop bus** goes to eight canyon overlooks west of the Bright Angel, making all stops westbound but only three on the way back; and the **Yaki Point/South Kaibab shuttle,** stopping at Bright Angel Lodge, the Maswik Transportation Center, and Yavapai Lodge, goes to the Yaki Point overlook and the nearby trailhead for the South Kaibab Trail (see "Active Views: Getting Down in the Canyon," in this chapter). All three routes begin an hour before sunrise; the Village Loop, the Energizer Bunny of the bunch, just keeps on going until 10:30 p.m., while the other two give it a rest an hour after sunset. During most of the day, figure on waiting about 10 to 15 minutes for a bus on the Village and West Rim lines, half an hour on the Yaki Point line.

Grand Canyon Car Talk

I don't generally like it when my advice goes out of date, but I'm happy that this bit will be obsolete as soon as the South Rim's light rail system is complete. In the meantime, for a safe drive around the canyon:

✔ **Make sure your car is in good shape.** The **Grand Canyon Garage,** east of the Grand Canyon National Park Lodges' General Offices, in Grand Canyon Village (☎ 520-638-2631, exit 6502), is open for repairs from 8 a.m. to noon and 1 to 5 p.m. and has 24-hour emergency service, but it's the only game in town; you never know how long it'll take for your part to come in.

✔ **Always carry an extra set of car keys** with you (they're not much help inside your hotel room). The canyon does not have a resident locksmith.

✔ **Fill 'er up before you enter.** Gas stations aren't exactly clustered on every canyon corner. Only one station, **Desert View Chevron,** is inside the national park near the eastern park entry and it's not always open in winter. A service station is available in Tusayan, and there's another station just outside the south entrance to the park near Moqui Lodge and one at Cameron.

✔ **Carry water,** especially in summer when your car — and you — are more prone to overheat.

✔ **Don't even think about trying to park at the popular spots** like the El Tovar Lodge. Alternatives include the lot in front of Babbitt's General Store near Yavapai Lodge (you enjoy a scenic hike along the rim to the historic part of the village) and the Maswik Transportation parking lot, where you can pick up the Village Loop shuttle.

But don't worry: You don't have to remember any of this. The park service publication called *The Guide* (see "Fees & Information" in the following section) will tell you everything you need to know about routes and schedules.

See "Getting There" under "The North Rim (And More)," later in this chapter, for information on the **Transcanyon Shuttle** service.

By Taxi

Strange but true: You can cab it to the canyon. The **Fred Harvey Transportation Company** (☎ **520-638-2631**, ext. 6563) runs round-the-clock taxi service from Tusayan to Grand Canyon Village and nearby — $5 per person, with a $10 minimum.

Fees and Information

It costs $20 per vehicle to enter the park, $10 per person for bikers and walkers. If you plan to visit other national parks anyway and come in high season, I suggest you invest $50 (in advance) in a National Parks Pass. Not only does the pass get you and your family into all the National Parks for an entire year, but this way also means you can thumb your nose at the other cars as you breeze through the express lane for seasonal pass holders (sometimes the wait is as long as half an hour). To order a pass, call ☎ **888-GO-PARKS** from 7 a.m. to 8 p.m., Pacific Time, every day or go online to www.nationalparks.org. Either way, you pay an additional $3.95 for regular mail service (7 to 10 days), $11.95 if you need the pass to arrive within 5 days.

As soon as you pay your park fee, you are handed a copy of *The Guide,* which has maps of the park, transportation schedules, lists of daily programs, warnings about all the dire things that can happen to you if you go hiking unprepared . . . your basic Grand Canyon bible. If your *Guide* isn't coffee stained and half shredded by the end of the day, you aren't consulting it enough.

When you drive into the park, you see signs directing you to the Grand Canyon Village parking areas, where you can catch the continuously running shuttles to **Canyon View Information Plaza** (☎ 520-638-7888), the new (opened late October 2000) orientation center, located about 150 feet from Mather Point. You can bypass it if you feel sufficiently informed, but taking the C-VIP shuttle is now the only way you can see the Mather Point overlook. Shuttles operate daily from an hour before dawn to an hour after dusk; you can't drive to C-VIP on your own.

If you drive in from the east, you pass the **Desert View Contact Station;** it's staffed by volunteers and doesn't always keep regular hours in winter. Between the trading post, cafeteria, service station, and bookstore in the Desert View Complex, you should be able to find out whatever it is you need to know.

Where to Stay

Beauty doesn't always come easy (as any cosmetician can tell you): The closer you want to be to the canyon, the harder it is to get a room. But if you want to be able to gaze out at the canyon as soon as possible after you wake up, it's definitely worth the effort.

If you visit anytime from April through October and want to be sure to have a bed inside the national park, **don't wait until the last minute to book** (and don't make me yell at you again). The best rooms at the El Tovar and Bright Angel lodge sell out as much as a year in advance. You have a better chance of getting something in Tusayan, the tourist village just south of the park, on short notice, but don't push your luck.

However, if you don't mind living on the edge — or maybe I should say really want to — it's not absolutely impossible to luck out inside the park at the last minute. Emergency cancellations and no-shows (from 15 to 30 a day in summer) always happen. Either call the park's same-day lodging switchboard at ☎ **520-638-2631** in the morning, or go to the front desk of the hotel you're interested in around 2:00 or 3:00 in the afternoon; by then, hotels know who has decided to check out a day early. And if you tried well in advance and couldn't get the hotel you had your heart set on, try again a month before you want to come: Large groups are required to cancel 30 days in advance in order to get their deposits refunded, so a block of rooms could suddenly get freed up.

You must book all the accommodations inside Grand Canyon National Park through the official parks concessionaire, **Amfac Parks & Resorts,** 14001 E. Iliff, Suite 600, Aurora, CO 80014 (☎ **303-29-PARKS**; Fax: 303-297-3175; Internet: www.grandcanyonlodges.com). The lodges all cluster on the western portion of Grand Canyon Village. For locations, see the Grand Canyon Village map, in this chapter. Only MC and V are accepted for rooms (shops, restaurants, and tour desks within the hotels also take DISC and DC).

Rates listed under "Rack rates" apply year-round. Check the Amfac Web site for seasonal specials (recently this included 30 percent off on Maswik Lodge) and packages (such as a honeymooners' special at the El Tovar).

The Top Hotels Inside the Park

Bright Angel Lodge & Cabins

$–$$ On the rim

My top pick inside the park. Designed in 1935 by Mary Colter, who was responsible for several of the park's most striking buildings, Bright Angel is a beauty (even if you don't stay here, drop in to look at the geologic fireplace and the wooden thunderbird over it). It's also a bargain. You get a room in the main lodge with a private or shared bath (some of these have only a sink, while others have both sink and toilet but no shower) or an individual cabin; four have rim views (as you can imagine, these get snapped up very, very fast). Furnishings are rustic but not shabby, and they suit the piney setting. This hotel isn't exactly serene during the day — it has a wildly busy tour desk, a museum, a coffeeshop, a steakhouse, and a soda fountain — but you're not going to be hanging around your room much then, are you?

Rack rates: $46–$54 with shared bath, $63 with bath, $73–$121 cabins.

El Tovar Hotel

$$–$$$ On the rim

The public areas of this 1905 native stone-and-pine building, a cross between a hunting lodge and a Norwegian villa, are wonderful, and the fine dining room has the best food on the South Rim (see "The Top Restaurants" in this chapter). I've always been underwhelmed by the guest rooms, though: The standard rooms are small, and the Victorian furnishings, faithful to a historic era when people liked to keep nature safely at bay, seem fussy now. Although the lodge sits near the rim, very few rooms have canyon views and you face crowds every time you venture beyond the corridor. Still, this is *the* great historic South Rim lodge, so it may just be worth it to say you stayed here.

Rack rates: $116–$130, $174 deluxe, $199–$284 suites.

Maswik Lodge

$–$$ West end of the village

You're not going to get rim views here — Maswik is in the woods, about 10 minutes from the edge — but you'll get a good choice of rooms and price ranges. Many of the units in Maswik North, built in the 1960s but with fresh carpets and updated furniture, have balconies looking out on the ponderosa pine forest. Those rooms in the slightly older Maswik South are less expensive because they're smaller and, in general, viewless. Least expensive of all are the rustic 1940s cabins — the furnishings are basic and they're closest to the road and therefore noisier. Conveniences include a transportation center, a decent cafeteria, and a sports bar/lounge.

Rack rates: $63 cabins, $73 Maswik South, $118 Maswik North.

The Runner-Up Hotels Inside the Park

Thunderbird and Kachina Lodges

$$ On the rim   The newest (late 1960s) lodges in the park, they've been slated for demolition. For the time being, both have fairly nice-size rooms with large windows and modern conveniences. Shell out the extra $10 for a second-floor "canyon view" — you won't necessarily see the rim, but at least you won't look out on the parking lot. *$114 park side, $124 canyon side.*

Miles to Go before You Sleep . . .

When people complain that it's a hike to their rooms, they're usually talking about an extra-long walk from the parking lot. But to get to **Phantom Ranch,** you either have to trek 9 miles to the bottom of the Grand Canyon, raft down a river, or get a mule to carry you. Lodgings, in wood-and-uncut river stone cabins designed by Mary Colter (these are mostly reserved for mule riders), or in newer gender-separated hiker dorms, are booked as much as a year in advance.

One-night mule trips to Phantom Ranch (and back . . .), including three meals, run $325.94 per person, $583.79 for two people. Hiker cabins cost $68.08 for the first person, $11.17 for an additional person; dorm bunks run $22.87 per person. Meals need to be reserved, too: $15.25 breakfast, $7.94 box lunch, $17.62–$29.20 dinner (the price depends on the entree). Like all the other national park bookings, these reservations must be made through Amfac (see "Where to Stay on the South Rim," in this chapter). Incidently, Colter named the ranch for a phantom who, according to Havasupai legend, emerged from the underworld at this spot and definitely liked what he saw.

Yavapai Lodges

$$ East end of the village   These lodges are a mile from the historic canyon district, but plenty of parking, a tour desk, a cafeteria, and a gift shop — as well as proximity to the visitors center/Bank One/general store complex — compensate. There are no rim views, but rooms in Yavapai East, which are larger and more pleasant in general, sit amidst pines and junipers. *$88 Yavapai West; $102 Yavapai East.*

The Top Hotels Outside the Park

Best Western Grand Canyon Squire Inn

$$$ Tusayan

Okay, so maybe it doesn't have the cachet of the older park lodges, but, hey, it has a bowling alley — not to mention a video arcade, billiards, coffee shop, restaurant, lounge, beauty salon (with massage room and tanning bed), pool, hot tub, sauna, tennis courts, exercise room, gift shop, guest laundry . . . even a small cowboy museum. The spacious, contemporary Southwest-style rooms come equipped with coffeemakers, too. If you like creature comforts nice and close to nature, this is the place.

Hwy. 64. ☎ *800-622-6966 or 520-638-2631. Fax: 520-638-0162. E-mail:* bestwestern@ thecanyon.com. *Internet:* www.grandcanyonsquire.com. *Rack rates: $135–$150. Children under 12 stay free. AE, DC, DISC, MC, V.*

The Cameron Trading Post Motel

$$ Cameron

This motel complex isn't all that close to the Grand Canyon — or to anywhere else in the world, for that matter — but its isolated Little Colorado Canyon location is part of its considerable appeal. Other parts include a Native American fine arts gallery; the largest modern trading post in northern Arizona, with room after room brimming with crafts and western goods; a historic restaurant serving primo Navajo tacos; and rooms arranged among lovely terraced gardens (many of their furnishings were handcrafted by the staff). The only drawbacks: You can't have a beer (or any other booze) because you're on the Navajo reservation, and you run the risk of never making it to the Grand Canyon because you need "just five more minutes" in that trading post.

Hwy. 89, ¼ mile north past the junction with Hwy. 64. ☎ 800-338-7385, ext. 414 or 520-679-2213. Fax: 520-679-2350. Rack Rates: Nov–Feb $59–$69, Mar–Apr $69–$79, May–Oct $74–$84. AE, MC, V.

Grand Hotel

$$$ Tusayan

Old West trappings plus modern plumbing — what could be bad? Tusayan's newest hotel was designed to resemble the national park lodges, with a high-ceiling lobby, lots of Native American rugs, wrought-iron lamps, antler chandelier . . . you get the picture. Guest rooms have beamed ceilings and, in some cases, small balconies (though there's not much to see from them but the parking lot). The hotel serves good Southwestern food and nightly Western entertainment in a dining room/lounge done up like a traditional Navajo hogan; Native American story tellers and dancers often entertain, too. Other pluses: An indoor pool and spa.

Hwy. 64. ☎ 888-63-GRAND or 520-638-3333. Fax: 520-638-3131. E-mail: THEGRAND@gcanyon.com. Internet: www.gcanyon.com. Rack rates: May–Oct $138, Nov–Apr $110. Ages 18 and under stay free in parent's room. AE, MC, V.

Grand Canyon Quality Inn and Suites

$$ Tusayan

A skylit atrium with a dining room, an 18-foot spa, and a lounge lends an open, relaxed feel to these canyon-area digs. The pastel-shaded guest rooms are restful, too; all have coffeemakers, and suites also have microwaves and refrigerators. Daily breakfast, lunch, and dinner buffets fortify you for (or replenish you after) a hard day of sightseeing, as do the outdoor pool and hot tub.

Hwy. 64. ☎ 800-221-2222 or 520-638-2673. Fax: 520-638-9537. Rack rates: Jan–Mar, Oct 20–Dec $68; Apr–Oct 19 $118; suites $118/$168. AE, DC, DISC, MC, V.

The Runner-Up Hotels Outside the Park

The Anasazi Inn

$$ Grey Mountain   Although neither close enough to the activities of Flagstaff nor in a setting as remote or scenic as Cameron, this is a decent motel with a good Native American gift shop that's convenient to the Grand Canyon's eastern approach. *40 miles north of Flagstaff on Hwy. 89.* ☎ *800-678-2214 or 520-679-2214.*

Holiday Inn Express Hotel and Suites

$$$ Tusayan   In 2000, this place took over the adjacent Grand Canyon Suites, so now, in addition to its more generic rooms, it also has large, well-equipped (microwave, coffeemaker, refrigerator, VCRs) rooms with fun themes such as Route 66 or Wild Bill Hickok. A good family getaway — if only it had a pool. *Hwy. 64.* ☎ **888-473-2269** *or 520-638-0123. Fax: 520-638-2747. Internet:* www.grandcanyon.com/holiday.

Moqui Lodge

$$ Between Tusayan and Grand Canyon National Park   Although the lodge has motel-like rooms, many of which look out on a parking lot, the setting is quiet and woodsy. Riding stables, a tour desk, a free breakfast buffet, and a good Mexican/American restaurants are other pluses. *Hwy. 64 (just south of the entrance to the Grand Canyon). For reservations, contact Amfac,* ☎ **303-29-PARKS;** *fax: 303-297-3175; Internet:* www.grandcanyonlodges.com. *Open Apr–Oct only.*

Where to Dine

While the Grand Canyon isn't a complete void, food-wise, the park does not exactly have a glut of good restaurants. Still, you can expect good hearty fare at reasonable prices in both the Grand Canyon Village and Tusayan. See the Grand Canyon Village map, in this chapter, for the locations of those restaurants within the park.

The Top Restaurants

Arizona Steakhouse

$$$ Grand Canyon Village   Steakhouse/American

The crowds come as much for the Grand Canyon views as for the meat, although the open-kitchen preparations of prime rib, chicken, steaks, and the like are good (I can't always say the same for the service). Come a few minutes before the 5 p.m. opening to avoid a long wait and to be settled in for the sunset; the lines start forming around 5:30 and tables aren't really worth a long wait after dark.

In the Bright Angel Lodge. ☎ **520-638-2631.** *Reservations not accepted. Main courses: $12.75–$22. Open: Dinner nightly; closed Jan and Feb. AE, DC, DISC, MC, V.*

El Tovar Restaurant

$$$ **Grand Canyon Village** **Continental/Southwestern**

You'd want to eat here even if it didn't involve the possibility of staring out at the Grand Canyon from huge picture windows: The rustic-elegant room with a soaring ceiling is drop-dead impressive, the service is top notch, and the food is a knockout, too. Rather than just catering to the lowest culinary common denominator, the menu mixes familiar Continental dishes such as filet mignon in peppercorns with more adventurous Southwestern fare such as Idaho trout with creole crab stuffing and jalapeño lobster sauces (don't worry, the fish is flown in fresh almost every day).

In the El Tovar Hotel. ☎ *520-638-2631, ext. 6432. Reservations required at dinner, not accepted for breakfast or lunch. Main courses: $15.75–$25.25. Open: Daily breakfast, lunch, dinner. AE, DC, DISC,MC, V.*

Cameron Trading Post Dining Room

$–$$ **Cameron** **American/Navajo**

You don't know where to look in this historic trading post dining room: The ornate pressed-tin ceiling, the huge antique sideboard, the colorful Navajo rugs on the wall, the splendid sandstone-and-sky views from the window? The (eventual) arrival of your food should solve the problem. The American dishes are fine, but why not go local with the Navajo tacos (see Chapter 21); they're among the best, anywhere, and they're huge, so unless you're training for a sumo wresling match, I suggest you share.

Hwy. 89 just south of the junction with Hwy. 64. ☎ *520-679-2231. Reservations not accepted. Main courses: $6–$15. Open: Daily breakfast, lunch, and dinner. AE, DC, MC, V.*

The Runner-Up Restaurants

Among the casual restaurants inside the park, the **cafeteria at the Maswik Lodge** ($) stands out for its inexpensive, tasty Tex-Mex selections. Park service employees like the **deli at Babbitt's General Store** ($) for its big sandwiches and good specials. The food at the **Bright Angel Coffeehouse** ($–$$) is nothing to write home about, but the view, if you're lucky enough to snag a window table, is. All are open for breakfast, lunch, and dinner (an early one, in the case of Babbitt's deli). The Maswik and Bright Angel take major credit cards but no reservations; the deli accepts neither.

In Tusayan, chains such as McDonald's, Subway, Taco Bell, and Pizza Hut help maintain family harmony, but the best full-service — notice I didn't say slow-food — restaurants are the **Coronado Dining Room** ($$), in the Best Western Canyon Squire Inn; the **Canyon Star** ($$), at The Grand Hotel; and the **Moqui Lodge Dining Room** ($$) (see "Top Hotels outside the Park," earlier in this chapter, for all three). All focus on Southwestern and American fare; the menu at the first two leans slightly toward fancy (spinach may turn up in the enchiladas, pine nuts in the salad), while the Moqui Lodge sticks with tried-and-true, cheese-smothered Tex-Mex. Prices for dinner entrees fall into the moderate range; all accept major credit cards.

Ode to Erosion: Some Grand Canyon Stats

The erosive action of the Colorado River formed the Grand Canyon, which continues to be shaped by the river, along with rain runoff, and snow melt. One of the world's seven natural wonders, it racks up some pretty impressive numbers:

- ✔ Grand Canyon National Park covers more than a million acres (1,218,375.54, to be exact).

- ✔ The canyon is 277 miles long, as the Colorado River flows.

- ✔ The distance between the South Rim and the North Rim at Grand Canyon Village is 10 miles, as the crow (or other bird of your choice) flies.

- ✔ At its lowest point from the rim, the canyon dips 6,000 vertical feet, but it's by no means the deepest canyon in the world — deeper ones include the Copper Canyon in Mexico and Hell's Canyon in Idaho.

- ✔ The oldest rocks exposed at the bottom of the canyon are close to 2 billion years old — which is only about half as old as the oldest rocks in the world. The canyon itself is a mere babe, just 5 or 6 million years old.

Exploring the South Rim

You can hover over the canyon in a helicopter, run a rim-to-rim marathon — or go for something in between the two; you're the best judge of the touring style that suits you. In general, the approaches to the canyon in the "Overviews" section are designed for day-trippers; many of the "Active Views" require a much greater time commitment.

No matter what you do, don't be surprised if you feel headachy and sluggish your first day in the Grand Canyon, especially if you don't spend any time beforehand in Flagstaff or Williams. Adjusting to the altitude (7,000 feet) takes a while.

One final thing before we take the plunge (as it were): The park rangers always have activities organized, even in winter — everything from geology talks to guided nature walks and grab bag question-and-answer sessions. Check *The Guide's* schedule of programs as soon as you get a copy so you don't find yourself leafing through it in late afternoon and muttering, "Darn, that sounded good. . . ."

Overviews: Driving around the Canyon

Rim drives are a great way to take in some of the canyon's best views. I highlight the two most popular drives — along the West and East Rims.

A (Forgettable) Kodak Moment

In 1937, Harold Anthony of the American Museum of Natural History decided to boldly go where he thought no man had ever gone before: to Shiva Temple, which he believed was completely isolated from the rest of the canyon. Rather than the independently evolved animal species he and his expedition expected to find there, however, they discovered only an empty Kodak film box.

Of the two paved drives that radiate to the rim from Grand Canyon Village, the **West Rim** is the shorter and, off-season, the more popular — so much so that it's closed to private cars from March to mid-October. During those months, you have to board a free shuttle (see "Getting Around," near the beginning of this section) to tour it. In summer, when people can drive to the **East Rim,** they do — which means you may have to wait to park your car at the various lookout points.

The **West Rim Drive** stands out for its overlooks of the Colorado River, while the **East Rim Drive** has wonderful central and eastern canyon vistas. But — I promise — neither has bad views. If you must choose between the two, go for the least crowded: Drive the West Rim in high season and the East Rim the rest of the year.

On the other hand, you may have enough time to drive one rim first and spend some time in Grand Canyon Village before driving the second rim. The break in between allows you to see the canyon in different lights and, I hope, prevents your eyes from glazing over from scenery overload.

✔ **Driving the West Rim:** Signs in Grand Canyon Village direct you to this 8-mile drive, first laid out in 1912, when horse-drawn buggies still outnumbered automobiles. The first stop is **Trailview I and II,** which looks down on the Bright Angel and Plateau Point hiking trails, and, in a lush cottonwood grove, Indian Gardens campground. The soaring San Francisco Peaks lie to the south, and if you gaze in you-know-which direction, you can also glimpse the North Rim. Look out from **Maricopa Point** to spot the remains of the 1893 Orphan Mine, which yielded a high grade of copper and, later, uranium — neither of which turned out to be very easy to transport, though the mine stayed open until 1966. The **Powell Memorial** pays tribute to one-armed Civil War veteran John Wesley Powell, who, in 1869, set out to document the then-uncharted canyons and creeks of the Colorado River (which, ironically, you can't see all that well from here). You can, however, get a good look at it from **Hopi Point,** where you can also stare out at exotically named formations such as the Tower of Ra and Osiris, Isis, and Shiva temples.

During a lull in the whirring of the videocams at **Mohave Point,** you may be able to hear the rushing waters of the Hermit Rapids; you can also see the Granite and Salt Creek rapids from here, along with the 5,401-foot-high Cheops Pyramid. While the other overlooks have you concentrating on the panoramic vistas, **The Abyss** lives up to its name by demonstrating the sheer sheerness of the cliffs — specifically, the Great Mohave Wall, which drops 3,000 feet (definitely a handrail gripper). At **Pima Point** you can see the remains of Hermit Camp, a tourist complex built by the Santa Fe Railway in 1911. It got its supplies via aerial tramway — which was also once used to ship a Ford to the bottom of the canyon (don't ask). The drive ends at **Hermits Rest,** named for Louis Boucher, a French-Canadian prospector who wasn't nearly as reclusive as his nickname suggests. Views of Hermit Rapids and the Supai and Redwall cliffs compete for your attention with a striking log-and-stone structure designed by Mary Colter: It sells souvenirs and snacks — and has the drive's only restrooms.

A leisurely round-trip drive of the West Rim, with a rest stop at Hermits, should take no more than an hour — unless you plan to set up a tripod at each stop.

The West Rim drive does not exit the park; you have to retrace your route. Because access to the overlooks is easy from both sides of the road, save half the stops for your return trip.

✔ **Driving the East Rim:** Most of this 23-mile drive is open to cars year-round except its first stop (if you're departing from Grand Canyon Village) **Yaki Point,** which is closed to traffic from April through September. If you want to see the Point during this time, you need to take a shuttle, which many hikers do in order to pick up the South Kaibab Trail, one of the three routes to the Inner Gorge. Wotan's Throne, an imposing flat-topped butte, is the lookout's most distinctive landmark. Large stands of oak, juniper, and ponderosa and piñon pine flourish at **Grandview Point,** which sits at a higher elevation than most of the East Rim. From here you can see Horseshoe Mesa, where, in the 1890s, the Last Chance Copper Mine and the Grand View Hotel both thrived. Painter Thomas Moran was especially fond of the light from **Moran Point,** which was named after him because his illustrations of the journals of John Wesley Powell helped convince Congress to establish the Grand Canyon as a national park. The free **Tusayan Museum,** built in 1932, explains the significance of the remains of the small pueblo nearby — one of 2,000 prehistoric Native American sites in the park. Take the time to walk around here for a bit; it's a nice, educational break from the old drive-stop-stare routine.

And the Sundown Winner Is. . . .

Because it juts out into the canyon, Hopi Point gets my vote as the best spot on the West Rim drive to watch the sun set. On the East Rim, it's Lipan Point, with views that extend all the way west. Check *The Guide* for the right time to arrive.

Rock Stars

The tilted stratum of bright red, black, and white rocks at Lipan Point is part of a sedimentary rock sequence called the **Grand Canyon Supergroup**; it goes back about a billion years (even longer than the Rolling Stones). And talk about your rebels: the supergroup's relation to the straighter sandstone layer that hangs over it is called the Great Unconformity.

From the canyon's widest vista, **Lipan Point,** you get a fix on both geologic and human history. Views include colored strata of sedimentary rock and the Unkar Delta, farmed by the ancestral Puebloan peoples (often called Anasazi) around 800 years ago.

Spanish conquistadors tried to get down to the Colorado River from **Navajo Point** in 1540 but couldn't manage it (then again, they couldn't find the seven gold cities that originally brought them to the area, either). The last, and arguably most dramatic vista of both drives, is **Desert View.** Pay a quarter to climb the 70-foot-high Watchtower and you see the Painted Desert, San Francisco Peaks, Marble Canyon, and the Colorado River spread out before you. But don't worry if you don't want to climb the tower: You're at the highest point of the South Rim, 7,522 feet, so the views from the ground are nothing to sneeze at, either. The first stop when you enter from the east, the Desert View complex includes an information center, cafeteria, and a (not open in winter) gas station. Top-quality Native American paintings and crafts are sold in the rough-hewn Desert View building, shaped like a sacred ceremonial chamber. Mary Colter (see the "Canyon History" sidebar, in this chapter) designed both Desert View and the Watchtower.

Most people drive the East Rim one way, either on the way into or out of the park. Assuming that you make half-hour stops at both the Tusayan Museum and at Desert View, it should take you at least 1¾ hours one way, 2½ hours if you retrace the path (you can't drive quickly on these roads, both because of speed limits and a need to watch out for canyon-dazed drivers).

Guided Views: Bus and Jeep Tours

If you'd rather let someone else take the wheel, consider a **Fred Harvey Transportation Co.** (☎ **520-638-2631**) bus tour, departing mornings and afternoons (schedules depend on the season) from the Bright Angel, Maswik, and Yavapai lodges — which is also where the transportation desks for booking them are located. Rates are $14.50 per person for a West Rim tour (2 hours); $26.50 for an East Rim tour (4 hours); and $31.50 for a combination of the two. Children under age 16 are half-price.

Less herdlike, more off-road, and (weather permitting) more open air — as well as more expensive — the **Grand Canyon Outback Jeep Tours** (☎ **800-320-JEEP** or 520-638-JEEP; Internet: www.grandcanyonjeeptours.com) possibilities include a 2-hour Canyon Pines Tour ($48 adult, $35 ages 12 and under) through the Kaibab National Forest to the rim via an 1880s stage coach trail; the Grand Sunset Tour (3 hours; $53 adults, $40 child), another forest-rim combo; and the 1½-hour Indian Cave Paintings Tour ($30 adult, $25 child), which never leaves the trees, but gives you a close-up view of ancient art. You can mix and match these tours, too.

Bird's-Eye Views: Flying over the Canyon

Your comfort level with small planes and helicopters — not to mention with spending lots of cash in a flash — will determine whether an air tour is for you. Plane crashes have occurred in the years since flights over the canyon started, but the overall safety records are good. Helicopters are twice as expensive as small planes, but the relative smoothness and stability of the flights may make it worth the extra cost for you. All flights depart from the Grand Canyon Airport in Tusayan.

Virtual Views: The Canyon without Parking Problems

I've heard rumors that people watch the IMAX film *Grand Canyon — The Hidden Secrets* at Tusayan's **National Geographic Theater** (☎ **520-638-2203**) and never bother going to the national park. That would be very, very bad (me — judgmental?), but the six-story-high surround-sound film is a good adjunct to the genuine item if you want simulated adventure (the ride on the rapids feels stomach-churningly real). Hour-long shows start on the half hour 365 days a year (Mar–Oct 8:30 a.m.–8:30 p.m., Nov–Feb 10:30 a.m.–6:30 p.m.); tickets cost $8.50 adults, $6.50 ages 3 to 11.

Canyon History

Sure, you come to bond with nature, but you can only gaze into the middle distance for so long. The **Grand Canyon Village Historical District**, with its wonderful architecture from the classic High Tourist era — otherwise known as the first three decades of the 1900s — is definitely worth a wander-through. Pick up a self-guided tour brochure at the visitors center to learn about the nine artfully rustic structures: Hotels, curio shops, photography studios, and the 1909 railway depot, which is back in use. Verkamps Curios, opened in 1898 as the Grand Canyon's first tchotchke shop, still looks pretty much as it did in 1905, and the Kolb studio, built between 1904 and 1926, was the domain of two brothers who captured early shots of the mule passengers.

Hopi House, Bright Angel Lodge, and Lookout Studio are prime examples of the work of Mary Colter, who was also responsible for Hermits Rest, Desert View, and Watchtower. Her designs, which mesh beautifully with the landscape, were ahead of their time — as was the very fact that Colter was a designing woman: Females were not issued architect's licenses in those days, so Colter didn't have one.

Whirlybird or Puddle-Jumper? Photo-Op Pros and Cons

Helicopters fly 500 feet lower than small planes and have large bubble windows all around, which means excellent visibility for photographers. Helicopter hovering — as opposed to plane banking and dipping — provides better shots, too. BUT not everyone in a helicopter is guaranteed a window seat as are passengers on small planes (which have windows designed to minimize glare). Ultimately, if you're not shy about leaning over someone should you be seated in the middle, the helicopter will probably allow you to take your best shot.

Air Grand Canyon (☎ 800-247-4726 or 520-638-2686; Internet: www. airgrandcanyon.com), **Grand Canyon Airlines** (☎ 800-528-2413 or 520-638-2407; Internet: www.thecanyon.com/gcair), and Sky Eye Air Tours (☎ 888-2-SKYEYE or 520-638-6454; E-mail: skyeyeair@hotmail.com, www.airstar.com) all offer comparably priced small plane tours at about $89 ($49 for children under 12) for a 50- to 60-minute flight, including the airspace fee.

Tours with **Kenai Grand Canyon Helicopters** (☎ 800-541-4537 or 520-638-2764; Internet: www.flykenai.com), **AirStar Helicopters** (☎ 800-962-3869 or 520-638-2622; Internet: www.airstar.com), and **Papillon Grand Canyon Helicopters** (☎ 800-528-2418 or 520-638-2419; Internet: papillon.com) run from around $95 for a 25- to 30-minute flight to $165 for a 40- to 45-minute flight; not all offer lower children's rates.

Active Views: Getting Down in the Canyon

Not content with admiring the canyon at a distance? Those who prefer the up-close-and-personal approach have a few options, from hiking to riding to rafting.

✔ **Hiking:** You don't necessarily have to spend the night in the canyon in order to appreciate it (though some people may disagree with me); if you're in good shape, though, I urge you to at least attempt a short trek below the rim, both to escape the crowds and to get up close and personal with some of the fauna and flora (don't worry, unless you're near the bottom, it won't be cactus).

If you want to sleep down deep, contact the **Backcountry Reservations Office,** Grand Canyon National Park, P.O. Box 129, Grand Canyon, AZ 86023 (☎ **520-638-7875 or 638-7888** [call between 1–5 p.m.]; Fax: 520-638-2125; Internet: www.thecanyon.com/nps), to request an overnight permit ($20, plus $4 per person per night), required for all except those booked at Phantom Ranch. Again, don't wait until the last minute — there are a limited amount of permits and eager backpackers typically snap them up 4 months in advance. If you arrive without a permit, but want to take a shot at getting one, head over to the Backcountry Information Center (open Mon–Fri 8 a.m.–noon and 1–5 p.m.), located at the Maswik Transportation Center, and sign on to the daily waiting list.

Some Hiking Tips

Remember, what goes down must come up: And that means *you*. For every hour you hike downhill, allow 2 hours for the return.

Wear comfortable shoes with good traction: Hiking boots are best, but rough-soled sneakers or walking shoes are okay too.

Always carry enough food and drink: In summer two quarts of electrolyte replacement fluid is minimum, and one gallon is recommended for every 8 hours of hiking. Munch on nutritious, high carb, salty snacks every 20 to 30 minutes.

Layer your clothing: It gets hotter the farther down you go; be prepared for rain and snow in winter.

Look at your copy of *The Guide* before you attempt a hike: The 4-H list of hiking hazards (heat stroke, heat exhaustion, hyponatremia [water intoxication], and hypothermia) may send you running to the IMAX theater for a virtual descent instead.

- **Easy hikes:** A level 10-mile-long trail runs along the edge of the canyon from the **Yavapai Observation Station** (northeast of Grand Canyon Village) west to Hermits Rest; beyond Maricopa Point, however, it's unpaved and can veer a bit close to the edge. If you want to plan your walk, check *The Guide* for the distances between the various lookout points. The short and mostly flat rim trek around the historic buildings of Grand Canyon Village is also fun; see the "Canyon History" sidebar, in this chapter, for more details. The C-VIP visitors center can give you information about other short hikes.

- **Hard hikes:** Originally a bighorn sheep path and later used by the Havasupai Indians, **Bright Angel Trail** is the most popular route into the canyon. Almost 8 miles long, it descends 4,460 feet from the trailhead near Grand Canyon Village to the river at Phantom Ranch. From May through September, there's drinking water at 1.5 miles (Indian Gardens) and 3 miles (Plateau Point) — good goals for a 3- and 6-mile hike, respectively. The 4.5-mile point always has water. The 9-mile-long **Hermit Trail** begins beyond Hermits Rest and drops more than 5,000 feet to Hermit Creek. It's steep, non-maintained, and waterless; don't try it unless you're a serious hiker (it's 5 miles round-trip to Santa Maria Spring, 6 miles round-trip to Dripping Springs). Also strenuous but rewarding for its terrific views is the **South Kaibab Trail,** which you can pick up at Yaki Point; it's a 7-mile trek from the trailhead to the Colorado River (where the trail crosses a suspension bridge and runs on to Phantom Ranch). The 4½-mile round trip to Cedar Ridge, where there are portable toilets but no water, is a good goal for a hard day's hike.

Remember, the only way to get to Yaki Point in high season is by shuttle; if you miss it, however, you can call the Fred Harvey taxi service (see "Getting Around," near the beginning of this section) to come and retrieve you; there's a pay phone at the South Kaibab trailhead (even if you have a cell phone, a signal is difficult to get here).

✔ **Mule rides:** For many, visiting the Grand Canyon without riding a mule would be like visiting Yellowstone without seeing Old Faithful (of course, for others, riding a mule into the canyon would be like sitting and getting soaked in Old Faithful for 6 hours). If you think you're in the former category, plan ahead; for some summer dates, rides get booked up as much as a year in advance.

Your choices include a 7-hour (round-trip) ride to Plateau Point, with lunch at Indian Gardens ($100.75 per person); a 5½-mile ride down to Phantom Ranch (see the "Miles to Go before You Sleep . . ." sidebar in this chapter), with a 4½-mile return the next day ($278.70 one person, $495.40 two people); and (winter only) the ride down and back, plus two nights in Phantom Ranch ($385.95 one person, $647.90 two people). For advance reservations, contact **Grand Canyon National Lodges** (☎ **303-39-PARKS;** Fax 303-297-3175; Internet: www.grandcanyonlodges.com). If you didn't book but decide to give it a last minute shot — occasionally folks don't show up — call **520-638-2631** or stop by the Bright Angel Transportation desk to put your name on a waiting list for the next day's ride.

If you want to do some mule riding, be aware that you aren't allowed to ride if you

- Weigh more than 200 pounds

- Are less than 4'7" tall

- Are pregnant

- Don't speak English

- Are rude to the tour operators (just checking to see if you're paying attention, though who knows?)

And, you shouldn't ride if you

- Are afraid of heights

- Are afraid of large animals (the mule is the love child of a female horse and a male donkey, and it's often bigger than a horse; don't confuse it with the smaller burro)

- Have heart or respiratory problems

- Don't think you can sit in a saddle for at least 6 hours, or go 2½ hours without a bathroom break

The Canyon for Kids

If your kids can't relate to nature that's not on a screen, don't worry — they get into it soon enough (just give that mouse hand a little time to stop twitching). Some quick ways to get the Internet set on line with the canyon include the following:

✔ **Have them take part in the Junior Ranger program.** This program gears its activities to everything from finding animal tracks to recycling aluminum cans. The program is available to three age groups —4–7, 8–10, and 11–14. Kids who successfully complete five steps get a Junior Ranger Patch ($1.50 to offset the price of the program). Ask at the visitors center for details.

✔ **Buy them a disposable camera.** Beware: You may create a photography monster.

✔ **Take them to watch the mules set off in the morning.** The mules begin their journeys (8 a.m. in summer, 9 a.m. in winter) from the corral just west of Bright Angel Lodge (and yes, let them tell ca-ca jokes).

✔ **Bring them to one of the kid-oriented ranger talks and walks.** These activities are offered daily in summer, less frequently off-season; check *The Guide* for meeting times.

✔ **Put them on horseback.** The Apache Stable at the Moqui Lodge has gentle animals that are used to kiddie ways.

✔ **Take them to the IMAX.** Hey, if you can't beat 'em (and you really shouldn't), join 'em.

✔ **Horseback rides:** Less stressful and less expensive than the mule rides, rides run by **Apache Stables,** Moqui Lodge, Hwy. 64 (just before the south entrance to the park; ☎ 520-638-2891; Internet: www.apachestables.com), don't dip into the canyon; most, in fact, don't even enter the national park. You trot around Kaibab National Forest during the 1-hour ($30.50), 2-hour ($55.50), and campfire ($40.50 by trail, $12.50 in a wagon) rides; only the 4-hour ride ($95.50) gets you a (rather brief) glimpse of the rim. The stables are usually open from March to early December, but sometimes close earlier or open later, depending on the weather. Both mules and horses are used, so when you get home you can say you rode a mule at the canyon, which is essentially true, if you don't get hung up on phrases like "down into" as opposed to "around."

✔ **River rafting:** The options for getting wet 'n' wild on the Colorado River are almost as dizzying as the rapids you're bound to encounter: You can do everything from paddling your own canoe to zipping along on a motorized raft on trips ranging from 3 days to almost 3 weeks. You may be happy to learn that not every Joe Schmo with an air pump can run river trips into the Grand Canyon; the National Park Service only authorizes outfitters with good credentials. You can get the most current listings by writing ahead for the *Trip Planner* (see "Quick Concierge: Grand Canyon's South Rim," in this chapter) or by clicking on "River Trips," then "Commercial," then "Concessionaires" at www.thecanyon/nps.

Most of the outfitters run trips from April to October and most depart from Lees Ferry near Page, although some start or finish at Phantom Ranch. Expect to pay anywhere from around $650 (including meals and tent) for a 3-day trip to approximately $3,000 for 16 days on the water. Book as far in advance as possible; those rafts fill up fast and not too many people bail once they sign on.

Don't do white water? See Chapter 18 for smooth water trips from Glen Canyon Dam in Page to Lees Ferry. If, on the other hand, you want to do it all on your own, contact the **River Permits Office,** Grand Canyon National Park, P.O. Box 129, Grand Canyon, AZ 86023 (☎ **800-959-9164** or 520-638-7843, Fax 520-638-7844) or go to the "Noncommercial" portion of the "River Trips" section of www.thecanyon/nps.

Quick Concierge: Grand Canyon's South Rim

Area Code: The area code for this entire region is **520.**

ATM: The only ATM at the South Rim is at the Bank One in Grand Canyon Village (in the post office complex near Yavapai Lodge).

Classes: If you think the Grand Canyon may be a cool place to go to school, check out the classes given by the Grand Canyon Field Institute, P.O. Box 399, Grand Canyon, AZ 86023 (☎ 520-638-2485; Fax 520-638-2484; Internet: www.grandcanyon.org/ fieldinstitute), from March through November. Possibilities range from intro to backpacking to mother-daughter rim-to-rim hiking trips (a Mother's Day special), and from sketching classes to hands-on archaeology digs. Prices in 2000 started at $75 for an introductory day hike, going up to $995 for a 3-day llama trek to Lake Powell's Rainbow bridge.

Dentist: There's a dentist available by appointment only; call ☎ 520-638-2395.

Emergency: Call ☎ **911** for fire, police, and ambulance; ☎ 638-2477 is an additional in-park emergency number.

Fees: $20 per vehicle to enter the park, $10 per person to enter by foot or bicycle. Passes are good for 7 days, and can be used at both rims. Sorry, no rain (or snow) checks.

Hospitals/Clinics: Grand Canyon Clinic, Grand Canyon Village (☎ 520-638-2551 or 520-638-2469) is open weekdays 8 a.m.– 5:30 p.m., Sat 9 a.m.–noon, with after-hours care and 24-hour emergency service.

Information: Before you go, call Grand Canyon National Park at ☎ 520-638-7888 to order a copy of the free *Trip Planner,* which includes camping, hiking, and activity details, plus plenty of general advice. Get the same information electronically by logging on to the National Park Service Web site, www.thecanyon.com/nps. The commercially sponsored www. AmericanParkNetwork.com is another useful pre-trip site, and you can pick up its affiliated publication, *Grand Canyon Magazine,* gratis, when you get near the park. See "Fees & Information" in this chapter, for places to obtain information within the park.

Lost and Found: Check in person at the visitors center or the Yavapai observation center or phone ☎ 520-638-7798 Tue–Fri 8 a.m.–5 p.m. For items lost or found at a hotel, restaurant, or lounge, ☎ 520-638-2631, ext. 6503.

Pharmacies: The Grand Canyon Clinic Pharmacy, in Grand Canyon Village (☎ 520-638-2460); is open Mon–Fri 8:30 a.m.–5:30 p.m., Sat 9 a.m.–noon.

Post Office: Near the Yavapai Lodge, in the shopping center between Babbitt's general store and the bank. Open Mon–Fri 9 a.m.–4:30 p.m., Sat 11 a.m.–1 p.m. Access to stamp machines 5 a.m.–10 p.m.

Road Conditions and Weather: Call ☎ 520-638-7888 (on the automated system, press selection 3, then selection 1 [for road conditions] or selection 2 [for weather]).

Safety: The safety concerns in the Grand Canyon are less linked to crime than to people ignoring the fact that they're in nature, not Disneyland. Most problems are heat related: In 1999 about a third of the park's 325 search-and-rescues were a result of dehydration (see the "Some Hiking Tips" sidebar, in this chapter). And, although it may seem like a no-brainer not to lean too far over the guardrail to ogle the scenery, people have done just that and toppled in (10 of them in 1993 — a banner year for stupidity). Finally, while theft may not be a major problem, don't put your expensive camera down and walk away or amble around with your purse open. In short, don't leave your common sense at home.

The North Rim (And More)

Let me hit you with a few statistics. The North Rim of the Grand Canyon gets only about one-tenth of the visitors of the South Rim. That doesn't mean you find yourself entirely alone up here — we're talking one-tenth of five million and it's estimated that each year, 5 percent more visitors descend on this side of the great northern Arizona divide than the year before (I'll let you do the math; it was never my best subject). But if you want to see the Grand Canyon, this is definitely the place to come.

The crowd control exists for one simple reason — the North Rim is harder to reach than the South Rim. Fewer services and hotel rooms are available once you arrive, so plan ahead. But the views are as good as those at the South Rim, so if you prefer bonding with nature to bonding with (or bouncing off) your fellow *homo sapiens,* the effort is worth it, no question.

You won't find a whole lot to do in the remote, starkly beautiful region that you drive through en route to the North Rim, nor in the Arizona Strip, the even more remote area to the west of the canyon. However, there are a few worthwhile stops to tell you about.

Plan to linger a bit in this area — a minimum of two nights to make it worth the trip. If your pulse gets rapid at the idea of river rafting or if you're hooked on fishing, spend some more time at Lees Ferry, the departure point for the Colorado River adventures.

Northern Exposure: Getting to Know a Little about the "Other" Rim

Some things are worth going out of your way for — among them, the Grand Canyon's North Rim. Just so you know what you're getting (or at least looking) into:

✔ At about 8,000 feet, the North Rim is approximately 1,000 feet higher than the South Rim.

✔ The North Rim receives about 27 inches of rain or snow annually, compared to 15 inches for the South Rim.

✔ It took Europeans 236 years longer to find the North Rim than it took them to find the South Rim: 1776 versus 1540.

✔ The land that the North Rim sits on was hotly contested by Utah and Arizona. A journalist named Sharlot Hall helped convince Arizonans to go to bat for the abyss.

 There are no ATMs or pharmacies on the North Rim. Credit cards are accepted at most of the facilities in the park, but it's always good to have a little of the green stuff, so come prepared with cash and a full supply of any medications you may need.

Also, the North Rim is only open for overnight stays from mid-May to mid- or late October (day use continues through November — or until the first heavy snow).

Getting There

Except for the shuttle from the South Rim — more on this in a minute — the North Rim does not have public transportation.

By Car

It's 210 miles from Flagstaff to the North Rim: Take Hwy. 89 north to Bitter Springs, then Hwy. 89A to the junction of Hwy. 67 at Jacob Lake; take Hwy. 67 south to the North Rim. It's a spectacular drive.

Flying into Page (see Chapter 18) is an even better option if you can afford the airfare: A scenic 25-mile drive south on Hwy. 89 will get you to Bitter Springs/Hwy. 89A, hooking you up with the Flagstaff route sketched above.

You can also get here from Las Vegas via I-15 north to Hwy. 9 west, and Hwy. 67 south — a total of 263 miles.

By Shuttle

From mid-May to October, the **Transcanyon Shuttle** (☎ 520-638-2820) makes one round trip a day between the North and South Rim. Vans depart the North Rim's Grand Canyon Lodge (or the campground or a trailhead if you put in a special request) at 7 a.m., arriving at the South Rim's Bright Angel Lodge at noon; the return shuttle leaves at 1:30 p.m., reaching the North Rim at 6 p.m. The one-way fare is $60 per person; round-trips cost $100. Reservations required.

Getting Around

You mostly have to rely on your own wheels to get around the park. The exception is the hiker shuttle to the North Kaibab trailhead, which leaves from the front of the Grand Canyon Lodge every day at 5:30 a.m. and 7:45 a.m. Tickets have to be purchased in advance from the lodge's front desk; it's $5 for the first person, $2 for each additional one.

Where to Stay

You're not exactly spoiled by choices when it comes to rooming near the North Rim. Only one place is available in the park itself; two more lodging options are within a 30-mile radius; and an additional three are near Lees Ferry — all of which are detailed below. Rooms in this area are modest, but that goes for the prices, too. And, these places, especially the ones in Lees Ferry, tend to generate an outpost-style camaraderie; don't be surprised if you make new friends here.

The Top Hotels

Grand Canyon Lodge

$–$$ At the North Rim

It's the only game in the national park, but you'd want to play even if it weren't. Of the variety of lodging configurations available here, the western cabins are closest to the rim and most luxurious (the four that actually look into the canyon are usually booked two years in advance). The Pioneer and Frontier cabins, although the most rustic, are right near the Transept Trail. The motel rooms are standard issue and the farthest from the lodge, but all have queen-size beds (the others have doubles and singles). But you won't spend much time in your room. You'll want to explore the canyon or hang around the historic log-and-limestone lodge, where a high-ceiling dining room serves surprisingly sophisticated food that (almost) competes with the rim views from its huge windows. The bar, cafeteria, gift shop, and transportation desk are the other prime congregating spots.

Reservations: Amfac Parks and Resorts, 14001 E. Iliff, Suite 600, Aurora, CO 80014. ☎ ***303-29-PARKS**. Fax 303-297-3175. Internet:* www.amfac.com. *Hotel switchboard:* ☎ ***520-638-2611**. Rack Rates: $74 Frontier Cabins, $82 motel rooms, $81 Pioneer Cabins, $95 western cabin. MC, V rooms (other facilities within the lodge also take AE, DC, and DISC). Closed mid-Oct–mid-May.*

Kaibab Lodge

$–$$ 5 miles north of the North Rim

A huge stone fireplace, sometimes lit in spring and early fall, makes a cheery gathering spot for guests at this homey 1926 lodge. Rooms in the (rather thin-walled) pine-paneled cabins are motel plain; the real draw is the setting, near the national park and the edge of the large DeMotte Park meadow. Other perks include a restaurant, bar (beer only), gift shop, hot tub, and mountain bike and hiking-equipment rentals.

Hwy. 67. ☎ *800-525-0924 (outside AZ) or 520-638-2389. Internet:* www. canyoneers.com. *Rack rates: $75–$95. DISC, MC, V. Mostly closed mid-Oct–mid-May (some services remain open).*

Jacob Lake Inn

$–$$ Jacob Lake

This is where the action — such as it is — is en route to the North Rim. Everyone heading for the national park stops here for groceries, gas, Native American crafts, or fresh baked cookies and milkshakes (hey, it's a long ride and you need fortification). Spend the night and either bunk in a shabby cabin with a private porch or in one of the nicer drive-up motel units. The complex sits on five acres of Kaibab Forest, but many of the rooms look out on a highway. If you want a good night's sleep, ask for a room behind the lodge.

At the junction of Hwys. 67 and 89A. ☎ *520-643-7232. Fax: 520-643-7898. Internet:* www.jacoblake.com. *Rack rates: May 15–Nov $69–$77 double in cabins, $85–$88 double in rooms; Dec–May 15 $42 cabins, $53–$55 rooms. AE, DISC, DC, MC, V.*

Cliff Dweller's Lodge

$ Lees Ferry/Marble Canyon

The rooms here are fine — the newer, blander, slightly pricier ones have bathtubs, the older ones have only showers but more character — but it's the Vermilion Cliff and Echo Cliff surroundings that make this a knocknout. Not surprisingly, most of the action takes place outside; you can book a hiking tour here in summer, or go next door to a river outfitter to plan a water adventure. If you don't feel like socializing with the river runners in the good bar and restaurant (see "Where to Dine on the North Rim," in this chapter), you can stock up on booze and snacks in the hotel's convenience store.

Hwy. 89A (9 mi west of Navajo Bridge). ☎ *800-433-2543 or 520-355-2228. Fax: 520-355-2229. Rack rates: Apr–Sept $60–$70, Oct–Mar $40–$45. DISC, MC, V.*

Lees Ferry Lodge

$ Lees Ferry/Marble Canyon

There's definitely something fishy about this place, where the Lees Ferry anglers tend to congregate, but the views of the Vermilion Cliffs from the garden patios are completely on the up and up (and up). Rooms in this

1929 native stone-and-wood building sit close to the road — no, 89A is not exactly the Santa Monica freeway — and their plumbing is erratic, but they have plenty of nice touches. See the Vermilion Cliffs Bar & Grill in "Where to Dine on the North Rim," in this chapter.

Hwy. 89A (3.5 mi west of Navajo Bridge). ☎ *520-355-2231. Fax: 520-355-2301. Rack rates: $50–$75. MC, V.*

Marble Canyon Lodge

$–$$ Lees Ferry/Marble Canyon

Zane Grey and Gary Cooper were among the many celebs who bedded down at this appealing hotel, opened the same day that the Navajo Bridge was dedicated in 1929. The newer units across the road are less interesting than those in the original lodge, which have brass beds and hardwood floors, but an apartment there sleeps up to eight. You can ease your Learjet down onto the landing strip, or just settle for gassing up your car. A restaurant, gift shop, and coin-op laundry are on the premises.

Half mile west of Navajo Bridge on AZ 89A. ☎ *800-726-1789 or 520-355-2225. Fax: 520-355-2227. Rack rates: $60–$125 for two. AE, DISC, MC, V.*

The Runner-Up Hotels

You come across a few low-key motels in Fredonia, Arizona, and Kanab, Utah (30 and 37 miles west of Jacob Lake, respectively), but they're a bit out of the way if you're not heading north. There are plenty more beds in Page (see Chapter 18), and nearby Lake Powell is a great destination, but doing a single-day round-trip to the park from there isn't very relaxing — and kicking back and smelling the pine cones is what the North Rim is all about.

Where to Dine

You pretty much eat where you sleep near the North Rim (I don't mean that literally, unless you take your munchies to bed; this is definitely *not* room service country). That's not generally a bad thing, though. This area is too remote for the fast food franchises, so most of the chow is of the hearty, home-cooked variety. The best — also the only — gourmet food in the area is at the **dining room of the Grand Canyon Lodge** ($$–$$$), where a Southwestern spin (chiles, blue corn) is sometimes put on otherwise classic American fare. You have to make a reservation to eat there; call as soon as you book a room. Among the low-key eateries in the area, the standouts are the **Canyon Dreamers Cafe** ($$) at the Cliff Dweller's Lodge, which makes its desserts and soups from scratch and brews a mean espresso; and the **Vermilion Cliffs Bar & Grill** ($$–$$$) at Lees Ferry Lodge, where there's a big selection of beer, your steak is cooked the way you order it, and the fish is fresh from the river.

Exploring

Without the glut of concessionaires that converge on the South Rim, exploring the chasm's northern reaches is a much more personal, and usually more tranquil, experience. No helicopters hovering here, or even tour operators to guide you; it's just you, your car, and a few road signs.

As soon as you drive up to the entry kiosks and pay your park fee — the fee is the same as on the South Rim — you are handed a North Rim version of *The Guide.* Use it early and often. The park rangers and Grand Canyon Association employees at the **North Rim Visitors Center,** near the Grand Canyon Lodge (☎ **520-638-2611**), should be able to answer any other questions you may have. It's open 8 a.m. to 6 p.m. daily, sometimes longer in summer.

Rim Drives

About 8 miles to the north of the Grand Canyon Lodge, the only road in the area forks off in two directions. Veer right (there's a sign to remind you) and drive another 3 miles to **Point Imperial** — it's the highest vista point on either rim at 8,803 feet. From here you can see the Painted Desert to the east, the Vermilion Cliffs to the north, Utah's Navajo Mountain to the northeast, and the Little Colorado River gorge to the southeast.

Turn left at the fork to reach **Cape Royal,** a total of 23 miles from the Grand Canyon Lodge. From the parking lot at the road's end, it's a short (.3 miles each way), piñon pine-lined walk to some of the most awe-inspiring vistas in the park. **Angel's Window,** a giant, erosion-formed hole, is carved into a rock outcropping along the rim. Peer through the opening below the formation to catch a slice of the lower canyon, including a ribbon-like Colorado River. (For a nice walk from here, see the Cliff Springs Trail under "Hikes," below.) En route, stop at the **Wallhalla Overlook** to see the remains of two ancestral Puebloan villages, and at **Roosevelt Point,** where you get an angle on the spot where Little Colorado River gorge and the Grand Canyon converge.

Hikes

The North Rim has fewer maintained hiking trails than the South Rim, but, then, you won't have to share them with as many other people. Check with the visitors center — see "Quick Concierge: Grand Canyon's North Rim," at the end of this chapter — for other suggestions. Before attempting the longer walks, see the "Some Hiking Tips" sidebar, in this chapter.

> ✔ **Easy hikes:** The most popular North Rim hike because it starts just behind the Grand Canyon Lodge (pick it up at the corner of the east patio), the ½ mile (round-trip) walk to **Bright Angel Point** is also one of the most breathtaking — literally. You stroll along a skinny peninsula that divides Roarings Springs and Transept canyons, with sheer drops just a few feet away on either side (don't worry if, like me, you get weak-kneed just thinking about that; there are metal railings to grab on to at the narrowest parts).

Bright Angel Point seems to deprive some shutterbugs of their common sense. Don't climb any dangerous ledges to try for your best shot — it could be your last.

Feel like a walk in the woods? The spot where you picked up the Bright Angel Point trail also marks the start of the 3-mile (round-trip) **Transept Trail.** It edges the rim for a bit before plunging into the ponderosa pine forest, winding past a small ancestral Puebloan ruin, and ending up at the North Rim Campground and General Store.

There are also signs of the canyon's earlier inhabitants — the ones who preceded *Homo hikus* — on the **Cliff Springs Trail,** the 1-mile (round-trip) path through a forested ravine that begins at Angel's Window Overlook: About ¼ mile from the trailhead are the remains of an ancient granary. Narrow and precipitous where it hugs the north side of the Cliff Springs Canyon (so if you're scared of heights, pass this one up), the trail winds beneath several limestone overhangs before reaching Cliff Springs (and no, you can't drink the water).

✔ **Hard(er) hikes:** The only maintained trail to the bottom of the canyon from the North Rim, the **North Kaibab Trail,** which hooks up with the South Kaibab Trail (see "Exploring the South Rim," earlier in this chapter), is 14.4 miles long each way and descends nearly 6,000 feet before it reaches the Colorado River. Unless you're on the Olympic hiking team (is there even such a thing? but you get what I mean), you won't be able to do it in a day, but hiking part of it is a great way to dip below the rim and see Roaring Springs and Bright Angel canyons, among other things.

It's just 1.5 miles round-trip to **Coconino Overlook,** a sandstone clearing in a thick forest of aspen, Douglas fir, and gambel oak, but there are lots of switchbacks along this stretch. **Supai Tunnel,** about 2 miles from the trailhead, is an ideal turnaround point if you're more ambitious but don't want to push it; there are water and rest rooms here. You'd better be in really good shape — almost Olympic hiking team material — and head out really early if you want to make it all the way to Roaring Springs, the water source for both rims, and back. The 9.4-mile (round-trip) hike can take up to 8 hours.

Snoozing down in the canyon requires a backcountry permit; see "Exploring the South Rim," earlier in this chapter, for details.

If you want to trek with experts, check out **Canyon Rim Adventures** (☎ **800-897-9633;** Internet: www.canyonrimadventures.com), the only National Park Service-sanctioned tour operator specializing in the North Rim. They bring camping equipment, food, Dutch oven, and, if desired, mountain bikes; you bring your enthusiasm and your checkbook (prices range from $595 per person for a 3-day adventure to $995 for 5 days around and beneath the rim).

Some Restrictions Apply

In addition to the age minimums for the North Rim mule riders (I think different ones probably apply to the mules), weight and language rules apply: You can't weigh more than 220 pounds if you want to go around the rim or more than 200 if you'd like to dip into the canyon, and you have to speak English (sorry, the mules aren't bilingual).

Mule Rides

They're not as famous as their South Rim siblings — partly because of the area's lower profile, partly because they don't go the distance (to the bottom) — but the mules at the North Rim give the folks who hire them a good run (or at least trot) for their money. And the menu of options at **Grand Canyon Trail Rides,** at the Grand Canyon Lodge (☎ **435-679-8665,** ext. 222 preseason; 520-638-9875 after May 15 and until the North Rim closes in late fall), is larger. Every day from May 15 until the North Rim closes, there are 1-hour rim rides (for ages 7 and older) for $15; half-day trips — one stays on the rim, the other goes down to Supai Tunnel on the North Kaibab Trail — for $40 (minimum age 8); and full-day trips (minimum age 12) down to Roaring Springs for $95, lunch included. These rides don't need to be booked as far in advance as those on the South Rim, but they're very popular. Call or go over to the transportation desk of the lodge as soon as you know when you want to ride.

Exploring the North Rim

The road to the North Rim may be less traveled but it's definitely not boring. The scenery is amazing, there are a few interesting landmarks, and you can get some angling in if you're so inclined. Also beautiful is the Arizona Strip country, northwest of the national park. This area is even more isolated, punctuated by two small towns (Fredonia and Colorado City), the Kaibab-Pauite reservation, and a national monument (the only place where there's really anything to do).

En Route to the North Rim

As you drive north from Flagstaff on Hwy. 89, you see the **Painted Desert,** windswept plains and mesas colored with every pastel in the spectrum, to the east. The sandstone **Echo Cliffs,** with a more limited palate (soft pink to burnt umber), start putting in an appearance about 30 miles beyond the Cameron Trading Post (see "Where to Stay at the South Rim" in this chapter). You can't miss them: some are more than 1,000 feet tall. But it gets even grander. Keep going west from Navajo Bridge rather than detouring to Lees Ferry and you encounter the bright **Vermilion Cliffs,** topping off at more than 3,000 feet and with boulders surreally balanced on eroded columns of soil. Don't be surprised if you see a California condor around here; several pairs of the endangered birds were released in this area from 1996 through 1997 — no doubt because they look just mahr-velous swooping against those cliffs (and, okay, because they used to live here in prehistoric times; you can check out their progress online at www.peregrinefund.org). Stop at the **San Bartolome Historic Site** overlook to read about the 1776 Domínguez-Escalante expedition through this area or just to look at the scenery standing still (you, not the scenery). Once you are on the road again, you should begin to see forest rather than desert; you know you're climbing the **Kaibab Plateau,** more than 9,000 feet at its highest point.

Other high (and low) points of this region include

✔ **Spanning the canyon:** Listed on the National Register of Historic Places, the 834-foot-long steel Navajo Bridge, built in 1929, was the first — and until the bridge at Glen Canyon Dam was built in 1959, the only — way to get across the Grand Canyon; no other bridge before it crossed the Colorado River for the 600 miles from Moab, Utah, to the Hoover Dam. You can learn all about it at the Native American-staffed **Navajo Bridge Interpretive Center (☎ 520-355-2319),** opened in 1997. Keep an eye out for the building on your right, just beyond the new bridge (that's the one you drive across; the old one is pedestrian-only now). The building is hard to see because the native sandstone structure blends in beautifully with the Vermilion Cliffs backdrop. Pick up topographic maps, postcards, and books about the Grand Canyon, Lake Powell, Lees Ferry, and other area attractions here (free; open May 15–Oct 15 daily 8 a.m.–5 p.m.). Outside, vendors usually sell Native American jewelry.

✔ **Trouting around:** On a sharp bend in the Colorado River where the Echo Cliffs break — look for the turnoff just beyond Navajo Bridge on Hwy. 89A — **Lees Ferry** was long known as the river crossing for Mormon pioneers. Now it's famed for being mile zero — the coordinate from which all distances on the river system are measured. Straddling Glen Canyon upstream and Marble Canyon (the beginning of the Grand Canyon) downstream, it's also the point of departure for most Grand Canyon river rafting trips. Serious trout-fishers also spend time here because trophy-sized specimens often take the bait. You can pick up fishing gear and a guide at **Lees Ferry Anglers,** Marble Canyon, 3 miles west of Navajo Bridge (☎ **800-962-9755** or 520-355-2261). Guided fishing trips, including lunch, start at $250 per day for one person, $300 for two people, and $400 for (the maximum) three people. *Note:* This is the only guide service in the area that practices year-round catch and release.

✔ **Oh, give me a home . . . :** Arizona's largest herd of American bison roam around the **House Rock Buffalo Ranch,** operated by the Arizona Department of Game and Fish's wildlife division (☎ **520-774-5045).** On Hwy. 89A, about 17 miles west of Marble Canyon, is the turnoff for the 23-mile dirt road that leads to the ranchhouse (which is private, and has no interpretive center or other public facilities). Don't be disappointed if you don't see any buffalo, though: The range is huge (58,000 acres) and the 90 shaggy ones don't always cooperate by coming within photo-op distance of your car (which can be a good thing: those babies are BIG but move fast and en masse). You're likely to see antelope, mule deer, and jackrabbits, though. *Note:* This drive is not a good idea if you don't have a high clearance or four-wheel drive vehicle, especially in the rain or snow.

The Original Love Boat

After ferry service was established at Lees Ferry (you knew there was a good reason for the name, didn't you?) in 1873, the landing became part of the Honeymoon Trail, followed by Mormon couples who had tied the knot in Arizona but wanted their union sanctified at the Temple of Latter-Day Saints in St. George, Utah.

West of the North Rim

If you don't turn south toward the North Rim at Jacob Lake junction — okay, so I'm being very hypothetical; why else would you drive all the way up here? — you head into the Arizona Strip, the 12,000-square-mile spread of northwest Arizona that has been dubbed the American Tibet, and not because there are any yaks here. You can see hundreds of miles in all directions on this lunar landscape, where lava outcroppings and cinder cones rise up among the more familiar (by now) red rock and sandstone cliffs. It's beautiful, but desolate; only some members of the Kaibub-Paiute tribe and a few Mormon families live out here. The area's sole two sightseeing possibilities:

- ✔ **Put some spring in your step: Pipe Spring National Monument,** 45 miles west of Jacob Lake on Hwy. 389, Fredonia (☎ **520-643-7105**), makes a good, if surreally midwestern-looking, break from all that surrounding desert. The site's natural spring is one of the area's few consistent water sources; the Mormons built a fortress here in 1871, but it soon became a dairy farm and Arizona territory's first telegraph station. Summer mornings feature living history exhibits. Open: Memorial Day through Labor Day 7:30 a.m.–5:30 p.m., 8 a.m.–5 p.m. the rest of the year. $2 per adult; ages 16 and under free.

- ✔ **Make rock reservations:** During the busy season, members of the Kaibab Paiute tribe, who have a small reservation in the Arizona Strip, offer easy, guided hikes to nearby petroglyph sites for $10 per person; in theory they're offered regularly on weekday mornings, by advance arrangement on the weekends. It's not always easy to reach the tribal office by phone (☎ **520-643-7245**), however; your best bet is to stop in at the office, which is on Hwy. 389, just before the turn off to Pipe Spring National Monument (see above).

Quick Concierge: Grand Canyon's North Rim

Area Code: The area code for this entire region is **520**.

Clinic: The North Rim Clinic, adjacent to the Grand Canyon Lodge complex, Cabin 5 (☎ 520-638-2611, ext. 222), open Wed–Mon 9–noon and 3–6 p.m., Tues 9 a.m.–noon and 2–5 p.m., is staffed by a nurse practitioner and physician's assistant. Park rangers are trained in emergency medical procedures.

Emergency: For an ambulance, to report a fire or to get the police call ☎ **911.**

Garage/Gas Station: The Chevron Service Station on the access road to the North Rim Campground (☎ 520-638-2611) sells gas and does minor auto repairs. The next nearest gas is 5 miles north of the park boundary, at the Country Store & Gas Station; you can also get tanked up at Jacob Lake.

Information: You can order the free Trip Planner, which includes general information, by calling Grand Canyon National Park at ☎ 520-638-7888; the planner is also available electronically at the National Park Service Web site, www.thecanyon.com/nps. The North Rim Visitors Center, near the Grand Canyon Lodge (☎ 520-638-2611), is open 8 a.m. to 6 p.m. daily, sometimes longer in summer. The Kaibab Plateau Visitors Center at Jacob Lake, 30 miles north of the park boundary (☎ 520-643-7298), is open May 15–late Oct daily 8 a.m.–5:30 p.m. daily.

Lost and Found: Contact the National Park Service information desk at the visitors center.

Post Office: Grand Canyon Lodge complex, open Mon–Fri 8–11 a.m. and 11:30 a.m.–4 p.m., Sat. 8 a.m.–2 p.m.

Road Conditions and Weather: Call ☎ 520-638-7888.

Chapter 18

Northeast Arizona: Hopi and Navajo Country

- -

In This Chapter

▶ Flooded canyons, Hollywood buttes, and condo cliffs: Navajo Nation Northwest

▶ More canyons (dry) and a trading post: Navajo Nation East

▶ A triple (mesa) treat: The Hopi Heartland

▶ Some dead wood, a famous corner, an artful desert, and more: Along Old Route 66

- -

*W*hen you're raising Arizona — in your head, that is — there's a good chance that the vast open spaces and eerie rock formations of the northeast reel across your mind's videocam. But this region isn't just the rugged, photogenic face of classic western flicks. Home to the Navajo and Hopi and their ancestors, northeastern Arizona is also the spiritual heart of the Southwest. If this description sounds a little too serious for you, don't worry. A key way to experience local culture is shopping. And you can play as hard here as anywhere else in the state, whether you're water-skiing on Lake Powell, four-wheeling in Monument Valley, or horsing around at the bottom of Canyon de Chelly.

The only two places where you're likely to want to linger are the Page/Lake Powell area and the Canyon de Chelly region. Otherwise, your sleepovers may pretty much be limited to one night stands, although I can see spending two nights at Goulding's, a historic trading post/hotel near Monument Valley. Nonetheless, you can easily stay at least a week in this spectacular, spread-out region. Just prepare to forgo some luxuries during your visit.

Northeast Arizona

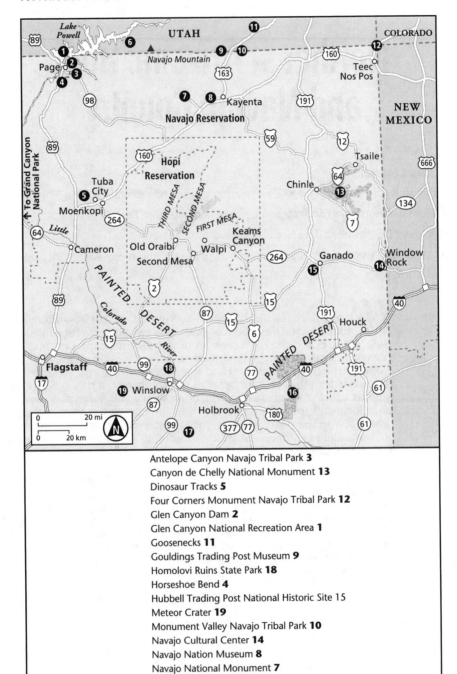

Antelope Canyon Navajo Tribal Park **3**
Canyon de Chelly National Monument **13**
Dinosaur Tracks **5**
Four Corners Monument Navajo Tribal Park **12**
Glen Canyon Dam **2**
Glen Canyon National Recreation Area **1**
Goosenecks **11**
Gouldings Trading Post Museum **9**
Homolovi Ruins State Park **18**
Horseshoe Bend **4**
Hubbell Trading Post National Historic Site 15
Meteor Crater **19**
Monument Valley Navajo Tribal Park **10**
Navajo Cultural Center **14**
Navajo Nation Museum **8**
Navajo National Monument **7**
Petrified Forest National Park **16**
Rainbow Bridge **6**
Rock Art Canyon Ranch **17**

What's Where? Northeast Arizona and Its Major Attractions

From flooded canyons and ancient settlements to fiberglass dinosaurs, plan to see a variety of attractions in this corner of Arizona.

Navajo Nation Northwest

The Navajo inhabit one of Arizona's most multifaceted stretches of real estate. Trading posts, fossil footsteps, and corkscrew-shaped canyons complement the main attractions, including:

- ✔ **Page/Lake Powell:** a water-sports mecca with a European flavor; the only part of this region that's not on the Navajo reservation.

- ✔ **Navajo National Monument:** the desert-meets-forest canyon home of the ancestral Puebloans.

- ✔ **Monument Valley Navajo Tribal Park:** the famous setting for numerous Hollywood Westerns.

Navajo Nation East

The region where Arizona, New Mexico, Utah, and Colorado square off with one another and where the Navajo Nation's capital resides may not have many tourist sights, but the quality, not the quantity, counts at:

- ✔ **Canyon de Chelly:** one of the most gorgeous gorges in the state with a rich Native American past — and presence.

- ✔ **The Hubbell Trading Post National Historic Site:** the country's oldest continuously operating trading post and a Navajo-rug mecca.

TIP

Time after Time

The whole state of Arizona is on a strange time trip — the state, which is in the Mountain Time zone, doesn't go for daylight saving time like most states. Time tracking gets a bit curious in the Northeast. The Navajos *do* observe daylight saving time (which is only logical because their reservation crosses into New Mexico and Utah), while the neighboring Hopi do not. Say you're going from Page to Monument Valley to the Hopi Mesas, you, would theoretically have to switch your watch three times. (You probably don't have any pressing engagements to worry about though.)

TIP

You Don't Need a Passport, But . . .

Traveling on an Indian reservation is similar to visiting a foreign country. The Navajo Nation is the largest sovereign, self-governing community within U.S. boundaries. Both the Navajos and the Hopis have their own customs, laws, and even languages. (Don't worry; you don't need to learn their languages — but don't be surprised if you hear the Navajo language spoken.) For example, you don't see any street addresses because house-to-house postal delivery is not available; everyone retrieves mail from a P.O. box. When in doubt about directions, just ask; locals are happy to help. You, in turn, are expected to behave politely. (See the "Indian Etiquette: Some Reservation Dos and Don'ts" sidebar in this chapter.)

The Hopi Mesas

The three mesas on which most of the Hopi villages perch are lands that time (but not tourists) forgot. They are:

- ✔ **First Mesa** features a tour of a village with amazing vistas — but no electricity.
- ✔ **Second Mesa,** the center of visitor activity, has the Hopi reservation's only hotel.
- ✔ **Third Mesa** is the site of Old Oraibi, home to the Hopi since the twelfth century.

Around Old Route 66

Old Route 66 connects two main towns between New Mexico and Arizona: Winslow and Holbrook. Now these towns are nostalgia-inducing destinations, but in the past, the Mother Road was a means, not an end, to such attractions as:

- ✔ **Petrified Forest National Park:** crystallized logs, dino bones, and a pastel-colored desert.
- ✔ **Meteor Crater:** a very large, quick-impact abyss.

Navajo Nation Northwest

This part of the state has some of the country's weirdest and most wonderful scenery, including the series of wet 'n' wild canyons that comprise Lake Powell; the skinny, strangely convoluted Antelope Canyon; and the mounds and spires of Monument Valley that set the scene for westerns ranging from *The Searchers* to *Thelma and Louise.*

The area is also rich in cultural sites like the cliff dwellings at Navajo National Monument and assorted historic trading points. Plan on spending a minimum of 3 days to give this area its due. In fact, if you enjoy playing on the water and/or if you detour to the Grand Canyon's North Rim (see Chapter 17), you may decide to spend your entire vacation here.

Getting There

It couldn't be easier to get from Flagstaff to Page: Just keep driving north on Highway 89 for 138 miles. When you reach Bitter Springs, where Highway 89A branches off from Highway 89, keep driving on Highway 89; Page is just 25 more miles up the road. The scenery along the way is spectacular; see Chapter 17 for details of what you see leading up to Bitter Springs. About 5 miles beyond the Bitter Springs turn-off, at mile marker 527, you come to the Big Cut. You may pull off the road to gaze at the sweeping vista of the Vermilion Cliffs and the Colorado River canyon on the Marble Plateau spread out below. (You can find more information about the Horseshoe Bend overlook later in this chapter.)

Sunrise Airlines (☎ 800-347-3962) has three flights a day from Phoenix to the Page Municipal Airport, (1 mile east of town on Highway 98; ☎ 520-645-2494). The carrier also offers regular service to Page from Las Vegas. You may rent a car at the airport from **Avis** (☎ 800-331-1212 or 520-645-2024). The drive is longer from the Flagstaff Pullium Airport, but this airport gives you a few more car rental and flight options; see Chapter 17 for more details.

Getting Around

Driving around and taking in the scenery are enjoyable ways to spend your time in this area. If you come via the Flagstaff-Page route, take Highway 98 west to Highway 160, which leads to the turnoffs for Navajo National Monument (Highway 564) and Monument Valley (Highway 163). If you fly into Page, you gain convenience but miss some terrific vistas, so take the less direct but more scenic route via Highway 89 past the striking sandstone Echo Cliffs on your way to Highway 160.

The **Navajo Transit System** (☎ 520-729-4002 or 520-729-5457) operates around the reservation (which doesn't include Page) — but not frequently and not swiftly. Unless you need to kill lots of time, you're better off soaking up local culture in other ways.

Page is the only major town in this area (population: 8,000-ish). En route to Glen Canyon Dam and Lake Powell, Highway 89 sweeps around Page in a business loop known as Lake Powell Boulevard; most of the main streets run off from it (or in the case of Navajo Boulevard, makes an intersecting loop through Lake Powell Boulevard). No public transportation is available but you can call **Lake Powell Taxi** (☎ 520-645-8540).

Go Toe to Toe with a Dinosaur

On the first stretch of Highway 160 beyond Highway 89 (just beyond mile marker 316), a turnoff for **Dinosaur Tracks** takes you to one of only two sets of dilophosaurus footprints ever found — and the other set is in China. The *dilophosaurus,* or "running dinosaur" got some pretty bad press in the movie *Jurassic Park,* where it had a nasty habit of spewing venom before polishing off its prey. No proof exists to show us that the dilophosaurus was either poisonous or that it spat. (I think dino laws against spitting in public places were on the books.)

You're likely to be approached by a local Navajo kid in the parking lot and asked if you want a tour. If you agree — and there's no reason why you shouldn't — you're expected to tip a dollar or two.

Where to Stay in Navajo Nation Northwest

Most of the lodgings in this area are of the chain-chain-chain persuasion but several notable exceptions are available — including a historic trading post and moveable rooms that aren't on wheels. Unless I say otherwise, you may expect to find a modest restaurant serving Navajo/American fare on all the Navajo reservation properties.

Where to Stay in Page/Lake Powell

The town of Page and Wahweap Marina at Lake Powell offer the best beds in the region. In addition to the chain motels described below, two other **Best Westerns, two Holiday Inns, a Day's Inn, an Econolodge,** and a **Super 8** (see the Appendix for the toll-free numbers) are available; several modest independent motels join their ranks on Page's main drags.

I don't necessarily recommend hostels, but Page draws a very continental crowd — two thirds of its visitors are French, German, or Italian — so the **Lake Powell International Hostel** ($), (141 8th Ave.; ☎ 520- 645-3898), is a great place for a foreign exchange. Because of zoning restrictions, most of the B&Bs in Page are of the small, homey persuasion — you know, someone else's clothes hanging in your closet — **DreamKatchers** ($$) Highway 89, just outside of Page in Big Water, Utah (☎ 888-479-9419; Internet: www.dreamkatchersbandb.com) was built from the ground up as a guest nest. This B&B, which opened in 1999, is brand spanking new, nicely furnished, and has panoramic views of the surrounding cliffs.

Book as far ahead as you can if you visit in spring or summer; in winter, you enjoy your pick of rooms — and at very good prices.

Best Western Arizona Inn
$$ Page

Great lake and desert vistas are the main draws of this hotel, where rooms are comfortable, but generic. Pluses include an airport shuttle, a whirlpool and pool with views, and a small exercise room. Don't think you'll be spending much time looking out your window? Consider sister property Best Western at Lake Powell (☎ **888-794-2888** or 520-645-5988), across the road, with slightly nicer rooms and good breakfasts included in its somewhat lower rates.

716 Rimview Dr. (the first hotel as you enter town on Highway 89). ☎ 800-826-2718 or 520-645-2466. Fax: 520-645-2053. Internet: www.bestwestern.com. Rack rates: Apr–May $69–$92, June–Oct $89–$101, Nov–Mar $45–$55. Jan–May and Sept–Dec 5, children 12 and under stay free with adult. Discounts for military and ages 55+. AE, DC, DISC, MC, V.

Courtyard by Marriott
$$ Page

This chain hotel has the fanciest bunks in Page and the Lake Powell National Golf Course in its backyard. Upscale perks not generally found in this area include room service (until 9 p.m.), laundry, exercise room, and a spa — plus the requisite pool. The big, comfy rooms have coffeemakers, hair dryers, and ports for your computer hookups; rooms with views of the golf course and/or Lake Powell cost extra. The on-site Peppers ($$) restaurant is a local favorite for buffet breakfasts, including a make-your-own Belgian waffle bar.

600 Country Club Dr. (at Lake Powell Blvd. and Highway 89). ☎ 800-851-3855 or 520-645-5000. Fax: 520-645-5004. Rack rates: Jan–Mar $69; April–May, Oct 15–Dec $79–$99; June, Oct 1–Oct 14 $89–$109; July–Sept $99–$119. Golf packages available. AE, CB, DC, DISC, MC, V.

Wahweap
$$$ Wahweap Marina

The closest digs to Lake Powell without actually being on it. (See the "Here B&B Means Bed and Boat" sidebar in this chapter.) The rooms are no big deal; a touch of Southwest styling puts them a cut above a standard motel. What you're paying for is (for better or worse) being in the heart of the water sports and tour boat action at Lake Powell's biggest marina. In some rooms, you are able to gaze out at the lake from your window. A casual restaurant (in season), gift shop, and tour desk cater to your material needs, but the vistas from the Rainbow Room restaurant (see "Where to Dine in Page/Lake Powell," in this chapter) and the adjacent bar and deck soothe your soul.

100 Lakeshore Dr. (4 miles north of Glen Canyon Dam). ☎ 800-528-6154 or 520-645-2433. Internet: www.visitlakepowell.com/lodging. Rack rates: Apr–Oct $159–$169, suites $155; Nov–Mar $111–$118; suites $227. B&B and touring packages available. AE, DC, DISC, MC, V.

Here B&B Means Bed and Boat

If you want to tour Lake Powell without straying more than a few feet from your fridge, go ahead — join the houseboating hordes. Don't worry if the closest you usually come to things nautical is riding the Staten Island Ferry. These babies are easy (and fun) to steer and you get plenty of training before anyone lets you go sliding away from the slip.

Prices range from $645 for 3 days on a 36-foot standard class houseboat (sleeping up to 6 people) to $4,495 for a week on a 56-foot sport class model (which sleeps up to 12). The more space you share, the lower the per-person cost; just make sure all of you really want to spend that much time on a boat together. Contact **Lake Powell Resorts and Vacations** (☎ **800-528-6154** or 520-645-1111 [don't even try the toll-free number in summer if your time is worth more than your dime]; Internet: www. visitlakepowell.com/lodging) for reservations.

Where to Stay around Navajo National Monument

Anasazi Inn at Tsegi

$$ **Tsegi**

This spot is convenient to both Navajo National Monument and Monument Valley. The rooms are small, basic, and phoneless; if you get a room in the back, looking out at soaring Tsegi Canyon, you may not mind the lack of amenities.

Highway 160 at Tsegi Canyon (about halfway between Navajo National Monument and Kayenta). ☎ *520-697-3793. Fax: 520-697-8249. Rack rates: May–Oct $80; Nov–Apr $59–69. AE, CB, DISC, MC, V.*

Where to Stay around Monument Valley

The closest town to Monument Valley (23 miles south) and the largest (which isn't saying much) in this region, Kayenta, isn't exactly quaint but the town has dueling gas stations, a supermarket, several casual restaurants, and three motels. In addition to the two motels I list, a Holiday Inn is available (see the appendix for the toll-free number). For a unique accommodation in this area, see also the "Hogan (That's _hoh-gahns_) Heroes" sidebar in this chapter.

Best Western Wetherill Inn Motel

$$ **Kayenta**

In a slightly quieter location than the other two chains that are also smack in the center of Kayenta, this motel is older and has fewer amenities. It has a bit of roadside character, though, and the rooms are comfortable enough.

Highway 163 (1.5 miles north of the junction at Highway 160). ☎ **800-528-1234** *or 520-697-3231. Fax: 520-697-3233. Rack rates: May–Oct 15 $98; Oct 16–Nov 15 and Mar 13–Apr $70; Jan–Mar 12 and Nov 16–Dec $55. AE, CB, DC, DISC, MC, V.*

Goulding's Lodge

$$ **Monument Valley**

Director John Ford's former stomping ground is still a Hollywood magnet. If you see a pickup truck commercial on television with a big sky/big rocks background, the film crew and actors from the ad probably bunked at Goulding's. The rooms are comfortable, with freshened-up Southwest-rustic decor. An on-site museum details the history of this former trading post. Other pluses include great craggy cliffs views from the balconies of many rooms, a tour desk, coin-op laundry, gas station, and an airstrip (where else would Hollywood types land their Learjets?).

On Indian Rte. 42 (intersects at Highway 163 some 27 miles north of Kayenta; take Indian Rte. 42 west (left) 2 miles). ☎ **435-727-3231.** *Fax: 435-727-3344. Internet:* www.gouldings.com. *Rack rates: Mar 15–Oct 15 $101–$140; Oct 16–March 14 $68–$79. AE, CB, DC, DISC, MC, V.*

The Hampton Inn

$$ **Kayenta**

Kayenta's newest (July 1999) sleep stop has the freshest, most attractive rooms (light-wood furniture, Navajo print bedspreads) plus a nice outdoor heated pool. A tour-bus haven near two highway crossroads, the location isn't terribly peaceful, but you're right next to the Navajo Cultural Center, which I talk about later in this chapter.

Highway 160 at Highway 163 (next door to the Burger King). ☎ **800-Hampton** *or 520-697-3170. Fax: 520-697-3189. Internet:* www.hampton-inn.com. *Rack rates: summer $99–106, winter $66–$72. Rates include continental breakfast buffet. AE, CB, DC, DISC, V.*

Where to Dine in Navajo Nation Northwest

Page has the area's greatest number of fast food franchises (Kayenta has a couple, too). In addition, Page is the only town in the region that even makes a stab at gourmet cuisine (but don't expect to find mixed baby mesclun greens dressed with a nicely aged raspberry vinaigrette).

Where to Dine Around Page/Lake Powell

I mention Peppers in the Courtyard by Marriott (see "Where to Stay in Page/Lake Powell," in this chapter) as a good place for breakfast; Peppers is also fine for lunch or dinner and has a Southwest flair (and view), too. In addition to Peppers, Page has a branch of Strombolli's ($–$$), 711 N. Navajo Dr. (☎ **520-645-2605**), described in Chapter 17;

this Strombolli's has the same good calzones and you can dine on a terrific deck. See also the next section, "Exploring Navajo Nation Northwest" in this chapter for information regarding dinner at the Navajolands Academy.

Garden Café

$ Page Café

The closest thing to froufrou in this part of Arizona, the Garden Café is great for when your inner yuppie emerges and starts demanding cappuccino. Try any of the baked goods and the veggie panini with mushrooms, olives, Swiss cheese, and pesto served warm on herbed foccacia bread. The cheesecake goes fast, so if you see a piece, grab it.

809 N. Navajo (just northeast of Lake Powell Blvd.). ☎ *520-645-6666. No reservations. Sandwiches: $5.30–$5.80. Open: summer Mon–Sat 8 a.m.–3 p.m., shorter hours in winter. MC, V.*

Dam Bar & Grill

$$–$$$ Page American/Italian/Southwest

The dam theme dominates only the front section of this cavernous restaurant but the fun atmosphere (and the puns) prevails throughout. The menu's pretty eclectic — ranging from fish and chips and filet mignon to tequila lime chicken and vegetarian lasagna — but everything tastes fresh and portions are more than generous.

644 N. Navajo (in the Dam Plaza). ☎ *520-645-2161. Reservations recommended in summer. Main courses: $9.95–$23.95. Open: Mon–Sat lunch and dinner, Sun dinner only. AE, MC, V.*

Ken's Old West

$$–$$$ Page Steakhouse

This is your quintessential wood-front steakhouse. Prime rib rules, but huge steaks — as rare as you want 'em — are here too. For the health conscious, light chicken entrees and a huge salad bar are available. Stick around for the nightly live country and western music.

718 Vista Ave. (behind the Best Western at Lake Powell). ☎ *520-645-5160. Reservations suggested during high-season weekends. Main courses: $10–$22. Open dinner nightly. MC, V.*

The Rainbow Room

$$–$$$ Wahweap Marina American/Southwest

Circular shape aside, all resemblance to Manhattan's swank dinner palace begins and ends with the name. That's okay. You don't dress to the teeth to eat here, you don't exceed your credit limit, and you enjoy amazing lake views from this room's panoramic windows. The food's good, too, especially the house specialty: pine nut–crusted trout. The

only similarities I'd like to import from New York are snappier service —
and a policy of accepting reservations.

*Wahweap Lodge, 100 Lakeshore Dr. ☎ 520-645-2433. Reservations not accepted
(and you may face a wait in summer if you want to eat anywhere near a normal
hour). Main courses: $12–$19. Open: daily breakfast, lunch, and dinner. AE, DC,
DISC, MC, V.*

Where to Dine around Monument Valley

I can't note many differences among the restaurants in the Monument
Valley area. You can expect reasonable versions of casual American
dishes and a few good Mexican and Navajo selections in Kayenta's
three motel restaurants and at the Haskéneini dining room at
Monument Valley (named after an early-twentieth-century Navajo
leader); the latter has great views and a terrific build-your-own Navajo
taco buffet, but the dining room is not always open during the off
season. The dining room at Goulding's is a cut above the rest in terms
of selection, quality, and view (though not necessarily service).

The entire Navajo Nation is dry; you can't buy or bring any booze
(including beer and wine) on the reservation.

Exploring Navajo Nation Northwest

You can easily spend a week in this area, which has tons of things to
see and do. An activity that involves a deliberate expenditure of energy
goes into "The Active Life" section, while an excursion that benefits by
the direction of an outside guide slips into the "Guided Tours" section.

Exploring Page/Lake Powell

Page was started in 1956 as a construction site for Glen Canyon Dam,
built to harness hydroelectric power from the Colorado River. The
dam's secondary result was a bit more splendid: After 17 years of slowly
flooding nearly 100 dramatic sandstone canyons (most of them in
Utah), the huge reservoir known as Lake Powell was created. Stretch
out its 1,960 miles of shoreline and you end up with more waterfront
property than exists on the entire West Coast of the United States.

The lake is only a small part of the huge Glen Canyon National
Recreation Area. Three smaller marinas on Lake Powell offer recreation, but Wahweap, 6 miles north of Page, is water-sports central.

Lots of folks spend their time here hanging off the side of their rented
houseboats or getting wet in other ways (see "The Active Life," in this
chapter). If you're a landlubber — or just want to dry out for a bit —
other options include:

> ✔ **Give a dam:** You don't have to care about hydroelectric energy to
> be impressed by the gigantic **Glen Canyon Dam,** Highway 89, 2
> miles west of Page (☎ **520-608-6404**); only Hoover Dam is taller
> (by 16 feet). You enjoy great Lake Powell views at the Carl Hayden
> Visitors Center, where an excellent bookstore stocks information

about the area's many natural attractions. Open daily (except Thanksgiving, Christmas, and New Year's Day) from 8 a.m. to 7 p.m. mid-May to mid-September, daily 8 a.m. to 5 p.m. the rest of the year. Free hour-long guided tours of the dam run every half hour between 8:30 a.m. and 4:30 p.m. in high season, less frequently in low season.

✔ **Explore an explorer:** The **John Wesley Powell Memorial Museum** (6 N. Lake Powell Blvd. at N. Navajo Dr.; ☎ 520-645-9496), celebrates the life and journeys of the one-armed Civil War hero who led the first (1869) river expedition along the entire length of the Grand Canyon. He named the canyon and many other landmarks in the area and, in turn, had lots of stuff — including Lake Powell — named after him. The museum doubles as a visitor center. Open daily 8 a.m. to 6 p.m., May through September; Monday through Friday 9 a.m. to 5 p.m., October to mid-December and mid-February through April; closed mid-December through mid-February. Admission: $1 adults, 50¢ children.

✔ **Dine with the Diné:** At the living history museum run by the **Navajolands Academy** (531 Haul Road, about a mile south of Page between Hwys. 89 and 98; (☎ **888-597-6873** or 520-660-0304), you learn a lot about the traditions of the Diné — as the Navajo call themselves. Crafts demonstrations take place during the day from 9 a.m. to 3 p.m. ($10 adults, $7 ages 6 to 13, 5 and under free). The dinner program includes a dance performance and you are assigned a clan and a clan brother or sister who is your cultural guide throughout the evening. The full program, from 4 to 8 p.m., costs $49.95 for adults, $34.95 for children. Two shorter programs, beginning at 5 p.m. and 6 p.m., last an hour and include shorter presentations as well as dancing; costs are $24.95 to $18.95 plus an additional $5 for all ages for dinner.

✔ **Go over the rainbow:** The world's largest (height: 290 feet, span: 275 feet) natural arch, the spectacular sandstone **Rainbow Bridge** is Lake Powell's most famous landmark. Long held sacred by the area's native peoples, the bridge is in a remote canyon at the foot of Navajo Mountain, some 50-lake miles north of Wahweap Marina. The hike is 26 miles round-trip from the nearest land point and you need a permit, so you probably want to go by boat (see "Guided Tours," in this chapter).

✔ **Get the skinny:** In Lower Antelope Canyon, sand dunes from an ancient sea solidified over millennia into what are variously known as skinny caves, wind caves, slot canyons, corkscrew canyons . . . well, you get the picture — and so does every professional or aspiring shutterbug. The narrow beams of light that stream into the caves from above offer a great photo op. The entrance station to **Antelope Canyon Navajo Tribal Park,** about 3 miles east of Page on Highway 98 at milepost 299 (☎ **520-698-3347**), is open April to September from 8 a.m. to 5 p.m., and October through November from 9 a.m. to 3 p.m. You can't enter without a guide, but you can get a ride in a four-wheel drive vehicle from the gate ($17.50 adults, $15.50 children, including the $5 entrance fee) or book a tour from Page (see "Guided Tours," in this chapter), a more reliable option because the four-wheelers operate irregularly.

✔ **Take a scenic toss:** To reach **Horseshoe Bend,** a stunning over-look of the Colorado River that makes — what else? — a complete horseshoe bend around a soaring sandstone butte, take Highway 89 about 5 miles south from the Carl Hayden Visitors Center to mile marker 545, turn west on the dirt road, and park at the base of the hill or on the wide pulloff by the highway; you'll be oohing and aahing in less than half a mile.

Navajo National Monument

Between Tuba City and Kayenta

The Navajo National Monument is a dazzler, with two sets of wonderfully preserved cliff dwellings in a sublime high-desert setting of soaring ochre cliffs punctuated by thick stands of fir and aspen trees. These dwellings are now on Navajo land but the people who settled in the two communi-ties preserved here, **Betatakin** *(beh-tat-uh-kin)* and **Keet Seel** — from about A.D. 950 to A.D. 1300 and A.D. 1250 to A.D. 1300, respectively — are forebears of the Hopi. (These people used to be called the *Anasazi,* which likely means "ancient enemy" in Navajo, but archaeologists now prefer the term *ancestral Puebloans.*) Because Navajo National Monument is not as well known as some of the other ancient sites in the Southwest, crowd control is not a problem.

The 1-mile **Sandal Trail** loop that leads to a spectacular overlook of Betatakin involves a bit of an upward slope on the return trip; if you take it slow you shouldn't have a problem, even if most of your hiking is done from the television to the refrigerator. (For harder treks, see "The Active Life," in this chapter.) The Sandal Trail loop takes about 45 minutes to complete; allot another 45 minutes if you also want to hike the short but steep **Aspen Forest Overlook trail,** which branches off from the Sandal Trail. And — I admit it — I always end up spending at least half an hour at the great gift shop (see "Shopping," in this chapter) next to the visi-tor's center.

On Highway 264, 9 miles north of the Highway 160 turnoff (where the pavement ends). ☎ *520-672-2366. Admission: Free. Open: Daily 8 a.m.–5 p.m., except Christmas, Thanksgiving, and New Year's Day.*

Monument Valley Navajo Tribal Park

Near Kayenta

The deep rust sandstone buttes, mesas, and spires of the 50-square-mile Monument Valley are the ultimate icons of the West — perhaps because they seem to exist on a different planet than urban and suburban America. The rock formations are strangely shaped to begin with — they're named after everything from mittens to elephants — but what makes the formations even more striking is that they rise up suddenly from a practically flat stretch of plain.

The only way to see Monument Valley on your own is to take the 17-mile unpaved — and unmaintained — loop drive. The drive takes about 2 hours, assuming you're going the 15-mile speed limit (definitely a smart plan) and just stopping quickly at the 11 signed turnoffs.

Most people make this drive in a rental car, so they don't care deeply about what happens to its shock absorbers. If you're in your own car — and especially if it's a low clearance one like mine — I'd suggest taking a pass on the self-guided ride. The Navajo consider Monument Valley a sacred spot, so going with a local guide is a great way to get the lore behind the rocks anyway. (See "Guided Tours" in this chapter.)

3 miles off Highway 163; take Highway 160 to Kayenta and drive north 27 miles until you see the sign on the right side of the road. ☎ *435-727-3287 or 727-3353. Admission: $2.50 adults, $1 seniors over 60, ages 7 and under free. Open: May–Sept daily 8 a.m.–7 p.m., Oct–Apr daily 8 a.m.–5 p.m., Thanksgiving 8 a.m.–noon, closed Christmas. National Park passes not accepted.*

Other Cool Things to See and Do

Great views, Navajo history, and dinosaur footprints — the Navajo Nation Northwest has much more to offer visitors:

- **Do the twist:** Drive north on Highway 163 from Monument Valley and then turn west on Highway 161 (4 miles past Mexican Hat, Utah) to reach the overlook for the wildly convoluted, erosion-created San Juan River canyons called **Goosenecks.** During the week, especially off-season, there's often no one at this remote outlook point except perhaps a jewelry vendor or two.

- **Trade on the past:** The **Goulding's Trading Post Museum** (see "Where to Stay around Monument Valley," in this chapter), in the store that Harry Goulding established in the 1920s, includes Native American artifacts and mementos from director John Ford's films. Upstairs, you can visit the Gouldings' former living quarters. Open April through October daily from 7:30 a.m. to 9 p.m., closed the rest of the year. Suggested donation: $2. See also in this chapter the Oljato and Tuba trading posts in "Shopping."

- **Learn some Navajo history:** In Kayenta, the **Navajo Cultural Center,** on Highway 160 just west of the Burger King (no ☎), includes several traditional structures — two *hogans* (the hexagonal buildings that serve as both homes and ceremonial chambers), a sweat house, and a shade house with displays about Navajo customs and religious beliefs; sometime there are crafts or dance exhibitions. See also the "Hogans'(That's *hoh-gahns*) Heroes" sidebar in this chapter for information on displays at the nearby Burger King.

- **Track down some dinosaurs:** See the "Go Toe to Toe with a Dinosaur" sidebar in this chapter.

Guided Tours

Whether you prefer to tour by air, boat, jeep, or even horse, you're sure to find an option here that suits you. See also the section, "The Active Life," later in this chapter for guided hikes to Navajo National Monument and guided hikes and river rafting trips in Page.

If you want to hover above the crowds at Rainbow Bridge, see spectacular formations that aren't accessible by boat or road, or just save some time, consider taking one of these air tours. **Classic Helicopter Tours** (☎ 520-645-5356; Internet: www.classicaviation.org) offers tours that range from 10-minute buzzes over Tower Butte for $39 to 55-minute excursions to the more remote Escalante River arm of Lake Powell for $160; it'll run you $96 to see Rainbow Bridge and return in 35 minutes. Flights via the small planes of **Lake Powell Air** (☎ 800-245-8668, ext. 5 or 520-645-2494) start at $79 for a 30-minute Rainbow Bridge jaunt and go up (and up and away) to $245 for a 2½-hour Lake Powell, Grand Canyon, and Monument Valley tour. (Ground-air tours of Monument Valley are available too, and there are discount fares for kids who fly with two adults.) Both companies operate out of Page Airport.

Four different concessionaires give you Antelope Canyon entry and guidance: **Lake Powell Jeep Tours,** 104 S. Lake Powell Blvd. (☎ 520-645- 5501; Internet: www.jeeptour.com); **Roger Ekis's Antelope Canyon Tours,** 22 Lake Powell Blvd. (☎ 520-645-9102; Internet: www. antelopecanyon.com); **Overland Canyon Tours,** Empire House Motel, 107 S. Lake Powell Blvd. (☎ 520-608-4072); and **Grand Circle Adventure Scenic Tours,** 48 S. Lake Powell (☎ 520-645-5594). All charge $25 for adults and $15 for children for their basic 1½-hour tours. The first two tours operate in open-sided four-wheel drive vehicles while the latter two tours use enclosed SUVs; you decide whether you like the wind in your hair or prefer air-conditioning. Other distinguishing features: Roger Ekis is known for his photographic skills and Overland Canyon is Navajo-run, giving you an insider's take on the area.

Hogans' (That's *hoh-gahns*) Heroes

Not a well-known fact: A secret code devised by a group of Navajos for the United States in World War II was the only code that the Japanese never broke. Introduced at Iwo Jima, their system of encryption — based on, but not exactly the same as, the complex Navajo language — helped the Allies win a victory that many consider the war's turning point. By the end of WWII, the Navajo Code Talkers, as the Navajo soldiers were called, numbered some 425. About 150 are still alive today.

The fact that the code wasn't declassified until 1968 is one reason these heroes have remained relatively unsung. That mistake is likely to be corrected soon, however. In 2000, Hasbro released a Navajo Code Talker GI Joe action figure and the next project of director John Woo *(Face Off, Mission Impossible II)* is slated to be *Windtalkers,* a World War II thriller highlighting this historic episode.

Meanwhile, you may learn more about these men in Kayenta's Burger King, Highway 160, just west of the Highway 160/163 intersection (☎ 520-697-3534); Richard Mike — son of Code Talker, King Mike — displays related photographs and memorabilia.

Lake Powell Resorts and Marina (☎ 520-645-1070; Internet: www.visitlakepowell.com) offers a variety of **boat trips** from Wahweap Marina. Those trips on the company's two-deck cruisers, which have a snack bar on board, include full-day excursions to Rainbow Bridge and at least one side canyon ($99 adult, $69 ages 12 and under; includes a box lunch); half-day tours to Rainbow Bridge without detour and lunch ($75 to $55); and shorter trips to Antelope Canyon and Navajo Canyon ($39 to $32 for a 2½-hour tour, $32 to $25 for 1½ hours). The company also runs excursions around Wahweap Bay on two paddle wheelers, the *Canyon King,* a nineteenth-century riverboat, and the newer *Desert Shadow* ($11 for adults, $8 for children during the day, and $60 per person [no matter the age] for an evening dinner cruise). All excursions (on cruiser and paddle wheelers) are offered year-round, but schedules vary by season, so check ahead.

Navajo-led tours around **Monument Valley** range from 1½-hour jeep jaunts (around $20 per person) to overnight horseback excursions ($150). Hiking tours that last 3½ hours to Mitchell Mesa ($45); full-day tours that divide their times between Monument Valley and Mystery Valley, where you can see cliff dwellings and petroglyphs ($90); sunrise ($35) and sunset ($30) tours on four wheels or four feet; and tours where photography is the main focus (from $25 an hour) are also available. **Sacred Monument Tours** (☎ 435-727-3218; Internet: www.sacredtoursmv.com) puts its full array of services online; **Ed Black** (☎ 800-749-4226 or 435-739-4226) is well-known in the valley for horseback rides; and Betty Jackson, who comes from a long line of Monument Valley residents, started **Jackson Tour** (☎ 435-727-3353) three decades ago. All have kiosks near the Monument Valley visitor's center. You may also call Lake Powell Air for information about the Monument Valley flights departing from the air strip at Goulding's Lodge, which also books trips into the valley (see "Where to Stay around Monument Valley," in this chapter).

When you drive to the dirt parking area just past the visitor's center, you see rows of concessionaire's booths. Don't make yourself crazy by comparison shopping. The park superintendent fixes the prices for all the tour groups so the sellers can't go above the advertised rates (they can dip a little below). In addition, I advise that you decide in advance what kind of tour you want to take, in what kind of vehicle (or nonvehicle), and when. Establishing your preferences gives you a sound basis for choosing a guide service.

Keeping Active

I cover horseback riding and hiking in Monument Valley in "Guided Tours" immediately previously; except for hiking in Navajo National Monument, all the following activities take place in the Page/Lake Powell area.

> ✔ **Fishing:** Lake Powell, like hell, never freezes over — which makes it an angler's heaven. Large- and small-mouth bass, striped bass, catfish, carp, walleye, and crappie abound year-round. Because Lake Powell straddles both Arizona and Utah, you need two licenses

(fees: $7 in Arizona, $3 in Utah), unless you're sure your fish don't cross state lines. You can get all your paperwork and buy tackle and bait at Wahweap Marina (☎ **520-645-1111**), where you can also rent a boat (see the "Water Sports" bullet later in this section).

Bubba's Guide Service (☎ **888-741-2822** or 520-645-3506; Internet: www.bubbasguide.com) can lead you to all the prime angling spots, including the tight ones, on sleek, fast bass boats. The price — $400 per 9-hour day for the first two people, $50 each additional person — includes everything except ground transportation and licenses.

✔ **Golfing:** The 27-hole **Lake Powell National Golf Course,** 400 N. Clubhouse Drive (behind the Marriott; ☎ **520-645-2023**; Internet: www.lakepowellgolf.com), is one of the most stunning places in the state to tee off; the lush, rolling greens contrast with the surrounding red and buff sandstone and startling blue-green lake. Green fees are reasonable, too, ranging from $36 to $60 from May to September, including cart, and dipping even lower the rest of the year, when the course also runs frequent specials.

✔ **Hiking:** Hikes to the major ruins at Navajo National Monument are permitted only between Memorial Day and Labor Day. During this period, rangers lead difficult 5-hour treks to Betatakin every morning at 8:15; these hikes are on a first-come, first-served basis and limited to 25 per group. To get up close and personal with Keet Seel, you need to reserve a backcountry permit and take the 17-mile (round-trip) trek on your own. These hikes, restricted to 20 people a day, are very popular, so call as soon as you know when you're going to visit; reservations are taken up to 2 months in advance by the visitor's center at Navajo National Monument (☎ **520-672-2366**).

Looking to explore some amazing sandstone bluffs? The Carl Hayden Visitors Center (see "Exploring Navajo Nation NorthWest" in this chapter) is a great source for trail information, and you may pick up a map of the 8-mile hiking, biking, and jogging trail that surrounds the mesa on which Page sits at the Page–Lake Powell Chamber of Commerce (see "Quick Concierge: Navajo Nation Northwest," in this chapter).

Vermillion Cliffs Tours (☎ **520-645-3961**; Internet: vermillioncl@aztrail.com) offers everything from guided sunset walks near Page in summer ($30 per person, with a two-person minimum and maximum of seven) to full-day hikes through the Vermillion Cliffs Wilderness and the dry parts of the Glen Canyon National Recreation Area in fall, winter, and spring ($200 for one or two people, $50 per person for third person and up).

✔ **River Rafting:** This activity offers open water without the fear, but not without the excitement. From mid-May to mid-September, **Wilderness River Adventure,** 50 S. Lake Powell Blvd. (☎ **800-528-6154** or 520-645-3279), runs smooth water rafting trips from Glen Canyon Dam to Lees Ferry. You float along an undeveloped section of the Colorado River past sandstone cliffs and Native American petroglyphs. From mid-May to mid-September, a full-day trip departs at 9 a.m. and returns at 3 p.m. ($77 adults, $69 11 and under); two half-day trips head out at 7:30 a.m. and 1:30 p.m. ($55–$47). The weather is too cold for boat floating from November to February but from mid-September to October and March to mid-May, one half-day trip departs at 11 a.m., returning to Page at 3:30 p.m.

✔ **Water Sports:** Lake Powell is not exactly serene in summer; every motorized or human powered contraption you can imagine zips in and out (and sometimes under) every inlet and cove.

If you can't beat the throngs, join 'em at the **Wahweap Marina** (☎ **520-645-1111**) where you can rent your favorite water toy: Tiger Shark, kind of like a water motorcycle ($235 a day, for two people), wakeboard ($24); ski tube ($20); or kneeboard ($22). A 14-foot power boat that holds up to five people costs $25 per hour or $125 a day; the rate is $60 per hour and $295 per day for a 19-foot craft that holds ten. A one-person kayak runs you $30 a day.

Renting your water-sports equipment in town is cheaper. At **Lake Powell Waterworld,** 920 Hemlock St. (☎ **520-645-8845,** Internet: www.lakepowellwaterworld.com), for example, you can rent comparable water toys for less, if you don't care about playing with the latest model. But . . . and it's a big BUT . . . the toys are big and you must get them to the water. Even with the cost of rent-ing a truck from the shop, the rate still comes out cheaper.

The Caribbean this ain't, but if you want to get a peek at what Glen Canyon looked like before water was added, **Twin Finn,** 811 Vista Ave. (☎ **520-645-3114,** Internet: www.twinfinn.com), may pro-vide you with the means. Scuba-diving packages — including two tanks, regulator, wet suits, weight belts, flags, and buoys — cost only $45; the rental rate is even less expensive ($8) if you only want to rent a snorkel, mask, and fins for snorkeling. The staff don't take you out on the water but they advise you on the best spots to take the plunge. They also make sure that you're certi-fied, so bring proof with you.

Shopping

Native American crafts, especially those crafts made by the Navajo, are sold all over Page, but you're better off going directly to the source: the reservation. You aren't automatically guaranteed high quality or low prices on the reservation, but at least you don't pay extra for a middle-man's commission. Also, keep in mind that if you buy from one of the open-air vendors near practically every natural attraction, you don't pay extra for their real-estate overhead.

Impromptu outdoor markets are hit and miss. Sometimes you see goods that look mass produced, other times you find treasures (I once bought a prized and unique key chain at the bottom of the Canyon de Chelly). Bargaining is acceptable; just find the comfort zone between not wanting to be taken advantage of and not being the one who's taking advantage. Remember, you're likely to pay a lot more for these crafts at home.

Health — Check? Car — Check?

The Navajo and Hopi reservations are not ideal destinations if you or your wheels are not in shipshape condition. A few modern medical facilities or up-to-date car repair or parts shops are scattered around but the region is large and remote, so assistance isn't always quick. For details, see the Medical, Pharmacies, Phones, and Road Service sections of "Quick Concierge" for the "Navajo Nation Northwest," "Navajo Nation East," and "Hopi Mesas" sections in this chapter.

In Kayenta, the hotel gift shops and the visitor's center all carry a good array of Navajo-made items; also, a branch of the cooperative **Navajo Arts and Crafts Enterprise** is on Highway 160, east of the intersection with Highway 163 (just beyond the Thriftway supermarket) (☎ **520-697-8611**). The **gift shop in Navajo National Monument** (see "Exploring Navajo Nation Northwest," in this chapter) carries items you're not likely to see anywhere else on the reservation, created by Native American artists from all around Arizona and New Mexico, some represented by major big-city galleries.

At the **Tuba Trading Post** (on the corner of Main and Moenave streets in Tuba City; ☎ **800-644-8383** or 520-283-5441; closed Sunday), built in 1906 in the shape of a six-sided Navajo hogan, locals still trade crafts for necessities. Along with jewelry, belts, rugs, and the like, you find creative T-shirts and books about the Southwest. Near Monument Valley, some 15 miles beyond Goulding's — take the same road west around Hoskininni Mesa — the remote **Oljato Trading Post** (☎ **435-727-3210**; Internet: www.a-aa.com/monumentvalley/) is on the National Register of Historic Places. Established in 1921, the trading post has shelves stocked as they were in the old days; a small museum and bookstore are open daily to the public.

Quick Concierge: Navaho Nation Northwest

Area code: Dial **520** for listings in this chapter.

ATMs: Page is the best place to find money machines, but Wells Fargo has branches with ATMs in Kayenta and Tuba City.

Information: Page/Lake Powell Chamber of Commerce, 644C N. Navajo Dr., Suite C

(☎ 888-261-7243 or 520-645-2741; Internet: http://page-lakepowell.com/Chamber.html), open high season Mon–Sat 8 a.m.–7 p.m., Sun 10 a.m.–6 p.m., shorter hours in winter; or Page's John Wesley Powell Museum and Visitors Center (☎ 888-597-6873 or 520-645-9496, Internet: www.powellmuseum.org), open high season Mon–Fri 8:30 a.m.–

5:30 p.m., winter 9 a.m.–5 p.m. The Kayenta Visitors Center, on Highway 160 just east of the Burger King (☎ 520-697-3572), open high season Mon–Sat 9 a.m.–7 p.m., Sun 10 a.m.–5 p.m.; winter Mon–Sat 8 a.m.–5 p.m. For advance information, contact Navajo Tourism, P.O. Box 663, Window Rock, AZ 85615 (☎ 520-871-6436; Internet: www.navajo. org). For current events, check the Web at www.thenavajo-times.com.

Internet Access: In Page, you can check your e-mail at Radio Shack, 609 E. Elm St. (☎ 520-645- 6664), across from the post office for $5 per hour.

Maps: The excellent *Guide to Indian Country,* published by the Automobile Club of Southern California, is available at local AAA offices and at most gas stations or hotel gift shops in Page and on the Navajo reservation.

Medical: Page Hospital, 501 N. Navajo Ave. (☎ 520-645-2424), is your best bet in case of a medical emergency. On the Navajo reservation, U.S. Public Health Service Indian hospitals in Tuba City (☎ 520-283-2501) and Kayenta (☎ 520-697-3211) are available; locate these hospitals via the blue "H" road signs (or ask locally). Only Native Americans get free medical care but others are welcome to use the hospitals' services; many insurance plans are accepted.

Pharmacies: In Page, Safeway, 650 Elm St. at S. Lake Powell Blvd. (☎ 520-645-5714), is open weekdays 9 a.m.–9 p.m., Saturday 9 a.m.–6 p.m., Sun 10 a.m.–4 p.m. No pharmacies on the Navajo reservation are available; if you need emergency medical supplies visit one of the hospitals.

Phones: Unless you have satellite service, you're likely to have a tough time getting your cell phone to work outside of the Page area. You find pay phones at most gas stations, hotels, and convenience stores/supermarkets on the Navajo reservations.

Police: Page: ☎ **911**; Kayenta: ☎ 520-697-5600; Tuba City: ☎ 520-283-3111.

Post Office: Page: 44 6th Ave. at Elm (☎ 520-645-2571). On the reservation, ask for the nearest mail depot; in many towns, postal services operate out of convenience stores.

Restrooms: No public restrooms or rest areas are available on the reservations. Don't leave a hotel, restaurant, or tourist attraction without using the facilities — you may not get to another one for a while.

Road Service: Your car isn't likely to be fixed quickly in the Navajo Nation. Also, keep in mind that there are no car rental agencies except in the border towns. Ask at your hotel for a referral to the best local auto repair or towing service or, as the Navajo tourism office suggests, contact the police (see above) for information. If you're a AAA member, call ☎ 800-222-4357 for towing service. Because of the distances involved between the reservations and service stations, the towing charge is likely to be very high.

Safety: Not much crime against tourists occurs on the reservations, but these areas are not high-income. Don't leave valuables in plain view in your car (what did you think those trunks with the locks were for, anyway?).

Time Zone: Mountain. But Arizona doesn't do the daylight saving time thing. See the "Time after Time" sidebar earlier in this chapter.

Navajo Nation East

This remote area doesn't have many landmark or attractions, but those it does have are completely wonderful. In addition to **Canyon de Chelly** (one of my all-time favorite spots) and the **Hubbell Trading Post** (a wonderfully preserved and still functioning historic retail hub), this region encompasses **Window Rock,** the Navajo Nation's capital, and the **Four Corners Monument,** one place you should visit — at least once.

You may spend two leisurely days at the Canyon de Chelly: hiking, four-wheeling, horseback riding, and perhaps taking a short side trip to Window Rock. You may choose to see the canyon in a very long morning or afternoon by just driving along one of the two rim routes. The Four Corners Monument isn't on the way to anywhere in Arizona, so you need to detour to get there (unless you are heading to Colorado). The Hubbell Trading Post, on the other hand, is en route to almost everywhere you're likely to visit, requiring just a few miles of backtracking. All in all, if you're on the move, you may cover the entire area comfortably in about a day and a half. Plan to spend the night near Canyon de Chelly, not only because the spot is beautiful, but also because the hotels have the nicest rooms on the Navajo reservation.

Getting There

If you come from the north (from around Monument Valley), take Highway 160 east. The distance is 40 miles from Kayenta to Mexico Water; turn south onto Highway 199 and drive 60 miles to reach Chinle, the closest town to Canyon de Chelly. (Alternatively, keep going another 40-odd miles on Highway 160 beyond Mexico Water and you arrive at the Four Corners Monument. If you're thinking of going there, now's the time!) You journey another 30 miles south on Highway 191 from Chinle to the Highway 264 turnoff to reach Ganado, home of the Hubbell Trading Post. The Highway 264 stretch is actually a 6-mile interruption in Highway 191, which you take south another 38 miles to get to I-40.

The intersection of Highway 191 and I-40 is 140 miles east of Flagstaff. If you approach via the southern I-40 route, just follow these instructions backwards. (There won't be any hidden references to Satan if you repeat them at high speed, I promise.)

Getting Around

I describe your basic sightseeing route through this area in "Getting There." The only town you deal with is Chinle, which is a breeze. Highway 191 takes you through most of Chinle; Highway 64 and Indian Route 7, which branches east from 191 to become the North Rim Drive and South Rim Drives of Canyon de Chelly, respectively, are Chinle's only other thoroughfares. (Since you'll have wheels, you won't need to use the town's slow public bus.)

Where to Stay

I recommend Chinle as your main place to hole up in this area. Chinle doesn't have a loser among its lodgings; the accommodations aren't fancy, but all are very pleasant and convenient to the Canyon de Chelly.

In Window Rock (see "More Cool Things to See and Do," in this chapter), the **Navajo Nation Inn** ($), 48 W. Highway 264 at Highway 12 (☎ **800-662-6189** or 520-871-4108, Fax: 520-871-5466) — an oldish motel, not really an inn — is clean and reasonably efficient.

The Thunderbird Lodge

$$ Canyon de Chelly

You have it all here — history, nature, and shopping. The only roofed bunk within the park's boundaries, this one-time trading post sits nestled in a lovely cottonwood grove. Rooms, in pink pueblo-style buildings, are updated rustic with all modern amenities. Other perks include a great gift shop, a tour desk, and a Navajo rug–draped dining room.

Off Indian Route 7 (South Rim Drive), inside Canyon de Chelly (about half a mile southwest of the visitor's center). ☎ *800-679-2473 or 520-674-5841. Fax: 520-674-5844. Internet:* www.tbirdlodge.com. *Rack rates: Apr–Oct $96–$101, $138 suites; Nov–Mar $65, $91 suites. AE, CB, DISC, MC, V.*

Holiday Inn Canyon de Chelly

$$ Chinle

Built in 1992, this Holiday Inn holds on to a bit of Old West history: It incorporates the trading post built on this site in the 1880s into the main lobby. The hotel restaurant and gift shop go way beyond generic, too. Rooms, on the other hand, are pastel bland, but have all the modern requisites. The hotel sometimes hosts outdoor music and dance performances, and although you're not inside the park, you're actually closer to the start of both rim drives than you are at the Thunderbird Lodge.

Indian Rte. 7, about 3 miles east of the junction with Highway 191 (½ mile from the park entrance). ☎ *800-HOLIDAY or 520-674-5000. Fax: 520-674-8264. Rack rates: May–Aug $94–$109, Sept–Apr $64–$99. AE, CB, DC, DISC, MC, V.*

Best Western Canyon de Chelly Inn

$ Chinle

The farthest from the canyon of the three hotels recommended here (but still less than 4 miles from the park entrance), and without any sort of trading post on its grounds, this motel compensates with an indoor pool and rooms that have a bit of Southwest flair as well as my favorite, uh, perk: coffeemakers. The on-site Junction Café is a local hangout.

On Indian Rte. 7, about 1/4 of a mile east of the junction with Highway 191. ☎ *800-327-0354 or 520-674-5875. Fax: 520-674-3715. Rack rates: May–Oct $106, Nov–Apr $66. AE, CB, DC, DISC, MC, V.*

Oh, Give Me a Hogan

Staying in a hogan is camping raised to an art (and cultural) form. You sleep in a traditional six-sided log, dirt, and cement structure with a small hole in the center (in Manhattan, the locals call the hole a skylight). Smoke from a wood-burning stove escapes through the hole; you glimpse the stars while you're lying on a cot, sleeping bag, or sheepskins. In the morning, your host serves you coffee and an authentic Navajo breakfast, which may include blue corn pancakes. (Sorry — no indoor plumbing — another reason this experience is like camping.)

Coyote's Pass Hospitality, near the Canyon de Chelly (☎ **520-724-3383;** Internet: www.navajocentral.org/cppage.htm) was one of the first lodgings to offer this type of accomodation. Close to Monument Valley, the **Country of Many Hogan Bed & Breakfast** (☎ **888-291-4397,** pin 4617; Internet: http://navajoland.com/cmh; E-mail: zenbah@hotmail.com) is also available. At both locations, the accommodations run about $125 for two people. For information about other Navajo B&Bs, contact **Largo Navajoland Tours** (☎ **888-726-9084;** Internet: www.navajolandtours.com).

Where to Dine

Not much is available in the way of fine dining in this region but you enjoy lots of local flavor around the Canyon de Chelly. (Remember that the Navajo Nation bans alcohol.) Food in the **Thunderbird Lodge restaurant** ($–$$) — the original trading post building lined with old photos — is served cafeteria style, which works well for vegetarians who get a nice choice of side dishes and desserts. **Garcia's** ($–$$) in the Holiday Inn is the closest this area comes to fine dining, with good versions of traditional Navajo dishes — such as mutton stew — along with American standards; Garcia's offers daily breakfast buffets. Locals frequent both of these restaurants — there aren't many other restaurants around except for a few fast food places. The low-key **Junction Café** at the Best Western, serving decent American, Mexican, and Navajo coffee-shop grub, gets the lunch and breakfast townie regulars. You'd be hard pressed to spend more than $10 here.

In Ganado, **Café Sage** ($), on the grounds of the Sage hospital (☎ 520-755-3411), is fine for a cafeteria-style lunch. Fans of Tony Hillerman's mysteries may want to check out the restaurant in Window Rock's **Navajo Nation Inn,** where fictional Navajo police detectives, Joe Leaphorn and Jim Chee, drink endless cups of coffee. The standard American/Navajo fare is pretty good.

If you buy a snack from one of the vendors near the Four Corners Monument (corn dogs or fry bread, for example), you can pig out in four states. Now don't say I never tell you how to have a good time!

Exploring Navajo Nation East

You should find something to satisfy your interests here, whether you buy rugs, hike the canyons, or splay yourself around four states.

The Top Things to See and Do

Canyon de Chelly

Chinle

The Grand Canyon is, well, grander, but cold and remote compared with the softer, more accessible grace of these gorges. Here soaring red sandstone cliffs, brushed with a translucent black wash called desert varnish, rise from canyon floors laced with gently flowing streams and dotted with cottonwoods. The Navajo speak in the Blessing Way ceremony about walking in beauty, and the Canyon de Chelly (*de-shay*) is such a place. Many dwellings of the ancestral Puebloans are found here and the Navajo still farm and graze sheep on the canyon floor. (And, inviting as the area is, it's relatively uncrowded.)

You can choose from two rim drives. The first is a 37-mile round-trip South Rim drive with seven dramatic overlooks into the Canyon de Chelly — the name of one of the three gorges that meet here, as well as the name of the national monument. The second is a 34-mile North Rim drive with four vistas overlooking the adjoining Canyon del Muerto. Both drives branch off from the same road (Highway 64/Indian Rte. 7) just beyond the visitor's center. The South Rim drive takes at least 2 hours when you add in the time you spend gazing from each viewpoint. Because the North Rim drive has fewer viewpoints, the drive's a bit shorter; you can cover this drive in about 1½ hours.

Only have time for one drive? If you're most interested in the vistas, choose the South Rim drive with eye-popping overlooks like Spider Rock. The North Rim, with sites such as Antelope House and Massacre Cave, is ideal for history buffs. Get details on both drives from the visitor's center, where you can also check out the available activities — such as the ranger talks given in the hogan.

You can hike unattended to the White House Ruin. (The hike takes about 1½ hours round trip and isn't arduous if you're reasonably fit; it's a gradual slope down. I rate it moderate.) For other hikes, as well as horseback rides and jeep tours, you need a Navajo guide.

At Indian Rte. 7 and Highway 64 (3 miles east of Highway 191). ☎ *520-674-5500; Internet:* www.nps.gov/cach. *Admission: Free. The visitor's center is open daily Oct–Apr 8 a.m.–5 p.m., May–Sept 8 a.m.–6 p.m. You may drive along the paved canyon rims any time, weather permitting; you just don't see anything when it's dark.*

Hubbell Trading Post

Near Ganado

I'm happy when I merge two of my prime interests — history and retail — so I'm in hog heaven here. This trading post was puchased by John Lorenzo Hubbell in 1878 and operated by the Hubbell Family until 1967, when the post was sold to the National Park Service. The trading post looks (and works) much the same as it did a century ago, although now the post is not-for-profit and trader Bill Malone manages it.

Southwest crafts of all types are available to browse. Unless you're planning on buying a Navajo rug (see Chapter 19), which could take half the day, you will probably find that you want to spend more time here in the summer than in the winter. During the summer, more events are usually going on. Call ahead — especially during the off season — to get a schedule for the Hubbell home tours, weaving demonstrations, lectures, or tours of the 160-acre grounds.All of the activities are interesting — and free. A house tour plus the standard amount of rug and craft ogling takes about 1½ to 2 hours.

One mile west of Ganado, on Highway 264. ☎ *520-755-3475. Internet:* www.nps.gov/hutr. *Admission: Free. Open: Daily summer 8 a.m.–6 p.m., winter 8 a.m.–5 p.m. Closed Thanksgiving, Christmas, and New Year's Day. Tours of the Hubbell home are given on the hour (usually every hour) during the summer, less frequently in winter.*

More Cool Things to See and Do

✔ **Get a window on Navajoland:** Window Rock is the hole-y sandstone cliff that gave the Navajo Nation's capital its name; find the formation 2 miles north of Highway 264, near the government administration center. Besides this sandstone cliff, the top thing to see in Window Rock is the modern **Navajo Nation Museum,** at Highway 264 and Post Office Loop Road (☎ **520-871-7941**). The museum is still a work in progress as the permanent collections evolve and expand; expect to see everything from historic photographs to contemporary Navajo art. Free; open Monday to Friday, 8 a.m. to 5 p.m. (until 8 p.m. on Thursday); Saturday, 9 a.m. to 5 p.m., June to August; no Saturday hours September to May.

✔ **Survey a cartographic quirk:** Did you know the Native Americans own the piece of America where Arizona, New Mexico, Utah, and Colorado meet? The site is officially called **Four Corners Monument Navajo Tribal Park,** ¼ mile north of Highway 160 (6 miles beyond the Hwy 164 junction at Teec Nos Pos; ☎ **520-871-6647**). The monument isn't much more than a bronze plaque on a concrete slab with four state seals, but you must come, if only to see people splay out weirdly in order to be photographed in four states — and to get yourself strapped in a similarly compromising pose. Snack and souvenir stands are set up and — breathe a sigh of relief — restrooms are available (because you have been driving in the middle of nowhere for ages).

Keeping Active

The only unescorted hike you may take into the Canyon de Chelly is on the 2.5-mile round-trip White House Ruin trail, which leads from the White House overlook on the South Rim to the White House Ruin. The hike is moderately difficult with a winding descent of 600 feet to the canyon floor, where you can see a two-level ancestral Puebloan cliff dwelling. The cliff dwelling and the footholds carved into the steep canyon walls that allow access to this early condo date back to around A.D. 1060.

The tours of the Hubbell Trading Post are covered in this chapter in "Exploring Navajo Nation East;" all of the following tours refer to the Canyon de Chelly.

✔ **Hiking:** On all Canyon de Chelly hikes except the White House Ruin trail (see preceding section), a Navajo guide is required. At the visitor's center (☎ **520-674-5500**), you find members of the **Tsegi Guide Association,** who take you (and 14 others, max) trekking for $15 per person, per hour (minimum of 3 hours). **Canyon Hiking Service,** ¼ mile north of Thunderbird Lodge (☎ **520-674-1767**), makes similar arrangements. For all hikes, decide with the help of your guide where you want to trek based on your interests (say, ruins or petroglyphs) and fitness level.

Don't be macho (or macha). If you don't hike much, make this point clear to your guide. A hike that is easy for your guide, who may run up and down the canyon to visit relatives routinely, may be very difficult for you. If you have a fear of heights (or, more accurately, edges), discuss that concern too. (Hiking up doesn't generally bother me, but I found myself terrified by the sheer rock ledges involved in the descent.)

✔ **Four (or six) wheel tours:** The Thunderbird Lodge (see "Where to Stay," in this chapter) runs tours of the canyon in six-wheel-drive flatbed trucks outfitted with padded seats. A full-day version of these tours is available from spring to late fall, road conditions permitting ($59.50, including lunch). Half-day tours are available year-round, departing at 9 a.m. and 1 or 2 p.m., depending on the season ($37 adults, $28.50 ages 12 and under). Reserving a spot in the summer is a good idea.

De Chelly Tours into the canyon may be booked at the gift shop of the Holiday Inn (see "Where to Stay," in this chapter)) or by contacting the company directly (☎ **520-674-3772** or 674-5433; Internet: www.dechellytours.com); tours cost $125 for 3 hours in a Jeep Wrangler driven by a guide that holds three passengers, $150 for a larger vehicle with room for up to four people, and $175 for jumbo-sized four wheelers that carry from five to seven people. In all cases, an additional $30 per hour (per vehicle) is charged if you want to tour longer than 3 hours. These tours, which include **Antelope House** and the **White House Ruin,** depart twice daily in high season, less frequently in winter. Three-hour tours in a Unimog army truck cost $40 per person, but these tours only operate if all 12 spaces are filled. Call ahead to book all tours.

You still must follow a Navajo leader if you drive your own all-terrain vehicle, but the tour is less expensive. De Chelly Tours and the Tsegi Guide Association (see "Hiking," above in this list) lead you (and up to four more vehicles) for $15 to $20 per hour (3-hour minimum).

> ✔ **Horseback tours: Justin's Horse Rental,** South Rim Drive near the park entrance; (☎ 520-674-5678), and **Totsonni Ranch,** South Rim Drive 1.3 miles east of the Spider Rock turnoff, where the pavement ends; (☎ 520-755-6209), charge about $10 per person, per hour, with an additional $15 per hour charge for the guide. No minimum charge is set, but if you want to get into the canyon rather than just riding the rims, figure on at least 3 hours.

Shopping

You don't have to go beyond the area's two main attractions to shop. At the Canyon de Chelly, the **Thunderbird Lodge** and the **Holiday Inn** run excellent gift shops; the latter is smaller, but has some unusual, high-quality pieces. And although rugs are its specialty, you may find pretty much any type of craft you're looking for at the **Hubbell Trading Post.** If you're visiting Window Rock, check out the **Navajo Arts & Crafts Enterprise,** Highway 264 and Rte. 12 (☎ 520-871-4090), and the gift shop at the Navajo Nation Museum (see "Navajo Nation East/Exploring Navajo Nation East/More Cool Things to See and Do," in this chapter), which has a huge collection of Native American tapes and CDs that you may listen to before you buy.

Indian Etiquette: Some Reservation Do's and Don'ts

Forgive me if you think I'm stating the obvious, but you may be surprised to know how many people seem to leave their manners — and sense — back home.

- ✔ **Don't enter a home uninvited.** How would you feel if someone wandered into your living room or knocked on your door, asking for a tour?

- ✔ **Don't enter any areas marked off-limits.** In addition, stay on designated trails or routes unless a Native American tour guide accompanies you. Driving or hiking back roads or trails on your own is forbidden.

- ✔ **Don't litter.**

- ✔ **Don't bring alcohol, drugs, or firearms onto the reservation.**

- ✔ **Observe outdoor as well as indoor privacy.** On the Navajo reservation, ask for permission to photograph, videotape, sketch, or audiotape any event or person. (If you are granted permission, you're expected to tip the grantee a dollar or two.) On the Hopi reservation, no photography and other types of reproduction — either personal or commercial — are allowed. Period.

- ✔ **Make sure your attendance at a ceremony is permitted.** Just because an event is held outside doesn't necessarily mean that it's open to the public. And if you're granted permission to attend, stand politely in the back unless you're invited to do otherwise. (Imagine attending an outdoor wedding where strangers shove in front of the immediate family to get a better view of the ceremony.) And don't applaud.

Quick Concierge: Navajo Nation East

Also see "Quick Concierge: Navajo Nation Northwest."

Hospitals: A hospital is available in Chinle (☎ 520-674-7001), but Sage Memorial Hospital in nearby Ganado (☎ 520-755-3411) has better facilities.

Information: The visitor's center of the Canyon de Chelly and the Hubbell Trading Post are your best resources; in Window Rock, the Navajo Nation Visitors Center, open Mon–Fri 8 a.m.–5 p.m., is in the Navajo Nation Museum. For the locations of these places, see "Exploring Navajo Nation East," in this chapter.

Police: In Chinle, ☎ 520-674-2111; in Window Rock, ☎ 520-871-6111.

The Hopi Mesas

The small Hopi reservation is entirely surrounded by Navajo land, but the size of their real estate holdings is not the only distinguishing feature between the two nations. The Navajo, who migrated from Canada in the fifteenth century, are relative newcomers to this area, whereas ancestors of the Hopi have been in the Four Corners region since prehistoric times. The Hopi established the village of Old Oraibi in the twelfth century, when upstart settlements like Boston or even St. Augustine, Florida, weren't even gleams in European explorers' eyes.

The Hopi reservation has no Safeways, McDonald's, or Holiday Inns; one of the villages, Walpi, isn't even wired for electricity. And, although the *pueblos* (villages) and the three mesas on which they perch are picturesque, few natural or archaeological attractions are in the area. You come here for a glimpse of an ancient culture's living traditions. Tourism is a mixed blessing for the Hopi as an economic necessity and, at times, a pain in their necks (see the "Indian Etiquette: Some Reservation Dos and Don'ts" sidebar in this chapter).

Strolling around the villages and browsing the shops takes you no more than a half to a full day. The one hotel on the reservation isn't exactly hopping after dark. If you're up for a peaceful evening, spend the night; otherwise, make Hopi a day visit.

Getting There

Highway 264, which extends from Tuba City to the Arizona/New Mexico border, links the Hopi reservation with the outside world. Highway 191 is its easternmost link. The southern roads connecting Highway 264 with I-40 are Highway 77 (just east of Holbrook); Highway 87 (at Winslow); Highway 99; and Indian Rte. 15 (both Highway 99 and Indian Rte. 15 hook up with Indian Rte. 2 at Leupp).

If you're en route from (or to) Flagstaff, Indian Rte. 15 to Indian Rte. 2 is a scenic shortcut that takes you right into the heart of Hopi land, between the Second and Third Mesas.

Getting Around

Highway 264 runs through the entire Hopi reservation, from Keams Canyon on the east to Moenkopi on the west; all the small, unnamed roads that lead to the three Hopi mesas branch off from Highway 264. For all (tourist) intents and touring purposes, no public transportation is available.

Where to Stay

To say your choice of lodgings is limited is an understatement; only one lodging is available on the reservation. If you don't bed down here, your next best bet is Winslow (see "Along Old Route 66/Where to Stay," in this chapter), some 70 miles away.

The Hopi Cultural Center Motel

$$ Second Mesa

How can you resist a motel that lists as its location "the Center of the Universe?" This motel's definitely at the center of the Hopi tourist world with the best restaurant on the reservation (see the next section, "Where to Dine"), a museum that doubles as an informal visitor's center, and the only lodging available. The guest rooms are modest but clean and have some nice Native American decor touches, as well as TVs and phones.

On the north side of Highway 264, west of the junction with Highway 87. ☎ ***520-734-2401,*** *Fax: 520-734-6651. Internet:* www.psv.com/hopi.html. *Rack rates: Mar 15–Oct 15 $95, Oct 16–Mar 14, $65–$70. MC, V.*

Where to Dine

In the **Keams Canyon shopping center,** a coffee shop dishes out burgers, sandwiches, and Native American dinner fare (although the fry bread pileup isn't called a Navajo taco here, as it is elsewhere). Unless you're really hungry, hold out for the **Hopi Cultural Center restaurant** ($) on Second Mesa. There you find everything from BLTs to Philly cheesesteaks on the menu, but go for the local dishes such as Nöqkwivi — a lamb and hominy stew served with green chiles — which comes with light and flaky blue-corn piki bread, baked over hot stone.

Remember, no alcohol is permitted on the Hopi reservation.

Exploring the Hopi Mesas

Most of the Hopi villages are clustered on three mesas that are about 10 miles apart from each other and which extend, fingerlike, from the huge Black Mesa to the north. Two other tours that aren't on the mesas and have little to interest are **Moenkopi**, 40 miles to the west of Third Mesa, and nearby **Keams Canyon**, 15 miles east of First Mesa.

Although they are physically close, the villages differ in their histories and are governed by different clans; you can't necessarily expect someone on Third Mesa to be able to give you information about First Mesa. You may stroll around all the villages except Walpi — accessible by guided tour only — but you don't find bronze "Historic Landmark" plaques on the old houses and small shops (nor do you find signs with town names, for that matter). Don't worry, getting lost is not a problem; each mesa has only one road and you may figure a cluster of houses is a village. Be courteous and park outside the towns, not on the narrow streets.

Making the Hopi Cultural Center on Second Mesa your first stop is a good idea. You are introduced to Hopi traditions and you may browse the posted notices about the events on the different mesas. After that, drive over to Walpi on First Mesa for one of the daily tours and finish off with a stroll around Old Oraibi on Third Mesa. Alternatively, if you want to arrive in time for lunch at the Hopi Cultural Center (really the only place to eat), begin your day with the Walpi tour, a good initiation into Hopi culture.

The Hopi are renowned for their elaborate religious ceremonial dances — but don't be disappointed if you don't get to see one. Because of visitors' disrespectful behavior, the famous snake dances are completely barred to outsiders, and access to the katsina dances is restricted; only those on Second and Third mesas are occasionally open to non-Indians now.

Katsina dances are religious ceremonies, very elaborate and colorful, with masked and costumed dancers representing the katsina spirits. They are held most weekends from December to July, but no set times or places for these dances are set; even the locals don't know until a day or two in advance exactly where and when these dances occur. If you're determined to see a dance, your best bet is to show up on a weekend during katsina season, find out if a dance is scheduled, and ask permission to attend. (And if you do get to go, behave yourself!)

Exploring First Mesa

At the foot of First Mesa you find **Polacca,** a town founded in the late 1800s as an offshoot of **Walpi.** Walpi is the most interesting of this mesa's towns, both for its old sandstone homes and its amazing views (see "Guided Tours" below in this chapter). Established on the side of the mesa as early as A.D. 900, Walpi moved to the hilltop for protection purposes after the 1680 Pueblo Revolt against the Spanish. The steep road that snakes up to Walpi also passes **Sichomovi** and **Hano/Tewa,** both established after the 1680 revolt, the former by the people of Walpi, the latter by two successive groups of non-Hopi puebloan peoples.

Exploring Second Mesa

The **Hopi Cultural Center Museum,** on the north side of Highway 264, just west of the junction with Highway 87 (☎ 520-734-6650), is the main draw of Second Mesa. The museum is open weekdays 8 a.m.–5 p.m; weekends mid-May through mid-October, 9 a.m.– to 4 p.m., closed weekends the rest of the year (admission $3). The oldest village on the mesa is

Shungopavi, which lies to the south of Highway 264, on the road west of the Hopi Cultural Center. **Sipolauvi** and **Mishongnovi,** on a paved road that heads north from Highway 264 just east of the cultural center, were both created soon after the 1680 Pueblo Revolt. You see the **Corn Rock shrine,** a natural monument, in Mishongnovi.

Exploring Third Mesa

Old Oraibi, founded around 1150, claims to be the oldest continuously occupied town in the United States. You see the ruins of a Spanish mission here, as well as lots of ancient houses intermingled with newer ones. (If you choose to wander around, you may want to do the locals the courtesy of politely introducing yourself at the shop called **Hamana so'oh,** which is an informal visitor's center.) All the other Third Mesa towns derive from Old Oraibi: **Hotelvilla** was formed after an internal clan schism in 1906, **Bacavi** was a 1907 offshoot of Hotelvilla, and **Kykmostmovi,** at the base of the mesa, was founded soon afterward by villagers who wanted to be closer to the main road. Kykmostmovi is the home to the Hopi Tribal offices (see "Quick Concierge: The Hopi Mesas," in this chapter). Although it's 40 miles northwest, **Moenkopi** is also a satellite town of Oraibi and considered part of Third Mesa.

Guided Tours

Guided walking tours of Walpi on First Mesa run from 30 to 45 minutes and are given daily between 9 a.m. and 4 p.m. except when religious ceremonies are being held ($5 per person). No set starting times are scheduled for the walks; tour guides wait at the First Mesa Visitors Center (☎ 520-737-2262) — just keep driving up the hill until you see the sign for the center — until about 10 people gather or until the guides determine that no one else is going to turn up.

On the tour, the guides ask if you want to visit any artisans' houses. You may decline but, if you say yes, you're under no obligation to buy anything. However, you may have a tough time walking away empty-handed, especially because many of the artists are poor. Don't let guilt be your guide. If you don't like what you see at the first home, you're bound to find something you really want to purchase later.

Left Handed Hunter (☎ **520-734-2567,** E-mail: lhhunter58@ hotmail.com) tours, run by Gary Tso — a reservation resident who's half Hopi–half Navajo — provides a unique perspective on both societies. Tso takes visitors to the homes of top artisans on all three mesas, to Old Oraibi, and to an amazing petroglyph site that's off limits to anyone without a Hopi guide and archaeological license. The tour rates — $175 for the first person, $245 for two, and $275 for three (arrangements can be made for larger groups) — include lunch at the Hopi Cultural Center and an authorized tour of Walpi. The steep price is worth the bucks if you want to take part in something akin to a private Hopi culture tutorial. (The tours you get off the reservation may cost less — as low as $100 — but they are not given by native guides.)

Shopping

Many of the shops on the Hopi mesas are literally mom and pop opera-tions: Crafts are sold out of their homes (look for signs that say some-thing like "Pottery sold here"). Log on to www.hopimarket.com for a preview of the goods and the prices you're likely to find. See also Chapter 19.

Among the more traditional shops, my favorite is **Tsakurshovi,** Second Mesa, 1½ miles east of the Hopi Cultural Center on Highway 264 (☎ 520-734-2478), with a great collection of high-quality and unusual crafts. The staff is extremely knowledgeable — and the Tsakurshovi is the only place to find owner Janet Day's original "Don't Worry, Be Hopi" tee shirts. **McGee's Indian Art** in Keams Canyon (☎ 520-738-2295) is a good place to shop for katsina dolls, and the **Hopi Silver Crafts Cooperative,** just west of the Hopi Cultural Center (☎ 520-734-2463), has a large selection of belt buckles, jewelry, and other decorative items.

Quick Concierge: The Hopi Mesas

Also in this chapter, see the sections "Quick Concierge: Navajo Nation Northwest" and "Quick Concierge: Navajo Nation East." (You may note little difference between the Navajo and Hopi reservations' services.)

Hospitals: The Public Health Service Hospital in Keams Canyon (☎ 520-739-2211), mostly serves the Hopi and Navajo people; the reservation's only pharmacy is located here.

Information: The Hopi Tribal Council (☎ 520-734-3000 [main switchboard]) and the Hopi Cultural Preservation Office (☎ 520-734-2244, 734-3750) are both in

Kykotsmovi on Third Mesa. The official Hopi Web site is www.hopi.nsn.us.

Police: ☎ 520-738-2233 (or extensions -2234, -2235, or -2236)

Road Service: The Texaco Station, approxi-mately ¼ mile past the junction of Hwys. 264 and 87, has a garage.

Along Old Route 66

When you drive on the stretch of I-40 that borders southern Indian Country from its intersection with Highway 191 to its eastern approach to Flagstaff, the journey itself — or, more precisely, the road — is the attraction. With the exception of **Petrified Forest National Park** and **Meteor Crater Natural Landmark,** this area's main draw is old Route 66, which was bypassed by I-40 in 1965 and runs roughly parallel to it. (you need to exit off the road to towns like Winslow and Holbrook).

Route 66, the first interstate stretching from Chicago to California, repre-sented the lure of the West to many; John Steinbeck dubbed this early free-way the "Mother Road." It no longer exists in its entirety — much of it was destroyed or has fallen into disrepair — so the long stretches preserved here are significant. Lined with neon signs and classic kitsch store-fronts, Route 66 embodies tourism nostalgia.

The region's two main towns, Holbrook and Winslow, are good bases for exploring Indian Country and these towns offer economical stopovers if you're road weary. You may cover this area in a single day if you just want to hit the main sights.

You're off the reservations here. All the usual rules apply.

Getting There

Simply put, the road itself is the attraction. Pretty much everything you want to see is off an I-40 exit ramp — including **Historic Route 66,** which parallels I-40 along several stretches. See "The Hopi Mesas" section in this chapter, for the roads that feed into it from the north.

From Phoenix, Highway 87, the old Beeline Highway, is the most direct route northeast to Winslow. This stretch of highway is a bit up and down — though not frighteningly mountainous — and two lane in many stretches. But it is scenic; if you take Highway 87, be sure to stop at **Tonto Natural Bridge State Park.**

Getting Around

What's a road trip without wheels? You may rent a car at the two deal-erships in town: **Ames Ford (☎ 520-289-3354)** and **Cakes Chevrolet (☎ 520-289-4681).** (If you drive, you may pass [or be passed by] a few classic cars on the highway; this area is a magnet for these roadsters.) Keep in mind that in Holbrook, Route 66 is called Hopi Drive; in Winslow, the Mother Road goes under the name 2nd Street.

However, travelers may walk next door to the terrific La Posada hotel (see "Where to Stay," the next section). If train travel appeals to you, call **Amtrak (☎ 800-872-7245)** for more information. If you prefer taking a bus, **Greyhound (☎ 800-231-222)** has service from Phoenix to Winslow.

This area is also home to a different kind of wheels — a major rail route for the old Atcheson, Topeka, and Santa Fe line, and a passenger train still stops at the original station in Winslow. These days, the station is unattended and train travelers arrive in the middle of the night.

Where to Stay

Motel franchises replace most of the funky Route 66 lodgings in Holbrook and Winslow, although some great old neon signs announce some not so great (I suspect) old rooms for $19.99 per night. The chains in Holbrook include **Best Western, Budget Inn, Comfort Inn,**

Day's Inn, Econo Lodge, Holiday Inn Express, Ramada Limited, Super 8, and **Travel Lodge.** In Winslow, **Best Western, Day's Inn, Econo Lodge, Holiday Inn Express, Motel 6, Super 8,** and **Travelodge** are available. See the Appendix for toll-free numbers for these chains.

The towns are only about 25 minutes from each other, so your choice may depend on which of the following two lodgings appeals most to you.

Wigwam Village Motel

$ Holbrook

A Route 66 classic, this 1940's holdover was revamped in 1988. The Wigwam's not fancy — what do you expect at these prices? — but you sleep in an individual wigwam-shaped unit with the original rustic furniture. The units don't have phones (try smoke signals), but they are equipped with remoteless cable televisions. And best of all — they're clean.

811 W. Hopi Dr. ☎ *800-414-3021 or 520-524-3048. Internet:* www.cybertrails. com/wigwam/. *Rack rates: high season $33–$38, lower rates in low season. MC, V.*

La Posada

$–$$ Winslow

Charles Lindbergh and Clark Gable were among the glitterati who bunked at this grand Spanish rancho-style hotel, designed for the Santa Fe Railway in 1930 by Mary Colter. The rooms, gardens, and ornately detailed lobby are slowly being restored and a restaurant (see the next section, "Where to Dine") opened in the fall of 2000. You don't find the modern comfort of the chains — the rooms don't have phones, for example — but this hotel is a prime pick for anyone who hankers for historic character.

303 E. 2nd St. at Highway 87. ☎ *520-289-4366, Fax: 520-289-3873. Internet:* www.laposada.org. *Rack rates: $79–$89, $99 suites. AE, DC, DISC, MC, V.*

Where to Dine

Fans of diner fare and down-home cooking are in hog heaven here, but gourmands better hightail it back to Phoenix. Also, plenty of fast-food places are available; if your children are hungry, finding kiddie eats around here is no trouble.

In Holbrook, **Joe & Aggie's Café** ($), 120 W. Hopi Dr. (☎ **520-524-6540**), is the prime spot for a Route 66 decor and comfort food fix; the Mexican dishes are fine, too. At dinnertime, the **Butterfield Stage Co.** ($$–$$$), 609 W. Hopi Dr. (☎ **520-524-3447**), serves good steaks in a fun Old West atmosphere.

In Winslow, **Falcon** ($), 1113 E. Third St. (☎ **520-289-2342**), opened in 1955 and is still in the same family. Falcon is the place to go for blue plate specials and great pie. The newest entry on the restaurant scene, the **dining room at La Posada** (see the above section, "Where to Stay"), wasn't yet open as this book went to press, but the menu was slated to include American comfort food classics, new Southwestern cuisine, and Native American–inspired dishes; you may want to check out the dining room for the decor alone.

Exploring along Old Route 66

Although the road is the attraction, you may take the occasional exit ramp for a few good reasons.

The Top Things to See and Do

Petrified Forest National Park

Reality check: Don't expect to see a turned-to-stone version of Redwood National Forest (like I did the first time I visited). The petrified wood is in log form and it's lying on the ground. And, although this park has magnificent vistas of the Painted Desert at its north end, this area isn't the only place that offers you views of that multihued sandstone wonderland. The Painted Desert begins east of the Grand Canyon; if you come from that direction, you experience great stretches of the desert.

This 93,000-acre park is as remarkable for its past as for its present. At the **Rainbow Forest Museum and Visitors Center,** you see vestiges of the days when the park was a forest primeval roamed by dinosaurs. "Gertie," an ancestor of the tyrannosaurus, about the size of a crocodile, is one of the three Triassic period dino skeletons on display, along with fossils of other animals and plants. The area's human history, dating back more than 2,000 years, is evident at sites like **Newspaper Rock,** with its large concentration of petroglyphs, and the **Puerco Indian Ruins,** home to many rock artists until A.D. 1400.

A 27-mile road with more than 20 overlooks connects the park's two visitor's centers; if you're on a mission, you can complete the drive in less than an hour. If you can spare a bit more time and arrive in the morning, start out from the south end: Peruse the Rainbow Forest visitor's center and museum, stroll the three easy self-guided trails, and stop at the scenic overlooks. By the time you reach the Painted Desert Visitors Center in the north, you're ready for lunch at the cafeteria or a picnic at nearby Kachina Point (where you can also visit the museum in the Painted Desert Inn). Alternatively, start out at lunchtime on the north side and end up at the south visitor's center's snack bar in the late afternoon. Hikers may easily spend an entire day in the nearby wilderness areas; campers need to obtain a free overnight permit from either of the visitor's centers.

North entrance: exit 311 off I-40 (30 miles east of Holbrook). South entrance: off Highway 180 (19 miles southeast of Holbrook). ☎ *520-524-6228. Admission: $10 per vehicle, good for 7 days. All National Park discount passes honored. Park and visitor's centers open daily (except Christmas), summer 7 a.m.–7 p.m., winter 8 a.m.–5 p.m.*

You Wooden, Wood You?

Despite the posted warnings and the testimonials from people who claim that cadging wood from the Petrified Forest ruined their lives — you may peruse a wonderful collection of cautionary "I've been hexed" letters in the Rainbow Forest Museum's "Guilt Book" — some 12 tons of fossilized wood are stolen from the Petrified Forest every year. Resist the temptation.

Exploring Holbrook

You come to this classic Route 66 town, with one of the country's few remaining wigwam motel courts (see "Where to Stay," in this chapter), miles of neon, and towering dinosaur replicas on its main drag, to ogle the kitsch and browse the shops selling rocks, petrified wood, and Mother Road-o-bilia (see "Shopping," later in this chapter). The town's one real sight is, conveniently, also its visitor's center (see "Quick Concierge: Along Route 66," in this chapter): a free historical museum in the 1898 Navajo County Courthouse, containing replicas of an early drugstore/soda fountain and a jail cell replete with prisoner graffiti.

Exploring Winslow

This town's stretch of Route 66 doesn't offer quite as many nostalgia-inducing shops and signs as Holbrook, but you can:

- **Take it easy:** So many people asked about the fictional Winslow intersection immortalized by The Eagles in the song "Take It Easy" that the "Standin' on the Corner" park was dedicated at 2nd and North Kinsley streets in 1999. Highlight: John Pugh's trompe l'oeil mural, complete with a girl in a flatbed Ford, permanently slowed down to take a look at you.

- **Get your kicks:** Much of the Route 66 stuff missing from the streets of Winslow seems to have ended up at the free **Old Trails Museum,** 212 N. Kinsley St. (☎ 520-289-5861; hours vary — call ahead). Also here are artifacts from the town's heydey as a hub for the Santa Fe Railway, much of it derived from **La Posada Hotel** (see "Where to Stay," in this chapter). The La Posada Hotel is also well worth touring (pick up a self-guided pamphlet in the lobby), even without all of its original plates and cutlery (many of which are on display at the museum).

Meteor Crater

You may be annoyed to learn that this crater is privately owned, fronted by a cheesy rock shop, and costs eight bucks to see. But nowhere else do you get such a graphic view of what could — and did — happen if a meteorite were to strike Earth. Talk about deep impact: The mega-million-ton hunk of rock that hurtled down at a speed of 45,000 mph about 50,000 years ago left a hole 570-feet deep and wide enough to fit 20 football fields. NASA used this place to test moonwalks, as the films and exhibits at the visitor's center show. You can't enter the crater but you may take a guided hike along the rim trail (daily 9 a.m.–2 p.m.).

20 miles west of Winslow (exit 233 of I-40). ☎ *520-289-2362. Internet:* www. meteorcrater.com. *Open: daily, May 15–Sept 15 6 a.m.–6 p.m., Sept 16–May 14 8 a.m.–5 p.m.. Admission: $8 adults, $7 seniors (over 60), $4 ages 5–17, 4 and under free.*

More Cool Things to See and Do

✔ **See some artful stones:** You may visit an incredible array of pictographs and petroglyphs at **Rock Art Canyon Ranch** at Chevelon Canyon, about 15 miles south of I-40 between Holbrook and Winslow (☎ 520-288-3260); the ranch also has the last remaining bunkhouse of the largest U.S. ranching operation in the nineteenth century. Call to get a brochure with a map and arrange to meet owner Brantley Baird at the ranch house; he points out the highlights of the canyon, which you may explore on your own. You pay what you like; proceeds go to maintaining the ranch museum. If you gather a group of 30 or more together (May 1 to mid-October), a hayride and cowboy dinner are options.

✔ **Get windswept:** You may explore more than 300 remains of ancestral Puebloan dwellings at **Homolovi Ruins State Park,** 3 miles northeast of Winslow (☎ 520-289-4106) You may find it hard to imagine that people lived on this rather bleak plain; the winds always seem to howl. Several hiking trails lead through the ruins, which include prehistoric pit houses, fourteenth-century pueblos, and a variety of petroglyphs. Admission: $4 per vehicle (up to four people; $1 per person after that). The ruins are open sunrise to sunset, the visitor's center daily 8 a.m. to 5 p.m. To get to the park, take I-40 to exit 257; then go 1.3 miles north on Highway 87.

Shopping

Three miles west of Holbrook, the **International Petrified Forest/ Dinosaur Park,** 1001 Forest Dr. (exit 292 off I-40, ☎ 520-524-9178), is a huge warehouse chock-a-block with petrified wood, rocks, and fossils. You see additional rock shops and places to buy Route 66 mementos on Holbrook's main street, Navajo Boulevard. Navajo Boulevard is also where you find **McGees,** 2114 E. Navajo Blvd. (☎ 520-524-1977), featuring high-quality jewelry, baskets, katsinas (dolls), and other Native American crafts at reasonable prices. **Jack Rabbit Trading Post,** near Joseph City between Winslow and Holbrook (take exit 269 off I-40, ☎ 520-288-3230), is loaded with Route 66 kitsch and more rocks; enjoy some cherry cider and get yourself photographed with a giant black-and-yellow rabbit. In Winslow, head for **Moore's,** 1020 W. 3rd St., (☎ 520-289-3871), a combination hardware store and pawn shop with a great selection of turquoise-studded Navajo bracelets and squash-blossom necklaces (heavy silver necklaces with horseshoe-shaped pendants).

Quick Concierge: Along Route 66

Area code: 520.

Hospitals: Holbrook does not have a hospital; for medical emergencies, go to Winslow Memorial Hospital, 1501 Williamson Ave. (☎ 520-289-4691).

Information: Holbrook Chamber of Commerce, Old West Courthouse, 100 E. Arizona (☎ 800-524-2459 or 520-524-2459; Internet: http://ci.holbrook.az.us/ Chamber), open daily 8 a.m.–5 p.m. Winslow Chamber of Commerce and Visitors Center, 300 W. North Rd. (☎ 520-289-2434; Internet: www.winslowarizona.org), open daily 8 a.m.–5 p.m. in summer, usually closed weekends during the off season.

Pharmacies: Holbrook: Safeway, 702 W. Hopi Dr. (☎ 520-524-2661), Mon–Sat 9 a.m.–7 p.m. Winslow: Safeway, 1601 N. Park Dr. (☎ **520-289-4615**) Mon–Fri 9 a.m.–7 p.m., Sat 9 a.m.–5 p.m., Sun 10 a.m.–4 p.m.

Police: Call ☎ **911.**

Post Office: Holbrook, 100 W. Erie St. (☎ **520-524-3311**). Winslow: 223 Williamson Ave. (☎ **520-289-2131**).

Part V
The Part of Tens

The 5th Wave   By Rich Tennant

"Of all the stuff we came back from Arizona with, I think these adobe bathrobes were the least well-thought-out."

In this part. . .

*T*he parts of this book are like children — you pour your heart into getting them to be the best they can, and then they go out into the world (the ingrates!) — so I don't like to play favorites, but let's just say this one has loads of personality and is very organized to boot. It consists of three fun topics — crafts, food, and local quirks — presented in a "top ten" format. What's not to like?

Chapter 19

The Top Ten Crafts to Buy in Arizona

. . . .

In This Chapter

▶ Getting Native American goods

▶ Wrangling Western wares

▶ Shopping for south-of-the-border stuff

. . . .

Shopping for crafts is one of Arizona's great recreational activities. Don't let anyone try to tell you that no skill is involved. Identifying the best items to buy and the best places to find them takes savvy, sleuthing — or scanning the following list.

What did it take for the crafts to make the top ten ranking? Locality, for one thing. I concentrate on items either indigenous to Arizona or — if nothing like it is made in the state — to immediate neighbors New Mexico and Mexico. (Sorry, nothing from Nevada, I figure you have enough fuzzy dice.) Also, port-ability or ship-ability: Why buy some-thing special that's not going to arrive home intact or that's prohibi-tively expensive to send safely? Finally, value for money. Some of the things I recommend are quite costly, but these items are investments in works of art as well as in continuing traditions.

In general, if you want to be sure that a Native American craft is gen-uine rather than mass-produced or a cheap knockoff, look for the name of the artisan on it, or ask the seller, who should be able to tell you. Small irregularities are also a tip-off that an item is handmade.

For a preview of Hopi crafts and their prices, log on to www. hopimarket.com; for a quick introduction to Navajo rugs, check out http://navajorugs.spma.org. The *Field Guide to Southwest Indian Arts and Crafts* by Susanne and Jake Page (Random House) is an excel-lent all-around resource and Phoenix's Heard Museum is the best single stop in the state for those interested in Native American crafts. To learn more about goods created south of the border, get a hold of *Arts and Crafts of Mexico* by Chloë Sayer (Chronicle Books).

Unless I say otherwise, expect to find listings for specific places to buy the crafts discussed in the "Shopping" sections of Chapters 11 through 18. And now (drum roll) the list . . .

Hopi Katsina Dolls

To the Hopi people, *katsinas* (less accurately called "kachinas" and pronounced *kat-see-nuhs*) are the spiritual aspect of all material phenomena including plants, animals, rain . . . you name it; there are some 400 different kinds in all. Naturally, as spirits, the spirits can't be seen, but their representations are made visible through such things as ceremonial masks, headgear, costumes worn by katsina dancers, and, most famously, dolls. Katsina dolls were (and still are) used as toys and teaching tools for young girls. Craftspeople now make many katsina dolls to be sold to outsiders.

Hopi katsina dolls are intricately carved and painted and always made of cottonwood root; knockoffs are generally cruder and created from other materials. Buy these dolls on the Hopi Mesas, either directly from the artisans or at one of the small shops, in order to guarantee authenticity and good prices. (Middleman or expensive rent costs are not factored into the prices on the Hopi Mesas as these costs are factored into the prices at Native American craft boutiques in the big cities.) The smallest katsina dolls start at about $50; you may pay $500 or more for larger, very detailed figures.

Hopi Overlay Silverwork

A relatively new craft — originating in the mid-1950s — Hopi overlay silverwork is just what is sounds like: Intricate designs are cut with a fine tool out of a flat layer of silver, which is soldered onto a second layer of approximately the same size, but slightly thinner. Both layers are oxidized but only the top layer is polished, which makes it stand out in contrast with the black layer below. The back may be (but isn't always) stamped with a personal hallmark — usually the artist's name or clan symbol and you should expect to find a "sterling" stamp (unless of course, the item is made of gold — which some of the younger artists are now using).

This double-layered silver is fashioned into decorative items — everything from earrings to watch bands and belt buckles — as varied as the Hopi universe-oriented designs. The Hopi mesas are the best place to buy this work but you may find good pieces throughout the state. Prices start at about $15 for a simple pair of earrings and go up from there.

Navajo Rugs

The 300-year history of Navajo rugs is a long and complicated one — and one that was strongly tied to western traders. In the late nineteenth century, those traders encouraged the Navajos to create patterns they knew would sell well to Anglos. Many of the distinct designs you find today — Two Grey Hills, for example, Crystal, and Ganado Red — are named for the trading posts where they originated.

The colors used in Navajo rugs vary widely and most of the patterns are abstract and purely decorative. Some rugs weave tall, skinny figures into their designs representing *yeis,* supernatural healers who act as intermediaries between the Navajos and their gods. Other rugs show *yeibichais* (look for the uplifted feet), Navajo dancers dressed as yei spirits. Rugs with pictorial scenes depict life on the reservation; details may include anything from pick-up trucks to soda machines.

Which is the best design? The one that really strikes your fancy. You pay a lot for the genuine item — rugs start at about $350 and go well into the thousands; large, antique ones fetch upwards of $25,000 — so you need to make a love connection with your selection. Ironically, now that the rugs are becoming prized for their great artistry, few skilled artisans are left. Most of the younger Navajos abandoned weaving for more potentially lucrative professions, and a large rug can take almost a year to finish.

You can trust the authenticity of anything you buy at the Hubbell Trading Post in Ganado (see Chapter 18) and at Garland's Navajo Rugs in Sedona (see Chapter 16), both of which have wide selections of contemporary and antique pieces.

Navajo Silverwork

Navajo silversmithing began in the mid-nineteenth century as a vehicle for incorporating much-prized pieces of turquoise — traditionally a lucky, healing stone — into decorative items such as necklaces and belts. These days, many pieces, especially wide bracelets, belt buckles, and squash blossom necklaces (the ones with the horseshoe-shaped pendants), still incorporate the blue stone. You may also find intricate designs on plain silver concha belts, earrings, and bracelets. Navajo silverwork is single layer, unlike that of the Hopi, and the stones incorporated (often coral as well as turquoise) tend to be rough-hewn and natural looking. Braided silver is common too, especially in antique pieces.

You find good pieces at trading posts and crafts shops all over the Navajo reservation; some of the older, heavily turquoise-studded ones are sold as "pawn" near the reservation in towns such as Flagstaff, Winslow, and Holbrook. Some of the most creative work is exported to Native American crafts boutiques in Greater Phoenix and Tucson. Prices range widely, starting at about $20 for small earrings and going up to the thousands for the larger items. The newer work should be marked (sometimes in ink) with the artist's name and stamped "sterling"; antique work won't necessarily have those signs of authenticity.

Zuni Carvings (Fetishes)

A *fetish* is a kind of talisman or personal charm. All tribes in the Southwest make use of fetishes, but the Zuni, a New Mexico puebloan people closely related to the Hopi, are particularly renowned for their skill at carving these small figurines.

According to legend, certain animals — mountain lions, bears, badgers, wolves, eagles, and moles — serve as protectors, as healers, and as messengers to and from the spirit world. Small stone representations of these sacred animals, believed to contain their spirit, are worn for protection from harm and to assure success. Those made for sale to non-Indians (the Zunis allude to them as "carvings" rather than fetishes) aren't imbued with any religious significance. These crafts are made out of a variety of carvable, colorful stones, including such semi-precious ones as turquoise, alabaster, and lapis. These fetishes represent many different animals in addition to the traditional ones, but the bear is still the most popular.

Because they're not native to Arizona, you can't find Zuni carvings in any particular place in the state; you locate them at most reputable Native American crafts shops. Prices start at about $15 and rarely go much beyond $40.

Tohono O'odham Baskets

The Tohono O'odham people, whose reservation near Tucson is the second largest in the country (after that of the Navajo), are the most prolific basket makers in the Southwest. Their traditional coiled baskets are prized for their artistry as well as for the complicated process involved in making them. To collect the natural materials used — willow, yucca, devil's claw (for the black color), and bear grass, to name a few — the Tohono O'odham often travel far and in different seasons. The labor is careful and painstaking, too, so it's no surprise that small baskets start at about $200.

The "Man in the Maze" design, which depicts a small figure at the head of a circular labyrinth, is the main tribal symbol. You may find several other patterns, including linked friendship dancers and a variety of desert plants and critters (even scorpions and snakes look charming when they're woven) as well.

Locating these baskets is easiest in Tucson, at shops in town selling Native American crafts, and at San Xavier Plaza. The San Xavier Plaza is directly across from the San Xavier Mission, built for the Tohono O'odham people centuries ago and still their prime place of worship. The largest selection, however, is at the gift shop at Kitt Peak National Observatory, which leases its lofty plot of land from the tribe. At Kitt Peak and San Xavier Plaza, which are both on the Tohono O'odham reservation, all the proceeds go to the tribe rather than the store owners.

Bola Ties

Arizona can't lay claim to having invented such standard Western items as cowboy boots or saddles — most of them are actually of Spanish/Mexican origin — but the state can take credit for the classic

Western string tie. In Wickenburg in 1949, as the story goes, Vic Cedarstaff caught a glimpse of his cowboy hat's "stampede strings" lying across his shoulders. He fixed the strings around his neck with an oval clasp of turquoise and silver and called his tie a "piggin' necklet," but for obvious reasons the name didn't catch on. Then he changed the name to "bola" — short for *boleadora,* a rope contraption used for reigning in cattle in South America — and a trend was born.

Turquoise and silver remain the most popular fastener materials, although styles now vary from copper to plastic and designs include everything from corporate logos to replicas of the state of Texas (where they no doubt claim they invented the tie). The bola was declared Arizona's official state neckwear in 1971.

Bola ties make great gifts for both men and women (worn with a simple, tailored shirt, these ties are a nice stand-in for a necklace). You find bola ties at every Western store and practically every Native American crafts shop in the state; both the Hopi and Navajo fashion bolas with elaborately designed silver clasps. Prices start at about $15 for mass-produced ones and go up from there depending on the materials used and artistry involved. Just don't buy one anywhere that uses the spelling "bolo" — you need to draw the line in the sand somewhere.

Western-Style Leatherwork

Unless you own a horse, you probably won't want to tote a saddle home. Few places are around where you can get much play out of a full set of chaps (except maybe some leather bars with a cowboy bent), but other hand-tooled, stitched, studded, and stamped leather items say West in a way most people can use. Belts, wallets, purses, and briefcases are the most obvious choices. If you're looking for purely decorative items, you may also consider a holster.

You can purchase factory-made leatherwork all over the state. If you want the real thing, follow the horse trail — though not literally, that could get messy — to places like Wickenburg, Tucson, and southeast Arizona where ranching still goes on. I mentioned William Brown Holster Co. in Tombstone (Chapter 15) and Ben's Saddlery in Wickenburg (Chapter 16); elsewhere, check the Yellow Pages under "Leather" and look for places that have "saddlery" in their names. Secondhand or antiques stores can also be a good source of leatherwork if you don't mind it a bit worn (just call it broken in). Estimating prices is difficult; these items are labor intensive and good leather doesn't come cheap. Expect to shell out at least $35 for something small — and without studs — like a wallet.

Mexican Tinwork

For inexpensive gifts, especially around the holidays, you may be hard pressed to find anything as pleasing as Mexican tinwork. You can choose from a variety of items — the colorful painted ornaments are a particularly good pick. These painted ornaments come in delightful, surprising shapes — angels, tropical fish, cactus, parrots, armadillos, cheerful Day of the Dead skeletons engaged in all manner of activities — most not overtly religious in subject matter. In Nogales, Mexico, where they're sold in practically every shop, these ornaments cost about $1 each, but at even twice or quadruple the price in crafts stores in Tucson or Greater Phoenix, they're still a bargain.

Also interesting and very transportable are the unpainted tin ex-votos called *milagros* (literally "miracles"). These small, charmlike representations of arms, legs, eyes, hearts, and other parts of the body that may be cured through divine intervention are often sold inexpensively in bins for about 75¢ each. You may also find many of these milagros incorporated into works of devotional folk art in Mexico and southern Arizona.

Candlesticks and decorative boxes fashioned from unpainted tins are also a good deal; plain ones in each category start at about $5 in Nogales. The more ornate tinwork mirrors, which often incorporate colored tile, are gorgeous, but not nearly as portable. Still, you may consider a small one, so long as you wrap it carefully and can store it easily under an airplane seat; expect to pay about $40 for these in Nogales.

Piñatas

Dating back to the days of the Aztecs, piñatas have been a mainstay at Hispanic celebrations for centuries. These hollow papier-mâché sculptures, stuffed with candy and toys, are great energy releasers for children. The kids are blindfolded and spun around; then they try to whack the piñata open with a stick. Piñatas are increasingly popular with other cultures, too (even Hallmark puts out a line now). If you want the authentic version, go to the source: Mexico, or the Mexican-American communities in southern Arizona. Just comb the stalls in Nogales or look in the Phoenix and Tucson Yellow Pages under "Party Supplies" (store names like La Piñata in Tucson are a dead giveaway; if you're in doubt about other shops, phone and ask).

Piñatas come in a variety of shapes — from the traditional donkeys to the latest cartoon characters — and can be custom designed. (I once saw a piñata version of a pink 1957 Chevy convertible.) The Guiness Book of World Records lists one that's 27-feet high and weighs 10,000 pounds, but most are a lot more portable and affordable. Prices start at about $6 in Mexico and $10 in the states — of course you pay considerably more for something like that Chevy. They can be a bit bulky, but smallish ones are available. What other item can you promise the kids they can break just as soon as they get home?

Chapter 20

The Top Ten Ways to Avoid Being Pegged As a Tourist

*P*assing for an Arizonan doesn't involve toning down that New Jersey or Louisiana accent; practically everyone who lives in the state is from somewhere else, anyway. You just need to master a bit of the lingo and style and get acquainted with some of the state's quirks. Follow these ten simple rules and you should be right into the swim of things. (Bonus tip #11: Remember, that's "swim" as in pool or lake, not ocean.)

Oh, yeah — this is true pretty much anywhere you travel with borrowed wheels — when parked, remain a discreet distance away from your car. You auto's bound to have license plates that shout "RENTAL."

Habla a Little Español

Remember, the conquistadors, not the pilgrims, were the first piratical real estate developers in these parts. And southern Arizona belonged to Mexico until 1853, when General Santa Anna sold it to the United States as part of the Gadsden Purchase (as a result of which he was charged with high treason). All this to say, Arizona comes by its Iberian pretensions honestly.

Take street names, for example. Everything's "Cañon del Oro" (canyon of gold) this or "Via Linda" (pretty road) that — even if there isn't a canyon of gold within a hundred miles of the spot or if the road couldn't be any less beautiful. Homes that no self-respecting horse would approach are often called "ranchos." In fact, if you're acquainted with Spanish, you probably find the Housing Development dialect pretty amusing.

On the other hand, Mexican Menu Spanish is not at all silly and extremely helpful when it comes to getting fed throughout the state; see Chapter 21 for a few details.

In general, if a word seems to be of Spanish origin, watch your "j's" (sometimes pronounced "h" if at the beginning of a word, as in "javelina"); "g's" (sometimes silent, as in "saguaro," or pronounced like "h," as in "gila monster"); and "n's" that have funny squiggly things called tildes on top of them (always pronounced "nyuh" — as in the aforementioned "Cañon del Oro").

Know Your Desert Critters

Yep, southern Arizona's Sonoran Desert is home to all kinds of creepy, crawly things — as well as to some very cute creatures. The trick is to distinguish among the good, bad, and the ugly. Here are ten of the more exotic creatures you're likely to encounter — though not necessarily up close and personally and almost definitely, not in your hotel room:

✔ **Coyotes:** These wild animals pretty much keep to themselves during the day, so you may not see any. (Large wolf-like dogs are often mistaken for coyotes.) Don't be suprised if you hear coyotes howling at night. And, no, they don't wear bandanas.

✔ **Hummingbirds:** Southern Arizona is hummingbird heaven; nowhere else in North America do you find such a wide variety. These birds look adorable — flitting and hovering, helicopter-like, around flowers. What they're actually doing is pigging out. With the highest metabolic rate of any warm-blooded vertebrate, hummingbirds eat all day long to keep from starving.

✔ **Jackrabbits and desert cottontails:** What can I say? Every day is Easter in the desert. You're most likely to see jackrabbits and their cousins, the desert cottontails (the latter's ears are smaller, and they have cute fluffy tails), hopping around at dawn or dusk. Both types are, well, pigs; they nibble voraciously on a variety of plants, including cactus.

✔ **Javelinas:** (That's *hav-uh-lee-nuhs,* also called collared peccaries.) These animals resemble small wild boars — though they're not actually in the pig family (or related to spears, for that matter). Javelinas are the desert version of racoons: They like to root through the garbage in the more remote housing developments. Several resorts in Greater Phoenix and Tucson have resident javelina families; they're cute, but my, what big teeth they have (the better to nibble on cactus, prickles and all), so steer clear.

✔ **Lizards:** Small, pinkish, and delicate **geckos** are notable for the round pads on their fingers and toes — the better to climb the walls, literally. These lizards are far more common — you may be relieved to hear — than the two-feet-long, black-and-orange-striped **gila** (that's *hee-la*) **monster.** The largest native lizard in the United States, the gila monster is the only venomous animal protected by state law. Don't be deceived by their placid, sluggish demeanor; gila monsters can bite with a vise-like grip. Pick one up and you may need to pry it off with a screw driver; then head for the nearest emergency room. Gila monsters aren't considered deadly to humans, but you don't really want to test that hypothesis.

✔ **Quails:** These chubby, plumed birds tend to cross the road together in family groups *(coveys)*. The mother quail shepherds a bunch of her babies. These birds may also turn up on your dinner plate — but I won't discuss that here.

✔ **Rattlesnakes:** Arizona public relations people like to point out the fact that rattlers are present in nearly every state in the United States. What the public relations folks may not mention is the fact that the Southwest has more species of rattlesnakes than any other single region in the Americas. The good news: Rattlers don't really want to tussle with you; that rattling sound means "go away." Nor do they want to waste venom on you — you're too large to kill and eat. If you do get bit, chances are 50/50 that it's a dry (nonpoisonous) bite. The bottom line: Watch where you step in the wild but don't get hung up on worrying. You're 20 times more likely to be struck by lightening than to be bit by a rattlesnake.

✔ **Roadrunners:** I spotted one of these large (about two feet long), crested birds sprinting across a parking lot of my accountant's office in Tucson. I've never seen one being pursued by a coyote, however, or heard one go "beep, beep." They eat rattlesnakes whole, they prefer to run rather than fly, and they can sprint as fast as 15 miles per hour. Roadrunners live in the deserts and other hot arid parts of the Southwest and the Southern great plains, and I see them pretty often — not only in my accountant's parking lot — so I'd say they're pretty common.

✔ **Scorpions:** These miniature lobsters like to hang out in dark, dry spots. All varieties are nearly invisible in the dark (though they glow under ultraviolet light). If your shoes are under your bed all night, shaking them out before sticking your feet back into them is not a bad idea. The scorpion's bite is painful, but not dangerous. Their sting is venomous, but they only sting humans in self-defense, and most species' stings just cause a painful swelling. The exception (out of the 20 species common to the Southwest) is the small bark scorpion, which can cause convulsions and, occasionally, heart failure. Unfortunately, this book doesn't tell you how to identify this particular type. Just don't try to start a conversation with a scorpion by asking, "What's your sign?"

✔ **Spiders:** Big, hairy **tarantulas** are the most conspicuous of the desert spiders, but they're harmless — honest; some people even keep them as pets. The spiders you really want to give a wide berth to are the much smaller, but far more poisonous black widows. The bite of a black widow spider can be deadly but, fortunately, they're not aggressive, so just don't go poking your fingers in their faces, or into dark corners. You can recognize the venomous females by the bright red, hourglass-shaped markings on their chests.

Wear Lots of Clinking, Chunky Silver Stuff

This tip goes for both men and women. And the bigger the item, the better — turquoise-studded belt buckles that could eat Chicago, earrings that could draw your lobes so low you could turn up in a *National Geographic* photo. Sure, accessories like these may weigh you down while you sightsee, but you can use them as weapons if you're ever in a fix.

Get Tattooed

True, tattoos are not a fashion statement throughout Arizona, and investing in one can be both permanent and expensive. However, when Arizonans go in for body decoration, they often do it with a vengeance. For example, Earl Kenneth Kaufmann, a computer salesman from Minneapolis (his wife and many friends attest that he is a very nice person), moved to Tucson, got tattooed over 85 percent of his body, opened up three tattoo shops, and had his name officially changed to "The Scary Guy."

Don't Ask, "Where Are the Trees?"

Everyone knows that the real ones are in northern Arizona, decorating the area near the Grand Canyon (Mother Nature must have thought that big ol' hole could use a little softening around the edges) or on top of mountains. Deduction: Act like most of southern Arizona's plants are unapproachable, to the point of removing these plants from your person and clothing with tweezers if you get too close to them.

Learn to Repeat the Words, "But It's a Dry Heat"

Everyone in southern Arizona becomes a pseudo-Buddhist in the hotter months, when this phrase is used continuously as a mantra.

Bone Up on the Latest Political Scandal (Or Weirdness)

Since the mid-1980s alone, Arizona has been involved in the federal savings and loan debacle, with Phoenix financier Charles Keating jailed for securities fraud; had two governors convicted of finance-related felonies (Ev Mecham, who was impeached and thrown out of office, and Fife Symington, who resigned); and had 18 people, including six state legislators, indicted on charges of accepting bribes in return for supporting casino gambling (five were locked up). Arizona passed a vegetable libel law (a statute making it illegal to malign agricultural products). This state also decided to forgo daylight saving time, and the Maricopa County sheriff, Joe Arpaio, gained national attention for making inmates work on chain gangs and wear pink underwear. Check around: You're bound to join in some good conversations where folks are dishing some dirt during your visit.

Don't Worry about Slipping on Slickrock

Unless you're a klutz who slips on everything, Slickrock isn't slick, though it's bare of plants. The strikingly beautiful, eroded, rust orange and buff sandstone of northern Arizona's Colorado Plateau got its name because it's often covered with a slightly shiny desert varnish. The sheen isn't actually varnish but a thin blue-black veneer formed by seeping water, wind, and a variety of microbes. Slickrock served as the original Etch-a-Sketch for Native American artists, who pecked or scratched their designs onto the dark surface to reveal the lighter rock below (creating what are now called *petroglyphs*).

Don't Say, "I'm Looking for a Shaded Parking Spot"

Shaded parking spots don't exist. Arizonans have more space than sense.

Don't Be Put Out If You're Called a "Zonie"

Congratulations. You're not being accused of being a member of a cult; rather, you're accepted — and only slightly insulted — as an Arizonan. "Zonie" is probably one of the fonder names that Californians (who tend to descend on Arizona en masse come summer) call a resident in their next-door neighbor state.

Chapter 21

Arizona's Top Ten Food Groups

In This Part

▶ Standards with an Arizona twist: Beans, beef, bread, corn, and veggies

▶ Unique southwest favorites: Cacti, chiles, chimichangas, cilantro, and topopo salad

The beans are black, the corn is blue. Arizonans eat cacti and sometimes prepare their steaks dry — on purpose. So, the local cuisine, with its strong Native American and Mexican influences, can occasionally seem a little weird to outsiders. Familiarity breeds contentment when it comes to food; you may enjoy Arizona's specialties, too, once you figure out exactly what it is you're sinking your teeth into.

I realize the folks responsible for the health-related food pyramid may not agree with some of the following categories. You just try telling an Arizonan that the chimichanga is not a major food group.

Beans

Beans play a big role in northern Mexican and cowboy cooking alike (the famous campfire scene from *Blazing Saddles* may come to mind). Arizona has beans in every form you can imagine. Kidney beans are cooked in tangy barbecue sauce and served with ribs, chicken, and the like in casual steakhouses. The tonier New Southwestern restaurants embrace the rich, smoky-flavored black bean (also known as the turtle bean) for soups and dips. *Frijoles* — the Mexican menu bean of choice — are more commonly called pintos and turn up as *frijoles refritos* — refried and topped with cheese.

Beef

Arizona does steaks in all cuts and sizes — this was, after all, cattle country not so long ago — with preparations ranging from roadside pan-fried to big-city butter sautéed. The most common (and most delicious) way to get your big meat fix, however, is mesquite-grilled; you practically think the cows here are crossbred with the wood of a fragrant tree.

In the days before ice cube–dispensing refrigerators with double freezers were common, dried meat was a staple of the Southwest diet. That tradition lives on in statewide convenience stores, where beef jerky sits next to the cash registers. And dehydrated beef also comes in a much more palatable, Mexican variety: *Carne seca* is sun-dried, shredded, and spiced before being sautéed and served as filling for tacos, burritos, and enchiladas.

Bread

Forget sourdough, wheat, and Wonder. Sure, Arizona has those but what the state does best is *tortillas* (mostly corn and flour, though yuppie whole wheat versions have snuck in) and *Indian fry bread,* flat discs of deep-fried dough served with a variety of toppings. When lettuce, cheese, tomatoes, and ground beef are piled on fry bread, you have a *Navajo taco* — similar to the Mexican variety, only flat. Another Native American specialty is *piki bread,* a delicious light, flaky variety prepared from blue cornmeal (see "Corn," later in this chapter) and baked over a hot stone. Piki bread is generally only available on the Hopi reservation.

Cacti

No, Arizonans don't eat all kinds and the locals don't eat the spines, but pretty much everything else is fair game on the prickly pear cactus. The plant's tender young pads, called *nopales,* turn up on Mexican menus in southern Arizona, mostly sliced and diced and scrambled with eggs. Occasionally, nopales are roasted or served marinated in salads. These goodies are also sold in supermarkets as *nopalitos* — small pickled strips. You don't detect a really strong taste in napoles; they're kind of like okra (which they resemble in texture too, unfortunately). Napoles are loaded with vitamins, minerals, antioxidants, and amino acids; they're even touted as diet aids because their fibers slow down digestion.

The sweet, kiwi-sized fruit of the prickly pear, filled with seeds, is called a *tuna* (though there's nothing fishy about it). Ranging in color from pale pink and lavender to deep red, the fruit is made into jams, jellies, marinades, and sweet syrup (often used to create a mighty pretty margarita).

Chiles

First things first: There's no such thing as a chile pepper. According to chef Mark Miller's *The Great Chile* book, the mix-up dates back to Christopher Columbus, who thought he brought a new type of black pepper to the Old World; he actually introduced a plant of an unrelated genus, *capsicum.* Second, the chile plant is spelled with an "e," not an "i." Chili, the stew made of meat and (sometimes) beans and usually containing fresh chiles, is a whole other food group — but not an Arizonan one. Third, not all chiles are hot.

The chiles you most often come across in Arizona are the fairly mild anaheims and poblanos, which tend to turn up stuffed (relleno); anaheims are also dried and strung together in chile strings known as *ristras*. The medium-hot jalapeño (called chipotles when they're dried and smoked) is used in a lot of recipes, too. You sometimes find dishes that include serranos, farther up still on the heat scale (it's got a bit of an after-kick) but you rarely encounter the incendiary habernero, estimated to be 30 to 50 times hotter than the jalapeño. Frankly, much as I hate to admit it, Arizonans are generally wusses, chile-wise — especially when compared to neighboring New Mexico. No need to be scared of your salsa here.

Chimichangas

As opposed to Tex-Mex or New Mexican, Arizona's version of Mexican cuisine isn't all that distinct from the hearty, cheese-smothered fare of northern Mexico. Although filling and tasty, Arizona's Mexican-inspired edibles are not wildly exciting. This state did, however, originate two excellent south-of-the-border spin-offs: the chimichanga and the topopo salad (see later in this chapter). The chimi — as it's known to its fans — consists of a large flour tortilla filled with meat, deep-fried, and topped with guacamole, cheese, and salsa. Can anything *be* more fattening — or yummy? Like that of the Caesar salad and of the fajita, the exact genesis of the chimi is widely disputed, but El Charro restaurant in Tucson stakes a pretty strong claim.

Cilantro

The herb derived from the lacy leaves of the coriander plant, also called Chinese parsley and related to the American kind, definitely rules. Nothing says Mexican/Southwest like cilantro. Don't be surprised if you come across a menu item like crabmeat enchiladas with jalapeno-cilantro pesto sauce, for example. I'd like to add that Cilantro isn't the only seasoning in Arizona — in addition to the usual suspects such as garlic and salt, chefs cooking in the New Southwest tradition love exotic spices like achiote (made from the musky, dark-red seeds of the annatto tree) and epazote (sometimes called Mexican tea, and similar in taste to winter savory).

Some people absolutely despise cilantro, which is hard for the many who adore its fresh, bracing taste to understand. Turns out, a scientific fact may explain: Just as folks have allergies to peanuts, dairy, and other foods, the body chemistry of some people reacts with the herb so that it literally tastes like soap. If you fall into this group (you'll know the first time you try anything with cilantro) and you dine at a Mexican or New Southwest restaurant, be sure to ask your server if cilantro is included in a dish you may order. It's strong stuff.

Corn

Another New World food, corn is a staple of both American Indian and Mexican diets. Corn turns up in everything from tortillas and piki bread to soups and stews that use hominy (corn from which the hull and germ have been removed). Even the husks (think tamales) are called into service by both cultures.

The so-called Indian corn, with its multicolored kernels, is mostly decorative these days, although one native corn hue has become synonymous with Southwest food — blue. Grown by many Pueblo tribes and especially important to the Hopi for whom it is part of a creation myth, blue corn isn't eaten on the cob, but dried and ground into a cornmeal. This blue cornmeal is somewhat more flavorful — and definitely more attractive — than the regular kind. Chic Southwest chefs adore blue corn because it exemplifies two key cooking tenets: drawing on local traditions and providing aesthetic pleasure. Expect to find blue corn tortilla chips or blue corn taco shells on some of the priciest plates in the state.

Topopo Salad

No one's exactly sure where the name came from, how the salad turned up in Tucson, or why you won't find it anywhere else (except in a few restaurants that have imported it from the Old Pueblo). But everyone pretty much agrees that the topopo salad is a treat. Lots of variations of the salad are served, but generally, you can expect a crispy corn tortilla spread with refried beans and topped with lettuce, tomato, chicken, cheese, and often, sour cream (yep, this pig-out is one you can rationalize by saying, "But I only had a salad"). Most of Tucson's South Fourth Avenue Mexican restaurants list the topopo on their menus.

Vegetables

Shredded lettuce is probably the most popular vegetable in the state; in fact, Yuma, Arizona, is the country's largest producer of the much maligned iceberg variety. Shredded lettuce is particularly prized as a garnish for cheese and beans. And squash is the darling of New Southwest cuisine, because it's indigenous to the Western hemisphere and the chefs love to use unpronounceable ingredients. Two favorite squashes are calabaza, a yellow squash similar in sweetness and firmness to butternut squash, and chayote, the mild-tasting (think cucumber), pear-sized gourd that was a principal food of the Aztecs and the Mayas. Another hard-to-say veggie star is jicama (that's _heek-uh-muh_), a member of the root family most often used raw in salads. Jicama has the crunchy consistency of a water chestnut but a sweeter taste.

And I suppose you're going to try to tell me that guacamole is not a vegetable. It's green, isn't it?

Appendix

Quick Concierge

● ●

*T*his handy section presents a wrap up of the practical information you need to plan a stress-free vacation — from A to Z facts to a phone list of airlines and hotel chains — plus, for the over-achievers among you, some additional resources to consult. Another bonus: There's no need to tip this concierge.

Arizona A to Z: Facts at Your Fingertips

AAA

For emergency road service, call ☎ 800-AAA-HELP (800-222-4357). To locate the AAA offices in Arizona — most are in Greater Phoenix, but there are also two in Tucson and one in Prescott — log on to www.aaa.com.

American Express

For cardholder services, call ☎ 800-528-4800; for lost or stolen travelers checks, call ☎ 800-221-7282. Phoenix: 2508 E. Camelback Road, Biltmore Fashion Park (☎ 602-468-1199). Scottsdale: 6900 E. Camelback Rd., Scottsdale Fashion Square (☎ 480-949-7000). Tucson: 3573 E. Sunrise Dr. (☎ 520-577-0550).

ATMs

There are automatic teller machines everywhere in Arizona — including, in some places, drive-throughs — and all the major ATM networks are represented. Call ☎ 800-424-7787 or 800-4CIRRUS for Cirrus, and ☎ 800-843-7587 for Plus. See Chapter 9 for additional cash machine details.

Business Hours

Business hours vary throughout Arizona and are often more relaxed — as in "I feel like closing my store this afternoon, so I will" — than in other parts of the country, but you can use the following as a guideline. Note, too, that business tends to be conducted on the early, rather than the late side: You're likely to have better luck reaching someone in an office at 8 a.m. than finding that person at his or her desk a few minutes before 5 p.m. Banks: Monday through Friday from 9 a.m. to 5 p.m. (in the Greater Phoenix and Tucson, many banks are also open on Saturday from 9 or 10 a.m. to noon or 1 p.m.). Retail Stores: Monday through Saturday from 9 or 10 a.m. to 5 or 6 p.m.; malls usually stay open Monday through Saturday until 9 p.m., and operate Sundays from 10 a.m., 11 a.m., or noon until 6 p.m. Bars: Most places don't open their doors until 11 a.m. or noon, but drinking establishments are legally allowed to let souses in Monday through Saturday from 6 a.m. to 1 a.m., Sunday from 10 a.m. to 1 a.m.

Credit Cards

Information numbers for American Express are listed above. MasterCard's general information number is ☎ 800-307-7309. For Visa, call ☎ 800-847-2911.

Drugstores

You'll find **Walgreen** (☎ 800-WALGREENS) and **Osco** (☎ 800-888-443-5701 or Internet: www.oscodrug.com) pharmacies all over the state, many with 24-hour service. Just punch in the zip code of the phone you're calling from to find the branch nearest you (or, in the case of Osco, type it in when you log on).

Emergencies

In most parts of the state, call ☎ 911 to report a fire, contact the police, or get an ambulance. The numbers for emergency services on the Indian reservations are given in the Fast Facts sections of Chapter 18, but you're not likely to remember where to find them in a hurry so just call "0" and have the operator connect you.

Fishing

Fishing licenses for nonresidents are available for one day ($12.50), five days ($26), four months ($37.50), and one year ($51.50); fees for the shorter permits include a trout stamp, but if you want to angle for bigmouth all year long, it's a whopping $49.50 extra. For more details, contact the Arizona Game and Fish Department, 2222 W. Greenway Rd., Phoenix, AZ 85021 (☎ 602-942-3000). The Indian reservations have a different license and fee structure; get in touch directly with the Hopi and Navajo tribes (see Information in the Quick Concierge section of Chapter 18).

Health

It can't be emphasized too much: Wear sunscreen and drink lots of water when you're traveling in Arizona. The sun is surprisingly strong, even in the north, and it's easy to get sunburned and dehydrated before you know it. The major metropolitan areas have excellent and plentiful medical facilities; that's not the case, however, on the Indian reservations

in northeast Arizona, where health centers are sparser and less modern. See Chapter 10 for additional details on health-related matters, including what to do in case of medical emergencies.

Information

See "Finding More Information," at the end of the appendix.

Internet Access and Cyber Cafes

You can get direct Internet access via a local call on AOL and Earthlink in these Arizona cities: Flagstaff, Greater Phoenix, Prescott, Sedona, and Tucson. You can access your e-mail at most Kinko's and some Radio Shack locations (check the telephone directory) and at the following cyber cafes (rates range from about $6–$9 an hour): Flagstaff: CyberCafe, in Bookman's, 1520 S. Riordan Rd. (☎ 520-774-0005; Internet: www.bookmans.com/html/cyber_cafe.html); Phoenix: Gypsy Java, 3321 E. Bell Rd. (☎ 602-404-9779; Internet: www.gypsyjava.com); Sedona: Innhouse Video & Cybercafe, 160a Coffee Pot Dr. (☎ 520-282-7368; Internet: www.inhousevideo.com); Tucson: Library of Congress, Hotel Congress, 311 E. Congress St. (☎ 520-622-2708; Internet: www.hotcong.com/libcong/).

Liquor Laws

The legal age for buying or consuming alcoholic beverages is 21. Hours to purchase booze are the same as those of bars: You can't buy alcoholic drinks Monday through Saturday between 1 and 6 a.m. and Sunday between 1 and 10 a.m. Liquor stores tend to have the most specialized selections but you can get the hard stuff as well as wine and beer at most major supermarkets and drugstores. Convenience stores generally only sell beer and wine coolers.

Mail

To find the address and hours of operation of the U.S. Post Office nearest you, phone ☎ 800-275-8777. Be prepared to know what ZIP code you're calling from.

Maps

Most gas stations, convenience stores, and supermarkets sell maps, and they tend to be better than the ones you can get at the local tourist offices, though those often indicate the popular tourist sights. If you're a member of AAA, you can also get excellent maps in advance at your local AAA office. Mapquest, www.mapquest.com, will plot you a route from point A to point B; it's a good online resource if you know exactly where you're coming from and where you're going, but it's no help for the clue-or computer-less.

Newspapers/Magazines

See "Finding More Information," at the end of the appendix.

Pets

Lots of hotels and motels in Arizona accept pets, especially small ones, for an extra fee. Always check in advance; even if a place won't allow your pooch to live in your room, the desk clerk is likely to be able to provide a recommendation for a nearby kennel. Never leave your pet in a locked car, even for what seems like a short period, and even with the window cracked open; temperatures can rise to fatal limits within minutes.

Photography

Shoot it out in sunny Arizona with a slower film — that is, one with a lower ASA number — in order to get sharper pictures. Serious shutterbugs with more than point-and-shoots may also want to invest in a polarizer, which reduces contrast, deepens colors, and eliminates glare; they're especially useful for the high-altitude north. Never, ever, leave your camera and/or film behind in a car in the sun or they may melt (just kidding, but film is heat sensitive and your images may well be damaged).

Restrooms

There are clean, safe rest stops along most Arizona roads — some of them are extremely scenic, and several have dog-walking areas — and you can generally find gas stations, restaurants, or convenience stores close to the exits every 25 miles or so. The exception is in Indian country, where you may drive longer distances without coming to facilities of any sort. There are almost no public restrooms in the cities, but an abundance of malls and accommodating restaurants compensates.

Safety

You need to take the usual common sense precautions for your personal safety and that of your belongings as you would anywhere else in the U.S. (see Chapter 9 for information about what to do if your money does get lost or stolen), but in Arizona you also have to think about the road — and the elements. See Chapter 7 for details about driving around Arizona, and the individual destination chapters for tips relating to touring desert or high-altitude areas.

Smoking

Arizona may look like Marlboro Country, but not as many people light up in the state as they did in the past. Some businesses and public buildings ban smoking entirely and restaurants tend to have separate smoking areas or restrict puffing to outdoor terraces. That said, only Tucson and Mesa (in Greater Phoenix) have blanket laws against smoking in restaurants or, in the case of Mesa, all public places. Everywhere else, smoking policies are set on a business-by-business basis.

Taxes

The state sales tax is 5.5 percent, and all the individual counties and towns tack additional tariffs on your purchases; you usually won't pay more than 8½ percent on anything you buy, however. Not so for car rental taxes, which range from 10 percent to more than 20 percent, or hotel room taxes, which run from around 6 percent to 14 percent (depending on which pet projects each city decides to have tourists help finance — but don't say you read that here).

Time Zone

You got to love a state ornery enough to just say no to daylight saving time — hey, the one thing we've got more than enough of here is daylight — but bucking the temporal tide does wreak havoc with our time zones. Arizona is on Mountain Time, but when the rest of the country goes on daylight saving time, the state is, in effect, on Pacific Time. To compound the confusion, the Navajo reservation does observe daylight saving time, while the Hopi reservation, which it encircles, doesn't.

Tipping

Tipping in Arizona is no different from tipping in any other U.S. city except that the service personnel and other potential tippees usually remain polite, even if they get stiffed. See Chapter 4 for details.

Weather Updates

For the best weather reports on line — replete with satellite pictures and loads of other great trivia for meteorological junkies — log on to the National Weather Service Web site at www.wrh.noaa.gov/. Cable subscribers may also be able to get the Weather Channel, one of the more soporific stations on TV — unless, of course, a hurricane is predicted for your destination (not likely in Arizona, where you'll usually find gradations of sunny, sunnier, and sunniest). There's no central number for state weather reports; see the Fast Facts sections of the destination chapters for your preferred prognostication.

Toll-Free Numbers & Web Sites

Airlines

Aeromexico
800-237-6639
www.aeromexico.com

Air Canada
800-776-3000
www.aircanada.ca

Air Jamaica
800-523-5585
www.airjamaica.com

Alaska Airlines
800-426-0333
www.alaskaair.com

America West Airlines
800-235-9292
www.americawest.com

American Airlines
800-433-7300
www.americanair.com

American Trans Air
800-435-9282
www.ata.com

British Airways
800-247-9297, 0345-222-111 (in Britain)
www.british-airways.com

Continental Airlines
800-525-0280
www.continental.com

Delta Air Lines
800-221-1212
www.delta.com

Frontier
800-432-1359
www.flyfrontier.com

Midwest Express
800-452-2022
www.midwestexpress.com

Northwest Airlines
800-225-2525
www.nwa.com

Scenic Air
800-634-6801
www.scenic.com

Southwest Airlines
800-435-9792
www.iflyswa.com

Sun Country
800-752-1218
www.suncountry.com

Trans World Airlines (TWA)
800-221-2000
www.twa.com

United Airlines
800-241-6522
www.ual.com

US Airways
800-428-4322
www.usairways.com

Car-Rental Agencies

Advantage
800-777-5500
www.arac.com

Alamo
800-327-9633
www.goalamo.com

Avis
800-331-1212 (in Continental U.S.)
800-TRY-AVIS (in Canada)
www.avis.com

Budget
800-527-0700
www.budgetrentacar.com

Courtesy
800-368-5145
www.courtesyleasing.com

Dollar
800-800-4000
www.dollarcar.com

Enterprise
800-325-8007
www.pickenterprise.com

Hertz
800-654-3131
www.hertz.com

National
800-CAR-RENT
www.nationalcar.com

Payless
800-PAYLESS
www.paylesscar.com

Rent-A-Wreck
800-535-1391
www.rent-a-wreck.com

Resort
800-289-5343
www.resortcards.com

Thrifty
800-367-2277
www.thrifty.com

Major Hotel & Motel Chains

Baymont Inns & Suites
800-301-0200
www.baymontinns.com

Best Western International
800-528-1234
www.bestwestern.com

Clarion Hotels
800-CLARION
www.hotelchoice.com

Comfort Inns
800-228-5150
www.hotelchoice.com

Courtyard by Marriott
800-321-2211
www.courtyard.com

Days Inn
800-325-2525
www.daysinn.com

Doubletree Hotels
800-222-TREE
www.doubletreehotels.com

Econo Lodges
800-55-ECONO
www.hotelchoice.com

Fairfield Inn by Marriott
800-228-2800
www.fairfieldinn.com

Hampton Inn
800-HAMPTON
www.hampton-inn.com

Hilton Hotels
800-HILTONS
www.hilton.com

Holiday Inn
800-HOLIDAY
www.basshotels.com

Homewood Suites
800-225-5466
www.homewood-suites.com

Howard Johnson
800-654-2000
www.hojo.com

Hyatt Hotels & Resorts
800-228-9000
www.hyatt.com

ITT Sheraton
800-325-3535
www.sheraton.com

La Quinta Motor Inns
800-531-5900
www.laquinta.com

Marriott Hotels
800-228-9290
www.marriott.com

Motel 6
800-4-MOTEL6 (800-466-8536)
www.motel6.com

Quality Inns
800-228-5151
www.hotelchoice.com

Radisson Hotels International
800-333-3333
www.radisson.com

Ramada Inns
800-2-RAMADA
www.ramada.com

Red Roof Inns
800-843-7663
www.redroof.com

Residence Inn by Marriott
800-331-3131
www.residenceinn.com

Rodeway Inns
800-228-2000
www.hotelchoice.com

Travelodge
800-255-3050
www.travelodge.com

Super 8 Motels
800-800-8000
www.super8motels.com

Wyndham Hotels and Resorts
800-822-4200
www.wyndham.com

Finding More Information

Tourist Info

Call or write the **Arizona Office of Tourism,** 2702 N. Third St., Suite 4015, Phoenix, AZ 85004 (☎ 800-842-8257 or 602-230-7733), for a copy of *Arizona Journeys,* a glossy publication that details attractions, activities, and lodgings throughout the state. You can also phone with specific questions; if the friendly representatives can't tell you what you want to know about the state, they'll refer you to someone who can. The office of tourism's Web site, www.arizonaguide.com, is the prime source of online information, with links to Arizona cities and regions and to lots of special interest sites (for example, ones relating to golf and adventure travel). See also the "Fast Facts" sections of the individual destination chapters for the local tourism offices and for additional useful Web sites.

Newspapers and Magazines

If a peek at *Arizona Highways* magazine doesn't make you want to visit the state, nothing will; it's hard to find more spectacular photography anywhere (of course, the landscape lends a hand by being incredibly photogenic). See the "Photography" section of Chapter 5 for the photo workshops run by the magazine. Single copies are available at newsstands for $3.50, or you can opt for a subscription, which is available for $19 for 12 issues. An online teaser of the magazine can be found at www.arizonahighways.com. Newspapers and magazines relating to Greater Phoenix and Tucson are detailed in the Fast Facts section of chapters 11 and 13.

State Guides

Frommer's Arizona is a great complement to this book, covering destinations not included in these pages and offering additional details on many that are. Another excellent resource is www.frommers.com, which is full of travel tips, on-line booking options, and a daily e-mail newsletter, updated daily by Arthur Frommer himself, filled with bargains and travel advice.

Fare Game: Choosing an Airline

Travel Agency: _____ Phone: _____

Agent's Name: _____ Quoted Fare: _____

Departure Schedule & Flight Information

Airline: _____ Airport: _____

Flight #: _____ Date: _____ Time: _____ a.m./p.m.

Arrives in: _____ Time: _____ a.m./p.m.

Connecting Flight (if any)

Amount of time between flights: _____ hours/mins

Airline: _____ Airport: _____

Flight #: _____ Date: _____ Time: _____ a.m./p.m.

Arrives in: _____ Time: _____ a.m./p.m.

Return Trip Schedule & Flight Information

Airline: _____ Airport: _____

Flight #: _____ Date: _____ Time: _____ a.m./p.m.

Arrives in: _____ Time: _____ a.m./p.m.

Connecting Flight (if any)

Amount of time between flights: _____ hours/mins

Airline: _____ Airport: _____

Flight #: _____ Date: _____ Time: _____ a.m./p.m.

Arrives in: _____ Time: _____ a.m./p.m.

Notes

Making Dollars and Sense of It

Expense	Amount
Airfare	
Car Rental	
Lodging	
Parking	
Breakfast	
Lunch	
Dinner	
Babysitting	
Attractions	
Transportation	
Souvenirs	
Tips	
Grand Total	

Notes

Sweet Dreams: Choosing Your Hotel

Enter the hotels where you'd prefer to stay based on location and price. Then use the worksheet below to plan your itinerary.

Hotel	Location	Price per night

Places to Go, People to See, Things to Do

Enter the attractions you most want to see to help plan your schedule. Then use the worksheet below to plan your itinerary.

Attractions	Amount of time you expect to spend there	Best day and time to go

Menus & Venues

Enter the restaurants where you'd most like to dine. Then use the worksheet below to plan your itinerary.

Name	Address/Phone	Cuisine/Price

Going "My" Way

Itinerary #1

☐ _____
☐ _____
☐ _____
☐ _____

Itinerary #2

☐ _____
☐ _____
☐ _____
☐ _____

Itinerary #3

☐ _____
☐ _____
☐ _____
☐ _____

Itinerary #4

☐ _____
☐ _____
☐ _____
☐ _____

Itinerary #5

☐ _____
☐ _____
☐ _____
☐ _____

Itinerary #6

- ☐ _____
- ☐ _____
- ☐ _____
- ☐ _____

Itinerary #7

- ☐ _____
- ☐ _____
- ☐ _____
- ☐ _____

Itinerary #8

- ☐ _____
- ☐ _____
- ☐ _____
- ☐ _____

Itinerary #9

- ☐ _____
- ☐ _____
- ☐ _____
- ☐ _____

Itinerary #10

- ☐ _____
- ☐ _____
- ☐ _____
- ☐ _____

Index

• *N* •

• T •

IDG BOOKS WORLDWIDE
BOOK REGISTRATION

Register
This Book
and Win!

We want to hear from you!

Visit **http://my2cents.dummies.com** to register this book and tell us how you liked it!

- ✔ Get entered in our monthly prize giveaway.

- ✔ Give us feedback about this book — tell us what you like best, what you like least, or maybe what you'd like to ask the author and us to change!

- ✔ Let us know any other *For Dummies*® topics that interest you.

Your feedback helps us determine what books to publish, tells us what coverage to add as we revise our books, and lets us know whether we're meeting your needs as a *For Dummies* reader. You're our most valuable resource, and what you have to say is important to us!

Not on the Web yet? It's easy to get started with *Dummies 101*®: *The Internet For Windows*® *98* or *The Internet For Dummies*® at local retailers everywhere.

Or let us know what you think by sending us a letter at the following address:

For Dummies Book Registration
Dummies Press
10475 Crosspoint Blvd.
Indianapolis, IN 46256

™

BESTSELLING
BOOK SERIES